Accounting for Senior Cycle

Davin Kielthy
Christy Tyrrell

First published 2013
The Educational Company of Ireland
Ballymount Road
Walkinstown
Dublin 12
www.edco.ie

A member of the Smurfit Kappa Group Plc

ISBN 978-1-84536-567-7

Editor: Simon Coury
Design: Graham Thew
Layout: Compuscript
Cover design: Identikit
Cover illustration: istockphoto
Project Editor: Lucy Taylor

Web references in this book are intended as a guide for teachers. At the time of going to press, all web addresses were active and contained information relevant to the topics in this book. However, the Educational Company of Ireland and authors do not accept responsibility for the view of information contained in these websites. Content and addresses may change beyond our control and pupils should be supervised when investigating websites.

09S18

Foreword

Many years' experience both teaching and examining Leaving Certificate accounting has made it clear to us that students need a clear and concise explanation of accounting theory followed by graded exercises designed to reinforce their understanding of the theory and its practical application.

In writing this book the students' needs have been paramount, resulting in the extensive number of graded exercises attached to each chapter.

This textbook covers all the requirements of the Leaving Certificate syllabus at both Ordinary and Higher Level. It contains many worked examples to illustrate accounting principles and practices. The exercises are graded to suit the needs of the Ordinary and Higher Level syllabuses. It also includes new practice exercises to aid students' understanding of the more difficult adjustments one by one before attempting complete and complex exercises.

This book gives a comprehensive coverage of all aspects of the Leaving Certificate Ordinary and Higher Level syllabus and contains:

- New full-colour student-friendly layout, well structured and attractively designed
- Fully updated text with all new exercises throughout
- Gradual and clear progression to more complex topics
- Emphasis on theory as required by the Leaving Certificate examination
- Examples in each chapter in accordance with best accounting practice
- Step-by-step approach to difficult adjustments and related exercises
- Tips for answering examination questions
- Important points highlighted for easy revision

We wish to express our sincere thanks to all those who helped us to complete this book. We are grateful to all at Edco, but in particular to Lucy Taylor, Simon Coury, Emer Ryan and Declan Dempsey for the countless hours spent editing and designing.

We wish to acknowledge the help and inspiration provided by our colleagues who reviewed and tested the material for us.

Special thanks to our families who were exceptionally patient and understanding.

About the Authors

Christy Tyrrell has many years' experience in both teaching and examining Leaving Certificate accounting.

Davin Kielthy is an Accounting and Business Studies teacher in Templeogue College, Dublin. He has 16 years' experience of teaching accounting.

Contents

1 Introduction to Accounting – Concepts, Bases and Policies

Objectives

On completion students should be able to:

- Understand the objectives and qualities of financial information;
- List and explain the different users of financial information;
- List and explain the four fundamental accounting concepts;
- List and explain other accounting concepts;
- Distinguish between an accounting base and an accounting policy.

Accounting is the art of preparing financial information for all organisations, from the sole trader to large companies, as well as non-profit-making organisations and other institutions such as farms. Accounting enables a large number of financial transactions to be summarised and reported in a simple fashion.

The objectives of financial information

There are two main accounting areas – **financial** and **management**.

1. Financial accounting

Financial accounting focuses on **past** events. This is where financial information about an organisation's past financial transactions is collected and recorded. These financial statements show:

- the performance of the organisation over the accounting period (generally one year)
- the financial position of the organisation at the end of the accounting period.

The financial statements prepared consist of:

- a **trading account**
- a **profit and loss account**
- a **balance sheet**
- a **cash flow statement**.

The main **objectives of financial accounting** are:

- To provide financial information which can be used for the purpose of assessing the organisation and making decisions.
- To prepare the relevant financial statements in accordance with the rules and regulations as laid down by the accounting regulatory bodies.

2. Management accounting

Management accounting, unlike financial accounting, is concerned with **future** financial decisions as well as past transactions. It provides information so that the organisation can plan, control and make decisions.

Management accounting will be dealt with in Chapters 20 to 24.

The qualities of financial information

In order for financial information to benefit an organisation and its users the information must have four main qualities. It must be:

- **Relevant** – the information should meet exactly the requirements of the user(s).
- **Reliable** – the information should be certified by either a director or an auditor.
- **Comparable** – the information should be prepared on a consistent basis from one accounting period to the next, so that results can be compared from year to year and/or from business to business.
- **Understandable** – the information should be clear, concise and capable of being easily understood by the user(s).

The users of financial information

There are many different groups that are interested in the financial affairs of a company for different reasons.

Users	Users' interests
Banks and other lending institutions	Can interest payments be met? Can loans and overdrafts be repaid? Should new loans be granted? What security (collateral) is available?
Trade creditors	Is there enough working/liquid capital to repay amounts owed? Will credit terms be met? Will they have priority for payment?
Ordinary shareholders	Is the company profitable? Is the company viable/liquid? What dividend (if any) will be paid? What is the value of shares?
Potential shareholders	Is this company a good investment opportunity? What is the share price? What is the company's dividend policy and yield? Are there sufficient profits to cover dividends?
Directors and senior management	How profitable is the company? Is the company liquid? Is it solvent? How are managers performing?
Employees and trade unions	Can the company maintain current wage levels? Can the company afford wage increases? Can the company maintain or increase staff levels?
Competitors	To compare performance To see if a takeover is possible
The Revenue Commissioners/ government	To charge the correct amount of taxation To allocate government or EU grants To offer government contracts

The four fundamental accounting concepts

There are four main accounting concepts which must apply to all financial information. There is a presumption that accounts are prepared with these accounting concepts in mind. The four main concepts are:

- **Going concern**
- **Accruals (matching)**
- **Consistency**
- **Prudence**.

Going concern

When preparing accounts it must be assumed that the business will continue in its present form for the foreseeable future – i.e. there is no intention or need for the business to close down or go into liquidation.

Accruals (matching)

This means that all items of income and expenditure that belong to a given accounting period must be included in the financial statements for that period regardless of whether they are paid/ received or not. For example, items sold on credit must be treated as income/gain immediately and not when the money is actually received.

Consistency

This means that accounting items must be treated in exactly the same way from one accounting period to the next. This enables the business to compare like with like.

Prudence

When preparing accounts, caution should be exercised. This means that losses can be anticipated but gains cannot. This ensures that profits will not be overstated and losses will not be understated. The prudence concept overrides the accruals concept in cases where they may clash.

Other accounting concepts and principles

There are other concepts and principles which apply along with the four main ones above. These are:

- **Entity concept**
- **Money measurement concept**
- **Materiality concept**
- **Realisation concept**
- **Double entry principle**
- **Period of account convention**
- **Objectivity concept.**

Entity

The business exists in its own right, separate from its owners. A clear distinction is made between the owners' business and their private affairs. The capital of a business is owed to the owners.

Money measurement

Only items that have a monetary value can be included in the financial accounts of an organisation. Items such as staff morale or the state of industrial relations are not included as these cannot be measured in monetary terms.

Materiality

This takes into account the fact that some items may be too small to be regarded as materially significant. The size of the expense or the gain is considered relative to the size of profits. As a general rule most accountants would regard an item as material if it is greater than 5% of overall profit.

Realisation

This means that profit is earned at the time the goods or services pass to the customer and not when they are paid for.

Double entry

The basic principle of double-entry bookkeeping is adhered to, that for every debit there is a corresponding credit. For example, if a business purchases a delivery van on credit from JD Garages, the asset Motor Vehicles is increased (debit side) while at the same time a liability to JD Garages is increased (credit side).

Period of account

The length of time of one accounting period should be consistent with the next accounting period. Most businesses will prepare their accounts on an annual basis. This convention allows businesses to compare like with like.

Objectivity

This means that the accounts are prepared without any personal bias on the part of the accountant that compiles them. All figures should be independently backed up with documents such as invoices and receipts.

Accounting bases

There are a number of different procedures and policies for preparing accounts. These vary from firm to firm and an organisation is free to choose which one suits them best. The different ways in which items can be treated are known as **accounting bases**.

For example, a company may depreciate fixed assets by either the straight line method or the reducing balance method (see Chapter 4). These are both accounting bases.

Accounting policies

When a business decides which base they are going to use, this becomes the **accounting policy** of the firm. These are usually explained in the notes to the accounts. These explanations should be clear, fair and as brief as possible.

1

If the accountant for the firm decides to choose the reducing balance method of depreciation, then this is accounting policy for that business in relation to depreciation of fixed assets.

Other areas where an accounting policy must be chosen include:

- the method of stock valuation
- the use of historical cost convention.

Exercises

Theory

Q1 **What are the main objectives of financial accounting?**

Q2 **There are a number of different users of financial information. For example, the Revenue Commissioners will want to see the profit and loss account of a business for the purpose of checking their tax liabilities for the year. They carry out a tax audit on the business's accounts on a regular basis.**

Name five other main users of financial accounts, giving reasons as to why they would want to examine and have an interest in the accounts of a business.

Q3 **Name the four fundamental accounting concepts, and in each case explain your answer.**

Q4 **Name and explain five other accounting concepts, giving an example in each case.**

Q5 **Define an accounting base.**

Q6 **Define an accounting policy. Give one example.**

Q7 **Distinguish between an accounting base and an accounting policy.**

Q8 **What are the qualities that financial statements should have?**

Exam Tip

- Theory is becoming more important in the Accounting exam. Theory needs to be learnt well, revised and applied throughout the syllabus.

2 Accounting Records

Objectives

On completion students should be able to:

- Understand the purpose of financial records;
- Understand basic record keeping;
- List and explain the main day books and ledgers including their source documents;
- Explain what VAT is and how the VAT system operates;
- Prepare a cash book and petty cash book;
- Explain what a trial balance is;
- List and explain the main final accounts;
- Understand the difference between capital and revenue income and expenditure;
- Explain statutory deductions;
- Define, understand and know how to treat bad debts, provision for bad debts and bad debts recovered.

The purpose of accounting records is to inform the owners of:

- how much the business **owes**
- how much is **owed** to the business
- the value of the **assets** of the business
- whether the business is making a **profit** or a **loss**.

The information is provided by setting up and maintaining an accurate set of records.

Accounting records are dealt with in this chapter as follows:

Part A: Basic record-keeping (including the treatment of VAT)
Part B: Capital and revenue income and expenditure
Part C: Statutory deductions
Part D: Accruals and prepayments
Part E: Treatment of bad debts and provision for bad debts

Part A: Basic Record-Keeping

The starting point of any set of financial information is the books of first entry. From this point records are kept right up to and including the final accounts.

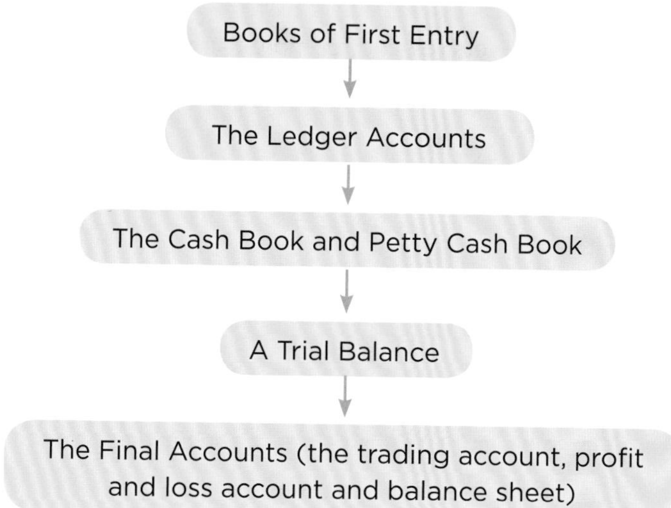

Double-entry bookkeeping

The basic principle of double-entry bookkeeping is that for every **debit** entry there must be a corresponding **credit** entry. In other words, there must always be a **receiver** and a **giver**. When all recording is completed the total of all the debits must be equal to the total of all the credits.

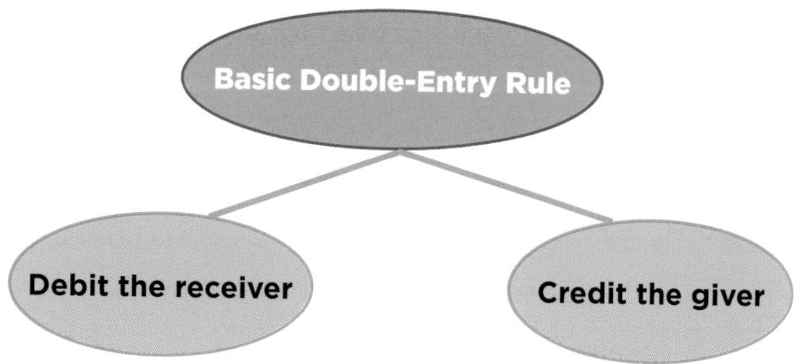

There are two types of transaction: a **credit** transaction and a **cash/cheque** transaction.

It is also important to be aware of the type of goods that the business is dealing in. This will vary from firm to firm. These are referred to as **goods for resale**. Other goods purchased would be treated differently.

For example, if a sweet shop purchased a display cabinet it would be treated as the purchase of an asset, whereas if a furniture store purchased tables and chairs they would be treated as purchases for resale as it trades in this type of good.

Ledger Account

Debit	Credit
An entry here indicates that the item named on the account has been received.	An entry here indicates that the item named on the account has been given.

2

Basic definitions

Term	Explanation
Asset	An item that the business **owns** There are four types of asset: Intangible assets – e.g. patents, goodwill Tangible fixed assets (owned for more than a year) – e.g. vans, buildings Financial assets – e.g. investments Current assets (owned for less than a year) – e.g. debtors, stock
Liability	An item that the business **owes** There are three main types of liability: Current (amounts due to be repaid within one year) – e.g. creditors Long-term (amounts due to be repaid after a year) – e.g. loans Capital (amounts owed to the owners of the firm)
Capital	The amount invested by the owner(s) of the business (and therefore owed to them)
Expenses	The day-to-day costs of running the business
Gains	The income of the business
Debtor	Someone to whom the business has sold goods on credit
Creditors	Someone from whom the business has bought goods on credit

The books of first entry (day books)

There are four main books of first entry. These are used for **credit** transactions. They are:

- the **sales book**
- the **sales returns book**
- the **purchases book**
- the **purchases returns book**.

The book of first entry for cash/cheque transactions is the **cash book**.

The book of first entry for unusual items is the **general journal**.

Information is taken from the books of first entry and entered in the ledger accounts using the double-entry system.

The ledgers

The ledgers can be divided into three types:

- the **debtors ledger (DL)** – also referred to as the personal ledger or customers ledger
- the **creditors ledger (CL)** – also referred to as the personal ledger or suppliers ledger
- the **general ledger (GL)** – also referred to as the nominal ledger.

Each debtor has his/her own personal account in the debtors ledger.

Each creditor has his/her own personal account in the creditors ledger.

The general ledger is used for recording information about things rather than information about people.

Summary of the books of first entry/day books

Book	Contents	Source document	Rules for posting
Purchases (PDB)	Goods for resale bought on credit	Invoices received	Debit purchases Credit supplier a/c
Purchases returns (PRDB)	Goods returned previously purchased on credit	Credit notes received	Debit supplier a/c Credit purchases returns
Sales (SDB)	Goods sold on credit	Copies of invoices sent	Debit customer's a/c Credit sales
Sales returns (SRDB)	Goods returned previously sold on credit	Copies of credit notes sent	Debit sales returns Credit customer's a/c
Cash book (CB)	All cash transactions	Receipts book	Debit cash book with all receipts Credit appropriate ledger a/c
Cheque payments (CP)	All Cheque payments	Cheque counterfoils	Credit cash book with payments Debit appropriate ledger a/c
Petty cash (PC)	Small cash payments for everyday items	Petty cash vouchers Receipts	Credit with all payments Debit appropriate ledger a/c
General journal (GJ)	Unusual transactions which require an explanation	Notes from manager requesting the entry	Debit the debit column with the item received Credit the credit column with the item given

VAT (Value Added Tax)

Under the Statement of Standard Accounting Practice (SSAP) 5 VAT is a tax on the supply of goods and services that is collected at each stage of the production and distribution chain but that is eventually borne by the final consumer. Therefore the treatment of VAT in the accounts of a trader should reflect his/her role as a collector of tax and should not be included in income or expenditure.

NOTE

VAT is a tax on goods and services.

Not all transactions are subject to VAT.

- Some goods/services are exempt from VAT – for example, necessities such as bread.
- Some businesses may be exempt from VAT – for example, schools, universities and other organisations that supply recognised educational services.
- Some businesses are too small to be registered for VAT.

Summary

Organisation	Treatment of VAT
Taxable companies	Add VAT onto cost of sales and pay VAT on purchases Difference is sent to the Collector General Refund is made if VAT on payments is bigger
Exempt companies	Do not charge VAT on sales Do not receive a refund on purchases
Zero-rated companies	Do not charge VAT to their customers They can reclaim VAT on their purchases

2

VAT on fixed assets and expenses is treated as follows:

- If VAT is paid and is reclaimable then the items should be shown net of VAT in the accounts.
- If VAT is paid and is not reclaimable then the items should be shown inclusive of VAT in the accounts.

Treatment of VAT in the accounts

Example

From the following details prepare the purchases and purchases returns books of Sam Ltd and post to the ledgers for the month of April 20-3. Goods were purchased on credit and VAT is added at 20%.

April 1	Purchased goods from O'Halloran Ltd	€20,000	Invoice no. 234
April 6	Purchased goods from P. Wall	€30,000	Invoice no. 345
April 10	Purchased goods from C. O'Toole	€15,000	Invoice no. 565
April 23	Returned goods to P. Wall	€5,000	Credit note no. 123
April 28	Returned goods to O'Halloran Ltd	€8,000	Credit note no. 657

The above transactions are exclusive of VAT figures.

Solution

Purchases Book

Date	Details	Invoice no.	Folio	Net	VAT	Total
April 1	O'Halloran Ltd	234	CL 3	20,000	4,000	24,000
April 6	P. Wall	345	CL 9	30,000	6,000	36,000
April 10	C. O'Toole	565	CL 23	15,000	3,000	18,000
	Total			65,000	13,000	78,000
				GL 31	GL 54	

Purchases Returns Book

Date	Details	Credit note no.	Folio	Net	VAT	Total
April 23	P. Wall	123	CL 9	5,000	1,000	6,000
April 28	O'Halloran Ltd	657	CL 3	8,000	1,600	9,600
	Total			13,000	2,600	15,600
				GL 5	GL 54	

The Creditors Ledger

O'Halloran Ltd Account (3)

Dr.							Cr.
Date	**Details**	**Folio**	**€**	**Date**	**Details**	**Folio**	**€**
April 28	Returns	PRB	9,600	April 1	Purchases	PB	24,000
April 30	Balance c/d		14,400				
			24,000				24,000
				May 1	Balance b/d		14,400

P. Wall Account (9)

Dr.							Cr.
Date	**Details**	**Folio**	**€**	**Date**	**Details**	**Folio**	**€**
April 23	Returns	PRB	6,000	April 6	Purchases	PB	36,000
April 30	Balance c/d		30,000				
			36,000				36,000
				May 1	Balance b/d		30,000

C. O'Toole Account (23)

Dr.							Cr.
Date	**Details**	**Folio**	**€**	**Date**	**Details**	**Folio**	**€**
				April 10	Purchases	PB	18,000

The General Ledger

Purchases Account (31)

Dr.							Cr.
Date	**Details**	**Folio**	**€**	**Date**	**Details**	**Folio**	**€**
April 30	Creditors	PB	65,000				

Purchases Returns Account (5)

Dr.							Cr.
Date	**Details**	**Folio**	**€**	**Date**	**Details**	**Folio**	**€**
				April 30	Creditors	PRB	13,000

VAT Account (54)

Dr.							Cr.
Date	**Details**	**Folio**	**€**	**Date**	**Details**	**Folio**	**€**
April 30	Creditors	PB	13,000	April 30	Creditors	PRB	2,600
				April 30	Balance c/d		10,400
			13,000				13,000
May 1	Balance b/d		10,400				

NOTE

The amounts inclusive of VAT are always recorded in the personal accounts as these are the amounts due to be paid (or received).

NOTE

The VAT figure is always recorded in the VAT account on the same side as the item on which the VAT is charged.

2

2

Summary

Book of first entry (including VAT)	Treatment in ledgers
Purchases book	Debit purchases account with total of net column Debit VAT account with total of VAT column Credit personal accounts with personal totals
Purchases returns book	Debit personal accounts with personal totals Credit purchases returns with total of net column Credit VAT account with the total of VAT column
Sales book	Debit personal accounts with personal totals Credit sales with total of net column Credit VAT account with the total of VAT column
Sales returns book	Debit sales returns with total of net column Debit VAT account with total of VAT column Credit personal accounts with personal totals

Other books

The receipts and payments/cash book

Most businesses prefer to record their receipts and payments in separate books, namely a cheque payments book and a cash receipts and lodgement book.

With **cash transactions** the rule is:

Debit the cash/receipts book with cash received/lodged.

Credit the cheque payments book/cash book with any payments made.

All money received by a business is debited in the cash book and subsequently credited in the appropriate ledger accounts.

All money paid by the business is credited in the cash book and subsequently debited in the appropriate ledger accounts.

Cash Book

Debit Side	Credit Side
Any cash coming into the business is entered here (using appropriate headings for analysed cash book)	Any cash going out of the business is entered here (using appropriate headings for analysed cash book)

The petty cash book

The petty cash book is used for recording small day-to-day expenses on a cash-only basis. It operates under what is known as the **imprest system**. This is where the petty cashier begins each week or month with the same amount (float). The amount spent is reimbursed at the end of the period.

It is a book of first entry and contains a receipts column and a payments column, as well as analysis columns for the most common expenses. It is part of the double-entry bookkeeping system.

The petty cash book is written up from petty cash vouchers.

Example

Prepare a petty cash book on the imprest system from the following details using the headings: Postage, Stationery, Travel, Cleaning and Other.

Mar 1	Opening balance €35
Mar 1	Restored imprest to €300
Mar 2	Paid for stamps €23
Mar 3	Bus fare €5
Mar 5	Cleaner's wages €32
Mar 6	Parcel post €43
Mar 7	Tea and coffee for the office €12
Mar 10	Courier fees €21
Mar 21	Envelopes €14
Mar 21	Taxi fare €44
Mar 22	Photocopying paper €45
Mar 25	Train ticket €34
Mar 28	Flowers for the office €21
Mar 31	Reimbursed expenses for the month

2

Solution

Date	Details	€	Date	Details	€	Postage	Stationery	Travel	Cleaning	Other
Mar 1	Balance	35	Mar 2	Stamps	23	23				
Mar 1	Bank	265	Mar 3	Bus fare	5			5		
			Mar 5	Cleaner's wages	32				32	
			Mar 6	Parcel	43	43				
			Mar 7	Tea/coffee	12					12
			Mar 10	Courier	21	21				
			Mar 21	Envelopes	14		14			
			Mar 21	Taxi fare	44			44		
			Mar 22	Paper	45		45			
			Mar 25	Train fare	34			34		
			Mar 28	Flowers	21					21
			Mar 31	Total paid	294	87	59	83	32	33
			Mar 31	Balance	6	GL1	GL2	GL3	GL4	GL5
		300			300					
Apr 1	Balance b/d	6								
Apr 1	Bank c/d	294								

The totals of each of the analysis columns are posted to the debit side of their respective accounts in the general ledger.

The general journal

This is the book of first entry for unusual transactions and entries which may require an explanation. Such entries would include:

2

- Opening entries when setting up a business, i.e. assets, liabilities, capital
- Correction of errors and transfers betweeen accounts
- Drawings (when the owner takes some item of value from the business for his/her private use, e.g. stock)
- Purchase and sale of fixed assets on credit
- Other items that can't be entered in other books of first entry, e.g. losses and gains.

When posting from the general journal to the ledgers, the debit side of the journal is posted to the debit side of the appropriate account in the ledger and likewise the credit side of the journal is posted to the credit side of the appropriate account in the ledger.

Example

Ruth Ltd had the following assets and liabilities on 1 March 20-2:

Assets: Premises €200,000; cash €50,000; debtors €35,000; stock €15,000
Liabilities: Creditors €20,000

Prepare the general journal of Ruth Ltd.

Solution

General Journal of Ruth Ltd on 1 March 20-2

	Debit	Credit
Premises	200,000	
Cash	50,000	
Debtors	35,000	
Stock	15,000	
Creditors		20,000
Capital		280,000
Being assets, liabilities and capital on this date	300,000	300,000

The debit entries above will be entered on the debit side of the relevant ledger accounts.

The credit entries above will be entered on the credit side of the relevant ledger accounts.

The trial balance

The trial balance itself is not part of the double-entry system. It is, however, a check on the accuracy of the double-entry system. If each transaction is entered correctly then for every debit there should be a corresponding credit.

It follows therefore that the sum of all the debits must be equal to the sum of all the credits. The trial balance is a list of all these balances both debit and credit at any given moment in time. If the total of the debits does not equal the total of all the credits then an error has been made in the bookkeeping records.

Not all errors will be revealed by a trial balance.

2

The final accounts

The final accounts are prepared at the end of the accounting period and are drawn up from the accounts prepared and records kept. The final accounts consist of:

Accounts	Explanation
1. The Trading, Profit and Loss Account	Shows the profit or loss for the period. It contains all revenue receipts and revenue expenditure.
2. The Balance Sheet	Sets out the balances in the ledger accounts at the end of the accounting period.
3. Cash Flow Statement (see Chapter 17)	Sets out the cash inflows and outflows for the accounting period. Remember: cash is not always equal to profit.

Example

R. Thorton had the following assets and liabilities on 1 January, 20-3:

Assets: Premises €230,000; motor vehicles €45,000; furniture €24,000; debtor (J. Dunne) €12,000; cash at bank €10,900

Liabilities: Creditor (D. Hammond) €9,800

During the month of January the following transactions took place:

Jan 2 Purchased goods on credit from F. Flannery €2,500 (invoice no. 234)
Jan 3 Purchased goods on credit from D. Hammond €5,000 (invoice no. 298)
Jan 6 Cash sales €23,000
Jan 9 Sold goods on credit to J. Dunne €4,500 (invoice no. 650)
Jan 12 Received a cheque from J. Dunne €10,000
Jan 15 Sold goods on credit to I. Howey €3,500 (invoice no. 654)
Jan 19 Purchased goods €10,000 by cheque
Jan 23 Cash sales €20,000
Jan 25 Paid insurance €2,000 by cheque
Jan 28 Returned goods to D. Hammond €2,000 (credit note no. 567)
Jan 29 I. Howey returned goods €1,000 and settled his account (credit note no. 1)
Jan 29 Purchased goods on credit from D. Hammond €4,000. (invoice no. 456)
Jan 30 Paid D. Hammond €2,500 on account

VAT is to be charged at 10%

Record the above transactions in the books of R. Thorton.

Solution

Step 1

Enter the transactions in the appropriate books of first entry.

2

General Journal

Details	Debit	Credit
Premises	230,000	
Motor vehicles	45,000	
Furniture	24,000	
Debtors (J. Dunne)	12,000	
Bank	10,900	
Creditors (D. Hammond)		9,800
Capital		312,100
Being assets, liabilities and capital at 1 January 20-3	321,900	321,900

Purchases Book

Date	Details	Invoice no.	Folio	Net €	VAT €	Total €
Jan 2	F. Flannery	234	CL 4	2,500	250	2,750
Jan 3	D. Hammond	298	CL 76	5,000	500	5,500
Jan 29	D. Hammond	456	CL 76	4,000	400	4,400
	Total			11,500	1,150	12,650

Purchase Returns Book

Date	Details	Cr. note no.	Folio	Net €	VAT €	Total €
Jan 28	D. Hammond	567	CL 76	2,000	200	2,200
	Total			2,000	200	2,200

Sales Book

Date	Details	Invoice no.	Folio	Net €	VAT €	Total €
Jan 9	J. Dunne	650	DL 89	4,500	450	4,950
Jan 15	I. Howey	654	DL 34	3,500	350	3,850
				8,000	800	8,800

Sales Returns Book

Date	Details	Cr. note no.	Folio	Net €	VAT €	Total €
Jan 29	I. Howey	1	DL 34	1,000	100	1,100
				1,000	100	1,100

Cash Book (debit side) or receipts (Cheque Lodgements Book)

Date	Details	Folio	Total €	Debtors €	Sales €	VAT €	Other €
Jan 1	Balance		10,900				
Jan 6	Sales		25,300		23,000	2,300	
Jan 12	J. Dunne	DL 89	10,000	10,000			
Jan 23	Sales		22,000		20,000	2,000	
Jan 29	I. Howey	DL 34	2,750	2,750			
			70,950	12,750	43,000	4,300	
Feb 1	Balance b/d		55,450		GL64	GL32	

Cash Book (credit side) or Cheque Payments Book

Date	Details	Folio	Total €	Creditors €	Purchases €	VAT €	Other €
Jan 19	Purchases		11,000		10,000	1,000	
Jan 25	Insurance	GL 17	2,000				2,000
Jan 30	D. Hammond	CL 76	2,500	2,500			
Jan 31	Balance c/d		55,450				
			70,950	2,500	10,000	1,000	2,000
					GL16	GL32	

Step 2

Having entered each transaction into its appropriate book of first entry, they are now posted to their relevant ledger accounts.

Debtors Ledger

Dr. J. Dunne Account (89) Cr.

Date	Details	Folio	€	Date	Details	Folio	€
Jan 1	Balance b/d		12,000	Jan 12	Cash book	CB	10,000
Jan 9	Sales	SDB	4,950	Jan 31	Balance c/d		6,950
			16,950				16,950
Feb 1	Balance b/d		6,950				

Dr. I. Howey Account (34) Cr.

Date	Details	Folio	€	Date	Details	Folio	€
Jan 15	Sales	SDB	3,850	Jan 29	Sales Returns	SRDB	1,100
				Jan 29	Cash book	CB	2,750
			3,850				3,850

Creditors Ledger

Dr. D. Hammond Account (76) Cr.

Date	Details	Folio	€	Date	Details	Folio	€
Jan 28	Returns	PRDB	2,200	Jan 1	Balance b/d		9,800
Jan 30	Cash	CB	2,500	Jan 3	Purchases	PDB	5,500
Jan 31	Balance c/d		15,000	Jan 29	Purchases	PDB	4,400
			19,700				19,700
				Feb 1	Balance b/d		15,000

F Flannery Account (4)

Dr. Date	Details	Folio	€	Date	Details	Folio	€ Cr.
				Jan 2	Purchases	GL 16	2,750

2

General Ledger

Premises Account (23)

Dr. Date	Details	Folio	€	Date	Details	Folio	€ Cr.
Jan 1	Balance		230,000				

Motor Vehicles Account (25)

Dr. Date	Details	Folio	€	Date	Details	Folio	€ Cr.
Jan 1	Balance		45,000				

Furniture Account (84)

Dr. Date	Details	Folio	€	Date	Details	Folio	€ Cr.
Jan 1	Balance		24,000				

Capital Account (90)

Dr. Date	Details	Folio	€	Date	Details	Folio	€ Cr.
				Jan 1	Balance		312,100

Purchases Account (16)

Dr. Date	Details	Folio	€	Date	Details	Folio	€ Cr.
Jan 31	Creditors	PDB	11,500				
Jan 31	Cash book	CB	10,000	Jan 31	Balance c/d		21,500
			21,500				21,500
Feb 1	Balance b/d		21,500				

VAT Account (32)

Dr. Date	Details	Folio	€	Date	Details	Folio	€ Cr.
Jan 31	Creditors	PDB	1,150	Jan 31	Creditors	PRDB	200
Jan 31	Debtors	SRDB	100	Jan 31	Debtors	SDB	800
Jan 31	Cash	CB	1,000	Jan 31	Cash	CB	4,300
Jan 31	Balance b/d		3,050				
			5,300				5,300
				Feb 1	Balance c/d		3,050

Purchase Returns Account (48)

Dr. Date	Details	Folio	€	Date	Details	Folio	€ Cr.
				Jan 31	Creditors	PRDB	2,000

Sales Account (64)

Dr. Date	Details	Folio	€	Date	Details	Folio	€ Cr.
				Jan 31	Debtors	SDB	8,000
Jan 31	Balance		51,000	Jan 31	Cash	CB	43,000
			51,000				51,000
				Feb 1	Balance		51,000

Dr.		Sales Returns Account (90)					Cr.
Date	Details	Folio	€	Date	Details	Folio	€
Jan 31	Debtors	SRDB	1,000				

Dr.		Insurance Account (97)					Cr.
Date	Details	Folio	€	Date	Details	Folio	€
Jan 31	Cash	CB	2,000				

2

Step 3

We can now extract a trial balance.

Trial Balance

Details	Debit	Credit
Insurance	2,000	
Sales returns	1,000	
Sales		51,000
Purchase returns		2,000
VAT		3,050
Purchases	21,500	
Capital		312,100
Furniture	24,000	
Motor vehicles	45,000	
Premises	230,000	
Flannery		2,750
Hammond		15,000
Dunne	6,950	
Cash/bank	55,450	
	385,900	385,900

Since the total of the debit column is equal to the total of the credit column the double entries for these transactions have been completed correctly.

Practice Questions 2.1

Q1 T. Black is a taxable firm. The following is a list of purchases and sales on credit for the month of March 20-2.

20-2	Details	Invoice no.	€
March 1	Sold goods to T. Robin	201	800
March 4	Purchased goods from J. Tobin	340	1,600
March 6	Sold goods to D. O'Shea	202	900
March 10	Bought goods from N. Mowlan	389	2,400
March 12	Sold goods to R. Roche	203	4,500
March 14	Bought goods from S. Sheehy	234	2,100
March 16	Bought goods from M. Malley	256	1,500
March 23	Sold goods to D. O'Shea	204	1,560
March 24	Sold goods to T. Robin	205	3,500
March 27	Bought goods from J. Tobin	390	1,600
March 31	Sold goods to T. Robin	206	3,400

2

VAT is to be charged on all items at a rate of 20%.

You are required to:

- Prepare the purchases book for the month of March 20-2.
- Prepare the sales book for the month of March 20-2.
- Post all transactions to the ledger accounts.

Q2 B. Cullen is a taxable firm. The following is a list of purchases and purchases returns on credit for the month of June 20-3.

June 1	Bought goods from P. Healy	Invoice no. 123	€10,000
June 4	Bought goods from B. Brady	Invoice no. 125	€15,000
June 8	Bought goods from E. Carroll	Invoice no. 245	€21,000
June 12	Returned goods to B. Brady	Credit note no. 125	€4,000
June 24	Returned goods to E. Carroll	Credit note no. 189	€3,500
June 26	Bought goods from P. Healy	Invoice no. 454	€12,000
June 30	Bought goods from E. Carroll	Invoice no. 786	€9,000

VAT is to be charged on all items at a rate of 20%.

You are required to:

- Prepare the purchases book for the month of June 20-3.
- Prepare the purchases returns book for the month of June 20-3.
- Post all transactions to the ledger accounts.

Q3 P. Larkin is a taxable firm. The following is list of sales and sales returns on credit for the month of August 20-3:

August 2	Sold goods to B. Hanley	Invoice no. 15	€20,000
August 9	Sold good to M. O'Rourke	Invoice no. 16	€8,000
August 16	Sold goods to H. Black	Invoice no. 17	€50,000
August 22	B. Hanley returned goods	Credit note no. 56	€5,000
August 24	H. Black returned goods	Credit note no. 57	€2,000
August 28	Sold goods to H. Black	Invoice no. 18	€15,000
August 29	Sold goods to B. Hanley	Invoice no. 19	€80,000
August 31	H. Black returned goods	Credit note no. 58	€4,000

VAT is to be charged on all transactions at the rate of 10%.

You are required to:

- Prepare the sales book for the month of August 20-3.
- Prepare the sales returns book for the month of August 20-3.
- Post all transactions to the ledger accounts.

Q4 Explain what is meant by double-entry bookkeeping. What is the basic rule?

Q5 Explain the term VAT. How should VAT be treated by taxable company?

Q6 Explain the terms: assets, liabilities, expenses and gains.

Q7 Explain what is meant by the term 'imprest system' as it operates in relation to the petty cash book.

Q8 Name two types of organisation that are exempt from VAT.

Q9 Name two situations where the general journal should be used as a book of first entry, and give examples.

Part B: Capital and Revenue – Receipts and Expenditure

2

Receipts and expenditure can be classified into two types, namely
- **Capital**
- **Revenue**.

Capital expenditure is expenditure on items which will generally bring benefit to the business for **more than one** financial year. This usually arises from sources other than the normal trading of the business. An example of this would be the purchase of fixed assets.

Revenue expenditure, also known as **current expenditure**, is the day-to-day spending on the running the business. It includes items which occur almost daily and recur many times throughout the financial year. Examples are purchases of trading goods, diesel, insurance, light and heat.

There are also capital and revenue **receipts.**

Capital receipts are once-off receipts. Examples include the sale of fixed assets, further capital introduced by the owner(s), bank loans, government grants.

Revenue receipts are receipts that arise from the day-to-day transactions of the business such as sales, rent received, discounts received and investment income.

NOTE

It is important to remember that any costs involved in the initial setting up of a business or in the purchase of a fixed asset are deemed to be part of the purchase price and are therefore capital expenditure. For example, if a business buys new shop fittings but pays its own staff wages to install these fittings, these wages are deemed to be capital expenditure as it is a cost involved in the purchase of the new fittings.

It is also important to distinguish between capital and revenue for the purpose of final accounts. An incorrect allocation between capital and revenue will distort both the profits and the value of assets in the balance sheet.

Capital items will affect the **balance sheet**. For example, the purchase of a new van will increase the value of delivery vans.

Revenue items will be treated in the **profit and loss account**. For example, the purchase of new tyres for the van will be treated as a selling and distribution expense.

Practice Questions 2.2

2

Q1 The following expenses were incurred for January 20-4 by E. Blackburn, who runs a lumber yard. Classify the items as capital or revenue expenditure.

1. Purchase of timber for use in the factory
2. Payment of wages to workers in the factory
3. Payment of wages to office staff
4. Purchase of a photocopier for factory office
5. Purchase of a facsimile (fax) machine for the general office
6. Paid postage
7. Payment for the servicing of the factory machinery

Q2 For the business of F. Spencer, a wholesale grain merchant, classify the following as either capital or revenue expenditure.

1. Building a new warehouse
2. Painting the new warehouse
3. Carriage on paint for the new warehouse
4. Wages to own workers for painting new warehouse
5. Carriage paid on sales
6. Purchase of new lorry
7. Insurance premium paid on building
8. Architect's fees for planning new building
9. Purchase of new fittings for the office
10. Painting new fittings

Q3 Jane Blackwood owns a garage. The following items appear in her books during the year. State which items are capital expenditure and which are revenue expenditure.

1. Bought new cars for use of car sales personnel
2. Purchase of new cars for resale
3. Purchase of new car wash on credit
4. Purchased petrol
5. Cost of the annual service of the compressor
6. Purchase of a new hydraulic jack
7. Cost of installing the new jack
8. Cost of cleaning materials and soaps for the car wash
9. Cost of replacement brushes for the car wash
10. Petrol costs for car sales personnel

Part C: Statutory Deductions

Statutory deductions are the compulsory deductions that must be made by employers when paying employees' wages.

2

PAYE (Pay As You Earn)

PAYE is a system of deducting income tax from employees' wages and salaries as they are paid. This spreads tax payable equally over the year.

For each employee, the employer is given a tax certificate which contains enough details for the employer to deduct the correct amount of tax for each employee after applying the employee's tax credits.

The government uses this money for running the country on a day-to-day basis - for example, the payment of the wages of civil servants.

PAYE is treated in the accounts as follows:

- Debit wages account with the gross wage (i.e. the full wage bill before any deductions are made).
- Credit bank account with net pay (i.e. the amount of money the employee takes home).
- Credit PAYE account with the appropriate amount of income tax payable.

PRSI (Pay-Related Social Insurance)/ USC (Universal Social Charge)

PRSI is the amount payable by employees and employers to cover the employees' entitlements to state pensions. The USC is a tax paid by employees, and must be deducted by the employer, in the same way as PRSI.

PRSI/USC is treated in the accounts as follows:

- Debit wages account.
- Credit PRSI/USC account.

Both PAYE and PRSI (USC) are forwarded to the Revenue Commissioners on a regular basis. When this payment happens it is treated as follows:

- Debit PAYE/PRSI/USC accounts.
- Credit bank account.

NOTE

PAYE and PRSI (USC) due at the end of the year are shown in the balance sheet as a current liability (Creditors: amounts falling due within one year).

There are also voluntary deductions from pay. These are amounts that the employee chooses to pay from his/her wages.

Some of the main examples of voluntary deductions include:

- health insurance (VHI, Aviva, etc.)
- pension contributions (private)
- trade union subscriptions
- savings schemes.

Voluntary deductions are treated as follows in the accounts:

- Debit wages/salaries account with the amount of voluntary contribution.
- Credit relevant account for voluntary deduction.

2

Example

The following details were taken from the books of Looney Ltd for the month of March 20-2:

Gross Pay	46,000
PAYE	12,000
Employees' PRSI	4,000
Employer's PRSI	2,500
Pension	5,000

You are required to prepare:

- the wages book
- the ledger accounts.

Solution

Note: Folio references have been added for the sake of clarity.

Wages Book

Date	Name	Gross pay	PAYE	USC/ PRSI	Pension	Total deductions	Net pay	Employers' PRSI
March 12	All employees	46,000	12,000	4,000	5,000	21,000	25,000	2,500

Dr. **Wages Account (4)** Cr.

Date	Details	Folio	€	Date	Details	Folio	€
March	Bank	CB	25,000				
	PAYE	GL 67	12,000				
	PRSI (employees')	GL 64	4,000				
	Pension	GL 54	5,000				
	PRSI (employer's)	GL 64	2,500				
			48,500				

Dr. **Bank Account (CB)** Cr.

Date	Details	Folio	€	Date	Details	Folio	€
				March	Wages	GL 4	25,000

Dr. **PAYE Account (67)** Cr.

Date	Details	Folio	€	Date	Details	Folio	€
				March	Wages	GL 4	12,000

Dr. **PRSI Account (64)** Cr.

Date	Details	Folio	€	Date	Details	Folio	€
				March	Wages (employee)	GL 4	4,000
				March	Wages (employer)	GL 4	2,500
							6,500

Dr. **Pension Account (54)** Cr.

Date	Details	Folio	€	Date	Details	Folio	€
				March	Wages	GL 4	5,000

Practice Questions 2.3

2

Q1 The following details were taken from the books of Bonner Ltd for the month of April 20-3:

Gross Pay	56,700
PAYE	23,500
Employees' PRSI	12,000
Employer's PRSI	4,500
VHI	3,000

You are required to show:

- the wages book
- the ledger accounts.

Q2 The following details were taken from the books of Harper Ltd for the month of July 20-2:

Gross Pay	34,500
PAYE	9,000
PRSI/USC	2,300
Employer's PRSI	1,500
Pension	1,500
Union fees	500

You are required to show:

- the wages book
- the ledger accounts.

Q3 The following details were taken from the books of Robinson Ltd for the month of October 20-2:

Gross Pay	67,900
PAYE	23,000
Employees' PRSI	8,000
Employer's PRSI	2,350
Pension	7,000
VHI	4,500

You are required to show:

- the wages book
- the ledger accounts.

Part D: Accruals and Prepayments

2

The matching concept

The **matching concept** is where income and expenditure are matched to the period to which they relate and not the period in which they were actually received or paid. The adjustments for amounts due (accrued) and prepaid appear in many other topics throughout the syllabus, including:

- Final accounts (sole trader, company, manufacturing, departmental)
- Club, service and farm accounts
- Tabular statements
- Incomplete records
- Published accounts.

Accrual: this is the amount of an expense due from the business at the end of the accounting period but not yet paid – for example, electricity due €200.

An accrual can also be receipts due to the business – for example, rent receivable due €400.

Prepayment: this is the amount of an expense prepaid by the business at the end of the accounting period – for example, advertising prepaid €300. This is for the next accounting period.

A prepayment can also be a receipt prepaid to the business – for example, rent receivable prepaid €500.

Treatment of accruals and prepayments

The adjustments for such items must be made when preparing accounts at the end of the accounting period. A summary of the adjustments is listed in the table below:

	Opening Balances (statement of reserves, accumulated fund, capital)	**Trading, Profit & Loss Account**	**Balance Sheet**
Expenses due start	liability	subtract	not applicable
Expenses due end	not applicable	add	liability
Expenses prepaid start	asset	add	not applicable
Expenses prepaid end	not applicable	subtract	asset
Gains due start	asset	subtract	not applicable
Gains due end	not applicable	add	asset
Gains prepaid start	liability	add	not applicable
Gains prepaid end	not applicable	subtract	liability

NOTE

The adjustments above must be made in order to arrive at the correct figures for net profit in the profit and loss account and to include the correct accruals and prepayments in the balance sheet.

Expense accounts

An example of an expense account would look like this:

Dr. Expense Account	Cr.
Balance PREPAID at start	Balance DUE at start
Amount paid during the year	Amount charged to profit and loss account
Balance DUE at end	Balance PREPAID at end

2

Gain accounts

An example of a gain account would look as follows:

Dr. Gain Account	Cr.
Balance DUE at start	Balance PREPAID at start
Amount included in profit and loss a/c	Amount received during the year
Balance PREPAID at end	Balance DUE at end

Example 1

Abbot Ltd had the following entries in relation to its light and heat for the year ended 31/12/20-0:

> Opening stock of oil €350; electricity due at 1/1/20-0 €200; light and heat paid €890; closing stock of oil €150; closing electricity due €120.

Calculate the amount to be charged to profit and loss and show the relevant entries in the profit and loss account and balance sheet.

Solution

Dr. Light and Heat Account Cr.

Date	Details	€	Date	Details	€
1/1/20-0	Balance (oil start)	350	1/1/20-0	Balance due	200
31/12/20-0	Bank (paid)	890	31/12/20-0	Profit and loss a/c	1,010
31/12/20-0	Balance due (electricity)	120	31/12/20-0	Balance (oil)	150
		1,360			1,360
1/1/20-1	Balance	150	1/1/20-1	Balance	120

Profit and Loss Account (extract)

Expenses (administration)	
Light and heat	€1,010

Balance Sheet (extract)

Current assets	
Stock of oil	€150
***Less* Liabilities due within 1 year**	
Electricity due	€120

2

Another way of looking at this is to consider the period during which the item is used or consumed by the business.

In the above example the opening stock of oil is included **(added)** because it is used in the current accounting period. The electricity due at the end of the year is also included **(added)** because it is used during the year but not yet paid for.

Likewise the electricity due at the start of the year is excluded **(subtracted)** because it was used during the previous accounting period. The closing stock of oil at the end is excluded **(subtracted)** because it won't be used until the next accounting period.

Always start with the amount paid and then adjust it for accruals and prepayments as per the adjustment chart.

Amount paid	€890	
Add Opening stock oil	€350	– add gains prepaid at start (used this year)
Less Electricity due start	(€200)	– less expenses due at start (last year)
Less Closing stock oil	(€150)	– less gains prepaid at end (next year)
Add Electricity due end	€120	– add expenses due at end (used this year)
Total amount for year	€1,010	

NOTE

This is applying the **matching concept**.

Example 2

Bruno Ltd had the following entries in relation to their rent receivable account for the year ended 31/12/20-9:

1/1/20-9	Rent receivable due €1,500
	Rent received during the year €8,000
31/12/20-9	Rent receivable prepaid €2,000

Calculate the amount of rent receivable for the year and show the relevant extracts from the final accounts (profit and loss account and balance sheet).

Solution

Dr. **Rent Receivable Account** **Cr.**

Date	Details	€	Date	Details	€
1/1/20-9	Balance due start	1,500	31/12/20-9	Bank	8,000
31/12/20-9	Transfer to profit & loss	4,500			
31/12/20-9	Balance prepaid end	2,000			
		8,000			8,000
			1/1/20-0	Balance	2,200

Profit and Loss Account (extract)

***Add* Other income**	
Rent received	€4,500

Balance Sheet (extract)

***Less* Liabilities due within 1 year**	
Rent receivable prepaid	€2,000

Or

Amount received	€8,000	Amount received during the year
Due 1/1/20-9	(€1,500)	This is subtracted as it is for last year
Prepaid 31/12/20-9	(€2,000)	This is subtracted as it is for next year
Total amount receivable for the year	€4,500	

2

Practice Questions 2.4

Q1 Cork Ltd had the following entries in relation to its heating and lighting for the year ended 31/12/20-3:

Opening stock oil €1,930; electricity due at 1/1/20-3 €240; light and heat paid €3,890; closing stock of oil €1,234; closing electricity due €560.

You are required to:

- Calculate the amount to be charged to profit and loss.
- Show the relevant entries in the profit and loss account and balance sheet as at 31/12/20-3.

Q2 Durrow plc had the following entries in relation to its advertising account for the year ended 31/12/20-2:

Prepaid balance at start €2,000.

Advertising paid during the year €36,000. This was to run from 1/9/-2 to 31/8/-3.

You are required to:

- Calculate the amount to be charged to profit and loss.
- Show the relevant entries in the profit and loss account and balance sheet.

Q3 Eastern Ltd had the following entries in relation to their interest receivable account for the year ended 31/12/20-4:

1/1/-4: Interest receivable due €3,400

Interest received during the year €28,000

31/12/-4: Interest receivable due €2,400

You are required to:

- Calculate the amount of interest receivable for the year.
- Show the relevant extracts from the final accounts (profit and loss account and balance sheet).

Q4 Frank Ltd had the following entries in relation to their commission receivable account for the year ended 31/12/20-3:

1/1/-3: Commission receivable due €3,500

Commission received during the year €18,000

31/12/-3: Commission receivable due €1,200

You are required to:

- Calculate the amount of commission receivable for the year.
- Show the relevant extracts from the final accounts (profit and loss account and balance sheet).

Part E: Bad Debts and the Provision for Bad Debts

2

Bad debts

Bad debts arise because the debtor is either unable or unwilling to pay the amount owed. This can happen when, in the opinion of the seller, the debt will not be recovered.

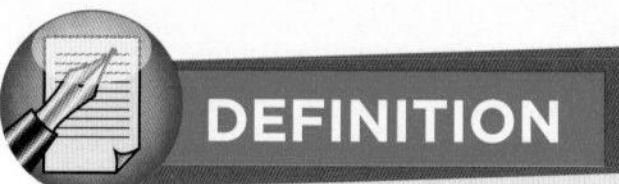

A **bad debt** is an expense (cost) to a business when a credit customer fails to pay the amount due.

Each year businesses which sell on credit more often than not end up having some customers who fail to pay the amount due. The amounts owed by these customers become a bad debt of the business, and this is treated as an **expense** in the profit and loss account.

When a bad debt **actually** occurs the amount of the bad debt is transferred from the debtors ledger account to a bad debts account and then, at the end of the financial year, to the profit and loss account, where the bad debt is charged against profit. This would be done by means of a journal entry.

Example

The debtors ledger of G. Byrne amounted to €43,000 on 31 December 20-2. On that date it was discovered that a debtor, D. Moore, who owed €2,300, was unable to meet his debt and it was decided to write it off in full.

Show how this will be recorded in the books of G. Byrne.

Solution

General Journal

Details	€	€
Bad debts a/c	2,300	
D. Moore a/c		2,300
Being write-off of a bad debt		

Dr. D. Moore Account Cr.

Date	Details	€	Date	Details	€
1/1/20-3	Balance b/d	2,300	31/12/20-3	Bad debts a/c	2,300

Dr. Bad Debts Account Cr.

Date	Details	€	Date	Details	€
31/12/20-3	D. Moore	2,300	31/12/20-3	Profit and loss a/c	2,300

Profit and Loss Account (extract)

Selling and distribution expenses	
Bad debt written off	€2,300

Provision for bad debts

Under the prudence concept (where you can anticipate a loss but not a gain) a business may create what is known as a **provision for bad debts**.

2

A provision for bad debts account can remain open from one financial year to another and the amount can increase or decrease by making adjustments based on the amount owed by debtors.

The treatment of this in accounts can be summarised as follows:

Item	Profit and Loss Account	Balance Sheet
Actual bad debt (given in trial balance)	Selling and distribution expense	No entry
Actual bad debt (given in additional information)	Selling and distribution expense	Reduce debtors by the amount of bad debt
Creation of a new provision for bad debts	Selling and distribution expense	Deduct new provision from debtors
An increase in the provision for bad debts	Selling and distribution expense (the increase only)	Deduct new provision from debtors
A decrease in the provision for bad debts	Enter under *Add* Other income (the reduction only)	Deduct new provision from debtors
No change in the provision for bad debts	No effect	Deduct existing provision from debtors

Example 1: an actual bad debt and an increase in the provision for bad debts

Sean Ltd had the following entries in their accounts for the last financial period:

Trial Balance (extract)

	€	€
Debtors	100,000	
Bad debts	2,000	
Provision for bad debts		5,000

The company decided to adjust the provision for bad debts to 6% of debtors.

You are required to:

- Calculate the amount of bad debts and provision for bad debts and show the relevant accounts.
- Show the relevant entries in the profit and loss account and balance sheet.

Solution

The actual bad debt of €2,000 happened during the year and has already been written off so this is treated as an expense in the profit and loss account and does not affect the balance sheet.

The provision for bad debts needs to be adjusted as follows:

100,000 x 6% = €6,000

This is an increase of €1,000 from the old provision of €5,000.

This is an expense (the amount of the increase only) while the new provision must be subtracted from debtors in the balance sheet.

Dr.		Debtors Account			Cr.
Date	Details	€	Date	Details	€
31/12/-1	Balance	102,000	31/12/-1	Bad Debt	2,000
			31/12/-1	Balance	100,000
		102,000			102,000

Dr.		Bad Debts Account			Cr.
Date	Details	€	Date	Details	€
31/12/-1	Debtors	2,000	31/12/-1	Profit and loss a/c	2,000

Dr.		Provision for Bad Debts Account			Cr.
Date	Details	€	Date	Details	€
			1/1/-1	Balance	5,000
31/12/-1	Balance	6,000	31/12/-1	Profit and loss a/c	1,000
		6,000			6,000
			1/1/-2	Balance	6,000

Profit and Loss Account (extract)

	€
Selling and distribution expenses	
Bad debts	2,000
Increase in provision for bad debts	1,000

Balance Sheet (extract)

	€	€
Current assets		
Debtors	100,000	
Less Provision for bad debts	(6,000)	94,000

Example 2: an actual bad debt and a decrease in the provision for bad debts

Gerard Ltd had the following entries in their accounts for the last financial period:

Trial Balance (extract)

	€	€
Debtors	96,000	
Provision for bad debts		8,000

The company decided to adjust the provision for bad debts to 5% of debtors.

At the end of year a debtor who owed the company €3,000 was declared bankrupt and this was written off as a bad debt on 31/12/20-1.

You are required to:

- Calculate the amount of bad debts and provision for bad debts and show the relevant accounts.
- Show the relevant entries in the profit and loss account and balance sheet.

2

Solution

In this case the actual bad debt happened after the trial balance was drawn up. The bad debt of €3,000 must still be treated as a bad debt in the accounts but also debtors must be adjusted before making the new provision.

The provision for bad debts will be as follows:

Debtors €96,000 less the actual bad debt of €3,000 = Debtors €93,000

€93,000 x 5% = €4,650

This is a reduction in provision of €8,000 - €4,650 = €3,350 (treated as other income).

Dr. **Debtors Account** **Cr.**

Date	Details	€	Date	Details	€
31/12/-1	Balance	96,000	31/12/-1	Bad Debt	3,000
			31/12/-1	Balance	93,000
		96,000			96,000

Dr. **Bad Debts Account** **Cr.**

Date	Details	€	Date	Details	€
31/12/-1	Debtors	3,000	31/12/-1	Profit and loss a/c	3,000

Dr. **Provision for Bad Debts Account** **Cr.**

Date	Details	€	Date	Details	€
31/12/-1	Profit and loss a/c	3,350	1/1/-1	Balance	8,000
31/12/-1	Balance (new provision)	4,650			
		8,000			8,000
			1/1/-2	Balance	4,650

Profit and Loss Account (extract)

	€
Selling and distribution expenses	
Bad debts	3,000
***Add* Other income**	
Decrease in provision for bad debts	3,350

Balance Sheet (extract)

	€	€
Current assets		
Debtors	93,000	
Less Provision for bad debts	(4,650)	88,350

Bad debts recovered/recoverable

Sometimes a debtor whose debt had previously been written off as bad subsequently pays back all or part of his debt. This is treated as follows:

2

1. Reinstate the debt	Debit the debtors account. Credit bad debts recovered account (with the amount of bad debt).
2. Record the amount received	Debit cash/bank. Credit debtors account with the amount received.
3. At the end of the financial year	Debit bad debts recovered account. Credit profit and loss account (with total of all bad debts recovered).

Example

During the year 20-8 in the books of E. Dunphy the following took place. A debt previously written off by Dunphy for €500 owed by a debtor E. O'Toole was recovered in full. Another debtor T. Roche, who owed Dunphy €300 and had been written off as a bad debt in 20-7, is now known to be fully recoverable. The debtor wishes to trade with Dunphy again, and has given his guarantee to repay the amount in January 20-9.

You are required to show the ledger accounts necessary to record the recovery of the bad debt and the bad debt recoverable.

Solution

Dr. **E. O'Toole Account** **Cr.**

Date	Details	€	Date	Details	€
Dec 20-8	Bad debt recovered a/c	500	Dec 20-8	Cash/bank a/c	500

Dr. **Bad Debts Recovered Account** **Cr.**

Date	Details	€	Date	Details	€
Dec 20-8	Profit and loss a/c	500	Dec 20-8	E. O'Toole a/c	500

Dr. **Bank Account** **Cr.**

Date	Details	€	Date	Details	€
Dec 20-8	E. O'Toole a/c	500			

Dr. **Bad Debts Recoverable Account** **Cr.**

Date	Details	€	Date	Details	€
Dec 20-8	Profit and loss a/c	300	Dec 20-8	T. Roche a/c	300

Dr. **T. Roche Account** **Cr.**

Date	Details	€	Date	Details	€
Dec 20-8	Bad debts recoverable a/c	300			

Profit and Loss Account for the year ended 31/12/20-8 (extract)

	€
Add **Other income**	
Bad debt recovered	500
Bad debt recoverable	300

2

Practice Questions 2.5

Q1 Outline three reasons why firms sell goods on credit.

Q2 Give three ways in which a business might be able to reduce the amount of bad debts it incurs.

Q3 Name three ways in which a business can check the creditworthiness of potential credit customers.

Q4 Baxter Ltd had the following entries in their accounts for the last financial period:

Trial Balance (extract)

	€	€
Debtors	156,000	
Bad debts	9,000	
Provision for bad debts		10,000

The company decided to adjust the provision for bad debts to 7% of debtors.

You are required to:

- Calculate the provision for bad debts (show ledger accounts).
- Show the relevant sections of the profit and loss account and balance sheet.

Q5 Farrell Ltd had the following entries in their accounts for the last financial period:

Trial Balance (extract)

	€	€
Debtors	35,600	
Bad debts	3,500	
Provision for bad debts		2,900

The company decided to adjust the provision for bad debts to 5% of debtors.

You are required to:

- Calculate the provision for bad debts (show ledger accounts).
- Show the relevant sections of the profit and loss account and balance sheet.

Q6 Chattan Ltd had the following entries in their accounts for the last financial period:

Trial Balance (extract)

	€	€
Debtors	84,000	
Provision for bad debts		4,500

The company decided to adjust the provision for bad debts to 9% of debtors.

At the end of year a debtor who owed the company €2,000 was declared bankrupt and this was written off as a bad debt on 31/12/20-3.

You are required to:

- Calculate the amount of bad debts and provision for bad debts (show ledger accounts).
- Show the relevant sections of the profit and loss account and balance sheet.

2

Q7 Kehoe Ltd had the following entries in their accounts for the last financial period:

Trial Balance (extract)

	€	€
Debtors	174,000	
Provision for bad debts		9,900

The company decided to adjust the provision for bad debts to 4% of debtors.

At the end of year a debtor who owed the company €12,000 was declared bankrupt and this was written off as a bad debt on 31/12/20-4.

You are required to:

- Calculate the amount of bad debts and provision for bad debts (show ledger accounts).
- Show the relevant sections of the profit and loss account and balance sheet.

Q8 Lynch Ltd had the following entries in their accounts for the last financial period:

Trial Balance (extract)

	€	€
Debtors	235,000	
Bad debts	11,000	
Provision for bad debts		19,000
Bank	54,000	

The company decided to adjust the provision for bad debts to 10% of debtors.

At the end of year a debtor who owed the company €9,000 was declared bankrupt and paid 25c in the euro, the remainder being written off as a bad debt on 31/12/20-5.

You are required to:

- Calculate the amount of bad debts and provision for bad debts (show ledger accounts).
- Show the relevant sections of the profit and loss account and balance sheet.

Exam Tips

- Topics covered in this chapter make up the workings for a lot of other areas of the syllabus.
- All workings should be clearly set out when answering examination questions and labelled clearly.
- When preparing workings always be careful with accruals and prepayments when calculating the amount of the expense/gain to be entered in the final answer.

3 Bank Reconciliation Statements

Objectives

On completion students should be able to:

- Explain the purpose of a bank reconciliation statement;
- Explain the reasons why there may be differences between the business's bank balance and that on the statement;
- Understand how such entries can affect the bank balance;
- Prepare an adjusted bank account;
- Prepare a bank reconciliation statement.

Purpose of bank reconciliation statements

At the end of each month a bank will send its business customers a statement showing all the transactions recorded in the current account since the previous statement. This is usually sent to personal customers on a regular basis. This is a **bank statement.**

When a bank statement arrives it should be compared with the business's own bank account in its own records. Both balances should agree if the same transactions are recorded in both statement and bank account. However, more often than not they are different. Hence the need to prepare a **bank reconciliation statement.**

A **bank reconciliation statement** reconciles the different balances in the bank statement and the business's bank account.

Reasons for differences

1. Time delays (lags)

There is sometimes a delay between the time of recording a transaction and its appearing on the bank's records. For example:

- A business makes a lodgement and records this in its own books immediately, but it will not be credited by the bank for a few days.
- A business pays a creditor by cheque and records this in his/her own books, but the creditor does not present the cheque for payment for up to six months.
- A direct payment made to the bank on behalf of a business is recorded on the statement. However, the business cannot record this in his/her bank account until the statement arrives.

3

2. Unknown entries

One party is unaware of a transaction. This might involve:

- a cheque dishonoured by the bank
- bank charges, bank interest
- standing orders, direct debits and credit transfers.

3. Errors

Errors can occur on either side, the bank or the business. These might involve:

- calculation errors
- entering incorrect amounts – for example, €356 entered as €653
- entering amounts on the incorrect side of the account or in the wrong account – for example, the bank debits P. Ryan's account instead of debiting T. Ryan's account.

How do entries affect the bank balance?

The bank balance **increases** when:

- any lodgements (cash, cheques) are made to the bank
- any amounts are lodged by others on behalf of the business – for example, interest receivable, dividends received, credit transfers.

When the bank balance is increased:

- The business will **debit** its bank account.
- The bank will **credit** the business's bank account.

The bank balance **decreases** when:

- any payments are made by cheque and honoured by the bank
- any payments are made by direct debit or standing order
- any cash withdrawals are made by the business
- any bank interest and other financial charges are made by the bank on behalf of the business.

When the bank balance is decreased:

- The business will **credit** its bank account.
- The bank will **debit** the business's bank account.

Procedure for preparing a bank reconciliation statement

A bank reconciliation statement is a formal way of showing the adjustments necessary to make the balances in the business's bank account and the balance on the bank statement agree.

Steps

1. Compare the debit side of the bank account with the credit side of the bank statement. Place a ✓ against the items common to each.

Be sure to check that the opening balances are the same.

2. Compare the credit side of the bank account with the debit side of the bank statement. Place a ✓ against the items common to both.
3. Prepare the business's adjusted bank account as follows:

Dr. **Adjusted Bank Account** Cr.

Date	Details	€	Date	Details	€
Balance as per bank account			Balance as per bank account if overdraft		
Place any unticked items from the credit side of the statement here, e.g. credit transfers.			Place any unticked items from the debit side of the statement here, e.g. direct debits or bank charges.		

3

NOTE

Errors made by the bank even though unticked should not be entered here.

4. Correct any errors made by the business in the business's bank account.
5. Prepare the bank reconciliation statement as follows:

Bank Reconciliation Statement

Balance as per bank statement
Add: Any lodgements not yet credited by the bank
Any debit entries made by the bank in error
Less: Any cheques paid not presented for payment
Any credit entries made by the bank in error
Balance as per adjusted bank account

Example 1

The following is the bank account of B. Mitchell as on 1 June 20-2:

Dr. **Bank Account** Cr.

Date	Details	€	Date	Details	€
July 1	Balance	4,800✓	July 2	L. Lorcan, Chq 23	3,400
July 4	L. Lurgan	840✓	July 3	T. Tyrrell, Chq 24	2,300✓
July 7	T. Tobin	1,680✓	July 6	C. Ryan, Chq 25	340✓
July 12	L. Jones	3,800✓	July 13	M. Breen, Chq 26	1,200✓
July 18	R. Taggart	5,200✓	July 15	P. Quinn, Chq 27	3,200
July 26	B. Stack	1,340	July 30	E. Daly, Chq 28	1,500✓
			July 31	Balance	5,720
		17,660			17,660
Aug 1	Balance	5,720			

On 31 July B. Mitchell's bank statement showing the following details:

Date	Details	Debit (€)	Credit (€)	Balance (€)
July 1	Balance			4,800✓
July 3	Cheque no. 24	2,300✓		2,500
July 4	Lodgement		840✓	3,340
July 7	Cheque no. 25	340✓		3,000
July 8	Lodgement		1,680✓	4,680
July 10	Direct debit	560		4,120
July 12	Cheque no. 26	1,200✓		2,920
July 15	Bank charges	120		2,800
July 21	Lodgement		3,800✓	6,600
July 23	Bank interest	100		6,500
July 25	Credit transfer		400	6,900
July 25	Lodgement		5,200✓	12,100
July 31	Cheque no. 28	1,500✓		10,600

Note: The credit transfer on 25 July was credited in error by the bank to B. Mitchell's bank account instead of P. Mitchell's bank account.

You are required to:

- Prepare adjusted bank account for B. Mitchell.
- Prepare a bank reconciliation statement as at 31/07/-2.

Solution

Step 1

Place a tick beside common items by comparing the debit column of the bank account with the credit side of the statement and vice versa.

Remember to check that both opening balances are the same.

Step 2

Prepare the adjusted bank account with the unticked items from the statement as follows:

- Debit the bank account with any unticked items in the credit column of the bank statement.
- Credit the bank account with any unticked items in the debit column of the bank statement.

Remember: errors by the bank do not go into the adjusted bank account.

Dr. **Adjusted Bank Account** **Cr.**

Date	Details	€	Date	Details	€
July 31	Balance	5,720	July 31	Bank charges	120
				Direct debit	560
				Bank interest	100
				Balance	4,940
		5,720			5,720
Aug 1	Balance	4,940			

Step 3
Prepare the bank reconciliation statement.

Bank Reconciliation Statement

			€
Balance as per bank statement			10,600
Add	Lodgement not yet credited by the bank		1,340
			11,940
Less	Cheques drawn not yet presented for payment		
	Cheque no. 23	3,400	
	Cheque no. 27	3,200	(6,600)
			5,340
Less	Error by bank		(400)
Balance as per adjusted bank account			4,940

3

Example 2

On 31 July 20-3, Eddie Bob's bank account showed a debit balance of €60,780. On the same date his bank statement showed a credit balance of €57,200. On investigation he discovered that:

(a) Bank charges, €120, had not been entered in the bank account.
(b) Cheques drawn by Bob, €670, had not been presented for payment.
(c) Standing orders, €2,350, had not been entered in his bank account.
(d) A cheque drawn by Bob, €560, had been entered in his bank account as €650.
(e) A lodgement of €430 had not been entered by the bank.
(f) A cheque issued by Bob, €780, has been entered on the incorrect side of the bank account.
(g) A cheque of €120 lodged by Eddie Tob had been entered by error by the bank to the credit of Bob's account.

You are required to:

- Adjust Bob's bank account as necessary.
- Prepare a bank reconciliation statement as at 31/07/20-3.

Solution

Step 1
Since there is no bank account or statement given, the first step is to bring the bank account up to date.

Dr. **Bank Account** **Cr.**

Date	Details	€	Date	Details	€
July 1	Balance	60,780	July	Bank charges (a)	120
	Cheque error (d)	90		Standing orders (c)	2,350
				Cheque error (f)	1,560
				Balance	56,840
		60,870			60,870
August	Balance	56,840			

Step 2

Prepare the bank reconciliation statement.

Bank Reconciliation Statement as at 31 July 2013

			€
Balance as per bank statement			57,200
Add	Lodgement made not yet credited by the bank (e)		430
			57,630
Less	Cheque drawn not presented for payment (b)	670	
	Error by bank (credit mistake) (g)	120	(790)
Balance as per adjusted bank account			56,840

3

Exercises – Ordinary Level

Q1 **Kim Farrell's bank account was as follows for the month of July 20-1:**

Dr. **Bank Account** **Cr.**

Date	Details	€	Date	Details	Cheque no.	€
July 1	Balance b/d	37,600	July 8	P. O'Shea	12	6,400
July 5	G. Bates	4,000	July 15	B. Doran	13	3,200
July 12	F. Rowe	17,600	July 19	Insurance	14	10,400
July 19	G. Short	14,400	July 24	P. York	15	9,600
July 31	G. Power	3,600	July 28	O. Joyce	16	5,000
			July 29	I. Neville	17	4,600
			July 31	Balance c/d		38,000
		77,200				77,200
Aug 1	Balance b/d	38,000				

Her bank statement on 31 July 20-1 was as follows:

Date	Details	Debit (€)	Credit (€)	Balance (€)
July 1	Balance			37,600
July 5	Lodgement		4,000	41,600
July 10	Cheque no. 12	6,400		35,200
July 14	Lodgement		17,600	52,800
July 19	Cheque no. 14	10,400		42,400
July 24	Cheque no. 15	9,600		32,800
July 28	Lodgement		14,400	47,200
July 29	Direct debit	32,000		15,200
July 30	Bank charges	200		15,000

You are required to:

- Adjust the bank account as necessary.
- Prepare a bank reconciliation statement as at 31 July 20-1.

Q2 **J.R. Ewing's bank account showed the following entries for October 20-2:**

Dr. **Bank Account** **Cr.**

Date	Details	€	Date	Details	Cheque no.	€
Oct 1	Balance	11,000	Oct 2	G. Long	345	567
Oct 3	L. Loby	4,560	Oct 5	A. Short	346	2,456
Oct 10	D. Orr	2,250	Oct 9	G. Harp	347	1,540
Oct 17	Cash sales	2,500	Oct 19	H. Kemp	348	500
Oct 22	R. Moore	2,800	Oct 23	Insurance	349	1,670
Oct 29	Cash sales	2,400	Oct 31	Y. Young	350	4,500
			Oct 31	Balance		14,277
		25,510				25,510
Oct 31	Balance	14,277				

His bank statement on 31 October was as follows:

Date	Details	Debit (€)	Credit (€)	Balance (€)
Oct 1	Balance			11,000
Oct 2	Cheque no. 345	567		10,433
Oct 3	Lodgement		4,560	14,993
Oct 6	Bank charges	130		14,863
Oct 10	Lodgement		2,250	17,113
Oct 13	Cheque no. 347	1,540		15,573
Oct 19	Lodgement		2,500	18,073
Oct 22	Lodgement		2,800	20,873
Oct 22	Cheque no. 348	500		20,373
Oct 26	Dishonoured cheque	2,800		17,573
Oct 28	Direct debit	1,340		16,233
Oct 31	Standing order	2,300		13,933
Oct 31	Credit transfer		1,707	15,640

You are required to:

- Adjust the bank account as necessary.
- Prepare a bank reconciliation statement as at 31 October 20-2.

3

Q3 Tom Moore's bank account showed the following entries for November 20-3:

Dr. Bank Account Cr.

Date	Details	€	Date	Details	Cheque no.	€
Nov 1	Balance	2,280	Nov 2	T. Bradley	396	1,365
Nov 4	Sales lodged	2,760	Nov 8	Rent	397	870
Nov 7	Lodgement	2,670	Nov 15	T. Grant	398	930
Nov 10	Sales lodged	1,560	Nov 18	T. Tolan	399	1,515
			Nov 22	K. Pilkington	400	1,110
			Nov 29	Advertising	401	360
			Nov 30	N. Jolly	402	420
			Nov 30	Balance		2,700
		9,270				9,270
	Balance	2,700				

His bank statement on 30 November was as follows:

Date	Details	Debit (€)	Credit (€)	Balance (€)
Nov 1	Balance			2,280
Nov 2	Dividends received		690	2,970
Nov 4	T. Bradley, 396	1,365		1,605
Nov 10	Rent, 397	870		735
Nov 11	Lodgement		2,670	3,405
Nov 12	T. Grant, 398	930		2,475
Nov 15	Dishonoured cheque	390		2,085
Nov 18	Lodgement		2,760	4,845
Nov 22	K. Pilkington, 400	1,110		3,735
Nov 30	Advertising, 401	360		3,375
Nov 30	Bank charges	75		3,300
Nov 30	Standing order	630		2,670
Nov 30	Y. Tong	435		2,235

Note: The €435 entered in the bank statement on November 30 was debited in error to Tom Moore's account instead of to Joe Moore's account.

You are required to:

- Show Tom Moore's adjusted cash book (bank column only) in ledger form and bring down the correct balance.
- Prepare a statement as on 30/11/-3 reconciling the adjusted cash book with the bank statement balance.

Q4 **June Wong's bank account showed the following entries for March 20-5:**

Bank Account

Dr.						Cr.
Date	**Details**	**€**	**Date**	**Details**	**Cheque no.**	**€**
Mar 1	Balance	3,600	Mar 5	B. Jones	0013	1,320
Mar 9	Sales lodged	4,200	Mar 7	B. Ewing	0014	1,860
Mar 17	Lodgement	3,840	Mar 9	Wages	0015	1,200
Mar 30	Sales lodged	7,350	Mar 11	D. Jiffy	0016	780
			Mar 13	Oil	0017	1,740
			Mar 16	F. Jeaney	0018	4,860
			Mar 26	Wages	0019	2,400
			Mar 27	G, Jeaney	0020	3,210
			Mar 28	H. Hogan	0021	630
				Balance		990
		18,990				18,990
Mar 31	Balance	990				

Her bank statement on 31 March was as follows:

Date	Details	Debit (€)	Credit (€)	Balance (€)
Mar 1	Balance			3,600
Mar 2	Dividends received		3,300	6,900
Mar 5	Cheque 0013	1,320		5,580
Mar 11	Cheque 0015	1,200		4,380
Mar 12	Lodgement		4,200	8,580
Mar 12	Interest received		1,500	10,080
Mar 15	Standing order	636		9,444
Mar 17	Lodgement		3,840	13,284
Mar 17	Cheque 0018	4,860		8,424
Mar 28	Cheque 0019	2,400		6,024
Mar 28	Cheque 0020	3,210		2,814
Mar 28	Bank charges	84		2,730
Mar 29	Credit transfer		300	3,030
Mar 31	Dishonoured cheque	1,230		1,800

Note: The €300 entered in the bank statement on March 29 was credited in error to June Wong's account instead of to Tony Wong's account.

You are required to:

- **Show June Wong's adjusted cash book (bank column only) in ledger form and bring down the correct balance.**
- **Prepare a statement as on 31/03/-5 reconciling the adjusted cash book with the bank statement balance.**

3

3

Q5 **Kyle Myle's bank account showed the following entries for January 20-4:**

Dr. **Bank Account** **Cr.**

Date	Details	€	Date	Details	Cheque no.	€
Jan 1	Balance	6,030	Jan 3	B. Poland	001	4,005
Jan 9	Sales lodge	7,740	Jan 6	Salaries	002	2,970
Jan 13	Lodgement	8,100	Jan 9	C. Coates	003	1,890
Jan 30	Sales lodge	3,150	Jan 13	F. Dwyer	004	990
			Jan 16	Cleaning	005	3,060
			Jan 17	J. Bones	006	3,825
			Jan 21	H. Healy	007	1,080
				Balance		7,200
		25,020				25,020
	Balance	7,200				

His bank statement on 31 January was as follows:

Date	Details	Debit (€)	Credit (€)	Balance (€)
Jan 1	Balance			6,750
Jan 3	Interest received		1,080	7,830
Jan 7	B. Poland	4,005		3,825
Jan 9	Salaries	2,970		855
Jan 11	Coates	1,890		1,035 Dr.
Jan 12	Lodgement		7,740	6,705
Jan 13	P. Prune	720		5,985
Jan 13	Dishonoured cheque	1,260		4,725
Jan 16	Lodgement		8,100	12,825
Jan 17	J. Bones	4,068		8,757
Jan 19	Cleaning	3,060		5,697
Jan 20	Bank charges	270		5,427
Jan 23	Standing order	1,620		3,807
Jan 31	W. Turner	1,107		2,700

Note: The €1,107 entered in the bank statement on Jan 31 was debited in error to Kyle Myle's account instead of to Kyle Myer's account.

You are required to:

- Show Kyle Myle's adjusted cash book (bank column only) in ledger form and bring down the correct balance.
- Prepare a statement as on 31/1/-4 reconciling the adjusted cash book with the bank statement balance.

Exercises – Higher Level

3

Q1 **On 30 June 20-6, Gary Ryan received his bank statement showing an overdraft of €3,572. His bank account on the same date showed a debit balance of €14,516. On investigation the following errors were revealed:**

(a) A cheque lodged in the bank, €1,292, had been entered in error by the bank as €1,140.
(b) A credit transfer for €760 had not been entered in the bank account.
(c) A cheque for €380 paid into the bank had been returned by the bank marked 'refer to drawer'.
(d) A standing order, €228, had not been entered in the bank account.
(e) A lodgement of €6,840 had not been credited by the bank.
(f) Bank charges of €152 did not appear in the bank account.
(g) The bank account balance had been brought down as a debit balance of €9,120 instead of a debit balance of €8,360 on 1 June 20-6.
(h) Cheques drawn, €304, had not been presented to the bank.
(i) A transfer to the An Post savings account of €11,400 had not been entered in the bank account.
(j) Cash paid into the bank, €760, had been entered in the bank account as €684.
(k) A cheque paid to G. Byrne, €2,584, had been entered in the bank account as €3,268.

You are required to:

- Show Ryan's adjusted bank account.
- Prepare a bank reconciliation statement as at 30 June 20-6.

Q2 **On 28 February 20-9 the bank account of Mark Delaney's cash book showed a debit balance of €5,100. His bank statement, however, showed a balance in the bank of €5,484. On examination of the cash book and bank statement the following discrepancies were revealed.**

(a) Cheques issued by Delaney amounting to €3,780 had not been presented for payment.
(b) A cheque issued by Delaney for €888 was entered on the incorrect side of the cash book.
(c) A cheque received for €2,460 and lodged by Delaney had been dishonoured by the bank.
(d) Interest received, €1,200, bank charges of €240 and a credit transfer received, €1,920, had not been entered in the cash book.
(e) A cheque for €540 lodged by Mary Delaney had been entered in error by the bank to the credit of Mark Delaney's account.
(f) Lodgements amounting to €480 had not been credited by the bank.
(g) Delaney had given his secretary cash sales of €2,100 to lodge to his business bank account, but when lodged his private bank account number was entered on the lodgement slip.

You are required to:

- Show Delaney's adjusted bank account.
- Prepare a bank reconciliation statement as at 28 February 20-9.

Exam Tips

- Read the question carefully when comparing the bank statement and the business bank account.
- Mark off items common to both.
- Ensure all unmarked items in the statement are entered in the corrected bank account.
- Ensure all unmarked items in the business bank account are entered in the bank reconciliation statement.
- When completed, the balance on the adjusted bank account and the bank reconciliation statement should be the same.

4 Depreciation and Revaluation of Fixed Assets

Objectives

On completion students should be able to:

For depreciation

- Define depreciation;
- Explain the causes of depreciation;
- Understand how depreciation is estimated;
- Explain and illustrate scrap value;
- Explain and illustrate both methods of depreciation – straight line and reducing balance;
- Prepare the relevant accounts necessary for depreciation account questions;
- Show the relevant extracts from the profit and loss account and balance sheet for depreciation;
- Understand why depreciation is charged as an expense in the accounts.

For revaluation

- Understand why it is necessary to revalue assets and why it is incorporated into the accounts;
- Prepare the relevant accounts necessary;
- Show the relevant extracts from the profit and loss account and balance sheet for revaluation.

Part A – Depreciation of Fixed Assets

What is depreciation?

Depreciation of a fixed asset is the measure of the loss in value of that asset over its useful economic life. The main causes of depreciation can be summarised as:

1. Natural usage (wear and tear)
2. Item being replaced by newer models (obsolescence)
3. End of its useful economic life – for example, extraction from a mine
4. Passage of time – for example, lease on a property.

Why do businesses depreciate fixed assets?

If depreciation is not charged, profits will be overstated and the balance sheet will not show the true value of the assets.

How is depreciation estimated?

The annual depreciation charge takes **four** factors into account:

- the cost of the asset
- the estimated economic life of the asset
- the estimated residual or scrap value of the asset
- the selection of an appropriate method of depreciation.

4

Methods of depreciation

There are **two** main methods of calculating depreciation:

1. **Straight line (or per-cost basis):** This method reduces the value of the asset by the **same amount each year**. It allocates the depreciation cost equally to each year over the estimated useful economic life of the asset. This means that the charge to the profit and loss account will be the same for each year.
2. **Reducing balance (written-down method):** This method reduces the value of the asset by a **smaller amount each year**. The amount of the depreciation decreases as the value of the asset drops.

Since the purchase of a fixed asset is classified as a capital expense, it cannot be entered as an expense in the profit and loss account all in one year. This is because the benefit of the asset is expected to last in the business for more than one financial year. Consequently, the cost of the asset is allowed to be written off against the business's profits over its useful economic life. The depreciation cost is treated as an expense in the business's profit and loss account with the net book value shown in the business's balance sheet.

Each of the above methods of depreciation is what is known as an **accounting base**. The one chosen by the business is said to be the business's **accounting policy** on depreciation.

Example

A simple distinction between the two methods can be illustrated as follows:

> Company A purchased a delivery van for €25,000 and its depreciation policy is to charge depreciation at the rate of 10% per annum using the straight line method.
>
> Company B purchased a delivery van for €25,000 and its depreciation policy is to charge depreciation at the rate of 10% per annum using the reducing balance method.

Calculate the depreciation charged by each company for the first **four** years of the delivery van's life, showing the net book value of the van at the end of year four in each case.

Solution

	Company A	Company B
Year 1	25,000 x 10% = **2,500**	25,000 x 10% = **2,500**
Year 2	25,000 x 10% = **2,500**	First we must subtract 2,500 25,000 - 2,500 = 22,500 22,500 x 10% = **2,250**
Year 3	25,000 x 10% = **2,500**	Again we must first subtract 2,250 22,500 - 2,250 = 20,250 20,250 x 10% = **2,025**
Year 4	25,000 x 10% = **2,500**	Again we must first subtract 2,025 20,250 - 2,025 = 18,225 18,225 x 10% = **1,823**
Total depreciation charged	Year 1: 2,500 Year 2: 2,500 Year 3: 2,500 Year 4: 2,500 Total: **€10,000**	Year 1: 2,500 Year 2: 2,250 Year 3: 2,025 Year 4: 1,823 Total: **€8,598**
Net book value Year 4	25,000 - 10,000 = **€15,000**	25,000 - 8,598 = **€16,402**

Scrap value

Sometimes, at the end of its useful economic life, an asset may have what is known as a residual value or scrap value. If this is the case then depreciation only takes place from the cost price down to this residual value.

Example

Darby Ltd purchased a new piece of machinery costing €12,000 which has a useful economic life of five years, after which time it will be valued at €2,000.

This means the asset will drop in value by €10,000 over its useful economic life and not the full €12,000.

Depreciation will therefore be:

Cost (€12,000) - Scrap value (€2,000) = €10,000

€10,000 / 5 years = €2,000 per annum

NOTE

Remember that the maximum amount that an asset can be depreciated by is its **cost price**.

Example

Vaughan Ltd purchased a new bus costing €75,000 and its policy is to depreciate its vehicles at a rate of 20% of cost per annum. The bus was purchased on 1/7/20-1. Show the depreciation charges for the years 20-1 to 20-7 inclusive.

Solution

Cost of vehicle €75,000
Depreciation rate 20% = €15,000 per annum

Year	Depreciation charge
20-1	(6 months) €7,500
20-2	€15,000
20-3	€15,000
20-4	€15,000
20-5	€15,000
20-6	€7,500
20-7	Nil

NOTE

Even though the company has the vehicle for a full year in 20-6, it can only charge €7,500 (or six months) as the asset will by then be fully depreciated and have a net book value of nil. Following this there also can be no depreciation charged on this asset in 20-7.

The accounts

The accounts and statements affected by depreciation are:

- the asset account
- the provision for depreciation account
- the disposal account
- the profit and loss account extract
- the balance sheet extract.

The accounts required will look as follows:

Dr. **Asset Account** **Cr.**

Date	Details	€	Date	Details	€
Year 1	Balance	xx	Year 1	Disposal of asset (if any)	xx
	New assets	xx		Closing balance Year 1	xx
		xx			xx
Year 2	Balance	xx			

Dr. **Provision for Depreciation Account** **Cr.**

Date	Details	€	Date	Details	€
Year 1	Total depreciation to date on asset sold	xxx	Year 1	Balance	xxx
	Balance	xxx		Depreciation charge	xxx
		xxx			xxx
			Year 2	Balance	

Dr. **Disposal Account** **Cr.**

Date	Details	€	Date	Details	€
	Cost price of asset sold	xx		Depreciation to date on the asset sold	xx
	Profit on sale (if any)	xx		All proceeds from sale	xx
				Loss on sale (if any)	xx
		xx			xx

Profit and Loss Account (extract)

	€
Expenses	
Depreciation of assets	xxxx

Balance Sheet (extract)

	Cost €	Depreciation €	Net Book Value €
Fixed assets			
Asset	xxxx	xxxx	xxxx

4

Sample Ordinary Level question

The following details were taken from the books of Fast Haulage Ltd:

1/1/-2	Lorries at cost, €300,000
1/1/-2	Provision for depreciation account balance, €45,000
1/6/-2	Purchased a new lorry for €60,000
31/12/-2	The depreciation charge for 20-2 was to be €25,000
1/7/-3	Sold for €12,000 a lorry which had cost €50,000 Depreciation to date on this vehicle was €30,000
31/12/-3	Depreciation for the year was to be 10% of the value of lorries at 31/12/20-3

4

You are required to show:

- the lorry account for the years ending 31/12/20-2 and 20-3
- the provision for depreciation account for the years ending 20-2 and 20-3
- the disposal account for the year ended 31/12/20-3.

Solution

Dr. **The Lorry Account** **Cr.**

Date	Details	€	Date	Details	€
1/1/-2	Balance	300,000	31/12/-2	Balance	360,000
1/6/-2	Bank	60,000			
		360,000			360,000
1/1/-3	Balance	360,000	1/7/-3	Disposal a/c	50,000
			31/12/-3	Balance	310,000
		360,000			360,000
1/1/-4	Balance	310,000			

Dr. **The Provision for Depreciation Account** **Cr.**

Date	Details	€	Date	Details	€
			1/1/-2	Balance	45,000
31/12/-2	Balance	70,000	31/12/-2	Profit and loss a/c	25,000
		70,000			70,000
1/7/-3	Disposal a/c	30,000	1/1/-3	Balance	70,000
31/12/-3	Balance	71,000	31/12/-3	Profit and loss a/c	31,000
		101,000			101,000
			1/1/-4	Balance	71,000

Dr. **Disposal Account** **Cr.**

Date	Details	€	Date	Details	€
1/7/-3	Lorry a/c	50,000	1/7/-3	Depreciation	30,000
			1/7/-3	Bank	12,000
			1/7/-3	Profit and loss a/c (loss)	8,000
		50,000			50,000

Sample Higher Level question (straight line method)

Rigney's Coach Company prepares its final accounts on 31 December each year. The company's policy is to depreciate its vehicles at the rate of 20% of cost per annum, calculated from the date of purchase to the date of sale, and to accumulate this depreciation in a provision for depreciation account.

On 1 January 20-7, Rigney's Coach Company owned the following vehicles:

- No. 1, purchased on 01/01/-4 for €80,000
- No. 2, purchased on 01/10/-5 for €100,000
- No. 3, purchased on 01/01/-6 for €120,000

On 1 July 20-7 vehicle no. 1 was traded in for a new vehicle costing €132,000. The trade-in allowance was €24,000. It should be noted that vehicle no. 1 had a DVD unit installed on 1 January 20-5 costing €32,000. This DVD unit should be depreciated at the rate of 30% for the first two years and thereafter at the same rate as vehicle no. 1.

On 1 May 20-8 vehicle no. 3 was involved in an accident and traded in for a new vehicle costing €144,000. Rigney's Coach Company received compensation from the insurance company to the value of €40,000 and the cheque paid for the new vehicle was €122,000.

You are required to show with workings for each of the two years 20-7 and 20-8:

- the vehicles account
- the provision for depreciation account
- the disposal account.

Solution

Step 1

Construct a table for calculations:

- Place years across the top starting with the earliest year.
- Place the vehicles down the side (usually 1-5) with a row for the extra asset or adjustment, in this case the DVD unit.

Vehicle	20-4	20-5	20-6	20-7	20-8	Total
No. 1 €80,000						
DVD unit (X) €32,000						
No. 2 €100,000						
No. 3 €120,000						
No. 4 €132,000						
No. 5 €144,000						

4

4

Step 2

Read the question carefully and place a line in any box where the asset did not exist in the business. Insert a small number to indicate the number of months the vehicle was owned in an incomplete year.

Vehicle	20-4	20-5	20-6	20-7	20-8	Total
No. 1 €80,000				{6}	———	
DVD unit (X) €32,000	———			{6}	———	
No. 2 €100,000	———	{3}				
No. 3 €120,000	———	———			{4}	
No. 4 €132,000	———	———	———	{6}		
No. 5 €144,000	———	———	———	———	{8}	

The small numbers inside the brackets indicate that there is less than a full year's depreciation to be charged in these years. The blank boxes will have a full year's depreciation.

Step 3

Fill in the depreciation figures in the boxes.

Vehicle	20-4	20-5	20-6	Total Dpr pre-20-7	20-7	20-8	Total
No. 1 €80,000	16,000	16,000	16,000	**48,000**	{6} 8,000	———	56,000
DVD unit (X) €32,000	———	9,600	9,600	**19,200**	{6} 3,200	———	22,400
No. 2 €100,000	———	{3} 5,000	20,000	**25,000**	20,000	20,000	
No. 3 €120,000	———	———	24,000	**24,000**	24,000	{4} 8,000	56,000
No. 4 €132,000	———	———	———	———	{6} 13,200	26,400	
No. 5 €144,000	———	———	———	———	———	{8} 19,200	
Totals				116,200	68,400	73,600	
				Opening depreciation	P & L charge	P & L charge	

Workings

No. 1	80,000 x 20% = 16,000	6 months = 8,000
No. 2	100,000 x 20% = 20,000	3 months = 5,000
No. 3	120,000 x 20% = 24,000	4 months = 8,000
No. 4	132,000 x 20% = 26,400	6 months = 13,200
No. 5	144,000 x 20% = 28,800	8 months = 19,200
X	32,000 x 30% = 9,600	$32,000 \times 20\% \times \frac{6}{12} = 3,200$

Step 4

Draw up the accounts using the figures from the tables you have constructed.

Dr. **Vehicles Account** Cr.

Date	Details	€	Date	Details	€
1 Jan 20-7	Balance (1 + 2 + 3 + X)	332,000	1 July 20-7	Disposal (1 + X) a/c	112,000
1 July 20-7	Bank (4)	132,000	31 July 20-7	Balance	352,000
		464,000			464,000
1 Jan 20-8	Balance	352,000	1 May 20-8	Disposal (3) a/c	120,000
1 May 20-8	Bank (5)	144,000	31 Dec 20-8	Balance	376,000
		496,000			496,000
1 Jan 20-9	Balance	376,000			

4

Dr. **Provision for Depreciation Account** Cr.

Date	Details	€	Date	Details	€
1 July 20-7	Disposal (1 + X) a/c	78,400	1 Jan 20-7	Balance	116,200
31 Dec 20-7	Balance	106,200	31 Dec 20-7	Profit and loss a/c	68,400
		184,600			184,600
1 May 20-8	Disposal (3) a/c	56,000	1 Jan 20-8	Balance	106,200
31 Dec 20-8	Balance	123,800	31 Dec 20-8	Profit and loss a/c	73,600
		179,800			179,800
			1 Jan 20-9	Balance	123,800

Dr. **Disposal Account** Cr.

Date	Details	€	Date	Details	€
1 July 20-7	Vehicles a/c	112,000	1 July 20-7	Depreciation a/c	78,400
			1 July 20-7	Trade-in allowance	24,000
			31 Dec 20-7	Profit and loss a/c (loss)	9,600
		112,000			112,000
1 May 20-8	Vehicles a/c	120,000	1 May 20-8	Depreciation a/c	56,000
			1 May 20-8	Bank a/c (insurance)	40,000
			1 May 20-8	Trade-in allowance	22,000
			31 Dec 20-8	Profit and loss a/c (loss)	2,000
		120,000			120,000

Sample Higher Level question (reducing balance method)

Kelleher Airport Transport Links Ltd prepares its final accounts on 31 December each year. The company's policy is to depreciate its vehicles at the rate of 10% on a reducing balance basis, calculated from the date of purchase to the date of sale, and to accumulate this depreciation in a provision for depreciation account.

On 1/1/20-8, Kelleher Airport Transports Links Ltd owned the following vehicles:

- No. 1, purchased on 01/01/-5 for €90,000
- No. 2, purchased on 01/7/-6 for €120,000
- No. 3, purchased on 01/08/-7 for €140,000

On 1 July 20-8 vehicle no. 1 was traded in for a new vehicle costing €180,000. The trade-in allowance was €64,000. It should be noted that vehicle no. 1 had a coffee machine installed on 1 January 20-6 costing €12,000. This unit should be depreciated at the rate of 20% for the first year and thereafter at the same rate as vehicle no. 1.

On 30 April 20-9 vehicle no. 2 was involved in an accident and traded in for a new vehicle costing €220,000. Kelleher Airport Transport Links received compensation from the insurance company to the value of €66,000, and the cheque paid for the new vehicle was €197,000.

4

You are required to show with workings for each of the two years 20-8 and 20-9:

- the vehicles account
- the provision for depreciation account
- the disposal account.

Solution

Step 1
Construct a table for calculations.

Steps 2 and 3
Read the question carefully and place a line in any box where the asset did not exist in the business. Insert a small number to indicate the number of months the vehicle was owned in an incomplete year.

Fill in the depreciation figures in the boxes.

Vehicle	20-5	20-6	20-7	Total Dpr pre-20-8	20-8	20-9	Total
No. 1 €90,000	9,000	8,100	7,290	**24,390**	{6} 3,281	______	27,671
Coffee machine (X) €12,000	______	2,400	960	**3,360**	{6} 432	______	3,792
No. 2 €120,000	______	{6} 6,000	11,400	**17,400**	10,260	{4} 3,078	30,738
No. 3 €140,000	______	______	{5} 5,833	**5,833**	13,417	12,075	
No. 4 €180,000	______	______	______	______	{6} 9,000	17,100	
No. 5 €220,000	______	______	______	______	______	{8} 14,667	
Totals				**50,983**	36,390	46,920	
				Opening depreciation	P & L charge	P & L charge	

Workings for this question are a bit more complicated as it involves the reducing balance method of depreciation. However, it is only the calculations that change; the placing of items in the accounts is exactly the same as for the straight line method.

Workings

Year	Vehicle 1	Vehicle 2	Vehicle 3	Vehicle 4	Vehicle 5	X
20-5	90,000 x 10% = 9,000	———	———	———	———	———
20-6	81,000 x 10% = 8,100	120,000 x 10% x $\frac{6}{12}$ = 6,000	———	———	———	12,000 x 20% = 2,400
20-7	72,900 x 10% = 7,290	114,000 x 10% = 11,400	140,000 x 10% x $\frac{5}{12}$ = 5,833	———	———	9,600 x 10% = 960
20-8	65,610 x 10% x $\frac{6}{12}$ = 3,281	102,600 x 10% = 10,260	134,167 x 10% = 13,417	180,000 x 10% x $\frac{6}{12}$ = 9,000	———	8,640 x 10% x $\frac{6}{12}$ = 432
20-9	———	92,340 x 10% x $\frac{4}{12}$ = 3,078	120,750 x 10% = 12,075	171,000 x 10% = 17,100	220,000 x 10% x $\frac{8}{12}$ = 14,667	———

Dr. **Vehicles Account** **Cr.**

Date	Details	€	Date	Details	€
1 Jan 20-8	Balance (1 + 2 + 3 + X)	362,000	1 July 20-8	Disposal (1 + X) a/c	102,000
1 July 20-8	Bank (4)	180,000	31 July 20-8	Balance	440,000
		542,000			542,000
1 Jan 20-9	Balance	440,000	30 Apr 20-9	Disposal (2) a/c	120,000
30 Apr 20-9	Bank (5)	220,000	31 Dec 20-9	Balance	540,000
		660,000			660,000
1 Jan 20-0	Balance	540,000			

Dr. **Provision for Depreciation Account** **Cr.**

Date	Details	€	Date	Details	€
1 July 20-8	Disposal (1 + X) a/c	31,463	1 Jan 20-8	Balance	50,983
31 Dec 20-8	Balance	55,910	31 Dec 20-8	Profit and loss a/c	36,390
		87,373			87,373
1 Apr 20-9	Disposal (3) a/c	30,738	1 Jan 20-9	Balance	55,910
31 Dec 20-9	Balance	72,092	31 Dec 20-9	Profit and loss a/c	46,920
		102,830			102,830
			1 Jan 20-0	Balance	72,092

4

Dr. **Disposal Account** **Cr.**

Date	Details	€	Date	Details	€
1 July 20-8	Vehicles a/c	102,000	1 July 20-8	Depreciation a/c	31,463
			1 July 20-8	Trade-in allowance	64,000
			31 Dec 20-8	Profit and loss a/c (loss)	6,537
		102,000			102,000
1 Apr 20-9	Vehicles a/c	120,000	1 May 20-9	Depreciation a/c	30,738
			1 May 20-9	Bank a/c (insurance)	66,000
			1 May 20-9	Trade-in allowance	23,000
			31 Dec 20-9	Profit and loss a/c (loss)	262
		120,000			120,000

4

Practice Questions

Q1 **X Ltd purchased a delivery van for €15,000 and its depreciation policy is to charge depreciation at the rate of 15% per annum using the straight line method.**

Y Ltd purchased a delivery van for €15,000 and its depreciation policy is to charge depreciation at the rate of 15% per annum using the reducing balance method.

Calculate the depreciation charged by each company for the first three years of the delivery van's life, showing the net book value of the van at the end of Year 3 in each case.

Calculations to be made to the nearest euro.

Q2 **Lite Ltd purchased furniture and fittings for €9,000 and its depreciation policy is to charge depreciation at the rate of 20% per annum using the straight line method.**

High Ltd purchased furniture and fittings for €9,000 and its depreciation policy is to charge depreciation at the rate of 20% per annum using the reducing balance method.

Calculate the depreciation charged by each company for the first four years of the furniture's life, showing the net book value of the furniture and fittings at the end of Year 4 in each case.

Calculations to be made to the nearest euro.

Q3 **Motion Ltd purchased a new vehicle for €110,000 with a useful economic life of nine years, at which time it will have a scrap value of €20,000. Calculate the depreciation charge per annum for this asset.**

Q4 **Tools Ltd purchased a new machine for €45,000 with a useful economic life of eight years, at which time it will have a scrap value of €5,000. Calculate the depreciation charge per annum for this asset.**

Q5 **Cleary Ltd purchased a computer stock system for €74,000 with a useful economic life of eight years, at which time it will have a scrap value of €2,000. Calculate the depreciation charge per annum for this asset.**

Q6 French Ltd purchased a photocopier for €27,000 with a useful economic life of six years, at which time it will have a scrap value of €3,000. Calculate the depreciation charge per annum for this asset.

Q7 Codd Ltd purchased a lorry for €58,000 with a useful economic life of ten years, at which time it will have a scrap value of €5,000. Calculate the depreciation charge per annum for this asset.

Q8 Moore Plc purchased a new van costing €96,000 and its depreciation policy is to depreciate its vehicles at a rate of 25% per annum. The van was purchased on 1 January 20-9. Show the depreciation charges for the years 20-9 to 20-4 inclusive.

Q9 Nolan Plc purchased a computer system €25,000 and its depreciation policy is to depreciate its equipment at a rate of 15% per annum. The computer system was purchased on 1 January 20-0. Show the depreciation charges for the years 20-0 to 20-7 inclusive.

Exercises – Ordinary Level

Q1 **The following details were taken from the books of Brew Enterprises Ltd:**

1/1/20-0	Vans at cost were €125,000.
1/4/20-0	Purchased a new van costing €35,000.
31/12/20-0	The depreciation charge for 20-0 was to be €13,000.
1/7/20-1	Purchased a new van costing €45,000.
31/12/20-1	The depreciation charge for 20-1 was to be €15,000.
1/9/20-2	Purchased a new van costing €55,000.
31/12/-2	The depreciation charge for the year was to be €17,000.

You are required to show:

- the van account for the years ending 31/12/20-0, 20-1 and 20-2
- the provision for depreciation account for the years ending 20-0, 20-1, 20-2.

Q2 **The following details were taken from the books of N. Cully Transport Ltd:**

1/1/20-9	Lorries at cost were €95,000.
1/1/20-9	The balance in the provision for depreciation account was €10,000.
1/6/20-9	Bought a new lorry costing €35,000.
31/12/20-9	The depreciation charged against profits was €6,000.
1/5/20-0	Bought a new lorry costing €60,000.
31/12/20-0	The depreciation charged against profits was €9,000.
1/8/20-1	Bought a new lorry costing €75,000.
31/12/20-1	The depreciation charged against profits was €16,000.

You are required to show:

- the lorry account for the years ending 20-9, 20-0, 20-1
- the provision for depreciation account for the years ending 20-9, 20-0 and 20-1.

Q3 The following details were taken from the books of Mark O'Neill Logistics Ltd:

1/1/20-9	The cost of trucks owned was €160,000.
1/1/20-9	The balance in the accumulated depreciation account was €16,000.
1/1/20-9	O'Neill purchased a new truck costing €60,000.
31/12/20-9	The charge for depreciation on trucks for 20-9 was to be €24,000.
1/7/20-0	Sold for €15,000 a truck which had cost €30,000 and which had a book value on the date of sale of €14,000.
31/12/20-0	The charge for depreciation on trucks for 20-0 was to be €23,000.

You are required to show:

- the trucks account for the years ending 20-9 and 20-0
- the provision for depreciation account for the years ending 20-9 and 20-0
- the disposal account for 20-0.

4

Q4 The following details were taken from the books of Eoin Walsh Couriers Ltd:

1/1/20-4	The balance on the vehicles account was €105,000.
1/1/20-4	The balance on the provision for depreciation account was €35,000.
1/1/20-4	Walsh purchased a new vehicle at a cost of €36,000.
31/12/20-4	The charge for depreciation against profits was €15,000.
1/8/20-5	Sold for €19,000 a vehicle which cost €40,000 and on which depreciation had been accumulated to date of €18,000.
31/12/20-5	Depreciation is to be 10% of the cost of vehicles held on 31/12/20-5.

You are required to show:

- the vehicles account for the years ending 20-4 and 20-5
- the provision for depreciation account for the years ending 20-4 and 20-5
- the disposal account for 20-5.

Q5 The following details were taken from the books of Glass Tours Plc:

1/1/20-3	The balance on the bus account was €345,000.
1/1/20-3	The balance in the provision for depreciation account was €69,000.
1/7/20-3	Purchased a new bus costing €96,000.
31/12/20-3	The depreciation charge for the year on buses was to be €35,000.
1/6/20-4	Sold for €25,000 a bus which had originally cost €46,000. The book value of this bus was €26,000.
31/12/20-4	Depreciation for the year was to be based on the cost price of buses held on 31/12/20-4, assuming they have a useful economic life of eight years and a scrap value of €15,000.

You are required to show:

- the bus account for the years ending 20-3 and 20-4
- the provision for depreciation account for the years ending 20-3 and 20-4
- the disposal account for 20-4
- the relevant extracts for the profit and loss account for 20-4 together with a balance sheet extract as at 31/12/20-4.

Exercises – Higher Level

4

Q1 Roche Freight Ltd prepares its final accounts to 31 December each year. The company's policy is to depreciate its vehicles at the rate of 10% of cost per annum, calculated from the date of purchase to the date of disposal, and to accumulate this depreciation in a provision for depreciation account.

On 1 January 20-5, Roche Freight owned the following vehicles:

- No. 1, purchased on 1/1/-2 for €50,000
- No. 2, purchased on 1/1/-3 for €60,000
- No. 3, purchased on 1/7/-3 for €70,000

On 1 July 20-5 vehicle no. 1 was traded in for a new vehicle costing €80,000. The company received a trade-in allowance of €26,000.

On 1 October 20-6 vehicle no. 2 was involved in an accident. The company received compensation to the value of €24,000. The vehicle was subsequently traded in for a new vehicle costing €90,000. The company received a trade-in allowance of €16,000.

You are required to prepare with workings, for each of the two years 20-5 and 200-6:

- the vehicles account
- the provision for depreciation account
- the disposal account.

Q2 Duck Transport prepares its final accounts to 31 December each year. The company's policy is to depreciate its vehicles at the rate of 20% of cost per annum, calculated from the date of purchase to the date of disposal, and to accumulate this depreciation in a provision for depreciation account.

On 1 January 20-8, Duck Transport owned the following vehicles:

- No. 1, purchased on 1/4/-5 for €45,000
- No. 2, purchased on 1/10/-6 for €60,000
- No. 3, purchased on 1/1/-7 for €72,000

On 1 April 20-8 vehicle no. 2 was traded in for a new vehicle costing €80,000. The company received a trade allowance of €43,000. Vehicle no. 2 had a refrigeration unit fitted on 1 January 20-7 which cost €12,000. This was to be depreciated at the rate of 25% for the first year and thereafter at 20% of cost per annum.

On 1 September 20-9 vehicle no. 3 was involved in an accident. The company received compensation to the value of €20,000. The vehicle was subsequently traded in for a new vehicle costing €84,000. The cheque paid for the new vehicle was €60,000.

You are required to prepare, with workings, for each of the two years 20-8 and 20-9:

- the vehicles account
- the provision for depreciation account
- the disposal account.

Q3 E. Murphy Couriers prepares its final accounts to 31 December each year. The company's policy is to depreciate its vehicles at the rate of 15% of cost per annum, calculated from the date of purchase to the date of sale, and to accumulate this depreciation in a provision for depreciation account.

On 1 January 20-2, E. Murphy Couriers owned the following vehicles:

- No. 1, purchased on 01/01/20-7 for €46,000
- No. 2, purchased on 01/10/20-9 for €64,000
- No. 3, purchased on 01/01/20-1 for €78,000

On 1 July 20-2 vehicle no. 2 was traded in for a new vehicle costing €84,000. The trade-in allowance was €34,000. It should be noted that vehicle no. 2 had a tachograph unit installed on 1 January 20-0 costing €22,000. This unit should be depreciated at the rate of 30% for the first year and thereafter at the same rate as vehicle no. 2.

On 1 October 20-3 vehicle no. 1 was involved in an accident and traded in for new a vehicle costing €90,000. E. Murphy Couriers received compensation from the insurance company to the value of €2,000 and the cheque paid for the new vehicle was €82,000.

You are required to show, with workings, for each of the two years 20-2 and 20-3:

- the vehicles account
- the provision for depreciation account
- the disposal account.

Q4 Acheson Haulage prepares its final accounts to 31 December each year. The company's policy is to depreciate its vehicles at the rate of 12.5% of cost per annum, calculated from the date of purchase to the date of sale, and to accumulate this depreciation in a provision for depreciation account.

On 1 January 20-0, Acheson Haulage owned the following vehicles:

- No. 1, purchased on 01/01/20-7 for €48,000
- No. 2, purchased on 01/09/20-8 for €64,000
- No. 3, purchased on 01/04/20-9 for €72,000

On 1 July 20-0 vehicle no. 3 was crashed and was traded in for a new vehicle costing €108,000. The company received compensation to the value of €35,000 and paid €56,000 for the new vehicle, the remainder being a trade-in allowance from a scrap dealer.

On 1 June 20-1 vehicle no. 2 was traded in for a new truck costing €96,000. The trade-in allowance was €33,000. It should be noted that vehicle no. 2 had a cooling unit fitted six months after it was first purchased. This unit cost €12,000. This cooling unit should be depreciated at the rate of 20% for the first 16 months and then as per vehicle no. 2.

You are required to show, with workings (to the nearest euro), for each of the two years 20-0 and 20-1:

- the vehicles account
- the provision for depreciation account
- the disposal account.

Q5 Guilmartin Buses prepares its final accounts to 31 December each year. The company's policy is to depreciate its vehicles at the rate of 10% per annum on a reducing balance basis, calculated from the date of purchase to the date of sale, and to accumulate this depreciation in a provision for depreciation account.

On 1 January 20-0, Guilmartin Buses owned the following vehicles:

- No. 1, purchased on 01/07/20-7 for €35,000
- No. 2, purchased on 01/09/20-8 for €45,000
- No. 3, purchased on 01/01/20-9 for €60,000

On 1 January 20-0 vehicle no. 2 was traded in for a new vehicle costing €72.000. The trade-in allowance was €44,000. It should be noted that vehicle no. 2 had a DVD unit installed on 1 January 20-9 costing €14,000. This DVD unit should be depreciated at the rate of 20% for the first year and thereafter at the same rate as vehicle no. 2.

On 1 August 20-1 vehicle no. 1 was involved in an accident and traded in for new a vehicle costing €78,000. Guilmartin Buses received compensation from the insurance company to the value of €23,000, and the cheque paid for the new vehicle was €56,000.

You are required to show, with workings (to the nearest euro), for each of the two years 20-0 and 20-1:

- the vehicles account
- the provision for depreciation account
- the disposal account.

Q6 Dimensions Ltd, a clothing manufacturer, owned the following machines on 1 January 20-2:

- Machine No. 123456H purchased on 7th July 20-9 for €70,652
- Machine No. 134568F purchased on 9th February 20-0 for €78,261
- Machine No. 158963E purchased on 17th August 20-1 for €104,348

4

You are provided with the following information:

It is the company's policy to depreciate its machinery on a straight line basis over ten years. Scrap value is estimated at 8% of the original cost of the machine. A full year's depreciation is charged in the year of acquisition and none in the year of disposal.

During the year ended 31 December 20-2 the following events occurred:

On 18 March, Machine 123456H was ruined by a fault which completely destroyed the motor. The insurance claim yielded €36,700 and €900 was received from the sale of the machine to a scrap dealer.

On 10 July, Machine No. 45690P was purchased for €165,000 in part exchange for Machine No. 134568F. The trade-in value of this machine was €32,400. The balance of the purchase price was paid immediately. It cost €5,000 to have the machine delivered and a further €435 to have it installed.

The following expenditure was also incurred during the year on Machine No. 158963E:

Servicing of the machine	€4,345
Replacement parts	€2,340
Insurance	€2,400
Costs of altering the motor to increase output levels	€5,850

You are required to show, with workings, the following accounts for the year ended 31/12/-2:

- the machinery account
- the provision for depreciation account
- the disposal account.

Theory

Q1 Define 'depreciation'.

Q2 Why does a company charge depreciation in calculating profit?

Q3 Name three causes of depreciation.

Q4 What factors should be taken into account in arriving at the annual depreciation charge?

Q5 Explain what is meant by the term 'useful economic life'.

Q6 What is meant by 'scrap value'? Illustrate your answer with an example.

Q7 Explain the factors to be considered when choosing a method of depreciation.

Q8 Distinguish between capital and revenue expenditure.

Part B – Revaluation of Fixed Assets

The revaluation of fixed assets is the process of entering the value of a company's assets in the accounts at their true market value. During periods of price increases, particularly on the open market when property prices are rising rapidly, the market value of an asset is likely to be more than what the asset would have cost the business initially. In order that the accounts of the business show a true and fair view, this market value should be incorporated into the accounts of the business.

Revaluation shows the asset at its new value, which can be useful because:

- it provides useful information to the user of accounts;
- it enables performance ratios to be calculated more satisfactorily.

4

Assets once revalued must then be depreciated based on the revalued amount. Revaluation brings increased depreciation and lower profits on disposal.

Freehold land does not normally require a provision for depreciation, unless it is subject to depletion – for example, the extraction of copper from the land if it is a mine.

It is important to remember that **land** is normally not depreciated.

The accounts

The accounts required for revaluation of fixed assets are:

- the asset account
- the provision for depreciation account
- the disposal account
- the revaluation reserve account
- the revenue reserve account
- relevant extracts from the profit and loss account and/or balance sheet.

Account templates

Dr. The Asset Account (always cost price or revalued price) Cr.

Date	Details	€	Date	Details	€
Year 1	Opening balance	xxxx	Year 1	Disposal (if any)	xxxx
Year 1	Increase if revaluation takes place	xxxx	Year 1	Closing balance	xxxx
Year 1	Any new assets or extensions at cost price	xxxx			
		xxxxx			xxxxx
Year 2	Opening balance	xxxx			

Dr. **Provision for Depreciation Account** Cr.

Date	Details	€	Date	Details	€
Year 1	Transfer balance to revaluation a/c if revaluation takes place	xxxx	Year 1	Opening balance	xxxx
Year 1	Transfer depreciation on asset sold to disposal a/c		Year 1	Depreciation charge for year	xxxx
Year 1	Closing balance				
		xxxx			xxxxx
			Year 2	Opening balance	xxxx

Dr. **Disposal Account** Cr.

Date	Details	€	Date	Details	€
Year 1	Cost of or revaluation value of any asset sold	xxxx	Year 1	Depreciation to date on any asset sold	xxxx
Year 1	Profit on sale if any	xxxx	Year 1	Any proceeds from the sale of fixed assets	xxxx
			Year 1	Loss on sale if any	xxxx
		xxxxx			xxxxx

Dr. **Revaluation Reserve Account** Cr.

Date	Details	€	Date	Details	€
Year 1	Revaluation to date on asset disposed of to revenue reserve a/c	xxxx	Year 1	Increase in value of asset from asset account	xxxx
Year 1	Closing balance	xxxx	Year 1	Depreciation to date on the asset revalued	xxxx
		xxxxx			xxxxx
			Year 2	Opening balance	xxxx

Dr. **Revenue Reserve Account** Cr.

Date	Details	€	Date	Details	€
			Year 1	Revaluation to date on asset disposed of	xxxx

Profit and Loss Account (extracts)

	€	€
Expenses		
Administration		
Loss on sale of assets	xxxx	
***Add* Other income**		
Profit on the sale of fixed assets	xxxx	

Balance Sheet (extract)

	Cost €	Aggregate Depreciation €	Net Book Value €
Fixed assets			
Premises	Cost or revalued price	Depends on date of revaluation	xxxx
Financed by			
Capital and reserves			
Revaluation reserve		xxxx	
Revenue reserve		xxxx	

4

Accounting procedure

- **Debit** the asset account with the increase in valuation.
- **Debit** the provision for depreciation account with the depreciation to date on the asset revalued.
- **Credit** the revaluation reserve account with the two **debits** above.

NOTE

There are two main rules you must remember when revaluing fixed assets:

1. When revaluation takes place you must transfer any depreciation on that revalued asset to the revaluation reserve account from the provision for depreciation account.
2. When the question gives a separate figure for land, land is not depreciated.

The date of revaluation

There is a major difference depending on whether revaluation takes place at the beginning or end of the year. Let us look at this difference.

Example

Company A has premises which cost €200,000 on which there is currently €25,000 depreciation.

Company B has premises which cost €200,000 on which there is currently €25,000 depreciation.

As you can see both companies are in the same position. However, Company A revalues its premises at 300,000 on 1 January 20-0 while Company B revalues its premises on 31 December 20-0. Both companies have a depreciation policy of 2% straight line.

Let us now show the differences in the calculations and the extracts of the profit and loss account and balance sheet.

Company A	Company B
Premises of 200,000 increases to 300,000, an increase of 100,000.	Premises of 200,000 increases to 300,000, an increase of 100,000.
Depreciation 25,000 cleared to revaluation reserve	A year's depreciation must be applied first as revaluation does not happen until the end of the year: 200,000 x 2% = 4,000 Depreciation is now 29,000 and this is cleared to revaluation reserve.
The charge for depreciation must be based on the revalued figure: 300,000 x 2% = 6,000	
Profit and Loss (extract) **Administration expenses** Depreciation of premises: €6,000	**Profit and Loss (extract)** **Administration expenses** Depreciation of premises: €4,000

Company A – Balance Sheet (extracts)

Fixed Assets	Cost €	Agg. Dpr. €	Net Book Value €
Premises	300,000	6,000	294,000

Capital and reserves
Revaluation reserve
100,000 + 25,000 = 125,000

Company B – Balance Sheet (extracts)

Fixed Assets	Cost €	Agg. Dpr. €	Net Book Value €
Premises	300,000	Nil	300,000

Capital and reserves
Revaluation reserve
100,000 + 29,000 = 129,000

So we can see there is a difference in the figures depending on the date of revaluation. The depreciation charge for the year is different, which also means a difference in the balance sheet in both fixed assets and the amount of revaluation reserve.

Ordinary Level questions

These require basic knowledge of where the entries go into the accounts. Few calculations are required – normally one: the charge for depreciation in Year 2.

Sample Ordinary Level question

The following details were taken from the books of Deadwood Plc:

1/1/-2	Premises at cost amounted to €1,500,000.
1/1/-2	The balance in the provision for depreciation account was €456,000.
1/09/-2	Purchased a building for €1,200,000.
1/09/-2	Sold for €900,000 a building which cost €650,000. The book value of this building was €480,000.
31/12/-2	The total depreciation charge for the year was €120,000.
1/1/-3	Revalued buildings at €2,900,000.
1/1/-3	Provide for depreciation at the rate of 2% of the value of the premises at 1/1/-3.

You are required to show:

- the premises account for the two years 20-2 and 20-3
- the provision for depreciation account for the two years 20-2 and 20-3
- the premises disposal account for the year ended 31/12/20-2
- the revaluation reserve account.

Solution

Dr. **Premises Account** **Cr.**

Date	Details	€	Date	Details	€
1/1/-2	Balance	1,500,000	1/9/-2	Disposal a/c	650,000
1/09/-2	Bank	1,200,000	31/12/-2	Balance	2,050,000
		2,700,000			2,700,000
1/1/-3	Balance	2,050,000			
1/1/-3	Revaluation a/c	850,000	31/12/-3	Balance	2,900,000
		2,900,000			2,900,000
1/1/-4	Balance	2,900,000			

4

Dr. **Provision for Depreciation Account** **Cr.**

Date	Details	€	Date	Details	€
1/9/-2	Disposal a/c	170,000	1/1/-2	Balance	456,000
31/12/-2	Balance	406,000	31/12/-2	Profit and loss a/c	120,000
		576,000			576,000
1/1/-3	Revaluation a/c	406,000	1/1/-3	Balance	406,000
31/12/-3	Balance	58,000	31/12/-3	Profit and loss a/c	58,000
		464,000			464,000
			1/1/2-4	Balance	58,000

Dr. **Disposal Account** **Cr.**

Date	Details	€	Date	Details	€
1/9/-2	Premises	650,000	1/9/-2	Depreciation	170,000
31/12/-2	Profit and loss a/c	420,000	1/9/-2	Bank	900,000
		1,070,000			1,070,000

Dr. **Revaluation Reserve Account** **Cr.**

Date	Details	€	Date	Details	€
31/12/-3	Balance	1,256,000	1/1/-3	Premises	850,000
			1/1/-3	Depreciation	406,000
		1,256,000			1,256,000
			1/1/-4	Balance	1,256,000

Higher Level questions

Higher Level Leaving Certificate questions involve the same accounts but the calculations become more difficult.

Always keep track of the changes in each piece of the property/land.

Sample Higher Level question

On 1 January 20-0 Mannion Road Holdings owned property and land which cost €320,000, consisting of land, €100,000, and buildings, €220,000. The company depreciates at the rate of 2% per annum using the straight line method. It is the company's policy to apply a full year's depreciation in the year of acquisition and no depreciation in the year of disposal. The property had been purchased ten years earlier and depreciation had been charged against profits in each of these ten years. (Land is not to be depreciated.)

The following details were taken from the firm's books:

1 Jan 20-0 Revalued property at €540,000, of which €140,000 was attributable to land.

1 Jan 20-1 Sold for €190,000 land which has cost €100,000 but was since revalued.

1 Jan 20-2 Purchased a new building for €320,000 and during the year a new extension was built adjoining these new premises. The company's own employees worked on this extension and their wages amounted to €30,000, while €90,000 was paid to a building contractor.

1 Jan 20-3 Revalued all property by 15%.

1 Jan 20-4 Sold for €619,000 the buildings owned on 1/1/20-0. All remaining buildings were revalued at €550,000.

4

You are required to:

- Prepare the relevant ledger accounts in respect of the above transactions for the years ended 31 December 20-0 to 31 December 20-4 (bank account and profit and loss account **not** required).

Solution

Step 1

Keep track of each individual piece of property.

Year	Original Building	Land	New Buildings	Total
20-0	220,000 to 400,000	100,000 to 140,000		320,000 to 540,000
20-1	400,000	Disposal (140,000)		400,000
20-2	400,000		320,000 + 30,000 + 90,000 = 440,000	840,000
20-3	400,000 + 15% = 460,000		440,000 + 15% = 506,000	966,000
20-4	Disposal (460,000)		506,000 to 550,000 = 44,000	550,000

Step 2

Calculate depreciation charges.

Value of Asset	Entry	Depreciation Charges	
320,000 to 540,000	Opening and closing balance 20-0	(540,000 – 140,000 =	400,000)
		400,000 x 2% =	8,000
400,000	Closing balance 20-1	400,000 x 2% =	8,000
840,000	Closing balance 20-2	840,000 x 2% =	16,800
966,000	Closing balance 20-3	966,000 x 2% =	19,320
550,000	Closing balance 20-4	550,000 x 2% =	11,000

The closing balance figure each year is the amount used to calculate the level of depreciation (except the first year when land has first to be deducted).

Step 3

Prepare the accounts.

Land and Buildings Account

Dr. | Cr.

Date	Details	€	Date	Details	€
1/1/-0	Balance	320,000	31/12/-0	Balance	540,000
1/1/-0	Revaluation a/c	220,000			
		540,000			540,000
1/1/-1	Balance	540,000	1/1/-1	Disposal a/c	140,000
			31/12/-1	Balance	400,000
		540,000			540,000
1/1/-2	Balance	400,000			
	Bank - new building	320,000			
	Bank - wages	30,000			
	Bank - contractor	90,000	31/12/-2	Balance	840,000
		840,000			840,000
1/1/-3	Balance	840,000			
1/1/-3	Revaluation a/c	126,000	31/12/-3	Balance	966,000
		966,000			966,000
1/1/-4	Balance	966,000	1/1/-4	Disposal a/c	460,000
1/1/-4	Revaluation a/c	44,000	31/12/-4	Balance	550,000
		1,010,000			1,010,000
1/1/-5	Balance	550,000			

Now let us look at the **provision for depreciation account**.

The depreciation charge for each of the years is calculated by the percentage of the closing balance in the asset account (except Year 1).

> The opening figure for depreciation is calculated by:
> Cost price of asset (excluding land) x Depreciation rate x Number of years held

Provision for Depreciation Account

Dr. | Cr.

Date	Details	€	Date	Details	€
1/1/-0	Revaluation a/c	44,000	1/1/-0	Balance (W1)	44,000
1/1/-0	Balance	8,000	31/12/-0	Profit and loss a/c	8,000
		52,000			52,000
			1/1/-1	Balance	8,000
31/12/-1	Balance	16,000	31/12/-1	Profit and loss a/c	8,000
		16,000			16,000
			1/1/-2	Balance	16,000
31/12/-2	Balance	32,800	31/12/-2	Profit and loss a/c	16,800
		32,800			32,800
1/1/-3	Revaluation a/c	32,800	1/1/-3	Balance	32,800
31/12/-3	Balance	19,320	1/1/-3	Profit and loss a/c	19,320
		52,120			52,120
1/1/-4	Disposal a/c (W2)	9,200	1/1/-4	Balance (W2)	19,320
1/1/-4	Revaluation a/c (W2)	10,120	31/12/-4	Profit and loss a/c	11,000
31/12/-4	Balance	11,000			
		30,320			30,320
			1/1/-5	Balance	11,000

Workings

W1 320,000 - 100,000 (land) = 220,000 x 2% x 10 years = 44,000

W2 The depreciation balance in the final year needs to be split because one building is sold and the other is revalued.

So the charge of €19,320 needs to be apportioned in proportion to the value of each building. This is easily done because we have kept track of each building. Let's look back at the table above:

Old building	460,000 x 2% =	9,200
New building	506,000 x 2% =	10,120
	Total	€19,320

This split becomes important again when working out the **revenue reserve**.

Dr. **The Revaluation Reserve Account** **Cr.**

Date	Details	€	Date	Details	€
1/1/-1	Revenue reserve a/c	40,000	1/1/-0	Land and buildings	220,000
1/1/-4	Revenue reserve a/c (W1)	308,000	1/1/-0	Depreciation	44,000
			1/1/-3	Land and buildings	126,000
			1/1/-3	Depreciation	32,800
			1/1/-4	Land and buildings	44,000
31/12/-4	Balance	128,920	1/1/-4	Depreciation	10,120
		476,920			476,920
			1/1/-5	Balance	128,920

The amount to be transferred to the revenue reserve account is all the revaluations to date including depreciation on the asset sold (the old building) and can be calculated as follows:

Workings

W1

1st revaluation: 220,000 - amount for land, 40,000 (140,000 - 100,000)	=	180,000
1st revaluation: all depreciation on old building	=	44,000
2nd revaluation old building: 400,000 x 15%	=	60,000
2nd revaluation depreciation: 400,000 x 2% x 3 years	=	24,000
Total	=	308,000

Dr. **Disposal of Land Account** **Cr.**

Date	Details	€	Date	Details	€
1/1/-1	Land and buildings a/c	140,000	1/1/-1	Bank (proceeds)	190,000
31/12/-1	Profit and loss a/c	50,000			
		190,000			190,000

Dr.		Disposal of Buildings Account			Cr.
DEBIT			**CREDIT**		
1/1/-4	Buildings a/c	460,000	1/1/-4	Bank (proceeds)	619,000
31/12/-4	Profit and loss a/c	168,200	1/1/-4	Depreciation	9,200
		628,200			628,200

Dr.		Revenue Reserve Account			Cr.
Date	**Details**	**€**	**Date**	**Details**	**€**
			1/1/-0	Revaluation a/c (land)	40,000
			1/1/-3	Revaluation a/c (buildings)	308,000

4

Practice Questions

In each of the following questions calculate the amount of revaluation reserve and the charge to the provision for depreciation account for the profit and loss for the year.

Q1 **Nelson Ltd owned property to the value of €140,000 on 1/1/20-2. On this date it decided to revalue this property at €200,000. Existing depreciation was €12,000 and the rate of depreciation is 2% per annum.**

Q2 **Colne Ltd owned property to the value of €360,000 on 1/1/20-3. On this date it decided to revalue this property at €410,000. Existing depreciation was €22,000 and the rate of depreciation is 4% per annum.**

Q3 **Beaufort Ltd owned property to the value of €540,000 on 1/1/20-2. On 31/12/20-2 it decided to revalue this property at €650,000. Existing depreciation was €72,000 and the rate of depreciation is 3% per annum.**

Q4 **Jack Ltd owned property to the value of €280,000 on 1/1/20-4. On this date it decided to revalue this property at €300,000. Existing depreciation was €42,000 and the rate of depreciation is 2% per annum.**

Q5 **Rose Ltd owned property to the value of €900,000 on 1/1/20-4. On 31/12/20-4 it decided to revalue this property at €1,200,000. Existing depreciation was €102,000 and the rate of depreciation is 5% per annum.**

Q6 **Pendle Ltd owned property to the value of €780,000 on 1/1/20-5. On this date it decided to revalue this property at €930,000. Existing depreciation was €82,000 and the rate of depreciation is 4% per annum.**

Exercises – Ordinary Level

Q1 **The following details were taken from the books of Cullen Plc:**

1/1/20-3	Premises at cost amounted to €900,000.
1/1/20-3	The balance in the provision for depreciation account was €135,000.
1/05/20-3	Purchased a building for €450,000.
1/05/20-3	Sold for €300,000 a building which cost €150,000. The book value of this building was €120,000.
31/12/20-3	The total depreciation charge for the year was €24,000.
1/1/20-4	Revalued buildings at €1,400,000.
31/12/20-4	Provide for depreciation at the rate of 2% of the value of the premises at 1/1/20-4.

You are required to show:

- the premises account for the two years 20-3 and 20-4
- the provision for depreciation account for the two years 20-3 and 20-4
- the premises disposal account for the year ended 31/12/20-3
- the revaluation reserve account.

Q2 **The following details were taken from the books of Parle Ltd:**

1/1/20-2	Premises at cost amounted to €860,000.
1/1/20-2	The balance in the provision for depreciation account was €135,000.
1/09/20-2	Purchased a building for €430,000.
1/09/20-2	Sold for €350,000 a building which cost €240,000. The book value of this building was €200,000.
31/12/20-2	The total depreciation charge for the year was €96,000.
1/1/20-3	Revalued buildings at €1,200,000.
31/12/20-3	Provide for depreciation at the rate of 4% of the value of the premises at 1/1/20-3.

You are required to show:

- the premises account for the two years 20-2 and 20-3
- the provision for depreciation account for the two years 20-2 and 20-3
- the premises disposal account for the year ended 31/12/20-2
- the revaluation reserve account.

Q3 **The following details were taken from the books of T. Wall Ltd:**

1/1/20-4	Premises at cost amounted to €790,000.
1/1/20-4	The balance in the provision for depreciation account was €234,000.
1/4/20-4	Sold for €230,000 a building which cost €150,000 on which €20,000 depreciation had been charged.
1/9/20-4	Built an extension to the premises which cost €450,000 to complete.
31/12/20-4	The total depreciation charge for the year was €165,000.
1/1/20-5	Revalued buildings at €1,200,000.
31/12/20-5	Provide for depreciation at the rate of 3% of the value of the premises at 1/1/20-5.

You are required to show:

- the premises account for the two years 20-4 and 20-5
- the provision for depreciation account for the two years 20-4 and 20-5
- the premises disposal account for the year ended 31/12/20-4
- the revaluation reserve account.

Q4 **The following details have been taken from the books of Gina Ltd:**

1/1/20-2	Buildings at cost amounted to €500,000.
1/1/20-2	The balance in the provision for depreciation account was €85,000.
1/4/20-2	Purchased buildings for €230,000.
1/4/20-2	Sold for €190,000 a building which cost €100,000. The book value on 1/4/20-2 was €91,000.
31/12/20-2	The total depreciation for the year ended 31/12/20-2 was €16,000.
1/1/20-3	The buildings were revalued at €820,000.
31/12/20-3	Provide for depreciation at the rate of 2% of the value of buildings on 1/1/20-3.

4

You are required to show:

- the buildings account for the two years 20-2 and 20-3
- the provision for depreciation account for the two years 20-2 and 20-3
- the buildings disposal account for the year ended 31/12/20-3
- the revaluation reserve account.

Q5 The following details were taken from the books of Cotton Candy Ltd:

01/01/20-4	Buildings at cost amounted to €450,000.
01/01/20-4	The balance in the provision for depreciation account was €68,000.
01/04/20-4	Purchased buildings for €250,000.
01/04/20-4	Sold for €280,000 a building which cost €130,000. The book value of this building on 1/4/20-4 was €92,000.
31/12/20-4	The total depreciation for the year ended 31/12/20-4 was €12,000.
01/01/20-5	The buildings were revalued at €750,000.
31/12/20-5	Provide for depreciation at the rate of 2% of the value of buildings on 01/01/20-5.

You are required to show:

- the buildings account for the two years 20-4 and 20-5
- the provision for depreciation account for the two years 20-4 and 20-5
- the buildings disposal account for the year ended 31/12/20-4
- the revaluation reserve account.

4

Exercises – Higher Level

Q1 On 1 January 20-9 Bolger Ltd owned property and land which cost €720,000, consisting of land, €190,000, and buildings, €530,000. The company depreciates at the rate of 4% per annum using the straight line method. It is the company's policy to apply a full year's depreciation in the year of acquisition and no depreciation in the year of disposal. The property had been purchased eight years earlier and depreciation had been charged against profits in each of these eight years. (Land is not to be depreciated.)

The following details were taken from the firm's books:

1 Jan. 20-9	Revalued property at €960,000, of which €260,000 was attributable to land.
1 Jan. 20-0	Sold for €320,000 land which has cost €190,000 but was since revalued.
1 Jan. 20-1	Purchased a new building for €520,000 and during the year a new extension was built adjoining these new premises. The company's own employees worked on this extension and their wages amounted to €40,000, while €80,000 was paid to a building contractor.
1 Jan. 20-2	Revalued all property by 10% in respect of each building.
1 Jan. 20-3	Sold for €835,000 the buildings owned on 1/1/20-9. All remaining buildings were revalued at €780,000.

You are required to:

- Prepare the relevant ledger accounts in respect of the above transactions for the years ended 31 December 20-9 to 31 December 20-3 (bank account and profit and loss account not required).

Q2 **On 1 January 20-1 Finney Property Ltd owned property and land which cost €460,000, consisting of land, €90,000, and buildings, €370,000. The company depreciates at the rate of 3% per annum using the straight line method. It is the company's policy to apply a full year's depreciation in the year of acquisition and no depreciation in the year of disposal. The property had been purchased six years earlier and depreciation had been charged against profits in each of these six years. (Land is not to be depreciated.)**

The following details were taken from the firm's books:

1 Jan. 20-1	Revalued property at €540,000, of which €120,000 was attributable to land.
1 Jan. 20-2	Sold for €145,000 land which has cost €90,000 but was since revalued.
1 Jan. 20-3	Purchased a new building for €230,000 and during the year a new extension was built adjoining these new premises. The company's own employees worked on this extension and their wages amounted to €80,000, while €120,000 was paid to a building contractor.
1 Jan. 20-4	Revalued all property by 12% in respect of each building.
1 Jan. 20-5	Sold for €505,000 the buildings owned on 1/1/20-1. All remaining buildings were revalued at €520,000.

You are required to:

- Prepare the relevant ledger accounts in respect of the above transactions for the years ended 31 December 20-1 to 31 December 20-5 (bank account and profit and loss account **not** required).

Q3 **On 1 January 20-9 Gibbons Ltd owned property and land which cost €1,200,000, consisting of land, €490,000, and buildings, €710,000. The company depreciates at the rate of 2% per annum using the straight line method. It is the company's policy to apply a full year's depreciation in the year of acquisition and no depreciation in the year of disposal. The property had been purchased 12 years earlier and depreciation had been charged against profits in each of these 12 years. (Land is not to be depreciated.)**

The following details were taken from the firm's books:

1 Jan. 20-9	Re-valued property at €1,560,000, of which €660,000 was attributable to land.
1 Jan. 20-0	Sold for €780,000 land which has cost €490,000 but was since revalued.
1 Jan. 20-1	Purchased a new building for €720,000 and during the year a new extension was built adjoining these new premises. The company's own employees worked on this extension and their wages amounted to €90,000, while €140,000 was paid to a building contractor.
1 Jan. 20-2	Revalued all property by 15% in respect of each building.
1 Jan. 20-3	Sold for €1,100,000 the buildings owned on 1/1/20-9. All remaining buildings were revalued at €1,120,000.

You are required to:

- Prepare the relevant ledger accounts in respect of the above transactions for the years ended 31 December 20-9 to 31 December 20-3 (bank account and profit and loss account **not** required).

Q4 **On 1 January 20-4 Chocolate Delight Ltd owned freehold buildings which cost €300,000 and adjacent land which cost €200,000. The company depreciates its buildings at the rate of 4% per annum straight line method. It is the company's policy to apply a full year's depreciation in the year of acquisition and nil depreciation in the year of disposal. This property had been purchased on 1/1/20-0 and depreciation had been charged against profits in each of these four years. (Land is not depreciated.)**

The following details were taken from the firm's books:

1 Jan. 20-4	Revalued land and buildings at €650,000. Of this revalued amount, €250,000 was attributed to land.

1 Jan. 20-5	Sold for €290,000 land which had cost €200,000 but was since revalued on 1/1/20-4.
1 Jan. 20-6	Purchased buildings for €500,000. During the year 20-6 €130,000 was paid to a building contractor for an extension to these recently purchased buildings. The company's own employees also worked on the extension and they were paid wages amounting to €70,000 by the company for this work.
1 Jan. 20-7	Revalued buildings owned at €1,210,000 (a 10% increase in respect of each building).
1 Jan. 20-8	Sold for €490,000 the buildings owned on 1/1/20-4. The remaining buildings were revalued at €800,000.

You are required to:

- Prepare the relevant ledger accounts in respect of the above transactions for each of the years ended 31 December 20-4 to 31 December 20-8 (bank account and profit and loss account **not** required).
- Show the relevant extract from the balance sheet as at 31/12/20-8.

4

Q5 On 1 January 20-2 Tiggy Ltd owned freehold property and land which cost €750,000, consisting of land, €280,000, and buildings, €470,000. The company depreciates its buildings at the rate of 2% per annum straight line method. It is the company's policy to apply a full year's depreciation in the year of acquisition and no depreciation in the year of disposal. This property had been purchased five years earlier and depreciation had been charged against profits in each of these five years. (Land is not depreciated.)

The following details were taken from the firm's books:

1 Jan. 20-2	Revalued property at €990,000. Of this revaluation, €340,000 was attributed to land.
1 Jan. 20-3	Sold for €440,000 land which cost €280,000 but was since revalued on 1/1/20-2.
1 Jan. 20-4	Purchased buildings for €310,000. During the year 20-4, €120,000 was paid to a building contractor for an extension to these recently purchased buildings. The company's own employees also worked on the extension and they were paid wages amounting to €170,000 by Tiggy for this work.
1 Jan. 20-5	Revalued buildings owned at €1,437,500 (a 15% increase in respect of each building).
1 Jan. 20-6	Sold for €810,000 the buildings owned on 1/1/20-2. The remaining buildings were revalued at €800,000.

You are required to:

- Prepare the relevant ledger accounts in respect of the above transactions for the years ended 31 December 20-2 to 31 December 20-6 (bank account and profit and loss account not required).
- Show the relevant extract from the balance sheet as at 31/12/20-6.

Q6 On 1 January 20-9 Dawn Ltd owned freehold property and land which cost €470,000, consisting of land, €150,000, and buildings, €320,000. The company depreciates its buildings at the rate of 3% per annum straight line method. It is the company's policy to apply a full year's depreciation in the year of acquisition and no depreciation in the year of disposal. This property had been purchased ten years earlier and depreciation had been charged against profits in each of these ten years. (Land is not depreciated.)

The following details were taken from the firm's books:

1 Jan. 20-9	Revalued property at €670,000. Of this revaluation €200,000 was attributed to land.
1 Jan. 20-0	Sold for €230,000 land which cost €150,000 but was since revalued on 1/1/20-9.
1 Jan. 20-1	Purchased buildings for €540,000. During the year 20-1, €220,000 was paid to a building contractor for an extension to these recently purchased buildings. The company's own employees also worked on the extension and they were paid wages amounting to €160,000 by Dawn for this work.

1 Jan. 20-2	Revalued buildings owned at €1,529,000 (a 10% increase in respect of each building).
1 Jan. 20-3	Sold for €650,00 the buildings owned on 1/1/20-9. The remaining buildings were revalued at €1,100,000.

You are required to:

- Prepare the relevant ledger accounts in respect of the above transactions for the years ended 31 December 20-9 to 31 December 20-3 (bank account and profit and loss account **not** required).
- Show the relevant extract from the balance sheet as at 31/12/20-3.

4

Theory

Q1 Why do firms revalue fixed assets?

Q2 Outline the two steps you must take when revaluation takes place.

Q3 What factors influence the price of property on the market?

Exam Tips

- Read the question carefully and identify which method of depreciation is being used.
- Use the table as illustrated to show all your calculations.
- Be very careful with the use of dates for acquisition and disposal.
- Any capital additions must also be included in depreciation calculations – including costs such as delivery and installation.
- Show all dates in each of the accounts in your solution.
- All calculations should be shown to the nearest whole euro – avoid decimals.
- In revaluation remember that land is not normally depreciated.
- When a revalued asset is sold, the amount of revaluation on that asset must be transferred to the revenue reserve account.
- Both revaluation and depreciation of assets appear as adjustments in other questions throughout the examination.

5 Control Accounts

Objectives

On completion students should be able to:

- Understand the purpose of control accounts;
- List the advantages of control accounts;
- Explain why a control account may have an unusual balance;
- Explain what is meant by a contra entry;
- Know the source documents for preparing control accounts;
- Explain what are bills receivable and bills payable;
- List the reasons why there may be differences between the control account balance and the balance on the schedule (list);
- Prepare a control account for debtors and/or creditors;
- Reconcile the balance on the control account and the schedule (list) (Higher Level only).

Introduction to control accounts

Purpose of control accounts

To find the total amount owed by debtors and the total amount owed by creditors, a **control account** is used. The totals of the books of first entry are used for the figures in the control account.

The purpose of control accounts is to check the accuracy of double-entry bookkeeping as it applies to **credit transactions**. Control accounts themselves are **not** part of the double-entry system. However, many large companies who have many credit customers and suppliers treat control accounts as an integral part of the double-entry system.

It is important to remember that control accounts are only used for credit transactions.

Control accounts are used to:

- locate errors quickly
- ensure the accuracy of debtors and creditors ledgers
- find out the amounts owed by debtors and to creditors quickly.

Preparation of control accounts

Debtors

The figures used in a debtors ledger control account are taken from the totals of the books of first entry, i.e. sales, sales returns, journal entries, cash receipts and lodgements book, which are ultimately entered in the general ledger.

The list of debtors is taken from the individual personal balances in the debtors ledger.

Creditors

The figures used in a creditors ledger control account are taken from the totals of the books of first entry, i.e. the purchases, purchase returns, journal entries and cheque payments book, which are ultimately entered in the general ledger.

The list of creditors is taken from the individual personal balances in the creditors ledger.

NOTE

Entries in a control account will appear on the same side as they appear in the debtors and creditors ledgers.

Advantages of control accounts

- They act as a check on the accuracy of the postings and totals of the individual ledger accounts.
- They allow amounts owed by debtors and amounts owing to creditors to be ascertained quickly by simply balancing the control accounts.
- They enable errors to be localised and found more speedily.
- They are very useful when preparing accounts from incomplete records.

5

The accounts

Debtors Ledger Control Account

DEBIT	CREDIT
Any item which **INCREASES** the amount owed **to** the business	Any item which **DECREASES** the amount owed **to** the business

The main entries in a debtors control account are as follows:

DEBIT	CREDIT
Opening balance	Opening credit balance (if any)
Sales (exclude cash sales)	Returns inwards (sales returns)
Discount disallowed	Cheques received from debtors (customers)
Interest charged by a business on overdue amounts	Cash received from debtors (customers)
Cheques received dishonoured	Discount allowed
Carriage charged to debtors	Bad debts written off
Bills receivable dishonoured	Transfer from debtors ledger to creditors ledger (contra entry: see below)
Closing credit balance (if any)	Bills receivable*
	Closing balance

NOTE

Bills receivable have the effect of reducing the amount owed by debtors.

Creditors Ledger Control Account

DEBIT	CREDIT
Any item which **DECREASES** the amount owed **by** the business	Any item which **INCREASES** the amount owed **by** the business

The main entries in a creditors control account are as follows:

DEBIT	CREDIT
Opening debit balance (if any)	Opening balance
Returns outwards (purchases returns)	Purchases (exclude any cash purchases)
Payments made to creditors both by cheque and cash	Interest charged by suppliers on overdue accounts
Discount received	Discount received disallowed
Bills payable*	Own cheques sent dishonoured
Transfer from creditors ledger to debtors ledger (contra)	Bills payable dishonoured
Closing balance	Carriage charged by suppliers
	Closing debit balance (if any)

5

Bills payable have the effect of reducing the amount owed to creditors.

Elements of control accounts

Opening and closing balances
A control account may have both a debit and credit opening balance and closing balance.

Cash sales and cash purchases
Sales and purchases for cash do not appear in control accounts.

Bad debt recovered
A bad debt recovered will only appear in the control account if the debt has been reinstated.

VAT
When preparing control accounts it is necessary to include the VAT elements of sales, sales returns, purchases and purchases returns.

Contra entry
When a debtor of the firm is also a creditor of the firm, the amounts owed to and by the firm can be written off against each other. This is known as a **contra entry**. A contra entry has the effect of reducing the amount owed by debtors while at the same time reducing the amount owed to creditors.

There is sometimes an unusual balance on a control account – a debit balance on a creditors and a credit balance on a debtors control account.

This can happen for a number of reasons:

- Where a payment has been made (creditors) or received (debtors), and later goods have been returned to or by the firm and hence a refund is now necessary.
- An error of some kind had been made involving the overpayment of a debt (either by or to the company).
- Full payment was made or received and then a discount was granted – for example, for early payment.

Sample Ordinary Level question

The following figures were taken from the books of D. Fitzpatrick during February 20-1:

Debtors ledger control account balance	€60,900
Debtors ledger control account balance (Cr.)	€900
Creditors ledger control account balance	€72,700
Creditors ledger control account balance (Dr.)	€1,240
Discount allowed	€3,200
Discount received	€2,345
Purchases (including cash purchases €12,200)	€198,900
Sales (including cash sales €23,100)	€212,790
Returns inwards	€4,600
Returns outwards	€2,450
Discount disallowed to Fitzpatrick	€3,560
Interest charged by Fitzpatrick on overdue accounts	€2,900
Cheques paid to suppliers	€56,900
Cheques received from customers	€123,450
Bad debts written off	€8,909
Cheques received dishonoured	€12,600
Transfer from debtors ledger to creditors ledger	€11,500
Bills receivable issued	€1,200
Bills payable accepted	€2,100
Debtors ledger balance 28/2/20-1	€5,600 Cr.
Creditors ledger balance 28/2/20-1	€4,500 Dr.

You are required to prepare for February 20-1:

- debtors ledger control account
- creditors ledger control account.

Solution

Step 1
Establish whether each entry relates to debtors or creditors, and

Step 2
Establish whether the amount has an increasing or decreasing effect.

This can be done by placing a D or C beside each entry followed by a + or –.

The question above would then look as follows:

The following figures were taken from the books of D. Fitzpatrick during February 20-1:

Debtors ledger control account balance	€60,900	D+
Debtors ledger control account balance (Cr.)	€900	D–
Creditors ledger control account balance	€72,700	C+
Creditors ledger control account balance (Dr.)	€1,240	C–
Discount allowed	€3,200	D–
Discount received	€2,345	C–
Purchases (including cash purchases €12,200)	€198,900	C+
Sales (including cash sales €23,100)	€212,790	D+

5

Returns inwards	€4,600	D–
Returns outwards	€2,450	C–
Discount disallowed to Fitzpatrick	€3,560	C+
Interest charged by Fitzpatrick on overdue accounts	€2,900	D+
Cheques paid to suppliers	€56,900	C–
Cheques received from customers	€123,450	D–
Bad debts written off	€8,909	D–
Cheques received dishonoured	€12,600	D+
Transfer from debtors ledger to creditors ledger	€11,500	D–/C–
Bills receivable issued	€1,200	D–
Bills payable accepted	€2,100	C–
Debtors ledger balance 28/2/20-1	€5,600 Cr.	D+
Creditors ledger balance 28/2/20-1	€4,500 Dr.	C+

5

The accounts should then look like this:

Dr. **Debtors Ledger Control Account** **Cr.**

Details	€	Details	€
Balance b/d	60,900	Balance b/d	900
Sales (less cash sales 23,100)	189,690	Discount allowed	3,200
Interest	2,900	Returns inwards	4,600
Dishonoured cheques	12,600	Cheques received	123,450
Debtors credit balance c/d	5,600	Bad debts written off	8,909
		Bills receivable	1,200
		Contra	11,500
		Balance c/d	117,931
	271,690		271,690
Balance b/d	117,931	Balance b/d (Cr.)	5,600

Dr. **Creditors Ledger Control Account** **Cr.**

Details	€	Details	€
Balance b/d	1,240	Balance b/d	72,700
Discount received	2,345	Purchases (less cash purchase 12,200)	186,700
Returns outwards	2,450	Discount disallowed	3,560
Cheques paid	56,900	Balance (Dr.)	4,500
Bills payable	2,100		
Contra	11,500		
Balance c/d	190,925		
	267,460		267,460
Balance	4,500	Balance b/d	190,925

Schedule (list) of debtors and creditors (Higher Level)

The total debtors figure arrived at in the debtors control account should equal the sum of the individual account balances in the debtors ledger (list of debtors). If the totals of the control account and the list do not agree it will be necessary to find the errors in one or both and set out the adjustments in a **reconciliation statement**. The individual ledger accounts and the schedule or list should be corrected as necessary. The control account should also be corrected where necessary. The same applies to creditors.

These differences arise for the following reasons:

- Errors or mistakes have been made in the preparation of either the control account or the schedule (list) or both.
- A breakdown in the double-entry system, where the debits and credits were incorrect.
- An error when totalling the day books (books of original entry) and these totals (incorrect) transferred to the control account and the list.

5

The **control account** is drawn up from the **books of first entry totals** or the general ledger, which contains accounts such as sales, purchases, returns, interest, discount.

The **list/schedule** is drawn up from the **personal ledger account balances** of the firm's customers and suppliers.

Debtors control account questions

If any of the following words appear –

debtor's account, customer's account, personal account

– then you need to correct the schedule (list).

Creditors control account questions

If any of the following words appear –

creditor's account, supplier's account, personal account

– then you need to correct the schedule (list).

All other entries will affect the control account.

NOTE

The following errors need to be corrected in both the control account and the list/schedule:

- Errors of omission
- Errors in day books double-entered in the ledgers.

Most common errors and their correction

Lets us now look at some of the more common errors and adjustments which can occur. These arise in both creditors and debtors questions.

For each correction you should remember **A B C**:

A = Actual - what was actually (and incorrectly) entered in the books

B = Should Be - what should have been entered in the books

C = Correction - the adjustment that you should make in the control account and/or schedule

Problem 1: interest and interest reduction

5

A creditor had charged interest of €80 on an overdue account. The only entry made in the books for this interest was €35 debited to the creditor's account. Following a protest this charge had been reduced to €40 but this reduction had not been reflected in the accounts.

Solution

Since the creditor's account was affected then the correction needs to be in the schedule (list) of creditors.

The €35 is on the incorrect side: it decreased the amount due instead of increasing it.

The charge should be €40 instead of €80, therefore the entry needs to be changed to what it should be. This will affect both the schedule (list) and the control account.

	Schedule (list)	Control Account
Actual entry	-35 (debit side of account)	0
Should **B**e - correct entry	+80 then changed to +40	+80 then changed to +40
Correction required	To get from -35 to +40 you need +75	To get from 0 to +40 you need +40 (i.e. credit the control account)

Problem 2: discount

Discount disallowed by a supplier of €32 had been treated as discount received in the books.

Solution

This should have been an increase in amount owed of €32. Instead of that it was treated as a decrease so therefore we need to double the amount to get the correct answer. To go from -32 to +32 we need to add 64.

Because it says 'in the books', this means a correction is needed in both the schedule (list) and the control account.

	Schedule (list)	Control Account
Actual entry	-32	-32
Should **B**e	+32	+32
Correction required	+64	+64

Problem 3: invoice errors

P. Dunne received an invoice from a supplier for €150. This was entered in the appropriate day book as €510. However, when posting from this book to the ledger, no entry was made in the supplier's account.

Solution

An invoice should increase the amount owed to the supplier. Therefore it should be +150.

There was an incorrect figure of €510 used in the accounts, which is a difference of €360.

Because there was no entry in the supplier's account the original entry is nil.

	Schedule (list)	Control Account
Actual entry	0	+510
Should **Be**	+150	+150
Correction required	+150	-360

5

Problem 4: credit notes

A credit note was sent to a customer for €220. The only entry was €22 debited to the customer's account.

Solution

A credit note has the effect of reducing the amount owed. Therefore it should be a minus of €220.

A debit entry in a customer's account is an increase, therefore we need to subtract this €22, plus €220, which is a minus of €242.

There was no entry in the control account, therefore we need to credit it (decrease it by €220).

	Schedule (list)	Control Account
Actual entry	+22	0
Should **Be**	-220	-220
Correction required	-242	-220

Problem 5: cash and credit transactions

Cash sales of €1,200 and credit sales of €3,200 had both been entered on the credit side of a customer's account.

Solution

The cash sales should not be included. Since we credited the account (-) we must debit it back (+).

The credit sales are on the incorrect side, so we need to debit it twice, once to cancel the credit and once to put it right.

	Schedule (list)	Control Account
Actual entry	-4,400	+3,200
Should **Be**	+3,200	+3,200
Correction	+7,600	0

Problem 6: restocking charge errors

This is perhaps the most difficult error to correct and usually means a change in both the Actual and the Should Be parts before we can do the final correction.

Goods worth €640 were returned to a supplier. This was entered correctly in the books. However, a credit note arrived showing a reduction for a restocking charge of 10%. The total amount of this credit note was entered on the credit side of the personal account. This was the only entry in the books in respect of this credit note and restocking charge.

Solution

First credit note

	Schedule (list)	Control Account
Actual entry	-640	-640
Should **B**e	-640	-640
Correction	0	0

5

Since this was entered correctly no corrections need to be made.

Second credit note

The Should Be has to change to -640 + 10% of 640 (+64) = -576.

This €576 was credited to the personal account in error, when it should have been debited.

	Schedule (list)	Control Account
Actual entry	-640 + 576 = -64	-640
Should **B**e	-640 + 64 = -576	-640 + 64 = -576
Correction required	-64 to -576 = -512	-640 to -576 = +64

Sample Higher Level question

The debtors ledger control account of J. Keenan showed the following balances on 31 December 20-1: €64,555 Dr. and €700 Cr. These figures did not agree with the schedule (list) of debtors balances extracted from the debtors ledger on the same date. An examination of the books revealed the following:

(a) A credit note was sent to H. Henry for €430. The only entry made in the books was €340 debited to the debtors account.

(b) An invoice was sent to a debtor, Colm Curran, showing the sale of goods for €1,200, less trade discount of 20%. This had been entered correctly in the appropriate day book but had not been posted to the personal account.

(c) A debtor, Jim Cullen, had been charged interest to the amount of €560 on an overdue account. The only entry in Keenan's books was €56 credited to the personal account. After a complaint by Cullen this interest was reduced to €400 but this reduction had not been reflected in the accounts.

(d) Discount disallowed to a customer had been treated in the books as discount allowed, €60.

(e) Cash sales of €200 and credit sales of €300 had both been credited to the personal account of a customer, M. Houlihan.

(f) Keenan had accepted sales returns to the value of €2,300 from a customer. This return was correctly entered in the books. The accounts clerk forgot to deduct a 10% restocking charge and when this error was discovered another credit note was sent for €2,070. The only entry in the books in respect of this credit note was €2,070 credited to the personal account.

You are required to prepare:

- the adjusted debtors control account
- the adjusted schedule of debtors balances.

Solution

Workings

		Schedule (list)	Control Account
(a)	**A**ctual entry	+340	0
	Should **B**e	-430	-430
	Correction required	-770	-430
(b)	**A**ctual entry	0	+960
	Should **B**e	+960	+960
	Correction required	+960	0
(c)	**A**ctual entry	-56	0
	Should **B**e	~~+560~~ + 400	~~+560~~ + 400
	Correction required	+456	+400
(d)	**A**ctual entry	-60	-60
	Should **B**e	+60	+60
	Correction required	+120	+120
(e)	**A**ctual entry	-500	+300
	Should **B**e	+300	+300
	Correction required	+800	0
(f)	**A**ctual entry	-2,300 - 2,070 = -4,370	-2,300
	Should **B**e	~~-2,300~~ -2,070	~~-2,300~~ -2,070
	Correction required	+2,300	+230

Dr. **Debtors Control Account** **Cr.**

Details	€	Details	€
Balance b/d	64,555	Balance b/d	700
Interest (c)	400	Credit note (a)	430
Discount (d)	120	Balance c/d	64,875
Restocking (f)	230		
Balance c/d	700		
	66,005		66,005
Balance b/d	64,875	Balance b/d	700

Schedule (List) of Debtors

	€	€
Balance as per list		60,309
Add		
Invoice (b)	960	
Interest (c)	456	
Discount (d)	120	
Restocking charge (f)	2,300	
Cash sales (e)	800	4,636
Less		64,945
Credit note (a)		(770)
Net balance as per control account (64,875 - 700)		64,175

5

Exercises - Ordinary Level

Q1 The following figures were taken from the accounts of J. Keville for the month of April 20-2:

Debtors ledger control account balance €67,000
Debtors ledger control account balance .... €8,800 Cr.
Creditors ledger control account balance €57,000
Creditors ledger control account balance .... €7,500 Dr.
Payments received from debtors €100,966
Sales (including cash sales €34,800) €134,600
Discount allowed €33,400
Discount received €23,100
Interested charged by Keville on overdue accounts €23,900
Discount disallowed to Keville €11,230
Bills payable €3,490
Bills receivable €2,456
Transfer from debtors ledger to creditors ledger €900
Bad debts €4,500
Returns outwards €4,600
Cheques paid to suppliers €90,000
Purchases (including cash purchases €23,560) €102,000
Cheques received dishonoured €5,700
Debtors ledger balance .... €4,566 Cr.
Creditors ledger balance .... €6,790 Dr.

You are required to prepare for April 20-2:

- **the debtors ledger control account**
- **the creditors ledger control account.**

Q2 **The following figures were taken from the accounts of J. Barron for the month of April 20-3:**

Debtors ledger control account balance	€98,000
Debtors ledger control account balance	€5,600 Cr.
Creditors ledger control account balance	€68,900
Creditors ledger control account balance	€3,400 Dr.
Sales (including cash sales €54,900)	€187,400
Discount allowed	€23,900
Discount received	€12,400
Interest charged by Barron on overdue accounts	€34,600
Discount disallowed to Barron	€22,345
Bills payable	€4,560
Bills receivable	€3,298
Transfer from debtors ledger to creditors ledger	€2,100
Returns inwards	€3,400
Returns outwards	€4,900
Cheques paid to suppliers	€101,000
Purchases (including cash purchases €22,900)	€98,000
Cheques received dishonoured	€4,300
Payments received from debtors	€133,000
Debtors ledger balance 31/4/-3	€2,334 Cr.
Creditors ledger balance 31/4/-3	€4,567 Dr.

You are required to prepare for April 20-3:

- the debtors ledger control account
- the creditors ledger control account.

Q3 **The following figures were taken from the books of Gerry Daly during July 20-3:**

Debtors ledger balance 1/7/-3	€45,600
Creditors ledger balance 1/7/-3	€32,670
Discount allowed	€4,509
Returns outwards	€1,240
Purchases (including cash purchases of €8,760)	€56,760
Cash paid to suppliers	€23,690
Bad debts written off	€3,450
Cheques received dishonoured	€730
Sales (including cash sales €21,809)	€87,409
Returns inwards	€2,670
Discount received	€4,390
Cheques received from customers	€76,900
Interest charged by Daly on overdue accounts	€1,280
Transfer from debtors ledger to creditors ledger	€908
Debtors ledger balance at 31/7/-3	€450 Cr.
Creditors ledger balance 31/7/-3	€650 Dr.

You are required to:

- Prepare the debtors ledger control account and a creditors ledger control account for July 20-3.

5

Q4 **The following figures are taken from the books of Pat Kenny during October 20-3:**

Debtors ledger balance 1/10/-3 .... €81,900
Creditors ledger balance 1/10/-3 .... €64,001
Returns outwards €550
Discount allowed €410
Discount received €720
Returns inwards €130
Bills payable accepted €2,150
Bills receivable issued €2,460
Purchases (including cash purchases €4,900) €67,300
Sales (including cash sales €21,100) €74,900
Discount disallowed to Kenny €590
Cheques paid to suppliers €26,900
Cheques received from customers €18,200
Cheques received dishonoured €450
Bad debts written off €270
Transfer from debtors ledger to creditors ledger €303
Debtors ledger balance 31/10/-3 .... €604 Cr.
Creditors ledger balance 31/10/-3 .... €202 Dr.

You are required to:

- Prepare the debtors ledger control account and a creditors ledger control account for October 20-3.

Q5 **The following figures were taken from the books of Mark Hughes during April 20-4:**

Debtors ledger balance 1/4/-4 .... €65,300
Creditors ledger balance 1/4/-4 .... €35,800
Debtors ledger balance 1/4/-4 .... €8,100 Cr.
Creditors ledger balance 1/4/-4 .... €7,000 Dr.
Discount allowed €4,300
Discount received €8,500
Purchases (including cash purchases €21,100) €84,100
Sales (including cash sales €25,600) €93,500
Returns inwards €9,700
Returns outwards €4,200
Interest charged by Hughes on overdue accounts €7,100
Discount disallowed to Mark Hughes €800
Cheques paid to suppliers €65,900
Cheques received from customers €72,800
Bad debts written off €6,300
Cheques received dishonoured €5,100
Transfer from debtors ledger to creditors ledger €9,200
Bills receivable issued €5,900
Bills payable accepted €4,700
Debtors ledger balance 30/4/-4 .... €300 Cr.
Creditors ledger balance 30/4/-4 .... €700 Dr.

You are required to:

- Prepare the debtors ledger control account and a creditors ledger control account for April 20-4.

Q6 **The following figures were taken from the books of Mike Murphy during December 20-4:**

Debtors ledger balance 1/12/-4	€32,600
Debtors ledger balance 1/12/-4	€900 Cr.
Creditors ledger balance 1/12/-4	€21,100
Creditors ledger balance 1/12/-4	€700 Dr.
Sales (including cash sales €11,000)	€65,000
Purchases on credit	€34,500
Sales returns	€4,500
Purchase returns	€5,400
Discount allowed	€800
Discount received	€870
Dishonoured cheque by Murphy to a supplier	€1,340
Bills receivable accepted	€2,100
Bills payable issued	€6,100
Cheques received from customers	€34,500
Customers cheques dishonoured	€5,600
Discount disallowed to Murphy	€1,560
Interest charged by Murphy on overdue accounts	€3,450
Transfer from debtors ledger to creditors ledger	€340
Cheques paid to suppliers	€43,200
Debtors ledger balance 31/12/-4	€400 Cr.
Creditors ledger balance 31/12/-4	€530 Dr.

You are required to:

- Prepare the debtors ledger control account and a creditors ledger control account for December 20-4.

Practice Questions

Q1 **In each of the following show the treatment necessary to correct the errors involving interest charges and reductions.**

(a) O'Shea was charged interest on an overdue account to the amount of €67. The only entry in the books was €79 debited in the personal account. After a protest, this interest was reduced to €35, but this reduction was not reflected in the accounts.

(b) Montoya charged interest on an overdue account to the amount of €90. The only entry in the books was €9 credited in the debtors account. After a protest, this interest was reduced to €65 but this reduction was not reflected in the accounts.

(c) Flatt was charged interest on an overdue account to the amount of €92. The only entry in the books was €29 debited in the supplier's account. After a protest, this interest was reduced to €30 but this reduction was not reflected in the accounts.

Q2 In each of the following show the treatment necessary to correct the errors involving discount received and discount allowed.

(a) Discount disallowed by a supplier of €54 had been treated as discount received in the books.

(b) Discount disallowed by a supplier of €104 had been treated as discount received in the books.

(c) Discount disallowed to a customer of €98 had been treated as discount allowed in the books.

(d) Discount disallowed by a supplier of €39 had been treated as discount received in the books.

(e) Discount disallowed to a customer of €123 had been treated as discount allowed in the books.

(f) Discount disallowed by a supplier of €79 had been treated as discount received in the books.

Q3 In each of the following show the treatment necessary to correct the errors involving invoices.

(a) A. Barrington sent an invoice to a customer for €780. This had been entered in the appropriate day book as €960. However, when posting from this book to the ledger no entry had been made in the debtor's account.

(b) S. Alderdyce sent an invoice to a customer for €560. This had been entered in the appropriate day book as €340. However, when posting from this book to the ledger no entry had been made in the customer's account.

(c) M. O'Leary received an invoice from a supplier for €950. This had been entered in the appropriate day book as €1,202. However, when posting from this book to the ledger no entry had been made in the creditor's account.

5

Q4 In each of the following show the treatment necessary to correct the errors involving credit notes.

(a) A credit note was received from a supplier for €345. The only entry in the books in respect of this credit note was €435 credited to the supplier's account.

(b) A credit note was sent to a customer for €240. The only entry was €42 debited to the customer's account.

(c) A credit note was received from a supplier for €124. The only entry in the books in respect of this credit note was €134 credited to the supplier's account.

(d) A credit note was sent to a customer for €680. The only entry was €86 debited to the customer's account.

(e) A credit note was received from a supplier for €610. The only entry in the books in respect of this credit note was €160 credited to the supplier's account.

Q5 In each of the following show the treatment necessary to correct the errors involving cash and credit transactions.

(a) Cash sales €600 and credit sales €2,400 had both been entered on the credit side of a customer's account.

(b) Cash purchases €1,600 and credit purchases €2,600 had both been entered on the debit side of a supplier's account.

(c) Cash sales €1,600 and credit sales €1,400 had both been entered on the credit side of a customer's account.

(d) Cash purchases €900 had been entered on the debit side of a supplier's account.

(e) Cash purchases €800 and credit purchases €1,900 had both been entered on the debit side of a supplier's account.

(f) Cash sales €2,600 had been entered on the credit side of a customer's account.

Q6 In each of the following show the treatment necessary to correct the errors involving restocking charges.

(a) Sales returns were accepted to the value of €600 from a customer and entered correctly in the books. However, the accounts clerk sent out the credit note with a 10% restocking charge but only made the necessary adjustment in the debtor's account. Later this charge was reduced to 5% but this reduction was not reflected in the accounts.

(b) Goods were returned to a supplier for €1,200. This was entered correctly in the books. However, a credit note arrived showing a reduction for a restocking charge of 15%. The total amount of this credit note was entered on the credit side of the personal account. This was the only entry in the books in respect of this credit note and restocking charge.

(c) Goods returned were accepted for €800 from a customer and this was entered correctly in the books. The accounts clerk sent out a credit note showing a restocking charge of 15% of sales price, but made the necessary adjustments only in the customer's account. Later this credit charge was reduced to 10% but this reduction was not reflected in the accounts.

Exercises – Higher Level

Q1 **The creditors ledger control account of P. O'Connell showed the following balances on 31 October 20-0: €76,000 Cr. and €900 Dr. These figures did not agree with the schedule (list) of creditors balances extracted from the creditors ledger on the same date. An examination of the books revealed the following:**

(a) P. O'Connell had received an invoice from a supplier for €1,020. This had been entered in the appropriate day book as €2,010. However, when posting from this book to the ledger no entry had been made in the supplier's account.

(b) A credit note was received from a supplier for €210. The only entry made in the books in respect of this was a credit entry in the creditor's account of €102.

(c) A creditor had charged O'Connell interest on an overdue account of €65. The only entry for this interest was €56 on the incorrect side of the interest account. This interest was later reduced to €50 but this reduction was not reflected in the accounts.

(d) Discount disallowed to O'Connell had been treated in the accounts as discount received €80.

(e) A credit note received for €4,500 had been entered on the incorrect side of the supplier's account.

(f) O'Connell returned goods to the value of €4,500 and had entered this correctly in the books. However, when the credit note arrived it showed a restocking charge of €300. This restocking charge was not reflected in the accounts.

You are required to prepare:

- the adjusted creditors control account
- the adjusted schedule of creditors balances.

Q2 **The debtors ledger control account of C. Power showed the following balances on 31 December 20-1: €87,000 Dr. and €650 Cr. These figures did not agree with the schedule (list) of debtors balances extracted from the debtors ledger on the same date. An examination of the books revealed the following:**

(a) A credit note was sent to C. Mannigan for €780. The only entry made in the books was €870 debited to the debtor's account.

(b) An invoice was sent to a debtor Billy Jones showing the sale of goods for €2,500, less trade discount of 25%. This had been entered correctly in the appropriate day book but had not been posted to the personal account.

(c) A debtor Ken Bates had been charged interest to the amount of €90 on an overdue account. The only entry in Power's books was €9 credited to the personal account. After a complaint by Bates this interest was reduced to €40 but this reduction was not reflected in the accounts.

5

(d) A debtor who owed Power €3,400 was declared bankrupt. He paid 40c for each €1 owed. No entry was made in the books in respect of this transaction.

(e) Cash sales of €800 and credit sales of €600 had both been credited to the personal account of a customer, M. Houlihan.

(f) Power had accepted sales returns to the value of €900 from a customer. This return was correctly entered in the books. The accounts clerk forgot to deduct a 10% restocking charge and when the mistake was noticed another credit note was sent for €810. The only entry in the books in respect of this credit note was €810 credited to the personal account. Following a complaint this restocking charge was reduced to 5% but this was not reflected in the accounts.

You are required to prepare:

- the adjusted debtors control account
- the adjusted schedule of debtors balances.

5

Q3 The debtors ledger control account of C. Jones showed the following balances on 31 August 20-3: €76,800 Dr. and €690 Cr. These figures did not agree with the schedule (list) of debtors balances extracted from the debtors ledger on the same date. An examination of the books revealed the following:

(a) A cheque for €1,350 received from a customer in full settlement of a debt of €1,400 had been entered correctly in the books. However, this cheque was dishonoured, but no entry had been made in the books relating to this cancelled cheque.

(b) The €690 owed to the debtor at the start was fully paid. This was not entered in the accounts.

(c) C. Jones sent an invoice to a customer for €2,400, less trade discount of 10%. This was entered in the appropriate day book at €2,400 and no entry had been made in the personal account.

(d) A credit note was sent to a customer for €234. The only entry in the books for this was €34 credited to the personal account.

(e) Cash sales €340 and credit sales €230 had both been entered on the credit side of the customer's account.

(f) Goods returned to a supplier had been treated as goods returned by a customer €600.

You are required to prepare:

- the adjusted debtors control account
- the adjusted schedule of debtors balances.

Q4 The creditors ledger control account of F. Clarke showed the following balances on 31 October 20-6: €43,211 Cr. and €433 Dr. These figures did not agree with the schedule (list) of creditors balances extracted on the same date. An examination of the books revealed the following:

(a) Cash purchases by Clarke of €450 had been debited to a supplier's account

(b) Discount disallowed to Clarke of €33 had been omitted from the books

(c) A credit note was received from a supplier for €144. The only entry in the books was €441 credited to the supplier's personal account.

(d) Clarke had received an invoice from a supplier for €780. This has been entered in the appropriate day book as €870. However, when posting from this book to the ledger no entry had been made in the personal account.

(e) Clarke had returned goods worth €120 to a supplier and entered this correctly in the books. However, a credit note arrived showing a deduction of 10% as a restocking charge. The total amount of this credit note was credited to the creditor's account. In relation to the credit note no other entry was made in the books.

(f) A creditor had charged Clarke interest amounting to €97 on an overdue account. The only entry in the books for this interest was €79 debited to the creditor's account. After a protest the interest was reduced to €30, but this reduction was not reflected in the accounts.

(g) The amount due on 31/10/-6 from a creditor was received. This entry was not reflected in the accounts.

You are required to prepare:

- the adjusted creditors ledger control account
- the adjusted schedule of creditors showing the original balance.

Q5 The schedule (list) of debtors balances of Darren Bishop showed a balance of €23,450 on 31 December 20-2. However, this figure did not agree with the debit balance on the debtors ledger control account on the same date. An examination of the books revealed the following errors (note: there was no credit balance on the control account):

(a) A cheque for €560 received from a customer in full settlement of a debt of €600 had been entered correctly in the books. However, this cheque was dishonoured but no entry had been made in the books relating to the dishonouring of the cheque.

(b) Bishop had sent an invoice to a customer for €1,230. This had been entered in the appropriate day book as €1,320 but when posting to the personal account it was entered as €2,320.

(c) A credit note received from a supplier for €340 was omitted from the books.

(d) Bishop had charged interest amounting to €150 to a customer on an overdue account. The only entry in the books for this was €15 entered on the incorrect side of the interest account. Following a complaint by the customer this interest was reduced by 40%, but this reduction had not been entered in the accounts.

(e) Cash sales of €340 and credit sales of €560 had both been entered by Bishop on the credit side of the personal account.

(f) Bishop had accepted sales returns of €300 from a customer and entered this in the books. However, a credit note was sent out showing a 10% reduction as a restocking charge. The accounts clerk only made the necessary adjustment in the personal account. Following a protest this restocking charge was reduced to 4%, but this was not reflected in the accounts.

(g) €200 was received from a debtor who was previously declared bankrupt and whose debt had been written off as bad. This represented 25% of the original debt. The debtor has undertaken to repay the remainder of the debt within one month and also bought goods on credit to the value €450, plus a mark-up of 20%. None of these transactions were reflected in the accounts.

You are required to prepare:

- the adjusted debtors control account
- the adjusted schedule (list) of debtors balances.

Q6 The following entries were taken from the books of G. McEvoy for the month of June 20-4:

Opening creditors balance	34,500
Credit purchases	67,000
Returns outwards	3,450
Cheques paid to suppliers	43,700
Discount received	3,500

Continued >

5

Contra	2,300
Interest charged on overdue account	1,670
Dishonoured cheque by McEvoy	130
Discount received disallowed	50
Amounts due from creditors on 30/6/-4	340

This creditors ledger control account when balanced did not agree with the balance on the schedule (list) of creditors extracted on the same date. An examination of the books revealed the following:

(a) An invoice received from A. Ferguson showing the purchase of goods for €1,400, less trade discount 25%, had been entered correctly in the appropriate day book but had not been posted to the personal account.

(b) Cash purchases by McEvoy of €800 had been debited to the supplier's account.

(c) Discount disallowed of €899 by a supplier had been treated as discount received in the books.

(d) A credit note was received from a supplier for €388. The only entry in the books was €83 credited to the creditor's account.

(e) A creditor had charged McEvoy interest of €105 on an overdue account. The only entry in the books for this interest had been €51 debited to the creditor's account. After a complaint by McEvoy this charge was reduced to €65, but this reduction had not been made on the books.

(f) McEvoy had returned goods worth €950 to a supplier and entered this correctly in the books. However, a credit note arrived showing a deduction of 10% as a restocking charge. The amount of this credit note was credited to the creditor's account but no other entry was made in the books.

You are required to:

- Prepare the original control account.
- Prepare the adjusted control account.
- Prepare the adjusted schedule (list) of creditors balances showing the original balance.

Q7 The following balances were extracted from the books of Michael Breen on 31 May 20-5:

Debtors ledger balance	23,780 Dr.	340 Cr.
Creditors ledger balance	16,890 Cr.	780 Dr.

These figures did not agree with the schedule (list) of debtors and creditors balances extracted on the same date. An examination of the books revealed the following:

(a) An invoice received from Gerard Murphy showing the purchase of goods for €4,680, less trade discount 10%, had been entered in the appropriate day book but had not been posted to the personal account.

(b) Cash purchases of €3,500 and cash sales of €2,400 had been credited to suppliers and customers respectively.

(c) Discount allowed of €1,100 had been entered on the incorrect side of the discount account, and no entry was made in the personal account.

(d) Interest charged to Breen of €250 had been entered on the incorrect side of the interest account and €520 debited in the personal account. Following a protest this interest was reduced by 60%. No entry had been made in the books with respect to this interest reduction.

(e) A credit note was sent to a customer Pat Power for €670. The only entry made in the books was €760 debited in the personal account.

(f) A contra item of €280 was omitted from the books.

(g) Bills receivable €2,800 were omitted from the books.

(h) Breen had returned goods worth €890 to a supplier and entered this as €980 in the books. However, the credit note arrived showing a restocking charge of 20% of invoice price. The accounts clerk made the necessary adjustment in the personal account. Following a complaint this restocking charge was reduced to 10% but this was not reflected in the accounts.

You are required to:

- Prepare the adjusted debtors control account.
- Prepare the adjusted creditors control account.
- Prepare the adjusted schedule (list) of debtors showing the original balance.
- Prepare the adjusted schedule (list) of creditors showing the original balance.

5

Theory

Q1 Explain why creditors control accounts are prepared.

Q1 Explain 'contra item'.

Q2 Explain why there could be a credit opening balance on a debtors control account.

Q3 Give reasons why the balance in the debtors control account may not agree with the balance in the schedule (list) of balances.

Q4 Which books of first entry are used in the production of debtors control accounts?

Q5 Explain the importance of control accounts.

Exam Tips

- For each entry identify clearly whether the error affects the control account or the schedule (list) or both.
- Use the ABC approach to find the necessary correction to reconcile the balances.
- Total figures will generally affect the control account while individual figures will generally affect the schedule (list).
- Errors of omission will affect both the control account and the schedule list.
- In debtors control accounts entries on the debit side increase the amount owed and entries on the credit side decrease the amount owed.
- In creditors control accounts entries on the debit side decrease the amount owed and entries on the credit side increase the amount owed.
- Cash sales and cash purchases are not entered in control accounts.

6 Final Accounts – Sole Trader

Objectives

On completion students should be able to:
- Understand what a sole trader is;
- Prepare a trading, profit and loss account for a sole trader business;
- Prepare a balance sheet for a sole trader business.

The sole trader

The sole trader is a type of business organisation where one person (the owner) is legally and personally responsible for the conduct of the business. A high percentage of Irish businesses today are sole traders despite the development of limited liability.

Limited liability means that an owner is liable only for the amount he/she has invested in the business. It applies only to companies.

Advantages

- The sole trader keeps all the profit.
- The sole trader makes all the decisions, such as opening hours, type of business.
- The business is easy to set up, with fewer legal procedures and setting up costs than other forms of business.

Disadvantages

- The sole trader suffers all losses (including personal loss because a sole trader does not have the protection of limited liability).
- There is likely to be a lack of capital for expansion.
- There is no one to help with decision-making.

Final accounts of a sole trader

The single aim of any business is to make a profit. Profit is when total revenue exceeds total costs incurred for the accounting period. A business will prepare a **trading, profit and loss account** to provide it with information regarding its profit or loss for a given period. A business will also prepare a **balance sheet** to provide information regarding its financial position at a particular point in time.

The trading account

The trading account establishes by how much the revenue received from sales exceeds the cost of these same goods.

The difference is called **gross profit**. However, if the cost of goods sold exceeds the revenue received, the difference is called **gross loss.**

Sales means all the cash and credit sales (less sales returns) of goods in which the trader normally deals.

Cost of goods sold is arrived at as follows:

Opening stock + Purchases - Closing stock = Cost of goods sold

The profit and loss account

The profit and loss account ascertains the net profit or loss of a business during a given accounting period.

When the gross profit and revenue receipts exceed the current expenditure (day-to-day running costs of a business) the difference is referred to as **net profit**. If this expenditure exceeds the gross profit then the difference is referred to as **net loss**.

DEFINITION

Operating profit is the profit on normal business activities before interest is deducted.

The balance sheet

The balance sheet provides a picture of the business on a particular day. It gives a list of all the assets and liabilities on that day, as well as the amount invested in the business by the owner. This amount invested is known as **capital**.

The balance sheet is not an account and so is not part of the double-entry system. It is a statement showing the financial position of the business at a particular point in time.

Classification of items in the balance sheet

Fixed assets
These are assets (owned by the business) held for more than one year. They are not for resale. Examples include buildings, motor vehicles and equipment.

Current assets
These are the assets whose values are constantly changing in line with the activity of the business. They are held for less than one year and include items such as debtors, stock, prepaid expenses, gains due, cash and bank balances.

Current liabilities (creditors: amounts falling due within one year)
These are the liabilities (amounts owed) that are payable within one year - for example, trade creditors, bank overdraft, expenses due and gains prepaid.

Net current assets (working capital)
This is the amount by which the current assets exceed the current liabilities and shows the ability of a firm to pay its debts as they fall due. This is referred to as **liquidity**.

Long-term liabilities (creditors: amounts falling due after more than one year)
These are the amounts owed by the business that do not have to be repaid for more than a year - for example, mortgages and term loans.

Capital (owner's equity)
This is the total of the owner's investment in the business. It is the amount owed by the business to its owner. In a sole trader business it is the amount invested plus the profit (if any), less any drawings.

Drawings is the amount of cash, stock or other items of value taken from the business for private use.

Basic adjustments to final accounts

The adjustments below apply to the final accounts of all organisations:

- Accruals and prepayments
- Changes in the provision for bad debts
- Depreciation calculations
- Provision for loan interest
- Apportionment (division) of expenses.

These adjustments will apply to all final accounts.

Accruals and prepayments

Income and expenditure (expenses and gains) must be entered in the accounting period in which they are incurred and not when they are received or paid (see Chapter 2, pp. 26–9).

6

Provision for bad debts

A change in provision for bad debts will affect the profit and loss account and balance sheet (see Chapter 2 pp. 30–34).

Depreciation

Depreciation is a cost which is allowable against profits for the purpose of taxation. It is therefore treated as an expense of the business (see Chapter 4).

Loan interest

The matching concept applies here. All interest payable/receivable for the accounting period must be entered in the trading, profit and loss account regardless of whether it is paid/received or not.

Example

An 8% loan for €120,000 was received on 1 July 20-4. Interest paid during 20-4 amounted to €3,400. Provide for loan interest due.

Solution

Firstly calculate the total interest payable on this loan:

120,000 x 8% x 6/12 =	€4,800	(The loan was received on 1/7/20-4 so interest is payable for six months only)
Less Interest paid	(€3,400)	
Interest due	€1,400	

€4,800 will be entered as interest payable in the profit and loss account.

€1,400 will be entered as interest due in the balance sheet.

Apportionment/division of expenses

Sometimes a cost or expense needs to be split among a number of different areas within a business – for example, between a business expense (profit and loss account) and a private expense (drawings). Carriage may need to be split between carriage inwards (trading account) and carriage outwards (selling and distribution expense).

Example

During the year €5,000 was paid for light and heat. However, the owner had a private apartment above the business premises and estimated that 20% of light and heat should be apportioned to this section of the building.

Show the necessary entries in profit and loss account and balance sheet.

Solution

Light and heat	5,000 x 80%:	**€4,000** entered in profit and loss account
Light and heat	5,000 x 20%:	**€1,000** entered in the balance sheet as drawings

Sample Ordinary Level question

The following trial balance was taken from the books of Amanda Smith at 31/12/20-4.

	€	€
Purchases	272,460	
Sales		447,250
Sales returns	7,250	
Purchases returns		12,660
Carriage inwards	1,800	
Stock 1/1/20-4	46,500	
Rent	7,000	
Rates	7,200	
Insurance	1,480	
Light and heat	16,300	
Discount allowed	3,500	
Discount received		860
Commission paid	10,950	
Salaries	58,540	
Debtors	27,600	
Creditors		34,690
Land and buildings	107,500	
Fixtures and fittings	12,500	
Motor vehicles	14,800	
Drawings	8,250	
Cash	1,380	
Bank	8,000	
USC		1,010
VAT		6,090
Bank term loan		50,000
Capital		60,450
	613,010	613,010

6

The following additional information should be taken into account:

(a) Stock at 31/12/20-4 was valued at €54,500.

(b) Rates prepaid amounted to €200.

(c) Rent due amounted to €700.

(d) Depreciate fixtures and fittings by 10%, motor vehicles by 20% and buildings by 2%.

You are required to prepare:

- the trading, profit and loss account for the year ending 31/12/20-4
- the balance sheet as at 31/12/20-4.

Solution

Trading, Profit and Loss Account for the year ended 31/12/20-4

	€	€	€
Sales		447,250	
Less Sales returns		(7,250)	440,000
***Less* Cost of sales**			
Opening stock		46,500	
Purchases	272,460		
Less Purchase returns	(12,660)	259,800	
Carriage inwards		1,800	
Cost of goods available for sale		308,100	
Less Closing stock		(54,500)	
Cost of goods sold			(253,600)
Gross profit			186,400
Less Expenses			
Administration			
Rent (W1)	7,700		
Rates (W2)	7,000		
Insurance	1,480		
Light and heat	16,300		
Salaries	58,540		
Depreciation fixtures (W3)	1,250		
Depreciation buildings (W5)	2,150	94,420	
Selling and distribution			
Depreciation motors (W4)	2,960		
Discount allowed	3,500		
Commission paid	10,950	17,410	(111,830)
			74,570
***Add* Other income**			
Discount received			860
Net profit			75,430

Balance Sheet as at 31/12/20-4

	Cost (€)	Aggregate Depreciation (€)	Net Book Value (€)
Fixed assets			
Land and buildings	107,500	2,150	105,350
Fixtures and fittings	12,500	1,250	11,250
Motor vehicles	14,800	2,960	11,840
	134,800	6,360	128,440
Current assets			
Stock		54,500	
Debtors		27,600	
Bank		8,000	
Cash		1,380	
Rates prepaid		200	
		91,680	
***Less* Creditors: amounts falling due within 1 year**			
Trade creditors	34,690		
VAT	6,090		
Universal Social Charge	1,010		
Rent due	700	(42,490)	
Net current assets			49,190
Total net assets			**177,630**
Financed by			
Creditors: amounts falling due after more than 1 year			
Bank term loan			50,000
Capital 1/1/20-4		60,450	
Add Net profit		75,430	
Less Drawings		(8,250)	127,630
Capital employed			**177,630**

Workings

W1 Rent

Rent paid	7,000	
Add Amount due	700	(current liability on balance sheet)
Charge to P & L	**7,700**	

W2 Rates

Rates paid	7,200	
Less Amount prepaid	(200)	(current asset on balance sheet)
Charge to P & L	**7,000**	

It is advisable to prepare workings like these when preparing final accounts.

W3 Depreciation of fixtures and fittings

12,500 x 10% **1,250** (expense in profit and loss account)

W4 Depreciation of vehicles

14,800 x 20% **2,960** (expense in profit and loss account)

W5 Depreciation of buildings

107,500 x 2% **2,150** (expense in profit and loss account)

Sample Higher Level question

Elements of this question may require an understanding of correction of errors and more difficult adjustments dealt with in Chapter 9.

The following trial balance was extracted from the books of Mike Baldwin on 31 December 20-9:

	€	€
Buildings (cost €656,000)	490,000	
Delivery vans (cost €90,000)	55,000	
12% Investments 1/6/-9	150,000	
9% Fixed mortgage (including an increase of €40,000 on 1/4/-9)		200,000
Patents (incorporating four months' investment income)	50,500	
Purchases and sales	505,000	784,000
Stocks 1/1/-9	52,600	
Commission	15,000	
Provision for bad debts		2,400
Salaries and general expenses	106,100	
Discount (net)		1,700
Rent		6,800
Mortgage interest paid for the first three months	4,500	
Insurance (incorporating suspense)	6,200	
Debtors and creditors	45,400	66,200
VAT		7,700
PRSI		1,800
Bank		15,900
Drawings	16,200	
Capital		410,000
	1,496,500	1,496,500

The following information and instructions are to be taken into account:

(a) Stock at 31/12/20-9 at cost was €51,000. This includes damaged stock which cost €5,000 but now has a net realisable value of €3,500.

(b) Provide for depreciation on vans at the annual rate of 15% of cost from the date of purchase to the date of sale. (**Note**: On 31/3/-9 a van which had cost €16,000 on 31/5/-5 was traded in against a new van which cost €20,000. An allowance of €7,000 was made on the old van. The cheque for the net amount of this transaction was incorrectly treated as the purchase of trading stock. This was the only entry in the books in respect of this transaction.)

(c) Patents incorporating four months' investment income received are to be written off over a five-year period commencing in 20-9.

(d) No record had been made in the books for goods in transit on 31/12/-9. The invoice for these goods had been received showing the recommended retail selling price of €12,500, which is cost plus 25%.

(e) The suspense figure arises as a result of the posting of an incorrect figure for mortgage interest in the mortgage interest account and discount received of €400 entered only in the creditors account. The correct interest figure was entered in the bank account.

(f) Provision should be made for mortgage interest due and investment income due.

(g) A new warehouse was purchased during the year for €60,000 plus VAT at 10%. The amount paid to the vendor was entered in the buildings account. No entry had been made in the VAT account.

(h) Provide for depreciation on buildings at the rate of 2% of cost per annum. It was decided to revalue the buildings to €850,000 on 31/12/-9.

(i) Provision for bad debts should be adjusted to 4% of debtors.

You are required to prepare:

- the trading, profit and loss account for the year ended 31/12/20-9
- the balance sheet as at 31/12/20-9.

Solution

Trading, Profit and Loss Account for Mike Baldwin for the year ended 31/12/20-9

	€	€	€
Sales			784,000
***Less* Cost of sales**			
Opening stock		52,600	
Purchases (W1)		502,000	
		554,600	
Less Closing stock (W2)		(59,500)	(495,100)
Gross profit			288,900
***Less* Expenses**			
Administration			
Salaries and general expenses	106,100		
Patents written off (W3)	11,300		
Insurance (W4)	7,500		
Depreciation of buildings (W5)	13,000	137,900	
Selling and distribution			
Commission	15,000		
Depreciation of vans (W6)	13,950	28,950	(166,850)
			122,050
***Add* Operating income**			
Profit on the sale of vans (W7)		200	
Reduction in provision for bad debts (W8)		584	
Rent		6,800	
Discount (W9)		2,100	9,684
Operating profit			131,734
Investment Income			10,500
			142,234
Less Mortgage interest (W10)			(17,100)
Net profit			**125,134**

6

Balance Sheet for Mike Baldwin as at 31/12/20-9

	Cost (€)	Aggregate Depreciation (€)	Net Book Value (€)	Total (€)
Intangible fixed assets				
Patents (56,500 - 11,300)				45,200
Tangible fixed assets				
Buildings (W11)	850,000	————	850,000	
Delivery vans (W12)	94,000	39,750	54,250	
	944,000	**39,750**	**904,250**	904,250
Financial fixed assets				
12% Investments				150,000
Current assets				1,099,450
Stock (W2)			59,500	
Debtors		45,400		
Less Provision for bad debts (W8)		(1,816)	43,584	
Investment income due			4,500	
			107,584	
Creditors: amounts falling due within 1 year				
Trade creditors (W13)		76,200		
Mortgage interest due (W10)		13,500		
VAT (W14)		1,700		
PRSI/USC		1,800		
Bank		15,900	109,100	
Net current assets				(1,516)
Total net assets				**1,097,934**
Financed by				
Creditors: amounts falling due after more than 1 year				
9% Fixed mortgage				200,000
Capital				
Capital 1/1/-9			410,000	
Add Net profit			125,134	
			535,134	
Less Drawings			(16,200)	
				518,934
Revaluation reserve (W15)				379,000
Capital employed				**1,097,934**

6

Workings

W1 Purchases

As per trial balance	505,000
Add Goods in transit	10,000
Less Payment for van	(13,000)
	502,000

W2 Closing stock

As given	51,000
Less Loss in value	(1,500)
Add Goods in transit	10,000
	59,500

W3 Patents

As per trial balance	50,500
Add Investment income	6,000
(12% of 150,000 x 4/12)	56,500
(56,500/5 = 11,300 written off)	

W4 Insurance

As per trial balance	6,200
Add Interest error	900
Add Discount error	400
	7,500

W5 Depreciation of buildings

656,000 - VAT 6,000 =	650,000
650,000 x 2% =	13,000

W6 Depreciation of vans

Old van 16,000 x 15% x 3/12	600
New van 20,000 x 15% x 9/12	2,250
Remainder 74,000 x 15%	11,100
	13,950

W7 Profit on sale of van

Cost price	16,000
Less Depreciation to date	(9,200)
Net value	6,800
Allowance	7,000
Profit	200

W8 Provision for bad debts

New 45,400 x 4% =	1,816
Less Old provision (TB)	(2,400)
Reduction	584

W9 Discount

As per trial balance	1,700
Add Error	400
	2,100

W10 Mortgage interest

160,000 x 9%	14,400
40,000 x 9% x 9/12	2,700
	17,100
Less Paid 160,000 x 9% x 3/12	(3,600)
Amount due	13,500

W11 Buildings

As per trial balance	656,000
Less VAT	(6,000)
	650,000
New value	850,000
Increase	200,000

W12 Delivery vans

Cost as per trial balance	90,000
Add New van	20,000
Less Old van	(16,000)
	94,000

Depreciation

As per trial balance	35,000
Add This year's charge	13,950
Less Disposal	(9,200)
	39,750

W13 Creditors

As per trial balance	66,200
Add Goods in transit	10,000
	76,200

W14 VAT

VAT as per VAT account	7,700
Less VAT on buildings	(6,000)
Vat due	1,700

W15 Revaluation reserve

Increase in value (W11)	200,000
Add This year's depreciation	13,000
Add Opening depreciation	166,000
	379,000

6

Practice Questions

6

Q1 Accruals and prepayments

(a) Advertising as per trial balance — €7,800

Advertising was for the year ended 31 March the following year.

Show the effect of this on the final accounts.

(b) Insurance as per trial balance — €8,400

Insurance was for the year ended 31 March the following year.

Show the effect of this on the final accounts.

(c) Cleaning as per trial balance — €9,400

Cleaning was for the year ended 31 March the following year.

Show the effect of this on the final accounts.

(d) Wages and salaries as per trial balance — €24,500

Wages due on 31 December amounted to €300.

Show the effect of this on the final accounts.

Q2 Bad debts and provision for bad debts

(a)

Trial Balance	**€**
Provision for bad debts	2,100
Debtors	45,000

Provision for bad debts should be adjusted to 4% of debtors.

Show the effects of this on the final accounts.

(b)

Trial Balance	**€**
Provision for bad debts	5,400
Debtors	96,000

Provision for bad debts should be adjusted to 3% of debtors.

Show the effects of this on the final accounts.

(c)

Trial Balance	**€**
Provision for bad debts	3,560
Debtors	104,000

Provision for bad debts should be adjusted to 5% of debtors.

Show the effects of this on the final accounts.

Q3 Loan interest

(a) 9% fixed loan received 1/4/20-1 — €240,000

Calculate the interest payable and show the relevant entries in the final accounts.

(b) 12% fixed loan received 1/7/20-2 — €96,000

Calculate the interest payable and show the relevant entries in the final accounts.

(c) 8% fixed loan received 1/10/20-3 — €102,000

Calculate the interest payable and show the relevant entries in the final accounts.

(d) 9% fixed loan received 30/09/20-4 — €66,000

Interest paid — €800

Calculate the interest payable and show the relevant entries in the final accounts.

Q4 Depreciation

(a) Roberts Ltd had the following entries in its trial balance on 31/12/20-1:

Buildings	340,000	
Motor vans	120,000	
Equipment	50,000	
Aggregate depreciation on vans		24,000
Aggregate depreciation on equipment		12,000

Provide for depreciation on assets as follows:

Buildings	2% of cost
Vans	20% of cost
Equipment	12% of book value

Calculate the amount to be charged as depreciation.

Show the relevant extracts from the balance sheet as at 31/12/20-1.

(b) Cruz Ltd had the following entries in its trial balance on 31/12/20-2:

Buildings	250,000	
Motor vans	100,000	
Furniture	35,000	
Aggregate depreciation on vans		16,000

Provide for depreciation on assets as follows:

Buildings	3% of cost
Vans	25% of book value
Furniture	10% of cost

Calculate the amount to be charged as depreciation.

Show the relevant extracts from the balance sheet as at 31/12/20-2.

(c) Samba Ltd had the following entries in its trial balance on 31/12/20-3:

Premises	870,000	
Motor vans	245,000	
Office machines	79,000	
Aggregate depreciation on vans		66,000
Aggregate depreciation on office machines		32,000

Provide for depreciation on assets as follows:

Buildings	4% of cost
Vans	25% of cost
Office machines	10% of book value

Calculate the amount to be charged as depreciation.

Show the relevant extracts from the balance sheet as at 31/12/20-3.

Q5 Apportionment of expenses

(a) Carriage €90,000

Carriage is to be split between sales and purchases in the ratio 5:4.

Show the effects of this adjustment on the final accounts.

(b) Light and heat €8,500

The owner has a private apartment above the business and has estimated that 25% of light and heat should be apportioned to the private section of the premises.

Show the effects of this adjustment on the final account.

6

(c) Light and heat €6,800

The owner has a private apartment above the business and has estimated that 10% of light and heat should be apportioned to the private section of the premises.

Show the effects of this adjustment on the final accounts.

Exercises – Ordinary Level

6

Q1 The following trial balance was extracted from the books of Ryan Malone, a sole trader, on 31 December 20-5:

	€	€
Buildings	280,000	
Delivery vans at cost	100,000	
Accumulated depreciation on vans		32,000
Fixtures and fittings (cost €40,000)	28,000	
Debtors and creditors	60,000	80,000
Stock 1/1/20-5	71,200	
Carriage inwards	4,800	
Purchases and sales	380,000	688,000
Salaries and general expenses	160,000	
Cleaning expenses	3,000	
Light and heat	5,200	
Insurance	6,800	
Advertising	3,800	
Bad debts	400	
Stationery	4,000	
Carriage outwards	2,000	
Long-term loan		120,000
Capital 1/1/20-5		180,000
Bank		9,200
	1,109,200	1,109,200

You are given the following additional information:

(a) Stock on 31/12/20-5 was valued at €56,000.

(b) Stock of heating oil on 31/12/20-5 was €800.

You are required to prepare:

- the trading, profit and loss account for the year ended 31/12/20-5
- the balance sheet as at 31/12/20-5.

Q2 **The following trial balance was extracted from the books of Cody Nicole, a sole trader, on 31 December 20-6:**

	€	€
Premises	375,000	
Delivery vans at cost	60,000	
Accumulated depreciation on delivery vans		18,000
Office equipment (cost €27,000)	15,000	
Debtors and creditors	33,000	48,000
Stock 1/1/20-6	46,500	
Custom duty	3,150	
Purchases and sales	300,000	555,000
Sundry expenses	50,250	
Wages and salaries	74,250	
Cleaning and repairs	1,800	
Light and heat	4,100	
Insurance	5,100	
Advertising	2,350	
Bad debts	600	
Stationery	3,750	
Carriage outwards	1,650	
Mortgage		120,000
Capital 1/1/20-6		225,000
Bank		10,500
	976,500	976,500

You are given the following additional information:

(a) **Stock on 31/12/-6 was valued at €41,000.**

(b) **Stock of stationery on 31/12/-6 was €300.**

(c) **Insurance prepaid was €600.**

(d) **Wages due €1,200.**

You are required to prepare:

- **the trading, profit and loss account for the year ended 31/12/20-6**
- **the balance sheet as at 31/12/20-6.**

6

Q3 **The following balances were taken from the books of Joe Ingles, a sole trader, on 31 December 20-7:**

	€	€
Buildings (cost €600,000)	450,000	
Delivery vans at cost	198,000	
Accumulated depreciation on vans		79,200
Computers and equipment	32,400	
Accumulated depreciation on computers		9,000
Goodwill	54,000	
Debtors and creditors	50,400	54,000
Capital 1/1/20-7		504,000
Mortgage 1/5/20-7		162,000
Purchases and sales	536,400	756,000
Carriage	14,400	
Wages and salaries	133,200	
Stock 1/1/20-7	86,400	
Returns	10,800	2,880
Stationery	3,360	
Provision for bad debts		3,600
Commission		12,060
Drawings	21,600	
General expenses	25,200	
Advertising	15,840	
Discount		5,040
Loan interest paid	7,200	
VAT		3,840
USC		5,220
Bank		42,360
	1,639,200	1,639,200

You are given the following additional information:

(a) **Stocks at 31/12/20-7 were: trading stock €116,400; stationery €720.**

(b) **Carriage is to be divided 70% for carriage on sales and 30% on purchases.**

(c) **Wages and salaries are to be divided 85% to workers and 15% to drawings.**

(d) **Depreciation is to be provided as follows:**

Buildings	**3% of cost**
Vans	**15% of cost**
Computers	**10% of book value**

(e) **Provide for interest on the mortgage at the rate of 8% per annum.**

(f) **Advertising was for the year ended 31/4/20-8.**

(g) **Provision for bad debts to be adjusted to 6% of debtors.**

You are required to prepare:

- **a trading, profit and loss account for the year ended 31/12/20-7**
- **a balance sheet as at 31/12/20-7.**

6

Q4 The following balances were extracted from the books of John Deere, a sole trader, on 31 December 20-8:

	€	€
Land and buildings	560,000	
Motor vehicles	182,000	
Office equipment	56,000	
Patents	86,800	
Accumulated depreciation on vehicles		72,800
Accumulated depreciation on office equipment		22,400
Capital 1/1/20-8		462,000
Purchases and sales	532,000	1,008,000
Custom duty	2,520	
Wages and salaries	117,600	
Debtors and creditors	105,000	50,400
Discount received		7,840
Term loan received 1/4/20-8		140,000
Loan interest paid	7,000	
Commission	9,800	
Returns	10,220	3,360
Cleaning and repairs	8,960	
General expenses	20,860	
Provision for bad debts		2,380
Insurance	33,600	
Bank		18,340
VAT		7,980
USC		14,000
Drawings	15,680	
Stationery	6,860	
Stock 1/1/20-8	54,600	
	1,809,500	1,809,500

You are given the following additional information:

(a) Stocks at 31/12/20-8 were €36,400.

(b) Stock of stationery was €420 on 31/12/20-8.

(c) Insurance was for the year ended 31/03/20-9.

(d) Provision should be made for interest due on the loan. The rate of interest is 10% per annum.

(e) Wages and salaries are to be divided 80% for employees and 20% for drawings.

(f) Depreciation is to be as follows:

Buildings	4% of cost per annum
Motor vehicles	15% of cost per annum
Office equipment	10% of net book value

(g) Provision for bad debts is to be adjusted to 8% of debtors.

6

You are required to prepare:

- the trading, profit and loss account for the year ended 31/12/20-8
- the balance sheet as at 31/12/20-8.

Q5 The following balances were extracted from the books of Annette Curtain, a sole trader, on 31 December 20-1:

	€	€
Premises	340,000	
Delivery vans	150,000	
Furniture and equipment	97,000	
Patents	160,000	
Accumulated depreciation on vans		63,000
Accumulated depreciation on furniture		12,000
Capital 1/1/20-1		401,000
Purchases and sales	298,000	825,600
Carriage	18,500	
Wages and salaries	98,000	
Debtors and creditors	74,600	89,000
Discount net	4,500	
Loan received 1/4/20-1		100,000
Loan interest paid	1,410	
Commission		4,900
General expenses	87,900	
Insurance	68,900	
Provision for bad debts		4,600
Bank		45,900
Stock 1/1/20-1	43,010	
Drawings	23,500	
Stationery	61,690	
VAT		13,400
PRSI and USC		2,500
Cleaning	34,890	
	1,561,900	1,561,900

You are given the following additional information:

(a) Stocks at 31/12/20-1 were €34,500 and stock of stationery €1,290.

(b) Cleaning expenses include a payment of €5,800 for January 20-2.

(c) Provide for loan interest at the rate of 8% per annum. Provide for the loan interest due.

(d) Carriage is 60% on sales and the remainder on purchases.

(e) Provide for depreciation on vans at 20%, furniture at 15% and premises at 3% of cost.

(f) Provision for bad debts should be adjusted to 7% of debtors.

You are required to prepare:

- the trading, profit and loss account for the year ended 31/12/20-1
- the balance sheet as at 31/12/20-1.

6

Exercises – Higher Level

Q1 The following trial balance was extracted from the books of John Lambert on 31 December 20-9:

	€	€
Buildings (cost €984,375)	727,500	
Delivery vans (cost €135,000)	82,500	
12% Investments 1/6/-9	225,000	
10% Fixed mortgage (including an increase of €60,000 on 1/4/-9)		300,000
Patents (incorporating 4 months' investment income received)	75,750	
Debtors and creditors	68,100	96,600
Purchases and sales	742,500	1,161,000
Stocks 1/1/20-9	71,400	
Commission	30,000	
Provision for bad debts		3,300
Salaries and general expenses	144,900	
Discount (net)		4,050
Rent		13,200
Mortgage interest paid for first 3 months	6,750	
Insurance (incorporating suspense)	10,800	
VAT		10,050
PRSI and USC		3,450
Bank		112,350
Drawings	43,800	
Capital		525,000
	2,229,000	2,229,000

The following information and instructions are to be taken into account:

(a) Stock at 31/12/20-9 at cost was €64,000. This figure includes damaged stock which cost €12,000 but which now has a net realisable value of €8,900.

(b) Provide for depreciation on vans at an annual rate of 12.5% of cost per annum from date of purchase to the date of sale. (**Note:** On 31/3/20-9, a delivery van which had cost €24,000 on 31/5/20-4 was traded in against a new van costing €32,000. An allowance of €10,500 was made for the old van. The cheque for the net amount of this transaction was incorrectly treated as the purchase of trading stock. This was the only entry made in the books in respect of this transaction.)

(c) Patents, which incorporate four months' investment income, are to be written off over a five-year period commencing in 20-9.

(d) No record had been made in the books for goods in transit on 31/12/20-9. The invoice for these goods had been received showing a recommended retail selling price of €18,750, which is cost plus 25%.

(e) The suspense figure arises as a result of the incorrect posting for mortgage interest in the mortgage interest account and discount received of €600 entered only in the creditors account. The correct interest was entered in the bank account.

6

(f) Provision should be made for mortgage interest due and investment income due.

(g) A new warehouse was purchased during the year for €75,000 plus VAT at 12.5%. The amount paid to the vendor was entered in the buildings account and no entry was made in the VAT account.

(h) Provide for depreciation on buildings at the rate of 3% of cost per annum. It was decided to revalue buildings at €1,150,000 on 31/12/20-9.

(i) Provision for bad debts should be adjusted to 5% of debtors.

You are required to prepare:

- the trading, profit and loss account for the year ended 31/12/20-9
- the balance sheet as at 31/12/20-9.

Q2 The following trial balance was extracted from the books of Emma O'Reilly on 31 December 20-7:

	€	€
Buildings (cost €693,750)	641,250	
Delivery vans (cost €97,500)	45,375	
6% Investments 1/6/20-7	120,000	
Patents (incorporating 3 months' investment income)	45,450	
5% Fixed mortgage (including increase of 6% €75,000 on 1/4/20-7)		225,000
Debtors and creditors	57,375	64,125
Purchases and sales	487,500	729,150
Commission	49,275	
Salaries and general expenses (incorporating suspense)	108,750	
Provision for bad debts		2,925
Discount (net)		5,625
Rent		9,000
Mortgage interest paid for the first 3 months	2,250	
Insurance	5,850	
VAT		3,225
PRSI and USC		4,800
Bank		45,600
Drawings	27,000	
Stock at 1/1/20-7	50,625	
Capital		551,250
	1,640,700	1,640,700

The following information and instructions are to be taken into account:

(a) Stock at 31/12/20-7 at cost was €55,000. No record had been made in the books for goods in transit on 31/12/20-7. The invoice for these goods had been received showing the recommended retail selling price of €5,250, which is cost plus 20%.

(b) Provide for depreciation on vans at an annual rate of 10% of cost per annum from date of purchase to the date of sale. (**Note:** On 31/3/20-7, a delivery van which had cost €30,000 on 30/9/20-4 was traded in against a new van costing €40,000. An allowance of €12,500 was made for the old van. The cheque for the net amount of this transaction was incorrectly treated as the purchase of trading stock. This was the only entry made in the books in respect of this transaction.)

6

(c) Patents, incorporating three months' investment income, are to be written off over a five-year period commencing in 20-7.

(d) The suspense figure arises as a result of the incorrect posting for mortgage interest in the mortgage interest account and discount received of €900 entered only in the creditors account. The correct interest was entered in the bank account.

(e) Provision should be made for mortgage interest due and investment income due.

(f) A new warehouse was purchased during the year for €150,000 plus VAT at 12.5%. The amount paid to the vendor was entered in the buildings account and no entry was made in the VAT account.

(g) Provide for depreciation on buildings at the rate of 2% of cost per annum. It was decided to revalue buildings at €800,000 on 31/12/20-7.

(h) Provision for bad debts should be adjusted to 4% of debtors.

You are required to prepare:

- the trading, profit and loss account for the year ended 31/12/20-7
- the balance sheet as at 31/12/20-7.

Q3 The following trial balance was extracted from the books of Tom Kehoe on 31 December 20-5:

	€	€
9% Investments (1/6/20-5)	320,000	
Buildings (cost €1,568,000)	1,492,800	
Delivery vans (cost €240,000)	128,800	
5% Fixed mortgage (including €320,000 5% on 1/4/20-5)		800,000
Patents (incorporating 4 months' investment income)	88,800	
Debtors and creditors	124,160	138,400
Purchases and sales	1,068,800	1,571,200
Stocks 1/1/20-5	108,320	
Commission	38,400	
Provision for bad debts		6,080
Salaries and general expenses	310,560	
Discount (net)		7,360
Rent		24,000
Mortgage interest paid for first 3 months	6,400	
Insurance (incorporating suspense)	13,920	
VAT		8,800
PRSI and USC		3,680
Bank		113,440
Drawings	60,000	
Capital		1,088,000
	3,760,960	3,760,960

The following information and instructions are to be taken into account:

(a) Stock at 31/12/20-5 at cost was €92,000. This figure includes damaged stock which cost €6,000 but which now has a net realisable value of €3,200.

(b) Provide for depreciation on vans at an annual rate of 15% of cost per annum from date of purchase to the date of sale. (**Note:** On 31/3/20-5, a delivery van which had cost €36,000 on 31/5/20-2 was traded in against a new van costing €54,000. An allowance of €17,000 was made for the old

6

van. The cheque for the net amount of this transaction was incorrectly treated as the purchase of trading stock. This was the only entry made in the books in respect of this transaction.)

(c) Patents, incorporating three months' investment income, are to be written off over a five-year period commencing in 20-5.

(d) No record had been made in the books for goods in transit on 31/12/20-5. The invoice for these goods had been received showing a recommended retail selling price of €21,250, which is cost plus 25%.

(e) The suspense figure arises as a result of the incorrect posting for mortgage interest in the mortgage interest account and discount received of €200 entered only in the discount account. The correct interest was entered in the bank account.

(f) Provision should be made for mortgage interest due and investment income due.

(g) A new warehouse was purchased during the year for €384,000 plus VAT at 12.5%. The amount paid to the vendor was entered in the buildings account and no entry was made in the VAT account.

(h) Provide for depreciation on buildings at the rate of 4% of cost per annum. It was decided to revalue buildings at €1,700,000 on 31/12/20-5.

(i) Provision for bad debts should be adjusted to 5% of debtors.

You are required to prepare:

- the trading, profit and loss account for the year ended 31/12/20-5
- the balance sheet as at 31/12/20-5.

6

Q4 The following trial balance was extracted from the books of Phil Lacey on 31 December 20-8:

	€	€
Buildings (cost €406,000)	339,500	
Delivery vans (cost €59,500)	51,100	
8% Investments (1/4/20-8)	91,000	
6% Fixed mortgage (including received €35,000 1/4/20-8)		105,000
Patents (incorporating 3 months' investment income)	36,680	
Debtors and creditors	28,000	79,100
Purchases and sales	358,680	510,300
Stock 1/1/20-8	45,920	
Commission	2,940	
Salaries and general expenses	59,500	
Provision for bad debts		840
Discount (net)	1,330	
Rent	6,300	
Mortgage interest paid for the first 3 months	875	
Insurance (including suspense)	4,305	
VAT		2,870
Bank		11,130
PRSI and USC		2,730
Drawings	25,340	
Capital		339,500
	1,051,470	1,051,470

The following information and instructions are to be taken into account:

(a) Stock at 31/12/20-8 at cost was €52,500. No record had been made in the books for goods in transit on 31/12/20-8. The invoice for these goods had been received showing the recommended retail selling price of €4,200, which is cost plus 25%.

(b) Provide for depreciation on vans at an annual rate of 15% of cost per annum from date of purchase to the date of sale. (**Note:** On 31/3/20-8, a delivery van which had cost €20,000 on 30/9/20-5 was traded in against a new van costing €25,200. An allowance of €10,000 was made for the old van. The cheque for the net amount of this transaction was incorrectly treated as the purchase of trading stock. This was the only entry made in the books in respect of this transaction.)

(c) Patents, incorporating three months' investment income, are to be written off over a five-year period commencing in 20-8.

(d) The suspense figure arises as a result of the incorrect posting for mortgage interest in the mortgage interest account and discount received of €140 entered only in the creditors account. The correct interest was entered in the bank account.

(e) Provision should be made for mortgage interest due. 20% of the mortgage interest for the year relates to the private section of the building.

(f) Goods with a retail value of €7,000 were returned to a supplier. The selling price was cost plus 25%. The supplier issued a credit note showing a restocking charge of 10% of cost price. No entry had been made in the books of the restocking charge.

(g) Provide for depreciation on buildings at the rate of 2% of cost per annum. It was decided to revalue the buildings at €560,000 on 31/12/20-8.

(h) Goods withdrawn by the owner for private use during the year with a retail value of €1,400, which is cost plus 25%, were omitted from the books.

(i) A cheque for €420 had been received on 31/12/20-8 in respect of a debt of €700 previously written off as bad. The debtor has agreed to pay the remainder with two months. No entry was made in the books in respect of this transaction.

You are required to prepare:

- the trading, profit and loss account for the year ended 31/12/20-8
- the balance sheet as at 31/12/20-8.

6

Q5 The following trial balance was extracted from the books of Mary Mosse on 31 December 20-6:

	€	€
Buildings (cost €744,000)	618,000	
Delivery vans (cost €108,000)	96,000	
4% Investments 1/7/20-6	144,000	
Patents (incorporating 3 months' investment income)	72,480	
6% Fixed mortgage (including increase of €96,000 on 1/4/20-6)		216,000
Debtors and creditors	60,000	144,000
Purchases and sales	558,240	791,580
Stock 1/1/20-6	75,840	
Commission	6,660	
Salaries and general expenses (including suspense)	90,000	
Provision for bad debts		2,160

Continued >

	€	€
Discount (net)	1,920	
Rent	9,600	
Mortgage interest paid for the first 3 months	1,680	
Advertising	2,880	
VAT		5,520
Bank		15,960
PAYE, PRSI and USC		6,480
Drawings	38,400	
Capital		594,000
	1,775,700	1,775,700

The following information and instructions are to be taken into account:

(a) **Stock at 31/12/20-6 at cost was €90,480. This figure includes damaged stock which cost €9,840 but which now has a net realisable value of €4,080.**

(b) **Provide for depreciation on vans at an annual rate of 12.5% of cost per annum from date of purchase to the date of sale. (Note: On 31/3/20-6, a delivery van which had cost €28,800 on 30/9/20-3 was traded in against a new van costing €57,600. An allowance of €14,400 was made for the old van. The cheque for the net amount of this transaction was incorrectly treated as the purchase of trading stock. This was the only entry made in the books in respect of this transaction.)**

(c) **Patents, incorporating three months' investment income, are to be written off over a five-year period commencing in 20-6.**

(d) **The suspense figure arises as a result of the incorrect posting for mortgage interest in the mortgage interest account and €1,200 paid for PAYE entered only in the bank account. The correct interest was entered in the bank account.**

(e) **Provision should be made for mortgage interest due. 10% of the mortgage interest for the year relates to the private section of the building.**

(f) **Goods with a retail value of €10,080 were returned to a supplier. The selling price was cost plus 20%. The supplier issued a credit note showing a restocking charge of 10% of cost price. No entry had been made in the books of the restocking charge.**

(g) **Provide for depreciation on buildings at the rate of 4% of cost per annum. It was decided to revalue the buildings at €1,020,000 on 31/12/20-6.**

(h) **The advertising payment is towards a 24-month campaign which began on 1/11/20-6.**

(i) **A cheque for €480 was received on 31/12/20-6 in respect of a debt of €1,080 previously written off as bad. The debtor has agreed to pay the remainder within a month. No entry was made in the books in respect of this transaction.**

You are required to prepare:

- **the trading, profit and loss account for the year ended 31/12/20-6**
- **the balance sheet as at 31/12/20-6.**

Q6 The following trial balance was extracted from the books of Maura Naughton on 31 December 20-5:

	€	€
Land and buildings (original cost €1,200,000)	1,500,000	
Computers and office equipment (cost €900,000)	750,000	
Drawings (incorporating rent received for the year)	40,000	
Capital		600,000
6% Investments received on 1/06/20-5	180,000	
VAT		24,000
PAYE, PRSI and USC		2,100
6.6% Fixed mortgage		300,000
Mortgage interest paid for the first 3 months	7,500	
Commission		3,000
Delivery vans at cost	300,000	
Accumulated depreciation on delivery vans		75,000
Debtors and creditors	48,000	72,000
Purchases and sales	841,350	1,935,000
Returns	8,850	
Stock 1/1/20-5	35,100	
Rent and rates	20,400	
Salaries and general expenses (incorporating suspense)	66,720	
Provision for bad debts		1,500
Light and heat	18,450	
Showroom expenses	26,850	
Revaluation reserve		300,000
Cash and bank	50,780	581,400
	3,894,000	3,894,000

The following information and instructions are to be taken into account:

(a) Stock at 31/12/20-5 at cost was €30,000. This includes stock of heating oil, €2,500.

(b) The suspense figure arises from the incorrect figure for mortgage interest entered in the mortgage interest account and discount allowed of €400 entered only in the debtors account. The correct figure for mortgage interest was entered in the bank account.

(c) Rent received for the year was €4,500, and one fifth of light and heat used was to be reclassified as drawings.

(d) The land had originally been purchased for €750,000. It was revalued at the end of 20-4. It was decided to revalue land again on 31/12/20-5 at €1,200,000. Buildings are to be depreciated at the rate of 2% of cost per annum.

(e) Sales include goods sold on a sale-or-return basis for €20,000. The debtor has indicated that the goods will be returned. The goods were sold at a mark-up of cost plus 25%.

(f) Provide for depreciation on office equipment at an annual rate of 20% from date of purchase to date of sale. (**Note:** On 30/9/20-5 computer equipment which cost €180,000 on 1/12/-3 was upgraded to a new system costing €225,000. An allowance of €90,000 was

6

made for the old system. The cheque for the net amount of this transaction was treated as the purchase of a delivery van. This was the only entry in the books in respect of this transaction.)

(g) Provide for depreciation on delivery vans at the rate of 30% of book value on 31/12/20-5.

(h) Provision should be made for mortgage interest payable and interest receivable due.

(i) Provision for bad debts should be adjusted to 5% of debtors.

You are required to prepare:

- the trading, profit and loss account for the year ended 31/12/20-5
- the balance sheet as at 31/12/20-5.

Q7 The following trial balance was extracted from the books of Michael Knight on 31/12/20-5:

	€	€
Land and buildings (cost €1,000,000)	900,000	
Delivery vans (cost €280,000)	200,000	
Drawings	34,500	
Light and heat	2,900	
Insurance	8,900	
Patents (incorporating 4 months' investment income)	92,000	
Purchases and sales	260,000	624,000
Rent	29,000	16,000
Bank deposit account	34,900	
Bank overdraft		45,000
6% Investments	80,000	
Stock (1/1/20-5) (including stock oil, €4,500)	28,700	
VAT		10,900
PRSI and USC		12,900
Debtors and creditors	108,000	93,490
8% Fixed interest mortgage (including an increase of €56,000 on 1/7/20-5)		246,000
Salaries and general expenses	68,500	
Showroom expenses (incorporating suspense)	3,800	
Provision for bad debts		3,400
Discount (net)	490	
Capital		800,000
	1,851,690	1,851,690

The following additional information is to be taken into account:

(a) Stock at 31/12/20-5 is valued at €32,400, which includes goods which cost €2,300 but have a net realisable value of 70% of cost, and stock of oil of €1,290.

(b) No record was made for goods in transit which were purchased for €8,000 plus VAT at 20%. The invoice was received.

(c) The suspense figure arises from the discount received of €310 entered only in the discount account.

6

(d) Provide for mortgage interest and investment interest due.

(e) During the year Knight took from stock goods to the value of €50 per week. However, owing to a computer error this was not recorded in the books.

(f) Drawings include €2,300 paid to Knight's daughter for summer work in the business.

(g) Provide for depreciation on buildings at the rate of 4% per annum. Knight revalued land and buildings at €1,200,000 on 31/12/20-5. Land had cost €200,000.

(h) During the year debts amounting to €3,500 were to be written off as bad and the provision for bad debts was to be adjusted to 4% of remaining debtors.

(i) Provide for depreciation on vans at the annual rate of 10% of cost from the date of purchase to the date of sale. (**Note:** On 1/4/20-5, a delivery van which had cost €34,000 on 1/10/20-2 was traded in against a new van costing €56,000. An allowance of €18,000 was made for the old van. The cheque for the net amount of this transaction was incorrectly treated as the purchase of trading stock. These were the only entries made in the books in respect of this transaction.)

(j) Knight estimated that 10% of light and heat used should be attributed to a private apartment based above the store.

You are required to prepare:

- the trading, profit and loss account for the year ended 31/12/20-5
- the balance sheet as at 31/12/20-5.

6

Exam Tips

- Know how to treat all accruals and prepayments correctly.
- Classify expenses as either administration or selling and distribution – this will be consistent with final accounts for other business organisations.
- Learn the layout for the preparation of these accounts.
- Assets and expenses are listed on the debit side of the trial balance.
- Liabilities and gains are listed on the credit side of the trial balance.
- Assets and liabilities are entered in the balance sheet.
- Expenses and gains are entered in the trading, profit and loss account.
- Practise the adjustments individually before attempting to prepare the final accounts. Develop a procedure for dealing with these adjustments.
- Make sure you write the titles of the accounts in full, including the year concerned.
- Avoid using abbreviations in your final answer.
- Be careful with the date of issue of loans and purchase of investments.
- The sole trader appears in Section A of the examination as one of the four possible final account questions carrying 120 marks.

7 Correction of Errors - Suspense Accounts

Objectives

On completion students should be able to:

- List and explain errors that do not affect the trial balance;
- Prepare journal entries to correct errors;
- Prepare the suspense account;
- Prepare a statement of corrected net profit;
- Prepare an adjusted balance sheet after the errors have been corrected.

The trial balance

Before preparing the final accounts of a business it is best practice to prepare a **trial balance**. This will ensure the accuracy of the double-entry bookkeeping system. If the double-entry principle is correctly applied then the total of all the debit entries should be equal to the total of the credit entries.

A **trial balance** is a list of balances taken from the ledger accounts.

To prepare a trial balance, the first step is to balance each of the ledger accounts and bring down the balances.

Then all the debit balances are listed under a column headed **Debit,** and all the credit balances are listed in a column headed **Credit**.

Here is a sample trial balance using entries from all the books of first entries.

Example

The following are the balances taken from the books of Phil Mitchell on 31/12/20-1:

Land and buildings €180,000; office equipment €50,000; carriage €600; discount received €200; discount allowed €100; rent payable €800; wages €49,000; cleaning €1,400; cash €1,000; bank €4,000; debtors €1,900; creditors €2,000; sales €406,000; purchases €240,000.

Prepare a trial balance.

Solution

Phil Mitchell Trial Balance as on 31/12/-1

	Debit €	Credit €
Land and buildings	180,000	
Office equipment	50,000	
Carriage	600	
Discount received		200
Discount allowed	100	
Rent payable	800	
Wages	49,000	
Cleaning	1,400	
Cash	1,000	
Bank	4,000	
Debtors	1,900	
Creditors		2,000
Sales		406,000
Purchases	240,000	
Capital (Phil Mitchell)		120,600
	528,800	528,800

7

Notes on the trial balance:

- The **capital** account balance is equal to the difference between debits and credits.
- The **assets** and **expenses/losses** accounts are on the **debit** side.
- The **liabilities** and **gains** accounts are on the **credit** side.
- The **asset** accounts (buildings, office equipment) are **real** accounts.
- The **losses** and **expenses** such as rent and wages are **nominal** accounts.
- The **debtors** and **creditors** are **personal** accounts.

In summary:

Debit	Credit	Entered in
Assets	**L**iabilities	Balance sheet
Expenses	**G**ains	Trading, profit and loss account

Errors revealed by the trial balance

Mathematical errors – errors of addition or subtraction

Double-entry errors – an entry on the debit side without a corresponding entry on the credit side or vice versa, or different amounts on the debit and credit sides

Misplaced entries – an entry entered on the incorrect side

Errors not revealed by the trial balance

- **Errors of omission**
- **Errors of principle**
- **Errors of commission**
- **Compensating errors**
- **Errors of original entry**
- **Complete reversal of entries**

Errors of omission

This is where the entries have been completely left out, hence nothing has been entered on the debit side or the credit side of the relevant accounts. For example, cash sales €300 omitted from the books. These entries are corrected by simply entering them into the books.

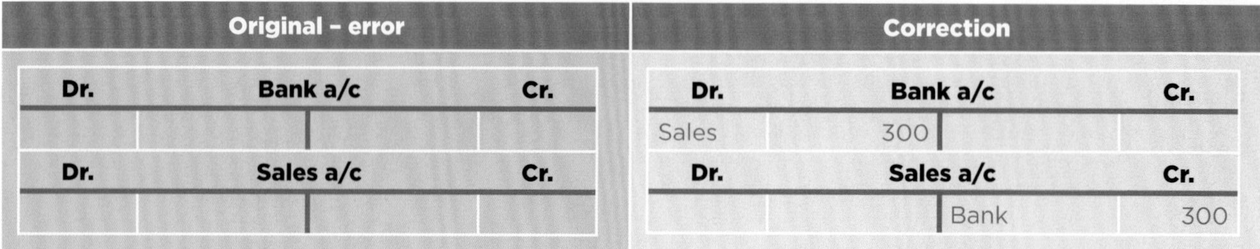

Original - error

Dr.	Bank a/c		Cr.

Dr.	Sales a/c		Cr.

Correction

Dr.	Bank a/c		Cr.
Sales	300		

Dr.	Sales a/c		Cr.
		Bank	300

Errors of principle

These are entries that are on the correct sides but in the wrong type (class) of account. An example of this is where an expense is treated as an asset. For example, repairs to vans €500 debited in error to the delivery vans account.

7

Original - error

Dr.	Delivery Van a/c		Cr.
Bank	500		

Dr.	Bank a/c		Cr.
		Repairs	500

Correction

Dr.	Delivery Van a/c		Cr.
Bank	500	Cancel	500

Dr.	Bank a/c		Cr.
		Bank	500

Dr.	Repairs a/c		Cr.
Correction	500		

Errors of commission

This is where entries are made in the correct type of account but in the incorrect account. For example, sales on credit to P. Ryan €700 debited to J. Ryan instead.

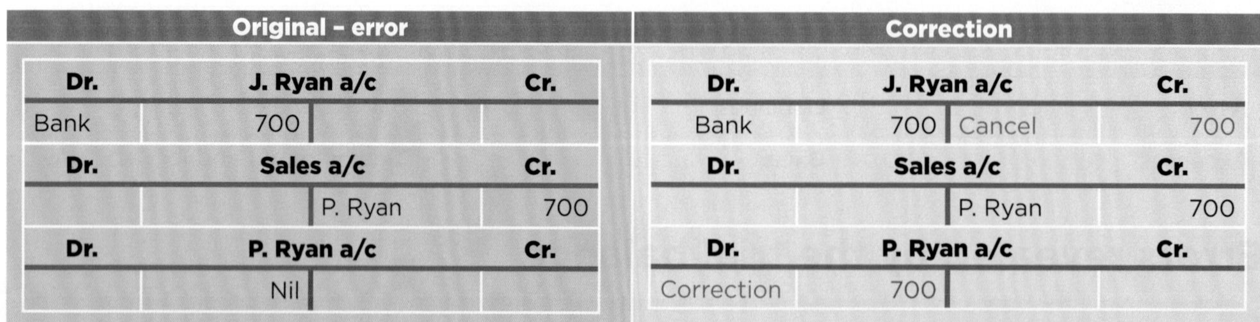

Original - error

Dr.	J. Ryan a/c		Cr.
Bank	700		

Dr.	Sales a/c		Cr.
		P. Ryan	700

Dr.	P. Ryan a/c		Cr.
	Nil		

Correction

Dr.	J. Ryan a/c		Cr.
Bank	700	Cancel	700

Dr.	Sales a/c		Cr.
		P. Ryan	700

Dr.	P. Ryan a/c		Cr.
Correction	700		

Compensating errors

This is where one error cancels another error. For example, a payment of €600 for cleaning entered as €60 on the debit of the cleaning account and on the credit side of the cash account.

Original - error				Correction			
Dr.	**Cleaning a/c**		**Cr.**	**Dr.**	**Cleaning a/c**		**Cr.**
Cash	60			Cash	60		
				Correction	540		
Dr.	**Cash a/c**		**Cr.**	**Dr.**	**Cash a/c**		**Cr.**
		Cleaning	60			Cleaning	60
						Correction	540

Errors of original entry

These are errors made in the books of first entry. For example, sales €207 treated as €702 in both the sales account and the cash account.

Original - error				Correction			
Dr.	**Bank a/c**		**Cr.**	**Dr.**	**Bank a/c**		**Cr.**
Sales	702			Sales	702	Correction	495
Dr.	**Sales a/c**		**Cr.**	**Dr.**	**Sales a/c**		**Cr.**
		Bank	702	Correction	495	Bank	702

Complete reversal of entry

This is where the correct accounts are used but both entries are on the incorrect sides of accounts. For example, rent paid €300 should be credited to bank a/c and debited to rent a/c, but these were entered incorrectly as a credit in rent a/c and debit in bank a/c.

Original - error				Correction			
Dr.	**Bank a/c**		**Cr.**	**Dr.**	**Bank a/c**		**Cr.**
Rent	300			Rent	300	Correction	600
Dr.	**Rent a/c**		**Cr.**	**Dr.**	**Rent a/c**		**Cr.**
		Bank	300	Correction	600	Bank	300

Suspense accounts

The six errors above and their corrections do not affect the balancing of the trial balance. However, when the trial balance fails to agree as a result of other types of error, the difference between the debit and credit sides is temporarily entered in a **suspense account**.

The suspense account is included as an account in the trial balance on the smaller side to make up the shortfall.

Errors that affect the balancing of the trial balance consist of:

- Errors in figures and additions
- Posting only one side of the double entry
- Entering one amount on the debit side of one ledger account and entering a different amount on the credit side of another ledger account or vice-versa.

When all the errors have been found and corrected, the balance on the suspense account will be eliminated and all the ledger accounts will then be correct. In a situation where draft final accounts are prepared before the errors are found, the following applies:

- If the suspense account balance is a debit balance it will be a current asset in the balance sheet.
- If the suspense account balance is a credit balance it will be a current liability in the balance sheet.

Procedure for dealing with errors

1. **Journalise** the necessary entries in the journal and provide a suitable narration which is a summary of the error and its correction.
2. Use **T-accounts** as follows:
   (i) Enter the original error(s) in the relevant account(s) in one colour.
   (ii) Enter the transaction as it should have been treated in the relevant account(s) – use separate T-accounts.
   (iii) Make the necessary adjustments in the relevant account(s) in a different colour, with the amounts necessary to arrive at the correct solution.
   (iv) Use a separate suspense account for each error. The overall suspense account will be a combination of each of these individual errors.
3. The **corrected entries** (those in the second colour) are the corrections that should be entered in the journal, as they are in the T-accounts.

Effects of errors on net profit

All errors in ledger accounts will affect either the profit and loss account or the balance sheet. If an expense or gain account is affected by an error and has to be adjusted this will affect the net profit.

To correct the profit and loss figure, a **statement of corrected net profit** is prepared. Only entries that affect expenses and gains will be entered in this statement.

7

Statement of Corrected Net Profit (template)

		€	€
Profit as per draft accounts			xxx
Add	Any **expense** account **credited** in the journal	xx	
	Any **gain** account **credited** in the journal	xx	xx
Less	Any **expense** account **debited** in the journal	xx	
	Any **gain** account **debited** in the journal	xx	(xx)
Corrected net profit			xxx

Effects of errors on the balance sheet (Higher Level)

We previously adjusted net profit for any expense or gain that was changed in the journal. We now look at the assets and liabilities we changed in the journal. Remember that the overall original suspense will also affect the account where the suspense figure was originally placed, for example in closing stock.

Summary of changes to assets and liabilities

	Debit	Credit
Asset will increase if	we debit the asset a/c	
Asset will decrease if		we credit the asset a/c
Liability will increase if		we credit the liability a/c
Liability will decrease if	we debit the liability a/c	

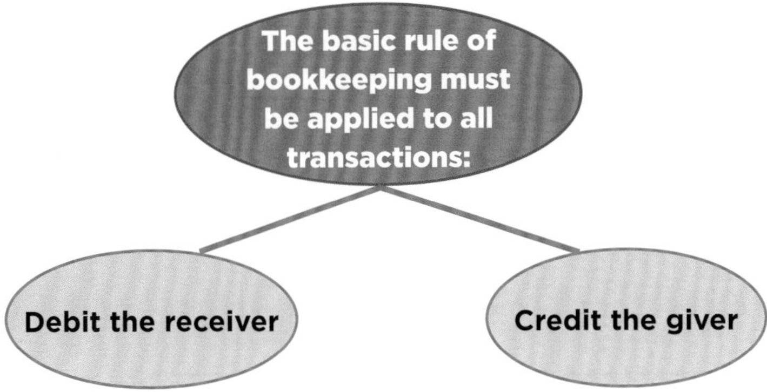

NOTE

Ensure that an account that incorporates the original suspense balance is also adjusted in the corrected balance sheet.

Sample Ordinary Level question

T. Kewell's trial balance failed to agree and the difference was entered in the suspense account. An examination of the books revealed the following errors:

(1) Goods sold on credit to John Jones for €1,200 had been posted to James Jones's account.

(2) Total of the purchases daybook, €24,000, had been posted to the purchases account as €42,000.

(3) Interest received, €230, had been treated as interest paid.

(4) Goods previously sold on credit, €190, were returned by a debtor. This return has been omitted from the books.

(5) Goods taken by Kewell, €230, for private use had not been entered in the books.

You are required to:

(a) Journalise the necessary corrections.

(b) Show the suspense account.

(c) Prepare a statement of corrected net profit if the profit as per accounts was €12,000.

Solution

Error 1

This is an error of commission. Since the debit and credit entries were correct, there will be no suspense account needed.

Since we need to transfer the figure from James Jones to John Jones, we credit James Jones and debit John Jones.

Sales a/c

Dr.			Cr.
		John Jones	1,200

James Jones a/c

Dr.			Cr.
Sales	1,200	Correction	1,200

John Jones a/c

Dr.			Cr.
Correction	1,200		

NOTE

Write down original entries in one colour.
Make necessary adjustments in a different colour.

Error 2

Here there is a difference between the debits and the credits so a suspense account will be needed. Enter the original entries and then place the difference in the suspense account.

We need to reduce purchases, hence we credit purchases and we debit suspense to cancel the original mistake.

Purchases a/c

Dr.			Cr.
Creditors	42,000	Correction	18,000

Creditors a/c

Dr.			Cr.
		Purchases	24,000

Suspense a/c

Dr.			Cr.
Correction	18,000	Original	18,000

Error 3

This is a complete reversal of entries and therefore no suspense account will be needed, as the debits and credits match.

Because the figures were reversed there will be a need to double them to make the position correct.

Dr.	Bank a/c		Cr.
Correction	460	Interest	230

Dr.	Interest a/c		Cr.
Bank	230	Correction	460

NOTE

The suspense account should be closed when all adjustments are made.

Error 4

This is an error of omission. Since it was not originally entered in the books both debit and credit are nil. Therefore the trial balance is not affected and there is no need for a suspense account.

Dr.	Debtor a/c		Cr.
		Correction	190

Dr.	Sales Returns a/c		Cr.
Correction	190		

Error 5

This is an error of omission, which means no suspense account is required.

Dr.	Drawings a/c		Cr.
Correction	230		

7

Dr.	Purchases a/c		Cr.
		Correction	230

(a) Journal

	€	€
John Jones (E1)	1,200	
James Jones		1,200
Being correction of error, incorrect debtor account posted with credit sales		
Suspense (E2)	18,000	
Purchases		18,000
Being correction of error, purchases day book incorrectly posted to the ledger		
Bank (E3)	460	
Interest		460
Being correction of error, interest received treated as interest paid		
Sales returns (E4)	190	
Debtors		190
Being correction of error, sales returned by a debtor omitted from the books		
Drawings (E5)	230	
Purchases		230
Being correction of error, stock used for private use omitted from the books		

(b) The suspense account

To draw up this account simply take all the suspense entries from the journal and place them on the same side.

Dr.	Suspense Account		Cr.
Error 2: day book error	18,000	Original error	18,000

(c) Statement of corrected net profit

The net profit is affected by changes to expenses and gains. For each expense or gain account adjusted in the journal you must make the necessary adjustment to the profit figure as follows:

If the expense account is DEBITED – this increases expenses so profits will go DOWN

If the expense account is CREDITED – this is a reduction in expenses so profits will go UP

If the gain account is DEBITED – this is a reduction in gains so profits will down DOWN

If the gain account is CREDITED – this is an increase in gains so profits will go UP

Applying these principles to this question:

Error 1 No expense or gain account is changed, therefore there is no effect on profits.

Error 2 Purchases are considered expenses (costs) which are entered on the debit side.
Since we credit purchases then purchases (costs) are going down.
Therefore profits will go up.

Error 3 Interest received is a gain (credit). This was treated as paid (expense).
Since we credit the gain, the gain is bigger, therefore profits will go up.

Error 4 Sales returns are a loss of sales revenue, so consider it a cost.
Costs are debits, so we are debiting the cost, therefore the cost is rising.
Since the cost is rising (loss of revenue) profits will go down.

Error 5 Since the owner took stock for private use it is not available for sale.
Therefore its cost can't be included in cost of sales (purchases).
This reduces our costs, therefore the profits will go up.

Statement of Corrected Net Profit

		€	€
Net profit as per original accounts (given in question)			12,000
Add	Purchases overcast (E2)	18,000	
	Interest received (E3)	460	
	Drawings (E5)	230	18,690
			30,690
Less	Sales returns (E4)		(190)
Corrected net profit			**30,500**

More difficult adjustments

Error 1: Incorrect side of an account

Example

A motor car purchased on credit from D. Foran (a garage owner) for €13,000 had been entered on the incorrect side of Foran's account as €1,300 and credited as €3,100 in the equipment account.

Dr.	D. Foran a/c		Cr.
Purchases	1,300	Cancel and correction	14,300

Dr.	Equipment a/c		Cr.
Cancel	3,100	D. Foran	3,100

Dr.	Purchases a/c		Cr.
Correction	13,000		

Dr.	Suspense a/c		Cr.
Original error	1,800	Cancel	1,800

Solution

- Foran's account needs to be credited with €1,300 to cancel the original error plus a further €13,000 to make the correct entry.
- Equipment needs to be debited with €3,100 to cancel the incorrect credit entry.
- Purchases needs to be debited with €13,000 so as to correctly record the purchase made on credit.
- Suspense needs to credited with €1,800 to cancel the original error.

7

See Practice Question 1 for exercises on the above adjustment.

Error 2: Returns and restocking charge

Example

Craddock had returned furniture, previously purchased on credit from a supplier for €8,800, and had entered this in the relevant ledger accounts incorrectly as €8,880. However, a credit note subsequently arrived from the supplier showing a transport charge of €200 to cover the cost of the return. The only entry made in the books in respect of this credit note was a credit of €8,600 in the creditor's account.

Dr.	Purchases Returns a/c		Cr.
Correction	280	Original	8,880

Dr.	Creditors a/c		Cr.
Original	8,880	Credit note	8,600
Correction	8,320		

Dr.	Suspense a/c		Cr.
Error	8,600	Cancel	8,600

Solution

- Purchases returns needs to be debited to take account of the restocking charge of €200 and error, €80.
- Creditors a/c needs to be debited with €8,320 to cancel the credit note and allow for the error of €80 and restocking charge of €200.
- Suspense needs to be credited with €8,600 to cancel the original error.

See Practice Question 2 for exercises on the above adjustment.

Error 3: A mistake where the entire original entry is incorrect

Example

Car parts previously sold on credit for €850 had been returned to Townsend (a garage owner). These returns had been entered incorrectly as €50 on the credit side of the equipment account and €580 on the debit side of the purchases account.

Solution

- The original entries were completely incorrect. Therefore these entries must first of all be completely cancelled.
- Then you correct the mistake by entering the correct figures in the correct accounts.

See Practice Question 3 for exercises on the above adjustment.

Equipment a/c

Dr.			Cr.
Cancel	50	Original	50

Purchases a/c

Dr.			Cr.
Original	580	Cancel	580

Suspense a/c

Dr.			Cr.
Cancel	530	Original	530

Sales Returns a/c

Dr.			Cr.
Correction	850		

Debtors a/c

Dr.			Cr.
		Correction	850

Error 4: Capital introduced into the business

This type of error can take many forms but is usually an omission from the accounts and therefore will not involve suspense. This, however, is not always the case.

Example

Reddington had won a private holiday prize for two worth €5,000 in total. One ticket had been given to a sales person as part of sales commission for the year and the other to an advertising firm as payment in full of a debt of €2,650. No entry had been made in the books.

Solution

- Since no entry was made in the books there will be no suspense, as both the debits and the credits are zero.
- Reddington is using private money to pay business debts; this is capital introduced.
- Each ticket is worth €2,500. Therefore since the advertising firm is accepting €2,500 for a debt of €2,650, the business is a receiving a discount of €150.

See Practice Question 4 for exercises on the above adjustment.

Capital a/c

Dr.			Cr.
		New capital	5,000

Discount Received a/c

Dr.			Cr.
		Advertising	150

Advertising a/c

Dr.			Cr.
Capital	2,650		

Sales Commission a/c

Dr.			Cr.
Capital	2,500		

Error 5: Private debts v. business debts

This can appear in two ways. Treat the owner as separate from the business as follows:

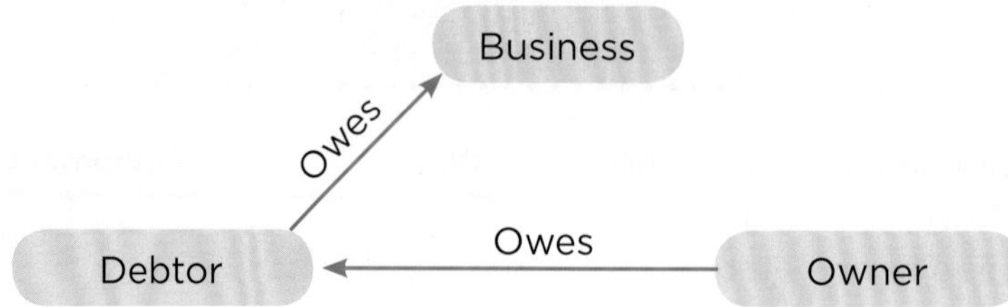

Here the business is owed money by a debtor. The owner privately owes the debtor money, therefore he/she uses business money to pay off a private debt. This is a drawing. Discount occurs when payment is less than the amount owed.

On the other hand, we can also have the following situation:

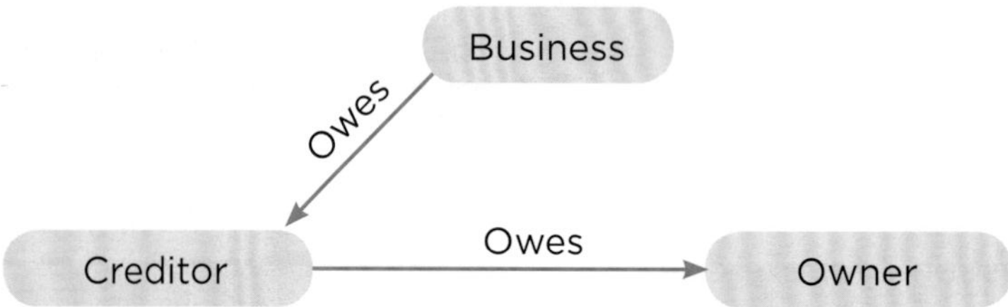

In this case the business debt is paid privately by the owner. The business should have paid the debt but he uses private money to pay off the business debt. This is capital introduced. Discounts may also apply here.

7

Example

A private debt for €1,200 owed by O'Shea had been offset in full against a business debt of €1,380 owed to the firm for car repairs previously carried out. No entry had been made in the books in respect of this offset.

Solution

- O'Shea is using business money to pay off private debts. This is a drawing (withdrawing of capital for private use).

NOTE

If the question says that no entry was made in the books, it means that no suspense account is required.

Dr. Drawings a/c Cr.

Correction	1,200		

Dr. Debtors a/c Cr.

		Correction	1,380

Dr. Discount Allowed a/c Cr.

Correction	180		

See Practice Question 5 for exercises on the above adjustment.

Sample Higher Level question

The trial balance of Pat Ryan, a cattle haulier and farmer, failed to agree on 31 December 20-2. The difference was entered in a suspense account and the following balance sheet was prepared:

Balance Sheet as at 31/12/20-2

	€	€	€
Fixed assets			
Land and buildings		750,000	
Trucks and equipment		250,000	1,000,000
Current assets			
Stock (including suspense)		95,000	
Debtors		24,000	
Cash		31,000	
		150,000	
***Less* Creditors: amounts falling due within one year**			
Bank overdraft	5,000		
Creditors	19,000	(24,000)	126,000
Total net assets			1,126,000
Financed by			
Capital		1,072,000	
Add Net profit		200,000	
Less Drawings		(146,000)	1,126,000
Capital employed			1,126,000

An examination of the books revealed the following errors and omissions:

(a) A milking machine, purchased on credit from J. Howlin for €13,000, had been entered on the incorrect side of Howlin's account as €2,600 and credited in the purchases account as €3,100.

(b) Ryan returned a trailer recently purchased from R. Doyle on credit for €12,000. This was entered as €21,000 by Ryan on the incorrect side of the correct accounts. However, a credit note subsequently arrived showing a restocking charge of 10% of invoice price. The only entry in respect of this credit note was a credit of €10,800 in the purchases returns account.

(c) Ryan had sent a cheque to a creditor for €1,200 in full settlement of a debt of €1,400. However, no entry had been made in the books for the subsequent dishonouring of this cheque. Ryan then paid €800 in cash on account.

(d) A private debt for €870 owed by Ryan had been offset in full against a business debt of €890 owed to Ryan's haulage firm for transport of horses to Goffs. There was no entry in the books in respect of this offset.

(e) A cheque for €1,248 paid by Ryan out of private funds for insurance on the business trucks for 16 months to the year ending 30/4/20-3 had not been entered in the books.

You are required to:

- Journalise the necessary corrections.
- Show the suspense account.
- Prepare a statement showing the correct net profit.
- Prepare a corrected balance sheet.

7

Solution

(a) Error 1

J. Howlin a/c

Dr.		Cr.	
Original error	2,600	Cancel and correction	15,600

Suspense a/c

Dr.		Cr.	
Original balance	500	Cancel	500

Purchases a/c

Dr.		Cr.	
Cancel	3,100	Original error	3,100

Trucks and Equipment a/c

Dr.		Cr.	
Correction	13,000		

(b) Error 2

Doyle (Creditors) a/c

Dr.		Cr.	
Cancel and correction	31,800	Original error	21,000

Purchases a/c

Dr.		Cr.	
Cancel	10,800	Original error	10,800

Trucks and Equipment a/c

Dr.		Cr.	
Original error	21,000	Correction	31,800

Suspense a/c

Dr.		Cr.	
Original error	10,800	Cancel suspense	10,800

(c) Error 3

Creditors a/c

Dr.		Cr.	
Original entry	1,400	Cancel	1,400
Correction	800		

Bank a/c

Dr.		Cr.	
Cancel	1,200	Original entry	1,200

Discount Received a/c

Dr.		Cr.	
Cancel	200	Original entry	200

Cash a/c

Dr.		Cr.	
		Correction	800

(d) Error 4

Drawings a/c

Dr.		Cr.	
Correction	870		

Discount Allowed a/c

Dr.		Cr.	
Correction	20		

Debtors a/c

Dr.		Cr.	
		Correction	890

(e) Error 5

Capital a/c

Dr.		Cr.	
		Correction	1,248

Insurance a/c

Dr.		Cr.	
Correction	312		

Profit and Loss a/c

Dr.		Cr.	
Correction	936		

Journal

	Details	Debit (€)	Credit (€)
(a)	Purchases a/c (E1)	3,100	
	Trucks and equipment a/c	13,000	
	Howlin a/c (creditor)		15,600
	Suspense a/c		500
	Being correction of error: equipment purchased on credit incorrectly entered in the books		
(b)	Doyle a/c (creditor) (E2)	31,800	
	Purchases a/c	10,800	
	Vehicles a/c		31,800
	Suspense a/c		10,800
	Being correction of error: equipment returned incorrectly treated in the accounts		
(c)	Creditors a/c (E3)	800	
	Discount received a/c	200	
	Bank a/c	1,200	
	Cash a/c		800
	Creditors a/c		1,400
	Being correction of error: dishonoured cheque omitted from books		
(d)	Drawings a/c (E4)	870	
	Discount allowed a/c	20	
	Debtors a/c		890
	Being correction of error: private debt offset against business debt omitted from the books		
(e)	Profit and loss account a/c – insurance (E5)	936	
	Debtor – insurance a/c	312	
	Capital a/c		1,248
	Being correction of error: business expenses paid out of private funds omitted from books		

Dr. **Suspense Account** **Cr.**

	€		€
Original balance – stocks	11,300	Equipment (E1)	500
		Vehicles (E2)	10,800
	11,300		11,300

7

Statement of Corrected Net Profit

	€	€
Profit as per original accounts		200,000
Add		
Less Purchases (E1)	3,100	
Purchases (E2)	10,800	
Discount received cancelled (E3)	200	
Discount allowed (E4)	20	
Insurance (E5)	936	(15,056)
Corrected net profit		184,944

Corrected Balance Sheet as at 31/12/-2

	€	€	€
Fixed assets			
Land and buildings		750,000	
Trucks and equipment		231,200	981,200
Current assets			
Stock		83,700	
Debtors		23,110	
Cash		30,200	
Insurance prepaid		312	
		137,322	
Less **Creditors: amounts falling due within 1 year**			
Bank overdraft	3,800		
Trade creditors	3,400	(7,200)	130,122
			1,111,322
Financed by (W7)			
Capital		1,073,248	
Net profit		184,944	
		1,258,192	
Less Drawings (W8)		(146,870)	1,111,322
			1,111,322

Workings

W7	Capital	1,073,248	
	Net profit	184,944	
		1,258,192	
W8	Less drawings	146,870	1,111,322
			1,111,322

W1	250,000	+	13,000	-	31,800		-		-		-		=	231,200
W2	95,000	-	11,300	-	-		-		-		-		=	83,700
W3	24,000	-	890	-	-		-		-		-		=	23,110
W4	31,000	-	800	-	-		-		-		-		=	30,200
W5	5,000	-	1,200	-	-		-		-		-		=	3,800
W6	19,000	+	15,600	-	31,800		-	800	+		1,400		=	3,400
W7	1,072,000	+	1,248	-	-		-		-		-		=	1,073,248
W8	146,000	+	870	-	-		-		-		-		=	146,870

Use either numbers or letters and be consistent with the question – preferably change the lettering or numbering in the question.

Exercises – Ordinary Level

Q1 The trial balance of J. Shields failed to agree and the difference was entered in the suspense account. An examination of the books revealed the following errors:

(a) Goods sold on credit to B. O'Reilly, €1,200, had been posted to S. O'Reilly's account.

(b) Total of the purchases day book, €12,000, had been posted to the purchases account as €32,000.

(c) Interest received, €700, had been treated as interest paid in the interest account.

(d) Goods previously sold on credit for €290 were returned by a debtor. This return has been omitted from the books.

(e) Goods taken by Shields, €900, for private use had not been entered in the books.

You are required to:

- Journalise the necessary corrections.
- Show the suspense account.
- Prepare a statement of corrected net profit if the profit as per accounts was €12,000.

Q2 J. Duggan's trial balance failed to agree and the difference was entered in the suspense account. An examination of the books revealed the following errors:

(a) Goods purchased on credit from T. Sheridan, €2,400, had been posted to K. Sheridan's account.

(b) Total of the sales day book, €23,000, had been posted the sales account as €32,000.

(c) Rent paid, €720, had been treated as rent received in the rent account.

(d) Goods previously purchased on credit for €450 were returned. This return has been omitted from the books.

(e) Cash taken by Duggan, €890, for private use had not been entered in the books.

You are required to:

- Journalise the necessary corrections.
- Show the suspense account.
- Prepare a statement of corrected net profit if the profit as per accounts was €12,000.

Q3 N. Hearn's trial balance failed to agree and the difference was entered in the suspense account. An examination of the books revealed the following errors:

(a) Goods sold on credit to J. Doyle, €1,200, had been posted to D. Doyle's account as €2,100.

(b) Total of the purchases day book, €34,000, had been posted to the purchases account as €42,000.

(c) Interest received, €980, had been treated as interest paid in the interest account. The bank account was correct.

(d) Goods previously sold on credit for €190 were returned by a debtor. This return has been omitted from the returns day book. The correct entry was entered in the debtor's account.

(e) Goods taken by Hearn for private use, €650, had not been entered in the books.

You are required to:

- Journalise the necessary corrections.
- Show the suspense account.
- Prepare a statement of corrected net profit if the profit as per accounts was €21,000.

Q4 K. Andrews's trial balance failed to agree and the difference was entered in the suspense account. An examination of the books revealed the following errors:

(a) Goods sold on credit to K. Downes, €1,400, had been posted to P. Downes's account.

(b) Total of the purchases day book, €21,000, had been posted in the purchases account as €12,000.

(c) Interest paid, €900, had been treated as interest received in the interest account.

(d) Goods previously sold on credit for €760 were returned. This return has been omitted from the books.

(e) Cash taken by Andrews for private use, €900, had not been entered in the books.

You are required to:

- Journalise the necessary corrections.
- Show the suspense account.
- Prepare a statement of corrected net profit if the profit as per accounts was €5,400.

Q5 S. Nichol's trial balance failed to agree and the difference was entered in the suspense account. An examination of the books revealed the following errors:

(a) Goods sold on credit to A. Hayes, €350, were returned. This return was not entered in the books.

(b) Nichol took cash amounting to €25 per week for private use during the year. This was treated as a general expense in the accounts.

(c) Nichol paid a creditor in full €350 for a business debt of €380. No entry was made in respect of this payment.

(d) The total of the sales day book was overcast by €3,400. The correct entry was made in the debtors account.

(e) Advertising for the year, €4,500, paid by cheque was correctly entered in the bank account but the accounts clerk forgot to post the relevant amount to the ledger.

You are required to:

- Journalise the necessary corrections.
- Show the suspense account.
- Prepare a statement of corrected net profit if the profit as per accounts was €9,000.

7

Practice Questions

Q1 In each of the following questions, journalise the necessary entries and show the effect on the final accounts. (Show T-accounts.)

(a) A bookcase purchased on credit by N. Donnelly for €12,000 had been entered on the incorrect side of the supplier's account and credited as €2,100 in the motor vans account. Donnelly's business is furniture sales.

(b) A motor car purchased on credit by E. Hayes for €14,400 had been entered on the incorrect side of the supplier's account as €4,400 and credited as €400 in the buildings account. Hayes is a garage owner.

(c) An oven purchased on credit by R. Montoya for €19,000 had been entered on the incorrect side of the Bakeware Suppliers Ltd account and credited as €91,000 in the furniture account. Montoya is a baker.

Q2 In each of the following questions journalise the necessary entries and show the effect on the final accounts. (Show T-accounts.)

(a) O'Shea (a garage owner) returned a motor car, previously purchased on credit from a supplier for €22,500, and entered this in the relevant ledger accounts incorrectly as €25,200. However, a credit note subsequently arrived from the supplier showing a transport charge of €500 to cover the cost of the return. The only entry made in the books in respect of this credit note was a credit of €22,000 in the creditor's account.

(b) O'Donnell (a garage owner) returned a motor car, previously purchased on credit from a supplier for €33,400, and entered this in the relevant ledger accounts incorrectly as €43,300. However, a credit note subsequently arrived from the supplier showing a transport charge of €400 to cover the cost of the return. The only entry made in the books in respect of this credit note was a credit of €33,000 in the creditor's account.

(c) Broderick (a baker) returned an oven, previously purchased on credit from a supplier for €44,600, and entered this in the relevant ledger accounts incorrectly as €66,400. However, a credit note subsequently arrived from the supplier showing a transport charge of €2,400 to cover the cost of the return. The only entry made in the books in respect of this credit note was a credit of €42,200 in the creditor's account.

Q3 In each of the following questions, journalise the necessary entries and show the effect on the final accounts. (Show T-accounts.)

(a) Car parts previously sold on credit for €960 were returned to Finnegan (a garage owner). These returns were entered incorrectly as €96 on the credit side of the equipment account and €69 on the debit side of the purchases account.

(b) Car parts previously sold on credit for €1,900 were returned to Byrne (a garage owner). These returns were entered incorrectly as €190 on the credit side of the buildings account and €910 on the debit side of the cleaning expenses account.

(c) Car parts previously sold on credit for €1,200 were returned to Foynes (a garage owner). These returns were entered incorrectly as €12 on the credit side of the furniture account and €21 on the debit side of the purchases account.

Q4 In each of the following questions, journalise the necessary entries and show the effect on the final accounts. (Show T-accounts.)

(a) McGuinness won a holiday for two worth €7,500 in total. One ticket was given to a sales person as part of sales commission for the year and the other to an advertising firm as payment in full of a debt of €3,950. No entry was made in the books.

(b) Igoe won a holiday for two worth €9,000 in total. One ticket was given to a sales person as part of sales commission for the year and the other to an advertising firm as payment in full of a debt of €4,600. No entry was made in the books.

(c) McGrath won a holiday for two worth €15,000 in total. One ticket was given to a sales person as part of sales commission for the year and the other to an advertising firm as payment in full of a debt of €8,500. No entry was made in the books.

Q5 In each of the following questions, journalise the necessary entries and show the effect on the final accounts. (Show T-accounts.)

(a) A private debt of €1,800 owed by Thompson was offset in full against a business debt of €1,900 owed to the firm from carpet repairs previously carried out. No entry was made in the books in respect of this offset.

(b) A private debt of €2,600 owed by O'Farrell was offset in full against a business debt of €3,000 owed to the firm from carpet repairs previously carried out. No entry was made in the books in respect of this offset.

(c) A private debt of €4,500 owed by Duignan was offset in full against a business debt of €5,400 owed to the firm from carpet repairs previously carried out. No entry was made in the books in respect of this offset.

Exercises - Higher Level

Q1 The trial balance of Sarah Powell, a garage owner, failed to agree on 31/12/20-1. The difference was entered in a suspense account and the final accounts were prepared. The accounts showed a net profit of €58,000. On checking the books, the following errors were revealed:

(a) A cheque for €6,000 paid by Powell out of private funds for 15 months' rent of a showroom up to 31/3/20-2 was not entered in the books.

(b) A motor car purchased on credit from S. O'Reilly on credit for €32,000 had been entered on the incorrect side of O'Reilly's account and credited as €23,000 in the equipment account.

(c) Car parts previously sold on credit for €340 had been returned to Powell. These returns were entered as €430 on the debit side of the equipment account and €340 on the debit side of the purchases account.

(d) Powell had won a private holiday for two worth €4,000. One ticket was given to a sales rep of the company and the other to an insurance company as full payment of a debt of €2,200. No entry had been made in the books.

(e) Powell returned a motor car, previously purchased on credit for €21,000, and this was incorrectly entered in the relevant accounts as €12,000. However, a credit note arrived showing a restocking charge of €2,100. The only entry in the books in respect of this credit note was €18,800 credited only in the creditor's account.

You are required to:

- Journalise the necessary corrections.
- Prepare the suspense account showing the original difference.
- Prepare a statement showing the corrected net profit.

7

Q2 The trial balance of Bobby Stack, a garage owner, failed to agree on 31/12/20-2. The difference was entered in a suspense account and the final accounts were prepared. The accounts showed a net profit of €32,400. On checking the books, the following errors were revealed:

(a) A cheque for €12,000 received from a debtor was correctly entered in the books. This was in full settlement of a debt of €12,300. However, there was no entry in the books for the subsequent dishonouring of this cheque and the payment on account of €2,300 by the debtor.

(b) A motor car purchased on credit from Syl Power on credit for €21,000 had been entered on the incorrect side of Power's account and credited as €2,100 in the furniture account.

(c) Car parts previously sold on credit for €280 had been returned to Stack. These returns were entered as €230 on the debit side of the equipment account and €210 on the debit side of the purchases account.

(d) Stack had won a private holiday for two worth €3,000. One ticket was given to a sales rep of the company and the other to an advertising agency as full payment of a debt of €1,650. No entry had been made in the books.

(e) Stack returned a motor car, previously purchased on credit for €19,000, and this was incorrectly entered in the relevant accounts as €91,000. However, a credit note arrived showing a restocking charge of €1,900. The only entry in the books in respect of this credit note was €17,100 credited only in the creditor's account.

You are required to:

- Journalise the necessary corrections.
- Prepare the suspense account showing clearly the original difference.
- Prepare a statement showing the corrected net profit.

Q3 **The trial balance of John Cassidy, a furniture retailer, failed to agree on 31/12/20-3. The difference was entered in a suspense account and the final accounts were prepared. The accounts showed a net profit of €21,300. On checking the books, the following errors were revealed:**

(a) A cheque for €4,500 paid by Cassidy out of private funds for 15 months' rent of a warehouse up to 31/3/20-4 was not entered in the books.

(b) A bookcase purchased on credit from Tom Sinnott on credit for €1,300 had been entered on the incorrect side of Sinnott's account and credited as €300 in the repairs account.

(c) Furniture shelves previously sold on credit for €140 had been returned to Cassidy. These returns were entered as €340 on the debit side of the wages account and €30 on the debit side of the motor vehicles account.

(d) Cassidy returned a wardrobe, previously purchased on credit for €800, and this was incorrectly entered in the relevant accounts as €880. However, a credit note arrived showing a restocking charge of €60. The only entry in the books in respect of this credit note was €740 credited only in the creditor's account.

(e) €200 received from the sale of an old office desk (book value €180) which was used by Cassidy to store private materials had not been entered in the books.

You are required to:

- Journalise the necessary corrections.
- Prepare the original suspense account.
- Prepare a statement showing the corrected net profit.

Q4 **The trial balance of Rodney Trotter, an independent trader and furniture retailer, failed to agree on 31/12/20-3. The difference was entered in a suspense account and the following balance sheet was prepared:**

Balance Sheet as at 31/12/20-3

	€	€	€
Fixed assets			
Buildings		925,000	
Equipment		135,000	1,060,000
Current assets			
Stock		79,000	
Debtors		33,000	
Cash (including suspense)		44,000	
		156,000	
***Less* Creditors: amounts due within 1 year**			
Expenses due	22,000		
Creditors	32,000	(54,000)	102,000
Total net assets			1,162,000
Financed by			
Capital			1,015,000
Add Net profit		189,000	
Less Drawings		(42,000)	147,000
Capital employed			1,162,000

An examination of the books revealed the following errors and omissions:

(a) Furniture purchased on credit from A. Trigger for €31,000 had been entered on the incorrect side of Trigger's account as €3,100 and credited in the premises account as €13,000.

(b) A debtor who owed Trotter €1,300 sent a cheque for €800 and €450 cash in full settlement of a debt. This was correctly entered in the books. However, no entry had been made in the books of the subsequent dishonouring of this cheque or the writing off of the remaining debt in full because of bankruptcy.

(c) Cash payments for advertising, €1,500, and €1,400 for private motor insurance had been credited to the creditors account and credited in the equipment account respectively.

(d) Trotter sold a private art collection to a debtor of the business on credit for €9,800. This had been incorrectly treated as the purchase of trading stock. Trotter had intended the proceeds from this sale to remain in the business.

(e) Trotter won a motor vehicle worth €22,000 in a local GAA lotto. He gave the vehicle to the business and instead took an old piece of equipment valued at €5,000 which was used for private purposes. The only entry in the books regarding either motor vehicle or equipment was a debit of €2,000 in the equipment account. The equipment had cost €6,500.

You are required to:

- Journalise the necessary corrections.
- Show the suspense account.
- Prepare a statement showing the correct net profit.
- Prepare a corrected balance sheet.

7

Q5 The trial balance of Aidan O'Leary, a car dealer, failed to agree on 31/12/20-4. The difference was entered in a suspense account and the following balance sheet was prepared:

Balance Sheet as at 31/12/20-4

	€	€	€
Fixed assets			
Land and buildings		1,200,000	
Equipment		60,000	
Delivery vans		120,000	1,380,000
Current assets			
Stock (including suspense)		196,800	
Debtors		44,600	
Cash		3,000	
		244,400	
***Less* Creditors: amounts due within 1 year**			
Bank overdraft	32,000		
Creditors	99,600	(131,600)	112,800
			1,492,800
Financed by			
Capital			989,000
Add Net profit		546,000	
Less Drawings		(42,200)	503,800
Capital employed			1,492,800

An examination of the books revealed the following errors and omissions:

(a) O'Leary sent a cheque in full settlement of a business debt of €1,200 and this was recorded correctly in the books. However, no entry has been made in the books of the subsequent dishonouring of this cheque and payment by O'Leary of €800 cash.

(b) O'Leary won a holiday for two to the USA worth €6,000. One ticket was given to car salesperson and the other was given to a creditor of the business in full settlement of a business debt of €3,450. No entry has been made in the books in respect of this.

(c) Cash payments of €650 for repairs to premises had been credited to the creditors account and also credited to the premises account.

(d) O'Leary returned a motor car previously purchased on credit from R. Doyle for €34,000. This was entered in the correct accounts as €43,000. However, a credit note arrived showing a transport charge of €700 in relation to the return. The only entry in the books in respect of this credit note was a credit of €33,300 in the premises account.

(e) A business debt of €3,400 owed to the company for car repairs was offset against a private debt of €3,200 owed by O'Leary to this debtor. This offset was omitted from the books.

You are required to:

- Journalise the necessary corrections.
- Show the suspense account.
- Prepare a statement showing the correct net profit.
- Prepare a corrected balance sheet.

Q6 **The trial balance of Warren Haworth, a grocer, failed to agree on 31/12/20-5. The difference was entered in a suspense account and the following balance sheet was prepared:**

Balance Sheet as at 31/12/20-5

	€	€	€
Fixed assets			
Land and buildings		430,000	
Equipment		120,000	
Fixtures and fittings		230,000	780,000
Current assets			
Stock		23,000	
Debtors (including suspense)		33,000	
Cash		12,000	
		68,000	
***Less* Creditors: amounts due within 1 year**			
Bank overdraft	2,300		
Creditors	6,700	(9,000)	59,000
Total net assets			839,000
Financed by			
Capital		928,000	
Add Net loss		(22,500)	
Less Drawings		(66,500)	839,000
Capital employed			839,000

An examination of the books revealed the following errors and omissions:

(a) Haworth decided to sell a private car to a debtor of the business for €11,500. On Haworth's instructions the debtor paid this amount directly to the business's bank account. The record keeper, however, misunderstood the nature of this transaction and treated it as a payment on account by the debtor. No other entry had been made in the books. This was the only entry made in the books in respect of this debit note.

(b) A debit note received from a creditor for €450 had been entered correctly in the day books but posted twice to the incorrect side of the creditor's account as €540.

(c) A private debt owed by Haworth for €545 had been offset in full against a business debt of €600 owed to the firm for groceries previously sold. No entry had been made in the books in respect of this offset.

(d) Haworth had won a private holiday prize to Blackburn and Burnley worth €3,000. One ticket had been given to a sales manager for outstanding performance and the other to an advertising firm in full payment of a bill of €1,750. No entry had been made in the books.

(e) Bank payments for repairs to refrigeration equipment, €450, and a roof of the personal dwelling, €230, had both been credited to the creditors account and also credited to the buildings account.

You are required to:

- Journalise the necessary corrections.
- Show the suspense account.
- Prepare a statement showing the correct net profit.
- Prepare a corrected balance sheet.

7

Theory

Q1 Explain with examples the difference between 'error of commission' and 'error of principle'.

Q2 Explain what is meant by 'misplaced entries'.

Q3 What is an error of original entry?

Q4 What is a compensating error?

Q5 Identify three types of errors that affect the balancing of a trial balance.

Exam Tips

- Always check the nature of the business involved in the question – for example, a garage. This will affect purchases, sales and related returns in particular.
- Use T-accounts to show the original entry and corrected entry – colour-code them.
- The corrected entries in the T-accounts should be transferred directly to the general journal.
- Expense and gain accounts in the journal will have an effect on the profit and loss account.
- Asset and liability accounts in the journal will have an effect on the balance sheet.
- When dealing with private debt adjustments, work out the business side of the debt first.
- Make sure you can list and explain the different types of error not revealed by the trial balance, as well as being able to provide examples.
- Don't forget to include the narration.
- This topic can appear in Section A or Section B of the exam paper.
- Suspense adjustments are often part of final accounts questions.

8 Regulatory Framework of Accounting

Objectives

On completion students should be able to:

- List and explain the accounting obligations of companies;
- List and explain the role of the accounting regulatory agencies;
- Classify a company as small, medium or large;
- Explain what is meant by an audit and the contents of an auditor's report;
- Understand the term 'true and fair view';
- Distinguish between a qualified and unqualified auditor's report.

Accounting obligations

Limited companies must annually publish a **profit and loss account** and a **balance sheet** together with explanatory notes.

Some companies are now also obliged to publish a **cash flow statement** (see Chapter 17).

In addition, a company must report its financial state of affairs to its shareholders (its owners). This report will also contain:

- a directors' report
- an auditor's report
- the published accounts (financial statements).

Limited companies must prepare financial statements which need to be audited (independently) and presented to shareholders at the Annual General Meeting (AGM). These accounts must also be filed with the Registrar of Companies.

Regulation

The accounts of a limited company are regulated so as to make sure that the required accounting information is available to the external users of the accounts and reports.

Regulation is the setting of **rules** about the content, preparation and presentation of financial reports and statements.

This will result in the accounts being:

- **Consistent** – the same year to year
- **Comparable** – so as they can be compared to other companies
- **Compliant** – in line with national and international law
- **Uniform** – reported the same way not just in Ireland but also in the European Union.

The regulatory agencies

There are four main agencies which are responsible for accounting regulation:

1. The Government – through legislation
2. The accounting profession – through Statements of Standard Accounting Practice (SSAPs) and Financial Reporting Standards (FRSs)
3. The European Union – through directives
4. The Stock Exchange – through its listing rules.

1. The Government

The Government controls how accounts and financial statements are prepared and presented through Acts of the Oireachtas (Parliament). The most significant of these are the Companies Acts 1963, 1990, 2003 and 2006. There have also been amendments to these Acts over the years.

Under these Acts different classifications of companies have been created. These are:

- public companies
- large private companies
- medium private companies
- small private companies.

A **private company** is one

- which has between 1 and 99 shareholders
- which has limited liability
- whose name ends with **Ltd**
- whose shares are not sold on the Stock Exchange.

A **public company** is one

- which has between seven and an unlimited number of shareholders
- which has limited liability
- whose name ends with **plc**
- whose shares are bought and sold on the Stock Exchange.

Company size

The size of a company is determined by **three** factors:

- the size of the balance sheet
- the annual turnover
- the number of employees.

It must meet **two** of the following criteria for consecutive years to be classified as small, medium or large.

Criteria	Small	Medium	Large
Balance sheet total	≤ €4.4 million	≤ €7.62 million	> €7.62 million
Annual turnover	≤ €8.8 million	≤ €15.24 million	> €15.24 million
Average no. of employees	≤ 50	≤ 250	> 250

Definitions

The **balance sheet total** is the sum of the fixed and current assets.

Turnover is the income from normal business activities, i.e. sales of what the company normally trades in (goods and services).

The **average number of employees** is the weekly average number employed by the company.

Financial reporting requirements

What a company needs to report in relation to disclosure of accounts depends on its size as classified above. This can be summarised as follows:

Profit and Loss Account

Report to	Small Companies	Medium Companies	Large (including all public companies)
Shareholders	Short	Short	Full
Registrar of Companies	None	Short	Full

Balance Sheet

Report to	Small Companies	Medium Companies	Large (including all public companies)
Shareholders	Abridged	Full	Full
Registrar of Companies	Abridged	Abridged	Full

8

Below is a summary of what each of these versions of accounts means:

Full	Abridged	Short
Trading account	**Trading account**	**No trading account**
Profit and loss account	**Profit and loss account**	**Profit and loss account**
Balance sheet	**Less detailed balance sheet**	**Balance sheet**
Explanatory notes	**Explanatory notes**	**Explanatory notes**

2. The accounting profession

The main contribution from the accounting profession (accountancy bodies) over the years has been to bring consistency to the preparation of accounts. This has been done by the issuing of two main items:

(i) Statements of Standard Accounting Practice (SSAPs)

An accounting standard is a statement on how certain transactions should be dealt with in the financial statements in order to give a true and fair view. An example would be the **valuation of stock**.

(ii) Financial Reporting Standards (FRSs)

These are newer standards which are being drawn up with the same goal as SSAPs. They are gradually replacing some older SSAPs as well as bringing in new ways in which accounts are prepared. One example is the **cash flow statement**.

The Financial Reporting Council (FRC)

This is the main body which regulates the preparation of accounts. The function of the FRC is to oversee the preparation and implementation of accounting standards (SSAPs and FRSs). The FRC also aims to improve confidence in financial reporting for investors and other interest groups.

There are six other bodies which report directly to the FRC. These are:

The Accounting Standards Board (ASB)

The ASB issues all new accounting standards and amends or withdraws the old accounting standards. The new standards are the FRSs.

The Review Panel

The review panel has the authority to request companies to:

- reissue financial statements if it believes that they do not show a true and fair view;
- take legal action if the company refuses to reissue financial statements.

The Urgent Issues Task Force (UITF)

The function of the UITF is to assist the ASB by responding promptly in areas where an accounting standard is being unsatisfactorily applied or interpreted and urgent action is required.

8

The Auditing Practices Board (APB)

The function of the APB is to develop auditing procedures and practice by ensuring that the highest standards of auditing are followed while meeting the developing needs of the different users of financial statements. This is also intended to build confidence in the entire auditing profession and process. (See also later note on the audit, p. 151.)

The Professional Oversights Board (POB)

The function of the POB is to monitor audits that take place by overseeing the regulation of the auditing profession and ensuring that this regulation is carried out by the professional accounting bodies.

The Accounting and Actuarial Disciplinary Board (AADB)

The function of the AADB is to deal with situations where there has been some kind of malpractice by an individual accountant or an accountancy firm.

The Irish situation

The Companies Act 2003 set up a new body called the Irish Auditing and Supervisory Authority (IAASA). The primary function of this organisation is to ensure that accounts are always prepared with adherence to the highest possible standards and to monitor the situation in relation to the classes of companies and other items as set out in the Companies Acts. Members of the Irish accounting bodies are obliged to abide by these standards.

3. The European Union

Ireland joined the EU in 1973 and since then the EU has had a major influence on the regulation of financial reporting in Ireland.

The EU Commission influences regulation by issuing **directives**. Directives are instructions to its member states. The member states are allowed a fixed period of time to incorporate the requirements of the directives into their own national legislation.

The EU is trying to harmonise or equalise accounting practice within member states.

EU directives

Directive	Content
Fourth	Amount of disclosure in the final accounts
Seventh	Consolidating company accounts (group companies)
Eighth	The qualification and regulation of auditors
2006 Directive	Amendments to the above

4. The Stock Exchange

Companies that have their shares quoted on the Stock Exchange (companies whose name ends with plc) must disclose extra information to the public and to shareholders so that the company's share price can be evaluated.

The Irish Stock Exchange (ISEQ) requires companies to:

- prepare half-yearly financial reports as a minimum, although many plc's publish them quarterly;
- disclose any financial arrangements or contracts that exist between the company and its directors;
- disclose any changes to capital structure (extra loans, for example) that could affect share price;
- provide a breakdown of all loans into short, medium and long term;
- provide a statement showing the interest of each director in the share capital of the company;
- disclose the principal country in which each subsidiary operates;
- provide a geographical breakdown of turnover and profit.

8

The audit

The role of the auditor is to express an opinion on the financial statements. The auditor will decide and report on whether the statements give a true and fair view of the state of affairs of the company and whether they comply with the Companies Acts.

An **audit** is an independent examination of a company's financial statements and the expression of an opinion on the preparation of accounts.

True and fair view

The accounts of a business will give a true and fair view if the auditor is satisfied that:

- All the information necessary to complete the audit and required by the Companies Acts is available and included.
- The fundamental accounting concepts have been adhered to when preparing the accounts.
- The accounts have been prepared in a way that is consistent with the previous accounting period.

The Companies Acts do not require the auditor to certify that the accounts are correct or accurate but that they give a true and fair view of the financial position of the business.

It is not the function of the auditor to discover errors or fraud. If fraud is detected, however, it is the duty of the auditor to report it.

Auditor's report

The auditors are appointed by and report directly to the shareholders. At the end of the audit, the auditors are required to report to the shareholders on the accounts which they examined.

Auditors must show:

- Whether they received all the information which they believed was necessary for the audit. An explanation of this information where required should also have been available.
- Whether in their opinion a proper set of accounts had been kept by the company.
- Whether the company's balance sheet and profit and loss accounts are in agreement with the books of account held by the company.
- Whether in their opinion the accounts provide all the information required by the Companies Acts and in such a way as required to give a true and fair view.
- That the company's balance sheet gives a true and fair view of the company's affairs at the end of its financial year.
- That the profit and loss account also gives a true and fair view of the profit or loss for its financial year.
- Whether in their opinion the company's net assets on the date of the balance sheet were less than 50% of the called-up share capital.
- Whether in their opinion the information in the directors' report (see Chapter 10) is consistent with the company's accounts for the year.

Qualifying reports

An **unqualified auditor's report**, often referred to as a **clean** report, is when the auditor can report that in his or her opinion the above conditions have been met.

A **qualified auditor's report** is the opposite of that. It is when an auditor states that in his or her opinion the accounts of the company do **not** comply with all these conditions. In other words, the business's financial statements do not give a true and fair view of the company's state of affairs. This report will state the elements of the accounts that are unsatisfactory. This is known as **qualifying** the report.

Not every accountant is an auditor but every auditor is an accountant.

Auditor's Report (example)

To: The Board of Directors, Shareholders of Hanley Plc

From: ABC Auditors

Re: Audit on Financial Statements of Hanley Plc

We have audited the financial statements of your company for the year ended 31/12/20-2 on pages 23 to 98 which have been prepared under the historical cost convention (as modified by the revaluation of certain assets) and the accounting policies as set out on page 102 of this report.

Respective responsibilities of directors and auditors

As described on page 67 of this report, the company's directors are responsible for the preparation of financial statements. It is our responsibility as auditors to form an independent opinion, based on our audit, on these statements and to report our opinion to you.

Basis of opinion

We conducted our audit in accordance with the Auditing Standards issued by the Auditing Practices Board. An audit includes examination, on a test basis, of evidence relevant to the amounts and disclosures in the financial statements. It also includes an assessment of the significant estimates and judgements made by the directors in the preparation of the financial statements and of whether the accounting policies are appropriate to the company's circumstances, consistently applied and adequately disclosed.

We planned and performed our audit so as to obtain all the information and explanations which we considered necessary in order to provide us with sufficient evidence to give reasonable assurance that the financial statements are free from material misstatement, whether caused by fraud or other irregularity or error. In forming our opinion we also evaluated the overall adequacy of the presentation of information in the financial statements.

Opinion

In our opinion the financial statements give a true and fair view of the state of the company's affairs as at 31 December 20-2 and its profit (loss) for the year then ended have been properly prepared with the Companies Acts of 1963 to 2006.

We have obtained all the information and explanations we consider necessary for the purposes of our audit. In our opinion, the company has kept proper books of account and the financial statements are in agreement with the books of account.

In our opinion, the information given in the directors' report on pages 45 to 56 is consistent with the financial statements.

The net assets of the company as stated in the balance sheet on page 90 are greater than 50% of the amount of its called-up share capital and in our opinion on that basis there did not exist at 31/12/20-2 a financial situation which, under Section 40 (1) of the Companies Amendment Act 1983, would require the convening of an extraordinary general meeting of the company.

CBA Auditors

Registered auditors

Signed [auditor]

Date

Theory

Q1 **What is meant by the regulatory framework of accounting? How does it operate?**

Q2 **What is the objective of regulation of financial reporting?**

Q3 **List the main regulatory bodies.**

Q4 **What is an accounting standard? Why are they issued? Discuss the arguments for their issue.**

Q5 **Explain how accounting standards are enforced in Ireland.**

Q6 **State the difference between an auditor's qualified and an unqualified report.**

Q7 **How does the Financial Reporting Council (FRC) help in the regulation of financial reporting?**

Q8 **What regulations must accountants observe when preparing financial statements for publication?**

Q9 **What is an audit? What is the role of the auditor?**

Q10 **How does an auditor safeguard the interests of shareholders?**

Q11 **Describe the obligations of limited companies with respect to their annual report.**

Q12 **Explain the term 'true and fair view'.**

Q13 **List the items on which auditors must express an opinion in their reports.**

Q14 **State the criteria that determine the size of (a) a small company and (b) a medium company.**

8

Exam Tips

- Theory is becoming more important in the accounting exam. Theory needs to be learnt well, revised and applied throughout the syllabus.
- The contents of this chapter often appears in conjunction with published account and cash flow statement questions.

9 Company Accounts (Internal Use)

Objectives

On completion students should be able to:

- Understand the term limited liability;
- Explain the two classes of company;
- List and explain the sources of finance for companies;
- Prepare a trading, profit and loss account for a company;
- Prepare a balance sheet for a company.

Limited companies

A limited company is a business owned by at least one shareholder, though it must have at least two directors. The owners are called **members** or **shareholders** and their investment is in the form of shares. Unlike the sole trader, the investors have the advantage of **limited liability**.

Limited liability means that liability of the owners is confined to the amount they invested in the company. It is a protection against total loss of private assets.

There are **two** classes of company.

1. Private companies

Some companies are obliged to have the word **Limited** or the letters **Ltd** after their names – for example, Inis Ltd, P. Kelly and Sons Ltd. The reason for this is to ensure that creditors (businesses and people who supply the company with goods or services on credit) are aware that the shareholders' liability is limited to their shares. A private company's ownership is limited to a maximum of 99 people.

2. Public companies

These companies' names must end with the letters **plc** (public limited company) – for example, Woodmaster plc, Total Direction plc. They must have at least seven shareholders/members and shares are publicly bought and sold on the stock exchange, for example on the ISEQ index or the Dow Jones.

Sources of finance

Share capital

In contrast to the sole trader, companies will have a number of owners. The amount invested by these owners is referred to as **share capital**. This is the main way in which companies raise finance to begin trading or for expansion as the business grows.

When a company is established (formed) the **authorised share capital** is set out in the Memorandum of Association. This is the total number of shares that the company can sell (issue). This is also known as the **nominal share capital**.

For example, Tiger Ltd had an authorised share capital of €400,000, broken into 300,000 ordinary shares at €1 each and 100,000 7% preference shares at €1 each.

The **issued share capital** is the part of authorised share capital that has actually been sold or issued. This can be equal to but never more than the authorised share capital figure.

NOTE

Both figures are shown in the balance sheet.

In summary, authorised share capital is the number of shares a company can sell at a particular price; the issued share capital is the amount actually sold.

If the company issued shares for the first time at a price above their nominal value the excess is known as **share premium.**

There are two classes (types) of share that a company can issue:

1. ordinary shares
2. preference shares.

NOTE

Shareholders get a reward for their investment in the form of a **dividend**, which is a portion of the profits paid out in any given year.

1. Ordinary (equity) shares

9

This is the most important and the most common type of share. The ordinary shareholders are the owners of the business. However, they also take on the risk. The main characteristics of ordinary shareholders are:

- They are the owners of the business.
- They have voting rights at the Annual General Meeting (AGM).
- They appoint the board of directors who in turn appoint a managing director.
- They decide on the amount of profits each year to be paid out to shareholders.

2. Preference shares

This class of share is simply a source of finance for a company and preference shareholders do not get a say in the running of the company. The main characteristics of preference shares are:

- They carry a fixed return and this must be paid before any profits (dividends) are paid to the ordinary shareholder (hence the name preference).
- They carry no voting rights at meetings, and therefore preference shareholders have no say in the day-to-day running of the company.
- If a company gets into financial difficulties, for example liquidation, the preference shareholders are entitled to be repaid their nominal value before any payment is made to ordinary shareholders.

- Most preference shares are **cumulative**, which means that if a dividend is not paid in any one year, it accumulates until the company is in a position to pay all the arrears of the dividend.
- There are also **redeemable preference shares**. These are shares which the company reserves the right to buy back, on or before a certain date. This should be duly noted in the balance sheet or on a note to the accounts.

Explanation of terms

Term	Definition
Dividends	This is the portion of profits paid to shareholders. This varies in the case of ordinary shares but is fixed for preference shares. In the case of ordinary shares it is a percentage of issued share capital and is decided by the Board of Directors. Sometimes a firm pays some dividends during the year and these are known as **interim dividends**.
Share premium	Profit gained by issuing shares at a price above their nominal value.
Reserves	The reserves belong to the ordinary shareholders and are part of the shareholders' funds. The main reserve is the profit and loss account balance. There are two types of reserve: **1. Capital reserves** are non-trading profits earned in some other way, such as share premium or revaluation reserve. These reserves cannot be used to pay dividends. **2. Revenue reserves** are profits retained by the company. These include general reserve, profit and loss reserve, debenture redemption reserve. These reserves can be used to pay dividends.
Shareholders' funds (equity funds)	This is the amount owed by the company to the ordinary shareholders. Shareholders' funds = Issued ordinary share capital + Reserves (including profit and loss balance)
Debentures	Debentures are long-term loans carrying a fixed rate of interest – for example, 8% debentures 20-8/20-9. They are usually for a fixed period of time and repayable within that period, which in the example above would be sometime between 20-8 and 20-9. The debenture is repaid in one lump sum. In the mean time only the interest is paid annually. Debentures are usually secured by a fixed or floating charge on the company's assets. This is similar to collateral on a bank loan. A **fixed charge** is on a specific asset – for example, the premises – whereas a **floating charge** is a charge on all the assets of the business. Prudent companies should transfer a portion of their annual profit into a **debenture redemption reserve** so that when the loan is due to be repaid in one lump sum they have the funds available to do so.

The accounts

Company final accounts presentation is similar to the trading, profit and loss account and balance sheet of the sole trader. There are, however, some new terms and items that are specific to company accounts. These can be summarised as follows:

Terms	Explanation	Treatment in the Accounts
Preliminary/ formation expenses	Expenses incurred in the formation of the company	An administration expense in the profit and loss account or against share premium
Auditor's remuneration	The fee paid to the auditor for carrying out the audit of the company's accounts	An administration expense in the profit and loss account If unpaid (accrued) it will also be a current liability in the balance sheet
Directors' remuneration	The fees, salaries and commission paid by the company to the directors for the accounting period	An administration expense in the profit and loss account If unpaid (accrued) it will also be a current liability in the balance sheet
Corporation tax	The tax paid on company profits	Deducted from net profit at the end of the profit and loss account If unpaid (accrued) it will also be a current liability in the balance sheet
Intangible fixed assets	These are items that have a value to the business but do not have a physical presence. They are, however, able to be sold. The main examples are goodwill and patents. They can be bought as an individual asset or as part of a group of assets – for example, goodwill if purchasing an adjoining business.	Entered separately in the balance sheet under the heading intangible fixed assets These assets have a useful economic life so therefore should be written off (amortised) over a number of years. This amount should be treated as an administration expense in the profit and loss account unless otherwise instructed.
Financial fixed assets	Long-term investments made by a business and loans given to other parties. Investments can be quoted or unquoted. Quoted investments can be sold and bought on the stock exchange.	Entered separately in the balance sheet under the heading financial fixed assets. Any income generated is treated as other income in the profit and loss account
Operating profit	This is the profit calculated after taking away the operating expenses and adding other operating income. It is the profit made before deducting any interest payable.	Entered in the profit and loss account after expenses and gains but before interest payments and dividends
Profit and loss balance	The company's retained profit is added to the profit and loss account (reserves) balance from the previous year	Last figure in the profit and loss account Included in reserves (shareholders' funds) in the balance sheet
Selling and distribution expenses	Any expense incurred in the selling of goods or supplying of services Examples include: commission payable, advertising, carriage out, sales staff wages + salaries.	Any amounts due are a current liability in the balance sheet Any amounts prepaid are a current asset in the balance sheet
Administration expenses	Any expense incurred in the running of the office and upkeep of premises and buildings (excluding any manufacturing expenses for manufacturing account questions)	Any amounts due are a current liability in the balance sheet Any amounts prepaid are a current asset in the balance sheet
Interest	Financial expense on debentures	Subtracted after operating profit

9

Sample Ordinary Level question

Hanley Ltd has an authorised capital of 600,000 ordinary shares at €1 each and 200,000 6% preference shares at €1 each. The company has already issued 400,000 of the ordinary shares and 150,000 6% preference shares. On 1/1/20-7 the company's general reserve account showed a balance of €35,000. Hanley Ltd had carried forward a profit of €56,000 from 20-6 and the accounts showed profits before interest and taxation of €140,000 for the year ended 31/12/20-7. During the year a total dividend of 8c per ordinary share was paid to ordinary shareholders and the total preference dividend for the year was paid to the preference shareholders.

On 31/12/20-7 the directors recommended that:

(a) interest of €21,000 be provided for

(b) taxation of €47,000 be provided for

(c) the general reserve be increased by €12,000.

You are required to:

- Show the profit and loss account for the year ended 31/12/20-7.
- Prepare a balance sheet showing the relevant accounts after making the above provisions and appropriations.

Solution

Profit and Loss Account of Hanley Ltd for the year ended 31/12/20-7

	€	€
Net profit for the year (operating profit)		140,000
Less Interest		(21,000)
Profit before tax		119,000
Less Taxation		(47,000)
Profit after tax		72,000
***Less* Appropriations**		
Increase in general reserve	12,000	
Ordinary dividend 8c per share	32,000	
Preference dividend for full year	9,000	(53,000)
Retained profit for year		19,000
Profit and loss balance 1/1/20-7		56,000
Profit and loss balance 31/12/20-7		75,000

9

Balance Sheet extract as at 31/12/20-7

	€	€	Total €
Fixed assets			740,000
Current assets			
***Less* Creditors: amounts falling due within 1 year**			
Interest due	21,000		
Taxation due	47,000	(68,000)	(68,000)
			672,000
Financed by			
Capital and reserves	**Authorised**	**Issued**	
Ordinary shares at €1 each	600,000	400,000	
6% preference shares at €1 each	200,000	150,000	
	800,000	550,000	
General reserve		47,000	
Profit and loss balance		75,000	672,000
Shareholders' funds			672,000

Sample Ordinary Level question – final accounts

The following trial balance was extracted from the books of Devon Ltd on 31/12/20-9. The company has an authorised share capital of €800,000 consisting of 800,000 €1 ordinary shares.

	€	€
Sales		972,000
Sales returns (inwards)	30,000	
Purchases	457,500	
Stock of goods 1/1/20-9	52,500	
Salaries sales staff	75,000	
Carriage outwards	3,000	
Salaries of administration staff	48,000	
Directors fees	7,500	
General expenses	64,500	
Discount allowed	9,000	
Audit fees	22,500	
Insurance	45,000	
Interest paid	10,500	
Discount received		15,000
Dividends paid for year	9,000	
Buildings (cost price)	825,000	
Investments (cost price)	150,000	
Patents	75,000	
Debtors	78,000	
Cash at bank	22,500	
Creditors		55,500
8% Debentures		150,000
Issued share capital		675,000
Profit and loss balance 1/1/20-9		120,000
Provision for bad debts		3,000
Delivery vans	180,000	
Accumulated depreciation on buildings		85,500
Accumulated depreciation on delivery vans		88,500
	2,164,500	2,164,500

9

You are given the following additional information and instructions:

(a) Stock at 31/12/20-9 was valued at €80,000.

(b) Provide for depreciation as follows:

Buildings, 2% of cost

Delivery vans, 25% of cost

(c) Provide for taxation due €98,000.

(d) Provide for debenture interest due.

(e) Provision for bad debts should be adjusted to 4% of debtors.

(f) Insurance was for the year ended 31/3/20-0.

You are required to prepare:

- trading, profit and loss appropriation account for the year ended 31/12/20-9
- balance sheet as at 31/12/20-9.

Solution

Trading, Profit and Loss Account of Devon Ltd for the year ended 31/12/20-9

	€	€	€
Sales			972,000
Less Returns inwards			(30,000)
			942,000
***Less* Cost of sales**			
Opening stock		52,500	
Purchases		457,500	
Cost of goods available for sale		510,000	
Less Closing stock		(80,000)	
Cost of goods sold			(430,000)
Gross profit			512,000
***Less* Expenses**			
Administration			
Salaries - administration	48,000		
Directors' fees	7,500		
General expenses	64,500		
Audit fees	22,500		
Insurance (W4)	33,750		
Depreciation - buildings (W1)	16,500	192,750	
Selling and distribution			
Salaries - sales staff	75,000		
Carriage outwards	3,000		
Increase in provision for bad debts (W3)	120		
Discount allowed	9,000		
Depreciation - delivery vans (W1)	45,000	132,120	(324,870)
			187,130
***Add* Other income**			
Discount received			15,000
Operating profit (profit before interest)			202,130
Less Interest payable (W2)			(12,000)

Continued >

	€	€	€
Profit before taxation			190,130
Taxation			(98,000)
Profit after taxation			92,130
Less Dividends			
Dividends paid			(9,000)
Retained profit for the year			83,130
Profit and loss balance 1/1/20-9			120,000
Profit and loss balance 31/12/20-9			203,130

Balance Sheet of Devon Ltd as at 31/12/20-9

	€	€	€	€
Intangible fixed assets				
Patents				75,000
Tangible fixed assets	**Cost**	**Aggregate depreciation**	**Net book value**	
Buildings	825,000	102,000	723,000	
Delivery vans	180,000	133,500	46,500	
	1,005,000	235,500	769,500	769,500
				844,500
Financial assets				
Investments at cost				150,000
				994,500
Current assets				
Closing stock		80,000		
Debtors	78,000			
Less Provision for bad debts (W3)	(3,120)	74,880		
Cash at bank		22,500		
Insurance prepaid (W4)		11,250	188,630	
***Less* Creditors: amounts falling due within 1 year**				
Trade creditors		55,500		
Taxation due		98,000		
Debenture interest due (W2)		1,500	(155,000)	
Net current assets				33,630
Total net assets				**1,028,130**
Financed by				
Creditors: amounts falling due after 1 year				
8% Debentures				150,000
Capital and Reserves		**Authorised**	**Issued**	
Ordinary share capital		800,000	675,000	
Profit and loss balance			203,130	
Shareholders' funds				878,130
Capital employed				**1,028,130**

9

Workings

W1 Depreciation: buildings

Cost	€825,000	
x Rate	2%	
Charge	**€16,500**	(administrative expense)

Depreciation: motor vehicles

Cost	€180,000	
x Rate	25%	
Charge	**€45,000**	(selling and distribution expense)

Total depreciation (balance sheet)

Buildings	85,500 + 16,500 = **€102,000**
Motor vehicles	88,500 + 45,000 = **€133,500**

W2 Debenture interest

150,000 x 8%	12,000
Less Paid	(10,500)
Amount due	**€1,500**

W3 Provision for bad debts

New provision (78,000 x 4%)	3,120	
Less Old provision	(3,000)	
Increase	**€120**	(selling and distribution)

W4 Insurance

Amount paid	45,000	
Less Prepaid (45,000 x 3/12)	(11,250)	
Charge	**€33,750**	(administrative expense)

Difficult adjustments

Adjustment 1: valuation of stock

Stock is always valued at the lower of cost or net realisable value. The loss in value of stock must always be taken away from the closing stock figure.

Example

Closing stock at 31/12/20-3 at cost was €85,000. This figure includes stock which cost €8,000 but has a net realisable value of 60% of cost.

The value of stock which lost value is now 8,000 x 60% = €4,800.

This is a loss in value of €3,200.

Therefore the closing stock must be reduced by €3,200, giving a new closing stock figure of €85,000 - €3,200 = **€81,800**

9

See Practice Question 1 for exercises on this adjustment.

Adjustment 2: investment income included in patents

The effect of placing a credit entry (the investment income) into the debit balance (the patent) makes the debit entry smaller. Hence if investment income is included in patents, it must be **added back** to the patents figure.

Investment income is a gain – credit entry (*debit* bank, *credit* investment income).

Patents are an asset (a debit balance).

Procedure

Step 1 Calculate the amount of investment for the period (e.g. three months, four months) that was included in the patents figure.

Step 2 Add this amount back to the patents figure before calculating the amount of the patent to be amortised (written off).

Step 3 Subtract this investment from the amount of investment interest the company is entitled to receive for the purpose of calculating the amount of interest due at the end of the year.

Example

Patents	€67,000
Investments (8% investments 1/5/20-1)	€150,000

Patents which incorporated three months' investment income are to be written off over a five-year period commencing in 20-1.

Solution

Step 1 **Find the amount of investment income included in patents.**

150,000 x 8% x 3/12 = **€3,000**

Step 2 **Add this amount back onto patents and find the amount to be written off.**

67,000 (trial balance) + 3,000 = 70,000/5 years = **€14,000** per annum

This will be treated as an administration expense in the trading, profit and loss account.

Step 3 **Subtract this investment from the amount of investment interest the company receives.**

Investment income 150,000 x 8% x 8/12 =	€8,000	(additional income)
Less Received	(3,000)	
Amount due (balance sheet)	**€5,000**	(current asset)

Summary

Expenses (administration)	**€14,000**	(patents w/o)
Patents balance sheet 70,000 – 14,000	**€56,000**	(intangible)
Current assets (investment interest due)	**€5,000**	

See Practice Question 2 for exercises on this adjustment.

Adjustment 3: depreciation of fixed assets

There are **five** figures we need to find:

1. the profit or loss on the sale of the fixed asset
2. the depreciation charge for the year
3. the cost price of assets in the balance sheet
4. the depreciation amount in the balance sheet
5. the new figure for purchases (if required).

9

There are usually **six steps** involved in this working. Step 6 may not be required.

Procedure

Step 1 Find the amount of depreciation to date on the asset sold.

Step 2 From step 1 find the profit or loss (expense or gain) on the sale of this asset.

Step 3 Find the cost of fixed assets for the purpose of the balance sheet.

Step 4 Find the depreciation charge for the year to be charged against profits.

Step 5 Find the net depreciation figure for the purpose of the balance sheet.

Step 6 Adjust the figure for purchases **if** the amount paid for the new asset has been treated as the purchase of trading stock. (This may not be in the question.)

Example

Delivery vans	€280,000
Depreciation of vans to date	€90,000
Purchases	€1,320,000

Provide for depreciation on delivery vans at the annual rate of 12.5% of cost from the date of purchase to the date of sale.

Note: On 31/3/20-6 a delivery van which cost €24,000 on 30/6/20-0 was traded in against a new van costing €56,000. An allowance of €10,000 was made for the old van. The cheque for the net amount of this transaction was incorrectly treated as the purchase of trading stock. This was the only entry in the books in respect of this transaction.

Solution

Step 1 Calculate the depreciation to date on the old van sold.

Old van purchased 30/6/20-0	6 months
20-1, 20-2, 20-3, 20-4, 20-5	5 full years
Sold on 31/3/20-6	3 months
Total time	5 years, 9 months = 69 months
24,000 x 12.5% x 69/12	= **€17,250**

Step 2 Calculate the profit or loss on the sale of this asset.

Cost of asset sold	€24,000	
Depreciation to date	(€17,250)	(from step 1 above)
Net book value	€6,750	
Trade-in allowance	€10,000	(from question)
Profit on sale	**€3,250**	(treated as gain in P & L)

Step 3 Calculate the cost price of vans for the purpose of the balance sheet.

Opening cost of assets	€280,000	(from trial balance)
Less Cost of old van	(€24,000)	
Add Cost of new van	€56,000	
Cost price for balance sheet	**€312,000**	

Step 4 Calculate the depreciation charge for the year.

Old van (3 months)	24,000 x 12.5% x 3/12 =	€750
New van (9 months)	56,000 x 12.5% x 9/12 =	€5,250
Vans held for year	(280,000 - 24,000) x 12.5% =	€32,000
Depreciation charge for the year		**€38,000**

Step 5 Calculate the net depreciation figure for the balance sheet.

Opening depreciation	€90,000	(trial balance)
Less Depreciation on old asset sold	(€17,250)	(from step 1)
Add This year's depreciation charge	€38,000	(from step 4)
Net depreciation for balance sheet	**€110,750**	

Step 6 Adjust the figure for purchases.

Purchases	€1,320,000	(from trial balance)
Less Amount paid for van	(€46,000)	
New purchases	**€1,274,000**	

Summary of entries for final answer

Trading Account (extract)

	€	
Purchases	1,274,000	(step 6)

Profit and Loss Account (extract)

	€	
Expenses		
Depreciation of vans	38,000	(step 4)
Add **Other income**		
Profit on sale of van	3,250	(step 2)

Balance Sheet (extract)

	Cost €	Aggregate Depreciation €	Net Book Value €
Fixed assets			
Delivery vans	312,000 (step 3)	110,750 (step 5)	201,250

See Practice Question 3 for exercises on this adjustment.

9

Adjustment 4: revaluation of fixed assets

Procedure

Step 1 Calculate this year's depreciation charge (if revaluation takes place at the end of the year). If revaluation takes place at the beginning, begin this adjustment at step 2.

Step 2 Bring the fixed asset being revalued up to its new value.

Step 3 Clear any existing depreciation to the revaluation reserve.

Step 4 Transfer total to the revaluation account which is entered in the balance sheet.

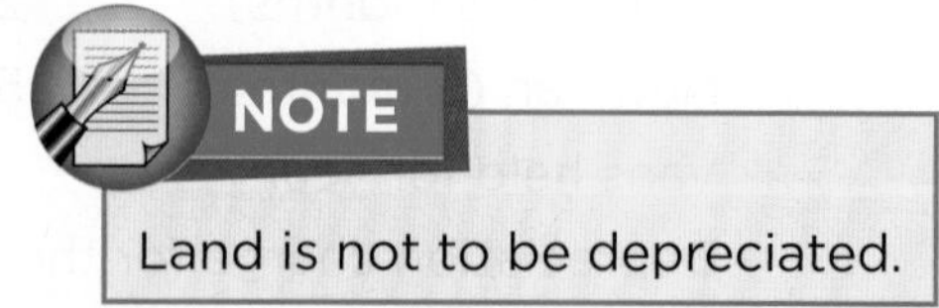

Land is not to be depreciated.

Example

Buildings	€580,000
Depreciation of buildings	€95,000

Provide for depreciation on buildings at the rate of 2% per annum. It was decided to revalue buildings at €800,000 on 31/12/20-7.

Solution

Step 1 Depreciation charge for 20-7.
580,000 x 2% = **€11,600** (administration expense)

Step 2 Bring asset up to new value.
580,000 up to 800,000 an increase of **€220,000**

Step 3 Clear all depreciation.

Opening depreciation (trial balance)	€95,000
This year's charge	€11,600
	€106,600

Step 4 Transfer total to the revaluation account.
220,000 + 106,600 = **€326,600**

Effects on final accounts

Profit and Loss Account (extract)

	€
Administration expenses	
Depreciation, land and buildings	11,600

Balance Sheet (extract)

	Cost €	Depreciation €	Net Book Value €
Fixed assets			
Land and buildings	800,000	Nil	800,000
Capital and reserves			
Revaluation reserve			326,600

See Practice Question 4 for exercises on this adjustment.

9

Other adjustments involving buildings

Apart from revaluation, adjustments involving buildings include:

- building of an extension
- damage to buildings
- VAT adjustments.

Extensions

Land and buildings may have to be adjusted for either the purchase of new buildings or the building of extensions. These extensions may involve using the company's own employees and materials taken from the firm's stocks. When this occurs the following adjustments are necessary:

Wages and salaries	**Decrease:** since the workers were paid to build the extension it is a capital expense not a revenue expense
Purchases	**Decrease:** the stock used to build the extension is not available for sale (non-trading goods)
Premises/buildings	**Increase:** the cost price of the extension is the total of the cost of materials and labour above (capital expenditure)

Example

Buildings cost	€440,000
Buildings depreciation	€45,000
Wages	€198,220
Purchases	€450,280

During 20-4 the company built an extension to the factory. This work was carried out by the company's own employees and the cost of their labour, €40,000, was included in wages. The cost of materials used, €18,000, was included in purchases. No entry had been made in the books in respect of this extension.

Any additions to buildings during the accounting period must be depreciated, as well as the original building.

Buildings are to be depreciated by 2% of cost at 31/12/20-4.

Show the effects of this adjustment on the final accounts.

Solution

Wages and salaries will decrease by 40,000	198,220 - 40,000 =	**€158,220**
Purchases will decrease by 18,000	450,280 - 18,000 =	**€432,280**
Buildings will increase by 18,000 + 40,000 = 58,000	440,000 + 58,000 =	**€498,000**
Depreciation of buildings 498,000 x 2%	=	**€9,960**

Trading, Profit and Loss Account (extract)

	€
Cost of sales	
Purchases	432,280
Expenses (administration)	
Wages and salaries	158,220
Depreciation of buildings	9,960

Balance Sheet (extract)

	Cost €	Depreciation €	Net Book Value €
Fixed assets			
Land and buildings	498,000	54,960	443,040

See Practice Question 5 for exercises on this adjustment.

9

Damage to buildings

This adjustment involves changing the value of the asset twice. Again depreciation on the asset must take account of these adjustments

Example

Land and buildings	€902,000
Purchases	€1,320,000
Wages and salaries	€199,600

During 20-6 a storeroom which cost €40,000 and stock which cost €12,000 were destroyed by fire. A new store was built by the firm's own workers. The cost of their labour, €19,000, was treated as a business expense and the materials costing €51,000 were taken from the firm's stocks. The insurance company agreed to contribute €52,000 in compensation for the fire damage. No adjustment was made in the books in respect of the old or new store.

Buildings to be depreciated by 2% of cost.

Show the effects of this adjustment on the final accounts.

Solution

Buildings increase and decrease – decrease by the cost of the old store and increase by the cost of the new store.

902,000 + 70,000 (51,000 + 19,000) – 40,000	=	**€932,000**
Depreciation of buildings	932,000 x 2% =	**€18,640**
Wage and salaries must decrease by €19,000	199,600 – 19,000 =	**€180,600**
Purchases must decrease by €51,000	1,320,000 – 51,000 =	**€1,269,000**
Purchases must also decrease by €12,000 (stock destroyed not available)	=	**€1,257,000**

The insurance company has not yet paid the compensation, therefore this €52,000 must be treated as a current asset in the balance sheet. Ensure that the compensation payable matches the cost of items lost (€40,000 + €12,000). You cannot make a profit from insurance.

Trading, Profit and Loss Account (extract)

	€	€
Cost of sales		
Purchases		1,257,000
Expenses		
Administration		
Buildings depreciation	18,640	
Wages and salaries	180,600	

Balance Sheet (extract)

	Cost €	Depreciation €	Net Book Value €
Fixed assets			
Land and buildings	932,000	18,640	913,360
Current assets			
Insurance compensation due		52,000	

See Practice Question 6 for exercises on this adjustment.

VAT

Example

Buildings	€980,000
Depreciation on buildings	€47,000 Cr.
VAT	€5,500 Cr.

Buildings must be included in the accounts at their VAT-exclusive amount.

A new warehouse was purchased during the year for €240,000 plus VAT at 12.5%. The amount paid to the vendor was entered in the buildings account. No entry was made in the VAT account.

Provide for depreciation on buildings at the rate of 2% of cost per annum. It was decided to revalue buildings at €1,100,000 on 31/12/20-2.

Solution

This adjustment will involve changes to buildings, VAT, expenses and revaluation reserve.

Step 1 Adjust the cost price of buildings for the VAT error.

240,000 x 12.5% = 30,000. This means an extra €30,000 was included in the cost of buildings.

Therefore the value of buildings is 980,000 - 30,000 = **€950,000**

Step 2 Adjust the VAT account.

From the trial balance, the company owed VAT of €5,500 (credit entry). Making the adjustment for €30,000 for VAT paid on buildings, this becomes a VAT refund of **€24,500**. This will be treated as a current asset in the balance sheet.

Step 3 Calculate the depreciation charge for the year.

New value of buildings (€950,000) x 2% = **€19,000** (administration expense)

9

Step 4 Revalue the buildings after the above adjustments.

Cost of buildings	€950,000 increased to €1,100,000, an increase of	€150,000
Clear opening depreciation	(from trial balance)	€47,000
Clear this year's depreciation	(from above)	€19,000
Revaluation reserve		**€216,000**

Effects on final accounts

Trading, Profit and Loss Account (extract)

	€	€
Expenses (administration)		
Depreciation of buildings	19,000	

Balance Sheet (extract)

	Cost €	Depreciation €	Net Book Value €
Fixed assets			
Buildings	1,100,000	Nil	1,100,000
Current assets			
VAT		24,500	
Capital and reserves			
Revaluation reserve			216,000

See Practice Question 7 for exercises on this adjustment.

Adjustment 5: debenture interest

The amount of interest that applies to a loan for the current financial year must be entered in the profit and loss account. This is in compliance with the matching principle.

Procedure

Step 1 Calculate the interest charge for the year.

The date on which the loan was taken out will determine the amount of interest to be charged. For example, if the loan was obtained on 1 April then nine months' interest must be entered in the profit and loss account.

Step 2 Subtract any interest paid from the interest chargeable for the year.

The amount of interest actually paid must be subtracted from this figure to find any interest still outstanding at the end of the financial year. This is entered in the balance sheet as a creditor amount falling due within one year.

Example

8% Debentures (including €100,000 8% debentures issued at par on 31/3/20-9): €350,000
Debenture interest paid: 3 months

9

Calculate the amount of interest payable for the year and any amount due at the end of the financial year.

Solution

Step 1 Calculate the interest charge for the year.

There are two separate loans, one for the full year and one for nine months of the year.

250,000 x 8%	=	€20,000	
100,000 x 8% x 9/12	=	€6,000	
Total debenture interest		**€26,000**	(P & L)

Step 2 Subtract any interest paid from the interest chargeable for the year.

250,000 x 8% x 3/12 = €5,000

Interest for the year is €26,000, amount paid is €5,000, therefore the amount due will be:

26,000 - 5,000 = **€21,000**

Trading, Profit and Loss Account (extract)

	€	€
Operating profit		
Less Debenture interest		26,000

Balance Sheet (extract)

	€	€
***Less* Creditors: amounts falling due within 1 year**		
Debenture interest due	21,000	

See Practice Question 8 for exercises on this adjustment.

Adjustment 6: bank account and bank statements

Adjustments made here can in turn affect further workings, for example bad debts.

Procedure

Step 1 Correct the company's bank account figure for the balance sheet.

Step 2 Reconcile this balance with the balance as per statement.

Step 3 Make the necessary adjustments elsewhere for each individual error.

Note: Cheques drawn but not presented for payment do not affect the firm's records as they have already been entered correctly in the business's books. It is the bank that needs to adjust its records.

Example

9

	€	€
Bank		44,000
Creditors		86,600
Debtors	100,400	
9% Investments (1/1/20-6)	320,000	
Provision for bad debts		3,200

The figure for bank in the trial balance (listed as €44,000 overdrawn) has been taken from the firm's bank account. However, a bank statement dated 31/12/-6 has arrived showing an overdraft of €42,760. A comparison of the bank account and the bank statement has revealed the following discrepancies:

(a) A cheque for €670 issued to a supplier had been entered in the books (cash book and ledger) as €760.

(b) A credit transfer of €750 has been paid direct to the firm's bank account on behalf of a debtor who had recently been declared bankrupt. This represents a first and final payment of 30c in the euro.

(c) A cheque for fees of €400 issued to a director has not been presented for payment.

Show the effects of these transactions on the final accounts.

Solution

Step 1 Correct the company's bank account figure for the balance sheet.

Bank balance as per trial balance	(44,000)	(overdraft)
Less Difference in cheque (760 – 670)	90	(cheque was too big)
Less Credit transfer received	750	(paid directly to bank)
Corrected bank balance	**(43,160)**	(balance sheet)

Step 2 Reconcile this balance with the balance as per statement.

Balance as per bank statement	(42,760)
Less Cheques not presented for payment	400
Balance as per adjusted cash book (step 1)	**(43,160)**

NOTE

This step has no effect on the final accounts.

Step 3 Make the necessary adjustments elsewhere for each individual error.

(a) Creditors were overpaid by €90, therefore they must increase by €90.

86,600 (trial balance) + 90 = **€86,690**

(b) €750 was received from a debtor which was 30c in the euro or 30% of the debt.

The full amount of the debt was therefore €2,500.

Debtors therefore will decrease by €2,500.

Since €750 was received, the remainder is a bad debt of **€1,750**.

(c) The cheque of €400 not presented for payment will not have any effect.

NOTE

If provision for bad debts is to be adjusted later, then this adjustment will also affect that calculation.

Profit and Loss Account (extract)

	€	€
Selling and distribution expenses		
Bad debts	1,750	

Balance Sheet (extract)

	€	€
Current assets		
Debtors		97,900
Creditors: amounts falling due within 1 year		
Creditors	86,690	
Bank	43,160	

See Practice Question 9 for exercises on this adjustment.

Adjustment 7: goods in transit

These are goods which were purchased during the year but have not yet been received by or delivered to the business. Therefore they are considered to be purchases for the year but were not included in closing stock as the goods were not physically present for the stock-take.

There are three changes or adjustments to be made for goods in transit:

1. **Increase** closing stock.
2. **Increase** purchases.
3. **Increase** creditors (if bought on credit) or **decrease** bank/cash (if paid for).

Stock must be valued at the lower of either cost or net realisable value.

Example

Stock at 31/12/20-5 at cost was €72,500. No record was made in the books for goods in transit on 31/12/20-5. The invoice for these goods had been received, showing a recommended selling price of €7,000, which is cost plus 25%.

Solution

Since the €7,000 is the selling price, the cost price must be found, as stock is always valued at the lower of cost or net realisable value:

7,000/125 x 100 = **€5,600**

Therefore in the final accounts:

1	Closing stock (trading a/c and balance sheet) will both increase by	€5,600
2	Purchases (trading a/c) will increase by	€5,600
3	Creditors (balance sheet) will increase by	€5,600

See Practice Question 10 for exercises on this adjustment.

Adjustment 8: goods sent on a sale-or-return basis

Under the **concept of prudence** you cannot anticipate a gain but you can anticipate a loss. Therefore goods sent on a sale-or-return basis cannot be included in the accounts as they are not officially sold.

Three changes are necessary in this adjustment:

1. Sales must **decrease** by the selling price.
2. Debtors must **decrease** by the selling price.
3. Closing stock must **increase** by the cost price.

Example

It was discovered that goods which cost €4,600 were invoiced to a customer on a sale-or-return basis. These goods had been entered in the books as a credit sale at cost plus 25%.

Solution

Cost €4,600 + 25% = selling price of €5,750

Therefore:

1. Debtors will decrease by €5,750.
2. Sales will decrease by €5,750.
3. Closing stock will increase by €4,600.

NOTE

Stock is increased as when stock-taking was carried out, these goods were with the customer.

See Practice Question 11 for exercises on this adjustment.

Adjustment 9: correction of errors

Correction of error adjustments involve the use of suspense accounts. These errors in relation to final accounts questions tend to involve mistakes regarding debenture/mortgage interest and discount received and allowed but can involve any asset, expense, liability or gain.

Procedure

Step 1 Make the necessary adjustments to cancel the suspense balance.

Step 2 Make the necessary adjustments to the accounts affected by the errors.

Step 3 Adjust the figure where the original suspense entry was entered.

NOTE

When the debit entries do not equal the credit entries the difference is entered in a **suspense account**.

Example

	€	€
Insurance (incorporating suspense)	6,150	
6% Fixed mortgage (including an increase of €50,000 on 1/4/20-7)		150,000
Mortgage interest paid for 3 months	1,250	
Bank		15,900
Discount (net)		1,200
Creditors		113,000

The suspense figure arises as a result of the posting of an incorrect figure for mortgage interest in the mortgage interest account and discount received €200 entered only in the creditors account. The correct interest was entered in the bank account.

Solution

1. Interest paid must be increased by €250, therefore the amount due in the balance sheet will decrease by €250.
2. Discount needs to be credited with €200, making it €1,400.
3. Since suspense was put into insurance, insurance needs to be credited with €50, decreasing insurance in the profit and loss account by €50 to €6,100.
4. No adjustments need to be made to either bank or creditors.

See Practice Question 12 for exercises on this adjustment.

9

Sample Higher Level question

Rocket Ltd has an authorised share capital of €1,700,000, divided into 1,300,000 ordinary shares at €1 each and 400,000 10% preference shares at €1 each. The following trial balance was extracted from its books on 31/12/20-6:

		€	€
Land and buildings at cost		942,000	
Delivery vans (cost €280,000)		220,000	
Stock 1/1/20-6		71,200	
Debtors and creditors		54,400	70,200
10% Investments		240,000	
10% Debentures			140,000
Bank			36,000
Purchases and sales		1,480,000	1,980,000
Salaries and general expenses		194,400	
Provision for bad debts			2,900
Discount (net)			4,200
Rent and rates (incorporating suspense)		22,000	
Directors' fees		17,200	
Advertising		6,200	
Debenture interest paid (3 months)		4,100	
Patents (incorporating investment income 3 months)		19,000	
Dividends paid		50,000	
Profit and loss balance 1/1/20-6		12,800	
Issued capital	900,000 ordinary shares @ €1 each		900,000
	200,000 10% preference shares		200,000
		3,333,300	**3,333,300**

9

The following information and instructions are to be taken into account:

(a) Stock at 31/12/20-6 at cost was €54,000. This figure includes damaged stock which cost €5,000 but which is now worth €1,600.

(b) Patents, which incorporates three months' investment, are to be written off over a five-year period commencing in 20-6.

(c) The suspense figure arises as a result of an incorrect figure for debenture interest (the correct figure was entered in the bank account, and discount allowed €200 entered only in the discount account).

(d) No record had been made in the books for goods in transit on 31/12/20-6. The invoice for these goods had been received showing a recommended retail price of €16,800, which is cost plus 20%.

(e) During 20-6 a store was destroyed by fire. A new store was built by the firm's own workers. The cost of their labour (€17,000) had been treated as a business expense and materials costing €43,000 were taken from the firm's stocks. The insurance company has agreed to contribute €50,000 to cover the complete cost of the destroyed store. No entry had been made in the books in respect of the old or new store.

(f) The directors recommended that:

- Provision should be made for debenture interest due.
- Delivery vans are to be depreciated at 15% of book value.
- Provision for bad debts should be adjusted to 6% of debtors.

You are required to prepare:

- trading, profit and loss account for the year ended 31/12/20-6
- balance sheet as at 31/12/20-6.

Solution

Trading, Profit and Loss and Appropriation Account for Rocket Ltd for the year ended 31/12/20-6:

	€	€	€
Sales			1,980,000
***Less* Cost of sales**			
Opening stock		71,200	
Purchases (W4 & W5)		1,451,000	
Cost of goods available		1,522,200	
Less Closing stock (W1 & W4)		(64,600)	
Cost of goods sold			**(1,457,600)**
Gross profit			522,400
***Less* Expenses**			
Administration			
Salaries and general expenses (W5)	177,400		
Directors' fees	17,200		
Rent and rates (W3)	22,800		
Patents written off (W2)	5,000	222,400	
Selling and distribution			
Depreciation - delivery vans (W8)	33,000		
Advertising	6,200		
Increase in provision for bad debts (W9)	352	39,552	(261,952)
			260,448
***Add* Other income (gains)**			
Investment income (W2)		24,000	
Discount received		4,200	28,200
Operating profit			288,648
Less Debenture interests (W7)			(14,000)
			274,648
***Less* Appropriations**			
Preference dividends (W6)		20,000	
Ordinary dividends (W6)		30,000	(50,000)
Retained profit for the year			224,648
Profit and loss balance 1/1/20-6			(12,800)
Profit and loss balance 31/12/20-6			**211,848**

9

Balance Sheet for Rocket Ltd as at 31/12/20-6

	Cost €	Agg. Dpr. €	NBV €	Total €
Intangible fixed assets				
Patents (W2)				20,000
Tangible fixed assets				
Buildings (W5)	952,000		952,000	
Motor vehicles (W8)	280,000	93,000	187,000	
	1,232,000	93,000	1,139,000	1,139,000
				1,159,000
Financial assets				
10% Investments				240,000
				1,399,000
Current assets				
Stocks (W1 & W4)		64,600		
Debtors	54,200			
Less Provision for bad debts (W9)	(3,252)	50,948		
Investment income due (W2)		18,000		
Amount due from insurance company		50,000	183,548	
***Less* Creditors: amounts falling due within 1 year**				
Trade creditors (W4)		84,200		
Bank overdraft		36,000		
Debenture interest due (W7)		10,500	(130,700)	
Net current assets				52,848
Total net assets				**1,451,848**
Financed by				
Creditors: amounts falling due after more than 1 year				
10% Debentures				140,000
Capital and reserves		**Authorised**	**Issued**	
Ordinary shares @ €1 each		1,300,000	900,000	
10% Preference shares @ €1 each		400,000	200,000	
		1,700,000	1,100,000	
Profit and loss balance 31/12/20-6			211,848	
Shareholders' funds				1,311,848
Capital employed				**1,451,848**

Workings

W1 Closing stock

As given	54,000
Less Loss in value	(3,400)
Closing stock	€50,600

W2 Patents and investment income

Amount received: 3 months' investment income

240,000 x 10% x 3/12 €6,000

This is the amount to be added back to patents.

Patents as per trial balance	19,000
Add Investment income	6,000
True value of patents	€25,000

This is to be written off over 5 years

25,000/5 = €5,000 (administration expense)

Balance sheet

Patents €20,000 (25,000 – 5,000)

W3 Correction of errors

Error 1

Debtors had no entry

Discount allowed	Dr €200
Suspense	Cr €200

Error 2

Debenture interest	Dr €4,100
Bank credit	Cr €3,500
Suspense	Cr €600

Corrections	
Debenture interest paid	€3,500
Debtors are reduced by	€200
Rent and rates increase by	€800

W4 Goods in transit

Selling price	€16,800
Cost price (16,800/120 × 100)	€14,000
Purchases will increase by	€14,000
Creditors will increase by	€14,000
Closing stock will increase by	€14,000

W5 Buildings

Buildings as given	942,000
Less Loss in fire	(50,000)
Add new building	60,000
New cost price	€952,000

Salaries and general expenses will decrease by	€17,000
Purchases will decrease by	€43,000
Insurance company due	€50,000

W6 Dividends

Preference	
Total 200,000 × 10%	€20,000
Ordinary	
Paid (50,000 - 20,000)	€30,000

W7 Debenture interest

Amount payable (140,000 × 10%)	€14,000
Less Amount paid	(€3,500)
Amount due	€10,500

W8 Depreciation of vans

Book value (220,000) × 15%	€33,000

W9 Provision for bad debts

New provision for bad debts = 6% of closing debtors

54,200 × 6% = 3,252

Less Old provision (2,900) (given in the trial balance)

Increase €352 (treated as a selling and distribution expense)

Exercises – Ordinary Level

Q1 Lewis Ltd has an authorised capital of 700,000 ordinary shares at €1 each and 290,000 6% preference shares at €1 each. The company has already issued 500,000 of the ordinary shares and 250,000 6% preference shares. On 1/1/20-8 the company's general reserve account showed a balance of €50,000. Lewis Ltd had carried forward a profit of €65,000 from 20-7 and the accounts showed profits before interest and taxation of €210,000 for the year ended 31/12/20-8. During the year an interim dividend of 5c per ordinary share was paid to ordinary shareholders and the full dividend for the year was paid to the preference shareholders.

On 31/12/20-8 the directors recommended that:

(a) The general reserve be increased to €75,000.

(b) Taxation of €24,000 be provided for.

(c) Interest of €14,000 be provided for.

You are required to:

- Show the profit and loss account for the year ended 31/12/20-8.
- Prepare a balance sheet showing the relevant accounts after making the above provisions and appropriations.

Q2 **The Real Deal Ltd has an authorised capital of €800,000, divided into 600,000 ordinary shares at €1 each and 200,000 7% preference shares at €1 each. The company has already issued 400,000 of the ordinary shares and 100,000 7% preference shares. On 1/1/20-9 the company's general reserve account showed a balance of €95,000. The Real Deal Ltd had carried forward a profit of €17,500 from 20-8 and the accounts showed profits before interest and taxation of €198,000 for the year ended 31/12/20-9. During the year an interim dividend of 4c per ordinary share was paid to ordinary shareholders and the full dividend for the year was paid to the preference shareholders.**

On 31/12/20-9 the directors recommended that:

(a) The general reserve be increased 10%.

(b) Taxation of €32,000 be provided for.

(c) Interest of €9,000 be provided for.

You are required to:

- Show the profit and loss account for the year ended 31/12/20-9.
- Prepare a balance sheet showing the relevant accounts after making the above provisions and appropriations.

Q3 **Final Fantasy Ltd has an authorised capital of €700,000 divided into 500,000 ordinary shares at €1 each and 200,000 9% preference shares at €1 each. The company has already issued 350,000 of the ordinary shares and 150,000 9% preference shares. On 1/1/20-4 the company's general reserve account showed a balance of €20,000. Final Fantasy Ltd had carried forward a profit of €24,000 from 20-3 and the accounts showed profits before interest and taxation of €104,000 for the year ended 31/12/20-4. During the year an interim dividend of 7c per ordinary share was paid to ordinary shareholders and the full dividend for the year was paid to the preference shareholders.**

On 31/12/20-4 the directors recommended that:

(a) The general reserve be increased to €25,000.

(b) Taxation of €12,000 be provided for.

(c) Interest of €10,000 be provided for.

You are required to:

- Show the profit and loss account for the year ended 31/12/20-4.
- Prepare a balance sheet showing the relevant accounts after making the above provisions and appropriations.

Q4 **Me2U Ltd has an authorised capital of €1,000,000, divided into 750,000 ordinary shares at €1 each and 250,000 5% preference shares at €1 each. The company has already issued 600,000 of the ordinary shares and 200,000 5% preference shares. On 1/1/20-5 the company's general reserve account showed a balance of €34,000. Me2U Ltd had carried forward a loss of €22,000 from 20-4 and the accounts showed profits before interest and taxation of €219,000 for the year ended 31/12/20-5. During the year an interim dividend of 7c per ordinary share was paid to ordinary shareholders and nine months' dividend was paid to the preference shareholders.**

On 31/12/20-5 the directors recommended that:

(a) The preference dividend due be paid

(b) A final dividend be paid on ordinary shares of 4c

(c) The general reserve be increased by €20,000

(d) Taxation of €23,000 be provided for.

Provide for interest of €15,000.

You are required to:

- Show the profit and loss account for the year ended 31/12/20-5.
- Prepare a balance sheet showing the relevant accounts after making the above provisions and appropriations.

Q5 The following information was extracted from the books of O'Gara Ltd on 31/12/20-6:

- O'Gara Ltd has an authorised share capital of 600,000 ordinary shares at €1 each and 200,000 5% preference shares at €1 each.
- The company has already issued 400,000 of the ordinary shares and 100,000 of the preference shares.
- On 1/1/20-6 the company's general reserve account showed a balance of €59,000.
- O'Gara Ltd carried forward a profit of €19,000 from 20-5 and the accounts showed profits of €120,000 before interest and taxation for the year ended 31/12/20-6.
- During the year a total dividend of 8c per ordinary share was paid to ordinary shareholders and the total preference dividend for the year was paid to the preference shareholders.

On 31/12/20-6 the directors recommended that:

(a) Interest of €13,000 be provided for.

(b) Taxation of €48,000 be provided for.

(c) The general reserve be increased by €12,000.

You are required to:

- Show the profit and loss account for the year ended 31/12/20-6.
- Prepare a balance sheet showing the relevant accounts after making the above provisions and appropriations.

Q6 The following information was extracted from the books of O'Heir Ltd on 31/12/20-2:

- O'Heir Ltd has an authorised share capital of 900,000 ordinary shares at €1 each and 300,000 6% preference shares at €1 each.
- The company has already issued 700,000 of the ordinary shares and 200,000 of the preference shares.
- On 1/1/20-2 the company's general reserve account showed a balance of €22,000.
- O'Heir Ltd carried forward a profit of €121,000 from 20-1 and the accounts showed profits of €234,000 before interest and taxation for the year ended 31/12/20-2.
- During the year a total dividend of 10c per ordinary share was paid to ordinary shareholders and the total preference dividend for the year was paid to the preference shareholders.

On 31/12/20-2 the directors recommended that:

(a) Interest of €16,000 be provided for.

(b) Taxation of €39,000 be provided for.

(c) The general reserve be increased to €30,000.

You are required to:

- Show the profit and loss account for the year ended 31/12/20-2.
- Prepare a balance sheet showing the relevant accounts after making the above provisions and appropriations.

9

Q7 **The following balances were extracted from the books of Higgins Ltd on 31/12/20-8:**

	€	€
Share capital		
Authorised: 800,000 ordinary shares @€1 each		
Issued: 600,000 ordinary shares @€1 each		600,000
Buildings	890,000	
Computers and office equipment	110,000	
Patents	160,000	
Accumulated depreciation computers and office equipment		12,000
Accumulated depreciation land and buildings		50,000
12% Debentures issued 1/7/20-8		150,000
Sales		990,600
Purchases	447,000	
Carriage inwards	3,500	
Wages and salaries	114,000	
Debtors and creditors	40,500	63,900
Stationery	6,700	
Stocks 1/1/20-8		
Goods for resale	42,800	
Stationery	2,600	
VAT		41,200
Directors' fees	32,000	
Profit and loss balance 1/1/20-8	20,100	
Cleaning	23,900	
Provision for bad debts		3,200
Bank	12,800	
Discount (net)	5,000	
	1,910,900	**1,910,900**

You are given the following additional information and instructions:

(a) Stocks at 31/12/20-8: Goods for resale, €54,800; stationery, €1,200.

(b) Depreciation is to be provided as follows:

Computers and office equipment: 15% of book value

Buildings: 6% of cost price

(c) Cleaning is paid in advance and is for the year ended 31/03/20-9.

(d) Provision should be made for debenture interest due.

(e) Wages due on 31/12/20-8 amounted to €2,500.

(f) Provide for corporation tax of €21,600.

You are required to prepare:

- the trading, profit and loss account for the year ended 31/12/20-8
- a balance sheet as at 31/12/20-8.

9

Q8 **The following balances were extracted from the books of Tatler Ltd on 31/12/20-7:**

	€	€
Share capital		
Authorised: 900,000 ordinary shares at €1 each		
Issued: 780,000 ordinary shares at €1 each		780,000
Patents	380,000	
Motor vehicles	220,000	
Premises	600,000	
Accumulated depreciation on vehicles		34,500
Accumulated depreciation on premises		60,000
Debtors and creditors	140,000	132,000
8% Debentures issued on 1/1/20-7		240,000
Purchases	450,000	
Sales		880,000
Wages and salaries	208,900	
Stocks 1/1/20-7		
Goods for resale	89,000	
Heating oil	1,000	
Profit and loss account balance 1/1/20-7		66,900
Returns inwards	4,000	
Light and heat	19,800	
Provision for bad debts		6,200
Commission		22,000
Dividends paid	65,000	
Insurance	32,000	
Advertising	28,900	
VAT		5,600
Debenture interest	10,500	
Bank		21,900
	2,249,100	**2,249,100**

You are given the following additional information and instructions:

(a) Stocks at 31/12/20-7: Goods for resale, €108,000; oil, €1,300.

(b) Provision for bad debts should be adjusted to 4% of debtors.

(c) Depreciation is to be provided as follows: Motor vehicles, 20% of cost; premises, 2% of cost.

(d) Provision should be made for debenture interest due.

(e) Advertising was for the year ended 31/3/20-8.

(f) Commission due at 31/12/20-7 was €2,340.

(g) Provide for corporation tax of €17,800.

You are required to prepare:

- **the trading, profit and loss account for the year ended 31/12/20-7**
- **a balance sheet as at 31/12/20-7.**

9

Q9 **The following balances were extracted from the books of Wizards Ltd on 31/12/20-0:**

	€	€
Share capital		
Authorised: 850,000 ordinary shares at €1 each		
Issued: 545,000 ordinary shares at €1 each		545,000
Patents	120,000	
Office equipment	40,000	
Buildings	900,000	
Accumulated depreciation on office equipment		16,000
Accumulated depreciation on buildings		160,000
Debtors and creditors	132,000	110,000
9% Debentures issued on 1/4/20-0		180,000
Purchases and sales	420,000	761,000
Stocks on 1/1/20-0		
Goods for resale	145,000	
Stationery	2,400	
Profit and loss balance 1/1/20-0		42,000
Returns	3,000	
Stationery	6,500	
Provision for bad debts		3,900
Commission		19,000
Directors' fees	46,900	
Advertising	25,000	
VAT		4,400
Light and heat	19,000	
Insurance	16,000	
Bank		34,500
	1,875,800	**1,875,800**

You are given the following additional information and instructions:

(a) Stocks at 31/12/20-0: Goods for resale, €98,600; stationery, €900.

(b) Provision for bad debts to be adjusted to 5% of debtors.

(c) Depreciation is to be provided as follows: Office equipment, 15% of book value; buildings, 3% of cost.

(d) Provision should be made for debenture interest due.

(e) Advertising was for the year ended 31/3/20-1.

(f) Provide for corporation tax of €14,600.

You are required to prepare:

- the trading, profit and loss account for the year ended 31/12/20-0
- a balance sheet as at 31/12/20-0.

9

Q10 **The following balances were extracted from the books of Taffe Ltd on 31/12/20-6:**

	€	€
Share capital		
Authorised: 1,600,000 ordinary shares at €1 each		
Issued: 1,000,000 ordinary shares €1 each		1,000,000
Buildings	1,200,000	
Motor vehicles	170,000	
Patents	150,000	
Accumulated depreciation, buildings		130,000
Accumulated depreciation, motor vehicles		40,000
8% Debentures issued on 1/4/20-6		100,000
Sales		1,280,000
Purchases	450,000	
Returns inwards	15,600	
Debtors	132,000	
Creditors		80,000
Carriage inwards	10,600	
Discount received		10,000
Wages and salaries	310,000	
Stationery	5,400	
Goods for resale on 1/1/20-6	98,700	
Dividends paid	90,000	
VAT		39,800
Insurance	23,000	
Bank		66,500
Stock of stationery 1/1/20-6	3,200	
Advertising	67,000	
Provision for bad debts		8,900
Profit and loss balance 1/1/20-6	29,700	
	2,755,200	**2,755,200**

You are given the following additional information and instructions:

(a) Stocks at 31/12/20-6: Goods for resale, €87,900; stationery, €900.

(b) Depreciation to be provided for as follows: Buildings, 5% of cost; motor vehicles, 10% of book value.

(c) Provision should be made for debenture interest due.

(d) Provision for bad debts should be adjusted to 8% of debtors.

(e) Advertising was for the year ended 31/3/20-7.

(f) Provide for corporation tax of €16,500.

You are required to prepare:

- the trading, profit and loss account for the year ended 31/12/20-6
- a balance sheet as at 31/12/20-6.

9

Q11 The following balances were extracted from the books of Venky Ltd on 31/12/20-2. The company's authorised share capital consisted of 500,000 ordinary shares at €1 each.

	€	€
Issued share capital: 350,000 ordinary shares @ €1 each		350,000
Premises	340,000	
Furniture and equipment	190,000	
Goodwill	5,000	
Accumulated depreciation		
Premises		23,000
Furniture and equipment		4,500
10% Debentures issued at par 1/4/20-2		80,000
Sales		360,000
Purchases	180,000	
Carriage	3,400	
Wages and salaries	56,000	
Debtors and creditors	61,000	32,000
Stationery	8,900	
Stocks 1/1/20-2	29,000	
VAT		5,600
Directors' fees	19,000	
Profit and loss balance 1/1/20-2		34,500
Returns	1,300	1,800
Advertising	4,900	
Bank		2,900
Commission		7,800
Cleaning expenses	3,600	
	902,100	**902,100**

9

You are given the following additional information and instructions:

(a) Stocks at 31/12/20-2: Goods for resale, €23,850, which included stock of cleaning materials, €450.

(b) Provide for depreciation as follows: Furniture and equipment, 10% reducing balance; premises, 3% on cost.

(c) Advertising was for the year ended 31/3/20-3.

(d) Provide for bad debts at a rate of 6% of debtors.

(e) Corporation tax is to be €12,000 for the year.

(f) Directors' fees due 31/12/20-2 were €2,100.

(g) Carriage is 60% on sales, the remainder on purchases.

You are required to prepare:

- trading, profit and loss account for the year ended 31/12/20-2
- balance sheet as at 31/12/20-2.

Q12 **The following balances were extracted from the books of Lawlor Ltd on 31/12/20-3:**

	€	€
Share capital		
Authorised: 700,000 ordinary shares @ €1 each		
Issued: 550,000 ordinary shares @ €1 each		550,000
Premises	640,000	
Equipment	160,000	
Debtors and creditors	34,000	23,000
Purchases and sales	179,000	434,000
Returns		9,400
Insurance	5,800	
Stationery	3,900	
Stock of goods 1/1/20-3	23,000	
PAYE and USC		13,400
Profit and loss balance 1/1/20-3		1,200
Bank	2,400	
Discount (net)		13,500
9% Debentures issued at par 1/7/20-3		120,000
Provision for bad debts		5,000
Wages and salaries	120,000	
Accumulated depreciation on equipment		16,300
Travel expenses	8,000	
Light and heat	5,900	
Custom duties	1,800	
Auditor's fees	2,000	
	1,185,800	**1,185,800**

You are given the following additional information and instructions:

(a) **Closing stock on 31/12/20-3 was €25,400 and this included stock of stationery of €400.**

(b) **Provide for depreciation on equipment at the rate of 15% on a reducing balance basis.**

(c) **Closing stock of oil on 31/12/20-3 was €1,400 while there was an electricity bill due of €340.**

(d) **Provide for auditor's fees due, €1,900, and corporation tax, €12,000.**

(e) **There were wages due of €12,500 at 31/12/20-3.**

(f) **The provision for bad debts was to be adjusted to 8% of debtors.**

You are required to prepare:

- trading, profit and loss account for the year ended 31/12/20-3
- balance sheet as at 31/12/20-3.

9

Practice Questions

Q1 In each case below calculate the value of closing stock to be included in the final accounts.

(a) Closing stock at 31/12/20-1 at cost was €66,000. This includes old stock which cost €7,000 but now has a net realisable value of 70% of cost.

(b) Stocks at 31/12/20-9 at cost were €105,200. This figure includes damaged stock which cost €9,000 but which now has a net realisable value of €4,400.

(c) Stocks at 31/12/20-0 at cost were €45,600. This figure includes damaged stock which cost €4,000 but which now has a net realisable value of €1,100.

(d) Stocks at 31/12/20-1 at cost were €95,000. This figure includes damaged stock which cost €12,000 but which now has a net realisable value of 55% of cost.

Q2 In each of the following questions calculate the amount of patents to be amortised in the relevant sections of the final accounts.

(a)	Patents	€24,000
	9% Investments 1/1/20-6	€320,000

Patents which incorporated three months' investment income are to be written off over a five-year period commencing in 20-6.

(b)	Patents	€93,000
	10% Investments 1/5/20-0	€70,000

Patents which incorporated three months' investment income are to be written off over a five-year period commencing in 20-0.

(c)	Patents	€76,000
	8% Investments 1/5/20-1	€50,000

Patents which incorporated three months' investment income are to be written off over a five-year period commencing in 20-1.

(d)	Patents	€85,000
	12% Investments 1/5/20-2	€125,000

Patents which incorporated four months' investment income are to be written off over a five-year period commencing in 20-2.

9

Q3 In each of the following questions calculate:

- **the profit or loss on the sale of an asset**
- **the amount of depreciation to be charged against profits for the year**
- **the figures for use in the balance sheet**
- **the adjustment to purchases in the trading account.**

(a)	E. O'Keeffe	Delivery vans	€168,000
		Depreciation of vans to date	€64,000
		Purchases	€510,000

Provide for depreciation on delivery vans at the annual rate of 20% of cost from the date of purchase to the date of sale.

Note: On 31/5/20-7 a delivery van which cost €50,000 on 1/1/20-4 was traded in against a new van costing €74,000. An allowance of €24,000 was made for the old van. The cheque for the net amount of this transaction was incorrectly treated as the purchase of trading stock. This was the only entry in the books in respect of this transaction

(b)	M. O'Hara	Delivery vans	€320,000
		Depreciation of vans to date	€70,000
		Purchases	€670,000

Provide for depreciation on delivery vans at the annual rate of 20% of cost from the date of purchase to the date of sale.

Note: On 31/3/20-5 a delivery van which cost €30,000 on 1/7/20-1 was traded in against a new van costing €65,000. An allowance of €12,000 was made for the old van. The cheque for the net amount of this transaction was incorrectly treated as the purchase of trading stock. This was the only entry in the books in respect of this transaction

(c)	M. Phelan	Delivery vans	€480,000
		Depreciation of vans to date	€80,000
		Purchases	€560,000

Provide for depreciation on delivery vans at the annual rate of 15% of cost from the date of purchase to the date of sale.

Note: On 1/4/20-6 a delivery van which cost €60,000 on 1/9/20-3 was traded in against a new van costing €84,000. An allowance of €23,000 was made for the old van. The cheque for the net amount of this transaction was incorrectly treated as the purchase of trading stock. This was the only entry in the books in respect of this transaction

Q4 Revaluation of assets adjustments: in each of the following show the relevant effects of these adjustments on the final accounts.

(a)	Land and buildings	€840,000
	Depreciation	€42,000

Provide for depreciation on buildings at the rate of 2% per annum. Land at cost was €140,000. It was decided to revalue buildings at €900,000 on 31/12/20-9.

(b)	Land and buildings	€350,000
	Depreciation	€40,000

Provide for depreciation on buildings at the rate of 3% per annum. It was decided to revalue buildings at €560,000 on 31/12/20-0. Land at cost was €50,000.

(c)	Buildings	€620,000
	Depreciation	€60,000

Provide for depreciation on buildings at the rate of 4% per annum. It was decided to revalue buildings at €750,000 on 31/12/20-9.

Q5 Other adjustments involving buildings – extensions: in each of the following show the relevant effects of these adjustments on the final accounts.

(a)	Buildings cost	€900,000
	Buildings depreciation	€50,000
	Wages	€300,000
	Purchases	€720,000

During 20-0 the company built an extension to the factory. This work was carried out by the company's own employees and the cost of their labour, €28,000, was included in wages. The cost of materials used, €32,000, was included in purchases. No entry had been made in the books in respect of this extension.

Buildings are to be depreciated by 4% of cost at 31/12/20-0.

(b) Buildings cost €570,000
Buildings depreciation €90,000
Wages €145,000
Purchases €390,000

During 20-1 the company built an extension to the factory. This work was carried out by the company's own employees and the cost of their labour, €46,000, was included in wages. The cost of materials used, €24,000, was included in purchases. No entry had been made in the books in respect of this extension.

Buildings are to be depreciated by 2% of cost at 31/12/20-1.

(c) Buildings cost €670,000
Buildings depreciation €74,000
Wages €231,000
Purchases €659,000

During 20-2 the company built an extension to the factory. This work was carried out by the company's own employees and the cost of their labour, €54,000, was included in wages. The cost of materials used, €56,000, was included in purchases. No entry had been made in the books in respect of this extension.

Buildings are to be depreciated by 5% of cost at 31/12/20-2.

Q6 Other adjustments involving buildings – damage: in each of the following show the relevant effects of these adjustments on the final accounts.

(a) Land and buildings €506,000
Purchases €234,000
Wages and salaries €123,000

During 20-0 a storeroom which cost €30,000 and stock which cost €16,000 were destroyed by fire. A new store was built by the firm's own workers. The cost of their labour, €12,000, was treated as a business expense and the materials costing €48,000 were taken from the firm's stocks. The insurance company agreed to contribute €46,000 in compensation for the fire damage. No adjustment was made in the books in respect of the old or new store.

Buildings are to be depreciated by 2% of cost.

9

(b) Land and buildings €805,000
Purchases €650,000
Wages and salaries €234,000

During 20-1 a storeroom which cost €25,000 and stock which cost €10,000 were destroyed by fire. A new store was built by the firm's own workers. The cost of their labour, €11,000, was treated as a business expense and the materials costing €19,000 were taken from the firm's stocks. The insurance company agreed to contribute €35,000 in compensation for the fire damage. No adjustment was made in the books in respect of the old or new store.

Buildings are to be depreciated by 2% of cost.

(c) Land and buildings €608,000
Purchases €450,000
Wages and salaries €123,000

During 20-2 a storeroom which cost €34,000 and stock which cost €24,000 were destroyed by fire. A new store was built by the firm's own workers. The cost of their labour, €24,000, was treated as a business expense and the materials costing €26,000 were taken from the firm's stocks. The insurance company agreed to contribute €58,000 in compensation for the fire damage. No adjustment was made in the books in respect of the old or new store.

Q7 Other adjustments involving buildings – VAT: in each of the following show the relevant effects of these adjustments on the final accounts.

(a) Buildings €560,000

Depreciation on buildings €40,000

VAT €6,000 Cr.

A new warehouse was purchased during the year for €72,000 plus VAT at 12.5%. The amount paid to the vendor was entered in the buildings account. No entry was made in the VAT account.

Provide for depreciation on buildings at the rate of 5% of cost per annum. It was decided to revalue buildings at €700,000 on 31/12/20-0.

(b) Buildings €670,000

Depreciation on buildings €50,000

VAT €9,000 Cr.

A new warehouse was purchased during the year for €300,000 plus VAT at 15%. The amount paid to the vendor was entered in the buildings account. No entry was made in the VAT account.

Provide for depreciation on buildings at the rate of 3% of cost per annum. It was decided to revalue buildings at €820,000 on 31/12/20-1.

(c) Buildings €780,000

Depreciation on buildings €56,000

VAT €3,400 Cr.

A new warehouse was purchased during the year for €180,000 plus VAT at 10%. The amount paid to the vendor was entered in the buildings account. No entry was made in the VAT account.

Provide for depreciation on buildings at the rate of 2% of cost per annum. It was decided to revalue buildings at €910,000 on 31/12/20-2.

Q8 Interest payable: in each of the following show the effect on the final accounts.

(a) 10% Debentures (including €120,000 10% debentures issued at par on 31/3/20-0) €420,000

Debenture interest paid 3 months

(b) 7% Debentures (including €70,000 7% debentures issued at par on 30/4/20-1) €270,000

Debenture interest paid 4 months

(c) 9% Debentures (including €150,000 9% debentures issued at par on 31/3/20-2) €450,000

Debenture interest paid 3 months

9

Q9 Bank account adjustments: in each of the following show the effect on the final accounts.

(a) **Matthews Ltd**

		€
Bank		16,800 Cr.
Creditors		23,000
Debtors		65,000

The figure for bank in the trial balance (listed as €16,800 overdrawn) has been taken from the firm's bank account. However, a bank statement dated 31/12/-3 has arrived showing an overdraft of €9,520. A comparison of the bank account and the bank statement has revealed the following discrepancies:

(i) Investment income of €2,500 had been paid directly to the firm's bank account.

(ii) A cheque for €680 issued to a supplier had been entered in the books (cash book and ledger) as €860.

(iii) A credit transfer of €600 has been paid direct to the firm's bank account on behalf of a debtor who had recently been declared bankrupt. This represents a first and final payment of 30c in the euro.

(iv) A cheque for fees of €4,000 issued to a director had not been presented for payment.

(b) **Jankl Ltd**

		€
Bank		56,000 Cr.
Creditors		34,500
Debtors		65,800

The figure for bank in the trial balance (listed as €56,000 overdrawn) has been taken from the firm's bank account. However, a bank statement dated 31/12/-0 has arrived showing an overdraft of €50,000. A comparison of the bank account and the bank statement has revealed the following discrepancies:

(i) A cheque for €870 issued to a supplier had been entered in the books (cash book and ledger) as €780.

(ii) A credit transfer of €950 has been paid direct to the firm's bank account on behalf of a debtor who had recently been declared bankrupt. This represents a first and final payment of 25c in the euro.

(iii) A cheque for fees of €5,140 issued to a supplier had not been presented for payment.

Q10 **Goods in transit: in each of the following show the adjustments to stock, purchases/sales and debtors/ creditors.**

(a) No record had been made in the books for goods in transit on 31/12/20-0. The invoice for these goods had been received showing the purchase price of €13,800.

(b) No record had been made in the books for goods in transit on 31/12/20-1. The invoice for these goods had been received showing the purchase price of €14,900.

(c) No record had been made in the books for goods in transit on 31/12/20-2. The invoice for these goods had been received showing the purchase price of €16,700.

(d) Stock at 31/12/20-3 at cost was €90,000. No record had been made in the books for goods in transit on 31/12/20-3. The invoice for these goods had been received showing a recommended selling price of €9,000, which is cost plus 20%.

Q11 **Goods on a sale-or-return basis: in each case show the effects on debtors, sales and stock.**

(a) It was discovered that goods which cost €8,700 were invoiced to a customer on a sale-or-return basis. These goods had been entered in the books as a credit sale at cost plus 20%.

(b) It was discovered that goods which cost €6,400 were invoiced to a customer on a sale-or-return basis. These goods had been entered in the books as a credit sale at cost plus 25%.

(c) It was discovered that finished goods which cost €9,100 to produce were invoiced to a customer on a sale-or-return basis. These goods had been entered in the books as a credit sale at cost plus 30%.

(d) It was discovered that finished goods which cost €12,300 to produce were invoiced to a customer on a sale-or-return basis. These goods had been entered in the books as a credit sale at cost plus 15%.

Q12 **Correction of errors: in each of the following show the effect on the final accounts.**

(a) Matlock Ltd

	€	€
Advertising (incorporating suspense)	9,600	
8% Fixed mortgage (including an increase of €70,000 on 1/4/20-0)		270,000
Mortgage interest paid for 3 months	1,350	
Bank		14,500
Discounts		4,500
Creditors		65,700

The suspense figure arises as a result of the posting of an incorrect figure for mortgage interest in the mortgage interest account and €500 discount received entered only in the creditors account. The correct figures were entered in the bank account

(b) James Bond Ltd

	€	€
Telephone and postage (incorporating suspense)	4,600	
10% Fixed mortgage (including an increase of €40,000 on 1/5/20-1)		220,000
Mortgage interest paid for 4 months	2,700	
Bank		89,000
Discount (net)		6,700
Creditors		86,500

The suspense figure arises as a result of the posting of an incorrect figure for mortgage interest in the mortgage interest account and €300 discount entered only in the creditors account. The correct figure for mortgage interest was entered in the bank account.

(c) Mr Gold

	€	€
Salaries and general expenses (incorporating suspense)	43,600	
12% Fixed mortgage (including an increase of €60,000 on 1/7/20-2)		340,000
Mortgage interest paid for 6 months	16,400	
Bank		73,000
Discount (net)		900
Debtors	356,000	

The suspense figure arises as a result of the posting of an incorrect figure for mortgage interest in the mortgage interest account and €500 discount allowed to a debtor entered only in the debtors account. The correct figure for mortgage interest was entered in the bank account.

9

Exercises – Higher Level

Q1 Heathfield Ltd has an authorised share capital of €2,000,000, divided into 1,400,000 ordinary shares at €1 each and 600,000 8% preference shares at €1 each. The following trial balance was extracted from the books at 31/12/20-9:

	€	€
Buildings at cost	804,000	
Delivery vans (cost €260,000)	200,000	
Discount (net)		11,500
Profit and loss balance 1/1/20-9	34,500	
Stock on hand 1/1/20-9	102,300	
Debenture interest for the first 3 months	4,500	
10% Investments 1/1/20-9	280,000	
Patents (incorporating 3 months' investment income)	34,000	
Purchases and sales	926,000	1,340,500
Dividends paid	32,000	
Bad debts provision		3,600
Debtors and creditors	89,500	76,000
Bank		46,000
Salaries and general expenses	201,900	
8% Debentures		220,000
Issued share capital		
Ordinary shares		900,000
Preference shares		200,000
Directors' fees	52,000	
Rent	21,300	
Advertising (including suspense)	15,600	
	2,797,600	**2,797,600**

9

The following information and instructions are to be taken into account:

(a) Stock at 31/12/20-9 at cost was €78,000. This figure includes damaged stock which cost €7,800 and now has a net realisable value of €2,300.

(b) Patents which incorporated three months' investment income are to be written off over a five-year period commencing in 20-9.

(c) Provide for depreciation on delivery vans at the annual rate of 15% of cost from date of purchase to date of sale.

Note: On 31/3/20-9 a delivery van which had cost €34,000 on 30/6/20-4 was traded in for a new van costing €72,000. An allowance of €12,000 was given for the old van. The cheque for the net amount of this transaction was incorrectly treated as the purchase of trading stock. This was the only entry in the books in respect of this transaction.

(d) The suspense figure arises as a result of the incorrect figure for debenture interest (although the correct entry had been made in the bank account), and discount received, €900, entered only in the creditors account.

(e) During 20-9 a storeroom which cost €50,000 and stock which cost €15,000 were destroyed by fire. A new store was built by the firm's own workers. The cost of their labour, €22,000, had been treated as a business expense and materials costing €48,000 were taken from the firm's stocks. The insurance company agreed to contribute €65,000 in compensation for the fire damage. No adjustment had been made in the books in respect of the old or new store.

(f) The figure for bank in the trial balance had been taken from the firm's bank account. However, a bank statement dated 31/12/20-9 has arrived showing an overdraft of €44,690. A comparison of the bank account and the bank statement has revealed the following discrepancies:

(i) A cheque for €760 issued to a supplier had been entered in the books (cash book and ledger) as €670.

(ii) A credit transfer of €800 had been paid direct to the firm's bank account on behalf of a bankrupt debtor who has recently been declared bankrupt. This represents a first and final payment of 40c in the euro.

(iii) A cheque for fees of €600 to a director had not been presented for payment.

(g) The directors recommend that:

(i) Provision should be made for both investment income and debenture interest due.

(ii) Provision for bad debts should be adjusted to 5% of debtors.

(iii) Buildings are to be depreciated by 3% of cost per annum.

You are required to prepare:

- the trading, profit and loss account for the year ended 31/12/20-9
- a balance sheet as at 31/12/20-9.

Q2 Waterveat Ltd has an authorised share capital of €3,000,000, divided into 2,000,000 ordinary shares at €1 each and 1,000,000 5% preference shares at €1 each. The following trial balance was extracted from the books at 31/12/20-8:

	€	€
Buildings at cost	900,000	
Delivery vans (cost €400,000)	330,000	
Discount (net)		12,300
Profit and loss balance 1/1/20-8	23,700	
Stock on hand 1/1/20-8	45,600	
Debenture interest for 2.4 months (one-fifth year)	3,800	
12% Investments 1/1/20-8	220,000	
Patents (incorporating 4 months' investment income)	38,900	
Purchases and sales	980,000	1,370,200
Dividends paid	40,000	
Bad debts provision		3,900
Debtors and creditors	130,500	67,000
Bank		34,500
Salaries and general expenses	245,900	
10% Debentures		200,000
Issued share capital		
Ordinary shares		900,000
Preference shares		500,000
Directors' fees	82,400	
Rent	21,500	
Advertising (including suspense)	25,600	
	3,087,900	**3,087,900**

9

The following information and instructions are to be taken into account:

(a) Stock at 31/12/20-8 at cost was €75,600 This figure includes damaged stock which cost €6,900 and now has a net realisable value of €1,800.

(b) Patents which incorporated four months' investment income are to be written off over a five-year period commencing in 20-8.

(c) Provide for depreciation on delivery vans at the annual rate of 10% of cost from date of purchase to date of sale.

Note: On 31/3/20-8 a delivery van which had cost €45,000 on 30/6/20-3 was traded in for a new van costing €80,000. An allowance of €15,000 was given for the old van. The cheque for the net amount of this transaction was incorrectly treated as the purchase of trading stock. This was the only entry in the books in respect of this transaction.

(d) The suspense figure arises as a result of the incorrect figure for debenture interest (although the correct entry had been made in the bank account), and discount received, €760, entered only in the creditors account.

(e) During 20-8 a storeroom which cost €20,000 and stock which cost €12,000 were destroyed by fire. A new store was built by the firm's own workers. The cost of their labour, €14,000, had been treated as a business expense and materials costing €36,000 were taken from the firm's stocks. The insurance company has agreed to contribute €32,000 in compensation for the fire damage. No adjustment had been made in the books in respect of the old or new store.

(f) The figure for bank in the trial balance had been taken from the firm's bank account. However, a bank statement dated 31/12/20-8 has arrived showing an overdraft of €27,190. A comparison of the bank account and the bank statement has revealed the following discrepancies:

(i) A cheque for €870 issued to a supplier had been entered in the books (cash book and ledger) as €780.

(ii) A credit transfer of €3,200 had been paid direct to the firm's bank account on behalf of a bankrupt debtor who has recently been declared bankrupt. This represents a first and final payment of 25c in the euro.

(iii) A cheque for fees of €4,200 to a director had not been presented for payment.

(g) The directors recommend that:

(i) Provision should be made for both investment income and debenture interest due.

(ii) Provision for bad debts should be adjusted to 4% of debtors.

(iii) Buildings are to be depreciated by 2% of cost per annum.

You are required to prepare:

- the trading, profit and loss account for the year ended 31/12/20-8
- a balance sheet as at 31/12/20-8.

Q3 Rio Ltd has an authorised share capital of €1,300,000 divided into 900,000 ordinary shares at €1 each and 400,000 10% preference shares at €1 each. The following trial balance was extracted from the books at 31/12/20-7:

	€	€
Buildings at cost	960,000	
Delivery vans (cost €320,000)	270,000	
Discount (net)		15,300
Profit and loss balance 1/1/20-7	21,300	
Stock on hand 1/1/20-7	78,000	
Debenture Interest for the first three months	3,700	

Continued >

	€	€
12% Investments 1/1/20-7	250,000	
Patents (incorporating 2 months' investment income)	42,000	
Purchases and sales	870,000	1,700,000
Dividends paid	30,000	
Bad debts provision		2,800
Debtors and creditors	82,300	65,000
Bank		49,400
Salaries and general expenses	189,700	
7% Debentures		150,000
Issued share capital		
Ordinary shares		700,000
Preference shares		200,000
Directors' fees	56,000	
Rent	12,800	
Advertising (including suspense)	16,700	
	2,882,500	**2,882,500**

The following information and instructions are to be taken into account:

(a) Stock at 31/12/20-7 at cost was €67,000. This figure includes damaged stock which cost €8,200 and now has a net realisable value of 60% of cost.

(b) Patents which incorporated two months' investment income are to be written off over a five-year period commencing in 20-7.

(c) Provide for depreciation on delivery vans at the annual rate of 15% of cost from date of purchase to date of sale.

Note: On 30/6/20-7 a delivery van which had cost €40,000 on 1/10/20-3 was traded in for a new van costing €78,000. An allowance of €9,000 was given for the old van. The cheque for the net amount of this transaction was incorrectly treated as the purchase of trading stock. This was the only entry in the books in respect of this transaction.

(d) The suspense figure arises as a result of the incorrect figure for debenture interest (although the correct entry had been made in the bank account) and discount received, €800, entered only in the discount account.

(e) During 20-7 a storeroom which cost €34,000 and stock which cost €10,000 were destroyed by fire. A new store was built by the firm's own workers. The cost of their labour, €16,000, had been treated as a business expense and materials costing €44,000 were taken from the firm's stocks. The insurance company has agreed to contribute €44,000 in compensation for the fire damage. No adjustment had been made in the books in respect of the old or new store.

(f) The figure for bank in the trial balance had been taken from the firm's bank account. However, a bank statement dated 31/12/20-7 has arrived showing an overdraft of €38,510. A comparison of the bank account and the bank statement has revealed the following discrepancies:

(i) A cheque for €450 issued to a supplier had been entered in the books (cash book and ledger) as €540.

(ii) A credit transfer of €1,200 had been paid direct to the firm's bank account on behalf of a bankrupt debtor who has recently been declared bankrupt. This represents a first and final payment of 50c in the euro.

(iii) A cheque for fees of €9,600 to a director had not been presented for payment.

9

(g) The directors recommend that:

(i) Provision should be made for both investment income and debenture interest due.

(ii) Provision for bad debts should be adjusted to 5% of debtors.

(iii) Buildings are to be depreciated by 2% of cost per annum.

You are required to prepare:

- the trading, profit and loss account for the year ended 31/12/20-7
- a balance sheet as at 31/12/20-7.

Q4 Sutton Ltd had an authorised share capital of €1,400,000 ordinary shares at €1 each and €420,000 8% preference shares at €1 each. The following trial balance was extracted from its books on 31/12/20-3:

	€	€
Land and buildings at cost	1,092,000	
Accumulated depreciation on buildings		54,600
Patents (incorporating 2 months' investment income)	81,480	
6% Investments 1/5/20-3	252,000	
Delivery vans at cost	240,800	
Accumulated depreciation on delivery vans		109,200
Stocks 1/1/20-3	107,240	
Purchases and sales	868,000	1,386,000
Directors' fees	112,000	
Salaries and general expenses	246,400	
Debenture interest paid	6,300	
Profit and loss balance 1/1/20-3		94,640
Debtors and creditors	103,460	113,400
Provision for bad debts		5,040
Dividends paid	56,000	
9% Debentures (including €112,000 issued at par 31/3/20-3)		322,000
VAT		23,100
Bank		7,700
Issued capital		
770,000 ordinary shares @ €1 each		770,000
280,000 8% preference shares @ €1 each		280,000
	3,165,680	**3,165,680**

The following information and instructions are to be taken into account:

(a) Stock at 31/12/20-3 at cost was €90,000. This figure includes damaged stock which cost €10,000 and now has a net realisable value of 40% of cost.

(b) Patents which incorporated two months' investment income are to be written off over a five-year period commencing in 20-3.

(c) Provide for depreciation on delivery vans at the annual rate of 20% of cost from date of purchase to date of sale.

Note: On 30/9/20-3 a delivery van which had cost €78,000 on 1/6/20-1 was traded in for a new van costing €100,000. An allowance of €39,000 was given for the old van. The cheque for the net amount of this transaction was incorrectly treated as the purchase of trading stock. This was the only entry in the books in respect of this transaction.

9

(d) Buildings are to be depreciated at the rate of 2% of cost per annum (land cost €192,000). At the end of 20-3 the company revalued the land and buildings at €1,200,000.

(e) The figure for bank in the trial balance had been taken from the firm's bank account. However, a bank statement dated 31/12/20-3 revealed the following discrepancies:

  (i) A cheque for €560 issued to a supplier had been entered in the books (cash book and ledger) as €650.

  (ii) A credit transfer of €900 had been paid direct to the firm's bank account on behalf of a bankrupt debtor who has recently been declared bankrupt. This represents a first and final payment of 30c in the euro.

  (iii) A cheque for fees of €3,600 to a director had not been presented for payment.

  (iv) Investment income of €4,000 had been paid direct to the firm's bank account

(f) The directors recommend that:

  (i) Provision should be made for both investment income and debenture interest due.

  (ii) Provision for bad debts should be adjusted to 5% of debtors.

  (iii) Corporation tax of €50,000 be provided for.

You are required to prepare:

- the trading, profit and loss account for the year ended 31/12/20-3
- a balance sheet as at 31/12/20-3.

Q5 Mays Ltd has an authorised capital of €2,000,000, divided into 1,250,000 ordinary shares at €1 each and 750,000 5% preference shares at €1 each. The following trial balance was extracted from its books on 31/12/20-4:

	€	€
Delivery vans at cost	420,000	
Accumulated depreciation on delivery vans		160,000
Land and buildings at cost	2,125,000	
Accumulated depreciation on land and buildings		190,000
Patents (incorporating 3 months' investment income received)	167,500	
8% Investments 1/5/20-4	375,000	
Stocks 1/1/20-4	152,500	
Purchases and sales	1,275,000	2,075,000
Directors' fees	155,000	
Salaries and general expenses	388,500	
Debenture interest paid for the first 3 months	7,500	
Debtors and creditors	176,250	212,500
Provision for bad debts		6,500
Dividends paid	80,000	
Profit and loss balance 1/1/20-4		126,000
8% Debentures (including 225,000 8% debentures issued at par on 31/3/20-4)		600,000
VAT		33,750
Bank		18,500
Issued capital		
1,150,000 ordinary shares at €1 each		1,150,000
750,000 5% preference shares at €1 each		750,000
	5,322,250	**5,322,250**

9

The following information and instructions are to be taken into account:

(a) Stock at 31/12/20-4 at cost was €165,000. This figure includes damaged stock which cost €12,000 and now has a net realisable value of 50% of cost.

(b) The figure for bank in the trial balance had been taken from the firm's bank account. However, a bank statement dated 31/12/20-4 revealed the following discrepancies:

(i) A cheque for €1,290 issued to a supplier had been entered in the books (cash book and ledger) as €1,920.

(ii) A credit transfer of €2,300 had been paid direct to the firm's bank account on behalf of a bankrupt debtor who has recently been declared bankrupt. This represents a first and final payment of 40c in the euro.

(iii) A cheque for fees of €2,000 to a director had not been presented for payment.

(iv) Investment income of €7,000 had been paid direct to the firm's bank account.

(c) Buildings are to be depreciated at the rate of 2% of cost per annum (land cost €725,000). At the end of 20-4 the company revalued the land and buildings at €2,300,000.

(d) Patents which incorporated three months' investment income are to be written off over a five-year period commencing in 20-4.

(e) Provide for depreciation on delivery vans at the annual rate of 20% of cost from date of purchase to date of sale.

Note: On 31/5/20-4 a delivery van which had cost €84,000 on 1/6/20-1 was traded in for a new van costing €120,000. An allowance of €22,000 was given for the old van. The cheque for the net amount of this transaction was incorrectly treated as the purchase of trading stock. This was the only entry in the books in respect of this transaction.

(f) The directors recommend that:

(i) Provision should be made for both investment income and debenture interest due.

(ii) Provision for bad debts should be adjusted to 5% of debtors.

(iii) Corporation tax of €80,000 be provided for.

You are required to prepare:

- the trading, profit and loss account for the year ended 31/12/20-4
- a balance sheet as at 31/12/20-4.

9

Q6 Bunny Ltd has an authorised share capital of €800,000, divided into 500,000 ordinary shares at €1 each and 300,000 8% preference shares at €1 each. The following trial balance was extracted from its books on 31/12/20-5:

	€	€
Land and buildings at cost	624,000	
Accumulated depreciation on land and buildings		54,000
Motor vehicles (cost €162,000)	127,800	
Patents (incorporating 3 months' investment income)	45,960	
Provision for bad debts		3,840
Purchases and sales	749,160	988,800
Salaries and general expenses	114,000	
9% Investments 1/5/20-5	144,000	
Stocks 1/1/20-5	51,000	
8% Debentures (including €72,000 12% debentures issued at par on 1/6/20-5)		180,000
Advertising	11,760	

Continued >

	€	€
Debtors and creditors	45,600	50,160
Debenture interest paid	2,880	
Bank		19,440
Directors' fees	12,600	
Dividends paid	39,480	
VAT		2,160
Profit and loss balance 1/1/20-5		9,840
Issued capital		
444,000 ordinary shares at €1 each		444,000
216,000 8% preference shares at €1 each		216,000
	1,968,240	**1,968,240**

The following information and instructions are to be taken into account:

(a) Stock at 31/12/20-5 at cost was €44,000. This figure includes damaged stock which cost €4,000 and now has a net realisable value of 20% of cost.

(b) The figure for bank in the trial balance had been taken from the firm's bank account. However, a bank statement dated 31/12/20-5 revealed the following discrepancies:

(i) A cheque for €880 issued to a supplier had been entered in the books (cash book and ledger) as €88.

(ii) A credit transfer of €4,500 had been paid direct to the firm's bank account on behalf of a bankrupt debtor who has recently been declared bankrupt. The represents a first and final payment of 60c in the euro.

(iii) A cheque for fees of €4,000 to a director had not been presented for payment.

(iv) Investment income of €3,000 had been paid direct to the firm's bank account.

(c) Buildings are to be depreciated at the rate of 2% of cost per annum (land cost €124,000). At the end of 20-5 the company revalued the land and buildings at €700,000

(d) Patents which incorporated three months' investment income are to be written off over a five-year period commencing in 20-5.

(e) Provide for depreciation on delivery vans at the annual rate of 25% of cost from date of purchase to date of sale.

Note: On 31/3/20-5 a delivery van which had cost €60,000 on 1/4/20-3 was traded in for a new van costing €80,000. An allowance of €25,000 was given for the old van. The cheque for the net amount of this transaction was incorrectly treated as the purchase of trading stock. This was the only entry in the books in respect of this transaction.

(f) The directors recommend that:

(i) Provision should be made for both investment income and debenture interest due.

(ii) Provision for bad debts should be adjusted to 6% of debtors.

(iii) Corporation tax of €10,000 should be provided for.

You are required to prepare:

- the trading, profit and loss account for the year ended 31/12/20-5
- a balance sheet as at 31/12/20-5.

9

Q7 **Rathangan Ltd has an authorised capital of €1,200,000, divided into 800,000 €1 ordinary shares and 400,000 8% preference shares at €1 each. The following trial balance was extracted from the books at 31/12/20-3:**

	€	€
Premises	804,000	
Delivery vans (cost €150,000)	120,000	
Rent	14,500	
Advertising	23,400	
Insurance incorporating suspense	12,900	
Stock 1/1/20-3	44,500	
Purchases and sales	189,000	590,200
Returns	2,400	4,300
Dividends paid	30,000	
Directors' fees	10,000	
Auditor's fees	5,400	
Issued share capital		
Ordinary shares @ €1 each		500,000
Preference shares @ €1 each		180,000
12% Debentures		230,000
Bank		115,400
Debtors and creditors	80,000	58,000
Provision for bad debts		4,700
Discount (net)		4,270
Profit and loss balance 1/1/20-3	9,000	
Salaries and general expenses	129,870	
Debenture interest (4 months)	9,900	
Patents incorporating 3 months' investment income	78,000	
10% Investments (1/4/20-3)	124,000	
	1,686,870	**1,686,870**

The following information and instructions are to be taken into account:

(a) **Stock at 31/12/20-3 at cost was €48,900, including damaged stock which cost €4,590 but now has a net realisable value of €2,090.**

(b) **Patents which incorporated three months' investment income are to be written off over a ten-year period commencing in 20-3.**

(c) **The suspense figure arises as a result of the incorrect figure for debenture interest. The correct interest was entered in the bank account and discount allowed of €1,800 entered only in the debtors account.**

(d) **A debtor whose debt had previously been written off now wishes to trade with Rathangan Ltd again. The amount of this debt was €12,000. He paid 55% and gave a guarantee to pay the remainder by 31/12/20-3. No entry was made in the books in respect of this transaction.**

(e) **Provide for depreciation on vehicles at the rate of 10% of cost per annum. Vehicles are depreciated by a full year in the year of acquisition and none in the year of disposal. All vehicles have a 5% scrap value of original cost.**

9

Note: During the year a vehicle which cost €25,000 in 20-1 was sold for €13,500. A new vehicle costing €40,000 was purchased. No entries had been entered in the books in respect of this transaction.

(f) The figure for bank in trial balance has been taken from the firm's own books. However, a bank statement dated 31/12/20-3 has arrived showing an overdraft which did not agree with the figure in the accounts. A comparison of the bank account and the bank statement showed the following discrepancies:

(i) A cheque for €890 issued to a supplier had been entered in the books (cash book and ledger) as €980.

(ii) A credit transfer of €900 had been paid direct to the firm's bank account on behalf of a bankrupt debtor. This represents 40c in the euro.

(iii) A cheque for €2,300 issued to a director had not been presented for payment.

(g) Provide for depreciation at the rate of 2% on premises. Premises were revalued at €900,000 on 31/12/20-3 and this revaluation is to be incorporated into the accounts.

(h) The directors recommend that:

(i) Provision should be made for debenture interest and investment income due.

(ii) Provision for bad debts should be adjusted to 6% of debtors.

(iii) Corporation tax of €29,000 should be provided for.

You are required to prepare:

- the trading, profit and loss account for the year ended 31/12/20-3
- a balance sheet as at 31/12/20-3.

Q8 The Long Ridge Company Ltd has an authorised capital of €1,500,000, divided into 1,000,000 ordinary shares at €1 each and 1,000,000 5% preference shares at 50c each. The following trial balance was extracted from the books on 31/12/20-5:

	€	€
Premises	1,100,000	
Delivery vans	234,000	
Accumulated depreciation on vans		42,000
Accumulated depreciation on premises		140,000
Patents incorporating 4 months' investment income	148,000	
Stock 1/1/20-5	84,000	
Purchases and sales	500,000	920,000
Directors' fees	45,000	
Salaries and general expenses	198,990	
Profit and loss balance 1/1/20-5		167,800
Provision for bad debts		3,900
Debenture interest paid (1 month)	3,210	
Insurance (incorporating suspense)	21,400	
7% Debentures (including €56,000 issued on 1/2/20-5)		134,000
VAT		2,700
Bank		155,600
Issued share capital		
700,000 ordinary shares		700,000
600,000 preference shares		300,000

Continued >

9

	€	€
Advertising	45,600	
Light and heat	32,800	
8% Investments 1/7/20-5	135,000	
Debtors and creditors	78,000	60,000
	2,626,000	**2,626,000**

The following information and instructions are to be taken into account:

(a) Stock on 31/12/20-5 at cost was €75,600, which included old stock which had cost €9,900 but has a net realisable value of 30% of cost. It also includes stock of stationery, €300.

(b) Patents are to be written off over five years commencing in 20-5.

(c) Premises were revalued on 1/1/20-5 at €1,500,000. This was to be incorporated in the books and you are required to provide for depreciation at the annual rate of 3%.

(d) The figure for suspense arises as a result of an incorrect figure for debenture interest. The correct interest was entered in the bank account.

(e) Goods were sent to a debtor on a sale-or-return basis. These goods had cost €5,000 and were invoiced at cost plus 50%.

(f) Provide for depreciation on delivery vans at the annual rate of 12% of cost price from date of purchase to date of sale.

Note: On 31/8/20-5 a delivery van which cost €26,000 on 1/6/20-2 was traded in for a new van costing €50,000. An allowance of €8,000 was made for the old van. The cheque for the net amount of this transaction was incorrectly treated as the purchase of trading stock. This was the only entry made in the books in respect of this transaction.

(g) The figure for bank in the trial balance did not agree with the bank statement which arrived on 31/12/20-5. A comparison of the bank account and the bank statement revealed the following discrepancies:

(i) Two months' investment income had been paid directly to the bank account.

(ii) A cheque received from a debtor for €4,500 had been dishonoured by the bank. It was also found that this debtor had been declared bankrupt and subsequently paid €0.25 in respect of each euro directly into the bank.

(iii) A credit transfer for rent of €2,400 had been paid into the firm's bank account for the annual rent of an office on 1/10/20-5.

(iv) A cheque for €2,000 paid to a director had not been presented for payment.

(v) A payment by cheque to a creditor for €2,890 had been entered in the books, cash book and ledger as €2,980.

(h) The directors recommended that:

(i) Debenture interest and investment income due should be provided for.

(ii) The provision for bad debts should be adjusted to 6% of debtors.

(iii) The managing director should be paid a bonus commission of 5% on sales in excess of €500,000 and a further 7% in respect of sales above €800,000.

You are required to prepare:

- the trading, profit and loss account for the year ended 31/12/20-5
- a balance sheet as as at 31/12/20-5.

Q9 The following information was extracted from the books of Aimee Ltd on 31/12/20-6:

(a) Amiee Ltd has an Authorised Capital of 600,000 Ordinary Shares at €1 each and 400,000 8% Preference Shares at €1 each. The company has already issued half of all shares (ordinary and preference).

(b) Amiee Ltd had carried forward a profit of €110,000 from 20-5 and the accounts showed profits of €140,000 before interest and taxation for the year ended 31/12/20-6

(c) On 1.1.20-6 the Company's General Reserve Account showed a balance of €25,000.

(d) During the year a total divided of 10c per ordinary share was paid to the Ordinary Shareholders and the total preference dividend for the year was paid to the Preference Shareholders.

(e) It was noted on 31/12/20-6 the following transactions were omitted from the books

   (i) A credit transfer of €600 had been paid direct to firm's bank account on behalf of a debtor who was recently declared bankrupt. This represents a first and final payment of 40c in €.

   (ii) During the year stock which cost €7,500 was destroyed by a fire. The Insurance Company has agreed to pay compensation of €6,000.

   (iii) A van which cost €24,000 and on which depreciation had been charged at 15% for 4 years was given to a creditor of the business in full settlement of a debt €11,500. There was no depreciation charged in 20-6 on the van sold during the year in line with the company's depreciation policy.

(f) On the 31/12/20-6 the directors recommended that:

   (i) Provision be made for debenture interest on 8% Debentures €200,000 (Including €50,000 9% Debenture issued on 1/7/20-6

   (ii) Taxation of €56,000 to be provided for

   (iii) The General Reserve to be increased by 25%.

   (iv) A provision for bad debts of 5% of debtors be created.

Other relevant figures provided on 31/12/20-6 include:

Creditors €45,000, debtors €50,600, closing stock €29,000, delivery vans €70,000, Depreciation on vans €20,000, bank €21,000, land and buildings €767,400 (cost €800,000)

You are required to prepare in as much detail as possible

- The Profit and Loss Account for the year ended 31/12/20-6
- The balance sheet showing the relevant accounts after making the above provisions and appropriations.

Exam Tips

- Make sure that you learn the layout for company final accounts.
- There are a number of adjustments to each question, so ensure that you have a complete and full understanding of these. Develop a technique for dealing with each adjustment that may appear.
- Ensure that you practise as many questions as possible.
- See also Chapter 6 for treatment of adjustments and tips.

9

10 Published Accounts – Financial Statements and Reports

Objectives

On completion students should be able to:

- List and explain the content of a company's annual report;
- Prepare a published profit and loss account;
- Prepare a published balance sheet;
- List and explain the responsibilities of directors;
- Discuss the content of a directors' report;
- List, explain and prepare the explanatory notes to the final accounts.

Introduction

All companies irrespective of size must by law produce company accounts and reports annually.

A company' s annual report will include:

- a **directors' report**
- an **auditor's report** (see Chapter 8)
- the **financial statements**, which include the published profit and loss account, balance sheet (including the explanatory notes) and a cash flow statement (see Chapter 17).

When a company prepares accounts for its own internal use, it can draft them in whatever way is most suitable to it. However, when a company prepares its accounts for presentation to its shareholders and for filing with the Registrar of Companies, it must follow the layout as outlined in the Companies (Amendment) Act 1986.

NOTE

The exact layout of the published profit and loss account and the published balance sheet must be learned.

To understand this chapter fully you should be aware of the regulations and framework of accounting as laid out in Chapter 8.

The directors

The shareholders of a company appoint the directors to manage the company on their behalf. The directors have a responsibility for:

- keeping a proper set of records which will enable a profit and loss account and balance sheet to be prepared in accordance with the Companies Acts
- safeguarding the assets of the company

- preparing annual financial statements
- selecting suitable accounting policies
- stating whether applicable accounting standards have been followed
- ensuring that all the financial statements are signed by two directors
- convening Annual General Meetings.

The directors' report

A directors' report must contain the following:

- the dividends recommended for payment
- the amount to be transferred to reserves
- a report of any changes in the nature of the company's business during the year
- a fair review of how the business developed during the year and of the position at the end of the year
- details of any important events affecting the company since the end of the year
- any likely future developments in the business
- an indication of activities in the field of research and development
- significant changes in fixed assets
- evaluation of the company's compliance with its safety statement
- details of directors' shareholdings and share dealings during the year.

Templates for the layout of published accounts

Profit and loss account

Profit and Loss Account for XYZ Ltd for year ended 20-1

1	Turnover	xxxxx
2	*Less* Cost of sales	(xxxx)
3	Gross profit (loss)	xxxxx
4	Distribution costs	(xxxx)
		xxxxx
5	Administrative expenses	(xxxx)
		xxxxx
6	Other operating income	xxxxx
7	Operating profit	xxxxx
8	Exceptional items	xxxxx
9	Income from financial assets	xxxxx
10	Amounts written off financial assets	(xxxx)
		xxxxx
11	Interest payable	(xxxx)
12	Profit on ordinary activities before taxation	xxxxx
13	Tax on profit on ordinary activities	(xxxx)
14	Profit on ordinary activities after taxation	xxxxx
15	Dividends paid	(xxxx)
16	Profit retained for the year	xxxxx
17	Profit (loss) brought forward at 1/1/20-1	xxxxx
18	Profit (loss) carried forward at 31/12/20-1	xxxxx

10

Explanation of terms

	Profit and Loss item	Explanation
1	Turnover	Net sales after returns
2	Cost of sales	Opening stock + Purchases – Closing stock
3	Gross profit	Net sales – Cost of sales
4	Distribution costs	Selling and distribution expenses
5	Administrative expenses	Administration expenses
6	Other operating income	Non-trading income such as rent/royalties receivable
7	Operating profit	Gross profit – Distribution expenses – Administrative expenses + Other operating income
8	Exceptional items	Profit or loss on the sale of material fixed assets
9	Income from financial assets	Interest received and dividends received
10	Amounts written off financial assets	The writing off of investments where such assets are worthless
11	Interest payable	Interest on loans, overdrafts and debentures
12	Profit on ordinary activities before taxation	Operating profit + Interest and dividends receivable – Interest payable
13	Tax on profit on ordinary activities	Tax due on this year's profits
14	Profit on ordinary activities after taxation	This is the profit available for appropriation
15	Dividends	Paid: interim dividends paid during the year
16	Profit retained for the year	Profits held over as reserves
17	Profit and loss 1/1/20-1	Last year's profit and loss balance
18	Profit and loss 31/12/20-1	Profit and loss figure for the balance sheet

DEFINITION

Ordinary activities are the normal day-to-day activities undertaken by a company. They include profit on the sale of land but exclude extraordinary activities.

Allocation of expenses

Cost of sales	Distribution costs	Administrative expenses
Opening stock	Selling expenses	Administrative salaries
Cost of manufacture	Bad debts and provisions	General expenses
Purchases	Advertising	Rent and rates
Purchases returns	Carriage outwards	Insurance
Carriage inwards	Depreciation of delivery vans	Directors' fees
Import duty	Commission payable	Auditor's fees
Closing stock	Showroom expenses	Discount
Manufacturing wages	Delivery van expenses	Depreciation of buildings
Depreciation of machinery	Depreciation of showroom	Depreciation of equipment

NOTE

This is a guide to help in distinguishing the different categories of expenses. It does not include all possible expenses that companies incur.

Published balance sheet

Balance Sheet for XYZ Ltd as at 20-1

	€	€	€
Fixed assets			
Intangible assets			xxxxxx
Tangible assets			xxxxxx
Financial assets			xxxxxx
			xxxxxx
Current assets			
Stocks	xxxxx		
Debtors	xxxxx		
Cash in hand and at bank	xxxxx	xxxxxx	
***Less* Creditors: amounts falling due within 1 year**			
Trade creditors	xxxxx		
Taxation and social welfare	xxxxx	(xxxxx)	
Net current assets			xxxxxx
Total assets less current liabilities			**xxxxxx**
Creditors: amounts falling due after more than 1 year			
Debentures			xxxxxx
Provisions for liabilities and charges			xxxxxx
Capital and reserves			
Called-up share capital		xxxxxx	
Share premium account		xxxxxx	
Revaluation reserve		xxxxxx	
Other reserves		xxxxxx	
Profit and loss account		xxxxxx	xxxxxx
			xxxxxx

NOTE

Only one figure needs to be shown on the balance sheet under the heading 'Creditors: amounts falling due within 1 year'. However, for examination purposes it is best to show it under the headings as above.

The Companies (Amendment) Act requires the profit and loss account and the balance sheet to be presented in the sequences shown and using these exact wordings. The above is the minimum that must be shown on the face of a published balance sheet.

NOTE

The format used here is Format 1. It is the format required for the Leaving Certificate and is the one used most commonly by companies.

Balance sheet – list of items for reference purposes

Heading	Explanation
Intangible fixed assets	Development costs, patents, trademarks and goodwill
Tangible fixed assets	Land and buildings, plant and machinery, equipment, motor vehicles, furniture, etc.
Financial assets	Shares in other companies Loans to other companies Investments other than loans Own shares
Current assets	Closing stocks Work in progress Raw materials and consumables Finished goods
Debtors	Trade debtors Amounts owed by other companies Other debtors Prepayments and accrued income
Cash at bank and in hand	Cash account balance Bank account balance
Creditors: amounts falling due within 1 year	Debenture loans due within 1 year Bank loans and overdrafts Trade creditors Amounts owed to other companies Other creditors, including tax and social welfare Accruals and deferred income Bills of exchange
Net current assets/liabilities	Current assets less current liabilities
Total net assets	Total assets less current liabilities
Creditors: amounts falling due after more than 1 year	Debenture loans due after 1 year Medium- and long-term bank loans Amounts owed to other companies
Provisions for liabilities and charges	Pensions and similar obligations Liabilities certain to be incurred (contingent)
Capital and reserves	Called-up share capital (issued and fully paid) Share premium account Revaluation reserve Other reserves – capital redemption reserve fund, reserves for own shares, reserves provided for by the Articles of Association
Profit and loss account	Balance from profit and loss account

Explanatory notes

These notes produced at the end of the published accounts of a company are used to give an explanation to the reader of the financial information which will show them the particular accounting policies used by the firm. These change from company to company and by including an explanation in the notes to the accounts, comparisons can be more easily made, for example by potential investors when deciding on which company to invest in.

The following notes are required for Leaving Certificate purposes. An explanation and example is given for each one. The structure of each note is rigid in nature. The text and figures in ***bold italics*** are examples of what could be entered in a published accounts exercise.

Explanatory notes accompany published profit and loss accounts and published balance sheets.

1. Accounting policy notes on tangible fixed assets and stock

Companies are required to disclose the particular accounting policies that have been used in the preparation of their financial statements. These include accounting policies for the valuation of fixed assets and stock.

Example

Buildings were revalued at the end of ***20-9***. These have been included in the accounts at their revalued amount. [Do not use if no revaluation took place.]

Assets	shown at cost

Depreciation is calculated in order to write off the value of the tangible fixed assets over their estimated useful economic life as follows:

Buildings	***3%***	per annum	***straight line*** basis
Delivery vans	***20%***	per annum	***straight line*** basis
Office machines	***10%***	per annum	***reducing balance*** basis

Stocks are valued on a ***first in, first out*** basis at the lower of cost or net realisable value.

10

2. Operating profit note

The operating profit note must show the amounts charged to the profit and loss account for the following items:

- directors' and auditor's remuneration
- depreciation and amortisation of intangible fixed assets
- exceptional items and staff costs.

Example

Operating profit is arrived at after charging:

Depreciation (including anything written off, either goodwill or patents)	***€25,000***
Auditor's fees	***€15,000***
Directors' fees	***€12,000***

3. Interest payable note

The amounts charged for interest on bank loans, overdrafts and debentures must be shown in this note, as well as an analysis of the interest as follows:

- amount of interest on loans repayable within five years by instalment
- amount of interest on loans repayable within five years but not by instalment
- amount of interest on all other loans.

Example

Interest payable on ***10%*** debentures of ***€100,000 = €10,000***

4. Dividends note

This note must separately show:

- the total dividends paid (interim)
- the dividend per share.

Example

Ordinary dividends

Interim paid ***2c per share*** ***€10,000***

Preference dividends

Interim paid ***5c per share*** ***€5,000***

5. Financial assets note

Details must be given in relation to:

- balance at the start of the year
- additions and disposals during the year
- directors' valuation and/or market value of investments at the end of the financial year.

Example

Financial assets	Start of period	End of period
Quoted investments	***€250,000***	***€250,000***
Unquoted investments	***€100,000***	***€100,000***
Total	***€350,000***	***€350,000***

6. Debentures note

A company must disclose information regarding:

- issue of debentures during the year
- details of any fixed or floating charge given as security.

Example

During the year ***20-1*** the company issued ***12%*** debentures to the value of ***€120,000*** repayable in the year ***20-7***. These debentures are secured by a ***fixed*** charge on the company's tangible fixed assets.

7. Tangible fixed asset note

A note on tangible and intangible fixed assets must show:

- value at the start of the year
- additions and disposals during the year
- depreciation charge
- revaluations
- aggregate depreciation and end-of-year value.

When fixed assets have been revalued, a company must disclose the date of valuation as well as the name and qualifications of the valuers.

Example

Details	Asset 1	Asset 2	Total
Assets			
Opening balance	***€200,000***	***€300,000***	***€500,000***
Disposal	***(€50,000)***	***Nil***	***(€50,000)***
Revaluation surplus 31/12	***Nil***	***€100,000***	***€100,000***
Closing balance	***€150,000***	***€400,000***	***€550,000***
Depreciation			
Opening depreciation	***€30,000***	***€50,000***	***€80,000***
Depreciation charge	***€20,000***	***€20,000***	***€40,000***
Transfer on revaluation	***Nil***	***(€70,000)***	***(€70,000)***
Closing balance 31/12	***€50,000***	***Nil***	***€50,000***
Net book value 1/1	***€170,000***	***€250,000***	***€420,000***
Net book value 31/12	***€100,000***	***€400,000***	***€500,000***

10

8. Exceptional item note

This note must show:

- amount entered in the profit and loss account
- figures used to arrive at the amount.

Exceptional items are items of significant size that must be disclosed separately. For the Leaving Certificate, exceptional items refer to the material profit or loss on the sale of fixed assets and very large bad debts.

Example

The company sold ***assets*** for ***€10,000*** more than they cost. Cost was ***€90,000.***

9. Capital expenditure commitments note

A company must disclose details of:

- any expenditure already contracted for
- expenditure that is agreed but not yet contracted for.

Example

The company has entered into a contract with ***Solar Ltd*** for the building of an extension to its premises for the sum of ***€390,000***.

10. Share capital note

A company must disclose:

- the amount of authorised ordinary and preference share capital
- details of the amount of allotted and called-up shares
- any shares issued during the year.

Example

Share Capital	Authorised €	Issued €
Ordinary shares	*1,000,000*	*800,000*
7% Preference shares	*500,000*	*200,000*
	1,500,000	*1,000,000*

11. Contingent liability or gain note

These are possible or probable liabilities or gains that have to be either entered in the accounts or treated in a note to the accounts.

10

When the contingent liability is probable:

- The estimated amount is provided for in the accounts.
- The nature of the loss is explained in the notes.

When the contingent liability is possible but unlikely it is not necessary to provide for it in the accounts. A note should be provided, showing:

- the nature of the liability
- the estimated amount
- an opinion regarding the outcome.

Example

The company is being sued by a ***former employee*** for ***unfair dismissal***. The company's legal team has advised that the company will ***not be liable*** under the terms of ***the Employee Dismissals Act***. They have also estimated that the amount of liability if any will be ***€50,000***.

Sample Higher Level question

Trial balance of Cleary plc as at 31/12/20-0

	€	€
Buildings at cost 1/1/20-0	1,400,000	
Building depreciation at 1/1/20-0		96,000
Debtors and creditors	278,000	482,000
Patents 1/1/20-0	336,000	
Purchases and sales	12,300,000	15,976,000
Rental income		104,000
VAT		164,000
Profit and loss balance 1/1/20-0		120,000
Fixed assets investments	600,000	
Stock 1/1/20-0	1,300,000	
8% Debentures 20-5/20-6		800,000
Distribution costs	1,220,000	
Administration expenses	1,484,000	
Provision for bad debts		46,000
Debenture interest paid	24,000	
Dividends paid	111,000	
Profit on the sale of land		160,000
Bank	295,000	
Issued capital		
Ordinary shares @ €1 each		800,000
7% Preference shares @ €1 each		600,000
	19,348,000	**19,348,000**

The following additional information and instructions are provided:

(a) Stock at 31/12/20-0 was €1,380,000.

(b) Depreciation to be provided for as follows: buildings 2% of cost per annum, and there were no additions or disposals of buildings during the year. However, land belonging to the business which cost €110,000 was sold for €270,000. Also take into account that at the end of 20-0, the company decided to revalue their premises at their true market value which was €1,500,000 and the directors decided that this value should be incorporated into the accounts of the business.

(c) The directors also proposed that provision should be made for directors' fees of €160,000, auditor's fees of €18,000.

(d) The company's corporation tax liability, as determined by the Revenue Commissioners, was set at €340,000.

(e) Provide for unpaid debenture interest due on 31/12/20-0.

(f) During the year the directors paid a dividend on shares as follows: a full year's dividend was paid to preference shareholders and the remainder to ordinary shareholders.

(g) The listed investments are in listed companies and have a current market value of €960,000 on the last day of the year. There were no new investments or investments sold during the year.

(h) On 12/12/20-0, the company received a letter from a customer of the business who had had a fall on the company's premises during the previous month. The customer is making a claim against the company for damages incurred as a result of this fall. The company's solicitors believe that the company is unlikely to be liable. They have estimated that any liability would be a maximum of €50,000.

(i) The patent was acquired a number of years ago and been amortised over ten years in equal instalments. It cost €480,000 originally and this amortisation should be included in cost of sales.

You are required to:

- Prepare the published profit and loss account for the year ended 31/12/20-0 and a balance sheet as at that date in accordance with the Companies Acts and latest accounting standards, showing the following notes:
  - **(i)** Accounting policy notes for tangible fixed assets and stock
  - **(ii)** Operating profit
  - **(iii)** Contingent liabilities
  - **(iv)** Dividends
  - **(v)** Tangible fixed assets.

Solution

Profit and Loss Account of Cleary plc for the year ended 31/12/20-0

	€
Turnover	15,976,000
Less Cost of sales (W1)	(12,268,000)
Gross profit	3,708,000
Distribution costs	(1,220,000)
	2,488,000
Administrative expenses (W2)	(1,690,000)
	798,000
Other operating income	104,000
Operating profit	902,000
Exceptional items	160,000
	1,062,000
Interest payable	(64,000)
Profit on ordinary activities before taxation	998,000
Taxation on profit on ordinary activities	(340,000)
Profit on ordinary activities after taxation	658,000
Dividends paid	(111,000)
Profit retained for the year	547,000
Profit brought forward 1/1/20-0	120,000
Profit carried forward 31/12/20-0	**667,000**

10

Balance Sheet as at 31/12/20-0

	€	€	€
Fixed assets			
Intangible assets			288,000
Tangible fixed assets			1,500,000
Financial assets			600,000
			2,388,000
Current assets			
Stock	1,380,000		
Debtors	232,000		
Cash in hand and at bank	295,000	1,907,000	
***Less* Creditors: amounts falling due within 1 year**			
Trade creditors	482,000		
Other creditors	218,000		
Taxation and social welfare	504,000	(1,204,000)	
Net assets less current liabilities			703,000
Total assets less current liabilities			**3,091,000**
Creditors: amounts falling due after 1 year			
8% Debentures 20/5/-6			800,000
Capital and reserves			
Called up share capital		1,400,000	
Revaluation reserve (W3)		224,000	
Profit and loss account		667,000	2,291,000
			3,091,000

Workings

W1 Cost of sales

Opening stock	1,300,000
Purchases	12,300,000
Less Closing stock	(1,380,000)
Add Patent amortised	48,000
Cost of sales	**€12,268,000**

W2 Administration expenses

From trial balance	1,484,000	
Depreciation	28,000	(1,400,000 x 2%)
Directors' fees	160,000	
Auditor's fees	18,000	
Total	**€1,690,000**	

W3 Revaluation reserve

Opening Depreciation	96,000
Add Increase in value	100,000
This year's charge	28,000
	€224,000

Other workings

Other creditors = Debenture interest due 40,000 + Directors' fees 160,000 + Auditor's fees 18,000 = **€218,000**

Taxation and social welfare = Corporation tax 340,000 + VAT 164,000 = **€504,000**

Debtors 278,000 – Provision for bad debts 46,000 = **€232,000**

Notes to the accounts

1. Accounting policy notes for tangible fixed assets and stock

Buildings were revalued at the end of 20-0. These have been included in the accounts at their revalued amount.

Depreciation is calculated in order to write off the value of the tangible fixed assets over their estimated useful economic life as follows:

Buildings	2% per annum	straight line basis

Stocks are valued on a first-in, first-out basis at the lower of cost or net realisable value.

2. Operating profit

Operating profit is arrived at after charging:

Depreciation on tangible assets	€28,000
Auditor's fees	€18,000
Directors' fees	€160,000
Patent amortised	€48,000

3. Contingent liability

The company is being sued by a customer for a fall on the company's premises. The company's legal team has advised that the company is unlikely to be liable under the terms of its public liability insurance policy. They have also estimated that the amount of liability if any will be €50,000.

4. Dividends

Clarification:

Ordinary dividends

Dividend paid 8.625c per share €69,000

Preference dividends

Dividend paid 7c per share €42,000

5. Tangible fixed assets

Details	Asset 1	Total
Assets		
Opening balance	1,510,000	1,510,000
Disposal	(110,000)	(110,000)
Revaluation surplus 31/12	100,000	100,000
Closing balance	**1,500,000**	**1,500,000**
Depreciation		
Opening depreciation	96,000	96,000
Depreciation charge	28,000	28,000
Transfer on revaluation	(124,000)	(124,000)
Closing balance	0	0
Net book value 1/1/20-0	1,414,000	1,414,000
Net book value 31/12/20-0	1,500,000	1,500,000

Exercises – Higher Level

Q1 The following figures were taken from the books of Bigbo Plc:

	€
Turnover	750,000
Stock 1/1/20-1	105,000
Purchases	450,000
Stock 31/12/20-1	135,000
Distribution costs	60,000
Administrative expenses	45,000
Dividends received	7,500
Discount received	22,500
Interest payable	42,000
Interest receivable	30,000
Corporation tax	76,000
Interim dividends paid	32,000
Final dividends paid	25,000
Profit and loss balance 1/1/20-1 (profit)	40,000

You are required to:

- **Prepare for the year ended 31 December 20-1 the profit and loss account for publication using Format 1.**

Q2 The following figures were taken from the books of Crimson Plc:

	€
Turnover	1,200,000
Stock 1/1/20-3	230,000
Purchases	600,000
Stock 31/12/20-3	190,000
Distribution costs	110,000
Administrative expenses	212,000
Interest receivable	14,000
Dividends receivable	10,000
Interest payable	21,000
Corporation tax	46,000
Loss on the sale of motor vehicles	17,000
Interim dividends paid	22,000
Final dividends paid	25,000
Profit and loss balance 1/1/20-3 (Profit)	28,000

10

You are required to:

- Prepare for the year ended 31 December 20-3 the profit and loss account for publication using Format 1.

Q3 The following figures were taken from the books of Kari Plc at 31/12/20-6:

	€
Turnover	980,000
Cost of sales	456,000
Distribution costs	122,000
Administrative expenses	102,000
Profit on the sale of land	88,000
Interest receivable	23,000
Losses due to the seizure of goods	11,000
Bank interest payable	45,000
Corporation tax	86,000
Interim dividends paid	110,000
Final dividends paid	90,000
Profit and loss balance 1/1/20-6 (loss)	22,000

You are given the following additional information:

(a) Number of ordinary shares issued during the year: 2,500,000.

(b) Distribution costs and administrative costs given above include the following items:

- Depreciation €35,000
- Directors' remuneration €22,000
- Auditor's remuneration €12,000

(c) A property which had cost €35,000 was sold for €123,000.

You are required to:

- Prepare for the year ended 31 December 20-6 the profit and loss account for publication using Format 1, together with the following notes to comply with the Companies Acts:
  - (i) Accounting policy note for stock
  - (ii) Operating profit
  - (iii) Dividends
  - (iv) Profit on the sale of property.

10

Q4 **The following figures were extracted from the books of Katie Hass Plc on 31/12/20-5:**

	€
Patents	30,000
Goodwill	90,000
Land and buildings	500,000
Computers and office machines	50,000
Plant and machinery	150,000
Delivery vans	200,000
Quoted investments (market value €42,000)	34,000
Unquoted investments (directors' value €30,000)	26,000
Stocks	30,000
Debtors and prepayments	56,000
Directors' loans repayable within 12 months	14,000
Bank deposit account	40,000
Creditors	56,000
Corporation tax due	44,000
PRSI and USC due	4,000
VAT due	16,000
10% Debentures 20-8/20-9	50,000
Bank term loan	150,000
Called-up share capital	800,000
Share premium	20,000
Revaluation reserve	48,000
Profit and loss account balance 31/12/20-5	32,000

You are required to:

- **Prepare as at 31 December 20-5 the balance sheet for publication using Format 1, together with the following notes to comply with the Companies Acts:**
  - **(i) Intangible fixed assets**
  - **(ii) Financial fixed assets**
  - **(iii) Stocks**
  - **(iv) Taxation due.**

10

Q5 **The following figures were extracted from the books of KHR Plc on 31/12/20-4:**

	€
Trademarks	20,000
Goodwill	50,000
Debtors	24,000
Creditors	48,000
Called-up capital	240,000
Profit and loss account balance 31/12/20-4	36,000
8% Debentures	50,000
10% Bank term loan	60,000
Delivery vans	150,000
Office equipment	50,000
Bank overdraft	18,000
Bills payable	12,000
PRSI and USC due	8,000
Corporation tax due	16,000
Revaluation reserve	424,000
Debenture reserve	20,000
Stocks	32,000
Land and buildings	500,000
Loans to employees due within 12 months	2,000
Loans to employees due after 12 months	4,000
Quoted investments (market value €140,000)	100,000

You are required to:

- **Prepare as at 31 December 20-4 the balance sheet for publication using Format 1, together with the following notes to comply with the Companies Acts:**
  - **(i) Accounting policy for stock**
  - **(ii) Financial fixed assets**
  - **(iii) Taxation due**
  - **(iv) Intangible fixed assets**
  - **(v) Debentures.**

Q6 The trial balance of French Plc as at 31/12/20-1 was as follows:

	€	€
Buildings at cost 1/1/20-1	1,075,000	
Buildings, depreciation at 1/1/20-1		66,000
Debtors and creditors	303,750	238,750
Patents 1/1/20-1	35,000	
Purchases and sales	1,675,000	2,506,250
Investment income		7,000
VAT		82,500
Profit and loss balance 1/1/20-1		105,000
7% Fixed assets investments	400,000	
Stock 1/1/20-1	101,250	
6% Debentures 20-7/20-8		375,000
Distribution costs	247,500	
Administrative expenses	265,000	
Provision for bad debts		18,125
Debenture interest paid	18,750	
Rental Income		60,000
Dividends paid	90,000	
Profit on the sale of land		90,000
Bank	78,625	
Patent royalties		13,750
Delivery vans at cost 1/1/20-1	350,000	
Depreciation on vans 1/1/20-1		140,000
Issued capital		
Ordinary shares @ €1 each		750,000
8% Preference shares @ €1 each		187,500
	4,639,875	**4,639,875**

The following additional information and instructions are provided:

(a) Stock at 31/12/20-1 was €111,250.

(b) Depreciation is to be provided for as follows: buildings at 2% of cost per annum, and there were no additions or disposals of buildings during the year. However, land belonging to the business which cost €75,000 was sold for €165,000. Also take into account that at the end of 20-1 the company decided to revalue their premises at their true market value, which was €1,187,500, and the directors decided that this value should be incorporated into the accounts of the business. **Note:** depreciation on buildings is to be apportioned 40% to distribution and 60% to administration costs.

(c) Depreciation on vehicles was to be 20% per annum straight line method.

(d) The directors also proposed that provision should be made for directors' fees of €50,000 and auditor's fees of €9,250.

(e) The company's corporation tax liability as determined by the Revenue Commissioners was set at €77,500.

(f) Provide for unpaid debenture interest due on 31/12/20-1 and investment interest due on the same date.

(g) The patent was acquired a number of years ago and is being amortised over six years in equal instalments. It had cost €105,000 originally and this amortisation should be included in the cost of sales.

(h) Included in administration expenses is the receipt of €21,250 for discount.

10

You are required to:

- Prepare the published profit and loss account for the year ended 31/12/20-1 and a balance sheet as at that date, in accordance with the Companies Acts and latest accounting standards, showing the following notes:
  - (i) Accounting policy notes for tangible fixed assets and stock
  - (ii) Operating profit
  - (iii) Interest payable
  - (iv) Tangible fixed assets.

Q7 **The trial balance of Codd Plc as at 31/12/20-1 was as follows:**

	€	€
Buildings at cost 1/1/20-1	560,000	
Buildings, depreciation at 1/1/20-1		38,400
Debtors and creditors	111,200	192,800
Patents 1/1/20-1	134,400	
Purchases and sales	4,920,000	6,390,400
Rental income		41,600
VAT		65,600
Profit and loss balance 1/1/20-1		48,000
Fixed assets investments	240,000	
Stock 1/1/20-1	520,000	
8% Debentures 20-5/20-6		320,000
Distribution costs	488,000	
Administration expenses	593,600	
Provision for bad debts		18,400
Debenture interest paid	9,600	
Interim dividends	19,200	
Profit on the sale of land		64,000
Bank	143,200	
Issued capital		
Ordinary shares @€1 each		320,000
7% Preference shares @ €1 each		240,000
	7,739,200	**7,739,200**

The following additional information and instructions are provided:

(a) Stock at 31/12/20-1 was €552,000.

(b) Depreciation is to be provided for as follows: buildings at 2% of cost per annum, and there were no additions or disposals of buildings during the year. However, land belonging to the business which cost €44,000 was sold for €108,000. Also take into account that at the end of 20-1 the company decided to revalue their premises at their true market value, which was €600,000, and the directors decided that this value should be incorporated into the accounts of the business.

(c) The directors also proposed that provision should be made for directors' fees of €64,000 and auditor's fees of €7,200.

(d) The company's corporation tax liability as determined by the Revenue Commissioners was set at €136,000.

(e) Provide for unpaid debenture interest due on 31/12/20-1.

(f) During the year the directors paid a dividend on shares as follows: a full year's dividend was paid to preference shareholders and the remainder to ordinary shareholders.

(g) The listed investments are in listed companies and have a current market value of €384,000 on the last day of the year. There were no new investments or investments sold during the year.

(h) On 12/11/20-1, the company received a letter from a former employee of the business who was dismissed during the previous month. The ex-employee is making a claim against the company for unfair dismissal. The company's solicitors believe that the company is unlikely to be liable. They have estimated that any liability would be a maximum of €20,000.

(i) The patent was acquired a number of years ago and is being amortised over ten years in equal instalments. It had cost €192,000 originally, and this amortisation should be included in cost of sales.

You are required to:

- Prepare the published profit and loss account for the year ended 31/12/20-1 and a balance sheet as at that date, in accordance with the Companies Acts and latest accounting standards, showing the following notes:
  - (i) Accounting policy notes for tangible fixed assets and stock
  - (ii) Operating profit
  - (iii) Interest payable
  - (iv) Tangible fixed assets
  - (v) Dividends
  - (vi) Financial fixed assets
  - (vii) Profit on the sale of fixed assets
  - (viii) Contingent liability.

Q8 Emerald Plc had an authorised share capital of €720,000, divided into 560,000 ordinary shares at €1 each and 160,000 8% preference shares at €1 each. The following trial balance was extracted from its books on 31/12/20-6:

	€	€
Patent	44,800	
9% Investments 1/1/20-6	96,000	
Land and buildings (re-valued on 1/7/20-6)	704,000	
Revaluation reserve		208,000
Delivery vans at cost	116,000	
Delivery vans - accumulated depreciation on 1/1/20-6		54,400
Debtors and creditors	149,600	78,400
Purchases and sales	556,800	884,000
Stocks 1/1/20-6	60,000	
Directors' fees	67,200	
Salaries and general expenses	141,600	
Discount		4,928
Advertising	16,800	
Investment income		6,480
Profit on sale of land		68,000
Rent	25,600	
Dividends Paid	21,600	
Profit and loss balance 1/1/20-6		58,960
8% Debentures (20/8/20-9) including €96,000 8% debentures issued on 1/8/20-6		216,000
Bank		14,192
VAT		6,640
Issued capital		
280,000 Ordinary shares @ €1 each		280,000
120,000 8% Preference shares		120,000
	2,000,000	**2,000,000**

10

The following information is also relevant:

(a) Stock on 31/12/20-6 was valued on a first-in, first-out basis at €61,600.

(b) The patent was acquired on 1/1/2-03 for €64,000. It is being amortised over ten years in equal instalments. The amortisation should be included in cost of sales.

(c) During the year the directors paid a dividend on shares as follows: a full year's dividend was paid to preference shareholders and the remainder to ordinary shareholders.

(d) On 1/7/20-6 land which had cost €72,000 was sold for €140,000. On this date the remaining land and buildings were revalued at €704,000. Included in this revaluation is land now valued at €144,000 but which originally cost €56,000. The revalued buildings had cost €440,000.

(e) Depreciation is to be provided for as follows: delivery vans at the rate of 20% of cost per annum; buildings at the rate of 2% of cost per annum until date of revaluation and thereafter at 2% per annum of revalued figure.

(f) Provide for debenture interest due, investment income due, auditor's fees of €6,160 and taxation, €26,400.

You are required to:

- Prepare the published profit and loss account for the year ended 31/12/20-6, in accordance with the Companies Acts and financial reporting standards, showing the following notes:
  - (i) Accounting policy note for stock and depreciation
  - (ii) Dividends
  - (iii) Interest payable
  - (iv) Operating profit
  - (v) Profit on sale of property.

Q9 **Brown Plc has an authorised capital of €1,200,000, divided into 900,000 ordinary shares at €1 each and 300,000 10% preference shares at €1 each. The following trial balance was extracted from its books on 31/12/20-5:**

	€	€
9% Investments 1/1/20-5	300,000	
Patent	96,000	
Land and buildings (re-valued on 1/7/20-5)	1,290,000	
Delivery vans at cost	210,000	
Delivery vans - accumulated depreciation on 1/1/20-5		96,000
Revaluation reserve		397,500
Debtors and creditors	300,000	142,500
Purchases and sales	1,050,000	1,831,500
Stock 1/1/20-5	105,000	
Directors' fees	133,500	
Salaries and general expenses	262,500	
Discount		9,390
Advertising	34,500	

Continued >

10

	€	€
Investment income		13,500
Profit on sale of land		120,000
Rent	45,000	
Dividends paid	43,500	
6% Debentures, including €150,000 issued on 1/8/20-5		420,000
Profit and loss balance 1/1/20-5		117,000
Bank		27,660
VAT		4,950
Issued capital		
450,000 Ordinary shares @ €1 each		450,000
240,000 10% Preference shares		240,000
	3,870,000	**3,870,000**

The following information is also relevant:

(a) Stock on 31/12/20-5 was valued on a first-in, first-out basis at €108,000.

(b) The patent was acquired on 1/1/20-3 for €120,000. It is being amortised over ten years in equal instalments. The amortisation is to be included in cost of sales.

(c) During the year the directors paid a dividend on shares as follows: a full year's dividend was paid to preference shareholders and the remainder to ordinary shareholders.

(d) On 1/7/20-5 land which cost €150,000 was sold for €270,000. On this date the remaining land and buildings were revalued at €1,290,000. Included in this revaluation is land now valued at €240,000 but which originally cost €75,000. The revalued buildings had cost €795,000.

(e) Depreciation is to be provided for as follows: delivery vans at the rate of 20% of cost; buildings at the rate of 2% of cost per annum until the date of revaluation and thereafter at 2% per annum of revalued figure.

(f) Provide for debenture interest due, investment income due, auditor's fees of €12,600 and taxation of €60,000.

You are required to:

- Prepare the published profit and loss account for the year ended 31/12/20-5, in accordance with the Companies Acts and appropriate reporting standards, showing the following notes:
  - (i) Tangible fixed assets
  - (ii) Stock
  - (iii) Dividends
  - (iv) Operating profit
  - (v) Profit on sale of property.

Q10 **Alison plc has an authorised share capital of €630,000, divided into 450,000 ordinary shares at €1 each and 180,000 8% preference shares at €1 each. The following trial balance was extracted from its books at 31/12/20-7:**

	€	€
Buildings at cost	585,000	
Buildings, accumulated depreciation on at 1/1/20-7		36,900
Vehicles at cost	180,000	
Vehicles, accumulated depreciation on at 1/1/20-7		34,200
Quoted investments at cost (market value €198,000)	180,000	
Unquoted investments at cost (directors' valuation €63,450)	54,000	
Debtors and creditors	249,300	177,300
Stock 1/1/20-7	58,500	
Patent 1/1/20-7	45,000	
Distribution costs	234,000	
Administrative expenses	144,000	
Purchases and sales	1,125,000	1,791,000
Rental income		45,000
Profit on sale of land		63,000
Dividends paid	38,700	
Bank	69,300	
VAT		63,000
8% Debentures 20-2/20-3		270,000
Profit and loss account at 1/1/20-7		45,000
Investment income received		
Quoted		9,000
Unquoted		2,700
Issued capital		
Ordinary shares		315,000
8% Preference shares		90,000
Provision for bad debts		18,000
Debenture interest paid	9,000	
Discount		11,700
	2,971,800	**2,971,800**

The following information is also relevant:

(a) **Stock on 31/12/20-7 was €199,800.**

(b) **During the year, land adjacent to the company's premises, which had cost €81,000, was sold for €144,000. At the end of the year the company revalued its buildings at €720,000. The company wishes to incorporate this value in this year's accounts.**

(c) **Provide for debenture interest due, auditor's fees of €7,200, directors' fees of €45,000 and corporation tax, €76,500.**

10

(d) Included in administrative expenses is the receipt of €7,200 for patent royalties.

(e) Depreciation is to be provided for on buildings at a rate of 2% straight line and is to be allocated 20% on distribution costs and 80% on administrative expenses. There was no purchase or sale of buildings during the year. Vehicles are to be depreciated at a rate of 20% of cost per annum.

(f) The patent was acquired on 1/1/20-3 for €81,000. It is being amortised over nine years in equal instalments. The amortisation is to be included in cost of sales.

You are required to:

- Prepare the published profit and loss account for the year ended 31/12/20-7, in accordance with the Companies Acts and appropriate accounting standards, showing the following notes:
  - (i) Accounting policy note for tangible fixed assets and stock
  - (ii) Operating profit
  - (iii) Financial fixed assets
  - (iv) Dividends
  - (v) Tangible fixed assets.

Q11 The following is the trial balance of Best Plc as at 31/12/20-7:

	€	€
Fixed asset investments	360,000	
Patent at 1/1/20-7	201,600	
Buildings at cost 1/1/20-7	840,000	
Buildings, accumulated depreciation 1/1/20-7		57,600
Stock 1/1/20-7	780,000	
Debtors and creditors	166,800	289,200
8% Debentures 20-8/20-9		480,000
Purchases and sales	7,380,000	9,585,600
Distribution costs	732,000	
Administrative expenses	890,400	
Rental income		62,400
Provision for bad debts		27,600
Debenture interest paid	14,400	
Dividends paid	28,800	
Profit on the sale of land		96,000
Bank	214,800	
VAT		98,400
Authorised and issued share capital		
Ordinary shares @ €1 each		480,000
7% Preference shares @ €1 each		360,000
Profit and loss at 1/1/20-7		72,000
	11,608,800	**11,608,800**

10

The following additional information is provided:

(a) Stock at 31/12/20-7 was €828,000.

(b) Depreciation is to be provided for as follows: buildings 2% straight line. (There were no purchases or sales of buildings during the year.) During the year land adjacent to the company's buildings which had cost €66,000 was sold for €162,000. At the end of the year the company revalued its buildings at €900,000. The company wishes to incorporate this value in this year's accounts.

(c) Provision should be made for:
- Directors' fees, €96,000
- Auditor's fees, €10,800
- Corporation tax, €204,000
- Debenture interest due at 31/12/20-7.

(d) The patent was acquired on 1/1/20-4 for €288,000. It is being amortised over ten years in equal instalments. The amortisation should be included in the cost of sales.

(e) During the year the directors paid a dividend on shares as follows: a full year's dividend was paid to preference shareholders and the remainder to ordinary shareholders.

(f) The fixed assets investments are in listed companies. The market value of these investments at 31/12/20-7 was €576,000. There were no purchases or sales of investments during the year.

(g) The debentures are secured by a fixed charge over the company's tangible fixed assets.

(h) On 14/11/20-7 the company received a letter from a former employee who was dismissed on 1/9/20-7. The employee is claiming compensation for unlawful dismissal. The company's legal advisors believe that company is unlikely to be liable under the terms of the employment contract and they estimate the maximum amount likely to be liable will be legal costs of €30,000.

You are required to:

- Prepare the published profit and loss account for the year ended 31/12/20-7 and a balance sheet as at that date, in accordance with the Companies Acts and latest accounting standards, showing the following notes:
  - (i) Accounting policy note for tangible fixed assets and stock
  - (ii) Operating profit
  - (iii) Contingent liabilities
  - (iv) Dividends
  - (v) Tangible fixed assets.

Q12 **Saff Blue Plc has an authorised capital of €1,120,000, divided into 840,000 ordinary shares at €1 each and 280,000 9% preference shares at €1 each. The following trial balance was extracted from its books at 31/12/20-4:**

	€	€
Vehicles at cost	308,000	
Vehicles, accumulated depreciation 1/1/2004		46,200
Investment income		14,000
Buildings at cost	980,000	
Buildings, accumulated depreciation 1/1/20-4		58,800
Debtors and creditors	404,600	228,200
9% Investments	336,000	
Stock at 1/1/20-4	102,200	
Patent at 1/1/20-4	56,000	
Administrative expenses	240,800	
Purchases and sales	1,610,000	2,632,000
Rental income		84,000
8% Debentures 20-8/20-9		280,000
Distribution costs	347,200	
Profit on sale of land		91,000
Bank	67,200	
VAT		99,400
Dividends paid	33,600	
Profit and loss at 1/1/20-4		72,800
Issued capital		
Ordinary shares		560,000
Preference shares		280,000
Provision for bad debts		37,800
Debenture interest paid	16,800	
Discount		18,200
	4,502,400	**4,502,400**

The following information is relevant:

(a) Stock on 31/12/20-4 was €134,400.

(b) The patent was acquired on 1/1/20-0 for €112,000. It is being amortised over eight years in equal instalments. The amortisation is to be included in cost of sales.

(c) During the year the directors paid a dividend on shares as follows: a full year's dividend was paid to preference shareholders and the remainder to ordinary shareholders.

(d) Provide for debenture interest due, investment interest due, auditor's fees of €13,300, directors' fees of €70,000 and corporation tax, €121,800.

(e) Depreciation is to be provided for on buildings at a rate of 2% straight line and is to be allocated 20% on distribution costs and 80% on administration expenses. There was no purchase or sale of buildings during the year. Vehicles are to be depreciated at the rate of 20% of cost.

(f) During the year land adjacent to the company's premises, which had cost €112,000, was sold for €203,000. At the end of the year the company revalued its buildings at €1,260,000. The company wishes to incorporate this value in this year's accounts.

(g) Included in administration expenses is the receipt of €16,800 for patent royalties.

You are required to:

- Prepare the published profit and loss account for the year 31/12/20-4 and a balance sheet as at that date, in accordance with the Companies Acts and appropriate accounting standards, showing the following notes:
  - (i) Accounting policy note for tangible fixed assets and stock
  - (ii) Operating profit
  - (iii) Interest payable
  - (iv) Dividends
  - (v) Tangible fixed assets.

Q13 **Tee Plc has an authorised capital of €1,330,000, divided into 910,000 ordinary shares at €1 each and 420,000 8% preference shares at €1 each. The following trial balance was extracted from its books at 31/12/20-8:**

	€	€
Vehicles at cost	392,000	
Vehicles, accumulated depreciation 1/1/20-8		156,800
Investment income		7,840
Buildings at cost	1,204,000	
Buildings, accumulated depreciation 1/1/20-8		73,920
Debtors and creditors	340,200	267,400
7% Investments	448,000	
Stock at 1/1/20-8	113,400	
Patents at 1/1/20-8	39,200	
Administrative expenses	296,800	
Distribution costs	277,200	
Purchases and sales	1,876,000	2,807,000
Rental income		67,200
6% Debentures 20/9/20-0		420,000
Profit on sale of land		100,800
Bank	88,060	
VAT		92,400
Dividends paid	100,800	
Profit and loss at 1/1/20-8		117,600
Issued capital		
Ordinary shares		840,000
Preference shares		210,000
Provision for bad debts		20,300
Debenture interest paid	21,000	
Patent royalties		15,400
	5,196,660	**5,196,660**

The following information is relevant:

(a) Stock at 31/12/20-8 was €124,600.

(b) The patent was acquired on 1/1/20-4 for €117,600. It is being amortised over six years in equal instalments. The amortisation is to be included in cost of sales.

(c) Provide for debenture interest due, investment interest due, auditor's fees of €10,360, directors' fees of €56,000 and corporation tax, €86,800.

(d) Depreciation is to be provided for on buildings at a rate of 2% straight line, and is to be allocated 40% distribution costs and 60% administrative expenses. There was no purchase or sale of buildings during the year. Vehicles are to be depreciated at the rate of 20% of cost.

(e) During the year land adjacent to the company's premises, which had cost €84,000, was sold for €184,800. At the end of the year the company revalued its buildings to €1,330,000. The company wishes to incorporate this value in this year's accounts.

(f) Included in administrative expenses is the receipt of €23,800 for discount.

You are required to:

- Prepare the published profit and loss account for the year 31/12/20-8 and a balance sheet as at that date, in accordance with the Companies Acts and appropriate accounting standards, showing the following notes:
  - (i) Accounting policy note for tangible fixed assets and stock
  - (ii) Operating profit
  - (iii) Interest payable
  - (iv) Tangible fixed assets.

Theory

Q1 How should a company deal with a contingent liability for which it is likely to be liable?

Q2 Explain the difference between an auditor's qualified and unqualified report.

Q3 What is meant by an exceptional item? Give an example.

Q4 State four items of information that you would find in a directors' report.

Q5 What regulations must be observed when preparing financial statements for publication?

Q6 What is an audit?

Q7 What are the criteria used to classify a company as large, medium or small?

10

Exam Tips

- Know the exact layout of the published profit and loss account.
- Know the exact layout of the published balance sheet.
- Prepare workings and be mindful of specific instructions.
- Revise the material covered in Chapter 8 – often used in conjunction with this topic.

11 Manufacturing Accounts

Objectives

On completion students should be able to:

- Understand prime cost and its components;
- Understand factory overheads;
- Explain terms associated with manufacturing accounts – for example, work in progress;
- Prepare a manufacturing account;
- Calculate the cost per unit produced.

Costs of manufacture

Manufacturing accounts are compiled in order to find out the cost of manufacturing a product. They enable the unit cost of production to be calculated. They deal with raw materials and manufacturing expenses.

There are two basic elements in the cost of manufacture:

1. **Prime cost**
2. **Factory overhead expenses**.

Prime cost

Prime cost is made up of:

- Direct materials
- Direct labour
- Direct expenses.

Direct Materials	Direct Labour	Direct Expenses
Cost of raw materials Carriage on raw materials Customs duties	Labour that is directly related to the manufacturing process – manufacturing/direct wages	Expenses directly related to the product – for example, royalties, hire of special machines/equipment

Factory overhead expenses

Factory overhead expenses are **indirect manufacturing costs** which cannot easily be traced to the product.

Indirect Labour	Depreciation of Fixed Assets	Indirect Expenses/Losses (Overheads)
Storekeepers' wages Supervisors' wages Wages of other staff involved in the manufacturing process	Factory buildings Factory plant and machinery Fork lift trucks, etc.	Factory rent Factory light and heat Factory insurance Factory repairs Loss on sale of manufacturing fixed assets

Prime cost = Direct materials + Direct labour + Direct expenses

Factory overheads = Indirect labour + Indirect losses (depreciation) + Indirect expenses

Cost of manufacture = Prime cost + Factory overheads

Work in progress

Most manufacturing firms will have partially completed goods during the accounting period. **Work in progress** is the term used to refer to these partially completed goods. In the accounts it is treated as follows:

Add Work in progress at the beginning of the accounting period.
Subtract Work in progress at the end of the accounting period.

Work in progress is normally entered after the factory overheads.

By-products and scrap materials

These materials arise as a result of the manufacturing process. They include items such as waste oil and wood chippings. These materials when sold reduce the overall cost of manufacture. Such sales should be deducted from the manufacturing costs.

Market value of manufactured goods

This is the amount that the firm would pay for the goods if they were to be purchased on the open market. By comparing this figure with the cost of manufacture, a firm can find out whether it is profitable for it to continue manufacturing.

If the market value of goods is greater than the cost of manufacture the difference is a manufacturing profit, and is transferred to the trading account – i.e. added to gross profit.

NOTE

The cost of manufacture is included in the **cost of sales**.

The accounts

Trading and profit and loss accounts

The **trading account** deals with finished goods – those manufactured by the firm and those bought in from outside.

The **profit and loss account** deals with the expenses incurred in selling these goods.

Balance sheet

The balance sheet of a manufacturing firm is presented in the same way as already illustrated for a sole trader or a company. When entering closing stocks there are three items of stock involved:

- Finished goods
- Raw materials
- Work in progress.

Example

The following figures were taken from the books of Ballymore Furniture Products Ltd on 31/12/20-8:

	€
Stock of raw materials 1/1/20-8	50,000
Purchase of raw materials	250,000
Carriage inwards on raw materials	10,000
Stock of raw materials 31/12/20-8	40,000
Manufacturing wages	150,000
Royalties for use of patent	20,000
Hire of special machines	30,000
Supervisor's salary	25,000
Factory rent	15,000
Depreciation of machines	10,000
Sale of scrap materials	2,000
Work in progress 1/1/20-8	24,000
Work in progress 31/12/20-8	26,000
Goods to be transferred from factory at current market value	600,000

You are required to:

- Prepare a manufacturing account for the year ended 31/12/20-8.
- Find the cost per unit if 10,000 units were produced.

Solution

Ballymore Furniture Ltd Manufacturing Account for year ended 31/12/20-8

	€	€
Direct materials		
Opening stock 1/1/20-8		50,000
Purchases of raw materials		250,000
Carriage inwards on raw materials		10,000
Cost of raw materials available		310,000
Less Closing stock of raw materials		(40,000)
Cost of raw materials used		270,000
Direct labour		
Manufacturing wages		150,000
Direct expenses		
Royalties (use of patent)	20,000	
Hire of special machines	30,000	50,000
Prime cost		**470,000**
Factory overheads		
Supervisor's salary	25,000	
Factory rent	15,000	
Depreciation of machinery	10,000	50,000
		520,000
Add Work in progress 1/1/20-8		24,000
		544,000
Less Work in progress 31/12/20-8		(26,000)
		518,000
Less Sale of scrap materials		(2,000)
Cost of manufacture		516,000
Profit on manufacture (add to gross profit in trading account)		84,000
Current market value (transferred to trading account)		**600,000**

Cost per unit: 516,000/10,000 = €51.60 per unit

Sample Ordinary Level question

The following figures were extracted from the books of Raven Ltd on 31/12/20-2:

	€	€
Factory buildings (cost €400,000)	304,000	
Machinery (cost €200,000)	112,000	
Trade debtors and creditors	50,000	38,000
Capital		154,000
8% Debentures		50,000
Stocks 1/1/20-2		
Raw materials	80,000	
Work in progress	10,000	
Finished goods	40,000	
Purchase of raw materials	520,000	
Manufacturing wages	160,000	
Hire of special machines	20,000	
Carriage on raw materials	30,000	
Factory supervisor's salary	60,000	
Factory rent and rates	6,000	
Purchases and sales – finished goods	70,000	1,400,000
Office salaries	54,000	
Telephone	6,000	
Debenture interest	4,000	
Sales staff salaries	72,000	
Sales staff commission	14,000	
Bank charges	2,000	
Advertising	8,000	
Office rent	12,000	
Office insurance	8,000	
	1,642,000	**1,642,000**

The following additional information is provided:

(a) Stocks at 31/12/20-2:

Raw materials	€70,000
Work in progress	€14,000
Finished goods	€36,000

11

(b) Goods are transferred to trading account at current market value of €1,000,000.

(c) Provide for depreciation as follows:

Factory buildings	€24,000
Machinery	€10,000

(d) 20,000 units were produced during the year.

You are required to:

- Prepare manufacturing and trading, profit and loss accounts for the year ended 31/12/20-2.
- Prepare a balance sheet as at 31/12/20-2.
- Calculate the manufacturing cost per unit.

Solution

Manufacturing Account of Raven Ltd for the year ended 31/12/20-2

	€	€
Direct materials		
Opening stock of raw materials	80,000	
Purchase of raw materials	520,000	
Carriage inwards on raw materials	30,000	
	630,000	
Less Closing stock of raw materials	(70,000)	
Cost of raw materials used		560,000
Direct costs		
Manufacturing wages	160,000	
Hire of special machines	20,000	180,000
Prime cost		**740,000**
Factory overheads		
Factory supervisor's salary	60,000	
Factory rent and rates	6,000	
Depreciation of building	24,000	
Depreciation of machinery	10,000	100,000
		840,000
Add Work in progress 1/1/20-2		10,000
		850,000
Less Work in progress 31/12/20-2		(14,000)
Cost of manufacture		836,000
Profit on manufacture		164,000
Current market value		**1,000,000**

Trading, Profit and Loss Account of Raven Ltd for the year ended 31/12/20-2

	€	€	€
Sales			1,400,000
***Less* Cost of sales**			
Opening stock (finished goods)		40,000	
Market value of goods manufactured		1,000,000	
Finished goods purchased		70,000	
		1,110,000	
Less Closing stock (finished goods)		(36,000)	(1,074,000)
Gross profit			326,000
Add Manufacturing profit			164,000
			490,000
***Less* Expenses**			
Administration			
Office salaries	54,000		
Telephone	6,000		
Bank charges	2,000		

Continued >

11

	€	€	€
Office rent	12,000		
Insurance	8,000	82,000	
Selling and distribution			
Salaries, sales staff	72,000		
Commission, sales staff	14,000		
Advertising	8,000	94,000	(176,000)
Operating profit			314,000
Less Debenture interest			(4,000)
Net profit			**310,000**

Balance Sheet of Raven Ltd as at 31/12/20-2

	Cost (€)	Aggregate Depreciation (€)	Net Book Value (€)
Fixed assets			
Factory buildings	400,000	120,000	280,000
Machinery	200,000	98,000	102,000
	600,000	218,000	382,000
Current assets			
Stock			
Raw materials	70,000		
Work in progress	14,000		
Finished goods	36,000	120,000	
Debtors		50,000	
		170,000	
***Less* Creditors: amounts falling due within 1 year**			
Creditors		(38,000)	
Net current assets			132,000
Total net assets			**514,000**
Financed by			
Creditors: amounts falling due after 1 year			
8% Debentures			50,000
Capital and reserves			
Issued share capital		154,000	
Profit and loss balance 31/12/20-2		310,000	464,000
Capital employed			514,000

Unit cost of manufacture: €836,000/20,000 = €41.80 per unit

Sample Higher Level question

Slaney Ltd has an authorised share capital of 750,000 ordinary shares at €1 each. The following trial balance was extracted from its books on 31/12/20-5:

	€	€
Buildings (cost €280,000)	245,000	
Plant and machinery (cost €100,000)	68,000	
Computers and office equipment (cost €25,000)	16,000	
Patents (cost €72,000)	45,000	
Profit and loss balance 1/1/20-5		31,400
Bank		39,400
Debtors and creditors	92,400	48,200
Purchases of raw materials	398,000	
Sales		737,600
Sale of scrap materials		9,000
Direct factory wages	133,200	
Factory power	11,600	
Insurance	6,400	
Production manager's salary	18,000	
Selling expenses	12,400	
Salaries and general expenses	70,000	
8% Debentures issued on 1/4/20-5		90,000
Stock on hand 1/1/20-5		
Finished goods	77,000	
Raw materials	44,000	
Work in progress	22,000	
Dividends paid	9,000	
Issued share capital		300,000
VAT		12,400
	1,268,000	**1,268,000**

The following information is to be taken into account:

(a) Stocks on hand at 31/12/20-5 were as follows: finished goods €86,000; raw materials €57,000; work in progress €25,000. Stocks of finished goods includes a batch of items which cost €7,500 to produce but have a net realisable value of €5,000.

(b) No record had been made in the books for raw materials costing €12,000 which were in transit on 31/12/20-5. The invoice for these goods had been received.

(c) Included in the sale of scrap materials is €3,000 received on 1/1/20-5 for the sale of obsolete machinery. This machinery had cost €25,000 on 1/1/20-0. The cheque had been entered in the bank account, but no other entry had been made in the books.

(d) General expenses, insurance and depreciation of buildings are to be allocated 75% to factory and 25% to office administration.

(e) Depreciation is to be provided as follows: plant and machinery 20% of cost; computers and office equipment 10% of cost; buildings 2% of cost per annum.

(f) Patents are being written off over a nine-year period and should be included in factory cost.

(g) During the year 20-5 Slaney Ltd built an extension to the warehouse. The work was carried out by the company's own employees. The cost of their labour (€10,000) is included in factory wages. The cost of the materials used (€20,000) is included in purchases.

11

(h) At 1/1/20-5 there were 800 units in production. During the year, work commenced on 8,000 units and 900 were still in production at 31/12/20-5. The work was halted on 200 units which were then sold as scrap. The remaining units were transferred to finished goods stocks.

(i) The directors are proposing that provision should be made for debenture interest due and corporation tax of €24,000.

You are required to:

- Prepare manufacturing and trading, profit and loss accounts for the year ended 31/12/20-5.
- Prepare a balance sheet as at 31/12/20-5.
- Calculate the unit cost of production per unit.

Solution

Manufacturing Account for Slaney Ltd for the year ended 31/12/20-5

	€	€
Raw materials		
Opening stock raw materials	44,000	
Purchase of raw materials (W1)	390,000	
	434,000	
Less Closing stock of raw materials (W2)	(69,000)	
Cost of raw materials consumed		365,000
Direct costs		
Direct wages (W3)		123,200
Prime cost		488,200
Factory overheads		
Factory power	11,600	
Insurance (W4)	4,800	
Productions manager's salary	18,000	
Patents amortised (W11)	8,000	
General expenses (W5)	52,500	
Depreciation of plant and machinery (W6)	15,000	
Depreciation of buildings (W7)	4,650	114,550
Factory cost		602,750
Add Work in progress 1/1/20-5		22,000
		624,750
Less Work in progress 31/12/20-5		(25,000)
		599,750
Less Sale of scrap materials	6,000	
Profit on the sale of machine (W8)	3,000	(9,000)
Cost of manufacture		**590,750**

Trading, Profit and Loss Account for the year ended 31/12/20-5

	€	€	€
Sales			737,600
***Less* Cost of sales**			
Opening stock (finished goods)		77,000	
Cost of manufacture		590,750	
		667,750	
Less Closing stock (finished goods) (W9)		(83,500)	(584,250)
Gross profit			153,350
***Less* Expenses**			
Administration			
Insurance (W4)	1,600		
General expenses (W5)	17,500		
Depreciation, office equipment (W10)	2,500		
Depreciation, buildings (W7)	1,550	23,150	
Selling and distribution			
Selling expenses		12,400	(35,550)
Operating profit			117,800
Debenture interest (W12)			(5,400)
Profit before taxation			112,400
Less Taxation			(24,000)
Profit after taxation			88,400
***Less* Appropriations**			
Dividends paid			(9,000)
Retained profit			79,400
Profit and loss balance 1/1/20-5			31,400
Profit and loss balance 31/12/20-5			**110,800**

Balance Sheet as at 31/12/20-5

	Cost (€)	Aggregate Depreciation (€)	Net Book Value (€)	Total (€)
Intangible fixed assets				
Patents (W17)				37,000
Tangible fixed assets				
Buildings (W14)	310,000	41,200	268,800	
Plant and machinery (W15)	75,000	22,000	53,000	
Computers and office equipment (W16)	25,000	11,500	13,500	
	410,000	74,700	335,300	335,300
				372,300
Current assets				
Stocks				
Raw materials (W2)	69,000			
Work in progress	25,000			
Finished goods (W9)	83,500	177,500		
Debtors		92,400	269,900	
***Less* Creditors: amounts falling due within 1 year**				
Trade creditors (W13)		60,200		
Debenture interest due (W12)		5,400		
Bank		39,400		
VAT		12,400		
Taxation		24,000	(141,400)	
Net current assets				128,500
Total net assets				**500,800**
Financed by				
Creditors: amounts falling due after 1 year				
8% Debentures				90,000
Capital and reserves		**Authorised**	**Issued**	
Ordinary shares @ €1 each		750,000	300,000	
Profit and loss account 31/12/20-5			110,800	
Shareholders' funds				410,800
Capital employed				**500,800**

11

Workings

W1 Purchase of raw materials

As per trial balance	398,000
Add Goods in transit	12,000
Less Goods for building	(20,000)
	390,000

W2 Closing stock raw materials

As per question	57,000
Add Goods in transit	12,000
	69,000

W3 Direct wages

As per trial balance	133,200
Less Building wages	(10,000)
	123,200

W4 Insurance

Amount paid	6,400
6,400 x 75% (man. a/c)	4,800
6,400 x 25% (adm. exp.)	1,600

W5 General expenses

Amount paid	70,000
70,000 x 75% (man. a/c)	52,500
70,000 x 25% (adm. exp.)	17,500

W6 Depreciation of plant and machinery

(100,000 – 25,000) x 20%	15,000

W7 Depreciation of buildings

280,000 + (extension) 30,000 =	310,000
310,000 x 2%	6,200
6,200 x 75% (man. a/c)	4,650
6,200 x 25% (adm. exp.)	1,550

W8 Profit on sale of machine

Cost	25,000
Less Depreciation (25,000 x 20% x 5)	(25,000)
Net book value	0
Proceeds	3,000
Profit on sale	3,000

W9 Closing stock, finished goods

As per question	86,000
Less Loss in value	(2,500)
	83,500

W10 Depreciation, office equipment

25,000 x 10%	2,500

W11 Patent amortised

72,000 / 9	8,000

W12 Debenture interest

90,000 x 8% x 9/12	5,400

W13 Creditors

As per trial balance (TB)	48,200
Add Goods in transit	12,000
	60,200

W14 Buildings

Cost as per TB	280,000
Add Extension	30,000
	310,000
Depreciation as per TB	35,000
Add This year's charge	6,200
	41,200

W15 Plant and machinery

Cost as per TB	100,000
Less Disposal	(25,000)
	75,000
Depreciation as per TB	32,000
Add This year's charge	15,000
Less Disposal	(25,000)
	22,000

W16 Computers and office equipment

Cost as per TB	25,000
Depreciation as per TB	9,000
Add This year's charge	2,500
	11,500

W17 Patents

As per TB	45,000
Less Amortisation charge	(8,000)
	37,000

11

Unit Cost of Production

$$\frac{\text{Total cost incurred in the production of finished goods}}{\text{Total number of units produced}}$$

(Number of units produced: 800 + 8,000 – 200 – 900 = 7,700)

$$\frac{590{,}750}{7{,}700}$$

Answer: €76.72

Exercises – Ordinary Level

Q1 The following balances were extracted from the books of Bolton Ltd on 31/12/20-1:

	€
Stock of raw materials at 1 January 20-1	11,200
Purchase of raw materials	68,800
Stock of raw materials at 31 December 20-1	16,000
Manufacturing wages	80,000
Factory supervisor's wages	32,000
Factory light and heat	11,200
Factory insurance	4,800

8,000 units were produced.

You are required to:

- **Prepare a manufacturing account for the year ended 31/12/20-1.**
- **Calculate the manufacturing cost per unit.**

Q2 The following balances were extracted from the books of Holloway Ltd on 31/12/20-2:

	€
Stock of raw materials at 1 January 20-2	28,000
Stock of raw materials at 31 December 20-2	22,600
Manufacturing wages	235,900
Supervisor's salary	32,500
Factory insurance	12,850
Factory light and heat	12,890
Hire of special machines	13,570
Depreciation, buildings	6,790
Depreciation, plant and machinery	5,600
Factory repairs	10,270
Carriage inwards on raw materials	3,450
Purchase of raw materials	145,600

5,000 units were produced.

You are required to:

- **Prepare a manufacturing account for the year ended 31/12/20-2.**
- **Calculate the manufacturing cost per unit.**

Q3 The following balances were extracted from the books of Coyle Ltd on 31/12/20-3:

	€
Work in progress at 1 January 20-3	11,800
Manufacturing wages	120,000
Depreciation of buildings	23,000
Purchase of raw materials	115,000
Stock of raw materials 1 January 20-3	10,500
Stock of raw materials 31 December 20-3	14,000
Factory rent	12,700
Storekeeper's wages	11,900
Factory insurance	3,400
Wages of forklift truck driver	10,900
Royalties for use of patent @ €1 per unit produced	14,000
Work in progress at 31 December 20-3	18,800
Carriage inwards on raw materials	600

14,000 units were produced.

You are required to:

- **Prepare a manufacturing account for the year ended 31/12/20-3.**
- **Calculate the manufacturing cost per unit.**

Q4 The following balances were extracted from the books of Seaside Ltd on 31/12/20-4:

	€
Purchase of raw materials	500,000
Sales	790,000
Manufacturing wages	101,500
Repairs to machinery	4,500
Stocks 1/1/20-4	
Raw materials	22,000
Work in progress	12,300
Finished goods	24,600
Factory rent and rates	4,900
Sale of scrap materials	3,600
Factory insurance	8,900
Factory light and heat	5,600
Stocks 31/12/20-4	
Raw materials	23,000
Work in progress	4,800
Finished goods	16,700

11

You are required to:

- Prepare a manufacturing account for the year ended 31/12/20-4.
- Prepare a trading account for the year ended 31/12/20-4.

Q5 The following balances were extracted from the books of Tram Ltd on 31/12/20-5:

	€
Purchase of raw materials	260,000
Sales	605,900
Repairs to machinery	6,500
Manufacturing wages	87,000
Stocks 1/1/20-5	
Raw materials	15,000
Finished goods	31,000
Work in progress	13,400
Returns outwards	2,300
Directors' fees	21,500
Showroom expenses	10,600
Carriage outwards	2,500
Dividend paid	12,000
Factory insurance	4,600
Discount received	6,700
Factory light and heat	12,340
Plant and machinery (cost €150,000)	90,000
Office equipment (cost €34,000)	30,000

You are given the following information and instructions:

(a) Stocks at 31/12/20-5 were: raw materials €23,000; finished goods €27,000; work in progress €17,800.

(b) Provide for depreciation as follows: plant and machinery €23,400; office equipment €3,400.

(c) Provide for taxation of €20,000.

You are required to:

- Prepare a manufacturing account for the year ended 31/12/20-5.
- Prepare a trading, profit and loss account for the year ended 31/12/20-5.

Q6 The following balances were extracted from the books of Morgan Ltd on 31/12/20-7:

	€	€
Share capital		
Authorised: 600,000 ordinary shares at €1 each		
Issued: 450,000 ordinary shares at €1 each		450,000
Plant and machinery (cost €330,000)	285,000	
Factory buildings at cost	450,000	
Delivery vans (cost €69,000)	51,000	
Patents	56,250	
Debtors and creditors	31,200	22,125
Stocks 1/1/20-7		
Raw materials	43,500	
Work in progress	24,750	
Finished goods	48,000	
Factory wages	97,500	
Purchase of raw materials	258,000	
Direct expenses	28,500	
Sales		735,000
Returns inwards	2,550	
Sale of scrap materials		6,000
Directors' fees	27,000	
Factory insurance	13,500	
Factory light and heat	32,550	
Profit and loss balance 1/1/20-7		65,250
10% Debentures (issued 1/4/20-7)		150,000
VAT		7,650
Stationery	4,050	
Provision for bad debts		2,100
Bank		20,475
Advertising	5,250	
	1,458,600	**1,458,600**

You are given the following additional information:

(a) Stocks at 31/12/20-7:

Raw materials	€36,750
Work in progress	€17,250
Finished goods	€55,500

(b) Depreciation is to be provided as follows:

Plant and machinery	20% of cost
Delivery vans	10% of book value
Factory buildings	3% of cost

(c) Factory wages are to be divided 75% for direct wages and 25% for supervisor's wages.

(d) Provision should be made for debenture interest due.

(e) Factory insurance was for the year ended 31/3/20-8.

(f) Finished goods are to be transferred from factory at current market value of €525,000.

(g) Provide for corporation tax of €9,000.

11

You are required to:

- **Prepare a manufacturing account for the year ended 31/12/20-7.**
- **Prepare the trading, profit and loss account for the year ended 31/12/20-7.**
- **Prepare a balance sheet as at 31/12/20-7.**

Q7 The following balances were extracted from the books of Grange Ltd on 31/12/20-4:

	€	€
Share capital		
Authorised: 480,000 ordinary shares at €1 each		
Issued: 400,000 ordinary shares at €1 each		400,000
Delivery vans (cost €33,600)	22,400	
Plant and machinery (cost €152,000)	108,000	
Factory building at cost	400,000	
Debtors and creditors	41,920	47,680
Patents	49,600	
12% Debentures issued 1/4/20-4		48,000
Purchase of raw materials	472,000	
Sales		688,000
Stocks 1/1/20-4		
Raw materials	36,800	
Work in progress	14,400	
Finished goods	25,600	
Factory wages	96,000	
Direct expenses	16,000	
Returns inwards	3,200	
Sale of scrap materials		10,240
Factory rent and rates	13,440	
Factory insurance	10,320	
Directors' fees	41,600	
VAT		16,320
Bank		45,440
Profit and loss balance 1/1/20-4		98,560
Showroom expenses	3,120	
Stationery	1,920	
Provision for bad debts		2,080
	1,356,320	**1,356,320**

You are given the following additional information:

(a) **Stocks at 31/12/20-4:**

Raw materials	**€35,200**
Work in progress	**€12,000**
Finished goods	**€39,200**

(b) **Depreciation is to be provided as follows:**

Delivery vans	**10% of book value**
Plant and machinery	**10% of cost**
Factory buildings	**4% of cost**

(c) **Wages are to be divided 80% for direct wages and 20% for supervisor's wages.**

11

(d) Provision should be made for debenture interest due.

(e) Factory insurance was for the year ended 31/4/20-5.

(f) Finished goods are to be transferred from factory at current market value of €640,000.

(g) Provide for corporation tax of €5,660.

You are required to prepare:

- manufacturing account for the year ended 31/12/20-4
- trading, profit and loss account for the year ended 31/12/20-4
- balance sheet as at 31/12/20-4

Q8 The following balances were extracted from the books of Riley Ltd on 31/12/20-7:

	€	€
Share capital		
Authorised: 1,000,000 shares at €1 each		
Issued: 675,000 shares at €1 each		675,000
Plant and machinery (cost €195,000)	165,000	
Office equipment (cost €30,000)	24,000	
Factory buildings at cost	600,000	
Patents	105,000	
Debtors and creditors	47,700	61,500
11% Debentures (issued 1/4/20-7)		120,000
Purchase of raw materials	495,000	
Sales		783,000
Wages	90,000	
Stocks 1/1/20-7		
Raw materials	37,500	
Work in progress	36,000	
Finished goods	58,500	
Profit and loss balance 1/1/20-7		34,500
Returns inwards	3,000	
Office expenses	3,300	
Provision for bad debts		2,400
Sale of scrap materials		12,000
Directors' fees	39,000	
Advertising	10,200	
Factory insurance	7,200	
Forklift driver's wages	13,800	
VAT		8,250
Bank		38,550
	1,735,200	**1,735,200**

You are given the following additional information:

(a) Stocks at 31/12/20-7 were as follows:

Raw materials	€42,000
Work in progress	€49,500
Finished goods	€64,500

(b) Wages are to be divided as follows: direct wages 60% and indirect wages 40%.

11

(c) Depreciation is to be provided as follows:

Plant and machinery	20% of cost
Office equipment	10% of book value
Buildings	2% of cost

(d) Provision should be made for debenture interest due.

(e) Factory insurance was for the year ended 31/2/20-8.

(f) Finished goods are to be transferred from factory at current market value of €720,000.

(g) Provide for corporation tax of €23,000.

You are required to:

- Prepare a manufacturing account for the year ended 31/12/20-7.
- Prepare the trading, profit and loss account for the year ended 31/12/20-7.
- Prepare a balance sheet as at 31/12/20-7.

Q9 The following balances were extracted from the books of Woods Ltd on 31/12/20-5:

	€	€
Share capital		
Authorised: 600,000 ordinary shares at €1 each		
Issued: 336,000 ordinary shares at €1 each		336,000
Computers and office equipment at cost	20,400	
Plant and machinery at cost	264,000	
Factory building at cost	240,000	
Debtors and creditors	36,000	48,000
Hire of special equipment	3,600	
10% Debentures		84,000
Accumulated depreciation on plant and machinery		33,600
Accumulated depreciation on computers and office equipment		7,200
Purchase of raw materials	192,000	
Sales		420,000
Stocks 1/1/20-5		
Raw materials	25,200	
Work in progress	17,400	
Finished goods	27,600	
Factory wages	90,000	
Carriage outwards	5,520	
Returns inwards	1,200	
Sale of scrap materials		5,640
Repairs	5,760	
Directors' fees	14,400	
Supervisor's salary	10,800	
USC		960
Bank		10,680
Profit and loss balance 1/1/20-5		12,600
Showroom expenses	2,160	
Stationery	840	
Factory light and heat	2,880	
Provision for bad debts		1,080
	959,760	**959,760**

You are given the following additional information:

(a) Stocks at 31/12/20-5:

Raw materials	€27,000
Work in progress	€19,200
Finished goods	€29,400
Stationery	€120

(b) Depreciation is to be provided as follows:

Computers	10% of cost
Plant and machinery	10% of cost
Factory buildings	2% of cost

(c) Provision should be made for debenture interest due.

(d) The provision for bad debts is to be adjusted to 5% of debtors.

(e) Finished goods are to be transferred from factory at current market value of €342,000.

(f) Provide for corporation tax of €6,000.

You are required to prepare:

- a manufacturing account for the year ended 31/12/20-5
- the trading, profit and loss account for the year ended 31/12/20-5
- a balance sheet as at 31/12/20-5.

Q10 The following balances were extracted from the books of King Ltd on 31/12/20-2. The company has an authorised share capital of 900,000 ordinary shares at €1 each.

	€	€
Issued share capital		760,000
Plant and machinery (cost €500,000)	440,000	
Buildings (including land €300,000) (cost €800,000)	750,000	
Motor vehicles at cost €100,000	94,000	
Patents	55,000	
Debtors and creditors	45,000	32,000
Stocks 1/1/20-2		
Raw materials	34,000	
Work in progress	56,000	
Finished goods	21,000	
Factory light and heat	34,600	
Factory wages	76,000	
Purchases (raw materials) and sales (finished goods)	490,000	1,200,000
Returns	400	1,200
Sale of scrap materials		3,700
Hire of special equipment	20,000	
Factory insurance	60,000	
Profit and loss balance 1/1/20-2		56,800
12% Debentures issued 1/7/20-2		100,000
Stationery	3,900	
VAT		2,900
Bank		23,000
Provision for bad debts		9,200
Showroom expenses	8,900	
	2,188,800	**2,188,800**

11

You are given the following information:

(a) Closing stock on 31/12/20-2:

Raw materials	€23,500
Finished goods	€34,900
Work in progress	€19,800

(b) Provide for depreciation as follows:

Buildings	2% of cost
Vehicles	20% of cost
Machinery	15% of cost

(c) Factory wages is to be split 90% for factory workers and 10% for supervisor.

(d) Provide for debenture interest due, and provision for bad debts should be adjusted to 8% of debtors.

(e) Provide for corporation tax of €24,000.

(f) Factory insurance is for the year ended 30/4/20-3.

(g) Finished goods are to be transferred from factory at current market value of €800,000.

You are required to prepare:

- a manufacturing account for the year ended 31/12/20-2
- the trading, profit and loss account for the year ended 31/12/20-2
- a balance sheet as at 31/12/20-2.

Exercises – Higher Level

Q1 **XXL Ltd, a manufacturing firm, has an authorised share capital of €1,520,000, divided into 1,040,000 ordinary shares at €1 each and 480,000 6% preference shares at €1 each. The following trial balance was extracted from its books on 31/12/20-5:**

	€	€
Factory buildings (cost €880,000)	809,600	
Plant and machinery (cost €416,000)	288,000	
Profit and loss balance 1/1/20-5		72,800
Bank		15,040
Debtors and creditors	135,200	93,120
Purchases of raw materials	739,040	
Sales		1,314,400
Sale of scrap materials		5,600
Direct factory wages	238,720	
General factory wages (incorporating suspense)	100,000	
Selling and distribution expenses	47,040	

Continued >

11

	€	€
Administration expenses	68,800	
8% Debentures (including €72,000 issued on 1/5/20-5)		240,000
Stocks on hand 1/1/20-5		
Finished goods	103,200	
Raw materials	65,600	
Work in progress	57,600	
Dividends paid	42,400	
Issued share capital		
Ordinary shares		608,000
6% Preference shares		320,000
VAT		26,240
	2,695,200	**2,695,200**

The following information and instructions are to be taken into account:

(a) Stocks on hand at 31/12/20-5:

Finished goods	€131,200
Raw materials	€78,400
Work in progress	€67,200

(b) No record had been made in the books for raw materials costing €17,600 which were in transit on 31/12/20-5. The invoice for these goods had been received.

(c) Included in the figure for sales is €3,200 received from the sale of an old machine on 30/6/20-5. This machine had cost €40,000 on 1/10/20-0. The cheque received had been entered in the bank account. These were the only entries in the books.

(d) It was discovered that goods which cost the company €11,520 to produce were sent to a customer on a sale-or-return basis. These goods had been charged in error to the customer at cost plus 25%.

(e) The suspense figure arises as a result of discount allowed, €960, entered only in the discount account.

(f) During 20-5 XXL Ltd built a new showroom. The work was carried out by the company's own employees. The cost of their labour (€35,200) is included in factory wages. The materials costing €44,800 were taken from stocks. No entry had been made in the books in respect of this showroom.

(g) Depreciation is to be provided for on fixed assets as follows: plant and machinery at 20% of cost per annum from date of purchase to date of sale; buildings at 2% of cost per annum for a full year (land at cost on 1/1/20-5 was €96,000). At the end of 20-5 the company revalued the land and buildings at €1,056,000.

(h) The directors are proposing that provision should be made for debenture interest due and corporation tax of €38,400.

You are required to prepare:

- a manufacturing account for the year ended 31/12/20-5
- the trading, profit and loss account for the year ended 31/12/20-5
- a balance sheet as at 31/12/20-5.

Q2 **Curvage Ltd, a manufacturing firm, has an authorised share capital of €720,000, divided into 495,000 ordinary shares at €1 each and 225,000 8% preference shares at €1 each. The following trial balance was extracted from its books on 31/12/20-4:**

	€	€
Factory buildings (cost €405,000)	364,500	
Plant and machinery (cost €234,000)	140,400	
Discount (net)		3,600
Profit and loss account balance 1/1/20-4		74,070
Stocks on hand 31/12/20-4		
Finished goods	76,950	
Raw materials	43,200	
Work in progress	21,735	
Sales		841,500
General factory overheads	45,270	
Patents	63,000	
Purchase of raw materials	405,252	
Sale of scrap materials		4,950
Hire of special equipment	10,800	
Debtors and creditors	84,960	51,930
Dividends paid	15,300	
Bank		10,305
Direct factory wages	178,398	
8% Debentures (including €27,000 issued on 1/4/20-4)		90,000
VAT		11,457
Issued share capital		
Ordinary shares		270,000
Preference shares		180,000
Carriage on raw materials	4,959	
Selling expenses	61,578	
Administration expenses (including suspense)	21,510	
	1,537,812	**1,537,812**

The following information and instructions are to be taken into account:

(a) **Stocks on hand at 31/12/20-4:**

Finished goods	**€82,800**
Raw materials	**€45,900**
Work in progress	**€25,695**

The figure for finished goods includes items which cost €6,300 to produce but now have a sales value of €4,050.

(b) **Included in the figure for sale of scrap materials is, €1,620, received from the sale of an old machine on 30/6/20-4. This machine had cost €19,800 on 1/4/20-0. The cheque had been entered in the bank account. This was the only entry made in the books.**

(c) **The suspense figure arises as a result of discount allowed, €900, entered only in the debtor's account.**

(d) **It was discovered that finished goods which cost €7,200 to produce were invoiced to a customer on a sale-or-return basis. These goods had been entered in the books as a credit sale at cost plus 20%.**

(e) **During 20-4 Curvage Ltd built an extension to the factory. The work was carried out by the company's own employees. The cost of their labour (€36,000) was included in factory**

11

wages. The cost of materials used (€16,200) is included in purchases. No entry was made in the books in respect of this extension.

(f) Depreciation is provided on fixed assets as follows: plant and machinery, 20% of cost per annum from date of purchase to date of sale; factory buildings, 2% of cost at 31/12/20-4.

(g) The directors are proposing that:

- Provision should be made for debenture interest.
- Corporation tax of €9,000 be provided for.

(h) Goods should be transferred from factory at current market value of €720,000.

You are required to prepare:

- a manufacturing account for the year ended 31/12/20-4
- the trading, profit and loss account for the year ended 31/12/20-4
- a balance sheet as at 31/12/20-4.

Q3 Kerry Ltd, a manufacturing firm, has an authorised share capital of €980,000, divided into 560,000 ordinary shares at €1 each and 420,000 4% preference shares at €1 each. The following trial balance was extracted from its books on 31/12/20-9:

	€	€
Factory buildings (cost €770,000)	616,000	
Plant and machinery (cost €336,000)	154,000	
Discount (net)		2,800
Profit and loss balance 1/1/20-9		50,960
Stocks on hand 1/1/20-9		
Finished goods	112,000	
Raw materials	69,300	
Work in progress	28,700	
Sales		1,540,000
Patents	140,000	
Carriage on raw materials	8,470	
Hire of special equipment	16,800	
Purchase of raw materials	616,700	
Dividends paid	42,000	
Sale of scrap material		8,400
Debtors and creditors	76,440	63,980
Bank		12,040
Direct factory wages	282,030	
Selling expenses (including suspense)	151,200	
9% Debentures (including €42,000 issued 1/4/20-9)		112,000
Issued share capital		
Ordinary shares		350,000
4% Preference shares		280,000
General factory overheads	70,560	
VAT	5,880	
Debenture interest paid for the first 3 months	1,400	
Administration expenses	28,700	
	2,420,180	**2,420,180**

11

The following information and instructions are to be taken into account:

(a) Stocks on hand at 31/12/20-9:

Finished goods	€119,000
Raw materials	€74,200
Work in progress	€35,700

The figure for finished goods includes items which cost €8,400 to produce but now have a sales value of €5,600.

(b) Patents are being written off over a period of ten years, which commenced in 20-7. This is to be included in factory cost.

(c) Included in the figure for sales is €5,600 received from the sale of an old machine. This machine had cost €33,600 on 1/10/20-4 and was sold on 30/6/20-9. The cheque had been entered in the bank account. This was the only entry in the books.

(d) The suspense figure arises as a result of discount received of €420 entered only in the creditor's account and of the posting of an incorrect figure for the debenture interest paid to the interest account. The correct interest was entered in the bank account.

(e) A bad debt of €630 should be written off and a provision for bad debts should be provided for at 5% of remaining debtors.

(f) It was discovered that goods which cost the firm €7,560 to produce were sent to a customer on a sale-or-return basis. In error these goods were charged to the customer at cost plus 25%.

(g) An invoice has been received for raw materials costing €21,000 which were in transit on 31/12/20-9. No record had been made in the books.

(h) Depreciation is provided for on fixed assets as follows: factory buildings at 2% of cost; plant and machinery at 20% of cost per annum from date of purchase to date of sale. At the end of 20-9 the company revalued the buildings at €910,000.

(i) The directors are proposing that:

- Provision should be made for debenture interest due.
- Corporation tax of €33,600 should be provided for.

You are required to prepare:

- a manufacturing account for the year ended 31/12/20-9
- the trading, profit and loss account for the year ended 31/12/20-9
- a balance sheet as at 31/12/20-9.

11

Q4 McGee Ltd, a manufacturing firm, has an authorised share capital of €720,000, divided into 480,000 ordinary shares at €1 each and 240,000 8% preference shares at €1 each. The following trial balance was extracted from its books on 31/12/20-6:

	€	€
Buildings (cost €336,000)	273,600	
Plant and machinery (cost €128,000)	89,600	
Profit and loss balance 1/1/20-6		44,400
Debtors and creditors	74,000	51,360
Sales		561,200
Sale of scrap materials		5,200
Purchases of raw materials	308,720	
Direct factory wages	108,160	

Continued >

	€	€
General factory expenses (incorporating suspense)	30,800	
Selling and distribution expenses	9,120	
Administration expenses	40,000	
9% Debentures (including €24,000 issued on 1/5/20-6)		64,000
Stock on hand 1/1/20-6		
Finished goods	61,600	
Raw materials	35,200	
Work in progress	16,800	
Dividends paid	20,800	
Issued share capital		
Ordinary shares		240,000
Preference shares		80,000
Bank		7,520
VAT		14,720
	1,068,400	**1,068,400**

The following information and instructions should be taken into account:

(a) Stock on hand at 31/12/20-6:

Finished goods	€63,200
Raw materials	€37,600
Work in progress	€19,200

(b) Included in the figure for sale of scrap materials is €400 received from the sale of obsolete machinery. This machinery had cost €1,600 on 1/4-20-2. The cheque had been entered in the bank account. These were the only entries made in the books.

(c) During 20-6, McGee Ltd built an extension to the warehouse. The work was carried out by the company's own employees. The cost of their labour (€12,800) is included in factory wages. The materials costing €19,200 were taken from stocks. No entry had been made in the books in respect of this extension.

(d) It was discovered that goods which cost the firm €4,000 to produce were sent to a customer on a sale-or-return basis. These goods were treated in the books as a credit sale at cost plus 20%.

(e) The suspense figure arises as a result of discount allowed of €320 entered only in the discount account.

(f) A full year's depreciation on fixed assets is to be provided for as follows:

Plant and machinery	20% of cost (the obsolete machine was sold on 1/1/20-6)
Buildings	2% of cost (cost of land €48,000)

(g) At the end of 20-6 the company revalued land and buildings at €440,000.

(h) The directors are proposing that:

- Provision should be made for debenture interest due.
- Provision should be made for corporation tax of €8,000.

You are required to prepare:

- a manufacturing account for the year ended 31/12/20-6
- the trading, profit and loss account for the year ended 31/12/20-6
- a balance sheet as at 31/12/20-6.

11

Q5 Silver Rider Ltd, a manufacturing firm, has an authorised share capital of €1,140,000, divided into 780,000 ordinary shares at €1 each and 360,000 8% preference shares at €1 each. The following trial balance was extracted from its books on 31/12/20-6:

	€	€
Buildings (cost €528,000)	494,400	
Plant and machinery (cost €192,000)	89,600	
Patent (cost €96,000)	57,600	
Profit and loss balance 1/1/20-6		66,600
Debtors and creditors	97,800	87,840
Sales		919,800
Sale of scrap materials		11,400
Purchases of raw materials	511,080	
Direct factory wages	169,440	
General factory expenses (incorporating suspense)	43,800	
Selling and distribution expenses	26,880	
Administration expenses	52,800	
Bank		82,080
9% Debentures (including €36,000 issued on 1/5/20-6)		96,000
Stock on hand 1/1/20-6		
Finished goods	82,800	
Raw materials	45,600	
Work in progress	27,600	
Cash	20,800	
Dividends paid	33,600	
Issued share capital		
Ordinary shares		360,000
Preference shares		120,000
VAT		10,080
	1,753,800	**1,753,800**

The following information and instructions should be taken into account:

(a) Stock on hand at 31/12/20-6:

Finished goods	€94,800
Raw materials	€56,400
Work in progress	€28,800

(b) Included in the figure for sale of scrap materials is €1,200 received on 1/1/20-6 from the sale of obsolete machinery. This machinery had cost €3,000 on 1/1/20-2. The cheque had been entered in the bank account. These were the only entries made in the books.

(c) During 20-6, Silver Rider Ltd built an extension to the warehouse. The work was carried out by the company's own employees. The cost of their labour (€31,200) is included in factory wages. The materials costing €40,800 were taken from stocks. No entry had been made in the books in respect of this extension.

(d) It was discovered that goods which cost the firm €6,000 to produce were sent to a customer on a sale-or-return basis. These goods were treated in the books as a credit sale at cost plus 20%.

(e) The suspense figure arises as a result of discount allowed of €240 entered only in the discount account.

(f) No record had been made in the books for raw materials costing €14,400 which were in transit on 31/12/20-6. The invoice for these goods had been received.

(g) A full year's depreciation on fixed assets is to be provided for as follows:

Plant and machinery	20% of cost
Buildings	2% of cost per annum based on year-end value.

11

(h) At the end of 20-6 the company revalued land and buildings at €720,000. Of this revaluation, land was valued at €120,000.

(i) The patent is being written off over ten years.

(j) The directors are proposing that:

- Provision should be made for debenture interest due.
- Provision should be made for corporation tax of €21,600.

You are required to prepare:

- a manufacturing account for the year ended 31/12/20-6
- the trading, profit and loss account for the year ended 31/12/20-6
- a balance sheet as at 31/12/20-6.

Q6 Sodor Ltd, a manufacturing firm, has an authorised capital of €1,200,000, divided into 900,000 ordinary shares at €1 each and 300,000 8% preference shares at €1 each. The following trial balance was extracted from its books on 31/12/20-4:

	€	€
Factory buildings (cost €750,000)	575,000	
Plant and machinery (cost €1,200,000)	1,100,000	
Discount (net)		5,900
Profit and loss balance 1/1/20-4		45,600
Factory overheads	82,300	
Administration expenses	34,500	
Wages and salaries (incorporating suspense)	98,900	
VAT		6,100
Carriage on raw materials	4,700	
Finished goods purchases for resale	45,900	
Stocks 1/1/20-4		
Raw materials	56,000	
Finished goods	12,800	
Work in progress	22,300	
Purchase of raw materials	176,000	
Sales		908,000
Bank		78,900
10% Debentures (including 12% debenture issued 1/10/20-4 at €60,000)		150,000
Debtors and creditors	86,000	85,500
Debenture interest paid for first 4 months	3,600	
Issued capital		
Ordinary shares		880,000
Preference shares		250,000
Delivery vans (cost €123,000)	100,000	
Light and heat	34,000	
Insurance	38,000	
Sale of scrap materials		28,100
Rent		31,900
	2,470,000	**2,470,000**

11

The following information and instructions are to be taken into account:

(a) Stocks on hand at 31/12/20-4:

Finished goods	€54,000
Raw materials	€32,900
Work in progress	€15,400

The figure for finished goods includes items damaged by fire which had cost €3,900 to produce. These were completed destroyed and the insurance company had agree to pay compensation to the value of their cost price. There was no entry in the books in respect of this damage.

(b) During the year Sodor Ltd purchased an adjoining business premises for €225,000. This includes VAT at 12.5%. The net amount to the vendor was entered in the buildings account with no entry in the VAT account.

(c) Included in the figure for sale of scrap materials is €1,200 received from the sale of an old machine. This machine had cost €6,500 on 1/1/20-2. The amount received was entered in the bank account. This was the only entry made in the books. The machine was sold on 1/7/20-4.

(d) During the year Sodor Ltd built an extension to the new premises at a cost of €120,000. The work was carried out by the company's own employees. The cost of their labour (€65,000) is included in wages and salaries and the cost of materials was taken from stocks. No entry had been made in the books in respect of this transaction.

(e) Depreciation is to be provided for as follows on fixed assets:

Buildings	2% of cost at 31/12/20-4
	(Note: 15% of the building is for office administration)
Plant and machinery	20% of cost from date of purchase to date of sale
Delivery vans	25% of book value.

(f) The suspense figure arises as a result of an incorrect figure for debenture interest.

(g) Goods which cost €8,000 to produce and which are sold with a mark-up of 25% of cost were sent to a customer on a sale-or-return basis. These goods were returned on 1/1/20-5.

(h) No entry had been made in the books in respect of raw materials purchased for €22,000, for which the invoice was received but which were in transit on 31/12/20-4.

(i) A customer whose debt amounting to €2,400 was previously written off as bad has paid 70c in the euro and given a guarantee to pay the remainder of the debt by end of the January 20-5. Also on the same date, goods were sold to this debtor for €4,500, which was cost plus 12.5%. No entry had been made in the books in respect of this recovered debt or the subsequent sale of goods on credit.

(j) The directors are proposing that:

- Provision should be made for debenture interest due.
- Corporation tax of €12,000 should be provided for.

11

You are required to prepare:

- manufacturing and trading, profit and loss accounts for the year ended 31/12/20-4
- a balance sheet as at 31/12/20-4.

Q7 **Bumblebee Ltd, a manufacturing company, has an authorised capital of €1,500,000, divided into 1,200,000 ordinary shares at €1 each and 600,000 5% preference shares at 50c each. The following trial balance was extracted from the its books on 31/12/20-6:**

	€	€
Factory buildings (cost €950,000)	825,000	
Plant and machinery (cost €450,000)	380,000	
Delivery vans (cost)	166,000	
Accumulated depreciation on vans		61,088
Profit and loss balance 1/1/20-6		34,500
Stocks 1/1/20-6		
Raw materials	56,000	
Finished goods	34,000	
Work in progress	12,500	
Sales		1,189,000
Wages and salaries	198,500	
Patents	246,000	
Hire of special machines	34,500	
Carriage on raw materials	12,500	
Debtors and creditors	56,000	67,000
Selling expenses	134,588	
Administration expenses	156,800	
Purchase of raw materials	246,000	
Sale of scrap materials		23,900
Bank		34,900
10% Debentures (including 15% debentures issued at par on 1/4/20-6 €90,000)		175,000
Insurance on buildings	34,500	
Diesel, oil and repairs on delivery vans	78,500	
Dividends paid	14,000	
Issued share capital		
Ordinary shares		800,000
Preference shares		300,000
	2,685,388	**2,685,388**

The following information and instructions are to be taken into account:

(a) Stocks on hand at 31/12/20-6:

Finished goods	€46,700
Raw materials	€42,000
Work in progress	€30,500

11

The figure for finished goods includes items which cost €5,000 to produce but now have a sales value of €2,400.

(b) During the year a delivery van which cost €32,000 two years previously was sold for €21,000 and a new van costing €45,000 purchased. It is the company's policy to depreciate its vans a full year in the year of acquisition and nil in the year of disposal. All vans have an estimated useful economic life of five years, at which time they will have a scrap value of 8% of original cost. No entry was made in the books in respect of this transaction.

(c) Included in the cost of van repairs is an alteration to the engine of a vehicle purchased two years earlier costing €2,100. This improves the fuel consumption of this vehicle.

(d) Finished goods which cost the company €16,000 to produce were sent to a customer on a sale-or-return basis. These goods had been treated in the books as a credit sale at cost plus 25%.

(e) During the year the company built an extension to the factory. The work was carried out by the company's own employees. The cost of their labour (€35,000) was included in factory wages. The cost of the materials used (€15,000) was taken from stocks. No entry was made in the books in respect of this extension.

(f) Provide for depreciation on buildings at 2% of cost on 31/12/20-6. The buildings are divided 90% factory and 10% office.

(g) Provide for depreciation on machinery at 20% of cost per annum from date of purchase to date of sale.

(h) The directors are proposing that:

- Debenture interest due be provided for.
- Corporation tax of €22,000 be provided for.

(i) Wages and salaries are divided 60% direct, 20% supervisor, 10% sales staff and 10% administration.

You are required to prepare:

- manufacturing and trading, profit and loss accounts for the year ended 31/12/20-6
- a balance sheet as at 31/12/20-6.

At the beginning of year there were 1,200 units of goods in production, a further 6,900 units were started and at the end of the year there were 1,160 units in production. A further 60 units were destroyed during the year. Calculate the unit cost of each good produced.

Exam Tips

- Learn the layout of the manufacturing account.
- Revise and be able to prepare adjustments covered in Chapter 6 and Chapter 9.
- Practise as many questions as possible.

12 Departmental Accounts

Objectives

On completion students should be able to:

- Explain what a departmental final account is;
- Explain the uses of departmental accounts and their role in making management decisions;
- Allocate and apportion expenses and gains among the individual departments;
- Prepare a departmental trading, profit and loss account;
- Prepare a balance sheet.

Introduction

Departmental accounts are prepared by companies whose activities are spread over a number of different areas of business, for example where a shop has a clothing section and a grocery section. They are prepared to provide management with information that can be used to make effective decisions and improve efficiency.

Management can compare the different departments and use this information to make decisions based on:

- the profit and loss of each department
- the profit and loss of each department in relation to the floor space it occupies
- the complementary (balancing) importance of each department.

This will enable management to make decisions such as:

- whether to expand or reduce a department's allocation of floor space
- whether to review salaries in each department, including bonus payments for reaching targets
- whether to close or sublet a department.

The information received from departmental accounts alone is unlikely to provide a full picture of the business.

The accounts

When the departmental day books and ledger accounts have been prepared and checked, departmental final accounts can be prepared. These consist of:

- a separate trading, profit and loss account for each department
- a balance sheet for the entire firm.

The balance sheet for departmental accounts is in the same format as those for sole trader and company final accounts.

Allocation and apportionment of expenses and gains

Management decides how the relevant expenses and gains should be allocated and apportioned (divided up) among the various departments. As a general rule, expenses are allocated and apportioned as follows:

1. Expenses that can be identified specifically with one department are allocated to that department – for example, salaries of personnel working in each department.
2. Expenses that are paid centrally but are capable of precise allocation, for example electricity where each department would have its own meter, are allocated according to use.
3. Expenses that are paid centrally but are not capable of precise allocation are apportioned in one of the following ways:
    - in proportion to sales of each department
    - in proportion to the floor area of each department
    - in proportion to the number of employees in each department
    - equally when no other suitable basis can be used.

NOTE

Profits and gains are allocated and apportioned in the same way as expenses.

Some expenses can be confined to one department, such as:

- tailoring expenses – clothing (drapery) department
- bad debts and provision for bad debts – departments that sell on credit
- repairs to sports equipment – sports department.

There can be a transfer of goods or expenses from one department to another. This is known as an **interdepartmental transfer**. It is treated as follows:

- Increase the cost in the receiving department.
- Reduce the cost in the transferring (giving) department.

Example

The drapery department transferred goods to the sports department:

- Increase purchases in the sports department
- Decrease purchases in the drapery department.

Examples of the bases according to which expenses are normally apportioned

Expense	Base	Expense	Base
Advertising	Sales	Canteen subsidy	No. of employees
Audit fees	Sales	Depreciation, vans	Sales
Depreciation, buildings	Floor space	Rent	Floor space
Showroom expenses	Sales	Stationery	Sales
General expenses	Sales	Insurance	Floor space
Rates	Floor space	Cleaning	Floor space
Provision for bad debts	Sales	Light and heat	Floor space

Sample Ordinary Level question

The retail business of April Corr is divided into two departments: food and clothing. The following trial balance was extracted from its books on 31/12/20-1:

	€	€
Buildings	200,000	
Shop equipment	80,000	
Delivery vans	60,000	
Debtors and creditors	20,000	40,000
Cash at bank	10,000	
Salaries, sales staff	96,000	
Rates	4,000	
Distribution expenses	2,800	
Bad debts	1,400	
Tailoring expenses	1,200	
Advertising	2,400	
Light and heat	5,000	
Food department		
Stock 1/1/20-1	15,000	
Purchases and sales	120,000	140,000
Carriage inwards	3,000	
Clothing department		
Stock 1/1/20-1	30,000	
Purchases and sales	240,000	420,000
Custom duties	6,000	
Capital		296,800
	896,800	**896,800**

You are given the following additional information:

(a) Stocks on 31/12/20-1 were: food, €20,000; clothing, €40,000.

(b) The floor space is divided food 20% and clothing 80%.

(c) During the year there was a transfer of purchases from the food department to the clothing department valued at €1,000.

(d) Expenses should be allocated between the departments on the basis of floor space or sales, whichever is more appropriate.

You are required to prepare:

- a departmental trading, profit and loss account for the year ended 31/12/20-1
- a balance sheet as at 31/12/20-1.

What decisions should be made by April Corr from the prepared final accounts?

12

Solution

As part of the workings, make out a table of the expenses to be allocated and state clearly the basis of apportionment used.

Always make adjustments (e.g. prepayments) before allocating expenses.

Expense	Amount	Basis	Food	Clothing
Sales staff salaries	96,000	Sales (1:3)	24,000	72,000
Rates	4,000	Floor space (1:4)	800	3,200
Distribution expenses	2,800	Sales (1:3)	700	2,100
Bad debts	1,400	Sales (1:3)	350	1,050
Advertising	2,400	Sales (1:3)	600	1,800
Light and heat	5,000	Floor space (1:4)	1,000	4,000

Departmental Trading, Profit and Loss Account of April Corr for the year ended 31/12/20-1

	Total	Food	Clothing	Total	Food	Clothing
Sales				560,000	140,000	420,000
***Less* Cost of sales**						
Opening stock	45,000	15,000	30,000			
Purchases	360,000	120,000	240,000			
Carriage inwards	3,000	3,000				
Custom duties	6,000		6,000			
	414,000	138,000	276,000			
Transfer goods		(1,000)	1,000			
Less Closing stock	(60,000)	(20,000)	(40,000)			
Cost of goods sold				(354,000)	(117,000)	(237,000)
Gross profit				206,000	23,000	183,000
***Less* Expenses**						
Administration						
Light and heat	5,000	1,000	4,000			
Rates	4,000	800	3,200			
Selling and distribution						
Salaries	96,000	24,000	72,000			
Distribution	2,800	700	2,100			
Bad debts	1,400	350	1,050			
Advertising	2,400	600	1,800			
Tailoring	1,200	———	1,200			
Total expenses				(112,800)	(27,450)	(85,350)
Net profit				**93,200**	**(4,450)**	**97,650**

12

Balance Sheet of April Corr as at 31/12/20-1

	Cost (€)	Aggregate Depreciation (€)	Net Book Value (€)	Total (€)
Fixed assets				
Buildings	200,000	——	200,000	
Shop equipment	80,000	——	80,000	
Delivery vans	60,000	——	60,000	
	340,000		340,000	340,000
Current assets				
Stocks			60,000	
Debtors			20,000	
Cash			10,000	
			90,000	
***Less* Creditors: amounts falling due within 1 year**				
Trade creditors			(40,000)	
Net current assets				50,000
Total net assets				**390,000**
Financed by				
Capital				
Balance at 1/1/20-1			296,800	
Profit and loss			93,200	390,000
Capital employed				**390,000**

What decisions should be made by April Corr from the above accounts?

It is obvious that the food department is making a loss on the year's trading. The loss on that department is 3.18% of sales compared to 23.25% profit for the clothing department.

Should the food department be closed down?

Before making such a decision, the figures from the previous years for this department should be examined in order to analyse the trend over the period. An evaluation will have to be made on whether the food department draws customers to the clothing department and what the likely effects would be on the clothing department if the food department were to close down.

Before deciding to close down, it will be necessary to calculate:

- the costs of making staff redundant and its effect on other staff
- the effects on cash flow and borrowing requirements brought by the loss of cash takings of €140,000 per annum
- what replacement income can be obtained from the area used by the food department – for example, should the clothing department be expanded or an alternative department be opened in place of the food department, such as sports equipment?

Sample Higher Level question

The firm Boyle Ltd is divided into two departments, grocery and hardware. The following balances were extracted from its books on 31/12/20-5:

	€	€
Share capital		
Authorised share capital: 600,000 ordinary shares @€1 each		
Issued share capital: 350,000 ordinary shares @ €1 each		350,000
Buildings at cost	500,000	
Delivery vans at cost	100,000	
Shop equipment at cost	25,000	
Accumulated depreciation on land and buildings		60,000
Accumulated depreciation in delivery vans		30,000
Accumulated depreciation on shop equipment		8,000
Debtors and creditors	64,000	37,500
10% Debentures		60,000
Grocery department		
Stocks 1/1/20-5	30,000	
Purchases and sales	415,000	600,000
Hardware department		
Stocks 1/1/20-5	26,000	
Purchases and sales	280,000	400,000
Profit and loss balance 1/1/20-5	13,000	
Salaries and general expenses	69,600	
Directors' fees	20,000	
Advertising	12,000	
VAT		3,600
USC		1,800
Light and heat	10,400	
Provision for bad debts		2,100
Bank		12,000
	1,565,000	**1,565,000**

You are given the following additional information:

(a) Stocks at 31/12/20-5:

Grocery €37,000
Hardware €28,000

(b) Hardware with a retail price of €7,200, which is cost plus 20%, was purchased in late December. The invoice was received for these goods and the goods were in transit on the date of stock valuation. No entry had been made in the books in respect of this transaction.

12

(c) During the year new shop equipment was installed. The materials, which cost €3,000, were taken from the stock in the hardware department, and the labour (€1,000) was provided by all the employees. No record had been made in the books in respect of this transaction.

(d) Provide for depreciation as follows:

Delivery vans	20% of cost
Shop equipment	10% of book value
Buildings	2% of cost

(e) Provision should be made for debenture interest due and taxation, €40,000.

(f) The floor space of the firm is divided: grocery, 80%; hardware, 20%.

(g) Expenses applicable to both departments should be divided on the basis of sales or floor space where appropriate.

You are required to prepare:

- a trading, profit and loss account for the year ended 31/12/20-5
- a balance sheet as at 31/12/20-5.

Solution

Trading, Profit and Loss Account of Boyle Ltd for the year ended 31/12/20-5

	Total	Grocery	Hardware	Total	Grocery	Hardware
Sales (W1)				1,000,000	600,000	400,000
***Less* Cost of Sales**						
Opening stock	56,000	30,000	26,000			
Purchases (W2)	698,000	415,000	283,000			
	754,000	445,000	309,000			
Less Closing stock (W3)	(71,000)	(37,000)	(34,000)			
Cost of sales				683,000	408,000	275,000
Gross profit				317,000	192,000	125,000
***Less* Expenses**						
Administration						
Salaries (W4)	68,600	41,160	27,440			
Directors' fees (W4)	20,000	12,000	8,000			
Depreciation, shop equipment (W4)	2,100	1,680	420			
Depreciation, buildings (W4)	10,000	8,000	2,000			
Light and heat (W4)	10,400	8,320	2,080			
Selling and distribution						
Advertising (W4)	12,000	7,200	4,800			
Depreciation vans (W4)	20,000	12,000	8,000			
Total expenses				(143,100)	(90,360)	(52,740)
Operating profit				173,900	101,640	72,260
Less Debenture interest (W4)				(6,000)	(4,800)	(1,200)
Profit before taxation				167,900	96,840	71,060
Less Taxation				(40,000)		
Retained profit for year				127,900		
Profit and loss 1/1/20-5				(13,000)		
Profit and loss 31/12/20-5				**114,500**		

12

Balance Sheet of Boyle Ltd for the year ended 31/12/20-5

	Cost (€)	Agg. Dpr. (€)	Net Book Value (€)	Total (€)
Tangible fixed assets				
Buildings	500,000	70,000	430,000	
Delivery vans	100,000	50,000	50,000	
Shop equipment	29,000	10,100	18,900	
	629,000	130,100	498,900	498,900
Current assets				
Stock grocery	37,000			
Stock hardware (W3)	34,000	71,000		
Debtors	64,000			
Less Provision for bad debts	(2,100)	61,900	132,900	
***Less* Creditors: amounts falling due within 1 year**				
Trade creditors (W1)		43,500		
USC		1,800		
VAT		3,600		
Taxation		40,000		
Debenture interest		6,000		
Bank		12,000	(106,900)	
Net current assets				26,000
Total net assets				**524,900**
Financed by				
Creditors: amounts falling due after more than 1 year				
10% Debentures				60,000
Capital and reserves		**Authorised**	**Issued**	
Ordinary share capital		600,000	350,000	
Add Profit and loss balance 31/12/20-5			114,500	464,900
				524,900

12

Workings

W1 Creditors

As given	37,500
Add Goods in transit	6,000
	43,500

W3 Closing stock hardware

As given	28,000
Add Goods in transit	6,000
	34,000

W2 Purchases

Hardware	280,000
Less Shop equipment materials	(3,000)
Add Goods in transit	6,000
	283,000

W4 Allocation of expenses

Expense	Basis	Amount	Grocery	Hardware
Salaries (N1)	Sales	68,600	41,160	27,440
Directors' fees	Sales	20,000	12,000	8,000
Dpr, equipment (N2)	Floor space	2,100	1,680	420
Dpr, buildings (N3)	Floor space	10,000	8,000	2,000
Advertising	Sales	12,000	7,200	4,800
Dpr, vans (N4)	Sales	20,000	12,000	8,000
Debenture interest (N5)	Floor space	6,000	4,800	1,200
Light & heat	Floor space	10,400	8,320	2,080

Notes to W4

Floor space:

Hardware	20%
Grocery	80%

Sales:

Hardware	600,000	
Grocery	400,000	3:2 ratio

N1	Salaries as given in TB	€69,600 *Less* Labour for equipment 1,000 =	€68,600
N2	Depreciation of equipment	€25,000 + 4,000 - 8,000 = 21,000 x 10% =	€2,100
N3	Depreciation of buildings	€500,000 x 2% =	€10,000
N4	Depreciation of vans	€100,000 x 20% =	€20,000
N5	Debenture interest	€60,000 x 10% =	€60,000

12

Exercises – Ordinary Level

Q1 **Frank McDonald runs a retail outlet which is divided into two departments, Children's Clothes and School Uniforms. From the following information prepare a departmental trading, profit and loss account for the year ended 31/12/20-1.**

		€
Stock 1/1/20-1	Children's Clothes	5,400
	School Uniforms	4,500
Sales	Children's Clothes	87,800
	School Uniforms	45,600
Purchases	Children's Clothes	34,600
	School Uniforms	23,700
Carriage inwards	Children's Clothes	1,400
	School Uniforms	2,300
Stocks 1/1/20-1	Children's Clothes	3,600
	School Uniforms	1,900

Q2 **Margaret Crowe divides her business into two departments, Clothing and Footwear. The following information is provided on 31/12/20-2. Prepare her departmental trading, profit and loss account for the year ended 31/12/20-2.**

	€	€
Clothing		
Purchases and sales	360,000	500,000
Import duty	23,000	
Stocks 1/1/20-2	54,600	
Stocks 31/12/20-2	57,800	
Footwear		
Purchases and sales	340,000	500,000
Import duty	27,700	
Stock 1/1/20-2	54,700	
Stock 31/12/20-2	48,200	
Salaries		
Clothing	125,000	
Footwear	96,700	
Discount allowed	12,000	
Cleaning expenses	21,000	
Advertising	28,000	
Rent and rates	50,000	
Telephone and broadband	21,800	
Insurance	16,000	

Expenses are to be apportioned as follows: rent, cleaning and insurance on the basis of floor space. All other expenses are to be apportioned on the basis of sales. The floor space is divided as follows: Clothing, 60%; Footwear, 40%.

Q3 **Billy Buckley runs a retail business which is divided into two departments, Menswear and Ladieswear. The following figures were extracted from its books on 31/12/20-3:**

	€
Salaries and general expenses	125,700
Repairs to buildings	7,200
Insurance	2,880
Advertising	2,040
Bad debts	350
Fees charged for alterations to men's suits	760 Cr.
Stationery	3,040
Provision for bad debts 1/1/20-3	2,400
Menswear Department	
Stock 1/1/20-3	29,600
Purchases	265,600
Sales	384,000
Carriage inwards	2,560
Ladieswear Department	
Stock 1/1/20-3	32,160
Purchases	102,400
Sales	256,000
Carriage inwards	2,240

You are given the following additional information:

(a) **Stocks at 31/12/20-3: Menswear €23,000**
Ladieswear €26,700.

(b) **Depreciation is to be provided as follows: Delivery vans €13,000**
Buildings €4,000.

(c) **Provide for debenture interest, €3,500.**

(d) **Advertising prepaid on 31/12/20-4 was €140.**

(e) **Provision for bad debts should be adjusted to €2,900.**

(f) **Stock of stationery on 31/12/20-4 was €340.**

(g) **The floor space is divided as follows: Menswear 75%**
Ladieswear €25%.

(h) **Expenses applicable to both departments should be divided on the basis of sales or floor space where appropriate.**

You are required to:

- **Prepare the trading, profit and loss account for each department, as well as for the entire firm for the year ended 31/12/20-3.**

12

Q4 The firm Pilkington Ltd is divided into two departments, Fashion and Sportswear. The following balances were extracted from its books on 31/12/20-0:

	€	€
Share capital		
Authorised: 770,000 ordinary shares at €1 each		
Issued: 649,000 ordinary shares at €1 each		649,000
Buildings (cost €825,000)	704,000	
Shop fittings (cost €220,000)	176,000	
6% Debentures (issued on 1/1/20-0)		154,000
Debtors and creditors	96,800	69,300
Fashion Department		
Stock 1/1/20-0	58,300	
Purchases and sales	319,000	660,000
Returns inwards	3,740	
Sportswear Department		
Stock 1/1/20-0	50,600	
Purchases and sales	173,800	330,000
Carriage inwards	5,500	
Insurance	35,200	
Salaries and general expenses	132,000	
Cleaning expenses	77,000	
Advertising	41,800	
VAT		11,990
Bank		14,960
USC		10,780
Directors' fees	33,000	
Profit and loss balance 1/1/20-0		6,710
	1,906,740	**1,906,740**

You are given the following additional information:

(a) Stocks at 31/12/20-0 were: Fashion €69,300
Sportswear €42,900.

(b) Depreciation is to be provided as follows: Buildings 2% of cost
Shop fittings 12.5% of book value.

(c) The floor space of the firm is divided as follows: Fashion 75%
Sportswear 25%.

(d) Provision should be made for debenture interest due on 31/12/20-0.

(e) Included in advertising is a cheque for an advertising campaign for year to 31/3/20-1. The cheque amounted to €8,800.

(f) Expenses applicable to both departments should be divided on the basis of sales or floor space where appropriate.

You are required to prepare:

- **a departmental trading, profit and loss account for the year ended 31/12/20-0**
- **a balance sheet as at 31/12/20-0.**

12

Q5 **The firm Tucker Ltd is divided into two departments, Sportswear and Footwear. The following balances were extracted from its books on 31/12/20-5:**

	€	€
Share capital		
Authorised: 720,000 ordinary shares at €1 each		
Issued: 540,000 ordinary shares at €1 each		540,000
Delivery vans at cost	162,000	
Buildings at cost	900,000	
Accumulated depreciation on delivery vans		28,800
Accumulated depreciation on buildings		63,000
10% Debentures		108,000
Debtors and creditors	194,400	263,160
Sportswear Department		
Stocks 1/1/20-5	113,400	
Purchases and sales	576,000	972,000
Carriage inwards	4,500	
Footwear Department		
Stocks 1/1/20-5	68,400	
Purchases and sales	252,000	648,000
Returns inwards	1,800	
Insurance	61,200	
Salaries and general expenses	144,900	
Directors' fees	90,000	
Light and heat	115,200	
Profit and loss balance 1/1/20-5		32,400
VAT		14,760
Cash and bank	2,520	10,080
PAYE and USC		6,120
	2,686,320	**2,686,320**

You are given the following additional information:

(a) **Stocks at 31/12/20-5: Sportswear €81,000**
Footwear €57,600.

(b) **Depreciation is to be provided as follows: Buildings 3% of cost**
Delivery vans 20% of cost.

(c) **Provision should be made for debenture interest due.**

(d) **Expenses applicable to both departments should be divided on the basis of sales or floor space where appropriate.**

(e) **The floor space is divided as follows: Sportswear 75%**
Footwear 25%.

(f) **Included in insurance is a cheque for €14,400 for buildings for the year to 31/12/20-6.**

You are required to prepare:

- **a departmental trading, profit and loss account for the year ended 31/12/20-5**
- **a balance sheet as at 31/12/20-5.**

12

Q6 **The firm Duffin Ltd is divided into two departments, Grocery and Hardware. The following trial balance was extracted from its books on 31/12/20-1:**

	€	€
Grocery Department		
Opening stock	33,600	
Purchases and sales	312,000	432,000
Carriage inwards	1,680	
Hardware Department		
Opening stock	24,000	
Purchases and sales	216,000	288,000
Returns outwards		1,920
Dividends paid	19,200	
Equipment (cost €57,600)	43,200	
Delivery vans (cost €192,000)	144,000	
Discount (net)		12,960
Profit and loss balance 1/1/20-1		24,000
Goodwill	144,000	
Provision for bad debts		3,120
11% Debentures (issued 1/10/20-1)		48,000
Commission		24,000
Debtors and creditors	48,000	43,200
Salaries and general expenses	72,000	
Bad debts	2,400	
Light and heat	5,760	
Stationery	4,320	
Bank		3,360
Advertising	21,600	
VAT		10,320
PAYE and USC		8,880
Share capital		
Authorised: 480,000 shares @ €1 each		
Issued: 192,000 shares @ €1 each		192,000
	1,091,760	**1,091,760**

The following additional information should be taken into account:

(a) Stocks at 31/12/20-1: Grocery €36,000
Hardware €26,400.

(b) Provision should be made for debenture interest.

(c) Provision for bad debts should be adjusted to 5% of debtors.

(d) Included in light and heat is a payment of €720 for repairs to an ice cream storage unit.

(e) The figure for carriage inwards includes a payment of €240 for delivery of groceries to customers.

(f) Depreciation is to be provided for as follows: Delivery vans 25% of cost
Equipment 10% of book value.

(g) The floor space of the premises is divided as follows: Grocery, two-thirds
Hardware, one-third.

(h) Expenses applicable to both departments should be apportioned on the basis of sales or floor space where appropriate.

(i) Provide for corporation tax of €12,000.

You are required to prepare:

- a departmental trading, profit and loss account for the year ended 31/12/20-1
- a balance sheet as at 31/12/20-1.

Q7 **The firm Coco Ltd is divided into two departments, Garden and Hardware. The following balances were extracted from its books on 31/12/20-2:**

	€	€
Share capital		
Authorised: 640,000 ordinary shares at €1 each		
Issued: 464,000 ordinary shares at €1 each		464,000
Premises	560,000	
Computers and shop equipment	68,000	
Delivery vans	96,000	
Accumulated depreciation on buildings		56,000
Accumulated depreciation on shop equipment		20,000
Accumulated depreciation on delivery vans		40,000
Garden Department		
Stock 1/1/20-2	28,800	
Purchases and sales	248,000	432,000
Returns outwards		5,600
Hardware Department		
Stock 1/1/20-2	19,200	
Purchases and sales	200,000	288,000
Carriage inwards	2,720	
Debtors and creditors	54,400	20,800
12% Debentures (issued 1/4/20-2)		96,000
VAT		3,040
Cash and bank	1,280	9,760
Profit and loss balance 1/1/20-2	34,800	
Salaries and general expenses	67,200	
Directors' fees	19,600	
Light and heat	20,800	
Insurance	14,400	
	1,435,200	**1,435,200**

You are given the following additional information:

(a) Stocks at 31/12/20-2: Garden €91,200
Hardware €64,800.

(b) Depreciation is to be provided for as follows: Premises 2% of cost
Show equipment 12% of cost
Delivery vans 20% of book value.

(c) Insurance was for the year ended 28/2/20-3.

(d) Provision should be made for debenture interest due.

(e) The floor space of the firm is divided as follows: Garden 25%
Hardware 75%.

(f) Expenses applicable to both departments should be divided on the basis of sales or floor space where appropriate.

12

You are required to prepare:

- a departmental trading, profit and loss account for the year ended 31/12/20-2
- a balance sheet as at 31/12/20-2.

Q8 **The firm O'Toole Ltd is divided into two departments, Toys and Clothing. The following balances were extracted from the books on 31/12/20-2:**

	€	€
Share capital		
Authorised: 800,000 shares @ €1 each		
Issued: 600,000 ordinary shares @ €1 each		600,000
Motor vehicles at cost	180,000	
Buildings at cost	900,000	
Accumulated depreciation on vans		20,000
Accumulated depreciation on buildings		40,000
12% Debentures issued on 1/1/20-2		140,000
Debtors and creditors	102,000	195,000
Toy Department		
Stock 1/1/20-2	60,000	
Purchases and sales	300,000	600,000
Carriage inwards	4,200	
Clothing Department		
Stock 1/1/20-2	40,000	
Purchases and sales	150,000	300,000
Returns inwards	5,000	
Cleaning expenses	40,000	
Salaries and general expenses	105,000	
Directors' fees	45,000	
Light and heat	34,000	
Profit and loss balance 1/1/20-2		35,000
VAT		10,300
Bank		34,000
Cash	12,100	
PAYE, PRSI and USC		3,000
	1,977,300	**1,977,300**

You are given the following information:

(a) Closing stock at 31/12/20-2: Toys €34,000
Clothing €36,000.

(b) Provide for depreciation on vehicles at the rate of 20% per annum straight line and on buildings at 4% on the same basis.

(c) Provide for debenture interest due.

(d) Expenses which are applicable to both departments should be divided on the basis of sales or floor space where appropriate. The floor space is divided as follows: Toys 70% and Clothing 30%.

(e) Included in light and heat is stock oil of €6,000 in the tank on 31/12/20-2.

You are required to prepare:

- a departmental trading, profit and loss account for the year ended 31/12/20-2 and a balance sheet as at that date.

Q9 **The firm Gurk Ltd is divided into two departments, Grocery and Hardware. The following balances were extracted from its books on 31/12/20-4:**

	€	€
Share capital		
Authorised: 500,000 ordinary shares @ €1 each		
Issued: 340,000 ordinary shares @ €1 each		340,000
Delivery vans at cost	120,000	
Accumulated depreciation on vans		10,000
Buildings	430,000	
Accumulated depreciation on buildings		25,000
7% Debentures issued on 1/1/20-4		80,000
Debtors and creditors	88,000	92,000
Grocery Department		
Stock 1/1/20-4	34,500	
Purchases and sales	99,900	320,000
Carriage inwards	8,700	
Hardware Department		
Stock 1/1/20-4	39,900	
Purchases and sales	84,000	160,000
Returns	1,400	
VAT		2,700
Cash and bank	22,000	15,600
PAYE, PRSI and USC		4,700
Profit and loss balance 1/1/20-4		12,000
Wages and salaries	63,000	
Insurance	16,000	
Dividends paid	42,000	
Directors' fees	12,600	
	1,062,000	**1,062,000**

You are given the following additional information:

(a) **Stocks as at 31/12/20-4: Grocery €28,900**
Hardware €45,800.

(b) **Provide for depreciation on buildings at 2% per annum of cost and on vans at 12.5% of cost.**

(c) **Provide for debenture interest due.**

(d) **Expenses applicable to both departments should be divided on the basis of sales or floor space where appropriate.**

(e) **The floor space is divided as follows: Grocery 60%**
Hardware 40%.

(f) **Included in insurance is €4,000 for buildings for the year ended 31/3/20-5. The remaining insurance is for vans.**

You are required to prepare:

- **a departmental trading, profit and loss account for the year ended 31/12/20-4**
- **a balance sheet as at 31/12/20-4.**

12

Exercises – Higher Level

Q1 The firm Nugent Ltd is divided into two departments, Grocery and Hardware. The following balances were extracted from its books on 31/12/20-5:

	€	€
Share capital		
Authorised: 600,000 ordinary shares @€1 each		
Issued: 300,000 ordinary shares @€1 each		300,000
Buildings at cost	450,000	
Delivery vans at cost	100,000	
Shop fittings and equipment	20,000	
Accumulated depreciation on buildings		54,000
Accumulated depreciation on delivery vans		30,000
Accumulated depreciation on shop fittings and equipment		3,000
Debtors and creditors	64,000	55,000
10% Debentures		60,000
Grocery Department		
Stocks 1/1/20-5	35,000	
Purchases and sales	420,000	600,000
Carriage inwards	5,000	
Hardware Department		
Stocks 1/1/20-5	26,000	
Purchases and sales	280,000	400,000
Returns outwards		2,000
Profit and loss 1/1/20-5	13,000	
Salaries and general expenses	66,600	
Directors' fees	23,000	
Discount (net)		1,500
Advertising	12,000	
VAT		2,100
USC		1,600
Provision for bad debts		2,300
Bank		13,500
Light and heat	10,400	
	1,525,000	**1,525,000**

You are given the following additional information:

(a) Stocks on 31/12/20-5 were as follows: Grocery €37,000
Hardware €28,000.

Due to bad weather a stock of barbecues which cost €5,600 are only valued at 50% of cost.

(b) During the year a coldroom was built onto the grocery department. The materials, costing €5,000, were taken from the hardware stock and the work, which cost €2,000, was carried out by all employees from both departments.

(c) Depreciation is to be provided for as follows:

Land and buildings	2% of cost (cost of land was €50,000)
Shop fittings and equipment	10% of book value
Delivery vans	20% of cost.

(d) Provide for debenture interest due.

(e) The payment for advertising is for the year ended 31/5/20-6.

(f) The floor space of the firm after the addition of the extension to the cold room was:

Grocery	80%
Hardware	20%.

(g) Expenses applicable to both departments should be divided on the basis of sales or floor space where appropriate

(h) The Revenue declared taxation of €50,000.

You are required to prepare:

- a departmental trading, profit and loss account for the year ended 31/12/20-5
- a balance sheet as at 31/12/20-5.

Q2 **The firm Charlie Ltd is divided into two departments, Grocery and Clothing. The following balances were extracted from its books on 31/12/20-9:**

	€	€
Share capital		
Authorised: 880,000 ordinary shares @ €1 each		
Issued: 650,000 ordinary shares @ €1 each		650,000
Premises	1,230,000	
Patents	66,000	
Shop equipment	20,000	
Delivery vans	240,000	
Accumulated depreciation on premises		30,000
Accumulated depreciation on shop equipment		5,000
Accumulated depreciation on delivery vans		40,000
Profit and loss balance 1/1/20-9	135,680	
Grocery Department		
Stocks 1/1/20-9	72,600	
Purchases and sales	792,000	990,000
Returns inwards	1,800	
Clothing Department		
Stocks 1/1/20-9	52,800	
Purchases and sales	284,000	495,000
Carriage inwards	10,000	
Salaries and general expenses	158,400	
Light and heat	26,400	
Provision for bad debts		3,000
Repairs to drinks cooler	24,560	
Insurance (incorporating suspense)	13,320	
Debenture interest paid (3 months)	14,300	
Fees for alteration of clothes		120,200
8% Debentures (1/4/20-9)		704,000
Bank	33,000	
VAT		39,660
Commission		115,000
Debtors and creditors	97,000	98,000
Interim dividends paid	18,000	
	3,289,860	**3,289,860**

You are given the following additional information:

(a) Stocks on 31/12/20-9 were: Grocery €90,000
Clothing €44,000.

(b) The suspense figure arises as the result of the posting on an incorrect figure for debenture interest paid. The correct figure was entered in the bank account.

(c) New shopping trolleys were purchased at a cost of €12,000. This was included in error as the purchase of stock in the grocery department. The cost of installing the trolley bays was €3,000, which is included in the overall wage bill of the firm.

(d) A delivery van was purchased during the year (1/7/20-9) for €44,000 plus VAT at 20%. The VAT-inclusive price was entered in the vans account with no entry in the VAT account.

(e) Depreciation is to be provided as follows:

Buildings	4% of cost
Equipment	15% of cost
Delivery vans	20% of cost (from date of purchase to date of sale).

(f) The directors recommend that:

- The provision for bad debts should be adjusted to €4,220.
- Provision should be made for debenture interest due.
- Provision should be made for corporation tax of €22,990.

(g) The floor space of the firm is divided as follows: Grocery 60%
Clothing 40%.

(h) Expenses should be allocated between the departments on the basis of floor space or sales, whichever is appropriate.

You are required to prepare:

- a departmental trading, profit and loss account for the year ended 31/12/20-9
- a balance sheet as at 31/12/20-9.

Q3 The firm Zak'n'Cody Ltd is divided into two departments, Carpets and Tiles. The following balances were extracted from its books at 31/12/20-5:

	€	€
Share capital		
Authorised: 640,000 ordinary shares at €1 each		
Issued: 480,000 ordinary shares at €1 each		480,000
Buildings	720,000	
Delivery vans	24,000	
Accumulated depreciation, buildings		115,200
Accumulated depreciation, vans		6,400
Debtors and creditors	137,600	49,600
Provision for bad debts		3,360
10% Debentures 1/5/20-5		96,000
Carpet Department		
Stocks 1/1/20-5	51,200	
Purchases and sales	432,000	579,000
Import duty	4,800	

Continued >

12

	€	€
Tiles Department		
Stocks 1/1/20-5	35,200	
Purchases and sales	256,000	384,000
Returns inwards	4,800	
Profit and loss balance 1/1/20-5		17,800
Salaries and general expenses	64,000	
Carpet fitting charges to customers		2,400
Directors' fees	51,200	
Advertising	9,760	
Debenture interest paid	4,000	
VAT		41,600
USC		1,920
Bank		17,280
	1,794,560	**1,794,560**

You are given the following additional information:

(a) Stocks at 31/12/20-5: Carpets €39,000
Tiles €32,000.
Tiles which cost €3,400 and were damaged during the year are now valued at €1,800.

(b) The provision for bad debts should be adjusted to 5%. It should be noted that a debtor who owed €3,400 was declared bankrupt and the company decided to write this off as a bad debt. No entry has yet been made in the books.

(c) Provide for depreciation as follows: Buildings 2% of cost
Vans 20% of cost.

(d) The company decided to revalue all buildings by 10% of cost at the end of 20-5. This adjustment has not been made in the books.

(e) Provision should be made for debenture interest due.

(f) The company's tax liability for the year is estimated at €23,000.

(g) During the year the carpet department was re-carpeted and the tile department was re-tiled. The carpets cost €2,500 and the tiles cost €3,400, both of which were taken from the firm's own stocks. The cost of labour for the work, €2,100, was included in general expenses. There are four employees in the carpet department and three employees in the tiling department.

(h) Carpets which cost €2,500 were sent to a customer on a sale-or-return basis at a mark-up on cost of 20%. These had been incorrectly entered in the books as a cash sale.

(i) No entry was made in the books for tiles purchased but still in transit. The invoice for these goods had been received showing a recommended retail price of €6,250, which is cost plus 25%.

(j) Expenses applicable to both departments should be divided on the basis of sales or floor space where appropriate.

(k) The floor space of the firm is divided as follows: Carpets 10,500 sq. ft
Tiles 15,750 sq. ft.

You are required to prepare:

- a departmental trading, profit and loss account for the year ended 31/12/20-5
- a balance sheet as at 31/12/20-5.

Q4 The firm Size-up Ltd is divided into two departments, Menswear and Ladieswear. The following trial balance was extracted from the books on 31/12/20-3. The authorised share capital is 800,000 €1 ordinary shares.

	€	€
Issued share capital: 550,000 ordinary shares @ €1 each		550,000
Buildings (cost €900,000)	750,000	
Shop equipment (cost €450,000)	400,000	
9% Debentures (including an 11% debenture €70,000 issued 1/4/20-3)		210,000
Debtors and creditors	175,200	89,000
Menswear Department		
Purchases and sales	445,000	810,000
Carriage inwards	16,600	
Stock 1/1/20-3	43,000	
Ladieswear Department		
Purchases and sales	330,000	540,000
Returns outwards		4,600
Stock 1/1/20-3	23,900	
Insurance	8,000	
Wages and selling expenses	45,000	
Light and heat	8,900	
Advertising	32,900	
VAT		5,700
Repairs to buildings	39,000	
Directors' fees	50,000	
Bank		56,200
Profit and loss balance 1/1/20-3		86,300
Alteration fees charged on men's suits		15,700
	2,367,500	**2,367,500**

You are given the following additional information:

(a) Closing stocks at 31/12/20-3 were as follows: Ladieswear €25,600
Menswear €54,000.

Included in the closing stock of menswear are items which cost €2,000 but only have a net realisable value of €1,300.

(b) Provide for depreciation of fixed assets as follows: Buildings 3% of cost
Shop equipment 15% of cost.

Note: Buildings were revalued at €1,100,000 on 1/7/20-3. This revaluation is to be incorporated into the accounts.

(c) Insurance was for the year ended 31/3/20-4.

(d) Provide for debenture interest due.

(e) Expenses applicable to both departments should be divided on the basis of sales or floor space where appropriate.

(f) The floor space of the firm is divided as follows: Menswear 30%
Ladieswear 70%.

(g) Included in the repairs to buildings is the cost of repainting the interior walls. The total cost of this paintwork was €26,000. Since the manager changed the colour in the menswear department, twice as much paint was used for painting the menswear department as was used for the ladieswear department.

12

(h) Commission is paid to the managers of each department at a rate of 8% of sales in excess of €540,000 for each department.

(i) Provide for corporation tax of €54,600.

(j) An invoice was received for a new delivery of ladies' shoes showing a recommended retail price of €10,000, which was cost plus 25%. These goods were in transit and this transaction had not been entered in the books.

You are required to prepare:

- a departmental trading, profit and loss account for the year ended 31/12/20-3
- a balance sheet as at 31/12/20-3.

Q5 The company Power 2 U Ltd is divided into two departments, Electrical and Furniture. The following balances were extracted from its books on 31/12/20-5:

	€	€
Premises (cost €800,000)	788,000	
Shop fittings and equipment	450,000	
Accumulated depreciation on equipment		198,000
Patents	60,000	
Debtors and creditors	83,000	199,000
Cash and bank	54,000	49,300
VAT		14,800
USC		2,500
Salaries and general expenses	332,500	
Light and heat	43,000	
Electrical Department		
Purchases and sales	378,000	780,000
Stock 1/1/20-5	32,000	
Carriage inwards	3,900	
Customs duties	3,800	
Furniture Department		
Purchases and sales	134,000	260,000
Stock 1/1/20-5	26,700	
Returns inwards	3,700	
Advertising	45,000	
Directors' fees	88,000	
Profit and loss balance	68,000	
10% Debentures, issued on 1/4/20-5		220,000
Share capital		
Authorised: 600,000 ordinary shares @ €2 each		
Issued: 500,000 ordinary shares @ €2 each		1,000,000
10% Investments	130,000	
	2,723,600	**2,723,600**

You are given the following additional information:

(a) Stocks at 31/12/20-5 were as follows: Electrical €43,500
Furniture €24,900
Oil €2,300.

(b) Included in the figure for advertising is an amount of €5,000 used for advertising in a well known interior design magazine called ***Interior Furniture Designs***.

(c) Expenses applicable to both departments should be divided on the basis of sales, floor space or number of employees where appropriate. The floor space is divided as follows: Electrical 45%, Furniture 55%. The company employs 22 full-time staff, 13 of whom work in Electrical and 9 in Furniture. There is also a manager who works between both departments equally. The manager's salary is 1.75 times the salary of other employees.

(d) Provide for debenture interest and investment income due.

(e) A customer of the furniture department who bought goods on credit for €4,500 was declared bankrupt. The customer paid 10c in the euro, and the remainder of the debt was written off as bad. There was no entry in respect of this transaction in the books, or the subsequent decision to create a provision for bad debts of 6% of the company's debtors.

(f) Provide for depreciation as follows: premises 2% of cost. Premises were revalued by 15% of original cost on 31/12/20-5. This revaluation was to be incorporated into the books.

(g) Provide for depreciation on shop equipment at the rate of 10% of cost. Depreciation is calculated from the date of purchase to the date of sale. **Note:** shop equipment which had cost €75,000 on 1/9/20-2 was sold for €42,000 on 28/2/20-5. New shop equipment was purchased for €95,000 on 1/7/20-5. It cost a further €7,000 to have this installed and €2,400 to repair a faulty part on this equipment during October 20-5. No entries had been made in the books in respect of any of these adjustments to equipment. The equipment sold was for camera display and photographic equipment.

(h) The directors recommend that:

- Directors' fees due of €13,000 be paid
- Auditor's fees due of €25,000 be paid
- Provision for corporation tax of €78,000 be made.

(i) The patent is in relation to the design of electrical goods and is to be amortised over the next 12 years.

(j) During the year a customer who was injured in the furniture department while testing a new bed has claimed for damages amounting to €30,000. The company's solicitors have advised that the company will be liable for damages.

You are required to prepare:

- a departmental trading, profit and loss account for the year ended 31/12/20-5
- a balance sheet as at 31/12/20-5.

Exam Tips

- Know the layout of a departmental trading, profit and loss account.
- Set out in a table the expenses/gains to the allocated department, stating clearly the basis of apportionment used.
- Make any necessary adjustments to the expenses/gains before making the final allocation to the individual departments.
- Ensure that you always include a Total column.
- The balance sheet should be prepared in the same way as learned in previous final account topics.

13 Club Accounts

Objectives

On completion students should be able to:

- List and explain the role and tasks of a club's treasurer;
- Prepare a receipts and payments account and book;
- Prepare an income and expenditure account and balance sheet;
- Explain the differences between an income and expenditure account and a receipts and payments account;
- Prepare special purpose profit and loss accounts;
- Explain terms associated with club accounts;
- Prepare a statement of accumulated fund;
- Offer advice to the club treasurer on a range of items.

Introduction

Clubs, societies and non-profit-making organisations are set up for the benefit of the members rather than for the purpose of making a profit.

A club's principal income comes from the subscriptions it receives from its members. Income is also earned from activities such as fundraising events.

Each year a club will hold an AGM (Annual General Meeting) and at this meeting the officers of the club will be appointed. The main officers of a club are:

- the chairperson
- the secretary
- the treasurer.

The treasurer

The **treasurer** has overall responsibility for the club's finances.

The main tasks of the treasurer include:

- collecting subscriptions and all other funds
- making all payments on behalf of the club
- making all lodgements to the bank on behalf of the club
- maintaining a proper set of financial records for all receipts and payments
- preparing the annual treasurer's report and presenting it at the AGM
- advising members of the financial implications of future planned expenditure, for example building a new clubhouse.

13

The accounts

All non-profit-making organisations should prepare accounts like any other business. Club accounts consist of:

1. Analysed receipts and payments book

This book is used to record the day-to-day receipts and payments of the organisation. It is similar to the analysed cash book kept by other businesses.

2. Receipts and payments account

This is a summary of the organisation's daily receipts and payments of cash for the period covered by the account.

The receipts and payments account, however, does not give the true financial position of the organisation owing to the following limitations:

- Amounts due and/or prepaid (expenses and gains) are not included.
- It does not distinguish between capital and revenue expenditure.
- It does not show whether there is enough income to cover expenditure.

Example

From the following cash receipts and cheque payments book of Fit 4 Life Sports Club, prepare a receipts and payments account for the month of January 20-1.

Analysed Receipts Book

Date	Details	Total Received €	Subscriptions	Lotto	Vending Machine
Jan 3	Subscriptions	1,600	1,600		
Jan 3	Lotto	800		800	
Jan15	Vending receipts	500			500
Jan 21	Subscriptions	1,600	1,600		
Jan 23	Lotto	900		900	
Jan 31	Vending receipts	680			680
		6,080	**3,200**	**1,700**	**1,180**

Analysed Payments Book

Date	Details	Total Paid €	Rent & Rates	Travel	Other Expenses
Jan 6	Rates	1,420	1,420		
Jan 7	Travel expenses	860		860	
Jan 14	Repairs	520			520
Jan 18	Rent	680	680		
Jan 23	Travel expenses	1,300		1,300	
Jan 25	Cleaning	420			420
		5,200	**2,100**	**2,160**	**940**

Solution

Receipts and Payments Account for January 20-1

Date	Receipts	€	Date	Payments	€
Jan 31	Subscriptions	3,200	Jan 31	Rent and rates	2,100
	Lotto	1,700		Travel expenses	2,160
	Vending	1,180		Other expenses	940
				Balance c/d	880
		6,080			**6,080**
Feb 1	Balance b/d	880			

3. Income and expenditure account

The income and expenditure account shows the difference between all income and all expenditure for the financial period.

The income and expenditure account is similar to a company's profit and loss account. This account must only take into account the actual income and expenditure for the year. It must therefore be adjusted for accruals and prepayments where necessary.

NOTE

The **income and expenditure account** reveals the true financial performance of the club over a period of time, showing a surplus income (profit) or deficit (loss).

It shows whether or not the organisation has enough income to pay for its activities.

Income and Expenditure Account (template)

	€	€
Income		
Subscriptions	xxxx	
Bar profit	xxxx	
Life membership written into income	xxxx	
Donations	xxxx	
Entrance fees	xxxx	
Sponsorship	xxxx	
Profit on raffle, disco, cake sale, etc	xxxx	xxxxx
***Less* Expenditure**		
Loan interest	xxxx	
Depreciation of assets	xxxx	
Wages and salaries	xxxx	
Light and heat/cleaning/postage, etc	xxxx	(xxxxx)
Surplus income over expenditure/expenditure over income		xxxxx

The table below sets out the differences between a receipts and payments account and an income and expenditure account.

Receipts and Payments Account	Income and Expenditure Account
Includes opening and closing cash and bank balances	Excludes opening and closing cash and bank balances
Capital income and expenditure included	Capital income and expenditure excluded
Non-cash items excluded	Non-cash items included, e.g. depreciation
Closing balance is entered in the balance sheet as a current asset/liability	Closing balance is either surplus income or surplus expenditure
Similar to a cash book	Similar to the profit and loss account
No adjustment for accruals and prepayments	Must include adjustments for accruals and prepayments

4. Statement of accumulated fund

The accumulated fund is a statement showing the list of assets less the liabilities at the beginning of the financial period.

The **accumulated fund** corresponds to the **capital** of a trading concern.

Statement of Accumulated Fund (template)

	€	€
Assets		
Clubhouse and courts/premises/pitches, etc	xxxxx	
Motor vehicles/equipment/lawnmowers etc	xxxxx	
Bank/cash	xxxxx	
Gains due and expenses prepaid	xxxxx	xxxxx
***Less* Liabilities**		
Loan/loan interest due	xxxxx	
Levy reserve fund	xxxxx	
Life membership	xxxxx	
Bank overdraft	xxxxx	
Prepaid gains and expenses due	xxxxx	(xxxxx)
Accumulated fund as at 31/12/xx		**xxxxx**

5. Special purpose profit and loss account

Sometimes non-profit organisations prepare a profit and loss account for activities that are carried out to make a profit. Such activities might include running a lotto, bingo or a disco. All expenses and revenues related to the particular activity are entered in the special profit and loss account and it is then transferred to the income and expenditure account.

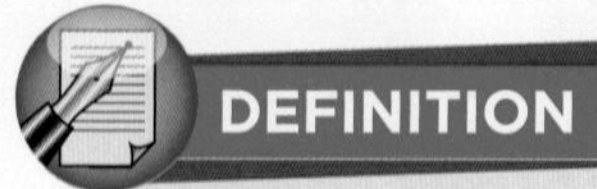

A **special purpose profit and loss account** is an account for a special activity being carried on by the club, usually a bar, café or restaurant.

Another example of such a special purpose profit and loss account is where the organisation runs a bar/restaurant/café which is intended to provide a profit and therefore contribute to the overall income of the organisation. In such cases, a bar/restaurant/café trading account should be prepared and the profit/loss from it transferred into the income and expenditure account.

Sample Bar Trading Profit and Loss Account for XY Club for the year ended 31/12/xx

	€	€
Sales (less opening debtors + closing debtors)		xxxxx
***Less* Cost of sales**		
Opening stock	xxxxx	
Purchases (less opening creditors + closing creditors + any payments to creditors)	xxxxx	
Cost of goods available	xxxxx	
Less Closing stock	(xxxxx)	
Cost of goods sold		(xxxxx)
Gross profit		xxxxx

NOTE

When items of a similar nature arise both as a receipt and a payment they should be netted and entered in the income and expenditure account.

For example, Catering receipts – Catering costs = Profit (loss) on catering

6. Balance sheet

A balance sheet for a club is laid out in similar fashion to the balance sheet for other organisations and shows the assets and liabilities of the club at the end of the financial period.

Special club receipts

There are a number of special items that apply only to club accounts.

Life membership

Since a life member will use the club's facilities for more than one year, the life membership is treated as a liability in the balance sheet and is normally written off to income over a stated number of years.

DEFINITION

Life membership entitles a member to use the facilities of the club for the remainder of his/her life.

Entrance fees

Entrance fees may be payable by new members in the first year of membership in addition to subscriptions for that year. These fees are treated as **income** in the year of receipt. Some clubs, however, have a policy of treating them as a capital receipt and consequently treat them as an increase to the accumulated fund in the balance sheet. These are also known as signing-on fees or joining fees.

13

Levies

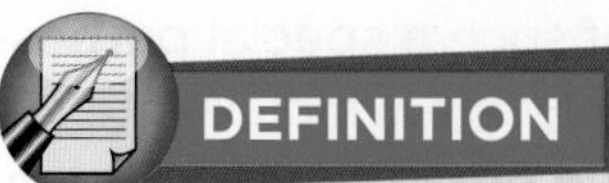

A levy must be used for the specific purpose for which it was collected. It is due to the members until it is used and is therefore a liability in the balance sheet.

DEFINITION

A **levy** is a payment made to a club by its members to fund a special project such as an extension.

Unpaid levies are treated as assets, as the money is due to be paid to the club.

Donations, gifts, winnings and annual grants

Small donations, gifts and annual grants should all be treated as income within the year of receipt and entered in the income and expenditure account.

Large donations, gifts, once-off grants and winnings (prize bonds) should be treated as capital receipts and consequently entered in the balance sheet as an addition to the accumulated fund.

NOTE

A donation is considered small if it is less than approximately 5% of total income.

Sponsorship

Commercial concerns regularly make contributions to sporting and other organisations. Sponsorship is now an annual income for most clubs and is treated as income in the income and expenditure account in the year of receipt.

Adjustments to club accounts

1. Life membership

Life Membership

Life membership at the start	xxxxxx
Plus any new life memberships issued during the year	xxxxxx
Total life membership	xxxxxx
Less Amount transferred to income	(xxxxxx)
Balance sheet entry	**xxxxxx**

Example

Life membership 1/1/20-2	€24,000
New life memberships	€6,000

Life membership is to be written off over a ten-year period commencing in 20-2. Show the relevant entries and adjustments for this.

Solution

Life memberships = 24,000 + 6,000 = €30,000

These are to be written off over 10 years = €3,000 per annum

Entries in the accounts would be as follows:

Income and expenditure account

Income €3,000

Balance sheet – Long-term liabilities

Life memberships €27,000 (30,000 – 3,000)

See Practice Question 1 for exercises on this adjustment.

2. Subscriptions

Adjustments to Subscriptions

Amount received during the year	xxxxxxx
Less Subscriptions due 1/1 (last year)	(xxxxxx)
Add Subscriptions prepaid 1/1 (this year)	xxxxxxx
Less Subscriptions prepaid 31/12 (next year)	(xxxxxx)
Add Subscriptions due 31/12 (this year)	xxxxxxx
Less Any life memberships included in subscriptions	(xxxxxx)
Less Any levies included in subscriptions	(xxxxxx)
Amount to be treated as income in the income and expenditure account	**xxxxxxx**

Example

Receipts and Payments Account (20-2)

Subscriptions received €34,000

Included in subscriptions are the following:

- Levy on 200 members of €30 each
- Subscriptions for 20-3: €4,500
- Subscriptions for 20-1: €2,300
- Life memberships – 2 new @ €3,000 each.

Calculate the amount for subscriptions to be included in the income and expenditure account and indicate the other adjustments necessary.

Solution

Item	Amount (€)	Other Adjustment
Amount received	34,000	
Less Levy for year	(6,000)	Added to any existing levy and placed in balance sheet under reserves
Less Subscriptions for 20-3	(4,500)	Current liability in balance sheet
Less Subscriptions for 20-1	(2,300)	Current asset in accumulated fund statement
Less Life memberships	(6,000)	Added to any existing life membership and placed in balance sheet under reserves
Amount to income	**15,200**	

See Practice Question 2 for exercises on this adjustment.

13

3. Bar/café trading account

Example

Calculate the profit/loss on the club's bar from the following extracts taken from the club's financial records:

	€
Bar receipts - sales	34,500
Opening stock	3,400
Bar purchases	12,400
Bar debtors 1/1	670
Bar creditors 1/1	1,230
Bar debtors 31/12	890
Bar creditors 31/12	1,120
Closing stock	4,300

See Practice Question 3 for exercises on this adjustment.

Solution

Bar Trading Account

	€	€
Bar sales (34,500 - 670 + 890)		34,720
***Less* Cost of sales**		
Opening stock	3,400	
Bar purchases (12,400 - 1,230 + 1,120)	12,290	
Less Closing stock	(4,300)	(11,390)
Gross profit on bar		**23,330**

4. Profit or loss on catering/disco/raffle

These figures are found in the receipts and payments account.

This is a small adjustment and generally involves simply taking the cost of catering or the disco or the raffle away from the receipts from the same event.

For example:

Raffle receipts	€4,600	
Raffle prizes	(€3,600)	
Profit on raffle	€1,000	(entered as income in I & E)

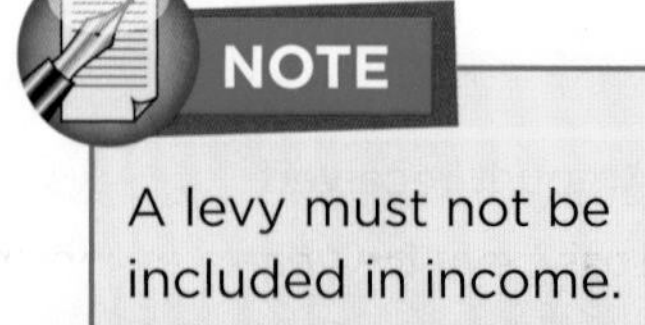

A levy must not be included in income.

5. Levy and levies due

Item	Treatment
Levy at beginning of year Levy reserve fund 1/1	**Liability** in statement of accumulated fund
Levy for current year	If included in subscriptions, **subtract** (Adjustment 2 above)
Levy due at start of year	**Asset** in statement of accumulated fund
Levy at end of year	Levy at start and levy for current year added together and entered in balance sheet as **reserve**

6. Loan interest and loan interest due

Loans and loan interest are found in the **receipts and payments account**.

Step 1 Separate the loan and interest.

Step 2 Separate the interest into the amount for the current year and previous years (this will depend on the date of repayment).

Item	Treatment
Loan	Entered as a **liability** in statement of accumulated fund
Interest due 1/1/xx	Entered as a **liability** in statement of accumulated fund
Interest for current year	Entered as an **expense** in the income and expenditure account

Example

A loan of €30,000 together with 18 months' interest, totalling €33,600, is to be repaid on 30/6/20-2 (in the current year).

Solution

Step 1 **Separate loan and loan interest.**

Repayment amount €33,600, less original loan €30,000 = Interest €3,600

Step 2 **Separate the interest into the amount for the current year and previous years.**

Since the interest is €3,600 for 18 months then 3,600/18 = €200 per month.

It was repaid on 30/6/20-2 so 6 months are for the current year.

This means interest due at the start was 12 months' worth.

Interest for current year	6 x 200 =	€1,200
Interest due at start	12 x 200 =	€2,400
Total interest		€3,600

This is then entered as follows:

Item	€	Treatment
Loan	30,000	**Liability** in accumulated fund statement
Loan interest due 1/1/xx	2,400	**Liability** in accumulated fund statement
Loan interest for current year	1,200	**Expense** in income and expenditure

See Practice Question 4 for exercises on this adjustment.

7. Investments and investment income

Investments are treated as **assets** in both the accumulated fund and the balance sheet. Any interest receivable on these investments is treated as **income** in the income and expenditure account.

Example

10% Investments	€25,000
Interest due 1/1/20-5	€400
Interest received	€1,800

Investments not given in the opening list of balances will have to be calculated using interest amounts and percentages given.

Show the necessary adjustments for this in the accounts.

Solution

The investments carry 10% interest, therefore 25,000 x 10% = €2,500 (income in income and expenditure).

The club received €1,800, of which €400 was due from the beginning, so received €1,400 for this year, which means that at the end of the year 2,500 - 1,400 = €1,100 still due.

Item	€	Adjustment
Investments	25,000	**Asset** in accumulated fund and balance sheet
Investment income due 1/1/-5	400	**Asset** in accumulated fund only
Investment income	2,500	**Income** in income and expenditure account
Investment income due 31/12/-5	1,100	**Asset** in balance sheet only

See Practice Question 5 for exercises on this adjustment.

8. Prize bonds and transfers to and from building societies

A **prize bond** is an asset that can be cashed in at any time for its original amount. Since prize bonds are an asset they must be entered in the balance sheet as a **current asset**.

A **transfer to a building society** is not an expense as cash is simply transferred from the bank account into the building society account. This will appear as an **investment (financial asset)** in the balance sheet.

A building society account can sometimes be a **hidden asset**. If a club makes a withdrawal from a building society account not mentioned in the opening list of balances, it should be assumed that this was the total amount on deposit in the building society. As well as being entered as a debit entry in the receipts and payments account, it should be entered as an asset in the statement of accumulated fund at the beginning of the accounting period.

9. Accruals and prepayments

These are similar to the adjustments for final accounts.

Sample Ordinary Level question

Included in the assets and liabilities of the Young Stars Football Club on 1/1/20-0 were the following:

Clubhouse and grounds €937,500; equipment €47,500; bar stock €15,750; 5% investments €75,000; bar creditors €2,250; members' subscriptions due €2,000; cash in hand €63,500.

The following is a summary of the club's receipts and payments for the year 20-0:

Receipts and Payments for the year ended 31/12/20-0

Receipts	€	Payments	€
Balance	63,500	Lotto prizes	32,500
Bar sales	96,250	Bar purchases	60,500
Lotto receipts	109,250	Purchase of equipment	6,250
Annual sponsorship	55,000	General expenses	35,750
Subscriptions	47,500	Prize bonds	250
Investment income	3,750	Balance	240,000
	375,250		**375,250**
Balance	240,000		

The treasurer also supplied the following information as at 31/12/20-0:

(a) Bar stock was €12,000.

(b) Bar creditors were €3,250.

(c) Subscriptions prepaid were €625.

(d) Expenses due were €2,250.

(e) Equipment held on 31/12/20-0 to be depreciated by 20%.

(f) Clubhouse and grounds to be depreciated by 2% of cost.

You are required to prepare:

- a statement showing the club's accumulated fund on 1/1/20-0
- the bar trading account for the year ended 31/12/20-0
- the income and expenditure account for the year ended 31/12/20-0
- the balance sheet as at 31/12/20-0.

Solution

Accumulated Fund

	€	€
Assets		
Clubhouse and grounds	937,500	
Equipment	47,500	
Bar stock	15,750	
Investments	75,000	
Subscriptions due	2,000	
Bank	63,500	1,141,250
***Less* Liabilities**		
Creditors	(2,250)	(2,250)
Accumulated fund		**1,139,000**

Bar Trading Account for the year ended 31/12/20-0

	€	€
Sales		96,250
***Less* Cost of sales**		
Opening stock	15,750	
Purchases	60,500	
Add Creditors 31/12/20-0	3,250	
	79,500	
Less Creditors 1/1/20-0	(2,250)	
	77,250	
Less Closing stock	(12,000)	(65,250)
Bar profit		**31,000**

Income and Expenditure Account for the year ended 31/12/20-0

	€	€
Income		
Subscriptions (W1)	44,875	
Bar profit	31,000	
Investment income	3,750	
Annual sponsorship	55,000	
Lotto profit (W2)	76,750	211,375
***Less* Expenditure**		
General expenses (W3)	38,000	
Depreciation of clubhouse (W5)	18,750	
Depreciation of equipment (W4)	10,750	(67,500)
Surplus income over expenditure		**143,875**

Balance Sheet of the Young Stars Football Club as at 31/12/20-0

	Cost (€)	Aggregate Depreciation (€)	Net Book Value (€)
Fixed assets			
Clubhouse and grounds (W5)	937,500	18,750	918,750
Equipment (W4)	53,750	10,750	43,000
	991,250	29,500	961,750
Financial assets			
Investments			75,000
Current assets			
Prize bonds		250	
Stock		12,000	
Bank		240,000	
		252,250	
***Less* Creditors: amounts falling due within 1 year**			
Creditors	3,250		
Subscriptions prepaid	625		
Expenses due	2,250	(6,125)	
Net current assets			246,125
			1,282,875
Financed by			
Accumulated fund 1/1/20-0			1,139,000
Surplus of income over expenditure			143,875
			1,282,875

Workings

W1 Subscriptions

Amount received	47,500
Less Due 1/12/20-0	(2,000)
Less Prepaid 31/12/20-0	(625)
Amount to income	**44,875**

W2 Lotto

Amount received	109,250
Less Lotto prizes	(32,500)
Amount to income	**76,750**

W3 General expenses

Amount paid	35,750
Add Due 31/12/20-0	2,250
Amount to expenditure	**38,000**

W4 Depreciation of equipment

Opening balance	47,500
Add New equipment	6,250
	53,750
53,750 x 20% =	**10,750**

W5 Depreciation of clubhouse

937,500 x 2% =	**18,750**

Sample Higher Level question

Included in the assets and liabilities of the Lakeside Golf Club on 1/1/20-9 were the following:

Clubhouse €304,000; bar stock €16,800; equipment (cost) €28,400; life membership €36,000; bar debtors €320; bar creditors €9,240; levy reserve fund €24,000; investment income due €2,400.

The club treasurer has supplied the following receipts and payments account for the year ended 31/12/20-9:

Receipts and Payments Account

Receipts	€	Payments	€
Balance	28,000	Bar purchases	110,960
Income from 6% Investments	4,800	Sundry expenses	44,800
Sale of equipment (cost €4,000)	1,800	Catering costs	5,600
Catering receipts	8,600	Equipment	5,200
Subscriptions	104,960	Transfer to building society	20,000
Bar receipts	150,000	Repayment of €32,000 loan on 31/12/20-9 with 1.5 years' interest	36,800
		Prize bonds	800
		Balance	74,000
	298,160		**298,160**

You are given the following additional information:

(a) Bar stock on 31/12/20-9 was €14,800.

(b) Equipment owned on 31/12/20-9 is to be depreciated at the rate of 25% of cost.

(c) Bar debtors and creditors on 31/12/20-9 were €420 and €8,840 respectively.

(d) Subscriptions include:

- one life membership, bringing the total life membership to 13 members
- levy of €80 due from 12 members since 20-8
- levy of €80 on this year's 300 members.

(e) Investment income due, €1,200.

You are required to prepare:

- the club's accumulated fund on 1/1/20-9
- the club's income and expenditure account for the year ended 31/12/20-9
- the balance sheet as at 31/12/20-9.

Solution

Accumulated Fund of Lakeside Golf Club on 1/1/20-9

	€	€
Assets		
Bank	28,000	
Clubhouse	304,000	
Equipment	28,400	
Bar stock	16,800	
Debtors	320	
Income receivable due	2,400	
Investments (W1)	60,000	
Levies due (W2)	960	440,880
***Less* Liabilities**		
Levy reserve fund	24,000	
Life membership	36,000	
Creditors	9,240	
Loan	32,000	
Loan interest due (W3)	1,600	(102,840)
Accumulated fund on 1/1/20-9		**338,040**

Income and Expenditure Account of Lakeside Golf Club for the year ended 31/12/20-9

	€	€
Income		
Subscriptions (W5)	77,000	
Bar profit (W4)	37,540	
Income on investments (W1)	3,600	
Catering profit (W7)	3,000	121,140
***Less* Expenditure**		
Sundry expenses	44,800	
Interest on loan (W3)	3,200	
Depreciation of equipment (W8)	7,400	
Loss on sale of equipment (W9)	2,200	(57,600)
Surplus income over expenditure		**63,540**

Balance Sheet of Lakeside Golf Club as at 31/12/20-9

	Cost (€)	Aggregate Depreciation (€)	Net (€)
Fixed assets			
Clubhouse	304,000		304,000
Equipment (W8)	29,600	7,400	22,200
	333,600	**7,400**	326,200
Financial assets			
6% Investments (W1)		60,000	
Building society		20,000	80,000
			406,200
Current assets			
Bar stock		14,800	
Prize bonds		800	
Debtors		420	
Investment interest due (W1)		1,200	
Bank		74,000	
		91,220	
***Less* Creditors: amounts falling due within 1 year**			
Creditors		(8,840)	
Net current assets			82,380
			488,580
Financed by			
Accumulated fund 1/1/20-9		338,040	
Add Surplus income over expenditure		63,540	401,580
Reserves			
Life membership (W6)		39,000	
Levy reserve fund		48,000	87,000
			488,580

Workings

W1 Investments and income

Amount received	4,800
Amount due 1/1/20-9	(2,400)
Amount due 31/12/20-9	1,200
Investment income	3,600

6% = 3,600

Therefore 100% = **€60,000**

W2 Levies due

Levy due from 20-8 (80 x 12)	**960**

W3 Loan and loan interest

Amount repaid	36,800
Less loan capital	(32,000)
Amount of interest for 18 months	4,800

4,800/18 months x 6	**1,600 due 1/1/-9**
4,800/18 months x 12	**3,200 expense**

W4 Bar trading account

Bar sales (150,000 – 320 + 420)		150,100
***Less* Cost of sales**		
Opening stock	16,800	
Purchases (110,960 – 9,240 + 8,840)	110,560	
	127,360	
Less Closing stock	(14,800)	(112,560)
Profit		**37,540**

W5 Subscriptions

Amount received	104,960
Less Levy 20-8 (W2)	(960)
Less Levy 20-9 (80 x 300)	(24,000)
Less Life membership (W6)	(3,000)
Amount to income	**77,000**

W6 Life membership

Existing life membership	36,000
12 existing members	12
Cost of 1 life membership	3,000
New life membership	**39,000**

W7 Catering

Amount received	8,600
Less Costs	(5,600)
Profit	**3,000**

W8 Depreciation of equipment

Opening balance	28,400
Less Cost equipment sold	(4,000)
New equipment purchased	5,200
Value at 31/12/20-9	29,600

29,600 x 25% = **7,400**

W9 Loss on sale of equipment

Cost price	4,000
Less proceeds	(1,800)
Loss	**2,200**

Exercises – Ordinary Level

Q1 The Riverside Hockey Club had a balance at the bank of €2,250 on 1 January 20-1. During the year the following transactions took place:

Receipts: sale of coffees €1,700; sale of raffle tickets €2,500; sale of club T-shirts €575; subscriptions €5,000

Payments: rent €1,300; cost of coffee €1,050; cleaning €375; cost of T-shirts €500; new hockey sticks €625; raffle prizes €800

You are required to prepare:

- a receipts and payments account for the year ended 31/12/20-1.

Q2 The following is a summary of the receipts and payments account of the Seaside Gymnastics Club for the year ended 31/12/20-2. They had an opening bank balance of €7,600.

Receipts: interest €9,200; subscriptions €86,500; restaurant receipts €121,200; competition receipts €7,690; raffle receipts €5,400

Payments: restaurant purchases €94,500; rent €4,800; purchase of equipment €54,000; general expenses €65,400; competition prizes €3,000.

The treasurer also supplied the following information on 31/12/20-2:

(a) Restaurant stock on 1/1/20-2 was €3,500 and on 31/12/20-2 was €4,200.

(b) Expenses prepaid on 31/12/20-2 amounted to €1,000.

(c) Subscriptions prepaid on 31/12/20-2 were €500.

(d) Depreciation of equipment for the year was €1,700.

You are required to prepare:

- **the club's receipts and payments account for the year ended 31/12/20-2**
- **the club's income and expenditure account for the year ended 31/12/20-2.**

Q3 **Included in the assets and liabilities of the Baldwinstown Football Club on 1/1/20-3 were the following: clubhouse and pitches €312,000; investments €98,800; equipment €38,480; bar stock €7,540; subscriptions prepaid €12,500.**

The following is a summary of the club's receipts and payments account for the year ended 31/12/20-3:

Receipts	€	Payments	€
Balance	2,860	Bar purchases	48,100
Investment income	6,240	Purchase of equipment	10,400
Subscriptions	63,180	General expenses	72,020
Bar sales	78,520	Competition prizes	3,900
Competition receipts	5,200	Balance	21,580
	156,000		**156,000**
Balance	21,580		

The treasurer supplied the following additional information on 31/12/20-3:

(a) Bar stock was €9,260.

(b) Bar creditors were €1,040.

(c) Expenses prepaid were €520.

(d) Subscriptions prepaid were €780.

(e) Equipment held to be depreciated by 20%.

You are required to prepare:

- **a statement of the club's accumulated fund on 1/1/20-3**
- **the club's income and expenditure account for the year ended 31/12/20-3.**

Q4 **Included in the assets and liabilities of the All-Terrain Mountaineering Club on 1/1/20-4 were the following: clubhouse €169,000; equipment €22,100; investments €13,000; café stock €3,120; expenses due €468; subscriptions due €195.**

The following is a summary of the club's receipts and payments account for the year ended 31/12/20-4:

Receipts	€	Payments	€
Cash in hand (balance)	2,782	Café purchases	25,610
Investment income	1,040	Equipment	6,760
Subscriptions	27,495	General expenses	33,930
Cafe sales	50,560	Competition prizes	2,730
Competition receipts	3,016	Cafe creditors	741
		Balance	15,122
	84,893		**84,893**
Balance	15,122		

The treasurer also supplied the following information as at 31/12/20-4:

(a) Café stock was €3,770.

(b) Café creditors were €559.

(c) Expenses prepaid were €312.

(d) Subscriptions prepaid were €390.

(e) Equipment held on 31/12/20-4 is to be depreciated by 20%.

(f) Clubhouse to be depreciated by 2%.

You are required to prepare:

- a statement of the club's accumulated fund on 1/1/20-4
- the club's income and expenditure account for the year ended 31/12/20-4.

Q5 **Included in the assets and liabilities of the Little Forest Golf Club on 1/1/20-5 were the following: clubhouse and courts €350,000; equipment €56,000; building society deposits €23,000; bar stock €2,300; wages due €2,100; prepaid subscriptions €350.**

The following is a summary of the club's receipts and payments account for the year ended 31/12/20-5:

Receipts	€	Payments	€
Balance	2,500	Wages and general expenses	35,600
Subscriptions	36,700	Bar purchases	23,400
Bar sales	32,500	Equipment	8,000
Sponsorship	3,000	Catering costs	3,400
Catering receipts	5,600	Coaching lessons	600
Entrance fees	600	Balance	9,900
	80,900		**80,900**
Balance	9,900		

The treasurer also supplied the following information on 31/12/20-5:

(a) Bar stock was €2,560.

(b) Bar creditors and debtors were €1,200 and €1,400 respectively.

(c) Wages due were €900.

(d) Subscriptions for 20-6 were €450.

(e) Equipment held on 31/12/20-5 to be depreciated by 20%.

(f) Clubhouse and courts to be depreciated by 3%.

You are required to prepare:

- a statement of the club's accumulated fund on 1/1/20-5
- the income and expenditure account for the year ended 31/12/20-5.

Q6 **Included in the assets and liabilities of the Rovers Wood Football Club on 1/1/20-6 were the following: clubhouse and pitches €450,000; equipment €70,000; minibus €24,000; bar stock €1,300; electricity due €500; subscriptions due €450.**

The following is a summary of the club's receipts and payments account for the year ended 31/12/20-6:

Receipts	€	Payments	€
Balance	8,900	Wages and general expenses	43,000
Subscriptions	43,000	Bar purchases	21,900
Bar sales	28,000	Equipment	2,500
Sponsorship	15,000	Raffle prizes	2,560
Raffle sales	6,000	Light and heat	2,400
Match day receipts	12,000	Printing of match day programmes	2,100
		Balance	38,440
	112,900		**112,900**
Balance	38,440		

The treasurer also supplied the following information on 31/12/20-6:

(a) Bar stock was €3,460.

(b) Bar creditors and debtors were €2,400 and €3,000 respectively.

(c) Heating oil stock was €800.

(d) Subscriptions for 20-7 were €900.

(e) Equipment held on 31/12/20-6 was valued at €65,000.

(f) Clubhouse and pitches to be depreciated by 2%.

You are required to prepare:

- a statement of the club's accumulated fund on 1/1/20-6
- the income and expenditure account for the year ended 31/12/20-6.

Q7 **Included in the assets and liabilities of the Little Swimmers Swimming Club on 1/1/20-7 were the following: equipment €37,800; investments €16,800; coffee bar stock €630; expenses due €2,560; subscriptions due €840.**

The following is a summary of the club's receipts and payments account for the year 31/12/20-7:

Receipts	€	Payments	€
Cash in hand 1/1/20-7	5,040	Rent of pool	25,200
Income for swimming gala	17,220	Equipment	7,350
Subscriptions	26,880	General expenses	41,790
Coffee bar sales	29,610	Competition prizes	3,780
Competition receipts	9,450	Coffee bar purchases	10,710
Sponsorship	13,650	Balance 31/12/20-7	13,020
	101,850		**101,850**
Balance	13,020		

The treasurer also supplied the following information as at 31/12/20-7:

(a) Coffee bar stock was €530.
(b) Coffee bar creditors were €670.
(c) Expenses prepaid were €520.
(d) Subscriptions prepaid were €1,350.
(e) Equipment held at 31/12/20-7 to be depreciated by 20%.
(f) Investment income due 10%.

You are required to prepare:

- a statement of the club's accumulated fund as at 31/12/20-7
- the coffee bar trading account for the year ended 31/12/20-7
- the income and expenditure account for the year ended 31/12/20-7.

Q8 Included in the assets and liabilities of St Anne's GAA Club on 1/1/20-8 were the following: clubhouse and pitches €544,000; equipment €14,400; investments €32,000; bar stock €4,640; wages due €1,152; subscriptions due €480; bar creditors €1,920

The following is a summary of the club's receipts and payments account for the year ended 31/12/20-8:

Receipts	€	Payments	€
Balance	6,240	Wages and general expenses	41,600
Subscriptions	45,280	Bar purchases	51,840
Bar sales	70,720	Equipment	10,400
Sponsorship	16,800	Disco and DJ costs	4,000
Disco receipts	15,040	Bar creditors	5,440
Investment income	640	Balance	41,440
	154,720		**154,720**
Balance	41,440		

The treasurer also supplied the following information as at 31/12/20-8:

(a) Bar stock was €3,840.
(b) Bar creditors were €1,184.
(c) Wages due were €720.
(d) Subscriptions for 20-9 were €1,440.
(e) Equipment held on 31/12/20-8 to be depreciated by 20%.
(f) Clubhouse and pitches to be depreciated by 2%.

You are required to prepare:

- a statement of the club's accumulated fund on 1/1/20-8
- the income and expenditure account for the year ended 31/12/20-8
- the club's balance sheet as at 31/12/20-8.

Q9 Included in the assets and liabilities of the West Coast Golf Club on 1/1/20-9 were the following: clubhouse and land €280,000; equipment €32,000; investments €40,000; bar stock €5,400; expenses due €480; subscriptions due €700.

The following is a summary of the club's receipts and payments account for the year ended 31/12/20-9:

Receipts	€	Payments	€
Balance	2,900	Bar purchases	34,800
Investment income	3,200	Equipment	7,200
Subscriptions	45,300	General expenses	51,400
Bar sales	56,800	Competition prizes	3,400
Competition receipts	3,640	Bar creditors	1,380
		Balance 31/12/20-9	13,660
	111,840		**111,840**
Balance	13,660		

The treasurer also supplied the following information as at 31/12/20-9:

(a) Bar stock was €6,500.

(b) Bar creditors were €620.

(c) Expenses prepaid were €400.

(d) Subscriptions prepaid were €1,200.

(e) Equipment held on 31/12/20-9 to be depreciated by 25%.

(f) Depreciate clubhouse and land by 4%.

You are required to prepare

- a statement showing the club's accumulated fund on 1/1/20-9
- a bar trading account for the year ended 31/12/20-9
- an income and expenditure account for the year ended 31/12/20-9
- a balance sheet as at 31/12/20-9.

Practice Questions

Q1 In each of the following adjustments show the treatment of life memberships in the income and expenditure account and the balance sheet.

(a) Life membership 1/1/20-2 €24,000
New life memberships €6,000
Life membership to be written off over a ten-year period commencing in 20-2.

(b) Life membership 1/1/20-3 €32,000
New life memberships €8,000
Life membership to be written off over an eight-year period commencing in 20-3.

(c) Life membership 1/1/20-4 €36,000
New life memberships €9,000
Life membership to be written off over a nine-year period commencing in 20-4.

13

Q2 **In each of the following questions calculate the amount of subscriptions for inclusion in the income and expenditure of a club and indicate the other adjustments necessary.**

(a) Year of account 20-1

Receipts and payments account: Subscriptions received, €56,000

Included in subscriptions are the following:

- Levy on 150 members of €90 each
- Subscriptions for 20-2, €3,500
- Subscriptions for 20-0, €3,900
- Life memberships, 3 new @ €6,000 each.

(b) Year of account 20-2

Receipts and payments account: Subscriptions received, €85,000

Included in subscriptions are the following:

- Levy on 200 members of €40 each
- Subscriptions for 20-1, €6,700
- Subscriptions for 20-3, €9,800
- Life memberships, 2 new @ €7,000 each
- Levy due from 50 members of €40 from 20-1.

Q3 **In each of following prepare the bar trading account from the extracts taken from the club's financial records, showing clearly the amount to be transferred to the income and expenditure account.**

(a)

	€
Bar receipts	45,790
Opening stock	2,340
Bar purchases	23,500
Bar debtors 1/1	1,230
Bar creditors 1/1	3,670
Bar debtors 31/12	1,450
Bar creditors 31/12	1,978
Closing stock	1,700

(b)

	€
Bar receipts	48,700
Opening stock	4,500
Bar purchases	23,690
Bar debtors 1/1	2,890
Bar creditors 1/1	3,450
Bar debtors 31/12	2,460
Bar creditors 31/12	3,910
Closing stock	5,680

Q4 In each of the following questions calculate the loan, loan interest due and loan interest for current year, stating clearly where each item will be entered in the accounts.

(a) Current year 20-3

Repayment of a €56,000 loan together with 15 months' interest on 30/9/20-3: €68,000

(b) Current year 20-4

Repayment of a €24,000 loan together with 2 years' interest on 31/12/20-4: €27,600

(c) Current year 20-5

Repayment of a €78,000 loan together with 3 years' interest on 30/9/20-5: €85,200

Q5 In each of the following show the necessary adjustments in relation to investment and investment interest due.

(a) 12% Investments, €14,000. Interest due, 1/1 €500. Interest received, €1,300.

(b) 8% Investments, €24,000. Interest due, 1/1 €600. Interest received, €1,600.

(c) Investment interest received €360 (9% for 3 months).

(d) Investment interest received €495 (11% for 3 months).

Exercises – Higher Level

Q1 Included among the assets and liabilities of the Hillview Golf Club on 1/1/20-0 were the following:

Clubhouse and fairways €736,000; bar stock €9,760; golf carts €99,200; life membership €28,800; bar debtors €592; bar creditors €4,320; prepaid subscriptions €960; 6% government investments €64,000; investment interest due €640; levy reserve fund €25,600; and wages due €2,560.

The club treasurer has supplied the following account of the club's activities during the year ended 31/12/20-0:

Receipts	€	Payments	€
Balance at bank	10,080	Bar purchases	65,680
Investment income	2,560	Sundry expenses	100,800
Entrance fees	14,960	Catering costs	23,600
Catering receipts	20,800	Golf carts	68,800
Annual sponsorship	36,800	Golf coaching lessons	3,040
Subscriptions	168,000	Repayment of €32,000 loan on 31/12/20-0 together with 15 months' interest	34,880
Bar sales	75,360	Balance	31,760
	328,560		**328,560**

You are given the following additional information and instructions:

(a) Bar stock at 31/12/20-0 was €13,040.

(b) Golf carts owned on 31/12/20-0 to be depreciated at the rate of 15% of cost.

(c) Clubhouse and fairways to be depreciated by 2%.

(d) Bar debtors and bar creditors on 31/12/20-0 were €664 and €4,880 respectively.

(e) Subscriptions include:

- six life memberships, bringing total life membership to 14
- subscriptions for 20-1 amounting to €2,560
- levy for 20-0 of €96 each on 250 members
- levy of €96 due from 8 members on 1/1/20-0.

(f) Life membership was to be written off over an eight-year period commencing in 20-0.

You are required to:

- Show the club's accumulated fund on 1/1/20-0.
- Show the income and expenditure account for the year ended 31/12/20-0.

What points would you as an ordinary member make concerning the proposed six-year levy scheme to fund a €90,000 extension to the clubhouse and bar?

Q2 Included in the assets and liabilities of the Mountmellick Basketball Club on 1/1/20-0 were:

Clubhouse and grounds €336,000; bar stock €22,120; equipment (at cost) €119,000; bar debtors €672; bar creditors €11,760; life membership €25,200; subscriptions due €840; levy reserve fund €21,000; wages prepaid €420.

The club treasurer has supplied the following information of the club's activities during the year ended 31/12/20-0:

Receipts	€	Payments	€
Bank current account balance	1,330	Bar purchases	53,480
Bar receipts	104,020	Equipment	8,400
Catering receipts	17,360	Sundry expenses	36,820
Income from 5% Gov. bonds	1,575	Catering costs	19,880
Subscriptions	58,191	Prize bonds	2,800
Sponsorship	9,100	Travel expenses	22,400
Sale of equipment (cost €5,600)	3,500	Repayment of €28,000 loan on 31/8/20-0 together with 1.5 years' interest	33,040
		Balance	18,256
	195,076		**195,076**

You are given the following additional information:

(a) Bar stock on 31/12/20-0 was €19,040.

(b) Equipment owned on 31/12/20-0 is to be depreciated at 25% of cost.

(c) Clubhouse and grounds are to be depreciated by 2%.

(d) Bar debtors and bar creditors on 31/12/20-0 were €504 and €12,880 respectively.

(e) Subscriptions include:
- three life memberships, bringing the total life membership to nine
- subscriptions for 20-1 amounting to €336
- levy for 20-0 of €35 on 300 members
- levy due 1/1/20-0 on nine members of €35 each.

(f) Life membership is to be written off over an eight-year period commencing in 20-0.

(g) Investment interest due on 31/12/20-0 was €175.

You are required to:
- Show the club's accumulated fund on 1/1/20-0.
- Show the income and expenditure account for the year ended 31/12/20-0.

Q3 Included in the assets and liabilities of Greengrass Tennis Club on 1/1/20-4 were the following:

Clubhouse and courts €600,000; equipment (cost) €60,000; 10% investments €50,000; life membership €16,000; bar debtors €3,500; bar creditors €6,700; bar stock €2,300; cleaning wages due €1,100; subscriptions prepaid €1,000; levy reserve fund €10,000; investment interest due €400.

The following is a summary of the club's receipts and payments account for the year ended 31/12/20-4:

Receipts	€	Payments	€
Balance	4,000	Bar purchases	35,000
Investment income	2,600	Cleaning expenses	31,000
Entrance fees	11,000	Raffle costs	1,600
Raffle income	4,500	Equipment	12,000
Sponsorship	22,000	General expenses	65,000
Transfer from building society	10,000	Repayment of a €30,000 loan together with 1.5 years' interest on 30/9/20-4	33,600
Bar sales	85,600		
Subscriptions	44,600	Balance	6,100
	184,300		**184,300**
Balance	6,100		

The treasurer has also supplied the following information and instructions as at 31/12/20-4:

(a) Bar stock was €4,500, which included stock of cleaning materials, €600.

(b) Electricity due was €250 and stock of heating oil, €870.

(c) Clubhouse and courts to be revalued on 1/7/20-4 at €800,000. Provision should be made for depreciation at a rate of 2% from date of revaluation. There was no depreciation prior to that date.

(d) Bar debtors and bar creditors on 31/12/20-4 were €2,100 and €2,500 respectively.

(e) Depreciate equipment at 20% of cost on 31/12/20-4.

(f) Life membership is to be written off over a ten-year period commencing in 20-4.

(g) Subscriptions include the following:
- three life memberships of €3,000 each
- subscriptions for 20-5 of €300
- levy of €100 on 100 members
- levy of €100 on 10 members due 1/1/20-4.

You are required to prepare:
- a statement of the club's accumulated fund on 1/1/20-4
- the income and expenditure account for the year ended 31/12/20-4.

Indicate the points you would make as treasurer to a proposal by the members at the AGM to reduce subscriptions by 10%.

Explain what a levy is. If it were proposed to introduce another levy for three years to fund a new clubhouse costing €300,000, what points would you as an ordinary member make?

Q4 Included in the assets and liabilities of the Glenside Golf Club on 1/1/20-6 were the following:

Clubhouse and land €295,500; bar stock €13,800; equipment at cost €23,400; life membership €27,000; bar debtors €255; bar creditors €7,530; investment income due €2,400; subscriptions prepaid €1,500.

The club treasurer has supplied the following bank records of the club's activities during the year ended 31/12/20-6:

Receipts	€	Payments	€
Balance current account	22,500	Sundry expenses	64,900
Income from 4% Gov. investments	4,800	Catering costs	21,300
Sale of equipment (cost €2,250)	1,485	Equipment	8,855
Catering receipts	7,050	Repayment of a €15,000 loan on 1/6/20-6 together with 3 years' interest	19,500
Subscriptions	48,720	Clubhouse extension	60,000
Bar sales	82,500	Bar purchases	67,500
Transfer from building society	45,000		
Balance	30,000		
	242,055		**242,055**

You are given the following additional information:

(a) Bar stock on 31/12/20-6 was €15,000.

(b) Equipment owned on 31/12/20-6 is to be depreciated at 20% of cost.

(c) Clubhouse is to be depreciated at the rate of 2%. **Note:** the value of land was €100,500.

(d) Bar debtors and bar creditors on 31/12/20-6 were €345 and €7,230 respectively.

(e) Subscriptions include life memberships of €6,750 and a levy for 20-6 of €15,000.

(f) Life membership is to be written off over a ten-year period commencing in 20-6.

You are required to:
- Show the club's accumulated fund on 1/1/20-6.
- Show the income and expenditure account for the year ended 31/12/20-6.
- Show the balance sheet as at 31/12/20-6.

State what points you would make as an ordinary member concerning a proposed 10% increase in the subscription rate for 20-7.

Explain the difference between capital and revenue expenditure, making reference to two of the above figures.

Q5 Included in the assets and liabilities of the Rings 'n' Hoops Basketball Club on 1/1/20-6 were the following:

Clubhouse and courts €925,000; café stock €4,750; equipment at cost €35,750; life membership €45,000; café debtors €190; café creditors €3,060; subscriptions for 20-6 €2,250; 7% investment bonds €50,000; investment income due €180; levy reserve fund €75,000; wages due €3,000.

The club treasurer has supplied the following account of the club's activities during the year ended 31/12/20-6:

Receipts	€	Payments	€
Bank	5,550	Café purchases	100,625
Investment income	1,810	General expenses	232,000
Lotto grant	21,250	Disco expenses	5,575
Disco receipts	8,310	Equipment	55,630
Annual sponsorship	41,250	Repairs to equipment	5,815
Subscriptions	317,750	Repayment of €37,500 loan on 31/12/20-6 together with 15 months' interest	43,125
Café sales	140,830	Transfer to building society	87,500
		Balance	6,480
	536,750		**536,750**

You are given the following additional information and instructions:

(a) Café stock on 31/12/20-6 was €5,375, which included damaged stock which cost €2,500 but has a net realisable value of €1,005.

(b) Equipment owned at the end of the year is to be depreciated at 10%.

(c) Clubhouse and courts are to be depreciated at 4% per annum. On 31/12/20-6 the clubhouse and courts were revalued at €1,100,000 and this revaluation is to be incorporated into the accounts.

(d) Café debtors were €140 and creditors were €3,460 on 31/12/20-6.

(e) Subscriptions include:
- two life memberships of €7,500 each
- subscriptions for 20-7 amounting to €3,000
- levy for 20-6 of €250 on 300 members
- levy for 20-5 of €250 on eight members.

(f) Life membership is to be written off over a 20-year period commencing in 20-6.

(g) During the year a person was involved in a fall while watching a basketball match. The person is suing the club for €25,000 compensation and the club's solicitors have advised that the club is likely to be liable.

You are required to:

- Show the club's accumulated fund on 1/1/20-6.
- Show the café trading account for the year ended 31/12/20-6.
- Show the club's income and expenditure account for the year ended 31/12/20-6.
- Show the club's balance sheet as at 31/12/20-6.

Q6 Included in the assets and liabilities of the Lakelands Tennis Club on 1/1/20-9 were the following:

Clubhouse and courts €1,020,000; bar stock 8,100; equipment (cost) €48,000; bar debtors €660; bar creditors €5,400; levy reserve fund €57,000; 8% government investments €90,000; investment income due €180; subscriptions prepaid €2,700; cleaning expenses due €4,350; life membership €63,000.

The club treasurer has supplied the following account of the club's activities during the year ended 31/12/20-9.

Receipts	€	Payments	€
Balance	10,665	Bar purchases	127,350
Investment income	4,860	Miscellaneous expenses	250,200
Tennis tournament fees	33,600	Cost of teas and minerals	7,800
Sale of teas and minerals	10,875	Equipment	49,200
Annual sponsorship	66,000	Coaching lessons	13,350
Subscriptions	255,300	Repayment of €60,000 loan on 31/12/20-9 with 16 months' interest	67,200
Bar sales	187,200	Transfer to building society	45,000
		Balance	8,400
	568,500		**568,500**

You are given the following additional information and instructions:

(a) Bar stock at 31/12/20-9 was €9,150.

(b) Equipment owned on 31/12/20-9 is to be depreciated by 15% of cost.

(c) Clubhouse and courts are to be depreciated by 2% per annum.

(d) Bar debtors and bar creditors on 31/12/20-9 were €780 and €6,300 respectively.

(e) Subscriptions include:
- three life memberships of €5,250 each
- subscriptions for 20-0 amounting to €5,400
- levy for 20-9 of €450 on 200 members
- levy for 20-8 on nine members at €450 each.

(f) Life membership is to be written off over a ten-year period commencing in 20-9.

You are required to:

- Show the club's accumulated fund on 1/1/20-9.
- Show the bar trading account for the year ended 31/12/20-9.
- Show the income and expenditure account for the year ended 31/12/20-9.
- Show the club's balance sheet as on 31/12/20-9.

Q7 Included in the assets and liabilities of the Moon and Stars Drama Club on 1/1/20-3 were the following:

Premises €464,000; props and stage equipment €17,600; life membership €38,400; restaurant stock €6,560; subscriptions prepaid €1,680; restaurant debtors €416; restaurant creditors €2,320; 8% government investments €40,000; investment income due €672; wages due €320; levy reserve fund €64,000.

The club treasurer has supplied the following account of the club's activities during the year ended 31/12/20-3:

Receipts	€	Payments	€
Restaurant receipts	19,840	Balance	2,960
Dance receipts	13,120	Restaurant purchases	14,768
Annual sponsorship	6,400	Drama lessons	1,920
Investment interest	2,720	Dance costs	9,952
Subscriptions	57,920	New props	12,800
Show sales	2,400	Repayment of €25,600 loan on 30/6/20-3 together with 1.5 years' interest	27,520
		Balance	32,480
	102,400		**102,400**

You are given the following additional information and instructions:

(a) Restaurant stock on 31/12/20-3 was €4,480.

(b) Props and stage equipment owned on 31/12/20-3 are to be depreciated at the rate of 10% per annum.

(c) Restaurant debtors and creditors on 31/12/20-3 were €224 and €400 respectively.

(d) Subscriptions include:
- three life memberships of €3,200 each
- subscriptions for 20-4 amounting to €2,880
- levy for 20-3 of €80 each on 40 members
- levy for 20-2 of €80 each on 20 members.

(e) Premises are to be depreciated at a rate of 2% of cost. Land was valued at €124,000.

(f) Life membership is to be written off over a ten-year period commencing in 20-3.

(g) The club had the premises including land revalued on 31/12/20-3 at €640,000.

(h) Wages due on 1/1/20-3 were owed to the drama teacher.

You are required to:

- Show the club's accumulated fund on 1/1/20-3.
- Show the restaurant trading account for the year ended 31/12/20-3.
- Show the income and expenditure account for the year ended 31/12/20-3.
- Show the balance sheet as on 31/12/20-3.

Indicate the points you as treasurer would make to a proposal to reduce the subscriptions by 10%.

Theory

Q1 Explain the differences between an income and expenditure account and a receipts and payments account.

Q2 Who is responsible for the production of a club's financial records?

Q3 Explain the differences between the balance in the income and expenditure account and the closing balance in the receipts and payments account.

Q4 Explain with an example what is meant by a special purpose profit and loss account.

Q5 Explain with examples, the difference between a levy on members and subscriptions.

Exam Tips

- These questions can be asked in section A or section B of the examination.
- Learn the layout of the different accounts associated with club accounts.
- When preparing the accumulated fund at the beginning, make sure you include the opening bank account balance and read the question in full, as there are often other hidden assets and/or liabilities further into the question.
- Prepare a special purpose profit and loss account for each activity – for example, bar trading account.
- Make adjustments for accruals and prepayments before entering figures in the accounts.
- Know where to place the items associated with club accounts – for example, life membership.
- Practise theory advice questions.

14 Service Firms' Accounts

Objectives

On completion students should be able to:

- List the reasons why service firms prepare accounts;
- Prepare a statement of capital/reserves for a service firm;
- Prepare a special purpose profit and loss account;
- Prepare a profit and loss account (income and expenditure account) for a service firm;
- Prepare a balance sheet.

Service firms

Service firms are businesses that are set up to earn a profit from providing a service rather than from buying and selling. They include: hairdressers, taxi firms, accountants, dentists, doctors, gymnasiums. Just like other businesses they should keep a proper set of accounts.

Service firms should keep records for the following reasons:

- to find out the profit or loss of the business
- to keep a record of amounts owing to and by them
- to find the value of assets and net worth of the business
- to find the value of closing stock of saleable items, if any
- to present to the Revenue Commissioners.

Service firms usually have few fixed assets and their main source of income is the fees they charge for their services. They often maintain a small number of products which they use in their profession, such as shampoo for use in a hair salon.

The accounts

Service firms usually prepare the following accounts:

- Statement of capital/reserves
- Special purpose profit and loss account
- Profit and loss account/income and expenditure account
- Balance sheet.

Statement of capital/reserves

This statement is prepared to find out the net worth/value of a service firm at a particular time.

It is similar to the statement of accumulated fund in a club account. It lists the assets and liabilities at the beginning of the accounting period. If it is a statement of reserves, the capital item is entered with the liabilities and the final figure is reserves.

Example

The Duffy family are involved in the tourist industry. They run a small guest house and holiday home. Included in their assets and liabilities on 1/1/20-1 were: guesthouse €235,000; holiday home €185,000; bicycles €1,200; linen €2,500; stock of heating oil €200; pre-booked deposits for holiday home €2,300; creditors for provisions €230. They also had a bank overdraft of €2,900.

Prepare a statement showing their total net assets (statement of capital) as at 1/1/20-1.

Solution

Statement of Capital for the Duffy family on 1/1/20-1

	€	€
Assets		
Guesthouse	235,000	
Holiday home	185,000	
Bicycles	1,200	
Linen	2,500	
Stock of oil	200	423,900
***Less* Liabilities**		
Store provisions/creditors	230	
Bank	2,900	
Advanced deposits	2,300	(5,430)
Capital 1/1/20-0		**418,470**

Special purpose profit and loss account

Service firms sometimes prepare a special purpose profit and loss account where they earn income from a different but related activity. For example, hair care products used in the salon and hair care products sold to clients.

NOTE

Most service firms do not prepare a trading account as they are not involved in buying and selling.

Income and expenditure account (profit and loss account)

The profit and loss account of a service firm is presented in the same way as an income and expenditure account of a club. It takes into account accruals and prepayments as for any other organisation.

NOTE

An income and expenditure account charges items such as depreciation and all revenue expenditure against income.

Balance sheet

The balance sheet of a service firm is presented in the same way as that of any other organisation.

Sample Ordinary Level question

The following were the assets and liabilities of Gary Byrne, a physiotherapist, on 1/1/20-0: buildings €230,000, equipment €45,000, motor car €21,000, amounts due from private patients €1,280, and stock of materials for use in the clinic €2,780. Cash at bank €1,900, amounts due from medical insurance scheme €3,400 and electricity charges due €430.

14

The following is a summary of his receipts and payments for the year ended 31/12/20-0.

Receipts	€	Payments	€
Private patient fees	94,800	Purchase of materials	23,000
Medical insurance scheme fees	197,800	Light and heat	6,900
		Insurance	3,500
		Telephone and postage	8,340
		Diesel for motor car	8,800
		Technician wages	10,800
		Magazines	800
		Equipment	24,000

The following information is to be taken into account on 31/12/20-0:

(a) Stock of materials for use in the clinic was €3,400.

(b) Insurance was for the year ended 31/3/20-1.

(c) Fees due from private patients and the medical insurance scheme were €2,670 and €5,600, respectively.

(d) Depreciate equipment by 25% of cost and buildings by 4% of cost.

(e) Depreciation is to be provided on motor vehicles at 15% of cost.

You are required to:

- Prepare G. Byrne's statement of capital on 1/1/20-0.
- Prepare Byrne's income and expenditure account for the year ended 31/12/20-0.

Solution

Statement of Capital of Gary Byrne on 1/1/20-0

	€	€
Assets		
Buildings	230,000	
Equipment	45,000	
Motor car	21,000	
Amounts due from private patients	1,280	
Stock of medical materials	2,780	
Cash at bank	1,900	
Fees due from medical insurance scheme	3,400	305,360
***Less* Liabilities**		
Electricity due		(430)
Capital on 1/1/20-0		**304,930**

Income and Expenditure Account of Gary Byrne for the year ended 31/12/20-0

	€	€
Income		
Private patient fees (W1)	96,190	
Fees, medical insurance scheme (W2)	200,000	296,190
Expenditure		
Materials (W3)	22,380	
Light and heat (W4)	6,470	
Insurance (W5)	2,625	
Telephone and postage	8,340	
Diesel for motor car	8,800	
Technician fees	10,800	
Magazines	800	
Depreciation of equipment (W6)	17,250	
Depreciation of buildings (W7)	9,200	
Depreciation of motor car (W8)	3,150	(89,815)
Net profit		**206,375**

Workings

W1 Private patient fees

Amount received	94,800
Less Due 1/1/20-0	(1,280)
Add Due 31/12/20-0	2,670
	96,190

W2 Medical insurance scheme

Amount received	197,800
Less Due 1/1/20-0	(3,400)
Add Due 31/12/20-0	5,600
	200,000

W3 Materials

Opening stock	2,780
Purchases	23,000
Less Closing stock	(3,400)
	22,380

W4 Light and heat

Amount paid	6,900
Less Electricity due 1/1/20-0	(430)
	6,470

W5 Insurance

Amount paid	3,500
Less Prepaid (3,500 x 3/12)	(875)
	2,625

W6 Depreciation of equipment

69,000 x 25% = **17,250**

W7 Depreciation of buildings

230,000 x 4% = **9,200**

W8 Motor car

21,000 x 15% = **3,150**

Adjustments (Higher Level)

1. Depreciation of fixed assets

NOTE

Fixed assets must be included in the statement of capital at their net book value.

Example

Topcare Health Services Ltd have the following assets at cost on 1/1/20-9: land and buildings €500,000; equipment €34,000; minibus €56,000. All fixed assets have three years' accumulated depreciation at the start of the year. During the year a piece of equipment which cost €4,000 was sold for €1,000.

Depreciation to be provided as follows: land and buildings 2% of cost, equipment and minibus 20% of cost.

Show the entries for fixed assets in the statement of capital and the relevant entries in the profit and loss account and balance sheet.

Solution

Asset	Statement of Capital	Profit and Loss Account	Balance Sheet
Land and buildings	500,000 x 2% x 3 = €30,000 depreciation 500,000 - 30,000 = **€470,000 net book value**	500,000 x 2% = **€10,000 expense**	Cost: €500,000 Depreciation: €40,000 NBV: €460,000
Equipment	34,000 x 20% x 3 = €20,400 depreciation 34,000 - 20,400 = **€13,600 net book value**	30,000 x 20% = **€6,000 expense** 4,000 x 20% x 3 = €2,400 depreciation 4,000 - 2,400 = NBV €1,600 Sold for €1,000 1,600 - 1,000 = **€600 expense**	Cost: €30,000 Depreciation: €24,000 NBV: €6,000
Minibus	56,000 x 20% x 3 = €33,600 depreciation 56,000 - 33,600 = **€22,400 net book value**	56,000 x 20% = **€11,200 expense**	Cost: €56,000 Depreciation: €44,800 NBV: €11,200

See Practice Question 1 for exercises on this adjustment.

2. Clients' fees

Client fees can be either from private clients or, in the case of dentists and doctors, there may also be public fees (fees from medical insurance scheme).

Clients' fees are adjusted for amounts due or prepaid at the beginning or end of the financial period.

NOTE

Clients' fees for the current financial year must be included. Clients' fees for past or future years must be excluded.

14

Example

The following is an extract taken from the accounts for the year ended 31/12/20-0:

Clients' fees due at the start	€350
Clients' fees received during the year	€203,560
Clients' fees prepaid at the end	€400
Clients' fees due at the end	€120

Note: A cheque received from a client for €230 was returned by the bank.
Calculate the clients' fees to be included in the company's profit and loss account.

Solution

Amount for inclusion in profit and loss account:

	€
Amount received	203,560
Less Due at start	(350)
Less Fees prepaid end	(400)
Add Amounts due at the end	120
Amount for profit and loss	202,930

If the client whose cheque was returned was declared bankrupt you must subtract it from the amount received and enter it as an expense in the profit and loss account as a bad debt.

See Practice Question 2 for exercises on this adjustment.

3. Materials used in the business

When there are opening and closing stocks of any material, a working should be shown to calculate the amount used during the year, e.g. dental materials used, medical materials used.

If these materials are bought and sold you should a prepare a trading account – for example, with hair care products in the salon, there must be a trading account prepared to find the profit or loss on the sale of these items.

Example

From the following extracts calculate the amount of materials used in the business during the year: opening stock of dental materials €3,400: purchases of dental materials €23,500; closing stock of dental materials €3,900; creditors at 31/12 for dental supplies amounted to €200.

Solution

	€	
Opening stock	3,400	**Asset** in statement of capital/reserves
Add Purchases + creditors	23,700	200 as **liability** in balance sheet
Less Closing stock	(3,900)	**Asset** in balance sheet
Amount used	23,200	**Expense** in profit and loss account

See Practice Question 3 for exercises on this adjustment.

4. Shop trading account

Sometimes a service firm will have to prepare a special purpose trading account when they buy and sell products. Expenses involved in selling these items must be apportioned between the shop and the main activity of the business.

14

Example

The following extracts are taken from the accounts of a service firm which also runs a shop:

Opening stock for shop	€3,400
Purchases for shop	€23,500
Closing stock for shop	€2,900

Other information includes:

Shop sales	€45,000
Wages and salaries	€75,600
Light and heat	€5,600
Telephone	€4,900
Insurance	€2,900

Wages and salaries include €15,000 paid to the receptionist who also runs the shop. It is estimated that 40% of this salary is attributable to the shop. Also it is estimated that 20% of light and heat, 30% of telephone and €800 of insurance is attributable to the shop.

Calculate the profit/loss on the shop.

Solution

	€	€
Sales		45,000
***Less* Cost of sales**		
Opening stock	3,400	
Purchases	23,500	
	26,900	
Less Closing stock	(2,900)	(24,000)
Gross profit		21,000
***Less* Expenses**		
Wages (40% of €15,000)	6,000	
Light and heat (20% of €5,600)	1,120	
Insurance	800	
Telephone (30% of €4,900)	1,470	(9,390)
Net profit on the shop		**11,610**

See Practice Question 4 for exercises on this adjustment.

5. Loans

These adjustments match those covered in Club Accounts and Final Accounts.

14

6. Statement of capital and/or reserves

Example

The assets and liabilities of S. Kean, a doctor, on 1/1/20-0 were as follows: surgery €240,000; medical equipment €45,000; motor car €20,000; stock of medical supplies €6,500; owed from medical insurance scheme €2,450; 5% investments €30,000; fees due from private patients €3,500; bank €9,100; creditors for medical supplies €2,800; capital 239,000.

The following additional information must be taken into account:

(a) On 1/5/20-0 €57,200 was paid to cover the repayment of a loan of €50,000 together with three years' interest.

(b) All fixed assets have been depreciated for two years prior to 20-0 as follows: equipment by 20% per annum of cost; surgery 2% per annum on cost; motor car 15% per annum on cost.

Prepare a statement of reserves as at 1/1/20-0.

Solution

Statement of Reserves as at 1/1/20-0

	€	€
Assets		
Surgery (240,000 - 9,600)	230,400	
Medical equipment (45,000 - 18,000)	27,000	
Motor car (20,000 - 6,000)	14,000	
Stock of medical supplies	6,500	
Owed from medical insurance scheme	2,450	
Investments	30,000	
Fees due from private patients	3,500	
Bank	9,100	322,950
***Less* Liabilities**		
Creditors for medical supplies	2,800	
Loan	50,000	
Loan interest due	6,400	
Capital	239,000	(298,200)
Reserves 1/1/20-0		**24,750**

See Practice Question 5 for exercises on this adjustment.

7. Other adjustments

Other adjustments in service firms include:

- investments and investment income due
- accruals and prepayments (for example, light and heat)
- division of expenses between the firm and the special purpose profit and loss account.

Sample Higher Level question

The following were included in the assets and liabilities of the Westside Gym Ltd on 1/1/20-1: buildings and grounds €416,000; equipment €60,000; vehicles at cost €48,000; stock in shop €2,880; stock of heating oil €1,440; 5% investments €32,000; contract cleaning prepaid €240; clients' deposits in advance €4,000; creditors for supplies €1,200; authorised share capital €320,000; issued share capital €280,000.

All fixed assets have three years' accumulated depreciation on 1/1/20-1.

The following is a receipts and payments account for the year ended 31/12/20-1:

Receipts	€	Payments	€
Bank balance	5,200	Laundry expenses	2,400
Clients' fees	256,000	Telephone	1,120
Investment income	880	Wages and salaries	67,440
Shop sales	33,600	Repayment of €24,000 loan on 1/4/20-1 with 1.25 years' interest	28,800
Balance	86,880	Equipment	16,000
		New extension 1/1/-1	176,000
		New vehicle	32,000
		Contract cleaning	2,720
		Light and heat	2,640
		Insurance	4,960
		Purchases - shop	20,800
		Purchases - supplies	27,680
	382,560		**382,560**

The following information and instructions are to be taken into account:

(a) Closing stock at 31/12/20-1: shop €1,280; heating oil €320.

(b) Cleaning is carried out under contract payable monthly in advance and includes a payment of €560 for January 20-2.

(c) Client fees includes fees for 20-2 of €4,400. Client fees in arrears at 31/12/20-1 were €480.

(d) Wages and salaries include €16,000 per annum paid to the receptionist who also runs the shop. It is estimated that 40% of this salary and €240 of the light and heat, €720 of the insurance and €320 of the telephone is attributable to the shop.

(e) Creditors for supplies at 31/12/20-1 were €1,600.

(f) Electricity due on 31/12/20-1 was €272.

(g) Provide for depreciation as follows:

Buildings	2% of cost for the full year
Equipment	10% of cost for the full year
Vehicles	20% of cost per annum from the date of purchase to date of sale.

Note: The vehicle held on 1/1/20-1 was purchased three years earlier and was traded in for a new vehicle on 1/7/20-1. The trade allowance was €6,400 against the new vehicle costing €38,400.

(h) On 31/12/20-1 the Westside Gym Ltd decided to revalue buildings at €680,000.

1. You are required to:

(a) Calculate the company's reserves (profit and loss balance) on 1/1/20-1.

(b) Calculate the profit/loss from the shop for the year ended 31/12/20-1.

(c) Prepare a profit and loss account of the Westside Gym Ltd for the year ended 31/12/20-1.

(d) Prepare a balance sheet as at 31/12/20-1.

2. The company now wishes to expand and build a new swimming pool at a cost of €120,000. Advise the company on how to fund this swimming pool.

Solution

14

1(a) Statement of Reserves of Westside Gym Ltd on 1/1/20-1

	€	€
Assets		
Buildings and grounds (W1)	391,040	
Equipment (W1)	42,000	
Vehicles (W1)	19,200	
Stock for the shop	2,880	
Stock of heating oil	1,440	
5% Investments	32,000	
Contract cleaning prepaid	240	
Bank	5,200	494,000
***Less* Liabilities**		
Clients' deposits in advance	4,000	
Creditors for supplies	1,200	
Loan (W6)	24,000	
Loan interest due (W6)	3,840	
Issued share capital	280,000	(313,040)
Reserves at 1/1/20-1		**180,960**

Fixed assets must be included here at their book value.

(b) Shop Trading, Profit and Loss Account for the year ended 31/12/20-1

	€	€
Sales		33,600
***Less* Cost of sales**		
Opening stock	2,880	
Purchases	20,800	
	23,680	
Less Closing stock	(1,280)	(22,400)
Gross profit		11,200
***Less* Expenses**		
Wages (W5)	6,400	
Light and heat	240	
Insurance	720	
Telephone	320	(7,680)
Net profit		**3,520**

(c) Income and Expenditure Account (profit and loss account) for the year ended 31/12/20-1

	€	€
Income		
Clients' fees (W2)	256,080	
Investment income (W3)	1,600	
Shop profit	3,520	261,200
***Less* Expenditure**		
Laundry expenses	2,400	
Telephone (W4)	800	
Wages and salaries (W5)	61,040	
Loan interest (W6)	960	
Depreciation of equipment (W12)	7,600	
Cleaning (W7)	2,400	
Light and heat (W8)	3,792	
Insurance (W9)	4,240	
Supplies (W10)	28,080	
Depreciation of buildings (W13)	11,840	
Depreciation of vehicles (W14)	8,640	
Loss on sale of vehicle (W11)	8,000	(139,792)
Net profit		121,408
Add Reserves 1/1/20-1		180,960
Reserves 31/12/20-1		**302,368**

(d) Balance Sheet as on 31/12/20-1

	Cost (€)	Agg. Dep. (€)	Net (€)
Fixed assets			
Buildings and grounds	680,000		680,000
Equipment	76,000	25,600	50,400
Vehicles	38,400	3,840	34,560
	794,400	29,440	764,960
Financial assets			
5% Investments			32,000
Current assets			796,960
Stock shop		1,280	
Stock oil		320	
Cleaning prepaid		560	
Clients' fees due		480	
Investment income due (W3)		720	
		3,360	

Continued >

14

14

	€	€	€
***Less* Creditors: amounts falling due within 1 year**			
Client fees in advance	4,400		
Electricity due	272		
Creditors for supplies	1,600		
Bank	86,880	(93,152)	(89,792)
			707,168
Financed by			
Capital and reserves	**Authorised**	**Issued**	
Ordinary share capital	320,000	280,000	
Revaluation reserve (W15)		124,800	
Profit and loss balance 31/12		302,368	707,168
			707,168

2. Advice regarding new swimming pool

The company has expanded during 20-1 with the building of an extension and the purchase of new equipment and a new bus, all without borrowing any money, as well as repaying a loan of €24,000 plus interest. However, it now has a bank overdraft in excess of €89,000 which may make borrowing in tough economic times difficult.

The company is profitable so should be able to sell the remaining shares, yielding €40,000. It could also sell its investments, which would yield a further €32,000. This leaves a shortfall of €48,000, which if the bank overdraft was reduced could be borrowed on a term loan from the bank.

Workings

W1 Opening value of fixed assets

	Cost	Years	Rate	Depreciation	Net Value
Buildings and grounds	416,000	3	2%	24,960	**391,040**
Equipment	60,000	3	10%	18,000	**42,000**
Vehicles	48,000	3	20%	28,800	**19,200**

W2 Clients' fees

Amount received	256,000
Add Prepaid 1/1/20-1	4,000
Less Prepaid 31/12/20-1	(4,400)
Add Due 31/12/20-1	480
	256,080

W3 Investment income

32,000 x 5%	1,600
Amount received	(880)
Amount due	**720**

W4 Telephone

Amount paid	1,120
Less Shop	(320)
	800

W5 Wages and salaries

Amount paid	67,440
Less Shop (16,000 x 40%)	(6,400)
	61,040

W6 Loan

Amount of loan	24,000
Repaid	28,800
Interest	4,800
4,800/15 months = 320 per month	
Due start 12 x 320	3,840
This year 3 x 320	**960**

W7 Contract cleaning

Amount paid	2,720
Add Prepaid 1/1	240
Less Prepaid 31/12	(560)
	2,400

W8 Light and Heat

Amount paid	2,640
Add Oil 1/1/20-1	1,440
Less Oil 31/12/20-1	(320)
Add Electricity due 31/12	272
Less Shop	(240)
	3,792

W9 Insurance

Amount paid	4,960
Less Shop	(720)
	4,240

W10 Supplies

Purchases	27,680
Less Creditors 1/1	(1,200)
Add Creditors 31/12	1,600
	28,080

W11 Sale of vehicle

Cost price	48,000
Depreciation	(33,600)
Book value	14,400
Proceeds	6,400
Loss on sale	**8,000**

W12 Depreciation of equipment

Cost price 1/1/20-1	60,000
Add New equipment	16,000
	76,000
76,000 x 10% =	**7,600**

W13 Depreciation of buildings

Cost price 1/1/20-1	416,000
Add Extension	176,000
	592,000
592,000 x 2% =	**11,840**

W14 Depreciation of vehicles

Old bus 48,000 x 20% x 0.5 =	4,800
New bus 38,400 x 20% x 0.5 =	3,840
	8,640

W15 Revaluation of Assets

Increase in value (680,000 – 592,000)	88,000
Add Opening depreciation	24,960
Add This year's depreciation	11,840
Revaluation reserve	**124,800**

Exercises – Ordinary Level

Q1 The following were the assets and liabilities of Sarah Wells, a dentist, on 1/1/20-9: premises €675,000; furniture €24,600; car €54,000; amounts due from private patients €1,800; cash at bank €16,800; dental equipment €42,000; electricity due €900.

The following details were taken from her records on 31/12/20-9:

Receipts	€	Payments	€
Fees from private patients	330,600	Dental equipment	18,000
Medical card receipts	157,350	Light and heat	21,750
		Dental supplies	51,300
		Insurance	9,000
		Telephone and internet	7,350
		Diesel and motor expenses	3,150
		Technician fees	37,050
		Newspapers and magazines	1,125

14

The following additional information should be taken into account on 31/12/20-9:

(a) Stock of dental supplies was valued at €5,100.

(b) Private patients owed Sarah €10,050.

(c) Prepaid insurance was €2,850.

(d) Provide for depreciation as follows: Dental equipment at 10% of cost
Car by 20% of cost.

You are required to prepare:

- Sarah's capital on 1/1/20-9
- an income and expenditure account for the year ended 31/12/20-9.

Q2 **The following were the assets and liabilities of Greg MacGyver, a doctor, on 1/1/20-5: buildings €568,000; furniture €10,240; car €35,200; due from medical card scheme €288; medical equipment €6,400; cash €20,000; telephone due €1,120.**

The following details were taken from his records on 31/12/20-5:

Receipts	€	Payments	€
Private patients' fees	152,160	Medical equipment	14,400
Medical card scheme	78,240	Telephone and internet	5,360
		Electricity and heating	10,320
		Wages and salaries	28,800
		Newspapers	960
		Diesel and motor expenses	17,840
		Audit fees	2,080
		Locum fees (substitute doctor)	23,200
		Cleaning	3,680
		Insurance	18,400

The following additional information is to be taken into account at 31/12/20-5:

(a) Telephone bill due was €720.

(b) Amount owed from the medical card scheme was €1,360.

(c) Wages due was €320.

(d) Provide for depreciation as follows: Car 10% per annum
Medical equipment 25% per annum.

You are required to:

- Calculate Greg's capital on 1/1/20-5.
- Prepare MacGyver's income and expenditure account for the year ended 31/12/20-5.

Q3 **The Butler family is involved in the tourist industry. They run a guesthouse and rent boats and a holiday home during the holiday season. Included among their assets and liabilities on 1/1/20-4 were the following: guesthouse €552,000; holiday home €144,000; boats €28,800; equipment €1,680; prepaid deposits from tourists for the holiday home €1,800; stock of coal €1,080.**

The following is a summary of the receipts and payments account for the year ended 31/12/20-4:

Receipts	€	Payments	€
Balance	1,452	Guest house provisions	17,040
Guest house receipts	34,320	Light and heat	3,840
Rent from boats	4,440	Drawings	1,104
Rent from holiday home	11,040	Wages	11,040
		Cleaning expenses	324
		Advertising	540
		Repairs to boats	2,112
		Balance	15,252
	51,252		**51,252**

The following information and instructions should be taken into account as at 31/12/20-4:

(a) Stock of coal and oil was €540.

(b) Depreciation is to be provided as follows: Boats 20% per annum
Equipment 25% per annum.

(c) Included in the receipts for the guest house were deposits of €1,800 for 20-5.

(d) It was estimated that 20% of provisions was for private use.

(e) There was €300 owed to the local shop for provisions.

You are required to prepare:

- a statement to show the total net assets of the Butler family business on 1/1/20-4
- an income and expenditure account for the year ended 31/12/20-4
- a balance sheet as at 31/12/20-4.

Q4 **Tom and Geri Hales are involved in a hairdressing business. Included in their assets on 1/1/20-2 were: buildings €540,000; equipment €195,000; car €54,000; stock of oil €2,550; fees due from customers €4,260; stock of shampoo and conditioners €7,200; and wages due to stylist €2,400.**

The following is a summary of the receipts and payments account for the year ended 31/12/20-2:

Receipts	€	Payments	€
Balance at bank	9,600	Advertising	27,600
Customers' fees	163,800	Purchase of shampoos	28,800
Sale of shampoos	47,400	New hair dryers	42,000
Loan from AIB bank	45,000	Light and heat	13,050
		Wages	48,600
		Drawings	57,000
		Cleaning	7,200
		AIB bank	9,000
		Insurance	18,900
		Balance	13,650
	265,800		**265,800**

14

The following information and instructions should be taken into account as at 31/12/20-2:

(a) Provide for depreciation on equipment owned on 31/12/20-2 at 15% per annum.

(b) Provide for depreciation on the car at 20% of cost per annum.

(c) The purchase price of shampoos is to be split evenly between the cost of shampoos for use in the salon and those for sale. All closing stocks of shampoo are for sale purposes only.

(d) Stock of shampoo and conditioners on 31/12/20-2 was valued at cost €11,400.

(e) Customers owed €9,720.

(f) Stock of heating oil was valued at €2,190.

(g) The loan received is repayable in five equal yearly instalments beginning on 1st July 20-2. This loan had 0% finance.

(h) It is estimated that 10% of cleaning was for family use.

You are required to prepare:

- a statement showing the total net assets of Tom and Geri's business on 1/1/20-2
- an income and expenditure account for the year ended 31/12/20-2
- a balance sheet as on 31/12/20-2.

Q5 **The following were the assets and liabilities of Jack Lord, a dentist, on 1 January 20-3: premises €240,000; fixtures and fittings €48,000; dental equipment €305,000; motor car €40,000; amounts due from private patients €8,500; prepaid insurance €400; electricity due €280; cash €5,460; stock of dental materials €1,516.**

The following details were taken from his records on 31/12/20-3:

Receipts	€	Payments	€
Patient fees (private)	120,660	Dental materials	10,530
Medical card scheme	40,220	Technicians' fees	18,840
		Anaesthetist's fees	13,150
		Rent and rates	9,650
		Insurance	10,140
		Electricity	6,780
		Newspapers and magazines	1,500
		Telephone and broadband	3,560
		Motor car running costs	12,340
		Audit fees	1,450
		Dental equipment	35,000
		Receptionist's salary	24,000

The following additional information is to be taken into account at 31/12/20-3:

(a) Stock of dental materials was valued at €2,430.

(b) He was owed €230 by private patients and €2,340 from the medical insurance scheme.

(c) He owed his receptionist wages of €300 per week for two weeks.

(d) Provide for depreciation as follows: dental equipment owned on 31/12/20-3 by 10% of cost and motor car by 20% of cost. Premises are to be depreciated by 5% per annum. (**Note:** land was valued at €40,000.)

You are required to:

- Calculate Jack Lord's capital on 1/1/20-3.
- Prepare Lord's income and expenditure account for the year ended 31/12/20-3.
- Prepare a balance sheet as at 31/12/20-3.

14

Q6 The following were the assets and liabilities of Aaron Spalling, a doctor, on 1/1/20-6: premises €300,000; fixtures and fittings €60,000; equipment €392,500; amounts due from private patients €10,750; prepaid rates €375; electricity due €350; cash at bank €6,400; stock of medicines €1,895; 10% investments €50,000.

The following details were taken from the records on 31/12/20-6:

Receipts	€	Payments	€
Fees from private patients	201,100	Medicines	13,170
		Drawings	40,000
		Rates to local council	815
		Medical insurance	1,935
		Light and heat	965
		Telephone and stationery	3,115
		Motor car expenses	5,600
		Cleaning expenses	2,150
		New surgical equipment	18,250
		Wages	30,000

The following additional information is supplied as at 31/12/20-6:

(a) Stock of medicines was valued at €6,860.

(b) Owed by private patients was €5,815.

(c) Wages due were €2,500.

(d) Depreciation was to be provided for at 10% of cost of equipment held on 31/12/20-6 and buildings at 5% of cost.

You are required to:

- Calculate Aaron's capital on 1/1/20-6.
- Prepare an income and expenditure account for Aaron Spalling for the year ended 31/12/20-6.
- Prepare a balance sheet as at 31/12/20-6.
- Advise Aaron regarding his financial position.

Q7 The Brady family are involved in the tourist industry. They run a guesthouse and also rent bicycles and a holiday apartment during the holiday season. Included in the assets and liabilities on 1/1/20-8 were the following: guesthouse €616,000; holiday apartment €156,000; bicycles €15,600; stock of heating oil €1,300; advance payments for rent of holiday apartment €2,600; linen and equipment €3,900.

14

The following is a summary of the receipts and payments account for the year ended 31/12/20-8:

Receipts	€	Payments	€
Balance	1,300	Guesthouse provisions	17,940
Guesthouse receipts	48,880	Light, heat and fuel	1,950
Rent from holiday apartment	16,900	Drawings	23,400
Receipts from bicycle hire	7,560	Wages	6,760
		Laundry costs	910
		Advertising	520
		Repairs to bicycles	1,820
		Balance	21,340
	74,640		**74,640**

The following information and instructions should be taken into account at 31/12/20-8:

(a) Bicycles are to be depreciated by 20% per annum, linen and equipment by 25% per annum.

(b) It is estimated that 20% of the provisions purchased were for family use.

(c) Included in the receipts for the guesthouse were deposits of €1,950 for 20-9.

(d) There was €1,170 worth of oil in the tank on 31/12/20-8.

(e) The Brady family owed the local supermarket €390 for provisions on 31/12/20-8.

You are required to prepare:

- a statement to show the total net assets of the Brady family on 1/1/20-8
- an income and expenditure account for the year ended 31/12/20-8
- a balance sheet as on 31/12/20-8.

Practice Questions

Q1 In each of the following show the entries for fixed assets in the statement of capital and the relevant entries in the profit and loss account and balance sheet.

(a) Land and buildings €350,000; equipment €90,000; furniture €80,000. All fixed assets have three years' accumulated depreciation at the start of the year. During the year a piece of equipment which cost €14,000 was sold for €10,000. Depreciation is to be provided for as follows: land and buildings 3% of cost; equipment and furniture 15% of cost.

(b) Land and buildings €650,000; equipment €45,000; computers €25,000. All fixed assets have four years' accumulated depreciation at the start of the year. Depreciation is to be provided for as follows: land and buildings 2% of cost, equipment and computers 15% of cost.

Q2 In each of the following calculate the amount of clients' fees to be included in the company's profit and loss account and indicate where the amount due/prepaid should be entered in the final accounts.

(a) Clients' fees due at the start €600; clients' fees received during the year €100,400; clients' fees prepaid at the end and due amounted to €900 and €690 respectively. **Note:** a cheque received from a client for €340 was returned by the bank.

(b) Clients' fees due at the start €800; clients' fees received during the year €76,400; clients' fees prepaid at the end and due amounted to €1,900 and €2,340 respectively. **Note:** a cheque received from a client for €1,450 was returned by the bank.

Q3 **From the following extracts calculate the amount of materials used in the firm during the year, stating clearly where the relevant amounts are entered in the final accounts.**

(a) Opening stock of medical supplies €4,500; purchases of medical supplies €32,400; closing stock of medical supplies €2,600; creditors for medical supplies at 31/12 amounted to €900.

(b) Opening stock of dental materials €6,000; purchases of dental materials €45,600; closing stock of dental materials €6,700; creditors for dental supplies at 31/12 amounted to €500. Creditors for materials 1/1 €340.

Q4 **In each of the following calculate the profit/loss on the shop.**

(a) The following extracts are taken from the accounts of a service firm which also runs a shop: opening stock for shop €6,500; purchases for shop €35,000; closing stock for shop €5,900. Other information includes:

Shop sales	€54,600
Wages and salaries	€90,000
Light and heat	€6,700
Telephone	€9,800
Insurance	€5,400
Debtors shop sales 31/12	€3,400

Wages and salaries include €18,000 paid to the receptionist who also runs the shop. It is estimated that 50% of this salary is attributable to the shop. Also it is estimated that 25% of light and heat, 40% of telephone and €1,800 of insurance is attributable to the shop.

(b) The following extracts are taken from the accounts of a service firm which also runs a shop: opening stock for shop €4,400; purchases for shop €32,000; closing stock for shop €3,100; opening creditors for shop €2,300; opening debtors for shop €1,200. Other information includes:

Shop sales	€89,800
Wages and salaries	€87,000
Light and heat	€9,800
Telephone	€9,600
Insurance	€6,000

Wages and salaries include €12,000 paid to the receptionist who also runs the shop. It is estimated that 30% of this salary is attributable to the shop. Also it is estimated that 10% of light and heat, 15% of telephone and €550 of insurance is attributable to the shop.

Q5 **In each of the following prepare a statement of capital/reserves.**

(a) The assets and liabilities of R. Harford, a dentist, on 1/1/20-1 were as follows: surgery €144,000; dental equipment €72,000; motor car €28,800; stock of dental supplies €6,480; owed from medical insurance scheme €6,840; creditors for dental supplies €4,840; 8% investments €96,000; fees due from private patients €2,520; bank €8,112. The following additional information must be taken into account:

(i) During 20-1, a loan of €48,000 was repaid on 1 May with three years' interest, totalling €52,320.

(ii) All fixed assets have been depreciated for two years prior to 20-1 as follows: equipment by 20% per annum of cost, surgery by 2% per annum on cost and motor car by 20% per annum on cost.

(b) The assets and liabilities of Healthline Ltd on 1/1/20-2 were as follows: premises €580,000; equipment €205,000; furniture €86,000; stock of health food €3,900; stock of heating oil €1,900; contract cleaning prepaid €900; creditors for supplies €2,870; clients' fees paid in advance €12,300; 10% investments €150,000; authorised share capital €800,000; issued share capital €500,000; bank account €8,900. The following additional information must be taken into account:

(i) During 20-2, a loan of €60,000 was repaid on 1 September with three years' interest, totalling €74,400.

(ii) All fixed assets have been depreciated for three years prior to 20-2 as follows: equipment by 25% per annum of cost, premises by 4% per annum on cost and furniture by 20% per annum on reducing balance.

Exercises – Higher Level

14

Q1 The following were included in the assets and liabilities of Helen Clarke, a dentist, on 1/1/20-6:
Surgery €256,000; equipment €175,000; motor car €57,600; creditors for dental supplies €7,680; stock of dental supplies €11,520; 12% investments €320,000; owed from the medical insurance scheme €30,400; 4% fixed mortgage €192,000; capital €555,240.

The following is her receipts and payments account for the year ended 31/12/20-6:

Receipts	€	Payments	€
Balance at bank	7,680	Dental supplies	38,400
Sale of equipment	19,200	Light and heat	7,040
Medical insurance scheme	56,576	Telephone and internet	8,320
Private patient receipts	240,000	Interest on mortgage	6,400
Investment income	28,800	Car expenses	14,720
		Insurance	8,640
		Sponsorship of local golf club	1,600
		Investment bonds (31/12/20-6)	128,000
		Drawings	68,224
		Balance	70,912
	352,256		**352,256**

The following additional information and instructions are to be taken into account:

(a) Stock of dental supplies on 31/12/20-6 was €13,120.

(b) The figure for bank balance on 31/12/20-6 does not take into account bank charges of €256 and a dishonoured cheque for €1,120 received from a private patient and lodged in late December.

(c) The figure for drawings includes wages of €3,200 for two weeks paid to a locum (substitute) dentist and you are required to provide for a further three weeks' wages due.

(d) It is estimated that 80% of light and heat and telephone and internet related to the dental practice and the remainder to a private residence above the surgery.

(e) Depreciation is to be provided for as follows:

Equipment	20% of cost
Motor car	20% of cost
Surgery	2% of cost.

Note: Fixed assets are given at cost and depreciation on them has been accumulated for two years up to 31/12/20-5. The equipment sold during the year had cost €51,200.

(f) Fees due from private patients and the medical insurance scheme on 31/12/20-6 were €1,230 and €28,780 respectively.

You are required to prepare:

- an income and expenditure account for the year ended 31/12/20-6
- a balance sheet as at 31/12/20-6.

14

Q2 **Included among the assets and liabilities of Steven Cox, a doctor, on 1/1/20-4 were:**

Surgery €600,000; equipment €125,000; motor car €30,000; furniture €120,000; creditors for medical supplies €11,500; stock of medical supplies €8,800; 4% investments €500,000; owed from medical insurance scheme €36,000; 5% fixed mortgage €300,000; capital €1,016,500.

The following is the receipts and payments account for the year ended 31/12/20-4:

Receipts	€	Payments	€
Balance at bank	17,000	Medical supplies	70,000
Sale of equipment (cost €60,000)	25,000	Light and heat	11,000
Medical insurance scheme	98,000	Telephone and postage	13,000
Receipts from private patients	460,000	Receptionist's salary	85,000
Investment income	15,000	Mortgage interest	12,500
		Motor car running costs	23,000
		Insurance	13,500
		Sponsorship	3,500
		Drawings	67,200
		Balance	316,300
	615,000		**615,000**

The following information and instructions are to be taken into account:

(a) Stock of medical supplies at 31/12/20-4 was €26,000.

(b) The figure for bank balance 31/12/20-4 does not take into account bank charges €450 and a dishonoured cheque for €1,800 received from a private patient and lodged in late December.

(c) The figure for drawings includes wages of €5,000 for two weeks paid to a relief doctor and you are required to provide for a further two weeks' wages due.

(d) It is estimated that 75% of light and heat, telephone and postage relates to the medical practice and the remainder is private.

(e) Provide for depreciation as follows:

Equipment	20% of cost
Motor car	20% of cost
Furniture	10% of book value
Surgery	2% of cost.

Note: Fixed assets are given at cost and depreciation on them has been accumulated for two years up to 31/12/20-3.

(f) Fees due from medical insurance scheme and private patients were €45,000 and €3,750 respectively on 31/12/20-4.

You are required to prepare:

- an income and expenditure account for the year ended 31/12/20-4
- a balance sheet as at 31/12/20-4.

Q3 **Michael and Bridget Cassidy operate a dental practice and on 1/1/20-2 their assets and liabilities were as follows:**

Surgery €400,000; dental equipment €137,600; furniture and fittings €51,200; car €38,400; stock of dental supplies €6,080; creditors for dental supplies €3,520; owed from the medical card scheme €3,360; 6% fixed mortgage €192,000; capital €450,784.

14

The following details were taken from their records on 31/12/20-2:

Receipts	€	Payments	€
Balance	16,960	Dental supplies	73,920
Fees from private patients	173,440	Technician's fees	19,840
Medical card scheme receipts	89,920	Rent and rates	6,720
Sale of equipment (cost €19,200)	16,000	Telephone and internet	19,680
		Insurance	32,000
		Receptionist's salary	29,760
		Equipment	8,960
		Drawings	14,720
		Light and heat	22,560
		Mortgage interest	9,280
		Balance	58,880
	296,320		**296,320**

The following additional information is to be taken into account as on 31/12/20-2:

(a) Stock of dental supplies was €7,040.

(b) The figure for cash drawings includes wages for two weeks for a substitute dentist at €1,280 per week.

(c) It is estimated that 80% of light and heat relate to the surgery and the remainder to a private dwelling above the premises.

(d) Fees due from the medical card scheme and private patients were €14,240 and €1,920 respectively.

(e) Provide for depreciation as follows:

Equipment	20% of cost
Motor car	10% of book value
Surgery	2% of cost.

Note: The car is given at cost and depreciation has been accumulated for two years on the above basis. It was the only fixed asset depreciated up to 1/1/20-2.

You are required to prepare:

- an income and expenditure account for the year ended 31/12/20-2
- a balance sheet as at 31/13/20-2

Q4 **The following were included among the assets and liabilities of the Glenbay Health Centre Ltd on 1/1/20-1:**

Land and buildings €910,000; equipment €104,000; minibus €54,600; stock of health food for sale €7,540; heating oil €780; creditors for supplies to health centre €4,030; 5% investments €97,500; prepaid cleaning €975; clients' fees paid in advance €5,460; authorised capital €975,000; issued capital €864,500.

All fixed assets have three years' accumulated depreciation on 1/1/20-1.

The following is the receipts and payments account for the year ended 31/12/20-1:

Receipts	€	Payments	€
Balance	16,640	Gardening expenses	4,706
Clients' fees	426,660	Wages and salaries	109,564
Investment income	4,160	Repayment of €104,000 loan on 1/7/20-1 with 20 months' interest	119,600
Shop sales	148,980	Equipment	15,600
Balance	4,940	Adjoining building and extension	195,000
		Cleaning (contract)	10,920
		Light and heat	11,570
		Insurance	21,320
		Telephone	3,380
		Purchases - shop	88,530
		Purchase of supplies	21,190
	601,380		**601,380**

The following information and instructions are to be taken into account:

(a) Closing stock at 31/12/20-1: shop €8,580; heating oil €1,066.

(b) Cleaning is done under contract and is payable monthly in advance and includes a payment of €702 for January 20-2.

(c) Client fees include fees for 20-2 of €8,320. Client fees in arrears at 31/12/20-1 were €1,040.

(d) The closing figure for bank does not take into account a dishonoured cheque for €390 received from a client and lodged in late December.

(e) Wages and salaries include €46,800 per annum paid to the receptionist who also runs the shop. It is estimated that 40% of this salary, €494 of the light and heat, €2,340 of the insurance and €533 of the telephone are attributable to the shop.

(f) Creditors for supplies to the health centre at 31/12/20-1 are €3,640.

(g) Electricity due on 31/12/20-1 was €455.

(h) Provide for depreciation as follows:

Buildings	2% of cost for a full year
Equipment	20% of cost for a full year
Minibus	20% of cost per annum.

(i) On 31/12/20-1 the Glenbay Health Centre decided to revalue land and buildings at €1,196,000.

You are required to:

- Calculate the company's reserves on 1/1/20-1.
- Calculate the profit/loss from the shop for the year ended 31/12/20-1.
- Prepare the profit and loss account of Glenbay Health Centre for the year ended 31/12/20-1.
- Prepare the balance sheet of Glenbay Health Centre on 31/12/20-1.

Q5 Included in the assets and liabilities of the Waistline Health and Leisure Centre on 1/1/20-2 were the following:

Buildings and grounds €780,000; equipment €135,000; furniture €37,500; health food stock for sale €2,250; stock heating oil €990; contract cleaning prepaid €450; creditors for supplies €2,175; clients' fees paid in advance €8,250; 6% investments €120,000; authorised capital €675,000; issued capital €480,000.

All fixed assets are given at cost and have three years' accumulated depreciation on 1/1/20-2.

14

The following is the receipts and payments account of Waistline Health and Leisure Centre Ltd for the year ended 31/12/20-2:

Receipts	€	Payments	€
Balance bank	11,340	Wages and salaries	132,360
Clients' fees	393,900	Insurance	9,450
Interest	3,240	Light and heat	4,350
Shop sales	100,500	Purchases - shop	61,950
Balance	14,250	Purchases - supplies	57,900
		Laundry expenses	6,150
		Extension	120,000
		Contract cleaning	4,050
		Telephone and stationery	2,820
		New treadmills	24,000
		Repayment of €90,000 loan on 1/6/20-2 with 17 months' interest	100,200
	523,230		**523,230**

You are given the following additional information and instructions:

(a) Closing stock at 31/12/20-2: shop €2,700; heating oil €540.

(b) Electricity due on 31/12/20-2 was €435.

(c) Cleaning is done by contract payable monthly in advance and includes a payment of €600 for January 20-3.

(d) Clients' fees include fees for 20-3 of €6,000. Clients' fees in arrears on 31/12/20-2 stood at €975.

(e) Wages and salaries include €24,000 per annum paid to the receptionist who also runs the shop. It is estimated that 40% of this salary, along with €330 of the light and heat, €900 insurance and €540 of the telephone and stationery, is attributable to the shop.

(f) The Waistline Health and Leisure Centre revalued its buildings and grounds at €1,050,000 on 31/12/20-2.

(g) Provide for depreciation as follows:

Buildings	2% of cost for a full year
Equipment	20% of cost per annum
Furniture	20% of cost per annum.

(h) Creditors for supplies to the health centre at 31/12/20-2 were €2,400.

You are required to:

- Calculate the company's reserves on 1/1/20-2.
- Calculate the profit/loss from the health shop for the year ended 31/12/20-2.
- Prepare the profit and loss account for the year ended 31/12/20-2.
- Prepare a balance sheet as at 31/12/20-2.

Q6 Included in the assets and liabilities of the Northside Nursing Home Ltd on 1/1/20-6 were the following:

Premises €440,000; equipment €120,000; furniture €40,000; stock for the shop €1,200; heating oil stock €1,060; contract cleaning prepaid €400; creditors for provisions €400; authorised capital €1,000,000; issued capital €400,000.

The following is the receipts and payments account for the year ended 31/12/20-6:

Receipts	€	Payments	€
Balance current a/c	4,720	Wages and salaries	154,200
Patients' fees	361,800	Insurance	3,880
Annual Health Board grant	40,000	Light and heat	5,640
Shop sales	24,400	Purchases - shop	14,400
Donations	10,000	Purchases - provisions	87,120
Balance	1,360	Laundry	10,480
		New extension	80,000
		Cleaning contractors	5,300
		Internet and telephone	1,460
		Rates	1,800
		Equipment	30,000
		Repayment of €30,000 loan on 1/5/20-6 together with 2 years' interest	48,000
	442,280		**442,280**

You are given the following additional information as at 31/12/20-6:

(a) Closing stocks were as follows: shop €1,260; heating oil €800; and there was an outstanding electricity bill for €600.

(b) The value of equipment held on 31/12/20-6 was €135,000.

(c) Cleaning is done by contract payable monthly in advance and includes a payment of €480 for January 20-7.

(d) Patient fees include €1,600 for 20-7, while there were fees outstanding for 20-6 of €840.

(e) Wages and salaries include €20,000 per annum paid to the receptionist who also runs the shop. It is estimated that 20% of this salary, along with €400 of the light and heat, €800 of the insurance and €600 of the internet fees, are attributable to the shop.

(f) Creditors for provisions at 31/12/20-6 were €440.

(g) Provide for depreciation on buildings of 2% of cost on 31/12/20-6.

You are required to:

- Calculate the reserves of the company on 1/1/20-6.
- Prepare a trading, profit and loss account for the shop for the year ended 31/12/20-6.
- Prepare an income and expenditure account for the year ended 31/12/20-6.
- Prepare a balance sheet as on 31/12/20-6.

Q7 Included in the assets and liabilities of the Young'n'Fit Health Farm Ltd on 31/12/20-8 were the following:

Buildings and grounds €680,000; equipment €180,000; furniture €32,000; stock of health food for resale €2,200; stock of heating oil €960; contract cleaning prepaid €800; creditors for supplies €1,800; authorised share capital €800,000; issued share capital €580,000; 6% investments €90,000; advance client fees €16,000.

All fixed assets have three years' accumulated depreciation on 1/1/20-8.

14

The following is the receipts and payments account for the year ended 31/12/20-8:

Receipts	€	Payments	€
Balance	8,920	Wages and salaries	184,240
Client's fees	362,200	Insurance	9,600
Competition entry fees	14,000	Light and heat	7,200
Investment income	5,000	Purchases shop	64,400
Shop sales	132,000	Purchases supplies	76,400
Balance	37,180	Competition prizes	10,200
		New swimming pool extension	100,000
		Cleaning contractor	7,800
		Internet and telephone	3,460
		Treadmills and weight lifts	24,000
		Repayment of €60,000 loan on 1/5/20-8 with 2 years' interest	72,000
	559,300		**559,300**

You are given the following additional information and instructions as at 31/12/20-8:

(a) Closing stocks were as follows: shop €1,870; general supplies €3,100; and heating oil €1,400. There was also an electricity bill outstanding of €600.

(b) Cleaning is done by contract payable monthly in advance and included a payment of €700 for January 20-9.

(c) Clients' fees include a payment of €2,000 for 20-9, while there are client fees due of €900 for 20-8.

(d) Wages and salaries include €22,000 per annum paid to the receptionist who also runs the shop. It is estimated that 50% of this salary, along with €1,400 of light and heat, €1,600 of insurance and €460 of the telephone bill, are attributable to the shop.

(e) Provide for depreciation as follows:

Equipment	20% of cost per annum
Buildings	2% of cost per annum
Furniture	15% of cost per annum.

(f) Creditors for general supplies were €1,500.

(g) The company decided to revalue buildings and grounds at €900,000 on 31/12/20-8. It is estimated that €90,000 of this is attributed to land which originally cost €50,000.

You are required to:

- Calculate the company's reserves on 1/1/20-8.
- Calculate the profit/loss from the shop for the year ended 31/12/20-8.
- Prepare a profit and loss account for the year ended 31/12/20-8.
- Prepare a balance sheet as at 31/12/20-8.

Exam Tips

- The accounts are very similar to club accounts.
- Assets must always be entered in the statement of capital (reserves) at their net book value.
- A sideline trading profit and loss account may be required.
- The profit and loss account will be presented in a similar way to the income and expenditure account from club accounts.

15 Farm Accounts

Objectives

On completion students should be able to:

- List the reasons why farms prepare accounts;
- Prepare a statement of capital/reserves of a farming enterprise;
- Prepare enterprise analysis accounts for each main farm activity;
- Prepare a general profit and loss account for the farm as a whole;
- Prepare a balance sheet.

Farming

Farming is a business and like any other form of business a farm should keep a proper set of financial records. The reasons farm accounts need be prepared include:

- to calculate the profit and loss of the farm
- to establish the net worth (value) of the farm
- to establish what is owing to and by the farm
- to apply for grants
- to apply for bank loans
- to facilitate planning and budgeting
- to ascertain the profit or loss on each farming activity – for example, sheep or cattle.

The accounts

Farming enterprises should prepare the following accounts:

1. Receipts and payments account (analysed cash book)
2. Statement of capital (reserves)
3. Enterprise analysis accounts
4. General profit and loss account
5. Balance sheet.

1. Receipts and payments account (analysed cash book)

Most farmers specialise in one or more type of enterprise – for example, dairy farming, tillage, sheep. All such farm enterprises should maintain an analysed cash book, where receipts and payments are recorded under headings for each enterprise and subheadings within each enterprise.

Example

Leo and Geraldine Bates, who run a mixed farming business, provided the following information from the counterfoils of their cheque and lodgement book for the month of June 20-6. All receipts are lodged.

15

Lodgements				Payments			
Date	**Details**	**Lodgement no.**	**€**	**Date**	**Details**	**Cheque no.**	**€**
Jun 1	Milk sales	301	4,800	Jun 4	Cattle	700	58,000
Jun 6	Sheep sales	302	20,000	Jun 6	Dairy wages	701	500
Jun 7	Cattle	303	46,000	Jun 9	Sheep	702	28,000
Jun 10	Single payment	304	7,600	Jun 10	Drawings	703	600
Jun 22	Rent conacre	305	1,920	Jun 10	General expenses	704	520
Jun 24	Crop sales	306	44,000	Jun 12	Seeds	705	800
				Jun 13	Dairy wages	706	500
				Jun 15	Repairs	707	440
				Jun 18	Sheep feed	708	840
				Jun 23	General expenses	709	520

Draw up an analysed receipts and payments account for the month of June. On 1 June 20-6 the family had a bank balance of €8,200.

Solution

Analysed Receipts and Payments Account (Dr. side) – receipts

Date	Lodgement no.	Details	Total	Milk sales	Sheep sales	Cattle sales	Gov. grant	Crop sales	Other
Jun 1		Balance c/d	8,200						
Jun 1	301	Milk	4,800	4,800					
Jun 6	302	Sales of sheep	20,000		20,000				
Jun 7	303	Cattle sales	46,000			46,000			
Jun 10	304	Single payment	7,600				7,600		
Jun 22	305	Rent	1,920						1,920
Jun 24	306	Crop sales	44,000					44,000	
		Total received	**132,520**	**4,800**	**20,000**	**46,000**	**7,600**	**44,000**	**1,920**
July 1		Balance b/d	**41,800**						

Analysed Receipts and Payments Account (Cr. side) – payments

Date	Cheque no.	Details	Total	Sheep	Cattle	Crops	Drawings	General	Other
Jun 4	700	Cattle	58,000		58,000				
Jun 6	701	Dairy wages	500		500				
Jun 9	702	Sheep	28,000	28,000					
Jun 10	703	Drawings	600				600		
Jun 10	704	General expenses	520					520	
Jun 12	705	Seeds	800			800			
Jun 13	706	Dairy wages	500		500				
Jun 15	707	Repairs	440						440
Jun 18	708	Feed for sheep	840	840					
Jun 23	709	General expenses	520					520	
July 1		Balance	41,800						
		Total paid	**132,520**	**28,840**	**59,000**	**800**	**600**	**1040**	**440**

2. Statement of capital (reserves)

A statement of capital for a farm is a list of opening assets and liabilities at the beginning of the financial year. It is presented in the same way as that of a club or a service firm.

See Practice Question 2 for questions based on the statement of capital/reserves.

15

3. Enterprise analysis accounts

An enterprise analysis account is a trading, profit and loss account for a particular enterprise.

The figures used in the enterprise analysis account are the analysis totals taken from the receipts and payments account columns. When separate enterprise analysis accounts are used it is necessary to prepare a general profit and loss account.

Farming enterprises may include:

- cattle and milk (including dairy and beef)
- sheep
- pigs
- tillage crops (including grain, beet, vegetables, potatoes)
- horses
- poultry
- deer.

NOTE

The contribution from an enterprise analysis account is transferred to the general profit and loss account.

Enterprise analysis accounts are presented in a similar way to the income and expenditure account of other organisations.

Example

From the following information prepare an enterprise analysis account for 'Cattle and Milk' and 'Sheep' for the year ended 31/12/20-0.

Stock of cattle at 1/1/20-0	€35,600
Stock of sheep at 1/1/20-0	€12,500
Other information	
Purchase of cattle	€58,000
Sale of wool	€12,000
Sale of lambs	€13,900
Purchase of sheep	€6,700
Milk sales	€76,500
Single payment beef	€3,400
Dairy wages	€12,500
General farm expenses	€45,600
Repairs	€4,600
Vet fees	€1,340
Sale of calves	€28,900

The following additional information should be taken into account:

(a) Lamb used by the family, €650; beef used by the family, €230.

(b) Milk cheque due on 31/12/20-0, €2,890.

(c) General farm expenses and vet fees are to be apportioned 75% to Cattle and Milk and 25% to Sheep.

(d) Other expenses are to be allocated equally between enterprises.

(e) Closing stock of cattle was €45,900; sheep, €12,390.

15

Solution

Enterprise Analysis Account for Cattle and Milk for the year ended 31/12/20-0

	€	€
Income – Sales and grants		
Milk sales (76,500 + 2,890)	79,390	
Sale of calves	28,900	
Single payment – beef	3,400	
Drawings – beef	230	111,920
***Less* Cost of sales**		
Opening stock – cattle	35,600	
Add Purchases – cattle	58,000	
Less Closing stock – cattle	(45,900)	(47,700)
Gross income (profit)		64,220
***Less* Expenses**		
Dairy wages	12,500	
General expenses	34,200	
Repairs	2,300	
Veterinary fees	1,005	(50,005)
Contribution from enterprise (net profit)		**14,215**

Enterprise Analysis Account for Sheep for the year ended 31/12/20-0

	€	€
Income – Sales and grants		
Sale of lambs	13,900	
Sale of wool	12,000	
Drawings – lamb	650	26,550
***Less* Cost of sales**		
Opening stock – sheep	12,500	
Add Purchases – sheep	6,700	
Less Closing stock – sheep	(12,390)	(6,810)
Gross income (profit)		19,740
***Less* Expenses**		
General expenses	11,400	
Repairs	2,300	
Veterinary fees	335	(14,035)
Contribution from enterprise (net profit)		**5,705**

4. General profit and loss account

A general profit and loss account is used to ascertain the overall profit or loss of a farm. Items that cannot be allocated directly to individual farm enterprises are included here.

5. Balance sheet

A balance sheet for a farm is presented in a similar way to the balance sheet of any other organisation.

Terms associated with farm accounts

Conacre

This is the official name for the rental of farming land. Conacre can be both a revenue (where the farmer rents out his/her land) or an item of expenditure (where the farmer requires extra land and rents it from other farmers). It is entered in the general profit and loss account. It generally refers to land rented out for tillage purposes, most commonly potatoes.

Set-aside land

This refers to land which is not in use and for which payments are made to farms. This system was introduced to reduce the overall supply of beef, milk, wine, etc. within the EU and help reduce the cost of keeping all this surplus produce - the beef mountains, wine lakes and so on. The system is no longer in use. It was also used to protect the environment.

Forestry premium

This is a premium paid to farmers to encourage the planting of trees.

Single payment

This a payment to farmers by the EU under the Common Agricultural Policy (CAP). It is a new system of direct payments and was introduced in 2005.

Dairy wages

This is the payment made to workers who work with cattle and cows on the farm. It is entered in the cattle and milk enterprise analysis.

Haulage

This is the term applied to the cost of transporting livestock. It is entered as an expense in the appropriate enterprise account.

Harvesting

These are amounts paid to contractors for harvesting crops.

REPS/AEOS

These are the Rural Environmental Protection Scheme and the Agri-Environment Options Scheme. Under these schemes payments are made to farmers to protect the environment within their own farms.

Drawings

Where the farmer uses things of value, including farm produce, for private use it is called drawings. Examples could include milk, beef, vegetables, light and heat.

Valuation of stock

The opening and closing stock of enterprises – for example, of cattle, sheep, pigs – is dealt with in the enterprise analysis accounts in one of two ways:

Option 1

- Enter all sales and grant items.
- Deduct all cost of sales items to arrive at gross income (profit).

15

Option 2

Find the difference between the opening and closing stock and enter as follows:

- If stocks have increased during the year the increase is treated as **income** – gain.
- If stocks have decreased during the year the decrease is treated as **expenditure** – loss.

Stocks are valued at the lower of cost or net realisable value, as with any other business.

In general practice, unharvested crops are valued at zero.

Other stocks

For other stocks on hand, such as diesel oil, fertilisers and feedstuffs, you are required to find out how much was actually consumed during the financial period. This is done using the following formula:

Opening stock + Purchases – Closing stock = Amount used

Consumption of farm produce

Farm produce consumed by the farmer is treated as **drawings**. It is entered in the drawings account and as a sale of the particular item (entered as income/sales) in the relevant enterprise analysis account.

Adjustments

1. Prepayments and accruals

The same rules apply here as under the matching principle. If the expense or gain is not for the current year it must be subtracted.

2. Allocation of expenses

Expenses must be allocated among the enterprises. Sometimes an expense will be allocated to general profit and loss.

For example, general farm expenses, vet fees, fence posts and wire might be allocated 60% to Cattle and Milk and 40% to Sheep.

Some expenses are exclusively related to a particular enterprise and should not to be allocated elsewhere. For example, dairy wages will be in Cattle and Milk only.

NOTE

Make adjustments to any expense/gain for accruals and prepayments before allocating to the relevant enterprise accounts.

15

3. Loans

Loans due and interest due at the start of the year need to entered in the statement of capital.

Example

Bank loan plus 18 months' interest at 4% per annum repaid on 30/4/xx: €9,540. Show how this would be treated in the final accounts.

Solution

In this example the original amount of the loan is not given. Hence we have to work it out backwards.

There has been 18 months' interest accumulated on the loan. Since the annual interest rate is 4% per annum, in this 18 months interest totaling 6% has been incurred.

Therefore 106% = 9,540 9,540/106 x 100 = €9,000 loan amount

Interest is €540 for 18 months, which is €30 per month. There are four months' interest for the current year, as it was repaid on 30/4/xx, and 14 months' for previous years.

Entries required:

Loan	€9,000	**Liability** in statement of capital at 1/1/xx
Interest due	€420 (14 x 30)	**Liability** in statement of capital at 1/1/xx
Interest for year	€120 (4 x 30)	**Expense** in general P & L (this year)

See Practice Question 1 for exercises based on this adjustment.

4. Drawings

Some expenses will have to be split between the farm and the household. The portion allocated to the household is treated as drawings – for example, light and heat, interest.

15

Sample Ordinary Level question

The following trial balance was extracted from the books of K. Windsor, a mixed farmer, on 31/12/20-0:

	€	€
Land and buildings (cost €480,000)	416,000	
Farm machinery (cost €96,000)	84,000	
Stocks 1/1/20-0		
Feedstuffs	2,880	
Fertiliser	1,280	
Cattle	76,800	
Grain crops	160	
Purchases		
Fertiliser	13,520	
Cattle	35,200	
Seeds for grain	5,440	
Feedstuffs	5,800	
Sale of cattle		188,000
Receipts from the creamery		101,040
Sale of crops		65,920
Electricity	10,336	
Veterinary fees	1,520	
10% Bank loan (1/1/20-0)		72,000
Cash drawings	6,400	
Loan interest paid	3,600	
Farm wages	45,120	
Bank overdraft		85,096
Capital		196,000
	708,056	**708,056**

The following additional information is available on 31/12/20-0:

(a) Closing stocks were livestock €59,200; fertiliser €720; feedstuffs €2,080; grain €220.

(b) Value of milk used by the family was €1,000.

(c) Both farm wages and fertilisers should be allocated 60% to Cattle and Milk and 40% to Crops.

(d) Provide for loan interest.

(e) Deprecation on buildings is to be 5% of cost and 15% of cost on machinery.

You are required to:

- Prepare enterprise analysis accounts for (i) Cattle and Milk and (ii) Crops.
- Prepare a general profit and loss account.
- Prepare the balance sheet.

Solution

Enterprise Analysis Account of K. Windsor for Cattle and Milk for the year ended 31/12/20-0

	€	€
Income – Sales and grants		
Sale of cattle	188,000	
Sale of milk	101,040	
Milk used by family	1,000	290,040
***Less* Cost of sales**		
Opening stock – cattle	76,800	
Add Purchases – cattle	35,200	
Less Closing stock – cattle	(59,200)	(52,800)
Gross income (profit)		237,240
***Less* Expenses**		
Feedstuffs (W2)	6,600	
Farm wages (W7)	27,072	
Fertiliser (W7)	8,448	
Veterinary fees	1,520	(43,640)
Contribution from enterprise (net profit)		**193,600**

Enterprise Analysis Account of K. Windsor for Crops for the year ended 31/12/20-0

	€	€
Income – Sales and grants		
Sale of crops		65,920
***Less* Cost of sales**		
Opening stock – crops	160	
Add Purchases – seeds	5,440	
Less Closing stock – crops	(220)	(5,380)
Gross income (profit)		60,540
***Less* Expenses**		
Farm wages (W7)	18,048	
Fertiliser (W7)	5,632	(23,680)
Contribution from enterprise (net profit)		**36,860**

General Profit and Loss Account of K. Windsor for the year ended 31/12/20-0

	€	€
Income		
Contribution from cattle and milk	193,600	
Contribution from crops	36,860	230,460
***Less* Expenditure**		
Loan interest (W4)	7,200	
Depreciation of machinery (W5)	14,400	
Depreciation of buildings (W6)	24,000	
Electricity	10,336	(55,936)
Net profit		**174,524**

15

Balance Sheet of K. Windsor as at 31/12/20-0

Fixed assets	Cost (€)	Aggregate Depreciation (€)	Net Book Value (€)
Buildings	480,000	88,000	392,000
Machinery	96,000	26,400	69,600
	576,000	114,400	461,600
Current assets			
Closing stock of feedstuffs	2,080		
Closing stock of fertilisers	720		
Closing stock of cattle	59,200		
Closing stock of grain	220	62,220	
***Less* Creditors: amounts falling due within 1 year**			
Bank	85,096		
Loan interest	3,600	(88,696)	
Net current assets			(26,476)
			435,124
Financed by			
Creditors: amounts falling due after more than 1 year			
Loan			72,000
Capital and reserves			
Capital		196,000	
Add Net profit		174,524	
		370,524	
Less Drawings (W3)		(7,400)	363,124
			435,124

Workings

W1 Fertiliser

Opening stock	1,280
Purchases	13,520
	14,800
Less Closing stock	(720)
Amount used	**14,080**

W2 Feedstuffs

Opening stock	2,880
Purchases	5,800
	8,680
Less Closing stock	(2,080)
Amount used	**6,600**

W3 Drawings

Cash drawings	6,400
Milk used by the family	1,000
	7,400

W4 Loan interest

72,000 x 10%	**7,200**

W5 Depreciation of machinery

96,000 x 15%	**14,400**

W6 Depreciation of buildings

480,000 x 5%	**24,000**

W7 Allocation of expenses: 60% and 40%

Expense	Amount	Cattle and Milk (60%)	Crops (40%)
Farm wages	45,120	27,072	18,048
Fertilisers (W1)	14,080	8,448	5,632

Sample Higher Level question

15

Included in the assets and liabilities of Kenneth and Deirdre Barden, who carry on a mixed farming business, on 1/1/20-0 were: farm buildings and land at cost €890,000; tractors and machinery €120,000; stock of heating oil €240; milk cheque due from creamery €4,900; value of cattle €80,700; value of sheep €23,000; and electricity charges due €900.

The following is a summary taken from their cheque payments and lodgement books for the year ended 31/12/20-0:

Lodgements	€	Cheque payments	€
Balance 1/1/20-0	66,300	Fertiliser	5,000
Milk sales	54,000	General farm expenses	23,400
Sheep sales	23,900	Dairy wages	4,500
Sale of cattle	32,000	Purchase of sheep	40,000
Sale of lambs	28,900	Purchase of cattle	32,000
Single payment - sheep	3,200	Machinery	12,000
Single payment - beef	3,800	Light and heat	1,800
Sale of wool	2,890	Veterinary fees	2,870
Forestry premium	2,810	Bank loan plus 18 months' interest at 4% per annum on 30/4/20-0	14,310
Six months' interest from 3% investment bonds	1,800	Repairs	2,100
Sale of calves	12,200	Balance	93,820
	231,800		**231,800**

The following information and instructions are to be taken into account:

(a) Value of livestock on 31/12/20-0 was: cattle €105,000; sheep €47,000.

(b) Farm produce used by the family during the year: milk €1,800; lamb €1,000.

(c) General farm expenses, fertiliser and vet fees should be apportioned 65% to Cattle and Milk; 35% to Sheep.

(d) Other expenses apart from depreciation are to be apportioned 75% to the farm and 25% to household.

(e) Provide for depreciation on the following: tractors at 10% of cost per annum and farm buildings at 3% per annum. (Land at cost was €230,000.)

(f) Veterinary fees includes a cheque for private healthcare of €370.

(g) On 31/12/20-0 there was a cheque due from the creamery for €3,200; creditors for fertiliser €2,300; stock of oil €200.

You are required to:

- Prepare a statement of capital for the farm 1/1/20-0.
- Prepare enterprise analysis accounts for (i) Cattle and Milk and (ii) Sheep for the year ended 31/12/20-0.
- Prepare a general profit and loss account for the year ended 31/12/20-0.

Solution

15

Statement of Capital of Kenneth and Deirdre Barden as on 1/1/20-0

	€	€
Assets		
Land and buildings	890,000	
Tractors and machinery	120,000	
Stock of heating oil	240	
Milk cheque due from the creamery	4,900	
Cattle	80,700	
Sheep	23,000	
Bank	66,300	
Investment bonds (W1)	120,000	1,305,140
***Less* Liabilities**		
Electricity charges due	900	
Loan (W2)	13,500	
Loan interest due (W2)	630	(15,030)
Capital as at 1/1/20-0		**1,290,110**

Enterprise Analysis Account of Kenneth and Deirdre Barden for Cattle and Milk for the year ended 31/12/20-0

	€	€
Income – Sales and grants		
Milk sales (W3)	52,300	
Sale of cattle	32,000	
Sale of calves	12,200	
Single payment beef	3,800	
Milk used by the family	1,800	102,100
***Less* Cost of sales**		
Opening stock – cattle	80,700	
Add Purchases – cattle	32,000	
Less Closing stock – cattle	(105,000)	(7,700)
Gross income (profit)		94,400
***Less* Expenses**		
Dairy wages	4,500	
General expenses (W4)	15,210	
Fertiliser (W4)	4,745	
Vet fees (W4)	1,625	(26,050)
Contribution from enterprise		**68,320**

Enterprise Analysis Account of Kenneth and Deirdre Barden for Sheep for the year ended 31/12/20-0

	€	€
Income – Sales and grants		
Sheep sales	23,900	
Lamb sales	28,900	
Sheep single payment	3,200	
Sale of wool	2,890	
Lamb used by family	1,000	59,890
***Less* Cost of sales**		
Opening stock – sheep	23,000	
Add Purchases – sheep	40,000	
Less Closing stock – sheep	(47,000)	(16,000)
Gross income (profit)		43,890
***Less* Expenses**		
Veterinary fees (W4)	875	
Fertiliser (W4)	2,555	
General expenses (W4)	8,190	(11,620)
Contribution from enterprise (net profit)		**32,270**

15

General Profit and Loss Account of Kenneth and Deirdre Barden for the year ended 31/12/20-0

Income	€	€
Contribution from cattle and milk	68,320	
Contribution from sheep	32,270	
Investment income	3,600	
Forestry premium	2,810	107,000
***Less* Expenses**		
Light and heat (W5) (W8)	705	
Loan interest (W2) (W8)	135	
Depreciation of tractors (W6)	13,200	
Depreciation of buildings (W7)	19,800	
Repairs (W8)	1,575	35,415
Net Profit		**71,585**

Workings

W1 Investments Bonds

€1,800 received for 6 months	
Therefore €3,600 is a full year	
3% = 3,600, so 100% =	**€120,000**

W2 Loan and Loan Interest

Interest 4% x 1.5 years = 6% interest	
Loan plus interest = 106%	
106% = 14,310, so 100% =	€13,500
14,310 - 13,500 =	€810
810/18 = 45 per month	
This year: 45 x 4 =	€180
Due at 1/1: 45 x 14 =	**€630**

W3 Milk sales

Amount received	54,000
Less Amount due 1/1/20-0	(4,900)
Add Amount due 31/12/20-0	3,200
	52,300

W4 Expenses to be split 65% and 35%

Expense	Amount	Cattle and milk (65%)	Sheep (35%)
General expenses	23,400	15,210	8,190
Fertiliser (Amount paid €5,000 + Creditors at 31/12/20-0 € 2,300)	7,300	4,745	2,555
Vet fees (€2,870, less €370 for private health)	2,500	1,625	875

W5 Light and heat

Amount paid	1,800
Add Stock oil 1/1/20-0	240
Less Electricity due 1/1/20-0	(900)
Less Oil 31/12/20-0	(200)
	940

W6 Depreciation tractors

120,000 + 12,000 = 132,000 x 10% **13,200**

W7 Depreciation of buildings

890,000 - 230,000 land = 660,000 x 3% = **€19,800**

W8 Expenses to be split 75% and 25%

Expense	Amount	Profit and loss (75%)	Drawings (25%)
Light and heat (W7)	940	705	235
Loan interest (W2)	180	135	45
Repairs	2,100	1,575	525

Exercises - Ordinary Level

Q1 **The Richards family carries on a mixed farming business with two main enterprises: cattle and sheep. The following is a summary of the receipts and payments account for the farm for the year ended 31/12/20-3:**

Receipts	€	Payments	€
Balance	11,400	Foodstuff sheep	6,600
Milk sales	150,000	General wages	21,000
Sheep sales	88,800	Conacre (rent)	13,200
Single payment - beef	16,200	Dairy wages	4,200
Sale of cows	66,000	Purchase of cows	96,000
Sale of calves	24,000	Repairs	24,600
Single payment - sheep	28,200	Purchase of sheep	19,800
Sale of wool	5,400	Light and heat	8,100
		Drawings	57,000
		Fertiliser	17,400
		Contractor expenses	22,800
		Foodstuff cattle	24,900
		Haulage	3,900
		Balance	70,500
	390,000		**390,000**
Balance	70,500		

The following information is also available:

(a) Value of livestock on 1/1/20-3 was: cattle €486,000; sheep €288,000.

(b) Milk used by the family during the year: €4,320.

(c) Lamb used by the family during the year: €2,190.

(d) General wages, haulage and rent to be allocated equally between the two enterprises. All other expenses are to be treated as general expenses for the farm.

(e) Value of livestock on 31/12/20-3 was: cattle €504,000; sheep €228,000.

You are required to:

- Prepare enterprise analysis accounts for Cattle and Milk and for Sheep for the year ended 31/12/20-3.
- Prepare a general profit and loss account for the year ended 31/12/20-3.

15

Q2 The Furlong family carries on a mixed farming business. The following is a summary of the receipts and payments account for the year ended 31/12/20-5:

Receipts	€	Payments	€
Balance	18,000	Feeding of cattle	15,000
Milk sales	85,000	Purchase of cattle	45,000
Sale of grain	67,500	Drawings	20,000
Single payment - beef	22,500	Fence posts and wire	1,000
Sale of cattle	130,000	Machinery	20,000
Conacre	6,000	Dairy wages	32,500
		Light and heat	8,500
		Wages	75,000
		Purchase of seeds	6,000
		Sowing of seeds	19,000
		Contractor for harvesting	21,000
		Repairs	12,500
		Insurance	3,500
		Haulage	10,000
		Balance	40,000
	329,000		**329,000**
Balance	40,000		

The following additional information is also available:

(a) Value of stock on 1/1/20-5 was: cattle €110,000; grain €20,000.

(b) Milk used by the family during the year was €3,500.

(c) Beef used by the family during the year was €12,500.

(d) General wages and haulage are to be divided equally between the enterprises.

(e) Value of stock on 31/12/20-5 was: cattle €105,000; grain €42,500.

You are required to:

- Prepare enterprise analysis accounts for Cattle and Milk and for Grain Crops for the year ended 31/12/20-5.
- Prepare a general profit and loss account for the year ended 31/12/20-5.

Q3 **The Gore family carries on a mixed farming business. The following is a summary of the receipts and payments of the farm for the year ended 31/12/20-7:**

Receipts	€	Payments	€
Balance	6,400	Feed for pigs	3,200
Milk sales	60,000	General wages	7,200
Pig sales	50,400	Rent – conacre	4,680
Single payment – beef	7,200	Dairy wages	2,400
Sale of cows	28,000	Purchase of cows	56,000
Sale of calves	13,600	Repairs	13,600
Forestry premium	14,400	Purchase of pigs	8,800
		Light and heat	3,560
		Drawings	28,000
		Fertiliser	9,200
		Insurance	17,600
		Haulage	1,600
		Balance	24,160
	180,000		**180,000**

The following information is also available:

(a) Value of livestock on 1/1/20-7 was: cattle €340,000; pigs €152,000.

(b) Milk used by the family during the year was €2,640.

(c) Bacon used by the family during the year was €880.

(d) General wages, haulage and rent are to be divided equally between the enterprises.

(e) Value of livestock on 31/12/20-7 was: cattle €348,000; pigs €156,000.

You are required to:

- Prepare enterprise analysis accounts for Cattle and Milk and for Pigs for the year ended 31/12/20-7.
- Prepare a general profit and loss account for the year ended 31/12/20-7.

Q4 **The following were the assets and liabilities of the Ferb family, who carry on a mixed farming business, on 1/1/20-0: land €480,000; farm buildings €224,000; machinery €60,000; sheep €19,200; cattle €54,400; electricity due €240; cash at bank €7,840.**

The following is a summary of the farm's receipts and payments account for the year ended 31/12/20-0:

Receipts	€	Payments	€
Sale of milk	25,600	Fertiliser	7,120
Sale of wool	1,040	Purchase of sheep	4,960
Sale of lambs	8,720	Purchase of cattle	7,760
Sale of cattle	66,400	Electricity	3,360
Single farm payment	13,120	Repairs	1,440
		Wages	20,960

The following additional information is to be taken into account as at 31/12/20-0:

(a) Closing stock: cattle €23,200; sheep €20,000.

(b) The single farm payment is to be allocated 75% to cows and 25% to sheep.

(c) Electricity due is €320.

(d) Fertiliser, repairs, wages and electricity are to be divided equally between the two enterprises.

(e) Milk used by the family during the year was €1,400.

(f) Lamb used by the family during the year was €400.

15

You are required to:

- Calculate the Ferb family's capital on 1/1/20-0.
- Prepare an enterprise analysis account for Cattle and Milk for the year ended 31/12/20-0.
- Prepare an enterprise analysis account for Sheep for the year ended 31/12/20-0.
- Explain two reasons why farmers should prepare accounts.

Q5 **The following trial balance was extracted from the books of S. Murphy on 31/12/20-2:**

	€	€
Capital		250,000
Sale of trees		9,000
Farm buildings	200,000	
Tractors and machinery	90,000	
Depreciation on tractors and machinery		45,000
Bank		17,070
Cash	30,000	
Opening stocks 1/1/20-2		
Cattle	78,000	
Horses	36,000	
Diesel oil	2,300	
Fertilisers	5,600	
Purchases		
Cattle	69,000	
Horses	78,000	
Diesel oil	4,600	
Fertilisers	8,870	
Wages	46,000	
Veterinary fees and medicines	6,700	
Tractor insurance	5,400	
Repairs to tractor	2,300	
Repairs to milking machine	8,900	
Loan interest	3,400	
Sales		
Cattle		150,000
Milk		24,500
Horses		132,000
Conacre		3,500
Bank term loan		60,000
Dairy wages	16,000	
	691,070	**691,070**

The following information is also available:

(a) Closing stocks: cattle €44,000; horses €24,000; fertilisers €6,500; diesel €3,780.

(b) Depreciate tractors by 15% on a reducing balance basis.

(c) There is €4,500 due from the creamery and €7,800 due from Goffs.

(d) Wages, diesel and veterinary fees are to be apportioned 60% to Cattle and Milk and 40% to Horses.

You are required to prepare:

- enterprise analysis accounts for Cattle and Milk and for Horses
- a general profit and loss account for the farm
- a balance sheet as at 31/12/20-2.

15

Q6 The following trial balance was extracted from the books of Anthony Kelly, a farmer, on 31/12/20-6:

	€	€
Farm buildings (cost €900,000)	780,000	
Machinery (cost €180,000)	157,500	
Stocks 1/1/20-6		
Livestock	144,000	
Seeds	300	
Fertiliser	2,400	
Feedstuffs	5,400	
Purchases		
Livestock	66,000	
Seeds	10,200	
Fertiliser	10,870	
Feedstuffs	25,350	
Sale of cattle		352,500
Sale of milk		189,450
Sale of crops and vegetables		123,600
Light and heat	19,380	
Veterinary fees	2,855	
Bank loan		135,000
Cash drawings	12,000	
Loan interest	6,750	
General farm wages	84,600	
Bank		159,555
Capital		367,500
	1,327,605	**1,327,605**

15

The following information is also available on 31/12/20-6:

(a) Closing stocks: livestock €111,000; fertiliser €1,350; feedstuffs €3,900; seeds €1,200.

(b) Value of milk used by the family during the year was €1,800.

(c) Farm wages and fertilisers should be divided equally between the enterprises.

(d) Provide for loan interest due. The loan interest was 10% APR.

(e) Provide for depreciation as follows: buildings 4% of cost; machinery 20% of cost.

You are required to prepare:

- enterprise analysis accounts for Cattle and Milk and for Grain for the year ended 31/12/20-6
- a general profit and loss account for the year ended 31/12/20-6
- a balance sheet as at 31/12/20-6.

Practice Questions

Q1 In each of the following calculate the amount of the original loan, the amount of interest due at the beginning and the amount of interest for the current year.

(a) Bank loan plus 15 months' interest at 8% per annum repaid on 30 April this year: €13,200.

(b) Bank loan plus 16 months' interest at 9% per annum repaid on 1 May this year: €12,320.

(c) Bank loan plus 27 months' interest at 12% per annum repaid on 30 April this year: €19,050.

Q2 In each of the following prepare a statement of capital.

(a) The following are the assets and liabilities of the Bridges family, who carry on a mixed farming business: farm premises €200,000; machinery €231,000; dairy wages due €1,238; milk cheque due from the creamery €9,800; value of cattle €221,000; value of deer €112,000; stock of fuel €900; bank €1,450; bank term loan including 18 months' interest at 8% per annum €50,400; EU premium due €22,000; conacre payable due €675.

Note: machinery is given at cost and has two years' accumulated depreciation to date at 15% of cost per annum.

(b) The following are the assets and liabilities of the McLaughlin family, who carry on a mixed farming business: land and buildings €580,000; machinery and equipment €120,000; electricity due €800; value of cattle €120,000; milk cheque due €4,800; stock of diesel €1,800; value of lambs €34,000; bank 4,900; investments €25,000; investment interest due €600; bank term loan with 18 months' interest at 6% per annum €32,700.

Note: machinery and equipment are given at cost and have been deprecated at 20% for the past three years on a reducing balance basis.

Exercises - Higher Level

15

Q1 **The following are the assets and liabilities on 1/1/20-5 of Jack and Ellie Ewing, who carry on a mixed farming business: farm buildings €278,400; farm land 185,600; machinery at cost €125,000; light and heat due €300; value of cattle €95,000; cheque due from creamery €3,500; value of pigs €22,000; prepaid insurance €700.**

The following is a summary taken from their cheque payments and lodgements books for the year ended 31/12/20-5:

Lodgements	€	Cheque payments	€
Balance	5,040	General expenses	27,000
Milk sales	50,400	Dairy wages	3,000
Sale of pigs	46,200	Fertiliser	5,700
Sale of cattle	23,000	Pigs - purchases	34,200
Forestry premium	22,900	Cattle - purchases	25,200
Sale of calves	10,620	Light, heat and fuel	6,100
Single payment cattle	4,500	Machinery	11,700
Rent - conacre	4,700	Bank loan plus 18 months' interest at 6% per annum on 1/5/20-5	29,430
6 months' interest from 8% investments	1,080	Veterinary fees and medicine	2,070
		Balance	24,040
	168,440		**168,440**

The following information and instructions are to be taken into account:

(a) Value of livestock on 31/12/20-5 was: cattle €65,000 and pigs €32,000.

(b) Farm produce consumed by the family during the year was: milk €990 and pigs €340.

(c) General farm expenses, fertiliser and vet fees are to be apportioned 60% to Cattle and Milk and 40% to Pigs.

(d) Other expenses apart from depreciation are to be apportioned 90% to the farm and 10% to the household.

(e) Provide for depreciation on machinery at the rate of 20% of cost per annum.

(f) Vet fees and medicine include a cheque for private health insurance for €770.

(g) On 31/12/20-5 there was a milk cheque due for €1,280; creditors for fertilisers were €1,400; and there was electricity due of €400.

You are required to:

- Prepare a statement of capital for the farm on 1/1/20-5.
- Prepare enterprise analysis accounts for Cattle and Milk and for Pigs for the year ended 31/12/20-5.
- Prepare a general profit and loss account for the year ended 31/12/20-5.

15

Q2 **Cliff and April Barnes carry on a mixed farming business. Among their assets and liabilities on 1/1/20-4 are: farm land €320,000; farm buildings €280,000; tractor €54,000; machinery €34,000; electricity due €300; milk cheque due €3,900; value of cattle €72,000; value of sheep €43,000; stock of fuel €1,250.**

The following is a summary taken from their cheque payments and lodgements book for the year ended 31/12/20-4:

Lodgements	€	Cheque payments	€
Balance	5,120	Sheep	41,600
Sale of lambs	14,240	Dairy wages	12,960
Milk sales	99,200	Light heat and fuel	13,440
Sale of sheep	49,600	Fertiliser	10,240
Sale of cattle	28,800	Cattle	25,600
Sale of calves	10,240	General expenses	51,200
Single payment - sheep	8,960	Drawings	14,720
Sale of wool	3,840	Repairs to milk tank	5,000
Single payment - beef	6,080	Veterinary fees and medicine	3,640
Forestry premium	2,240	Bank term loan and 18 months' interest at 8% per annum on 1/10/20-4	43,008
3 months' interest from 4% investments	800	Balance	7,712
	229,120		**229,120**

The following information and instructions are to be taken into account:

(a) Value of livestock on 31/12/20-4 was: cattle €65,000 and sheep €46,000.

(b) Farm produce used by the family during the year was: milk €900 and lamb €540.

(c) General farm expenses, fertiliser and veterinary fees are to be apportioned 80% to Cattle and Milk and 20% to Sheep.

(d) Other expenses apart from depreciation are to be apportioned 70% to the farm and 30% to the household.

(e) Provide for depreciation on farm machinery at the rate of 15% of cost per annum.

(f) Veterinary fees and medicines include a cheque to VHI for €440.

(g) On 31/12/20-4 there was a milk cheque due for €5,900; creditors for fertilisers amounted to €660; and there was a stock of heating oil of €900.

You are required to:

- Prepare a statement of capital for the farm on 1/1/20-4.
- Prepare enterprise analysis accounts for Cattle and Milk and for Sheep for the year ended 31/12/20-4.
- Prepare a general profit and loss account for the year ended 31/12/20-4.

Q3 **Jack and Jill Barry carry on a mixed farming business. Among their assets and liabilities on 1/1/20-8 are: farm land and buildings €780,000 (land at cost was €240,000); machinery at cost €134,000; electricity due €560; value of cattle €120,000; milk cheque due €3,100; stock of fuel €1,100; value of sheep €22,000.**

The following is a summary from their cheque payments and lodgements books for the year ended 31/12/20-8:

Lodgements	€	Cheque payments	€
Balance	79,500	Light, heat and fuel	8,640
Milk	69,600	General expenses	31,600
Lambs	34,320	Dairy wages	4,800
Sheep	57,600	Fertiliser	6,000
Cattle	38,400	Sheep	48,000
Calves	14,640	Machinery	16,800
Single payment - sheep	6,000	Repairs	15,800
Single payment - cattle	7,200	Veterinary fees and medicines	4,440
Sale of wool	3,360	Bank term loan including 18 months' interest at 4% on 30/4/20-8	22,896
6 months' interest from 6% investments	4,320	Balance	155,964
	314,940		**314,940**

The following information and instructions are to be taken into account:

(a) Value of livestock on 31/12/20-8 was: cattle €123,000 and sheep €26,000.

(b) Farm produce used by the family during the year was: milk €450 and lamb €800.

(c) General farm expenses, fertiliser and veterinary fees are to be apportioned 70% to Cattle and Milk and 30% to Sheep.

(d) Other expenses apart from depreciation are to be apportioned 80% to the farm and 20% to the household.

(e) Provide for depreciation on farm machinery at the rate of 20% of cost per annum.

(f) Provide for depreciation on farm buildings at the rate of 2% of cost per annum.

(g) Vet fees and medicines include a cheque for private health fees of €640.

(h) On 31/12/20-8 there was a milk cheque due for €2,400; creditors for fertilisers amounted to €1,000; and there was a stock of heating oil of €750.

You are required to:

- Prepare a statement of capital for the farm on 1/1/20-8.
- Prepare enterprise analysis accounts for Cattle and Milk and for Sheep for the year ended 31/12/20-8.
- Prepare a general profit and loss account for the year ended 31/12/20-8.
- Prepare the drawings account.

Which account other than drawings is affected by 'farm produce used by the family'?

15

15

Q4 Romeo and Juliet Caesar carry on a mixed farming business. Among their assets and liabilities on 1/1/20-1 are: land and buildings €400,000; farm machinery €210,000; value of grain €21,000; insurance prepaid €1,200; value of cattle €120,000; milk cheque due €4,500; stock of fuel €1,800.

The following is a summary taken from their cheque payments and lodgement book for the year ended 31/12/20-1:

Lodgements	€	Cheque payments	€
Balance	6,200	Dairy wages	20,130
Sale of cattle	51,200	Fertiliser	12,710
Sale of grain	89,900	General farm expenses	27,900
Sale of milk	111,600	Purchase of seeds	65,100
Sale of calves	26,300	Light, heat and fuel	22,900
Single payment - cattle	7,500	Insurance	12,300
Rent	8,150	Machinery	30,200
Forestry premium	8,900	Veterinary fees and medicine	8,300
Sale of straw	14,880	Bank term loan plus 18 months' interest at 8% on 31.3/20-1	104,160
6 months' interest from 12% investments	930	Balance	21,860
	325,560		**325,560**

The following information and instructions are to be taken into account:

(a) Value of stock on 31/12/20-1 was: cattle €136,000 and grain €19,500.

(b) Farm produce used by the family during the year was: milk €650 and vegetables €1,200.

(c) General farm expenses and fertiliser are to be apportioned 60% to Cattle and Milk and 40% to Grain and Vegetables.

(d) Other expenses apart from depreciation are to be apportioned 90% to the farm and 10% to the household.

(e) Provide for depreciation on farm machinery at the rate of 20% of cost per annum.

(f) Provide for depreciation on farm buildings at the rate of 2% of cost per annum. (**Note:** land at cost was €150,000.)

(g) Vet fees and medicines include a cheque for private health insurance of €700.

(h) On 31/12/20-1 there was a milk cheque due for €3,400; creditors for fertilisers amounted to €560; and there was a stock of heating oil of €1,340.

You are required to:

- Prepare a statement of capital for the farm on 1/1/20-1.
- Prepare enterprise analysis accounts for Cattle and Milk and for Grain and Vegetables for the year ended 31/12/20-1.
- Prepare a general profit and loss account for the year ended 31/12/20-1.

Q5 The following is the trial balance of Brian Pask, a farmer, on 31/12/20-4:

	€	€
Farm land and buildings	600,000	
Farm machinery at cost	90,000	
Accumulated depreciation on machinery		25,000
Sale of grain		280,000
Sale of cattle		135,500
Stocks at 1 January 20-4		
Livestock	87,000	
Grain	23,400	
Fertilisers	8,700	
Purchase of livestock	123,500	
Feeding stuffs	27,800	
Seeds	10,200	
Fertilisers	31,000	
Milk sales		78,000
General farm wages	24,500	
Insurance	12,400	
Light, heat and fuel	10,200	
Rent		15,000
Repairs to milking machine	5,600	
Veterinary fees and medicines	8,800	
Drawings	15,600	
Sub-contractors for harvesting	11,000	
Sale of potatoes		21,700
Bank		34,900
Loan interest paid	400	
Bank term loan 1/7/20-4		120,000
Capital 1/1/20-4		380,000
	1,090,100	**1,090,100**

The following additional information should be taken into account:

(a) The closing stocks on 31/12/20-4 were: grain €22,100; livestock €84,500; fertilisers €5,400.

(b) The value of farm produce used by the family was: milk €1,400 and potatoes €1,500.

(c) Provide for depreciation on farm machinery of 10% per annum, straight line basis.

(d) The milk cheque for December of €12,500 was due on 31/12/20-4.

(e) The insurance premium was for a 12-month period ending 31/3/20-5.

(f) Farm wages and fertilisers should be allocated equally between both enterprises.

(g) There was a month's rent of €1,200 which had not been received.

(h) Provide for interest on the bank term loan of 10% per annum.

(i) The bank loan is to be repaid over 20 years in equal instalments. The first payment is due 1/1/20-5.

15

You are required to:

- Prepare enterprise analysis accounts for Cattle and Milk and for Grain and Vegetables for the year ended 31/12/20-4.
- Prepare a general profit and loss account for the year ended 31/12/20-4.
- Prepare a balance sheet as on 31/12/20-4.
- Advise Brian on whether the two enterprises should be continued or not.

15

Q6 Stephen and Mary Skehan carry on a mixed farming business. Included in their assets and liabilities on 1/1/20-1 are:

Farm land and buildings €670,000 (land €170,000); machinery at cost €140,000; cattle €56,000; sheep €43,000; milk cheque due from the creamery €4,500; electricity due €900; stock of heating oil €560; and stock of fertiliser €1,230.

Note: all fixed assets (except land) are given at cost and deprecation on them has been accumulated for three years up to the 1/1/20-1.

The following is a summary taken from their cheque payments and lodgement book for the year ended 31/12/20-1:

Lodgements	€	Payments	€
Balance	3,400	Sheep	21,400
Sheep	23,500	Fertiliser	4,560
Milk	45,900	Dairy wages	6,500
Lambs	16,700	Cattle	10,900
Cattle	25,600	Drawings	5,700
Single payment - cattle	4,290	Repairs	8,760
Single payment - sheep	6,110	Light, heat and diesel	5,780
Wool	2,300	General farm expenses	23,400
Sale of machinery (cost €10,000)	3,500	Veterinary fees and medicines	6,600
Forestry premium	8,000	Bank term loan plus 20 months' interest at 6% per annum on 1/9/20-1	59,400
6 months' interest from 9% investments	2,700	Milk quota (hire)	6,500
Conacre	4,500		
Balance	13,000		
	159,500		**159,500**

The following additional information and instructions are to be taken into account:

(a) Value of livestock on 31/12/20-1 was:

	Cattle	Sheep
Cost	€54,000	€41,000
Market value	€55,000	€39,000

(b) Stock of fertiliser on 31/12/20-1 was €1,430.

(c) During the year the family consumed milk to the value of €800 and lamb to the value of €1,100.

(d) General farm expenses, fertiliser and veterinary fees are to be apportioned 70% to Cattle and Milk and 20% to Sheep.

(e) All costs associated with depreciation and sale of fixed assets are to be apportioned 100% to the farm. All other expenses are to be apportioned 80% to the farm and 20% to household.

(f) The machinery sold during the year was sold on 30/6/20-1 and you are required to provide for depreciation on machinery at a rate of 10% of cost per annum from date of purchase to date of sale.

(g) Provide for depreciation on land and buildings at a rate of 4% per annum from date of purchase and date of valuation. The land and buildings were revalued on 1/7/20-1 at €800,000, which now includes land valued at €200,000.

(h) On 31/12/20-1 there was a milk cheque due from the creamery for €1,800; creditors for fertilisers were €2,400; stock of heating oil was €1,100; and there was a cheque due for the sale of wool of €300.

(i) The milk quota payment was for ten months for the rent of a neighbour's milk quota to allow the production of more milk. Provide for the outstanding two months' rent due.

You are required to prepare:

- a statement of capital on 1/1/20-1
- enterprise analysis accounts for Cattle and Milk and for Sheep for the year ended 31/12/20-1
- a general profit and loss account for the year ended 31/12/20-1
- a balance sheet as on 31/12/20-1.

15

Exam Tips

- The accounts required are very similar to club accounts and service firms' accounts.
- When preparing a statement of capital, assets must be included at their net book value.
- Enterprise analysis accounts need to be prepared for the main farming activities. Everything related to that activity must be included and the overall contribution from the enterprise transferred to the general profit and loss account.
- Farm produce used by the farmer is treated as income (sales) in the enterprise analysis from which the produce was used. It is also treated as drawings in the balance sheet.
- An expense in one enterprise analysis account can be income in another.
- The general profit and loss account is presented in a similar way to the income and expenditure account of a club.
- Understand the different terminology involved in farm accounts - for example, single payments.

16 Incomplete Records

Objectives

On completion students should be able to:

- Prepare a trading, profit and loss account from incomplete information;
- Prepare a balance sheet from incomplete information;
- Understand the two main methods of completing final accounts from incomplete records;
- Give advice on the importance of keeping a proper set of records.

Introduction

Every business should keep proper accounting records, and all businesses will keep some records – for example, some form of cash account and a list of debtors and creditors.

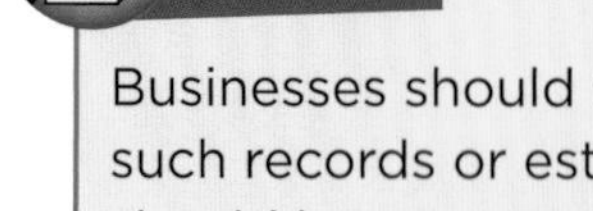

Businesses should not rely on such records or estimates and should keep a proper set of accounts and adhere to the double-entry principle.

Some smaller businesses, however, do not keep a proper set of accounts because they do not operate a double-entry system. These businesses are said to have records that are incomplete. Nevertheless, for reasons such as taxation these businesses must be able to prove and verify their profits/losses for the year.

As they do not keep ledger accounts, they will not have a record of their assets, liabilities, expenses and gains and hence they do not have a trial balance. As a result they are not able to prepare their final accounts in the normal way. Instead they use the figures they have and the relationship between them to ascertain their profit.

There are two main methods of dealing with incomplete records:

1: Control account/cash account method

2: Net worth/balance sheet method (including mark-up/margin)

1: Control Account/Cash Account Method

Most businesses will keep a record of cash and cheque receipts and payments and a list of debtors and creditors. Information about the business's assets and liabilities will also be held. From this information the final accounts can be drawn up as follows:

Procedure (Ordinary Level)

Step 1 **Prepare a statement of capital** – to ascertain the capital at the beginning of the period.

Step 2 **Prepare a debtors control account** – in order find credit sales.

Add cash sales to credit sales to find total sales.

If the cash sales figure is not given, prepare a cash account to find the figure.

Step 3 **Prepare a creditors control account** – in order to find credit purchases.

Add cash purchases to credit purchases to find total purchases.

Step 4 **Prepare any other necessary workings** – for example, accruals and prepayments.

Step 5 **Prepare the final accounts.**

16

Sample Ordinary Level question

I. Stokes did not keep a full set of accounts during the year ended 31/12/20-0. The following is a summary of the cash account for that period.

	€	€
Cash receipts		
Balance 1/1/20-0	9,490	
Debtors	101,660	
Rent received	5,850	
Cash sales	266,500	383,500
Cash payments		
Purchases	119,860	
Drawings	10,660	
Creditors	74,620	
General expenses	96,590	
Furniture	5,480	307,210

The following additional information is available:

	1/1/20-0	31/12/20-0
Land and buildings	1,092,000	1,092,000
Motor vehicles	88,400	88,400
Debtors	13,520	12,480
Creditors	11,310	6,370
Stock	15,990	18,460
Expenses due	676	780

Note: Depreciate motor vehicles by 25% of cost per annum.

You are required to:

- Prepare a statement of capital as on 1/1/20-0.
- Find Stokes's total purchases and total sales using control accounts.
- Prepare a trading, profit and loss account for the year ended 31/12/20-0.
- Prepare a balance sheet as at 31/12/20-0.

Solution

Step 1 Prepare a statement of capital

Statement of Capital as on 1/1/20-0

	€	€
Assets		
Cash	9,490	
Land and buildings	1,092,000	
Motor vehicles	88,400	
Debtors	13,520	
Stock	15,990	1,219,400
***Less* Liabilities**		
Creditors	11,310	
Expenses due	676	(11,986)
Capital as on 1/1/20-0		1,207,414

16

Step 2 Prepare a debtors control account

Dr. Debtors Control Account Cr.

Details	€	Details	€
Balance	13,520	Payments from debtors	101,660
Credit sales	**100,620**	Balance	12,480
	114,140		**114,140**

	€
Cash sales	266,500
Credit sales	100,620
Total sales	**367,120**

Step 3 Prepare a creditors control account

Dr. Creditors Control Account Cr.

Details	€	Details	€
Bank	74,620	Balance	11,310
Balance	6,370	**Credit purchases**	**69,680**
	80,990		80,990

	€
Cash purchases	119,860
Credit purchases	69,680
Total purchases	**189,540**

Step 4 Prepare any other necessary workings

Workings

W1 General expenses

Amount paid	96,590
Less Due 1/1/20-0	(676)
Add Due 31/12/20-0	780
	96,694

W2 Depreciation of motor vehicles

88,400 x 25% =	22,100

W3 Bank

Money received	383,500
Less Money spent	(307,210)
Balance	**76,290**

Step 5 Prepare the final accounts

Trading, Profit and Loss Account of I. Stokes for the year ended 31/12/20-0

	€	€
Sales (Step 2)		367,120
***Less* Cost of sales**		
Opening stock	15,990	
Purchases (Step 3)	189,540	
	205,530	
Less Closing stock	(18,460)	
Cost of goods sold		(187,070)
Gross profit		180,050
***Less* Expenses**		
Administration		
General expenses (W1)	96,694	
Selling and distribution		
Depreciation of vehicles (W2)	22,100	(118,794)
		61,256
***Add* Other income**		
Rent		5,850
Net profit		**67,106**

16

Balance Sheet of I. Stokes as on 31/12/20-0

	Cost (€)	Aggregate Depreciation (€)	Net Book Value (€)
Fixed Assets			
Land and buildings	1,092,000		1,092,000
Motor vehicles	88,400	22,100	66,300
Furniture	5,480		5,480
	1,185,880	22,100	1,163,780
Current Assets			
Debtors		12,480	
Stock		18,460	
Bank (W3)		76,290	
		107,230	
***Less* Creditors: amounts falling due within 1 year**			
Creditors	6,370		
Expenses due	780	(7,150)	
Net current assets			100,080
Total net assets			**1,263,860**
Financed by			
Creditors: amounts falling due after more than 1 year			
Capital and reserves			
Capital 1/1/20-0			1,207,414
Add Net profit			67,106
			1,274,520
Less Drawings			(10,660)
Capital employed			**1,263,860**

Procedure (Higher Level)

Step 1 **Prepare a statement of capital** (including goodwill) – to ascertain the capital at the beginning of the period.

Step 2 **Prepare two control accounts** as follows:

A debtors control account – in order to find credit sales

A creditors control account – in order to find credit purchases.

Step 3 **Prepare a cash account** – in order to find cash sales.

Prepare a bank account – in order to find bank balance at the end of the period.

Step 4 **Calculate total sales:** cash sales + credit sales = total sales.

Step 5 **Calculate total purchases:** cash purchases + credit purchases = total purchases.
Step 6 **Make adjustments for loan and investment funds.**
Step 7 **Make adjustments for all other expenses and gains.**
Step 8 **Make adjustments for drawings and ascertain the total drawings.**
Step 9 **Prepare the trading, profit and loss account.**
Step 10 **Prepare the balance sheet.**

Step 1: Statement of capital/goodwill

List all the assets less the liabilities. This will give the value of the business. This is compared to the amount paid for the business, which will either be the same as the value or more. The difference (if any) is goodwill.

If it is a new business there will be no goodwill.

16

Example

On 1/1/20-1 A. Shearer purchased for €737,500 a business that included the following assets and liabilities: buildings €700,000; debtors €15,000; three months' prepaid rates €2,000; creditors €22,750; cleaning due €3,250; and cash €250.

Prepare a statement of capital and calculate goodwill (if any).

Solution

	€	€
Assets		
Buildings		700,000
Debtors		15,000
Prepaid rates		2,000
Cash		250
		717,250
***Less* Liabilities**		
Creditors	22,750	
Cleaning	3,250	(26,000)
Value of business (net worth)		691,250
Price paid for business		737,500
Less Net worth		(691,250)
Goodwill		**46,250**

The price paid will always be equal to or greater than the net worth. There is no such thing as negative goodwill.

Step 2: Prepare the control accounts

There are **two** control accounts to be prepared, **debtors** and **creditors**.

Credit sales must be added to cash sales to find **total sales.**

Credit purchases must be added to cash purchases to find **total purchases** (subtract any stock taken by the owner for private use).

16

Example

From the following extracts from the books of S. McGrath, find his credit sales and credit purchases for the year.

Opening balances:	Debtors	€34,600	Creditors	€48,900
Payments made by debtors:		€328,900	Payments made to creditors:	€179,000
Closing balances:	Debtors	€32,700	Creditors	€51,900

Solution

Dr. **Debtors Control Account** Cr.

Details	€	Details	€
Balance	34,600	Bank (payments received)	328,900
Credit Sales	**327,000**	Balance	32,700
	361,600		**361,600**

Dr. **Creditors Control Account** Cr.

Details	€	Details	€
Bank (payments made)	179,000	Balance	48,900
Balance	51,900	**Credit purchases**	**182,000**
	230,900		**230,900**

Step 3: Prepare a cash account and a bank account

This involves setting up separate accounts for **cash** and **bank**.

Notes

- There may not be any opening cash (new business).
- Calculate the closing bank figure for the purpose of the balance sheet.
- The missing figure in the cash account will be cash sales.
- Put all entries through the bank account (especially any loans, transfers to investment funds, etc).

Example

During 20-0, McGrath did not keep a full set of accounts but was able to supply the following information:

Cash payments: Lodgements €234,000; general expenses €34,500; purchases €230,900

Bank payments: Vans €24,500; creditors €65,000; light and heat €4,800; interest €2,560; annual rent €12,000; equipment €35,000

Bank lodgements: Debtors €35,000; cash €234,000; lotto win €21,000

Notes: There was no opening cash and closing cash was €500.

Solution

Dr. **Cash Account** **Cr.**

Details	€	Details	€
Cash sales (balancing figure)	**499,900**	Bank (lodgements)	234,000
		General expenses	34,500
		Purchases	230,900
		Balance	500
	499,900		**499,900**

Dr. **Bank Account** **Cr.**

Details	€	Details	€
Debtors	35,000	Vans	24,500
Cash	234,000	Creditors	65,000
Lotto	21,000	Light and heat	4,800
		Interest	2,560
		Rent	12,000
		Equipment	35,000
		Balance	146,140
	290,000		**290,000**
Balance	**146,140**		

16

Step 4: Calculate total sales

	Cash sales from cash account (Step 3)	499,900
Add	Credit sales from debtors control account (Step 2)	327,000
	Total sales	**826,900**

Step 5: Calculate total purchases

	Cash purchases (from cash account)	230,900
Add	Credit purchases from creditors control account (Step 2)	182,000
Less	Any stock taken by the owner for private use	(0)
	Total purchases	**412,900**

Step 6: Loans and investment funds

You must:

- Debit the bank with the full amount of the loan received.
- Credit the bank with the amount spent on the new asset.

NOTE

If interest is earned by the fund, this interest is also entered under '*Add* Other income' in the profit and loss account.

This loan is repaid **either** in:

1. equal instalments

   or

2. the creation of an investment fund (financial asset in the balance sheet).

Example

Dalglish borrowed €360,000 from CD Finance Ltd on 1/9/20-0, part of which was used to purchase an adjoining premises and residence costing €310,000. It was agreed that Dalglish would pay interest on the last day of each month at the rate of 5% per annum. The capital sum was to be repaid in a lump sum in the year 20-9 and to provide for this the bank was to transfer €2,400 on the last day of each month from Dalglish's bank account into an investment fund, commencing on 30/9/20-0. €50 interest was earned on this fund to date on 31/12/20-0.

Show the effect of this on the final accounts.

Solution

Debit bank account:	€360,000	Credit CD Finance account:	€360,000
Debit premises account:	€310,000	Credit bank account:	€310,000

Interest 360,000 x 5% x 4/12 = €6,000 interest payable

Investment fund 2,400 x 4 = €9,600 (financial asset in balance sheet + €50 interest)

NOTE

The €50 interest earned is treated as a gain in the profit and loss account and included in the fund in the balance sheet.

Step 7: Adjustments to gains and expenses

All revenue and expenses must be recorded for the period to which they relate. This is in accordance with the **matching concept**. (See Chapter 2, Section D: Accruals and Prepayments.)

Step 8: Drawings

- Stock for private use: Increase drawings and reduce purchases.
- Cash for private use: Increase drawings and reduce cash.
- Other expenses: Apportion x% to drawings and y% to profit and loss, as instructed.

NOTE

Always distinguish between amount **used** and amount **paid/payable**.

Example

Sutton took goods from stock to the value of €120 per week and €145 cash per week for household expenses. Sutton also estimated that one-third of rent and 20% of light and heat **used** should be attributed to the private section of the premises.

Light and heat paid	€3,500
Electricity due at 31/12/20-0	€140
Stock of heating oil at 31/12/20-0	€540
Annual rent	€9,900

Calculate the amount of drawings applicable to Sutton.

Solution

Stock	52 x 120	=	€6,240
Cash	52 x 145	=	€7,540
Rent	9,900 x 1/3	=	€3,300
Light and heat	(3,500 + 140 - 540) = 3,100 x 20%	=	€620
Total drawings			**€17,700**

Steps 9 and 10

Prepare the trading, profit and loss account and balance sheet as per final accounts.

16

Sample Higher Level question

On 1/1/20-1, J. Lambert purchased a business for €340,000 consisting of the following tangible assets and liabilities: premises €260,000; stock €42,000; debtors €32,000; three months' insurance prepaid €1,200; trade creditors €31,800; and wages due €2,300.

During 20-1 Lambert did not keep a full set of accounts but was able to supply the following information on 31/12/20-1:

Cash payments: Lodgements €125,000; general expenses €35,700; purchases €78,000

Bank payments: Motor vans €32,000; creditors €54,000; light and heat €8,600; interest €1,800; annual insurance €2,400; covenant for charitable organisation €6,400; computers and equipment €39,000; annual rent €6,000

Bank lodgements: Debtors €57,800; cash €125,000; dividends €6,500

Lambert took goods from stock to the value of €120 and €90 cash per week for household expenses during the year.

Lambert borrowed €120,000 on 1/7/20-1 from ZY Finance Ltd, part of which was used to purchase an adjoining building costing €95,000. It was agreed that the amount borrowed be repaid in 12 equal instalments on 1st March each year beginning 1/3/20-2. Interest is to be charged at the rate of 5% per annum on the initial sum and paid monthly at the end of each month.

The figure for rent was in respect of an adjoining building rented by Lambert on 1/10/20-1. It was paid in advance and Lambert estimated that one-third of the building was used for private residence and that 25% of light and heat **used** should be attributed to the private section of the premises.

Included in the assets and liabilities of the firm on 31/12/20-1 were: stock €19,600 (including stock of heating oil €700); debtors €21,500; trade creditors €17,900; cash balance €980; electricity charges due €1,020.

You are required to show, with workings:

- the trading, profit and loss account for the year ended 31/12/20-1
- the balance sheet as at 31/12/20-1.

What additional information would be available if Lambert's accounts were prepared using the double-entry system?

Solution

Step 1: Statement of capital – to find goodwill

Statement of Capital for J. Lambert as on 1/1/20-1

	€	€
Assets		
Premises	260,000	
Stock	42,000	
Debtors	32,000	
3 months' prepaid insurance	1,200	335,200
***Less* Liabilities**		
Trade creditors	31,800	
Wages due	2,300	(34,100)
Net worth		301,100
Amount paid		340,000
Goodwill		**38,900**

16

Step 2: Debtors and creditors control accounts – to find credit sales

Dr. **Debtors Control Account** Cr.

Details	€	Details	€
Balance on 1/1/20-1	32,000	Bank	57,800
Credit sales	**47,300**	Balance on 31/12/20-1	21,500
	79,300		**79,300**

Dr. **Creditors Control Account** Cr.

Details	€	Details	€
Bank	54,000	Balance on 1/1/20-1	31,800
Balance on 31/12/20-1	17,900	**Credit purchases**	**40,100**
	71,900		**71,900**

Step 3: Cash and bank accounts

Dr. **Cash Account** Cr.

Details	€	Details	€
Cash sales	**244,360**	Lodgements	125,000
		General expenses	35,700
		Purchases	78,000
		Drawings (90 x 52)	4,680
		Balance	980
	244,360		**244,360**

Dr.		Bank Account	Cr.
Details	**€**	**Details**	**€**
Debtors	57,800	Motor vans	32,000
Cash	125,000	Creditors	54,000
Dividends	6,500	Light and heat	8,600
Loan	120,000	Interest	1,800
		Insurance	2,400
		Covenant	6,400
		Computers and equipment	39,000
		Annual rent	6,000
		Buildings	95,000
		Balance	**64,100**
	309,300		**309,300**

16

Step 4: Total sales

Cash sales (from Step 3)	244,360
Credit sales (from Step 2)	47,300
Total sales	**291,660**

Step 5: Total purchases

Cash purchases (Step 3)	78,000
Credit purchases (Step 2)	40,100
	118,100
Less Drawings (120 x 52)	(6,240)
Total purchases	**111,860**

Step 6: Loans and investments

Amount of loan	120,000
Interest chargeable (120,000 x 5% x 6/12)	3,000
Interest paid	(1,800)
Loan interest due	1,200

First instalment is due in March 20-2

120,000/12 =	**10,000**	(Creditors: amounts falling due within 1 year)
120,000 - 10,000 =	**110,000**	(Creditors: amounts falling due after 1 year)

Step 7: Adjustments for accruals and prepayments

W1 General Expenses

Amount paid	35,700
Less Wages due	(2,300)
	33,400

W2 Light and Heat

Amount paid	8,600
Less Stock oil	(700)
Add Electricity charges due	1,020
	8,920
Less Drawings (25%)	(2,230)
	6,690

W3 Insurance

Amount paid (12 months)	2,400
Add Prepaid start (3 months)	1,200
Less Prepaid end (3/12 of 2,400)	(600)
	3,000

W4 Rent

Amount paid	6,000
Less Drawings (1/3)	(2,000)
	4,000
Less Prepaid (9/12 of €4,000)	(3,000)
	1,000

Step 8: Drawings

Light and heat used (Step 7, W2)	8,920 x 25%	2,230
Rent (Step 7, W4)	6,000 x 1/3	2,000
Stock used by owner	120 x 52	6,240
Cash	90 x 52	4,680
Total drawings		**15,150**

16

Step 9: Trading, profit and loss account

Trading, Profit and Loss Account for the year ended 31/12/20-1

	€	€
Sales (Step 4)		291,660
***Less* Cost of sales**		
Opening stock	42,000	
Purchases (Step 5)	111,860	
Cost of goods available	153,860	
Less Closing stock (less stock of oil)	(18,900)	
Cost of goods sold		(134,960)
Gross profit		**156,700**
***Less* Expenses**		
Administration		
General expenses (Step 7) (W1)	33,400	
Light and heat (Step 7) (W2)	6,690	
Rent (Step 7) (W4)	1,000	
Insurance (Step 7) (W3)	3,000	
Covenant	6,400	(50,490)
Operating profit		106,210
Less Interest on loan (Step 6)		(3,000)
Net profit		**103,210**

Step 10: Balance sheet

Balance Sheet as on 31/12/20-1

	Cost (€)	Aggregate Depreciation (€)	Net Book Value (€)
Intangible fixed assets			
Goodwill (Step 1)			38,900
Fixed assets			
Land and buildings	355,000		355,000
Motor vans	32,000		32,000
Equipment	39,000		39,000
	426,000		464,900
Current assets			
Cash		980	
Bank (Step 3)		64,100	
Stock		18,900	
Stock oil		700	
Insurance prepaid (Step 7, W3)		600	
Debtors		21,500	
Rent prepaid (Step 7, W4)		3,000	
		109,780	
***Less* Creditors: amounts falling due within 1 year**			
Trade creditors	17,900		
Electricity charges due	1,020		
Loan interest due (Step 6)	1,200		
Loan instalment due (Step 6)	10,000	(30,120)	
Net current assets			79,660
Total net assets			**544,560**
Financed by			
Creditors: amounts falling due after more than 1 year			
Term loan (Step 6)			110,000
Capital and reserves			
Capital 1/1/20-1		340,000	
Add Net profit (Step 9)		103,210	
Add Capital introduced (dividends)		6,500	
		449,710	
Less Drawings (Step 8)		(15,150)	434,560
Capital employed			**544,560**

Advice

Lambert should keep a detailed cash book and general ledger supported by appropriate subsidiary day books. This would enable Lambert to prepare an accurate trading and profit and loss account and therefore would avoid reliance on estimates.

Exercises – Ordinary Level

16

Q1 **Matthew Hayes did not keep a full set of books during the year ended 31/12/20-1. The following is a summary of his cash account for that financial period:**

	€	€
Cash receipts		
Balance 1/1/20-1	56,700	
Commission	5,900	
Debtors	98,700	
Sales	234,500	395,800
Cash payments		
General expenses including wages	32,900	
Purchases	123,600	
Drawings	15,700	
Creditors	45,600	
Motor vehicles	34,000	251,800

The following additional information is also available:

	1/1/20-1	31/12/20-1
Buildings	345,000	345,000
Furniture	50,000	50,000
Debtors	21,300	19,600
Creditors	14,500	14,700
Stock	23,400	24,600
Expenses due	3,400	1,200

Note: Depreciate furniture by 10% of cost per annum.

You are required to:

- Calculate Matthew Hayes's capital on 1/1/20-1.
- Calculate Matthew Hayes's total purchases and total sales using control accounts.
- Prepare a trading, profit and loss account for the year ended 31/12/20-1.
- Prepare a balance sheet as at 31/12/20-1.

Q2 **Kari O'Sullivan did not keep a full set of books during the year ended 31/12/20-9. The following is a summary of her cash account for that period:**

	€	€
Cash receipts		
Balance 1/1/20-9	31,900	
Debtors	54,900	
Rent	5,800	
Sales	319,000	411,600
Cash payments		
Purchases	128,000	
Drawings	16,600	
Salaries and general expenses	8,900	
Creditors	21,100	
Office equipment	16,000	190,600

The following additional information is also available:

	1/1/20-9	31/12/20-9
Land and buildings	480,000	480,000
Delivery vans	82,000	82,000
Debtors	14,000	12,000
Creditors	11,500	13,900
Stock	10,700	14,500
Expenses due	100	1,100
Rent due		500

Note: Provide for depreciation on delivery vans at 25% of cost per annum.

You are required to:

- Calculate Kari O'Sullivan's capital on 1/1/20-9.
- Calculate Kari O'Sullivan's total purchases and total sales using control accounts.
- Prepare a trading, profit and loss account for the year ended 31/12/20-9.
- Prepare a balance sheet as at 31/12/20-9.

16

Q3 **Veronica Chapman did not keep a full set of books during the year ended 31/12/20-7. The following is a summary of her cash account for that financial period:**

	€	€
Cash receipts		
Balance 1/1/20-7	3,700	
Debtors	87,100	
Commission	5,400	
Sales	213,000	309,200
Cash payments		
Creditors	74,300	
Drawings	2,800	
Purchases	87,500	
General expenses	47,200	
Furniture	6,300	218,100

The following additional information is also available:

	1/1/20-7	31/12/20-7
Premises	460,000	460,000
Motor vehicles	86,000	86,000
Debtors	12,500	7,800
Creditors	10,800	15,400
Stock	13,200	12,400
Expenses prepaid	1,000	1,300

Note: Depreciate motor vehicles by 15% of cost per annum.

You are required to:

- **Prepare a statement of capital for Veronica Chapman as on 1/1/20-7.**
- **Calculate Chapman's total purchases and total sales using control accounts.**
- **Prepare a trading, profit and loss account for the year ended 31/12/20-7.**
- **Prepare a balance sheet as on 31/12/20-7.**

Q4 **Peter Roche did not keep a full set of books during the year ended 31/12/20-5. The following is a summary of his cash account for that financial period:**

	€	€
Cash receipts		
Balance 1/1/20-5	9,800	
Debtors	98,600	
Rent	10,800	
Sales	187,500	306,700
Cash payments		
Creditors	86,000	
Drawings	12,300	
Purchases	76,500	
Wages and general expenses	34,500	
Computers and office equipment	17,000	226,300

The following additional information is also available:

	1/1/20-5	31/12/20-5
Premises	321,000	321,000
Delivery vans	56,000	56,000
Debtors	23,400	19,700
Creditors	21,900	17,800
Stock	13,700	14,500
Expenses prepaid		2,400
Expenses due	1,500	

Note: Depreciate buildings by 2% of cost per annum and delivery vans at 20% per annum.

You are required to:

- Prepare a statement of capital for Peter Roche as on 1/1/20-5.
- Calculate Roche's total purchases and total sales using control accounts.
- Prepare a trading, profit and loss account for the year ended 31/12/20-5.
- Prepare a balance sheet as on the 31/12/20-5.

16

Exercises – Higher Level

Q1 **On 1/1/20-6, Samantha Hughes purchased a business for €708,000 which included the following tangible assets and liabilities: premises €670,000; stock €22,900; debtors €14,500; three months' prepaid rent €1,920; trade creditors €21,800; wages due €3,000; and cash €250.**

During 20-6 Hughes did not keep a full set of accounts but was able to supply the following information on 31/12/20-6:

Cash payments:	Lodgements €132,000; salaries and general expenses €89,000; purchases €114,800
Bank payments:	Computers €16,000; creditors €42,300; light and heat €6,500; interest €2,000; annual rent €12,000; furniture €22,000
Bank lodgements:	Debtors €69,000; cash €132,000; lotto win €1,200

Each week Hughes took goods from stock to the value of €120 and cash €180 for household expenses.

Hughes borrowed €200,000 on 1/7/20-6 part of which was used to purchase an adjoining premises costing €150,000. It was agreed that Hughes would pay interest on the last day of each month at a rate of 5% per annum. The capital sum was to be repaid in one lump sum in the year 20-9 and to provide for this the bank was to transfer €1,400 on the last day of each month from Hughes's business bank account into an investment fund, commencing on 31/7/20-6.

Hughes estimated that 20% of computers, 25% of interest **payable** and 15% of light and heat **used** should be attributed to the private section of the business.

Included in the assets and liabilities of the firm on 31/12/20-6 were: stock €23,000; debtors €15,600; trade creditors €22,300; cash €230; electricity due €500; and €60 interest earned by the fund to date.

You are required to:

- Prepare, with workings, the trading, profit and loss account for the year ended 31/12/20-6.
- Show the balance sheet as at 31/12/20-6.

16

Q2 On 1/1/20-2 Jordan Rhodes purchased a business for €500,000 consisting of the following tangible assets and liabilities: premises €430,000; stock €21,000; debtors €25,600; three months' prepaid advertising €660; trade creditors €29,000; and cleaning expenses due €2,300.

During 20-2 Rhodes did not keep a full set of accounts but was able to supply the following information on 31/12/20-2:

Cash payments:	Lodgements €78,000; general expenses €45,000; purchases €103,400
Bank payments:	Delivery van €34,000; light and heat €3,400; annual advertising campaign €1,800; trade creditors €47,800; interest €4,000; covenant for charitable organisation €2,400; office furniture €10,000
Bank lodgements:	Cash €78,000; debtors €62,500; dividends €1,200

During the year, Rhodes took from stock goods to the value of €2,300 per month and cash €1,200 per month.

Rhodes borrowed €140,000 on 1/4/20-2, part of which was used to build an extension costing €120,000. It was agreed that Rhodes would pay interest on the last day of the month at the rate of 12% per annum. The capital sum was to be repaid in one lump sum in the year 20-5 and to provide for this the bank was to transfer €1,300 each month from Rhodes's business bank account into an investment fund, beginning on 30/4/20-2.

Rhodes estimated that 20% of furniture and light and heat **used**, as well as 10% of interest **payable** for the year, should be attributed to the private section of the business.

Included in the assets and liabilities of the firm on 31/12/20-2 were: stock €19,800 which included stock of oil €700; debtors €27,600; trade creditors €23,500; cash €900; electricity due €200; and €150 interest earned by the fund to date.

You are required to:

- Prepare, with workings, the trading, profit and loss account for the year ended 31/12/20-2.
- Show the balance sheet as at 31/12/20-2.

Q3 On 1/1/20-3 Karl Jones lodged €340,000 into his business bank account and on the same day purchased a business for €294,000 consisting of the following tangible assets and liabilities: premises €260,000; stock €11,000; debtors €5,600; three months' prepaid insurance €450, trade creditors €9,000. and wages due €300.

During 20-3 Jones did not keep a full set of accounts but was able to supply the following information on 31/12/20-3:

Cash payments:	Lodgements €115,000; general expenses €43,200; purchases €66,700
Bank payments:	Furniture €14,000; light and heat €4,600; annual insurance €1,200; creditors €17,800; interest €1,100; college fees €3,400; delivery van €18,000
Bank lodgements:	Cash €115,000; debtors €25,500; dividends €2,100

During the year, Jones took from stock goods to the value of €300 per week and cash €900 per month.

Jones borrowed €60,000 on 1/10/20-3, part of which was used to buy an adjoining storeroom costing €50,000. It was agreed that Jones would pay interest on the last day of the month at the rate of 8% per annum. The capital sum was to be repaid in one lump sum in the year 20-8 and to provide for this the bank was to transfer €450 each month from Jones's business bank account into an investment fund, beginning on 31/10/20-3.

Jones estimated that 15% of furniture, 20% light and heat **used**, as well as 25% of interest **payable** for the year, should be attributed to the private section of the business. He also estimated that 50% of college fees was for his daughter and the remainder for an employee.

Included in the assets and liabilities of the firm on 31/12/20-3 were: stock €11,100 which included stock of oil €300; debtors €7,500; trade creditors €3,900; cash €400; electricity due €100; and €50 interest earned by the fund to date.

16

You are required to:

- Prepare, with workings, the trading, profit and loss account for the year ended 31/12/20-3.
- Show the balance sheet as at 31/12/20-3.

Q4 On 1/1/20-4, Steve McDonald purchased a business for €450,000 consisting of the following tangible assets and liabilities: premises €365,000; stock €32,000; debtors €28,700; three months' premises insurance prepaid €1,500; trade creditors €41,000; and wages due €5,000.

During 20-4 McDonald did not keep a full set of accounts but was able to supply the following information on 31/12/20-4:

Cash payments:	Lodgements €213,000; wages and general expenses €35,600; purchases €171,300.
Bank payments:	Delivery van €64,000; creditors €85,600; light and heat €13,400; interest €5,100; annual premises insurance €8,400; deposit for son's apartment €24,000; computers and equipment €32,100
Bank lodgements:	Debtors €71,300; cash €213,000; dividends €9,100

McDonald took from stock goods to the value of €160 and €205 cash per week for household use during the year.

McDonald borrowed €180,000 on 1/9/20-4, part of which was used to purchase an adjoining premises costing €160,000. It was agree that McDonald would pay interest on the last day of each month at the rate of 9% per annum. The capital sum was to be repaid in 12 equal instalments over six years. The first instalment is due on 1/1/20-5.

McDonald estimated that 20% of light and heat **used** and computers and equipment **paid**, as well as 30% of interest **payable**, should be attributed to the private section of the business.

Provide for depreciation on buildings at a rate of 2% of cost per annum on the value of buildings on 31/12/20-4.

Included in the assets and liabilities of the firm on 31/12/20-4 were: stock €34,000; debtors €44,500; trade creditors €62,000; cash €1,350, electricity due €1,020.

You are required to show with workings:

- the trading, profit and loss account for the year ended 31/12/20-4
- the balance sheet as at 31/12/20-4.

Q5 **On 1/1/20-7 Louise Cook purchased a business for €525,000 which consisted of the following tangible assets and liabilities: buildings €480,000; stock €33,000; debtors €34,500; five months' prepaid rent and rates €1,200; trade creditors €29,600; and electricity due €2.350.**

During 20-7 Cook did not keep a full set of accounts but was able to supply the following information on 31/12/20-7:

Cash payments:	Lodgements €87,800; general expenses €21,500; purchases €54,900
Bank payments:	Delivery van €34,000; light and heat €11,400; annual rent and rates €3,600; interest €1,200; wages €43,100; creditors €43,800
Bank lodgements:	Debtors €74,500; cash €87,800; lotto win €1,400

16

Each month, Cook took from stock goods to the value of €670 and cash €500 for household expenses.

Cook borrowed €100,000 on 1/7/20-7, part of which was used to build a new showroom at a cost of €70,000. The remainder of the loan was used to furnish this showroom. It was agreed that Cook would pay interest on the last day of the each month at a rate of 10% per annum. The capital sum was to be repaid in full in one lump sum during the year 20-9 and to provide for this the bank was instructed to transfer €1,400 at the end of each month into an investment fund from Cook's business bank account.

Cook estimated that 20% of light and heat **used**, 25% of furniture **purchased**, as well as 10% of interest **payable** for the year, should be attributed to the private section of the premises.

On 31/12/20-7 goods with a sales value of €12,000 which had been sold on credit at a mark-up of 20% of cost had not been recorded in the books. The goods were still in the warehouse and were included in closing stock.

Provide for depreciation as follows: buildings 4% of value on 31/12/20-7; delivery van 20% of cost per annum; furniture 15% of cost per annum.

Included in the assets and liabilities of the firm on 31/12/20-7 were: stock €33,500; stock of oil €550; debtors €32,000; trade creditors €21,500; cash €560; investment interest earned by the fund to date €235.

You are required to show with workings:

- the trading, profit and loss account for the year ended 31/12/20-7
- the balance sheet as at 31/12/20-7.

2: Net Worth/Balance Sheet Method (including Mark-up/Margin)

The principle of the net worth/balance sheet method is that unless cash or resources have been put into the business during the year the only way that capital/net worth can be increased is by making a profit.

This method is used to ascertain the net profit/loss when the organisation is unable to prepare a trading, profit and loss account because it does not have figures for sales, purchases, expenses, etc.

While this method does allow the profit to be found, it does not provide a full set of final accounts and will not give the owner enough details for analysis purposes. It is an unreliable method as it involves the use of estimates. A full trading, profit and loss account cannot be prepared as essential information, such as sales revenue and expenses incurred, is not available.

16

Net worth

> **Net worth** is the value of the business to the owners.
> Net worth = Total assets – Outside liabilities

The net worth of the business is calculated at both the beginning and end of the financial period.

If the closing net worth is **greater than** the opening net worth then it can be assumed the business made a profit.

If the closing net worth is **less than** the opening net worth then it can be assumed the business incurred a loss.

Procedure

Step 1 **Find the opening net worth of the business** by preparing a statement of capital as on that date.

Step 2 **Find the closing net worth of the business** after allowing for depreciation during the year.

Step 3 **Find the increase or decrease in the net worth**. If this is an increase the difference is assumed to be profit and if it is a decrease the difference is assumed to be a loss.

Step 4 **Make any necessary adjustments** for:

- drawings – anything of value the owner takes from the business
- capital introduced during the financial period
- expenses that have not yet been accounted for.

Sample Ordinary Level question

John Moran, a sole trader, had not been keeping a full set of accounts. The following figures relating to his business were supplied on 1/1/20-7:

Premises	€300,000
Delivery vans	€80,000
Fixtures and fittings	€10,000
Accumulated depreciation on vans	€12,500
Stock	€34,500
Debtors	€17,800
Insurance prepaid	€7,900
Creditors	€22,200
Wages due	€5,600
Bank overdraft	€19,000 (Cr.)

16

Moran also supplied the following additional information on 31/12/20-7:

(a) During the year Moran lodged €12,500, which he won privately on a club lotto, into his business account.

(b) During the year Moran paid €1,200 out of business funds for private expenses to his house and also took goods to the value of €120 per month for personal use.

Moran estimated that on 31/12/20-7 the business assets and liabilities were €491,000 and €45,800 respectively, before allowing for depreciation on delivery vans at 20% of book value and fixtures and fittings at 15% of cost and before allowing for expenses due, €1,300.

You are required to:

- Prepare a statement showing Moran's net worth/capital on 1/1/20-7.
- Prepare a statement showing Moran's profit or loss for the year ended 31/12/20-7.

Solution

Step 1 Find the opening net worth of the business

Statement of Net Worth/Capital as at 1/1/20-7

	€	€
Assets		
Premises	300,000	
Delivery vans (80,000 – 12,500)	67,500	
Fixtures and fittings	10,000	
Stock	34,500	
Debtors	17,800	
Insurance prepaid	7,900	437,700
***Less* Liabilities**		
Creditors	22,200	
Wages due	5,600	
Bank overdraft	19,000	(46,800)
Capital/net worth 1/1/20-7		**390,900**

Step 2 Find the closing net worth of the business

Statement of Net Worth/Capital as at 31/12/20-7

	€	€
Assets		491,000
Less Depreciation of delivery vans	13,500	
Depreciation of fixtures and fittings	1,500	(15,000)
Total assets		476,000
Less		
Liabilities	45,800	
Wages due	1,300	(47,100)
Net worth on 31/12/20-7		**428,900**

16

Steps 3 and 4 Find the increase/decrease in net worth and make any necessary adjustments

Statement of Net Profit/Loss for year ended 31/12/20-7

	€	€
Net worth on 31/12/20-7		428,900
Less Net worth on 1/1/20-7		(390,900)
Apparent profit for the year		38,000
Less Capital introduced		(12,500)
		25,500
Add Drawings		
Private expenses	1,200	
Stock (120 x 12)	1,440	2,640
Net profit for the year 20-7		**28,140**

Drawings are added in this method because if they had not been made, profit would have been higher.

Capital introduced is subtracted in this method because it has increased the net worth but not increased profit.

Alternatively this statement of profit and loss can be presented or calculated using a balance sheet format.

Prepare the balance sheet by entering all the assets and liabilities and hence find the net profit.

The net profit will be the balancing figure
- i.e. the difference between the assets and liabilities.

Balance Sheet as at 31/12/20-7

	€	€
Assets		491,000
Less Depreciation of delivery vans	13,500	
Depreciation of fixtures and fittings	1,500	(15,000)
Total assets		476,000
Less Liabilities	45,800	
Wages due	1,300	(47,100)
Net worth 31/12/20-7		428,900
Financed by		
Capital 1/1/20-7		390,900
Add Capital introduced		12,500
		403,400
***Less* Drawings**		
Private expenses	1,200	
Stock (120 x 12)	1,440	(2,640)
		400,760
***Add* Net profit (balancing figure)**		**28,140**
		428,900

Balance sheet - mark up/margin (Higher Level)

The mark-up or margin method depends on a knowledge of the relationship between the various figures that make up of the trading, profit and loss account and balance sheet.

Sales - Cost of goods sold (sales) = Gross profit
Opening stock + Purchases - Closing stock = Cost of sales
Gross profit - Expenses = Net profit

$$\textbf{Mark up} = \frac{\textbf{Gross profit} \times 100}{\textbf{Cost of sales}} \qquad \textbf{Margin} = \frac{\textbf{Gross profit} \times 100}{\textbf{Sales}}$$

16

Procedure

Step 1 **Prepare a statement of net worth/capital** (including goodwill, if any).

Step 2 **Make any necessary adjustments** for assets, expenses, gains, etc.

Step 3 **Prepare a balance sheet**, entering all the assets and liabilities to find the net profit/loss. This will be the balancing figure as outlined above.

Step 4 **Prepare a trading, profit and loss account** to find the gross profit. This will involve preparing a skeleton trading, profit and loss account by filling in the missing figures and then working upwards from net profit, which was taken from the balance sheet in Step 3 above.

Sample Higher Level question

16

On 1/1/20-5 Kerry Monaghan purchased a business for €854,000 consisting of premises €812,000; stock €14,150; debtors €11,200; creditors €9,800; insurance prepaid €840; and wages due €2,390. During 20-5 Monaghan did not keep a full set of accounts but was able to supply the following information on 31/12/20-5:

(a) On 1/1/20-5 Monaghan borrowed €516,000 from a MN Finance Ltd, part of which was used to purchase an adjoining warehouse and yard costing €450,000. It was agreed that this loan was to be repaid in 24 equal instalments over 12 years commencing on 1/6/20-5. In the meantime, interest is charged at 10% per annum on the initial sum payable at the end of each month.

(b) During 20-5 Monaghan inherited €20,000 and this was lodged to her business bank account. She also paid €12,000 out of the business bank account for her daughter's college fees.

(c) Monaghan has estimated that she took each month goods to the value of €900 and €500 cash for private use.

(d) The following payments were made by Monaghan during the year: cleaning €3,000; light and heat €13,600; insurance €6,600; salaries and general expenses €103,000; and interest €32,000.

(e) Monaghan and her family lived above the business's premises and she has estimated that 25% of insurance **paid** during the year, 20% of light and heat **used** and 15% of interest **payable** are attributable to the private section of the premises.

(f) Monaghan's gross profit is 50% of sales.

(g) On 31/12/20-5 stock was €47,600; debtors €36,400; creditors €3,500; electricity charges due €350; and there was a bank overdraft of €2,500.

You are required to:

- Prepare a statement showing Monaghan's profit and loss for the year ended 31/12/20-5.
- Prepare a trading, profit and loss account in as much detail as possible for the year ended 31/12/20-5.
- Indicate what advice you would give to Monaghan.

NOTE

In this type of question it is necessary first to find the net profit, and then work backwards from it.

16

Solution

Step 1: Prepare a statement of net worth

	€	€
Assets		
Premises	812,000	
Stock	14,150	
Debtors	11,200	
Insurance prepaid	840	838,190
***Less* Liabilities**		
Creditors	9,800	
Wages due	2,390	(12,190)
Net worth		**826,000**
Purchase price		854,000
Goodwill		**28,000**

Step 2: Make any necessary adjustments

Workings

W1 Premises

Original	812,000
Add New	450,000
	1,262,000

W2 Interest

516,000 x 10% x 12/12 =	51,600
Less Interest paid	(32,000)
Interest due	**19,600**

W3 Light and heat

Amount paid	13,600
Add Electricity due	350
	13,950
Less Drawings (20%)	(2,790)
	11,160

W4 Insurance

Amount paid	6,600
Add Prepaid 1/1	840
	7,440
Less Drawings (25%)	(1,650)
	5,790

(Note: 25% of 6,600 – amount paid)

W5 Interest – drawings

51,600 x 15% 7,740

Profit and loss **43,860** (51,600 – 7,740)

W6 Salaries and general expenses

Amount paid	103,000
Less Due 1/1/20-5	(2,390)
	100,610

W7 Drawings

Light and heat	2,790
Insurance	1,650
Interest	7,740
Stock (900 x 12)	10,800
Cash (500 x 12)	6,000
College fees	12,000
Total	**40,980**

NOTE

The balancing figure will be net profit or net loss.

Step 3: Prepare a balance sheet

Balance Sheet of Kerry Monaghan as on 31/12/20-5

	Cost (€)	Aggregate Depreciation (€)	Net Book Value (€)
Intangible fixed assets			
Goodwill (Step 1)			28,000
Tangible fixed assets			
Premises (Step 2 W1)	1,262,000		1,262,000
	1,262,000		1,290,000
Current assets			
Stock		47,600	
Debtors		36,400	
		84,000	
***Less* Creditors: amounts falling due within 1 year**			
Creditors	3,500		
Electricity due	350		
Bank	2,500		
Loan interest due (W2)	19,600		
Loan instalment due (21,500 x 2)	43,000	(68,950)	
Net current assets			15,050
Total net assets			1,305,050
Financed by			
Creditors: amounts falling due after more than 1 year			
Loan (21,500 x 22)			473,000
Capital and reserves			
Capital 1/1/20-5		854,000	
Add Capital introduced		20,000	
		874,000	
Less Drawings (W7)		(40,980)	833,020
			1,306,020
***Less* Net loss**			**(970)**
Capital employed			1,305,050

NOTE

All the figures for the balance sheet are given except net profit/loss. This figure can be ascertained by subtracting one section of the balance sheet from the other.

Step 4: Prepare the trading, profit and loss account

Trading, Profit and Loss Account of Kerry Monaghan for the year ended 31/12/20-5

	€	€
Sales (W8)		346,900
***Less* Cost of sales**		
Opening stock	14,150	
Purchases (W9) (217,700 - 10,800)	206,900*	
	221,050	
Less Closing stock	(47,600)	
Cost of goods sold		(173,450)
Gross profit		**173,450**
***Less* Expenses**		
Administration		
Light and heat (Step 2 W3)	11,160	
Insurance (Step 2 W4)	5,790	
Salaries and general expenses (Step 2 W6)	110,610	
Cleaning	3,000	(130,560)
Operating profit		42,890
Less Interest (Step 2 W5)		(43,860)
Net loss		**(970)**

*This figure is after allowing for drawings of stock, €10,800.

Net loss €970	Add back interest €43,860	=	Operating profit €42,890
Operating profit €42,890	Add back expenses €130,560	=	Gross profit €173,450

W8 Sales

Gross profit	173,450
Gross margin	50%
Therefore 173,450/50 x 100 =	Sales 346,900

W9 Purchases

Opening stock + Purchases - Closing stock	= Cost of sales
14,150 + Purchases - 47,600	= 173,450
Therefore Purchases = 173,450 + 47,600 - 14,150	= 206,900

Advice

Kerry should keep a detailed cash book and general ledger. All the accounts should be kept on the double-entry principle and supported by appropriate daybooks. This would enable her to prepare a trading, profit and loss account and therefore she would not have to rely on estimates.

Exercises – Ordinary Level

Q1 Robbie Savage, a sole trader, has not been keeping a full set of accounts. The following figures relating to his business were supplied on 1/1/20-8:

Premises	€550,000
Motor vehicles (at book value)	€31,900
Office equipment at cost	€51,000
Accumulated depreciation on office equipment	€17,700
Stock	€22,300
Debtors	€20,000
Insurance prepaid	€1,200
Creditors	€27,700
Wages due	€3,600
Bank	€26,475 (Cr.)

Savage supplied the following additional information on 31/12/20-8:

(a) During the year €8,000 was transferred from a personal bank account to the business bank account.

(b) During the year, Savage paid €3,500 out of business funds for private house expenses and also took goods to the value of €450 per month for private use.

Savage estimated that on 31/12/20-8 the business assets and liabilities were €720,000 and €60,000 respectively, before allowing for depreciation on office equipment at the rate of 20% of cost, depreciation on motor vehicles at the rate of 20% of book value, and before allowing for expenses due of €660.

You are required to:

- Prepare a statement showing Savage's net worth/capital on 1/1/20-8.
- Prepare a statement showing Savage's profit or loss for the year ended 31/12/20-8.

Q2 Lee Major, a sole trader, has not been keeping a full set accounts. The following figures relating to the business were supplied on 1/1/20-3:

Premises	€784,000
Furniture and equipment (cost price)	€132,800
Motor vehicles (book value)	€55,360
Depreciation on equipment	€41,920
Stock	€71,840
Debtors	€38,400
Advertising prepaid	€640
Creditors	€26,400
Expenses due	€2,880
Bank overdraft	€16,640

Major also supplied the following information on 31/12/20-3:

(a) During the year €19,200 was transferred from a personal bank account to the business bank account.

(b) During the year Major paid €4,160 out of business funds for private house repairs and had also taken goods to the value of €1,280 per month for private use.

Major estimated that on 31/12/20-3 the business assets and liabilities were €1,248,000 and €54,400 respectively, before allowing for depreciation on furniture and equipment at the rate of 20% of cost, depreciation of motor vehicles at the rate of 20% of book value, and before allowing for expenses due of €960.

You are required to prepare:

- a statement showing Major's net worth/capital on 1/1/20-3
- a statement showing Major's profit or loss for the year ended 31/12/20-3.

16

Q3 C. Stabler, a sole trader, has not been keeping a full set of accounts. The following figures relating to the business were supplied on 1/1/20-3:

Land and buildings	€444,000
Machinery at cost	€40,800
Delivery vans at cost	€25,560
Depreciation to date on machinery	€14,160
Stock	€19,560
Debtors	€16,200
Rates prepaid	€1,280
Creditors	€21,660
Wages due	€2,780
Bank	€21,180 (Cr.)

Stabler also supplied the following additional information on 31/12/20-3:

(a) During the year €6,600 was transferred from Stabler's personal bank account to the business bank account.

(b) During the year Stabler had paid €2,100 out of business funds for private expenses and he had also taken goods to the value of €480 per month for private use.

Stabler estimated that on 31/12/20-3 the business assets and liabilities were €576,000 and €48,000 respectively, before allowing for depreciation on machinery at the rate of 20% of book value and depreciation of delivery vans at the rate of 10% of cost, and before allowing for wages due of €528.

You are required to:

- Prepare a statement showing Stabler's net worth/capital on 1/1/20-3.
- Prepare a statement showing Stabler's profit or loss for the year ended 31/12/20-3.

Q4 Olivia Benson, a sole trader, has not been keeping a full set of accounts. The following figures relating to her business were supplied on 1/1/20-6:

Premises	€605,000
Machinery at cost	€56,000
Motor vehicles at cost	€45,600
Depreciation to date on motor vehicles	€14,600
Stock	€23,400
Debtors	€15,600
Prepaid insurance	€2,300

Creditors	€13,560
Rent due	€1,780
Bank	€32,800 (Cr.)

Benson also supplied the following additional information on 31/12/20-6:

(a) During the year €4,600 was transferred from Benson's personal bank account to the business bank account.

(b) During the year Benson had paid €3,400 out of business funds for private expenses and he had also taken goods to the value of €510 per month for private use.

Benson estimated that on 31/12/20-6 the business assets and liabilities were €672,000 and €54,000 respectively, before allowing for depreciation on machinery at the rate of 15% of cost per annum and depreciation on motor vehicles at the rate of 20% of book value, and before allowing for wages due of €1,200.

You are required to:

- Prepare a statement showing Benson's net/worth capital on 1/1/20-6.
- Prepare a balance sheet showing the net profit/loss for the year ended 31/12/20-6.

Q5 **Carter McKay, a sole trader, has not been keeping a full set of accounts. The following figures relating to his business were supplied on 1/1/20-5:**

Premises	€430,000
Motor vehicles (at book value)	€32,000
Office equipment at cost	€48,000
Accumulated depreciation on office equipment	€13,400
Stock	€32,600
Debtors	€23,670
Insurance prepaid	€1,760
Creditors	€29,800
Wages due	€6,570
Bank	€31,200 (Cr.)

McKay also supplied the following additional information on 31/12/20-5:

(a) During the year €12,100 was transferred from a personal bank account to the business bank account.

(b) During the year McKay paid €4,900 out of business funds for private house expenses and also took goods to the value of €320 per month for private use.

McKay estimated that on 31/12/20-5 the business assets and liabilities were €670,000 and €65,000 respectively, before allowing for depreciation on office equipment at the rate of 10% of cost, depreciation on motor vehicles at the rate of 25% of book value, and before allowing for expenses due of €780.

You are required to:

- Prepare a statement showing McKay's net worth/capital on 1/1/20-5.
- Prepare a balance sheet showing McKay's profit or loss for the year ended 31/12/20-5.

16

Exercises – Higher Level

16

Q1 On 1/1/20-0 Sam Dingle lodged €576,000 into a business bank account and on the same day purchased for €504,000 a business consisting of the following tangible assets and liabilities: buildings €480,000; stock €17,000; three months' rent prepaid €2,100; debtors €29,000; wages due €3,400; and trade creditors €58,800.

During 20-0 Dingle did not keep a full set of books but estimated that gross profit was 20% of sales and he was able to supply the following additional information on 31/12/20-0:

(a) Each week Dingle took from stock goods to the value of €200 and cash €150 to pay household expenses.

(b) On 1/1/20-0 Dingle borrowed €430,000, part of which was used to purchase an adjoining premises costing €330,000. It was agreed that interest would be paid on the last day of each month at the rate of 6% per annum. The capital sum was to be repaid in one lump sum in the year 20-7 and to provide for this the bank was instructed to transfer €5,700 on the last day of every month from Dingle's business account into an investment fund.

(c) During the year Dingle lodged €40,000 from a lotto win into his business bank account.

(d) Dingle also made the following payments by cheque: interest €2,800; light and heat €9,700; wages and general expenses €103,000; delivery van €15,000; rent for 12 months €10,800; and son's college fees €2,400.

(e) Dingle estimated that 20% of light and heat **used** and interest **payable** should be attributed to the private section of the premises.

(f) Included in the assets and liabilities of the firm on 31/12/20-0 were stock €18,000; debtors €34,500; trade creditors €32,100; electricity due €650; and €600 interest earned by the investment fund to date. The bank overdraft was €21,000.

You are required to:

- Prepare a statement/balance sheet showing Dingle's profit and loss account for the year ended 31/12/20-0.
- Prepare a trading, profit and loss account in as much detail as possible for the year ended 31/12/20-0.

Q2 Sean Kelly lodged €525,000 to a business bank account on 1/1/20-2 and on the same day purchased for €480,000 a business including the following assets and liabilities: buildings €435,000; stock €25,000; three months' insurance prepaid €3,600; debtors €48,700; salaries due €5,400; and trade creditors €87,000.

Kelly did not keep a full set of books during 20-2 but estimates that gross profit was 40% of sales and he was able to supply the following additional information on 31/12/20-2:

(a) Each week Kelly took from stock goods to the value of €150 and cash €180 for household expenses.

(b) On 1/10/20-2 Kelly borrowed €450,000, part of which was used to purchase an adjoining business premises worth €325,000. It was agreed that Kelly would pay interest on the last day of each month at the rate of 8% per annum. The capital sum was to be repaid in one lump sum in the year 20-9 and to provide for this the bank was instructed to transfer €3,200 on the last day of every month from Kelly's business account into an investment fund.

(c) During the year Kelly lodged dividends of €3,250 into the business bank account and made the following payments: light and heat €10,000; interest €4,200; salaries and general expenses €132,000; furniture and equipment €20,000; annual insurance premium €12,000; college fees €6,000.

(d) Kelly estimated that 25% of furniture, light and heat **used** and interest **payable** should be attributed to the private section of the premises. Kelly also estimated that 80% of college fees should be attributed to his daughter and the remainder to an employee.

(e) Included in the assets and liabilities of the firm on 31/12/20-2 were stock €21,800; debtors €68,700; trade creditors €34,500; bank €73,400; electricity due €800; and €80 interest earned by the investment fund to date.

You are required to prepare, with workings:

- a statement/balance sheet showing Kelly's profit or loss for the year ended 31/12/20-2
- a trading, profit and loss account, in as much detail as possible, for the year ended 31/12/20-2
- a summary of the advice you would give to Kelly in relation to the information given above.

16

Q3 James Quinlan lodged €624,000 to a business bank account on 1/1/20-8 and on the same date purchased a business for €430,000 consisting of the following tangible assets and liabilities: buildings €420,000; stock €34,800; three months' cleaning prepaid €1,920; debtors €58,800; expenses due €11,520; and trade creditors €91,200.

Quinlan did not keep a full set of books during 20-8 but estimates that gross profit was 40% of sales and was able to supply the following additional information on 31/12/20-8:

(a) Each week Quinlan took from stock goods to the value of €220 and cash €280 for household expenses.

(b) On 1/7/20-8 Quinlan borrowed €360,000, part of which was used to purchase an adjoining premises costing €288,000. It was agree that Quinlan would pay interest on the last day of the month at rate of 12% per annum. The capital sum was to be repaid in one lump sum in the year 20-0 and to provide for this the bank was instructed to transfer €2,880 on the last day of each month from Quinlan's business bank account into an investment fund.

(c) During the year Quinlan lodged an inheritance of €48,000 to the business bank account and made the following payments: light and heat €15,600; wages and general expenses €163,200; furniture €28,800; cleaning for 12 months €8,640; motor vehicles €34,000; college fees €9,600; interest €5,600.

(d) Quinlan estimated that 20% of furniture, light and heat **used** and interest **payable** should be attributed to the private section of the premises. He further estimated that 70% of college fees should be attributed to a family member and the remainder to an employee.

(e) Included in the assets and liabilities of the firm on 31/12/20-8 were stock €44,150; debtors €51,850; trade creditors €47,200; cash at bank €210,400; electricity due €1,500; and €160 interest earned by the investment fund to date.

You are required to prepare, with workings:

- a statement/balance sheet showing Quinlan's profit or loss for the year ended 31/12/20-8
- a trading, profit and loss account in as much detail as possible for the year ended 31/12/20-8.

Q4 On 1/1/20-2 Mary McCarthy purchased a business for €560,000 which included the following tangible assets and liabilities: buildings €408,800; stock €50,400; debtors €45,080; three months' advertising prepaid €630; furniture €28,000; trade creditors €49,980; cleaning expenses due €1,680; and 10% investments €70,000.

During 20-2 McCarthy did not keep a full set of accounts but estimates that gross profit was 25% of sales and was able to supply the following information on 31/12/20-2:

(a) Each week McCarthy took goods from stock to the value of €112 and cash €238 for private purposes.

(b) During the year McCarthy lodged to the business bank account: investment interest €3,500 and lotto win (private) €8,400.

(c) During the year McCarthy made the following payments from his business bank account: light and heat €10,500; furniture (1/7/20-2) €21,000; motor van (31/8/20-2) €42,000; general expenses €112,000; advertising for 12 months €10,500; interest €2,800. It should be noted that general expenses include petrol for his own private car to the value of €4,200.

(d) On 1/10/20-2 McCarthy borrowed €168,000, which was used to purchase an adjoining business premises. It was agreed that the sum borrowed would be repaid in 20 equal instalments over ten years. The first instalment will be due on 1/3/20-3. Interest was payable at the rate of 10% to be paid monthly at the end of each month.

(e) McCarthy invested private funds to the value of €42,000 which were used to purchase adjacent land to the buildings.

16

(f) McCarthy estimated that 20% of light and heat **used** and 10% of interest **payable** should be attributed to private use.

(g) McCarthy decided to create a provision for bad debts of 4% of debtors and to charge depreciation at 20% on vans and 10% on furniture held at the end of the year. Depreciation is charged from date of purchase to date of sale.

(h) Depreciation is charged on buildings at 2% per annum from date of purchase to date of sale.

(i) Included in the assets and liabilities of the firm on 31/12/20-2 were: stock €28,700, of which €420 was heating oil stock; debtors €47,600; creditors €48,300; bank overdraft €7,560; and electricity due €640.

You are required to prepare, with workings:

- a balance sheet showing McCarthy's profit or loss for the year ended 31/12/20-2
- a trading, profit and loss account in as much detail as possible for the year ended 31/12/20-2.

Q5 Jack Duckworth lodged €500,000 to a business bank account on 1/1/20-3 and on the same date purchased a business for €500,000 consisting of: buildings €505,000; stock €34,000; three months' insurance prepaid €6,300; debtors €24,500; wages due €2,300; and creditors €87,200.

Duckworth did not keep a full set of accounts during 20-3 but estimates that the gross profit was 50% of sales and he was able to supply the following additional information on 31/12/20-3:

(a) Each week Duckworth took from stock goods to the value of €210 and cash €170 for household expenses.

(b) On 1/10/20-3 Duckworth borrowed €160,000, part of which was used to purchase an adjoining premises costing €140,000. It was agreed that Duckworth would pay interest on the last day of the month at the rate of 5% per annum. The capital sum was to be repaid in one lump sum in the year 20-7, and to provide for this the bank was instructed to transfer €3,500 on the last day of every month from Duckworth's business account into an investment fund.

(c) During the year Duckworth lodged private funds of €12,000 to the business bank account and made the following payments: light and heat €10,500; interest €1,900; general expenses €108,900; office equipment €22,000; 12 months' insurance €12,000; and college fees €4,800.

(d) Duckworth estimated that 20% of office equipment, light and heat **used** and interest **payable** should be attributed to the private section of the business. He further estimated that 80% of college fees should be attributed to his daughter and the remainder to an employee for training purposes.

(e) Duckworth wishes to depreciate all buildings held at 2% per annum for the full year and office equipment at 12%.

(f) Included in the assets and liabilities of the firm on 31/12/20-3 were stock €19,000; debtors (net of new bad debts provision 5%) €14,250; creditors €35,900; cash at bank €76,400; electricity due €900; and the interest fund had earned €98 to date.

You are required to prepare, with workings:

- a balance sheet showing Duckworth's profit and loss account for the year ended 31/12/20-3
- a trading, profit and loss account in as much detail as possible for the year ended 31/12/20-3.

16

Exam Tips

- There are two methods that can be asked about – the control account method and the net worth (including the mark-up/margin) method.
- Follow the procedure to deal with each method.
- Show all workings for each adjustment.
- Be mindful when dealing with loans: the amount of the loan and the date received will be important when calculating the amount of interest payable.
- Make sure you check the repayment method of the loan – instalments or a lump sum (including investment funds).
- Be mindful of whether the gross profit is based on mark-up (percentage of cost of sales) or margin (percentage of sales).
- Covenants for family members are treated as drawings; for an employee it will be an expense.

17 Cash Flow Statements

Objectives

On completion students should be able to:

- Understand the purpose and importance of preparing a cash flow statement;
- Be able to distinguish between cash items and non-cash items;
- Understand that cash is not always equal to profit;
- Be able to prepare both reconciliation statements as required under FRS 1 (Revised);
- Be able to prepare a cash flow statement;
- Be able to prepare a cash flow statement when the abridged profit and loss account is not provided.

Introduction

The **cash flow statement** is a primary financial statement, along with the trading, profit and loss account and the balance sheet. It is used to assess past cash flows as well as helping to forecast future cash flows.

Cash flow statements are concerned with describing and examining the inflows and outflows of cash that lead to the change in the cash figure from one balance sheet to the next.

DEFINITION

Cash flow refers to the increase or decrease in the amount of cash held after a transaction has taken place.

The purposes for which cash flow statements are prepared include:

- to show cash inflows and cash outflows during the year
- to help forecast future cash flows
- to help with financial planning
- to aid in the assessment of a business's liquidity/solvency
- to show that profit and cash are not always equal.

DEFINITION

Cash refers to cash in hand, plus any deposits in banks and other financial institutions payable on demand, less any bank overdrafts.

Examples of cash flow

Inflow (cash received)	Outflow (cash paid)
Profits	Losses
Decrease/sale of stock	Increase/purchase of stock
Reduction in debtors	Increase in debtors
Increase in creditors	Decrease in creditors
Interest received	Interest paid
Dividends received/investment income	Dividends paid
Sale of fixed assets	Purchase of fixed assets
Issue of shares (capital introduced)	Cash drawings
Loans received/debentures issued	Loans repaid
Tax refunds/rebates	Taxation paid

Non-cash items

Non-cash items in the profit and loss account affect the net profit, but they do not change the cash situation.

Examples include:

- depreciation of fixed assets
- profit or loss on the sale of a fixed asset
- increase/decrease in the provision for bad debts.

These will affect the **net profit**, but they do not bring about a flow of cash in or out.

NOTE

Distinguish between an actual bad debt written off and bad debts provision. A bad debt written off will bring a reduction in debtors and therefore a cash outflow. The provision, on the other hand, does not reduce debtors so there is no change to cash inflow or outflow.

17

Cash does not always equal profit

It is important to realise that cash does not always equal profit. Some transactions will affect cash but will not affect the profit. For example:

- The purchase or sale of a fixed asset will increase or decrease cash but does not change profit.
- The introduction of capital or withdrawal of cash will affect cash flow but does not change profit.
- Non-cash items, as mentioned above, will affect profit but not cash.

Importance of cash flow statements

Cash flow information helps in assessing liquidity, viability/solvency and financial flexibility. It also gives a clear picture of the financial position of the business.

DEFINITION

Liquidity is the ability of a business to pay its current debts as they fall due.

Cash flow information provided by the cash flow statement will be relevant to the investment decisions of shareholders and lenders and can help by:

- allowing the business to assess its liquidity
- allowing the business to assess its future prospects and enable financial planning for the future
- allowing the business users to make decisions about the future of the business and their relationship with the business
- showing how the business can have a bank overdraft but yet earn a profit and vice-versa.

DEFINITION

Solvency is related to cash/assets. A solvent business is one that has adequate assets to pay all its debts.

Financial Reporting Standard 1 – FRS 1 (Revised)

FRS 1, revised in 1996, requires large companies to prepare a cash flow statement for each accounting period. It also requires that cash flow statements should be entered under certain standard headings according to the activity that gave rise to them (see template that follows).

The standard headings and sequence required are:

1. Operating activities
2. Returns on investments and servicing of finance
3. Taxation
4. Capital expenditure and financial investment
5. Equity dividends paid
6. Management of liquid resources
7. Financing.

Reconciliation notes

FRS 1 (Revised) requires that two reconciliation notes be prepared:

1. Reconciliation of operating profit to net cash flow from operating activities
2. Reconciliation of net cash flow to movement in net debt.

17

1. Reconciliation of operating profit to net cash flow from operating activities

The purpose of this reconciliation note is to find the net cash generated through operating profit.

Reconciliation of operating profit to net cash flow from operating activities (template)

Operating profit	xxxxxx	
Increase in debtors/prepayments	(xxx)	Outflow
Increase in stock	(xxx)	Outflow
Decrease in creditors/accruals	(xxx)	Outflow
Profit on sale of the fixed assets	(xxx)	Non-cash
Decrease in provision for bad debts	(xxx)	Non-cash
Decrease in debtors/prepayments	xxx	Inflow
Decrease in stock	xxx	Inflow
Increase in creditors/accruals	xxx	Inflow
Loss in the sale of fixed assets	xxx	Non-cash
Increase in provision for bad debts	xxx	Non-cash
Depreciation of fixed assets	xxx	Non-cash
Net cash inflow/outflow from operating activities	xxxxx	

An **increase** in a current asset has a **negative** impact on cash
A **decrease** in a current asset has a **positive** impact on cash

An **increase** in a current liability has a **positive** impact on cash
A **decrease** in a current liability has a **negative** impact on cash

2. Reconciliation of net cash flow to movement in net debt

This statement includes all cash flows in the main cash flow statement that affect the net debt position.

Reconciliation of net cash flow to movement in net debt (template)

Increase/decrease in cash (from cash flow statement)	xxxxxx
Cash used/received from liquid resources	xxxxxx
Cash used/received from debentures	xxxxxx
Change in net debt (funds)	xxxxxx
Net debt 1/1	xxxxxx
Net debt 31/12	xxxxxx

Net debt is all borrowings less cash and liquid resources
(Borrowings = Debentures + Loans + Overdrafts)
(Liquid resources = Cash + Current asset investments)

Net funds are cash and liquid resources less borrowings
(i.e. Cash + Current asset investments – Debentures, Overdraft, Loans)

17

Preparation of cash flow statements

Headings and entries

Cash Flow Statement (template)

	€	€
Operating activities		
Net cash inflow/outflow from operating activities		xxxxxxx
Returns on investments and servicing of finance		
Interest received	xxxxxx	
Interest paid	(xxxxxx)	
Dividends received	xxxxxx	
Preference dividend paid	(xxxxxx)	(xxxxxx)
Taxation		
Taxation rebate (overpayment)	xxxxxx	
Taxation paid	(xxxxxx)	(xxxxxx)
Capital expenditure and financial investments		
Receipts (proceeds) from the sale of fixed assets	xxxxxx	
Receipts (proceeds) from the sale of investments	xxxxxx	
Payments to acquire tangible fixed assets	(xxxxxx)	
Payments to acquire investments	(xxxxxx)	xxxxxx
Equity dividends paid		
Ordinary dividends paid	(xxxxxx)	(xxxxxx)
Net cash inflow/outflow before liquid resources and financing		**xxxxxx**

Continued >

	€	€
Management of liquid resources		
Sale of government securities/liquid assets	xxxxx	
Purchase of government bonds or securities	(xxxxx)	xxxxxx
Financing		
Issue of debentures	xxxxx	
Redemption of debentures	(xxxxx)	
Issue of shares	xxxxx	
Share premium	xxxxx	xxxxxx
Increase/decrease in cash		**xxxxxxx**

Procedure

17

Notes and workings will be required for items such as the purchase or sale of fixed assets, dividends and taxation paid, as well as non-cash item adjustments such as depreciation, provision for bad debts and profit/loss on the sale of fixed assets.

There are **five** steps to be taken in the approach to the preparation of cash flow statements:

Step 1 **Calculate the change in net cash and net debt** (funds).

Step 2 **Calculate the amount of dividends, taxation and interest paid.**

Step 3 **Calculate adjustments for increase/decrease in debtors, stock and creditors.**

Step 4 **Calculate the changes in fixed assets, including deprecation.**

Step 5 **Calculate the changes in the capital structure of the firm,** i.e. **shares and debentures.**

NOTE

It is the amount of dividends **paid** that is entered in the cash flow statement.

NOTE

Depreciation is a non-movement in cash. Calculations of the profit and loss on the sale of a fixed asset may also be required.

Sample Ordinary Level question

The following information has been extracted from the books of McCauley plc:

Profit and Loss extract for the year ended 31/12/20-9

	€
Operating profit	340,800
Interest	(33,600)
Profit before taxation	307,200
Taxation	(67,200)
Profit after taxation	240,000
Dividends for year	(76,800)
Retained profits for year	163,200
Profit and loss balance 1/1/20-9	103,200
Profit and loss balance 31/12/20-9	266,400

Balance Sheet

	as at 31/12/20-9		as at 31/12/20-8	
	€	€	€	€
Fixed assets				
Premises	2,112,000		1,680,000	
Less Accumulated depreciation	(312,000)	1,800,000	211,200	1,468,800
Current assets				
Stock	165,600		156,000	
Debtors	93,600		112,800	
Bank	8,400		6,800	
Cash	30,000		10,000	
	297,600		285,600	
***Less* Creditors: amounts falling due within 1 year**				
Creditors	108,000		100,800	
Taxation	67,200		86,400	
	(175,200)		(187,200)	
Net current assets		122,400		98,400
Total net assets		**1,922,400**		**1,567,200**
Financed by				
Creditors: amounts falling due after one year				
9% Debentures		432,000		360,000
Capital and reserves				
Ordinary share capital issued		1,224,000		1,104,000
Profit and loss account		266,400		103,200
		1,922,400		**1,567,200**

You are required to:

- Reconcile the operating profit to net cash flow from operating activities.
- Prepare the cash flow statement of McCauley Ltd for the year ended 31/12/20-9.
- Reconcile the net cash flow to movement in net debt.

Solution

Step 1: Calculate the change in net cash and net debt

Item	Opening figures	Closing figures	Net change
Cash	10,000	30,000	**20,000**
Bank	6,800	8,400	**1,600**
Net cash	16,800	38,400	**21,600**
Debentures	(360,000)	(432,000)	**(72,000)**
Net debt	(343,200)	(393,600)	**(50,400)**

17

Step 2: Calculate the amount of dividends, taxation and interest paid

Item	Opening figure	***Add*** This year's charge	***Less*** Closing figure	**Amount paid**
Taxation	86,400	67,200	(67,200)	**86,400**
Dividends	0	76,800	0	**76,800**
Interest	0	33,600	0	**33,600**

- The opening figures are taken from the balance sheet year ended 31/12/20-8.
- The closing figures are taken from the balance sheet year ended 31/12/20-9.
- The additional charges are taken from the profit and loss extract for the year.
- The amounts paid are entered in the cash flow statement.

Step 3: Calculate adjustments for increase/decrease in debtors, stock and creditors

17

Item	Opening balance	Closing balance	Change	Treat as
Debtors	112,800	93,600	**(19,200)**	**Positive**
Creditors	100,800	108,000	**7,200**	**Positive**
Stock	156,000	165,600	**9,600**	**Negative**

Step 4: Calculate the changes in fixed assets, including depreciation

Item	**Opening figure** (opening balance sheet)	***Add*** Any assets purchased during the period	***Less*** Any assets disposed of during the period	**Closing figure** (closing balance sheet)
Fixed assets	1,680,000	**432,000**	**0**	2,112,000
Depreciation	211,200	**100,800**	**0**	312,000

Step 5: Calculate the changes in the capital structure of the firm

Item	**Opening figure** (opening balance sheet)	***Add*** Any increase during the period	***Less*** Any decrease during the period	**Closing figure** (closing balance sheet)
Capital	1,104,000	**120,000**	**0**	1,224,000
Debentures	360,000	**72,000**	**0**	432,000

Reconciliation of operating profit to net cash flow from operating activities

	€
Operating profit	340,800
Increase in stock (Step 3)	(9,600)
Increase in creditors (Step 3)	7,200
Decrease in debtors (Step 3)	19,200
Depreciation (Step 4)	100,800
Net cash inflow from operating activities	**458,400**

Cash Flow Statement of McCauley plc

	€	€
Operating activities		
Net cash inflow from operating activities (from above)		458,400
Returns on investments and servicing of finance		
Interest paid (Step 2)		(33,600)
Taxation		
Taxation paid (Step 2)		(86,400)
Capital expenditure and financial investment		
Payments to acquire tangible fixed assets (Step 4)		(432,000)
Equity dividends paid		
Equity dividends paid (Step 2)		(76,800)
Net cash outflow before financing		**(170,400)**
Financing		
Receipts from issue of debentures (Step 5)	72,000	
Receipts from issue of shares (Step 5)	120,000	192,000
Increase in cash (Step 1)		**21,600**

Reconciliation of net cash flow to movement in net debt

	€
Increase in cash (from cash flow statement)	21,600
Receipts from issue of debentures (Step 5)	(72,000)
Change in net debt (Step 1)	**(50,400)**
Net debt 1/1/20-9 (Step 1)	(343,200)
Net debt 31/12/20-9 (Step 1)	(393,600)

Sample Higher Level question

The following are the balance sheets of Target Plc as at 31/12/20-7 and 31/12/20-8, together with an abridged profit and loss account for the year ended 31/12/20-8:

Abridged Profit and Loss Account for the year ended 31/12/20-8

	€
Operating profit	144,000
Interest	(12,000)
Profit before taxation	132,000
Taxation	(86,000)
Profit after taxation	46,000
Dividends for year	(70,000)
Retained loss for the year	(24,000)
Profit and loss balance 1/1/20-8	280,000
Profit and loss balance 31/12/20-8	256,000

17

17

Balance Sheet

	as at 31/12/20-8		as at 31/12/20-7	
	€	€	€	€
Fixed assets				
Buildings	700,000		800,000	
Less Accumulated depreciation	(80,000)	620,000	(86,000)	714,000
Delivery vans	400,000		320,000	
Less Accumulated depreciation	(135,000)	265,000	(104,000)	216,000
		885,000		930,000
Financial assets				
Quoted investments		80,000		50,000
		965,000		980,000
Current assets				
Stock	350,000		310,000	
Debtors	210,000		195,000	
Cash	6,000		4,000	
Bank	50,000		30,000	
	616,000		539,000	
***Less* Creditors: amounts falling due within 1 year**				
Trade creditors	180,000		165,000	
Taxation	175,000		134,000	
	(355,000)		(299,000)	
Net current assets		261,000		240,000
Total net assets		**1,226,000**		**1,220,000**
Financed by				
Creditors: amounts falling due after more than 1 year				
10% Debentures		120,000		160,000
Capital and reserves				
Ordinary shares at €1 each		850,000		780,000
Profit and loss account		256,000		280,000
Capital employed		**1,226,000**		**1,220,000**

The following information is also available:

(a) There were no disposals of delivery vans during the year but new delivery vans were acquired.

(b) There are no additions to buildings during the year but a warehouse was disposed of for €98,500.

(c) Depreciation charged for the year on buildings in arriving at operating profit was €12,500.

You are required to:

- Reconcile the operating profit to net cash flow from operating activities.
- Prepare the cash flow statement of Target Plc for the year ended 31/12/20-8.
- Reconcile the net cash flow to movement in net debt.

Solution

Step 1: Calculate the change in net cash and net debt

Item	Opening figures	Closing figures	Change
Bank	30,000	50,000	**20,000**
Cash	4,000	6,000	**2,000**
Net cash	34,000	56,000	**22,000**
Debentures	(160,000)	(120,000)	**40,000**
Net debt	(126,000)	(64,000)	**62,000**

17

Step 2: Calculate the amount of dividends, taxation and interest paid

Item	**Opening figure** (opening balance sheet)	***Add*** This year's charge (trading, profit and loss account)	***Less*** Closing figure (closing balance sheet)	**Amount paid** (entered in cash flow)
Taxation	134,000	86,000	(175,000)	**45,000**
Dividends	0	70,000	0	**70,000**
Interest	0	12,000	0	**12,000**

Step 3: Calculate adjustments for increase/decrease in debtors, stock and creditors

Item	**Opening Figure** (opening balance sheet)	**Closing figure** (closing balance sheet)	**Change** (trading, profit and loss account)	**Treat as**
Stock	310,000	350,000	**40,000**	**Negative**
Debtors	195,000	210,000	**15,000**	**Negative**
Creditors	165,000	180,000	**15,000**	**Positive**

Step 4: Calculate the change in fixed assets, including depreciation

(a) Premises

Item	**Opening figure** (opening balance sheet)	***Add*** Any assets purchased during the period	***Less*** Any assets disposed of during the period	**Closing figure** (closing balance sheet)
Buildings	800,000	**0**	**(100,000)**	700,000
Depreciation	86,000	**12,500**	**(18,500)**	80,000

Profit/loss on sale of building:

Cost price	€100,000
Less Depreciation	€(18,500)
Net book value	€81,500
Proceeds	€98,500
Profit on sale	**€17,000**

(b) Delivery vans

Item	Opening figure (opening balance sheet)	*Add* Any assets purchased during the period	*Less* Any assets disposed of during the period	Closing figure (closing balance sheet)
Delivery vans	320,000	**80,000**	**0**	400,000
Depreciation	104,000	**31,000**	**0**	135,000

17

Step 5: Calculate the changes in the capital structure of the firm

Item	Opening figure (opening balance sheet)	*Add* Any increase during the period	*Less* Any decrease during the period	Closing figure (closing balance sheet)
Capital	780,000	**70,000**	**0**	850,000
Debentures	160,000	**0**	**(40,000)**	120,000

Reconciliation of operating profit to net cash flow from operating activities

	€
Operating profit	144,000
Increase in debtors (Step 3)	(15,000)
Profit on sale fixed assets (Step 4)	(17,000)
Increase in stock (Step 3)	(40,000)
Increase in creditors (Step 3)	15,000
Depreciation, buildings (Step 4)	12,500
Depreciation, vans (Step 4)	31,000
Net cash inflow from operating activities	**130,500**

Cash Flow Statement of Target Plc

	€	€
Operating activities		
Net cash inflow from operating activities (from above)		130,500
Returns on investments and servicing of finance		
Interest paid (Step 2)		(12,000)

Continued >

	€	€
Taxation		
Taxation paid (Step 2)		(45,000)
Capital expenditure and financial investment		
Payments to acquire tangible fixed assets (Step 4)	(80,000)	
Payments to acquire financial investments	(30,000)	
Receipts from the sale of tangible fixed assets (Step 4)	98,500	(11,500)
Equity dividends paid		
Equity dividends paid (Step 2)		(70,000)
Net cash outflow before financing and liquid resources		**(8,000)**
Financing		
Repayment of debentures (Step 5)	(40,000)	
Receipts from issue of shares (Step 5)	70,000	30,000
Increase in cash (Step 1)		**22,000**

17

Reconciliation of net cash flow to movement in net debt

	€
Increase in cash (from cash flow statement)	22,000
Cash used to redeem debentures (Step 1)	40,000
Change in net debt (Step 1)	62,000
Net debt 1/1/20-8 (Step 1)	(126,000)
Net debt 31/12/20-8 (Step 1)	(64,000)

Cash flow statement when operating profit is not given

The first step here is to construct an abridged profit and loss account in as much detail as possible. The figures needed are:

- Profit and loss account balance at the beginning of the year
- Profit and loss account balance at the end of the year
- Dividends
- Taxation
- Interest (payable and receivable).

Procedure

1. Set out a skeleton profit and loss account.
2. Take the figures from the balance sheets and/or notes, starting at the bottom and working backwards to the top to find the operating profit.
3. Once you have completed the abridged profit and loss account, you can then proceed to answer the question in the same manner as before – using the **five steps** given above.

Sample Higher Level question (when no trading, profit and loss accounts are given)

The following are the balance sheets of Layla plc as at 31/12/20-4 and 31/12/20-5:

	31/12/20-5		31/12/20-4	
	€	€	€	€
Fixed assets				
Plant and machinery	500,000		470,000	
Less Accumulated depreciation	(60,000)	440,000	(40,000)	430,000
Furniture and equipment	320,000		210,000	
Less Accumulated depreciation	(40,000)	280,000	(15,000)	195,000
Financial assets				
Investments		120,000		80,000
		840,000		705,000
Current assets				
Stock	225,000		195,000	
Debtors	190,000		175,000	
Cash	4,000		6,000	
Bank deposit account	83,000		19,000	
Government securities	40,000			
	542,000		395,000	
***Less* Creditors: amounts falling due within 1 year**				
Trade creditors	125,000		102,000	
Taxation	82,000		55,000	
Bank overdraft	16,000		18,000	
Interest due	3,000		5,600	
	(226,000)		(180,600)	
Net current assets		316,000		214,400
Total net assets		**1,156,000**		**919,400**
Financed by				
Creditors: amounts falling due after more than 1 year				
10% Debentures		200,000		150,000
Capital and reserves				
Called-up share capital @ €1 each		850,000		650,000
Share premium		30,000		
Profit and loss account		76,000		119,400
Capital employed		**1,156,000**		**919,400**

The following information is also available:

(a) The debenture loan was issued on 1/7/20-5.

(b) Taxation paid during the year amounted to €43,000.

(c) 200,000 ordinary shares were issued at a premium of 15c per share.

(d) A dividend of 12c per share was paid on 1/12/20-5.

(e) Machinery which had cost €80,000 was sold during the year for €66,000.

(f) Equipment purchased during the year amounted to €190,000.

(g) Equipment sold during the year incurred a loss of €12,000.

(h) Depreciation charged for the year in arriving at operating profit was €45,000 on plant and machinery and €35,000 on equipment.

(i) The investments yield a fixed return of 10% and all monies were received during 20-5. The new investments were acquired on 1/1/20-5.

You are required to:

- Prepare an abridged profit and loss account for the year ended 31/12/20-5.
- Reconcile the operating profit to net cash flow from operating activities.
- Prepare a cash flow statement for the year ended 31/12/20-5.
- Reconcile the net cash flow to movement in net debt.

17

Solution

Abridged Profit and Loss account of Layla plc for the year ended 31/12/20-5

	€
Operating profit	134,100
Add **Other income**	
Investment income	12,000
	146,100
Less Interest payable	(17,500)
Profit before taxation	128,600
Taxation	(70,000)
Profit after taxation	58,600
Less Dividends	(102,000)
Retained loss for the year	(43,400)
Profit and loss balance 1/1/20-5	119,400
Profit and loss balance 31/12/20-5	76,000

Note 1

Interest payable:	150,000 x 10 %	=	15,000
	50,000 x 10% x .5	=	2,500
Total interest payable			**€17,500**

Note 2

Interest receivable 120,000 x 10% =**€12,000**

Step 1: Calculate the change in net cash and net debt

Item	Opening balance	Closing balance	Change
Bank	19,000	83,000	64,000
Bank overdraft	(18,000)	(16,000)	2,000
Cash	6,000	4,000	(2,000)
Net cash	7,000	71,000	64,000
Debentures	(150,000)	(200,000)	(50,000)
Government securities	0	40,000	40,000
Net debt	(143,000)	(89,000)	54,000

Step 2: Calculate the amount of dividends, taxation and interest

Item	Opening figure	*Add* This year's charge	*Less* Closing figure	Amount paid
Taxation	55,000	**70,000**	(82,000)	**43,000**
Dividends	0	102,000	0	**102,000**
Interest	5,600	17,500	(3,000)	**20,100**

17

Step 3: Calculate adjustments for increase/decrease in debtors, stock and creditors

Item	Opening figure	Closing figure	Change	Treat as
Stock	195,000	225,000	**30,000**	**Negative**
Debtors	175,000	190,000	**15,000**	**Negative**
Creditors	102,000	125,000	**23,000**	**Positive**

Step 4: Calculate the changes in fixed assets, including depreciation

(a) Plant and machinery

Item	**Opening figure** (opening balance sheet)	***Add*** Any assets purchased during the period	***Less*** Any assets disposed of during the period	**Closing figure** (closing balance sheet)
Plant machinery	470,000	**110,000**	**(80,000)**	500,000
Depreciation	40,000	**45,000**	**(25,000)**	60,000

Profit/loss on sale of machinery:

Cost price	€80,000
Less Depreciation	€(25,000)
Net book value	€55,000
Proceeds	€66,000
Profit on sale	**€11,000**

(b) Equipment

Item	**Opening figure** (opening balance sheet)	***Add*** Any assets purchased during the period	***Less*** Any assets disposed of during the period	**Closing figure** (closing balance sheet)
Equipment	210,000	190,000	**(80,000)**	320,000
Depreciation	15,000	35,000	**(10,000)**	40,000

Profit/loss on the sale of equipment:

Cost price of equipment sold	€80,000	
Less Depreciation to date	€(10,000)	
Net book value	€70,000	
Proceeds	€58,000	(balancing figure)
Loss on sale	**€12,000**	

Step 5: Calculate the changes in the capital structure of the firm

Item	**Opening figure** (opening balance sheet)	***Add*** Any increase during the period	***Less*** Any decrease during the period	**Closing figure** (closing balance sheet)
Capital	650,000	**200,000**	**0**	**800,000**
Share premium	0	**30,000**	**0**	**30,000**
Debentures	150,000	**50,000**	**0**	**200,000**
Liquid resources	0	**40,000**	**0**	**40,000**

17

Reconciliation of operating profit to net cash flow from operating activities

	€	€
Operating profit		134,100
Less		
Increase in debtors (Step 3)	15,000	
Profit on sale fixed assets (Step 4)	11,000	
Increase in stock (Step 3)	30,000	(56,000)
		78,100
Add		
Increase in creditors (Step 3)	23,000	
Loss on sale of fixed assets (Step 4)	12,000	
Depreciation, equipment (Step 4)	35,000	
Depreciation, machinery (Step 4)	45,000	115,000
Net cash inflow from operating activities		**193,100**

Cash Flow Statement of Layla plc

	€	€
Operating activities		
Net cash inflow from operating activities (from above)		193,100
Returns on investments and servicing of finance		
Interest paid (Step 2)	(20,100)	
Interest received	12,000	(8,100)
Taxation		
Taxation paid		(43,000)

Continued >

	€	€
Capital expenditure and financial investment		
Payments to acquire tangible fixed assets (Step 4)	(300,000)	
Payments to acquire financial investments	(40,000)	
Receipts from the sale of tangible fixed assets (Step 4)	124,000	(216,000)
Equity dividends paid		
Equity dividends paid (Step 2)		(102,000)
Net cash outflow before liquid resources and financing		**(176,000)**
Management of liquid resources		
Purchase of government securities		(40,000)
Financing		
Receipts from issue of debentures (Step 5)	50,000	
Receipts from share premium (Step 5)	30,000	
Receipts from share capital issued (Step 5)	200,000	280,000
Increase in cash (Step 1)		**64,000**

17

Reconciliation of net cash flow to movement in net debt

	€
Increase in cash (from cash flow statement)	64,000
Cash used to purchase liquid resources (Step 1)	40,000
Cash received from the issue of debentures (Step 1)	(50,000)
Change in net debt (Step 1)	**54,000**
Net debt 1/1/20-8 (Step 1)	(143,000)
Net debt 31/12/20-8 (Step 1)	(89,000)

Exercises – Ordinary Level

Q1 **The following information has been extracted from the books of Timmons plc:**

Profit and Loss (extract) for the year ended 31/12/20-1

	€
Operating profit	146,000
Interest	(12,000)
Profit before taxation	134,000
Taxation	(34,000)

Continued >

	€
Profit after taxation	100,000
Less Dividends	(35,000)
Retained profits for the year	65,000
Profit and loss balance 1/1/20-1	100,000
Profit and loss balance 31/12/20-1	165,000

Balance Sheet

	as at 31/12/20-1		as at 31/12/20-0	
	€	€	€	€
Fixed assets				
Land and buildings	568,000		538,000	
Less Depreciation	(34,400)	533,600	(25,400)	512,600
Current assets				
Stock	25,000		35,000	
Debtors	96,000		106,000	
Cash	23,400		22,500	
	144,400		163,500	
***Less* Creditors: amounts falling due within 1 year**				
Creditors	69,000		20,000	
Taxation	34,000		6,100	
	(103,000)		(26,100)	
Net current assets		41,400		137,400
Total net assets		**575,000**		**650,000**
Financed by				
Creditors: amounts falling due after 1 year				
10% Debentures		10,000		200,000
Capital and reserves				
Ordinary share capital		400,000		350,000
Profit and loss account		165,000		100,000
		575,000		**650,000**

You are required to:

- **Reconcile the operating profit to net cash inflow from operating activities.**
- **Prepare the cash flow statement of Timmons plc for the year ended 31/12/20-1.**
- **Reconcile the net cash flow to movement in net debt.**

17

Q2 **The following information has been extracted from the books of KGFK plc:**

Profit and Loss (extract) for the year ended 31/12/20-2

	€
Operating profit	56,500
Interest	(3,500)
Profit before taxation	53,000
Taxation	(12,500)
Profit after taxation	40,500
Less Dividends	(17,500)
Retained profits for the year	23,000
Profit and loss balance 1/1/20-2	31,500
Profit and loss balance 31/12/20-2	54,500

17

Balance Sheet

	as at 31/12/20-2		as at 31/12/20-1	
	€	€	€	€
Fixed assets				
Delivery vans	245,000		190,000	
Less Depreciation	(27,500)	217,500	(24,000)	166,000
Current assets				
Stock	65,500		54,500	
Debtors	41,000		33,500	
Bank	3,000		5,500	
	109,500		93,500	
***Less* Creditors: amounts falling due within 1 year**				
Creditors	42,500		36,000	
Taxation	30,000		27,000	
	(72,500)		(63,000)	
Net current assets		37,000		30,500
Total net assets		**254,500**		**196,500**
Financed by				
Creditors: amounts falling due after 1 year				
10% Debentures		50,000		35,000
Capital and reserves				
Ordinary share capital		150,000		130,000
Profit and loss account		54,500		31,500
		254,500		**196,500**

You are required to:

- Reconcile the operating profit to net cash inflow from operating activities.
- Prepare the cash flow statement of KGFK plc for the year ended 31/12/20-2.
- Reconcile the net cash flow to movement in the net debt.

Q3 **The following information has been extracted from the books of Wheelhouse plc:**

Profit and Loss (extract) for the year ended 31/12/20-3

	€
Operating profit	462,000
Interest	(45,000)
Profit before taxation	417,000
Taxation	(93,000)
Profit after taxation	324,000
Less Dividends	(84,000)
Retained profits for the year	240,000
Profit and loss balance 1/1/20-3	168,000
Profit and loss balance 31/12/20-3	408,000

17

Balance Sheet

	as at 31/12/20-3		as at 31/12/20-2	
	€	€	€	€
Fixed assets				
Furniture and fittings	2,265,000		2,085,000	
Less Depreciation	(420,000)	1,845,000	(375,000)	1,710,000
Current assets				
Stock	285,000		213,000	
Debtors	183,000		198,000	
Bank	21,000		36,000	
	489,000		447,000	
***Less* Creditors: amounts falling due within 1 year**				
Creditors	249,000		216,000	
Taxation	177,000		123,000	
	(426,000)		(339,000)	
Net current assets		63,000		108,000
Total net assets		**1,908,000**		**1,818,000**

Continued >

	as at 31/12/20-3		as at 31/12/20-2	
	€	€	€	€
Financed by				
Creditors: amounts falling due after 1 year				
10% Debentures		150,000		450,000
Capital and reserves				
Ordinary share capital		1,350,000		1,200,000
Profit and loss account		408,000		168,000
		1,908,000		**1,818,000**

You are required to:

- **Reconcile the operating profit to net cash inflow from operating activities.**
- **Prepare the cash flow statement of Wheelhouse plc for the year ended 31/12/20-3.**
- **Reconcile the net cash flow to movement in the net debt.**

17

Q4 The following information has been extracted from the books of Tom Haggard plc:

Profit and Loss (extract) for the year ended 31/12/20-8

	€
Operating profit	146,000
Interest	(17,000)
Profit before taxation	129,000
Taxation	(40,000)
Profit after taxation	89,000
Dividends paid	(26,000)
Retained profit for year	63,000
Profit and loss balance 1/1/20-8	174,000
Profit and loss balance 31/12/20-8	237,000

Balance Sheet

	as at 31/12/20-8		as at 31/12/20-7	
	€	€	€	€
Fixed assets				
Land and buildings	560,000		480,000	
Less Depreciation provision	(45,000)	515,000	(30,000)	450,000
Current assets				
Stock	65,000		45,000	
Debtors	50,000		32,000	
Cash	23,000		34,000	
	138,000		111,000	

Continued >

	as at 31/12/20-8		as at 31/12/20-7	
	€	€	€	€
***Less* Creditors: amounts falling due within 1 year**				
Creditors	12,000		10,000	
Taxation	34,000		30,000	
	(46,000)		(40,000)	
Net current assets		92,000		71,000
Total net assets		**607,000**		**521,000**
Financed by				
Creditors: amounts falling due after 1 year				
10% Debentures		170,000		167,000
Capital and reserves				
Ordinary share capital issued		200,000		180,000
Profit and loss account		237,000		174,000
Capital employed		**607,000**		**521,000**

17

You are required to:

- **Reconcile the operating profit to net cash inflow from operating activities.**
- **Prepare the cash flow statement of Tom Haggard plc for the year ended 31/12/20-8.**
- **Reconcile the net cash flow to movement in the net debt.**

Q5 The following information has been extracted from the books of Summer plc:

Profit and Loss (extract) for the year ended 31/12/20-7

	€
Operating profit	448,000
Interest	(6,000)
Profit before taxation	442,000
Taxation	(52,000)
Profit after taxation	390,000
Dividends paid	(40,000)
Retained profit for year	350,000
Profit and loss balance 1/1/20-7	40,000
Profit and loss balance 31/12/20-7	390,000

Balance Sheet

	as at 31/12/20-7		as at 31/12/20-6	
	€	€	€	€
Fixed assets				
Premises	900,000		450,000	
Less Depreciation provision	(100,000)	800,000	(50,000)	400,000
Current assets				
Stock	145,000		151,000	
Debtors	85,000		82,000	
Cash	70,000		18,000	
	300,000		251,000	
***Less* Creditors: amounts falling due within 1 year**				
Creditors	98,000		66,000	
Taxation	52,000		45,000	
	(150,000)		(111,000)	
Net current assets		150,000		140,000
Total net assets		**950,000**		**540,000**
Financed by				
Creditors: amounts falling due after 1 year				
5% Debentures		120,000		150,000
Capital and reserves				
Ordinary share capital issued		400,000		350,000
Share premium		40,000		
Profit and loss account		390,000		40,000
Capital employed		**950,000**		**540,000**

You are required to:

- **Reconcile the operating profit to net cash inflow from operating activities.**
- **Prepare the cash flow statement of Summer plc for the year ended 31/12/20-7.**
- **Reconcile the net cash flow to movement in the net debt.**

Exercises – Higher Level

Q1 **The following information has been extracted from the books of Britt plc:**

Profit and Loss (extract) for the year ended 31/12/20-9

	€
Operating profit	22,300
Interest for year	(20,000)
Profit before taxation	2,300
Taxation	(34,000)
Profit after taxation	(31,700)
Less Dividends	(50,000)
Retained profit for year	(81,700)
Profit and loss balance 1/1/20-9	135,700
Profit and loss balance 31/12/20-9	54,000

Balance Sheet

	as at 31/12/20-9		as at 31/12/20-8	
	€	€	€	€
Fixed assets				
Land and Buildings (cost)	580,000		426,000	
Less Accumulated depreciation	(42,000)	538,000	(33,000)	393,000
Equipment (cost)	270,000		300,000	
Less Accumulated depreciation	(45,000)	225,000	(30,000)	270,000
Financial assets				
Quoted investments		100,000		100,000
Current assets				
Stock	145,000		128,000	
Debtors	60,400		32,000	
Bank			23,700	
Cash	21,000		27,000	
	226,400		210,700	

Continued >

	as at 31/12/20-9		as at 31/12/20-8	
	€	€	€	€
***Less* Creditors: amounts falling due within 1 year**				
Creditors	32,000		27,000	
Interest due	5,000		8,000	
Bank	23,500			
Taxation	42,900		63,000	
	(103,400)		(98,000)	
Net current assets		123,000		112,700
Total net assets		**986,000**		**875,700**
Financed by				
Creditors: amounts falling due after 1 year				
8% Debentures		250,000		140,000
Capital and reserves				
€1 ordinary shares issued		670,000		600,000
Share premium		12,000		
Profit and loss account		54,000		135,700
Capital employed		**986,000**		**875,700**

The following information is also available:

(a) There were no disposals of buildings during the year but new buildings were acquired.

(b) There were no purchases of equipment during the year. Equipment was disposed of for €21,000.

(c) The debentures were issued on 1/1/20-9.

(d) Depreciation charged for the year on equipment in arriving at the operating profit was €20,000.

You are required to:

- **Reconcile the operating profit to net cash flow from operating activities.**
- **Prepare the cash flow statement of Britt plc for the year ended 31/12/20-9.**
- **Reconcile the net cash flow to movement in net debt.**
- **Explain why profit does not always mean a corresponding increase in cash.**
- **List two non-cash items.**

Q2 **The following information has been extracted from the books of Jade plc:**

Profit and Loss (extract) for the year ended 31/12/20-4

	€
Operating profit	172,600
Interest for year	(27,600)
Profit before taxation	145,000
Taxation	(58,000)
Profit after taxation	87,000
Less Dividends	(38,000)
Retained profit for year	49,000
Profit and loss balance 1/1/20-4	(18,000)
Profit and loss balance 31/12/20-4	31,000

17

Balance Sheet

	as at 31/12/20-4		as at 31/12/20-3	
	€	€	€	€
Fixed assets				
Premises (cost)	455,000		260,000	
Less Accumulated depreciation	(65,000)	390,000	(30,000)	230,000
Machinery (cost)	450,000		500,000	
Less Accumulated depreciation	(75,000)	375,000	(60,000)	440,000
Financial assets				
Quoted investments		90,000		50,000
Current assets				
Stock	102,000		98,000	
Government securities	80,000			
Debtors	35,600		44,500	
Bank			31,200	
Cash	41,400		42,300	
	259,000		216,000	
***Less* Creditors: amounts falling due within 1 year**				
Creditors	76,100		69,100	
Interest due	6,000		5,400	
Bank	35,900		23,500	
Taxation	61,000		58,000	
	(179,000)		(156,000)	
Net current assets		80,000		60,000
Total net assets		**935,000**		**780,000**

Continued >

	as at 31/12/20-4		as at 31/12/20-3	
	€	€	€	€
Financed by				
Creditors: amounts falling due after 1 year				
12% Debentures		230,000		168,000
Capital and reserves				
€1 ordinary shares issued		660,000		620,000
Share premium		14,000		10,000
Profit and loss account		31,000		(18,000)
Capital employed		**935,000**		**780,000**

The following information is also available:

(a) There were no disposals of premises during the year but new premises were acquired.

(b) The debentures were issued on 1/1/20-4.

(c) There were no purchases of machinery during the year. Machinery was disposed of for €19,600.

(d) Depreciation charged for the year on machinery in arriving at the operating profit was €24,000.

You are required to:

- Reconcile the operating profit to net cash flow from operating activities.
- Prepare the cash flow statement of Jade plc for the year ended 31/12/20-4.
- Reconcile the net cash flow to movement in net debt.
- Explain why cash flow statements are prepared.
- Identify a non-cash expense and a non-cash gain from the above question.

Q3 The following information has been extracted from the books of Bonny plc:

Profit and Loss (extract) for the year ended 31/12/20-7

	€
Operating profit	158,500
Interest for year	(12,000)
Profit before taxation	146,500
Taxation	(42,000)
Profit after taxation	104,500
Less Dividends	(40,000)
Retained profit for year	64,500
Profit and loss balance 1/1/20-7	34,000
Profit and loss balance 31/12/20-7	98,500

Balance Sheet

	as at 31/12/20-7		as at 31/12/20-6	
	€	€	€	€
Fixed assets				
Premises (cost)	550,000		500,000	
Less Accumulated depreciation	(63,000)	487,000	(50,000)	450,000
Delivery vans (cost)	260,000		310,000	
Less Accumulated depreciation	(43,000)	217,000	(24,000)	286,000
Financial assets				
Quoted investments		200,000		200,000
Current assets				
Stock	75,000		35,500	
Government securities	50,000			
Debtors	98,000		67,000	
Bank	204,000			
Cash	23,000		8,000	
	450,000		110,500	
***Less* Creditors: amounts falling due within 1 year**				
Creditors	85,000		87,000	
Interest due	11,000		9,000	
Bank			23,500	
Taxation	54,000		47,000	
	(150,000)		(166,500)	
Net current assets		300,000		(56,000)
Total net assets		**1,204,000**		**880,000**
Financed by				
Creditors: amounts falling due after 1 year				
8% Debentures		200,000		100,000
Capital and reserves				
Ordinary shares @€1 each		850,000		700,000
Share premium		55,500		46,000
Profit and loss account		98,500		34,000
Capital employed		**1,204,000**		**880,000**

The following information is also available:

(a) There were no disposals of buildings during the year but new buildings were acquired.

(b) Debentures were issued on 1/7/20-7.

(c) There were no purchases of delivery vans during the year. Delivery vans were disposed of for €31,000.

(d) Depreciation charged for the year on delivery vans in arriving at the operating profit was €28,000.

17

You are required to:

- Reconcile the operating profit to net cash flow from operating activities.
- Prepare the cash flow statement of Bonny plc for the year ended 31/12/20-7.
- Reconcile the net cash flow to movement in net debt.
- Explain the advantages of preparing cash flow statements.
- Explain the difference between a non-cash expense and a cash expense.

Q4 The following information has been extracted from the books of Candy plc:

Profit and Loss (extract) for the year ended 31/12/20-2

	€
Operating profit	136,600
Interest for year	(24,000)
Profit before taxation	112,600
Taxation	(19,600)
Profit after taxation	93,000
Less Dividends	(47,000)
Retained profit for year	46,000
Profit and loss balance 1/1/20-2	(11,000)
Profit and loss balance 31/12/20-2	35,000

Balance Sheet

	as at 31/12/20-2		as at 31/12/20-1	
	€	€	€	€
Fixed assets				
Land and buildings (cost)	472,000		360,000	
Less Accumulated depreciation		472,000	(45,000)	315,000
Equipment (cost)	320,000		230,000	
Less Accumulated depreciation	(27,000)	293,000	(15,000)	215,000
Financial assets				
Quoted investments		50,000		80,000
Current assets				
Stock	72,000		65,000	
Debtors	38,000		33,000	
Government securities	12,000			
Bank			6,000	
Cash	38,000			
	160,000		104,000	

Continued >

	as at 31/12/20-2		as at 31/12/20-1	
	€	€	€	€
***Less* Creditors: amounts falling due within 1 year**				
Creditors	54,000		41,000	
Interest	5,400		3,800	
Bank	8,000		2,800	
Taxation	37,600		50,400	
	(105,000)		(98,000)	
Net current assets		55,000		6,000
Total net assets		**870,000**		**616,000**
Financed by				
Creditors: amounts falling due after 1 year				
12% Debentures		70,000		200,000
Capital and reserves				
Ordinary shares @ €1 each		500,000		400,000
Share premium		46,000		27,000
Profit and loss account		35,000		(11,000)
Revaluation reserve		219,000		
Capital employed		**870,000**		**616,000**

The following information is also available:

(a) There were no disposals of equipment during the year but new equipment was acquired.

(b) There were no purchases of buildings during the year. A building which originally cost €50,000 was disposed of for €78,000. The book value on the date of sale was €40,000. Depreciation for the year on buildings was €22,000.

(c) The remaining buildings were revalued on 31/12/20-2 at €472,000.

(d) Debentures were redeemed on 31/12/20-2.

(e) The quoted investments were sold at their nominal value.

You are required to:

- Reconcile the operating profit to net cash flow from operating activities.
- Prepare the cash flow statement of Candy plc for the year ended 31/12/20-2.
- Reconcile the net cash flow to movement in net debt.
- Explain, with examples, items that affect cash and not profit and items that affect profit and not cash.

Q5 **The following are the balance sheets of Hyacinth Plc as at 31/12/20-0 and 31/12/20-1:**

	31/12/20-1		31/12/20-0	
	€	€	€	€
Fixed assets				
Land and buildings (cost)	485,000		400,000	
Less Accumulated depreciation	(55,000)	430,000	(34,000)	366,000
Equipment (cost)	350,000		210,000	
Less Accumulated depreciation	(60,000)	290,000	(36,000)	174,000
Financial assets				
Investments		50,000		50,000
Current assets				
Stock	102,000		95,000	
Debtors	83,000		65,000	
Government securities	40,000		32,000	
Investment income due	1,500		1,000	
Bank	183,500		49,000	
	410,000		242,000	
***Less* Creditors: amounts falling due with 1 year**				
Creditors	124,000		68,000	
Interest due	11,000		12,000	
Taxation	70,000		56,000	
	(205,000)		(136,000)	
Net current assets		205,000		106,000
Total net assets		**975,000**		**696,000**
Financed by				
Creditors: amounts falling due after 1 year				
10% Debentures		250,000		200,000
Capital and reserves				
€1 ordinary shares issued	600,000		400,000	
Share premium	80,000		60,000	
Profit and loss account	45,000	725,000	36,000	496,000
Capital employed		**975,000**		**696,000**

The following information is also available:

(a) Buildings which cost €70,000 were disposed of at a profit of €12,000.

(b) There were no disposals of equipment during the year.

(c) The investments yield a fixed return of 6% per annum.

(d) €50,000 debentures were issued on 1/7/20-1.

(e) The total dividend for the year was 7c per share paid in full.

(f) Depreciation charged for the year in arriving at operating profit included €35,000 on buildings.

(g) Corporation tax due at 31/12/20-0 was paid in full.

You are required to:

- Prepare an abridged profit and loss account to ascertain the operating profit for the year ended 31/12/20-1.
- Reconcile the operating profit to net cash flow from operating activities.
- Prepare the cash flow statement of Hyacinth Plc for the year ended 31/12/20-1.
- Reconcile the net cash flow to movement in net debt.
- Explain why profit does not always mean a corresponding increase in cash. Illustrate your answer with figures from this question.

17

Q6 **The following are the balance sheets of Lamppost plc as at 31/12/20-9 and 31/12/20-8:**

	31/12/20-9		31/12/20-8	
	€	€	€	€
Fixed assets				
Cost	1,020,000		800,000	
Less Accumulated depreciation	(64,000)	956,000	(55,000)	745,000
Financial assets				
Investments at cost		60,000		100,000
Current assets				
Stock	216,000		205,200	
Debtors	174,000		196,000	
Government securities	24,000		12,000	
Cash	61,000		6,000	
	475,000		419,200	
***Less* Creditors: amounts falling due within 1 year**				
Creditors	87,000		63,800	
General expenses due	15,000		18,000	
Bank	31,000		31,400	
Taxation	34,000		30,000	
	(167,000)		(143,200)	
Net current assets		308,000		276,000
Total net assets		**1,324,000**		**1,121,000**

Continued >

	31/12/20-9		31/12/20-8	
	€	€	€	€
Financed by				
Creditors amounts falling due after 1 year				
12% Debentures		370,000		340,000
Capital and reserves				
€1 ordinary shares issued	800,000		600,000	
Share premium	80,000		60,000	
Profit and loss account	74,000	954,000	121,000	781,000
Capital employed		**1,324,000**		**1,121,000**

The following information is also available:

(a) 200,000 shares were issued at €1.10 per share.

(b) Fixed assets which cost €85,000 and on which total depreciation of €34,500 had been provided were sold for €67,800.

(c) Debentures were issued on 1/1/20-9.

(d) Dividends paid during the year amounted to €80,000.

(e) Taxation charged on profits for the year was €37,000.

(f) Investments which cost were €40,000 were sold for cash at their book value.

You are required to:

- Prepare an abridged profit and loss account to ascertain the operating profit for the year ended 31/12/20-9.
- Reconcile the operating profit to net cash flow from operating activities.
- Prepare the cash flow statement of Lamppost plc for the year ended 31/12/20-9.
- Reconcile the net cash flow to movement in net debt.
- Write a note on the Accounting Standards Board and refer to how their role has influenced the preparation of cash flow statements.

Q7 The following are the balance sheets of Rose Plc as at 31/12/20-8 and 31/12/20-9:

	31/12/20-9		31/12/20-8	
	€	€	€	€
Fixed assets				
Land and buildings (cost)	780,000		670,000	
Less Accumulated depreciation	(45,000)	735,000	(30,000)	640,000
Financial assets				
Investments		150,000		150,000
Current assets				
Stock	56,000		37,000	
Debtors (95%)	64,600		57,000	
Government securities	90,000		45,000	
Insurance prepaid	12,000			
Bank	47,400		56,800	
	270,000		195,800	

Continued >

	31/12/20-9		31/12/20-8	
	€	€	€	€
***Less* Creditors: amounts falling due within 1 year**				
Creditors	75,000		65,800	
Taxation	48,000		43,000	
General expenses due	5,000			
Interest due	4,000		5,000	
	(132,000)		(113,800)	
Net current assets		138,000		82,000
Total net assets		**1,023,000**		**872,000**
Financed by				
Creditors: amounts falling due after 1 year				
12% Debentures		200,000		240,000
Capital and reserves				
€1 ordinary shares issued		800,000		560,000
Share premium		24,000		
Profit and loss account		(1,000)		72,000
Capital employed		**1,023,000**		**872,000**

The following information is also available:

(a) Buildings which cost €60,0000 were disposed of at a profit of €30,000.

(b) The debenture was redeemed on 1/1/20-9.

(c) The investments yield a fixed return of 10% per annum.

(d) The total dividend for the year was 12c per share.

(e) Depreciation charged for the year in arriving at operating profit included €25,000 on buildings.

(f) Corporation tax due at 31/12/20-8 was paid in full.

You are required to:

- **Prepare an abridged profit and loss account to ascertain the operating profit for the year ended 31/12/20-9.**
- **Reconcile the operating profit to net cash flow from operating activities.**
- **Prepare the cash flow statement of Rose Plc for the year ended 31/12/20-9.**
- **Reconcile the net cash flow to movement in net debt.**

Exam Tips

- Make sure you learn exactly the layout of each of the documents.
- Make sure you know all the headings.
- Follow closely the **five steps** in order to prepare the solution to the question.
- Step 1 can be used to give you the final figure in the cash flow statement – this will help guide you to get this question right.
- Make sure you are able to answer all theory questions – especially regarding the purpose and importance of cash flow statements, distinguishing between cash and non-cash items, and the difference between cash and profit.

18 Ratio Analysis and the Interpretation of Financial Statements

Objectives

On completion students should be able to:

- Interpret financial statements under various headings;
- Understand the limitations of ratios as a method of interpreting of financial statements;
- Understand and explain liquidity, solvency, profitability, gearing, dividend policy and investment policy;
- Understand improving and disimproving trends in relation to all ratios.

Introduction

Financial statements such as profit and loss accounts and balance sheets provide information about how a business is performing and about its financial position. This information needs to be analysed and interpreted.

Ratio analysis is the most widely used technique for analysing, interpreting and comparing financial statements.

The objective of ratio analysis is to:

- use key ratios to analyse the performance of the company from one year to the next
- use ratios from the current financial statements together with corresponding ratios from previous years to establish trend and patterns
- use the trends as an aid in decision-making
- use ratios to make comparisons with similar firms operating in the same type of industry.

This topic can be divided into three parts:

1. The manipulation of formulae (calculations)
2. The interpretation of formulae
3. Theory.

This chapter deals firstly with the calculations and secondly with interpretation. Theory is dealt with throughout.

Part A: The Manipulation of Formulae

Ratio classification

Ratios can be divided into the following groups:

- profitability and efficiency ratios
- asset/turnover ratios
- liquidity/solvency ratios
- activity ratios
- gearing ratios
- investment ratios.

1. Profitability and efficiency ratios

18

Ratio	Formula	Answer format
Return on capital employed (ROCE)	$\frac{\text{Profit before interest and tax x 100}}{\text{Capital employed}}$	percentage
Return on shareholders' equity funds	$\frac{\text{Net profit after tax and preference dividend x 100}}{\text{Shareholders' funds}}$	percentage
Gross profit mark-up percentage	$\frac{\text{Gross profit x 100}}{\text{Cost of sales}}$	percentage
Gross profit margin percentage	$\frac{\text{Gross profit x 100}}{\text{Sales}}$	percentage
Net profit percentage	$\frac{\text{Net profit before interest and tax x 100}}{\text{Sales}}$	percentage
Total expenses to sales	$\frac{\text{Total expenses x 100}}{\text{Sales}}$	percentage
Administration expenses to sales	$\frac{\text{Administration expenses x 100}}{\text{Sales}}$	percentage
Selling and distribution expenses to sales	$\frac{\text{Selling and distribution expenses x 100}}{\text{Sales}}$	percentage

Notes

1. **The figure for return on capital employed** should be compared with the return on risk-free investments, such as a bank deposit account, to see if the company is profitable. A company is regarded as profitable if the return is greater than the return from risk-free investments. This means that the shareholders get a higher reward from taking the risk of investing in the business. The profit before interest is used so that a comparison can be made between businesses which may have different borrowings.

Capital employed is the total net assets or the shareholders' funds plus long-term liabilities. It is the total of the balance sheet.

2. The **return on shareholders' funds** measures the return to the stakeholders after interest, taxes and preference dividends.

❸ **Gross profit percentage** indicates how much each euro of sales contributes to the company before selling expenses have been deducted.

If gross profit percentage is **falling**, the problem must lie with items that contribute to gross profit. This can be caused by, for example:

- falling sales price without a corresponding fall in the cost of sales
- increase in cost of sales without this increase being passed on to the final consumer
- cash losses – cash sales not recorded or theft from the till
- stock losses – pilferage of stock or stock becoming obsolete
- change in the sales mix – more low-margin and fewer high-margin items being sold
- increased competition in the market forcing down profit margins
- incorrect valuation of stock – overvaluing of opening stock and/or undervaluing of closing stock
- mark-downs during sales without an increase in sales.

❹ **Net profit percentage** indicates how much each euro of sales contributes to the business after expenses have been deducted. Since this ratio varies widely from one industry to the next it should only be used for comparing similar businesses within the same industry.

NOTE

Net profit = Gross profit less expenses

If the net profit percentage is **falling**, it means that the expenses as a percentage of sales must be increasing. This can be caused by:

- decreased efficiency of the sales manager and/or staff
- an increase in expenses without this being passed on to the final consumer
- an increase in the amount of slow-moving and obsolete stock.

This can be corrected in a number of ways, for example:

- increasing the selling price or increasing the volume of sales
- cutting back on unnecessary expenses or eliminating some altogether
- checking security systems against theft.

2. Asset/turnover ratios

These ratios indicate the efficiency with which a company uses its assets to generate sales.

Ratio	Formula	Answer format
Total assets turnover	$\frac{\text{Sales}}{\text{Total assets}}$	times
Fixed assets turnover	$\frac{\text{Sales}}{\text{Fixed assets}}$	times
Current assets turnover	$\frac{\text{Sales}}{\text{Current assets}}$	times
Working capital/net current assets turnover	$\frac{\text{Sales}}{\text{Net current assets}}$	times

Notes

1. A fall in the rate of **fixed assets turnover** may be caused by the underutilisation of the fixed assets. For example, the plant may be too big for the volume of goods being produced and sold.
2. A fall in the rate of the **current assets turnover** may be caused by a problem with current assets or sales – for example, a fall in sales without a corresponding decrease in working capital. This is known as **undertrading**.

3. Liquidity/solvency ratios

Liquidity measures the ability of a company to pay its **short-term debts** as they fall due.

Solvency is the ability of a company to pay **all its debts** as they fall due for payment (long term).

Ratio	Formula	Answer format
Current ratio	Current assets : Current liabilities	X : Y
Acid test/quick ratio/ liquid ratio	Current assets less closing stock : Current liabilities (liquid assets)	X : Y

18

Notes

1. The more **liquid** a company is the more likely it is to be able to pay its employees, suppliers and other short-term creditors.
2. **Solvency** is the most important indicator of a business's ability to survive. A business is solvent if its total assets exceed its outside liabilities.
3. The **current ratio** shows whether the working capital is adequate to meet the day-to-day costs of running the business. The recommended ratio by most businesses is **1.5 to 1** or higher, which means that for every €1 owed in the short term, the business has €1.50 available to pay it. If, however, this ratio is **too high** it could indicate that the business is making **inefficient** use of its resources or is building up too much stock.
4. The **acid test ratio** is a good indicator of liquidity as it includes only liquid assets, namely cash and debtors. It does not include closing stock as it may be difficult to turn it into cash quickly. Also the business may get a lower amount for this stock in the event of a quick sale, e.g. a liquidation sale. A ratio of **1 to 1** or slightly lower is acceptable. This means that the business has €1 readily available for each €1 owed in the short term.

Liquidity problems and overtrading

Problems of liquidity arise when working capital and liquid capital fall below desirable levels.

Overtrading is one of the main causes of liquidity problems.

Overtrading occurs when the business is trying to finance too high a volume of sales with too little working capital.

A business which is overtrading can at first glance seem to be doing very well. However, on closer examination there will be a large increase in debtors and creditors and a shortage of cash. When this happens creditors may insist on earlier payment and this may eventually lead to liquidation.

However, **a rising liquid ratio is not always a sign of prudent management**. It can mean that management is not putting cash to its most productive use. The cash could be used elsewhere to fund a higher level of activity and therefore earn more profit.

Liquidity problems can always be very quickly revealed by checking the **cash flow statement**.

Steps that can be taken to solve a liquidity problem

1. Enforce a strict credit policy by insisting that debtors pay earlier – offer cash discounts.
2. Issue any remaining shares from authorised share capital.
3. Borrow – long-term borrowing avoids repayments in the short term.
4. Keep stock levels to a minimum – for example, use JIT (Just In Time system).
5. Use sale and leaseback of assets (ones that have not already been mortgaged).
6. Postpone any planned capital projects.
7. Avoid paying dividends.

18

4. Activity ratios

Ratio	Formula	Answer format
Stock turnover	$\frac{\text{Cost of sales}}{\text{Average stock}}$	times
Average stock	$\frac{\text{Opening stock + Closing stock}}{2}$	euro
Average period of credit given to debtors	$\frac{\text{Trade debtors x 12 or 52 or 365}}{\text{Credit sales}}$	months/weeks/days
Average period of credit received from creditors	$\frac{\text{Trade creditors x 12 or 52 or 365}}{\text{Credit purchases}}$	months/weeks/days

Notes

1. **Stock turnover** is the number of times in a financial period (usually one year) that the average stock is sold. This can vary from one business to another. For example, stock turnover in a bakery would be a lot higher than in jewellery store. If stock turnover is falling this could mean that business is slowing down and there is a higher risk of stock becoming out of date or obsolete. However, a rising stock turnover could also mean that the business's stock policy is too tight and they run the risk of running out of stock and therefore stock shortages. This can lead to loss of customers and therefore loss of profits.
2. The **average period of credit given to debtors** is the average amount of time it takes a business to collect debts from debtors. The faster they can be collected, the better.

NOTE

The period of credit received from creditors should always be longer than the period of credit given to debtors. This means that a business can collect its debts before it has to pay its debts.

3. The **average period of credit received from creditors** indicates the average length of time it takes the business to pay its creditors. Having a long credit period will help a business finance its activities but a business may lose out on discounts by not paying debts on time.

5. Gearing ratios

Gearing refers to the capital structure of a company. It shows the level of risk borne by the equity shareholders. It compares fixed-interest capital and other capital of a business. The capital of a business is usually of two kinds:

1. Capital subscribed by the shareholders
2. Capital subscribed by outsiders which earns a fixed rate of return.

> **Fixed-interest capital** = term loans, debentures and preference shares
>
> **Equity capital** (owners' capital) = ordinary share capital and reserves

18

Ratio	Formula	Answer format
Fixed-interest capital to total capital	$\frac{\text{Loans + Debentures + Preference shares x 100}}{\text{Capital employed}}$	percentage or ratio
Fixed-interest capital to equity capital	$\frac{\text{Loans + Debentures + Preference shares x 100}}{\text{Ordinary share capital issued + Reserves}}$	percentage or ratio
Interest cover	$\frac{\text{Profit before interest and tax}}{\text{Interest charges for the year}}$	times

A **low-geared company** is a company where the fixed interest capital is less than 50% of the total capital or less than the equity capital.

A **high-geared company** is a company where the fixed-interest capital is greater than 50% of the total capital or is greater than the equity capital.

A **neutral-geared company** is a company where the fixed-interest capital and equity capital are almost the same.

Notes

1. A well-managed business will have a balance between the two types of capital. It is important that a business does not become too dependent on outside finance (borrowings), as interest and preference dividends must be paid whether profits are made or not.
2. The ability of a business to meet its interest costs out of current earnings is an indicator of its long-term solvency. A business whose operating profit covers its interest many times would be regarded as a satisfactory risk by long-term creditors.

6. Investment ratios

Shareholders (existing and potential) will be interested in the performance of the businesses shares. These ratios can help assess the performance of the business.

Ratio	Formula	Answer format
Earnings per share	$\frac{\text{Net profit (after preference dividend)}}{\text{Number of ordinary shares issued}}$	cent
Price earnings ratio	$\frac{\text{Market price of share}}{\text{Earnings per share}}$	years/times
Dividend per ordinary share	$\frac{\text{Ordinary dividends x 100}}{\text{Number of equity (ordinary) shares issued}}$	cent
Dividend cover (Dividend payout rate)	$\frac{\text{Net profit (after tax and preference dividend)}}{\text{Ordinary dividend}}$	times
Dividend yield	$\frac{\text{Dividend per ordinary share x 100}}{\text{Market price per ordinary share}}$	percentage
Price dividend ratio (period to recoup price at present payout rate)	$\frac{\text{Market price of share}}{\text{Dividend per share}}$	years

18

Notes

It is advisable to give answers to two decimal places where significant.

1. **Earnings per share (EPS)** is the profit in cents coming from each equity share. A trend in the EPS shows investors how well their investment has been used over the years. When comparing the performance of one year with another or with other businesses, the EPS should be calculated on the same basis.
2. **Price earnings ratio** indicates the **number of years** it would take to recover the share price, based on the **current earnings** of the business. The market price of the share is an indication of the investors' view of the future earning ability of the business. If the PE ratio is high this indicates that the business is expected to increase profits in the future. On the other hand, if it is low it shows that there is little confidence in the business's ability to be profitable in the future and it is a risky investment.
3. **Dividends per ordinary share** is the amount of dividend for the year expressed in cent on each ordinary share.
4. **Dividend cover** indicates the proportion of earnings retained by the business. It shows the level of risk to dividends in future years if profits were to decline. Retained earnings help to increase share value. Some shareholders prefer a high dividend cover as it helps to increase share value.
5. **Dividend yield** shows the return received by investors in the form of dividends as a result of share investment. This should be compared with the return from risk-free investments. It should also be noted, however, that this is not the complete earnings because total earnings are rarely paid out and instead are used to build up reserves for future needs.
6. **Period to recoup share price at payout rate** indicates how long it will take an investor to get his/her investment back based on the dividend payout policy of the business.

Limitations of ratio analysis

Ratio analysis, although very useful, has the following drawbacks:

1. Ratio analysis is concerned with past events – they can become quickly out of date.
2. Ratios can provide clues to the future but they do not show if a business is acting wisely.

3. Ratios do not allow for seasonal changes.
4. Accounting statements provide a limited picture of a business. Other important aspects of the business are not revealed in financial statements. The accounts alone cannot measure aspects which may be extremely significant such as monopoly position, economic climate, staff morale and management/staff relationships.
5. Businesses use different accounting bases when preparing financial statements – for example, depreciation of fixed assets and valuation of stock. As a result, inter-business comparisons can be misleading. In addition, businesses can vary greatly in size and in gearing.

Sample Ordinary Level question

The following is an extract from the books of Kian Plc for the year ended 31/12/20-1.

Trading, Profit and Loss Account for the year ended 31/12/20-1

	€	€
Sales (credit)		1,200,000
Less Cost of sales		
Stock 1/1/20-1	108,000	
Purchases	?	
Less Closing stock	(120,000)	?
Gross profit		800,000
Less Expenses (including interest)		(340,000)
Net profit		**460,000**

18

Balance Sheet as at 31/12/20-1

	€	€
Fixed assets		720,000
Current assets (including debtors €110,000)	232,000	
***Less* Creditors: amounts falling due within 1 year**		
Trade creditors	(32,000)	200,000
		920,000
Financed by		
Creditors: amounts falling due after more than 1 year		
10% Debentures		120,000
Capital and reserves		
Ordinary shares		340,000
Net profit balance		460,000
		920,000

You are required to calculate the following:

1. The amount of purchases
2. Return on capital employed

3. Acid test ratio
4. Period of credit given to debtors
5. Gross profit percentage
6. Net profit percentage
7. Period of credit received from creditors (assume all purchases are on credit)
8. Current ratio
9. Average stock
10. Stock turnover.

Solution

Question	Formula	Workings	Answer
1. Purchases	Sales – Cost of sales = Gross profit Cost of sales = Opening stock + Purchases – Closing stock	1,200,000 – Cost of sales = 800,000 Therefore cost of sales = 400,000 400,000 = 108,000 + Purchases – 120,000 Therefore purchases = 412,000	€412,000
2. Return on capital employed	$\frac{\text{Profit before interest} \times 100}{\text{Capital employed}}$	$\frac{(460{,}000 + 12{,}000) \times 100}{920{,}000}$	51.3%
3. Acid test ratio	Liquid assets : Current liabilities	232,000 – 120,000 : 32,000	3.5 : 1
4. Period of credit given to debtors	$\frac{\text{Debtors} \times 12}{\text{Credit sales}}$	$\frac{110{,}000 \times 12}{1{,}200{,}000}$	1.1 months
5. Gross profit %	$\frac{\text{Gross profit} \times 100}{\text{Sales}}$	$\frac{800{,}000 \times 100}{1{,}200{,}000}$	66.67%
6. Net profit %	$\frac{\text{Net profit} \times 100}{\text{Sales}}$	$\frac{460{,}000 \times 100}{1{,}200{,}000}$	38.33%
7. Period of credit received from creditors	$\frac{\text{Creditors} \times 12}{\text{Credit purchases}}$	$\frac{32{,}000 \times 12}{412{,}000}$	0.93 months
8. Current ratio	Current assets : Current liabilities	232,000 : 32,000	7.25 : 1
9. Average stock	$\frac{\text{Opening stock} + \text{Closing stock}}{2}$	$\frac{108{,}000 + 120{,}000}{2}$	€114,000
10. Stock turnover	$\frac{\text{Cost of sales}}{\text{Average stock}}$	$\frac{400{,}000}{114{,}000}$	3.5 times

Sample Higher Level question

The following figures were extracted from the books of Scallan Plc, a manufacturer in the computer industry. The company has an authorised share capital of €1,200,000, made up of 1,000,000 ordinary shares at €1 each and 200,000 10% preference shares at €1 each. Half of these preference shares had already been issued, along with 800,000 of the ordinary shares.

Trading, Profit and Loss Account for the year ended 31/12/20-0

	€
Sales	1,920,000
Opening stock	120,000
Closing stock	130,000
Cost of sales	(1,450,000)
Operating expenses	(280,000)
Profit before interest	190,000
Interest	(60,000)
Net profit	130,000
Dividends paid	(100,000)
Retained profits	30,000
Profit and loss balance 1/1/20-0	80,000
Profit and loss balance 31/12/20-0	110,000

Ratios for 20-9

Earnings per share	24c
Dividend per share	16c
Interest cover	4.7 times
Acid ratio	1.3 : 1
Gearing	41%
Dividend cover	1.5 times
Dividend yield	8.79%
Return on capital employed	12.4%
Market price of 1 share	€1.82

18

Balance Sheet as at 31/12/20-0

	€	€
Intangible assets		360,000
Tangible assets		1,040,000
Investments (market value €170,000)		240,000
		1,640,000
Current assets (debtors €90,000)	220,000	
Trade creditors	(154,000)	
Bank	(96,000)	(30,000)
		1,610,000
Financed by		
10% Debentures 20-7		600,000
Issued capital		
Ordinary shares	800,000	
10% Preference shares	100,000	
Profit and loss balance 31/12/20-0	110,000	1,010,000
		1,610,000

You are required to calculate the following for 20-0:

1. The interest cover
2. Return on capital employed
3. Earnings per share
4. Dividend per share
5. Dividend cover
6. The cash purchases if the average period of credit received from trade creditors is two months
7. Market price of one ordinary share if the price earnings ratio is 14
8. The dividend yield
9. Gearing
10. Current ratio
11. Acid ratio
12. Period to recoup share price at current payout rate.

Solution

Question	Formula	Workings	Answer
1. Interest cover	$\frac{\text{Profit before interest}}{\text{Interest}}$	$\frac{190{,}000}{60{,}000}$	3.17 times
2. Return on capital employed	$\frac{\text{Profit before interest} \times 100}{\text{Capital employed}}$	$\frac{190{,}000 \times 100}{1{,}610{,}000}$	11.8%
3. Earnings per share	$\frac{\text{Net profit after preference dividend}}{\text{Number of ordinary shares issued}}$	$\frac{130{,}000 - 10{,}000}{800{,}000}$	15c
4. Dividend per share	$\frac{\text{Total dividends} - \text{Preference dividend}}{\text{Number of ordinary shares issued}}$	$\frac{100{,}000 - 10{,}000}{800{,}000}$	11.25c
5. Dividend Cover	$\frac{\text{Net profit} - \text{Preference dividend}}{\text{Ordinary dividend}}$	$\frac{130{,}000 - 10{,}000}{90{,}000}$	1.33 times
6. Cash purchases	$\frac{\text{Creditors x 12}}{\text{Credit Purchases}}$ Opening stock + Total Purchases – Closing stock = Cost of sales Total Purchases = Cash Purchases + Credit Purchases	$\frac{154{,}000 \times 12}{\text{Credit Purchases}} = 2$ Credit Purchases = 924,000 120,000 + Total Purchases – 130,000 = 1,450,000 Total Purchases = 1,460,000 1,460,000 = Cash Purchases + 924,000 Cash Purchases = €536,000	€536,000
7. Market price	$\frac{\text{Market price}}{\text{Earnings per share}}$	$\frac{\text{Market price}}{15} = 14$	€2.10
8. Dividend yield	$\frac{\text{Dividend per share x 100}}{\text{Market price}}$	$\frac{11.25 \times 100}{210}$	5.36%
9. Gearing	$\frac{\text{Fixed interest capital x 100}}{\text{Total capital}}$	$\frac{700{,}000 \times 100}{1{,}610{,}000}$	43.5%
10. Current ratio	Current assets : Current liabilities	220,000 : 250,000	0.88 : 1
11. Acid ratio	Current assets – Closing stock : Current liabilities	220,000 – 130,000 : 250,000	0.36 : 1
12. Period to recoup at payout rate	$\frac{\text{Market price}}{\text{Dividend per share}}$	$\frac{210}{11.25}$	18.67 years

Exercises – Ordinary Level

In each of the following questions you are required to calculate:

- The amount of opening stock
- Return on capital employed
- Current ratio
- Acid test ratio
- Period of credit given to debtors
- Period of credit received from creditors
- Gross profit percentage
- Net profit percentage
- Stock turnover.

Q1 The following figures were taken from the books of Kasia plc for the year ended 31/12/20-2:

	€
Credit sales	980,000
Closing stock	75,000
Purchases	857,000
Gross profit	120,000
Expenses (including interest)	80,000
Fixed assets	360,000
Current assets (including debtors, €32,000)	160,000
Trade creditors	26,000
10% Debentures	25,000
Ordinary shares	429,000
Profit and loss balance 31/12/20-2	40,000

Q2 The following figures were taken from the books of M. O'Rourke for the year ended 31/12/20-3:

	€
Credit sales	260,000
Purchases	125,000
Closing stock	20,000
Gross profit	140,000
Expenses (including interest)	40,000
Net profit	100,000
Fixed assets	340,000
Current assets (including debtors, €25,000)	96,000
Trade creditors	66,000
5% Debentures	30,000
Ordinary shares	240,000

Q3 **The following information was taken from the accounts of G. Cahill for the year ended 31/12/20-4:**

	€
Credit sales	1,460,000
Purchases	1,080,000
Closing stock	152,000
Cost of sales	1,140,000
Expenses (including interest)	148,000
Fixed assets	884,000
Current assets (including debtors, €44,000)	324,000
Trade creditors	136,000
8% Debentures	200,000
Ordinary shares	700,000
Net profit 31/12/04	172,000

Q4 **The following information was taken from the books of D. Jones plc for the year ended 31/12/20-5:**

	€
Credit sales	900,000
Closing stock	88,000
Purchases	669,000
Gross profit	235,000
Expenses (including interest)	190,000
Net profit	45,000
Fixed assets	350,000
Current assets (including debtors, €58,000)	225,000
Trade creditors	125,000
12% Debentures	90,000
Ordinary shares	315,000

Q5 **The following information was taken from the accounts of Jack Walker plc for the year ended 31/12/20-6:**

	€
Sales (80% on credit)	980,000
Closing stock	45,000
Purchases (75% on credit)	640,000
Gross profit	350,000
Total expenses	340,000
Net profit	10,000
Fixed assets	560,000
Current assets (including debtors €50,000)	140,000
Trade creditors	110,000
12% Debentures	70,000
Ordinary shares	510,000

Exercises – Higher Level

In each of the following questions you are required to calculate:

- The interest cover
- Return on capital employed
- Return on shareholders' funds
- Earnings per share
- Dividend per share
- Dividend cover
- Dividend yield
- Gearing
- Current ratio
- Acid ratio
- Period to recoup share price at current payout rate
- Period to recoup share price at present activity level.

Additional information is provided on edcodigital.ie for questions 1 to 5

18

Q1 The following figures were extracted from the books of Duff Plc, a company operating in the leisure Industry.

	€
Sales	780,000
Cost of sales	345,000
Operating expenses	235,000
Interest	24,000
Net profit	176,000
Dividends paid	80,000
Intangible assets	145,000
Tangible assets	654,000
Investments (market value €98,000)	90,000
Current assets (debtors, €50,000)	135,000
Trade creditors	35,000
Bank overdraft	23,000
12% Debentures 20-5	200,000
Ordinary shares @ €1 each	500,000
10% Preference shares	170,000

Q2 **The following figures were extracted from the books of Costello plc, a manufacturer in the dairy industry. The company has an authorised share capital of €1,100,000 made up of 900,000 ordinary shares at €1 each and 200,000 12% preference shares at €1 each.**

	€
Sales	690,000
Cost of sales	450,000
Operating expenses	130,000
Interest	30,000
Net profit	80,000
Dividends	65,000
Retained profits	15,000
Intangible assets	111,000
Tangible assets	890,000
Investments (market value €98,000)	100,000
Current assets (debtors, €120,000)	390,000
Trade creditors	86,000
Bank overdraft	40,000
10% Debentures 20-9	300,000
Ordinary shares	850,000
12% Preference shares	200,000
Market price of one share	1.82

18

Q3 **The following figures have been taken from the final accounts of O'Riordan Plc, a manufacturer in the computer chip industry. The company has an authorised share capital of €1,000,000, made up of 800,000 €1 ordinary shares and 200,000 10% preference shares.**

	€
Sales	1,780,000
Cost of sales	1,390,000
Total operating expenses for year	240,000
Interest for year	40,000
Net profit	110,000
Dividends paid	96,000
Retained profits	14,000
Intangible assets	124,000
Tangible assets	640,000
Investments (market value €180,000)	210,000
Current assets (debtors €96,000 and stock €55,000)	196,000
Trade creditors	56,000
10% Debentures 20-1	400,000
Ordinary shares	600,000
10% Preference shares	100,000

Q4 **The following figures have been taken from the final accounts of Collins plc, a manufacturer in the computer chip industry. The company has an authorised share capital of €850,0000 made up of 500,000 €1 ordinary shares and 350,000 10% preference shares.**

	€
Sales	1,230,000
Cost of sales	980,000
Total operating expenses for year	120,000
Interest for year	10,000
Net profit	120,000
Dividends paid	40,000
Intangible assets	170,000
Tangible assets	340,000
Investments (market value €103,000)	100,000
Current assets (debtors €72,000)	224,000
Trade creditors	98,000
Bank overdraft	122,000
10% Debentures 20-2	100,000
Ordinary shares	352,000
10% Preference shares	82,000

18

Q5 **The following figures have been taken from the final accounts of White Plc, a manufacturer in the construction industry. The company has an authorised share capital of €1,200,000 made up of 1,600,000 50c ordinary shares and 400,000 8% preference shares at €1 each**

	€
Sales	2,340,000
Cost of sales	1,760,000
Total operating expenses for year	450,000
Interest for year	60,000
Net profit	70,000
Dividends paid	45,000
Retained profits	25,000
Intangible assets	190,000
Tangible assets	920,000
Investments (market value €120,000)	120,000
Current assets (debtors €75,000 and closing stock €48,000)	278,000
Trade creditors	168,000
Bank overdraft	50,000
15% Debentures 20-1	400,000
Ordinary shares	700,000
8% Preference shares	165,000

Part B: The Interpretation of Formulae

The interpretation of financial statements is used to show:

- the **performance** of a business
- the **state of affairs** of a business
- the **prospects** of a business.

The two most important areas to consider when assessing a business are its **profitability** and its **liquidity**. The main stakeholders will primarily be concerned with these two areas.

Interpretation of accounts – Ordinary Level

The financial statements of Brad Plc revealed the following information:

18

Current ratio	2.1 : 1
Acid ratio	1.2 : 1
Return on capital employed	18%
Return on shareholders' funds	14%
9% Debentures	€100,000

You are required to answer the following:

1. Would Brad Plc have fared better if it had sold out and invested its money in a financial institution for the past year? Give reasons for your answer.
2. If the current ratio and the quick ratio for the previous year were 1.3 : 1 and 0.7 : 1, comment on the liquidity of the firm.

Solution

1. Businesses take risks and for this they expect to earn more than they could by investing their money in risk-free securities. The return on capital employed for this year was 18%. The return currently available from banks and building societies is less than 4% so the business is performing well and is considered profitable. Therefore the business should not have sold out.
2. In the previous year the current ratio was 1.3 : 1 and the acid ratio was 0.7 : 1. This would be considered poor. In the current year these ratios are 2.1 : 1 and 1.2 : 1, so both have improved and are now near the industrial norms of 1.5 : 1 and 1 : 1, respectively. This indicates that the business is capable of paying its short-term debts as they fall due. This year the business has €1.20 available immediately for each €1 owed. The above firm would not have difficultly paying its debts.

Interpretation of accounts – Higher Level

Interpretation of accounts in more detail requires looking at all areas of the business, not only the profitability and liquidity but all other types of ratio, in order to assess properly the business's performance, state of affairs and prospects. The main stakeholders, namely the shareholders (existing and potential) and lenders (banks and debenture holders), along with management and employees, are interested in looking at the profitability and liquidity position of the firm and also at the investment and dividend policies adopted by the business.

When interpreting financial statements in more detail we can use the following main headings:

L Liquidity

I Interest cover and investment policy

P Profitability

G Gearing

L Level of dividends (dividend policy)

O Ordinary share market price

S Sector

S Security

NOTE

These are some of the main headings that can be used in interpreting financial statements, but they are not the only possible headings.

NOTE

Remember: **LIPGLOSS**

18

Starting points

A Shareholders (existing)
Shareholders would be happy (unhappy) with the performance, state of affairs and prospects for the company because...

B Shareholders (potential)
I would advise my friend to buy (not to buy) shares in the above company because...

C Debenture holders
Debenture holders would be happy (unhappy) with the performance, state of affairs and prospects for the company because...

D Banks
As manager of the bank I agree (do not agree) to grant the loan to the company because...

Example

Based on the figures calculated in the Scallan Plc example above, pp. 451–2), indicate if the ordinary shareholders would be satisfied with the performance, state of affairs and prospects of the company. Use relevant ratios and other information to support your answer.

Solution

Shareholders would be **unhappy** with the performance, state of affairs and prospects for the company because:

Liquidity

- The company is not liquid. This means that the company is **unable** to pay its debts as they fall due.
- The company currently has only 36 cent available in short-term assets to pay each €1 owed.
- The acid test ratio of 0.36 : 1 has **disimproved** since last year when the ratio was 1.3 : 1. This is a **negative trend**. It compares unfavourably with the industrial norm of approximately 1 : 1.
- The current test ratio of 0.88 : 1 compares **unfavourably** with the industrial norm of 1.5 : 1.
- Shareholders would **not be satisfied** with the liquidity of the company and its short-term safety is insecure.

Interest cover and investment policy

- The interest cover is 3.17 times. This means that the company can make its fixed interest payments on debentures 3.17 times. This has **disimproved** since last year. The trend is **negative**.
- Shareholders will be **happy** to see that interest payments will be met and that there is little risk from outside finance. However, the interest cover has **disimproved** from 4.7 times last year.
- The company has investments worth €170,000. These investments cost €240,000. This shows poor investment policy by management. These investments should be sold in order get their value before they drop further.
- These investments along with the true value of fixed assets should be examined. Is there enough security to cover existing loans or any new loans the company might need to take out?

Profitability

- The company is profitable. The return on capital employed is 11.8% . This compares to 12.4% last year. This has **disimproved** since last year. The trend is **negative**.
- The return on capital employed compares **favourably** with the return on risk-free investments of about 3% currently available from banks and other financial institutions.
- Shareholders would be **satisfied** with the above as they are getting more than the return from risk-free investments. Their return for taking the risk is adequate.
- However, the return has **disimproved** to 11.8% while the debenture holders are receiving a return of 10% and the preference shareholders are receiving a dividend of 10% when taking no risk. Ordinary shareholders would be showing some concern as they are only receiving 1.8% more of a return and yet taking all the risks.

18

Gearing

- The company is **low geared**. The current level of gearing is 43.5% and compares to a gearing of 41% last year.
- The company is therefore at little risk from outside creditors. Shareholders will be **happy** to see that most of the profits are not been taken up by fixed interest payments on loans and preference shares.

Level of dividends (dividend policy)

- The current dividend per share is 11.25c. This is only adequate and shareholders would be **unhappy** with this payout as it has **disimproved** from 16c last year.
- The dividend yield is 5.3%, which is below the 10% return on preference shares and the debenture loan. Shareholders would **not be satisfied** with this yield as they are getting less of a return for taking the risk.
- The dividend yield has **disimproved** from 8.79% last year, which is a **negative trend**. Shareholders will not want to keep their shares in the company, and this may make the company unstable. Debenture holders want a stable company because it gives more security to their loan as the company is at less risk of being subject to takeover.

Ordinary share market price

- The market price of one ordinary share is €2.10 The value of one share last year was €1.82 This is an **improvement** of 15.4%.
- The earnings per share have **disimproved** from 24c to 15c.
- The shares may be overpriced as it takes 18.67 years to recover their market price. Shareholders would not be happy with this situation.
- This would indicate a lack of confidence in the company and may discourage investment in the company in the future.

Sector

- The long-term prospects are not encouraging for the computer industry. During the current economic climate trading is difficult because there is a lack of disposal income available for discretionary expenditure.
- The company should try to develop overseas markets and also diversify into new technology products to take advantage of the advances made in tablet computers.

Security

- The security or collateral available for the current amount of loans and debentures is adequate.
- Shareholders would be **happy** as they know the company is not at threat from the outside investments.

Exercises – Ordinary Level

18

Q1 **The following information has been taken from the books of Ernie Ltd for the year ended 31/12/20-4:**

Trading, Profit and Loss Account for the year ended 31/12/20-4

	€	€
Credit sales		750,000
***Less* Cost of sales**		
Opening stock	105,000	
Purchases	570,000	
	675,000	
Less Closing stock	?	?
Gross profit		172,500
Less Expenses (including interest)		(79,500)
Net profit for year		93,000
Profit and loss account 1/1/20-4		39,000
Profit and loss account 31/12/20-4		132,000

Balance Sheet as at 31/12/20-4

	€	€
Fixed assets		540,000
Current assets (including debtors €54,000)	147,000	
Less Creditors: amounts falling due within 1 year	(51,000)	96,000
		636,000
Financed by		
Creditors: amounts falling due after more than 1 year		
4% Debentures 20-8/20-9		75,000
Capital and reserves		
Ordinary share capital		429,000
Profit and loss account 31/12/20-4		132,000
		636,000

(a) **You are required to:**

- Calculate the percentage mark-up on cost.
- Calculate closing stock.
- Calculate the period of credit given to debtors.
- Calculate the return on capital employed.

(b) **Explain the following:**

- Debentures 20-8/20-9
- Intangible assets
- Return on capital employed
- Rate of stock turnover.

(c) **Would the above firm have fared better if it had sold out and invested in a financial institution for the past year? Give reasons for your answer.**

(d) **If the current ratio and acid test ratio for 20-3 were 1.5 : 1 and 0.9 : 1, comment on the current liquidity of the firm.**

18

Q2 The following information has been taken from the books of King Ltd for the year ended 31/12/20-5:

Trading, Profit and Loss Account for the year ended 31/12/20-5

	€	€
Credit sales		624,000
***Less* Cost of sales**		
Opening stock	41,600	
Purchases	?	
	?	
Less Closing stock	(38,400)	?
Gross profit		208,000
Less Expenses (including interest)		(179,200)
Net profit for year		28,800
Profit and loss account 1/1/20-5		49,600
Profit and loss account 31/12/20-5		78,400

Balance Sheet as at 31/12/20-5

	€	€
Fixed assets		592,000
Current assets (including debtors €30,400)	164,800	
Less Creditors: amounts falling due within 1 year	(78,400)	86,400
		678,400
Financed by		
Creditors: amounts falling due after more than 1 year		
8% Debentures 20-7/20-8		120,000
Capital and reserves		
Ordinary share capital		480,000
Profit and loss account 31/12/20-5		78,400
		678,400

(a) **You are required to:**

- Calculate the figure for purchases.
- Calculate return on capital employed.
- Calculate the period of credit given to debtors.
- Calculate the acid test ratio.

(b) **Explain the following:**

- 8% Debentures 20-7/20-8
- Preference dividend
- Intangible assets
- Rate of stock turnover.

(c) **Would King Ltd have fared better if it had sold out and invested in a financial institution for the past year? Give reasons for your answer.**

(d) **If the current ratio and acid test ratio for 20-4 were 1.8 : 1 and 1.1 : 1, comment on the current liquidity of the firm.**

Q3 **The following information has been taken from the books of Laurel Ltd for the year ended 31/12/20-6:**

Trading, Profit and Loss Account for the year ended 31/12/20-6

	€	€
Credit sales		800,000
***Less* Cost of sales**		
Opening stock	?	
Purchases	468,000	
	?	
Less Closing stock	(57,000)	(524,000)
Gross profit		276,000
Less Expenses (including interest)		(154,000)
Net profit for year		122,000
Profit and loss account 1/1/20-6		28,000
Profit and loss account 31/12/20-6		150,000

Balance Sheet as at 31/12/20-6

	€	€
Fixed assets		556,000
Current assets	86,000	
***Less* Creditors: amounts falling due within 1 year**		
Trade creditors	(72,000)	14,000
		570,000
Financed by		
Creditors: amounts falling due after more than 1 year		
5% Debentures 20-9/20-0		170,000
Capital and reserves		
Ordinary share capital		250,000
Profit and loss account 31/12/20-6		150,000
		570,000

(a) **You are required to:**

- Calculate the figure for opening stock.
- Calculate the gross profit margin.
- Calculate the period of credit received from creditors.
- Calculate the acid test ratio.

(b) **Explain the following:**

- 5% Debentures 20-9/20-0
- Interest paid
- Liquid assets
- Shareholders' funds.

(c) **Would Laurel Ltd have difficulty paying its debts as they fall due? Give reasons for your answer.**

(d) **Calculate the return on capital employed. If this return was 14% in 20-5 comment on the current profitability of the company.**

Q4 **The following information has been taken from the books of Gray Ltd for the year ended 31/12/20-7:**

Trading, Profit and Loss Account for the year ended 31/12/20-7

	€	€
Credit sales		960,000
***Less* Cost of sales**		
Opening stock	84,000	
Purchases	?	
	?	
Less Closing stock	(82,000)	(593,000)
Gross profit		367,000
Less Expenses (including interest)		(231,000)
Net profit for year		136,000
Profit and loss account 1/1/20-7		(114,600)
Profit and loss account 31/12/20-7		21,400

Balance Sheet as at 31/12/20-7

	€	€
Fixed assets		880,000
Current assets (including debtors €61,000)	211,000	
Less Creditors: amounts falling due within 1 year	(91,600)	119,400
		999,400
Financed by		
Creditors: amounts falling due after more than 1 year		
6% Debentures 20-1/20-2		200,000
Capital and reserves		
Ordinary share capital		778,000
Profit and loss account 31/12/20-7		21,400
		999,400

(a) **You are required to:**

- Calculate the figure for purchases.
- Calculate return on capital employed.
- Calculate the period of credit given to debtors.
- Calculate the current ratio.

(b) **Explain the following:**

- 6% Debentures 20-1/20-2
- Ordinary dividend
- Intangible assets
- Capital employed.

(c) **Calculate the acid test ratio for 20-7. What information does this ratio give?**

(d) **If the return on capital employed for 20-6 was 12%, comment on the profitability for 20-7.**

Exercises – Higher Level

18

Q1 **The following figures have been taken from the final accounts of Keys plc, a manufacturer in the dairy industry, for the year ended 31/12/20-1. The company has an authorised capital of €900,000, made up of 700,000 ordinary shares at €1 each and 200,000 8% preference shares at €1 each. The company has already issued 500,000 ordinary shares and 150,000 of the 8% preference shares.**

Trading, Profit and Loss Account for the year ended 31/12/20-1

	€	€
Sales		980,000
Opening stock	40,000	
Closing stock	52,000	
Cost of goods sold		(560,000)
Operating expenses for year		(280,000)
Interest for year		(18,000)
Net profit for year		122,000
Dividends paid		(52,000)
Retained profit		70,000
Profit and loss balance 1/1/20-1		130,000
Profit and loss balance 31/12/20-1		200,000

Ratios and information for year ended 31/12/20-0

Earnings per share	16.74c
Dividend per share	6.2c
Interest cover	5.1 times
Quick ratio	1.5 : 1
Return on capital employed	11.1%
Market value of 1 share	€1.25
Gearing	38%
Dividend cover	2.7 times
Dividend yield	4.96%

Balance Sheet as at 31/12/20-1

	€	€	€
Fixed assets			
Intangible assets			200,000
Tangible assets			800,000
Investments (market value 31/12/20-1 €85,000)			100,000
			1,100,000
Current assets (including stock €52,000 and debtors €60,000)		160,000	
***Less* Creditors: amounts falling due within 1 year**			
Trade creditors	90,000		
Bank	120,000	(210,000)	(50,000)
			1,050,000
Financed by			
9% Debentures (20-6/20-7)			200,000
Capital and reserves			
Ordinary shares @ €1 each		500,000	
8% Preference shares @ €1 each		150,000	
Profit and loss balance		200,000	850,000
			1,050,000

The market value of one ordinary share at the end of 20-1 was €1.15.

(a) **You are required to calculate the following for 20-1:**

- The earnings per ordinary share
- The cash purchases if the average period of credit received from trade creditors is 2.4 months
- The dividend yield
- How long it would take one ordinary share to recoup (recover) its 20-1 market price assuming current performance is maintained
- Return on capital employed.

(b) **Indicate whether the ordinary shareholders would be satisfied with the performance, state of affairs and prospects of the company. Use relevant ratios, percentages and other information to support your answer.**

(c) **The gross profit percentage for 20-0 was 50%. Give five different explanations for the increase/decrease in 20-1.**

Q2 The following figures have been taken from the final accounts of Tiguan plc, a manufacturer in the sportswear industry, for the year ended 31/12/20-3. The company has an authorised capital of €800,000, made up of 600,000 ordinary shares at €1 each and 200,000 9% preference shares at €1 each. The company has already issued 450,000 ordinary shares and 100,000 of the 9% preference shares.

Trading, Profit and Loss Account for the year ended 31/12/20-3

Sales	540,000
Cost of goods sold	(320,000)
Operating expenses for year	(108,500)
Interest for year	(12,000)
Net profit for year	99,500
Dividends paid	(39,500)
Retained profit	60,000
Profit and loss balance 1/1/20-3	120,000
Profit and loss balance 31/12/20-3	180,000

Ratios and information for year ended 31/12/20-2

Earnings per share	11.6c
Dividend per share	5.8c
Interest cover	3 times
Acid test ratio	1 : 1
Return on capital employed	9.1%
Market value of 1 share	€1.61
Gearing	34%
Dividend cover	2 times
Dividend yield	3.6%

Balance Sheet as at 31/12/20-3

	€	€	€
Fixed assets			
Intangible assets			100,000
Tangible assets			600,000
Investments (market value 31/12/20-3 €95,000)			120,000
			820,000
Current assets (including stock €40,000 and debtors €80,000)		180,000	
***Less* Creditors: amounts falling due within 1 year**			
Trade creditors	100,000		
Bank	20,000	(120,000)	60,000
			880,000
Financed by			
8% Debentures (20-7/20-8)			150,000
Capital and reserves			
Ordinary shares @ €1 each		450,000	
8% Preference shares @ €1 each		100,000	
Profit and loss balance		180,000	730,000
			880,000

The market value of one ordinary share at the end of 20-3 was €1.70.

(a) **You are required to calculate the following for 20-3:**

- **The opening stock if the rate of stock turnover is 10 (based on average stock)**
- **Return on capital employed**
- **The earnings per share**
- **The dividend yield**
- **How long it would take one ordinary share to recover its value at present payout rate.**

(b) **Indicate whether the ordinary shareholders would be satisfied with the performance, state of affairs and prospects of the company. Use relevant ratios, percentages and other information to support your answer.**

(c) **Having assessed Tiguan plc, what actions would you advise the company to take?**

Q3 The following figures have been taken from the final accounts of Green Grove plc, a manufacturer in the solar panel industry, for the year ended 31/12/20-8. The company has an authorised capital of €900,000, made up of 700,000 ordinary shares at €1 each and 200,000 6% preference shares at €1 each. The company has already issued 700,000 ordinary shares and 150,000 of the 6% preference shares.

Trading, Profit and Loss Account for the year ended 31/12/20-8

	€
Sales	632,000
Opening stock	36,000
Closing stock	40,000
Cost of goods sold	(476,000)
Gross profit	156,000
Operating expenses for year	(105,000)
Profit before interest	51,000
Less Interest	(16,000)
Dividends paid	(23,000)
Retained profit	12,000
Profit and loss balance 1/1/20-8	33,000
Profit and loss balance 31/12/20-8	45,000

Projected ratios for year ended 20-9

Earnings per share	5.5c
Dividend per ordinary share	2.6c
Interest cover	3.6 times
Quick ratio	0.9 : 1
Price earnings ratio	17 : 1
Return on capital employed	8.1%
Gearing	26%

Balance Sheet as at 31/12/20-8

	€	€	€
Fixed assets			
Intangible assets			120,000
Tangible assets			800,000
Investments (market value 31/12/20-8 €170,000)			160,000
			1,080,000
Current assets		85,000	
***Less* Creditors: amounts falling due within 1 year**			
Trade creditors	60,000		
Bank	10,000	(70,000)	15,000
			1,095,000
Financed by			
8% Debentures (20-3 secured)			200,000
Capital and reserves			
Ordinary shares @ €1 each		700,000	
6% Preference shares @ €1 each		150,000	
Profit and loss balance		45,000	895,000
			1,095,000

18

The market value of one ordinary share at the end of 20-8 was €0.98.

(a) You are required to calculate the following:

- Cash purchases if the period of credit received from creditors is 2 months
- The interest cover
- The dividend cover
- How long it would take one ordinary share to recover its value at present payout rate
- The projected market value of one share in 20-9.

(b) Indicate whether the ordinary shareholders would be satisfied with the performance, state of affairs and prospects of the company. Use relevant ratios, percentages and other information to support your answer.

(c) Outline the limitations of ratio analysis.

Q4 **The following figures have been taken from the final accounts of Waverly plc, a business involved in the construction industry, for the year ended 31/12/20-5. The company has an authorised capital of €600,000, made up of 450,000 ordinary shares at €1 each and 150,000 6% preference shares at €1 each. The company has already issued 450,000 ordinary shares and 150,000 of the 6% preference shares.**

Trading, Profit and Loss Account for the year ended 31/12/20-5

	€
Sales	1,068,000
Cost of goods sold	(834,000)
Total operating expenses for year	(144,000)
Interest for year	(24,000)
Net profit	66,000
Dividends paid	(40,500)
Retained profit for year	25,500
Profit and loss balance 1/1/20-5	(47,500)
Profit and loss balance 31/12/20-5	(22,000)

Ratios and figures for year ended 31/12/20-4

Interest cover	6 times
Quick ratio	9.1 : 1
Earnings per share	17c
Return on capital employed	15.6%
Market value of 1 share	€1.62
Gearing	42%
Dividend per share	5c
Dividend cover	3.4 times

Balance Sheet as at 31/12/20-5

	€	€	€
Fixed assets			
Intangible assets			180,000
Tangible assets			480,000
Investments (market value 31/12/20-5 €108,000)			120,000
			780,000

Continued >

18

	€	€	€
Current assets (including debtors €58,000 and stock €52,000)		110,000	
***Less* Creditors: amounts falling due within 1 year**			
Trade creditors	34,000		
Bank	38,000	(72,000)	38,000
			818,000
Financed by			
10% Debentures 20-8/20-9 (secured)			240,000
Capital and reserves			
Ordinary shares @ €1 each		450,000	
6% Preference shares @ €1 each		150,000	
Profit and loss balance		(22,000)	578,000
			818,000

The market value of one ordinary share at the end of 20-5 was €1.40.

(a) You are required to calculate the following for the year 20-5:

- Interest cover
- Earnings per share
- Cash sales if the average period of credit given to debtors is 1.5 months
- How long it would take one ordinary share to recoup its 20-5 market price based on the current dividend payout rate
- Dividend yield on ordinary shares for 20-4.

(b) Indicate whether debenture holders would be satisfied with the performance, state of affairs and prospects of the company. Use relevant ratios, percentages and other information to support your answer.

(c) Advise the bank manager if a loan of €100,000 on which interest payable at a rate of 10% would be charged should be granted to Waverly plc for future expansion. Use relevant information to support your answer.

(d) A rising liquidity ratio is a sign of prudent management. Discuss.

18

Exam Tips

- Identify key figures – such as net profit, amount of dividends – before starting the question.
- Tackle part (a) by writing out the formulae and then substituting the figures. Show answers correct to two decimal places.
- Calculate all extra ratios as a working before attempting to interpret the accounts.
- Answer the interpretation question using the appropriate headings. Remember LIPGLOSS.
- Always make a clear decision in answering the interpretation question, i.e. shareholders would be happy or not be happy. Do not give a mixed answer.
- Know the limitations of ratios.
- In questions on the analysis of financial statements, definitions of terms related to ratio analysis and the accounts that are analysed are often required.

19 Tabular Statements – Effects of Transactions on the Balance Sheet

Objectives

On completion students should be able to:

- Complete a tabular statement showing the effects of transactions on the balance sheet;
- Show an understanding of the double-entry principle.

Tabular statements

A tabular statement shows the effect of transactions on the balance sheet.

A tabular statement is a continuous presentation of transactions as they occur. It shows how each transaction affects the assets and liabilities of the business. It is based on the double-entry principle. If a transaction increases one asset there is a corresponding decrease in another asset or a corresponding increase in a liability.

Procedure

A number of steps should be followed when preparing a tabular statement.

1. Make a list of all assets and enter them vertically on the upper section of the tabular statement. **Include fixed assets at their cost price and enter depreciation on these as a negative asset**. Use a similar approach with debtors less the provision for bad debts.
2. Make a list of all the liabilities and enter them vertically on the lower section of the tabular statement. **A bank overdraft may be treated as a negative current asset**.
3. **Check that the total assets equal the total liabilities**.
4. Leave **two** spare lines on the upper and lower sections of the tabular statement to allow for extra assets and/or liabilities that may need to be added, e.g. goodwill, revaluation reserve.
5. For the number of columns across to be used, count the number of transactions that have to be entered on the statement then **add five** more columns. This is to allow for:
   - the opening list of assets and liabilities in words
   - the opening list of assets and liabilities in figures
   - the closing total figures for the assets and liabilities after entering all the transactions
   - and two extra to allow for splitting up certain transactions – for example, rent received and prepaid.

6. Identify each asset and liability that is affected by each transaction and enter these on the tabular statement.
7. Total the assets and liabilities at the end of the financial period by adding the figures across the tabular statement.

The change as a result of a transaction in the upper section of the tabular statement must be equal to that in the lower section; the change in assets must correspond with the change in liabilities. However, the total change may be neutral. For example, when a debtor makes a payment, debtors decrease and cash increases by the same amount.

Sample Ordinary Level question

The following balance sheet shows the financial position of a sole trader, Percy Green, as at 1/12/20-1:

Balance Sheet as at December 1st 20-1

	€	€	€
Fixed assets			
Land and buildings		480,000	
Machinery		160,000	640,000
Current assets			
Stock		100,000	
Debtors		30,000	
Bank		25,000	
		155,000	
***Less* Creditors: amounts falling due within 1 year**			
Trade creditors	34,000		
Salaries and wages due	11,000	(45,000)	110,000
			750,000
Financed by			
Capital			750,000
			750,000

During the month of December the following transactions took place:

Dec 3 Received €900 from a debtor in full settlement of a debt of €920.
Dec 7 Purchased goods on credit for €2,300.
Dec 8 Paid the salaries and wages due at the start of the year.
Dec 10 Sold goods on credit for €5,000 which originally cost €4,800.
Dec 12 Paid €240 by cheque for repairs to a roof of private house.
Dec 23 Paid a creditor's account balance of €3,100 and received a discount of €100.
Dec 24 Bought a new machine costing €20,000. A deposit of 10% was paid by cheque and the remainder borrowed from Sodor Finance Company Ltd.
Dec 29 A debtor who owed Percy €3,000 was declared bankrupt and paid 40c in the euro.

You are required to record the above transactions and the effect they had on the assets and liabilities of Percy Green and to show the total assets and liabilities on 31/12/20-1.

Solution

	Dec 1	Dec 3	Dec 7	Dec 8	Dec 10	Dec 12	Dec 23	Dec 24	Dec 29	Total
Assets										
Land and buildings	480,000									**480,000**
Machinery	160,000							20,000		**180,000**
Stock	100,000		2,300		(4,800)					**97,500**
Debtors	30,000	(920)			5,000				(3,000)	**31,080**
Bank	25,000	900		(11,000)		(240)	(3,000)	(2,000)	1,200	**10,860**
Total assets	795,000	(20)	2,300	(11,000)	200	(240)	(3,000)	18,000	(1,800)	**799,440**
Liabilities										
Creditors	34,000		2,300				(3,100)			**33,200**
Wages (due)	11,000			(11,000)						**0**
Capital	750,000	(20)			200	(240)	100		(1,800)	**748,240**
Loan								18,000		**18,000**
Total liabilities	795,000	(20)	2,300	(11,000)	200	(240)	(3,000)	18,000	(1,800)	**799,440**

Sample Higher Level question

The financial position of Squeeze Ltd on 1/1/20-0 is shown in the balance sheet below:

Balance Sheet as at 31/12/20-0

	€	€	€
Fixed assets	**Cost**	**Aggregate Depreciation**	**Net Book Value**
Land and buildings	400,000	26,000	374,000
Delivery vans	69,000	30,000	39,000
	469,000	56,000	413,000
Current assets			
Stock		54,000	
Debtors (less 5% provision)		76,000	
Prepaid expenses (advertising)		5,000	
		135,000	
***Less* Creditors: amounts falling due within 1 year**			
Creditors	60,000		

Continued >

	€	€	€
Bank overdraft	19,000		
Wages due	1,000	(80,000)	55,000
			468,000
Financed by			
Capital and reserves			
Authorised share capital: 800,000 shares @ €1 each			
Issued share capital: 400,000 shares @ €1 each			400,000
Share premium			18,000
Profit and loss account			50,000
			468,000

The following transactions took place during 20-0:

Jan. On 1/1/20-0, Squeeze Ltd revalued land and bulidings at €480,000. This revaluation included land now valued at €90,000.

Feb. On 1/2/20-0 Squeeze Ltd bought an adjoining business which included premises €250,000; vehicles €70,000; stock €15,000; and creditors €22,000. The purchase price was discharged by granting the seller 300,000 shares in Squeeze Ltd at a premium of 20c per share.

April A payment of €1,610 was received from a debtor whose debt had previously been written off and who now wishes to trade with Squeeze Ltd again with immediate effect. This represents 70% of the original debt and the debtor undertook to pay the remainder of the debt by September.

May Received a bank statement on May 31 showing a direct debit of €6,000 to cover advertising for the year ended 31/5/20-1 and a credit transfer of €5,000 to cover ten months' rent in advance from May 1.

June Goods previously sold by Squeeze for €30,000 were returned. The selling price of these goods was cost plus 20%. Owing to a delay in returning these goods, a credit note was issued showing that a reduction of 15% of selling price was applied as a restocking charge.

July Received €125,000 from the issue of the remaining shares.

Aug. A vehicle which cost €14,000 was traded in for a new vehicle costing €26,000. An allowance of €8,000 was made for the old vehicle. Depreciation to date on the old vehicle was €5,600.

Sept. Received the remainder of the debt as promised from April.

Dec. The buildings depreciation charge for the year is to be 2% of book value. The depreciation is to be calculated from date of valuation and date of purchase. The depreciation charge on vehicles for the year was to be €13,200.

You are required to:

- Record on a tabular statement the effect each of the above transactions had on the relevant asset and liability and ascertain the total assets and liabilities on 31/12/20-0.

Solution

	Jan.	Jan.	Feb.	April	May	June	July	Aug.	Sept.	Dec.	Dec.	Total
Assets												
Premises	400,000	80,000	250,000									730,000
Depreciation	(26,000)	26,000								(12,383)		(12,383)
Vans	69,000		70,000					12,000				151,000
Depreciation	(30,000)							5,600		(13,200)		(37,600)
Stock	54,000		15,000			25,000						94,000
Debtors	80,000			690		(25,500)			(690)			54,500
Provision for bad debts	(4,000)											(4,000)
Advertising	5,000				6,000						(8,500)	2,500
Goodwill			47,000									47,000
Total assets	**548,000**	**106,000**	**382,000**	**690**	**6,000**	**(500)**	**0**	**17,600**	**(690)**	**(25,583)**	**(8,500)**	**1,025,017**
Liabilities												
Creditors	60,000		22,000									82,000
Bank	19,000			(1,610)	1,000		(125,000)	18,000	(690)			(89,300)
Wages	1,000											1,000
Ordinary share capital	400,000		300,000				100,000					800,000
Share premium	18,000		60,000				25,000					103,000
Profit and loss account	50,000			2,300		(500)		(400)		(25,583)	(4,500)	21,317
Revaluation reserve		106,000										106,000
Rent					5,000						(4,000)	1,000
Total liabilities	**548,000**	**106,000**	**382,000**	**690**	**6,000**	**(500)**	**0**	**17,600**	**(690)**	**(25,583)**	**(8,500)**	**1,025,017**

Exercises – Ordinary Level

19

Q1 **The following balance sheet shows the financial position of a sole trader, Thomas Stanley, as at 1/5/20-0:**

Balance Sheet as at May 1st 20-0

	€	€	€
Fixed assets			
Land and buildings		439,000	
Delivery vans		221,000	660,000
Current assets			
Stock		70,000	
Debtors		55,000	
Prepaid Insurance		5,000	
		130,000	
***Less* Creditors: amounts falling due within 1 year**			
Creditors	12,000		
Bank overdraft	8,000	(20,000)	110,000
			770,000
Financed by			
Capital			770,000
			770,000

During the month of May, the following transactions took place:

May	1	Bought goods on credit for €11,900.
May	2	A debtor who owed €1,200 was declared bankrupt and paid 20c in the euro.
May	8	Built an extension to the existing buildings costing €120,000. A deposit of €20,000 was paid by cheque and the remainder by a loan from High Finance.
May	10	Paid by cheque €2,600 repairs to a private motor car.
May	12	The insurance charge for the year was written off to profit and loss, €4,800.
May	22	Sold goods for €4,900 which originally cost €4,000. The amount was lodged.
May	23	Received a cheque for €3,400 from a debtor in full settlement of a debt of €3,800.
May	30	Paid a creditor by cheque €3,200 and received a discount of €200.

You are required to record the above transactions and the effect they had on the assets and liabilities of Thomas Stanley and to show the total assets and liabilities on 31/05/20-0.

Q2 **The following balance sheet shows the financial position of a sole trader, Elaine Fitzgerald, as on 1/12/20-2:**

Balance Sheet as at 1/12/20-2

	€	€	€
Fixed assets			
Premises		500,000	
Office equipment		190,000	690,000
Current assets			
Debtors		105,000	
Stock		90,000	
Bank		15,000	
		210,000	
***Less* Creditors: amounts falling due within 1 year**			
Creditors	25,000		
Expenses due	5,000	(30,000)	180,000
			870,000
Financed by			
Capital			870,000
			870,000

The following transactions took place during December 20-2:

Dec. 4 Received from a debtor a cheque for €930 in full settlement of a debt of €980.

Dec. 10 Paid by cheque expenses due at the beginning of the month.

Dec. 11 Purchased goods on credit, €9,500.

Dec. 17 Paid €2,000 by cheque for deposit on son's new apartment.

Dec. 21 Purchased a new computer network for €8,000. A deposit of €1,500 was paid by cheque and the remainder was borrowed from Sure Finance Ltd.

Dec. 28 A debtor who owed €1,200 was declared bankrupt and paid 75c in the euro by cheque.

Dec. 31 Paid by cheque a creditor's account balance of €1,500 and received a discount of €90.

You are required to:

- Record on a tabular statement the effect of each of the above transactions on the relevant assets and liabilities.
- Show the total assets and liabilities on 31st December 20-2.

19

Q3 **The following balance sheet shows the financial position of Dermot Moore Ltd as on 1/10/20-3:**

Balance Sheet as at 1/10/20-3

	€	€	€
Fixed assets			
Buildings		340,000	
Furniture and fittings		160,000	500,000
Current assets			
Debtors		68,000	
Stock		42,000	
Bank		11,500	
		121,500	
***Less* Creditors: amounts falling due within 1 year**			
Creditors	32,400		
Expenses due	3,100	(35,500)	86,000
			586,000
Financed by			
Capital			450,000
Profit and loss account			136,000
			586,000

The following transactions took place during October 20-3:

Oct. 2 Received from a debtor a cheque for €1,050 in full settlement of a debt of €1,100.

Oct. 4 Purchased goods on credit, €4,600.

Oct. 9 Paid the expenses due at the beginning of the month.

Oct. 11 Paid by cheque a creditor's account balance of €1,410 and received a discount of €60.

Oct. 15 Purchased new security system for €12,000. A deposit of €3,000 was paid by cheque and the remainder was borrowed from Pure Finance Ltd.

Oct. 19 Sold goods on credit for €5,600 which had cost €4,300.

Oct. 21 A debtor who owed €800 was declared bankrupt and paid 35c in the euro by cheque.

Oct. 26 Paid by cheque €150 for repairs.

You are required to:

- Record on a tabular statement the effect of each of the above transactions on the relevant assets and liabilities.
- Show the total assets and liabilities on 31st October 20-3.

Q4 **The following balance sheet shows the financial position of Wayne Scales Ltd as on 1/3/20-5:**

Balance Sheet as at 1/3/20-5

	€	€	€
Fixed assets			
Buildings		650,000	
Delivery vans		130,000	780,000
Current assets			
Debtors		48,000	
Stock		22,600	
Bank		25,600	
		96,200	
***Less* Creditors: amounts falling due within 1 year**			
Creditors	15,600		
Expenses due	3,600	(19,200)	77,000
			857,000
Financed by			
Capital			750,000
Profit and loss account			107,000
			857,000

The following transactions took place during March 20-5:

March	3	Received from a debtor a cheque for €3,400 in full settlement of a debt of €3,600.
March	9	Purchased goods on credit €11,500.
March	15	Paid the expenses due at the beginning of the month by cheque.
March	17	Paid by cheque a creditor's account balance of €6,470 and received a discount of €70.
March	19	Sold goods on credit for €18,900 which had cost €17,000.
March	23	A debtor who owed €1,700 was declared bankrupt and paid 50c in the euro by cheque.
March	26	Paid by cheque €180 for repairs.
March	29	Purchased an adjoining warehouse for €120,000. A deposit of 10% was paid by cheque and the remainder was borrowed from Total Finance Ltd.

You are required to:

- Record on a tabular statement the effect of each of the above transactions on the relevant assets and liabilities.
- Show the total assets and liabilities on 31st March 20-5.

19

19

Q5 **The following balance sheet shows the financial position of Yorkie Ltd as on 1/1/20-6:**

Balance Sheet as at 1/1/20-6

	€	€	€
Fixed assets			
Buildings		560,000	
Delivery vans		340,000	900,000
Current assets			
Debtors		50,000	
Stock		35,500	
Cash		15,600	
		101,100	
***Less* Creditors: amounts falling due within 1 year**			
Trade creditors	18,000		
Rent due	4,500		
Bank overdraft	6,600	(29,100)	72,000
			972,000
Financed by			
800,000 ordinary shares €1 each			800,000
Profit and loss account			172,000
			972,000

The following transactions took place during 20-6:

Jan.	Received from a debtor a cheque for €3,200 in full settlement of a debt of €3,300.
March	Purchased goods on credit, €14,500.
April	Paid the rates due at the beginning of the year by cheque.
May	Paid by cheque a creditor's account balance of €6,470 and received a discount of €70.
June	Sold goods on credit for €18,000, which is cost plus 20%.
Aug.	A debtor who owed €2,300 was declared bankrupt and paid 40c in the euro cash.
Sept.	Paid an interim dividend of 10c per share by cheque.
Dec.	Purchased an adjoining building for €200,000. A deposit of 10% was paid by cheque and the remainder was borrowed from Top Finance Ltd.

You are required to :

- Record on a tabular statement the effect of each of the above transactions on the relevant assets and liabilities.
- Show the total assets and liabilities on 31st December 20-6.

Exercises – Higher Level

19

Q1 **The financial position of Marlon Ltd on 1/1/20-5 is shown in the following balance sheet:**

Balance Sheet as at 1/1/20-5

	€	€	€
Fixed assets	**Cost**	**Aggregate Depreciation**	**Net Book Value**
Premises	300,000	15,000	285,000
Office equipment	150,000	10,000	140,000
Motor vehicles	60,000	20,000	40,000
	510,000	45,000	465,000
Current assets			
Stock		124,000	
Debtors		56,000	
		180,000	
***Less* Creditors: amounts falling due within 1 year**			
Trade creditors	104,000		
Bank	24,000		
Expenses due	6,000	(134,000)	
Net current assets			46,000
Total net assets			**511,000**
Financed by			
Capital and reserves			
	Authorised	**Issued**	
Ordinary shares @ €1 each	600,000	350,000	
Share premium		58,000	
Profit and loss account		103,000	511,000
Capital employed			**511,000**

The following transactions took place during 20-5:

Jan. Marlon Ltd bought an adjoining business which included premises €112,000, debtors €18,000 and creditors €12,500. The purchase price was discharged by granting the seller 100,000 shares in Marlon Ltd at a premium of 20c per share.

March A payment of €600 was received from a debtor whose debt had previously been written off and who now wishes to trade with Marlon Ltd again. This represents 30% of the original debt and the debtor has undertaken to pay the remainder of the debt by January 20-6.

May Goods previously sold for €500 were returned. The selling price of these goods was cost plus 25%. Owing to a delay in returning these goods a credit note for only €450 was issued.

June Received a bank statement on June 1 showing a direct debit of €800 to cover fire insurance for the year ended 31/3/20-6 and a credit transfer of €1,800 representing nine months' rent in advance from June 1.

Sept. Received €180,000 from the issue of the remaining shares.

Dec. A creditor who was owed €900 by Marlon Ltd accepted a bookcase, the book value of which was €740, in full settlement of the debt. The bookcase had cost €950.

You are required to:

- Record on a tabular statement the effect of each of the above transactions on the relevant assets and liabilities.
- Show the total assets and liabilities on 31st December 20-5.

Q2 **The financial position of Mitchell Ltd on 1/1/20-6 is shown in the following balance sheet:**

Balance Sheet as at 1/1/20-6

	€	€	€
Fixed assets	**Cost**	**Aggregate Depreciation**	**Net Book Value**
Goodwill			45,000
Premises	800,000	60,000	740,000
Delivery vans	150,000	70,000	80,000
	950,000	130,000	865,000
Current assets			
Stock		99,800	
Insurance prepaid		1,200	
Debtors		59,900	
		160,900	
***Less* Creditors: amounts falling due within 1 year**			
Trade creditors	87,800		
Bank	32,900		
Wages due	4,500	(125,200)	
Net current assets			35,700
Total net assets			**900,700**
Financed by			
Capital and reserves			
	Authorised	**Issued**	
Ordinary shares @ €1 each	1,000,000	700,000	
Share premium		80,000	
Profit and loss account		120,700	900,700
Capital employed			**900,700**

The following transactions took place during 20-6:

Jan. Mitchell Ltd bought an adjoining business on 1/1/20-6 which included premises €240,000, delivery van €48,000, and creditors €16,000. The purchase price was discharged by granting the seller 250,000 shares in Mitchell Ltd at a premium of 20c per share.

Feb. A creditor who was owed €10,100 by Mitchell Ltd accepted a delivery van, the book value of which was €9,500, in full settlement of the debt. The delivery van had originally cost €15,000.

March Received a bank statement on 1st March showing a direct debit of €6,000 to cover fire insurance for the year ended 31/3/20-7 and a credit transfer received of €9,900 to cover 11 months' rent receivable from March 1.

April Mitchell Ltd decided to revalue premises on 1/4/20-6 at €1,400,000.

July A delivery van which cost €22,000 was traded in against a new van costing €30,000. An allowance of €6,700 was made for the old van. Depreciation to date on the old van was €14,000.

Aug. A payment of €2,000 was received from P. Butcher, a debtor, whose debt had been previously written off and who now wishes to trade with Mitchell Ltd again. This represents 80% of the original debt and Butcher has undertaken to pay the remainder of the debt in January 20-7. On the same day goods valued at €800 were sold on credit to Butcher. This is a mark-up of 25%.

Dec. Depreciation on buildings is charged at the rate of 3% per annum of value at 1/4/20-6. The depreciation charge for the year on delivery vans was €31,200.

You are required to:

- Record on a tabular statement the effect of each of the above transactions on the relevant assets and liabilities.
- Show the total assets and liabilities on 31st December 20-6.

Q3 The financial position of Phineas Ltd on 1/1/20-2 is shown in the following balance sheet:

Balance Sheet as at 1/1/20-2

	€	€	€
Fixed assets	**Cost**	**Aggregate Depreciation**	**Net Book Value**
Goodwill			120,000
Land and buildings	480,000	24,000	456,000
Delivery vans	216,000	50,400	165,600
	696,000	74,400	741,600
Current assets			
Stock		148,800	
Debtors (provision for bad debts €3,600)		122,400	
		271,200	
***Less* Creditors: amounts falling due within 1 year**			
Creditors	132,000		
Bank	52,800		
Expenses due	10,800	(195,600)	75,600
			817,200
Financed by			
Capital and reserves			
Authorised share capital 840,000 shares @ €1 each			
Issued share capital 600,000 shares @ €1 each			600,000
Share premium			120,000
Profit and loss account			97,200
			817,200

The following transactions took place during 20-2:

Jan. Phineas purchased an adjoining business which consisted of buildings €192,000, office equipment €24,000, debtors €36,000, and creditors €52,800. The purchase price was paid by granting the seller, Ferb, 180,000 shares in Phineas Ltd at a premium of 25c per share.

Feb. Received €300 from a debtor who was declared bankrupt. This represented 30c in each euro owed.

March Sold for €25,000 goods which cost €21,500 (credit sales).

April The company received €75,000 from the issue of the remaining shares.

19

May Received a bank statement on May 31st showing a direct debit of €1,440 to cover fire insurance for the year ended 31/3/20-3 and a credit transfer of €3,888 representing nine months' rent in advance from 1/6/20-2.

July An interim dividend of 5c per share was paid.

Oct. Goods previously sold for €576 were returned. The selling price of these goods was cost plus 20%. Owing to a delay in returning these goods a credit note for only €500 was issued.

Nov. The directors decided that the provision for bad debts should be adjusted to 5% of debtors.

Dec. A delivery van which cost €38,400 was traded in against a new van costing €60,000. An allowance was made for the old van of €23,520. Depreciation to date on the old van was €18,000. The depreciation charge for the year on land and buildings was €5,000; equipment €7,600; and vans €34,600.

You are required to:

- Record on a tabular statement the effect of each of the above transactions on the relevant assets and liabilities.
- Show the total assets and liabilities on 31st December 20-2.

Q4 **The financial position of Guiney Ltd on 1/1/20-9 is shown in the following balance sheet:**

Balance Sheet as on 1/1/20-9

	€	€	€
Fixed assets	**Cost**	**Aggregate Depreciation**	**Net Book Value**
Premises and land	700,000	56,000	644,000
Delivery vans	140,000	50,000	90,000
	840,000	106,000	734,000
Current assets			
Stock		127,000	
Debtors		104,200	
Insurance prepaid		1,500	
		232,700	
***Less* Creditors: amounts falling due within 1 year**			
Trade creditors	102,000		
Bank	23,400		
Wages due	5,600	(131,000)	
Net current assets			101,700
Total net assets			**835,700**
Financed by			
Capital and reserves			
Authorised: 900,000 ordinary shares @ €1 each			
Issued: 600,000 ordinary shares @€1 each			600,000
Share premium		70,000	
Profit and loss account		165,700	235,700
Capital employed			**835,700**

The following transactions took place during 20-9:

Jan. On 1/1/20-9 Guiney Ltd decided to revalue premises and land at €950,000, which now includes land at €150,000.

April Guiney Ltd bought an adjoining business on 1/4/20-9 which consisted of premises €230,000, delivery vans €80,000, and creditors €48,000. The purchase price was discharged by granting the seller 230,000 shares in Guiney Ltd at a premium of 20c per share.

May Goods previously purchased for €5,000 by Guiney Ltd were returned. Owing to a delay in returning these goods a credit note was issued showing a deduction of 10% of invoice price as a restocking charge.

June A delivery van which cost €30,000 was traded in against a new van costing €55,000. An allowance of €14,000 was made for the old van. Depreciation to date on the old van was €17,600 and the depreciation charge for the year was to be €38,000.

Aug. Received a bank statement on May 31 showing a direct debit of €3,600 to cover fire insurance for the year ended 31/5/20-0.

Oct. A payment of €1,000 was received from a debtor whose debt had previously been written off and who wished to trade with Guiney Ltd again. This represents 50% of the original debt and the debtor undertook to pay the remainder of the debt in January 20-0.

Dec. The buildings depreciation charge for the year is to be 4% of book value. The depreciation charge is calculated from the date of valuation and the date of purchase.

You are required to:

- Record on a tabular statement the effect of each of the above transactions on the relevant assets and liabilities.
- Show the total assets and liabilities on 31st December 20-9.

Q5 The financial position of Weststar Ltd on 1/1/20-8 is shown in the following balance sheet:

Balance Sheet as at 1/1/20-8

	€	€	€
Fixed assets	**Cost**	**Aggregate Depreciation**	**Net Book Value**
Land and buildings	1,000,000	100,000	900,000
Motor vehicles	125,000	40,000	85,000
Furniture and equipment	90,000	30,000	60,000
	1,215,000	170,000	1,045,000
Current assets			
Stock		184,000	
Debtors (less provision 5%)		152,000	
		336,000	
***Less* Creditors: amounts falling due within 1 year**			
Trade creditors	130,000		
Bank	50,000		
Expenses due	6,000	(186,000)	
Net current assets			150,000
Total net assets			**1,195,000**
Financed by			
Capital and reserves			
Authorised: 700,000 ordinary shares @ €2 each			
Issued: 450,000 ordinary shares @ €2 each		900,000	
Share premium		180,000	
Profit and loss account		115,000	1,195,000
Capital employed			**1,195,000**

19

The following transactions took place during 20-8:

Jan.	Weststar Ltd decided to revalue land and buildings at €1,200,000 (which includes land valued at €200,000) on 1/1/20-8.
Feb.	Weststar Ltd bought an adjoining business on 1/1/20-8 which included a new warehouse €360,000, office computers €65,000, debtors €22,000 and creditors €54,000. The purchase price was discharged by granting the seller 170,000 shares in Weststar Ltd at a premium of 40c per share.
April	Management decided that the provision for bad debts should be increased to 8% of debtors.
May	A motor vehicle which had cost €33,000 was traded in against a new vehicle costing €50,000. An allowance of €22,000 was made for the old van. Depreciation to date on the old van was €8,500.
June	Received a bank statement on June 30 showing a credit transfer received of €9,000 to cover nine months' rent in advance from July 1 and direct debit of €3,000 to cover advertising for the year ended 31/3/20-9.
July	A payment of €1,460 was received from a debtor, Fred Perry, whose debt had been previously written off and who now wishes to trade with Weststar Ltd again. This represents 60% of the original debt and the debtor undertook to pay the remainder of the debt in January 20-9. On the same day goods to the value of €800, including a mark-up of 25%, were sold on credit to Perry.
Aug.	Goods previously sold for €1,500 were returned. The selling price of these goods was cost plus 25%. A credit note was issued showing a deduction of 10% of the selling price as a restocking charge.
Oct.	A creditor who was owed €1,700 by Weststar Ltd accepted a computer, the book value of which was €1,450, in full settlement of the debt. The computer had cost €1,600.
Nov.	A dividend of 6c per share was paid on all issued shares.
Dec.	Received €200,000 from the issue of the remaining shares.
	The buildings depreciation charge for the year is 2% of book value. The depreciation charge is calculated from the date of valuation and the date of purchase. The total depreciation charge on vehicles for the year was €32,000 and on computers and equipment it was €3,400.

19

You are required to:

- Record on a tabular statement the effect of each of the above transactions on the relevant assets and liabilities.
- Show the total assets and liabilities on 31st December 20-8.

Q6 The financial position of Spinner Ltd on 1/1/20-1 is shown in the balance sheet below:

Balance Sheet as at 31/12/20-1

	€	€	€
Fixed assets	**Cost**	**Aggregate Depreciation**	**Net Book Value**
Premises	300,000	65,000	235,000
Equipment	70,000	12,000	58,000
	370,000	77,000	293,000

Continued >

	€	€	€
Current assets			
Stock		25,000	
Debtors (less 6% provision)		47,000	
Prepaid expenses		8,000	
		80,000	
***Less* Creditors: amounts falling due within 1 year**			
Creditors	42,000		
Bank overdraft	3,500		
Wages due	1,500	(47,000)	33,000
			326,000
Financed by			
Capital and reserves			
Authorised: 500,000 shares @ €1 each			
Issued: 280,000 Shares @ €1 each			280,000
Share premium			25,000
Profit and loss account			21,000
			326,000

The following transactions took place during 20-1:

Jan. On 1/1/20-1 Spinner Ltd bought an adjoining business which included premises €140,000, debtors 10,000, stock €10,000, and creditors €23,000. The purchase price was discharged by granting the seller 130,000 shares in Spinner Ltd at a premium of 25c per share.

Feb. On 28/2/20-1, Spinner Ltd revalued premises at €470,000. This revaluation included land now valued at €50,000.

March The provision for bad debts was adjusted to 6% of debtors.

April A creditor who was owed €750 by Spinner accepted equipment with a book value of €680 in full settlement of the debt. The equipment had cost €800.

May Received a bank statement on May 31 showing a direct debit of €4,000 to cover insurance for the year ended 31/3/20-2 and a credit transfer of €9,600 to cover ten months' rent in advance from May 1.

June Goods previously purchased by Spinner for €3,000 were returned. Owing to a delay in returning these goods, a credit note was received showing a 10% reduction of purchase price as a restocking charge.

July Received €105,000 from the issue of the remaining shares.

Aug. A vehicle which cost €14,000, was traded in for a new vehicle costing €26,000. An allowance of €8,000 was made for the old vehicle. Depreciation to date on the old vehicle was €5,600.

Sept. An interim dividend of 4c was paid on all issued shares.

Nov A payment of €5,400 was received from a debtor whose debt had previously been written off and who now wishes to trade with Spinner Ltd again. This represents 60% of the original debt and the debtor has undertaken to pay the remainder of the debt in 20-2.

Dec The buildings deprecation charge for the year is to be 2% of book value at 28/2. The depreciation is to be calculated from date of valuation and date of purchase. The depreciation charge on vehicles for the year was to be €8,900.

You are required to:

- **Record on a tabular statement the effect of each of the above transactions on the relevant assets and liabilities.**
- **Show the total assets and liabilities on 31st December 20-1.**

Q7 The financial position of Coady Ltd on 31/1/20-5 is shown in the following balance sheet:

Balance Sheet as at 1/1/20-5

	€	€	€
Fixed assets	**Cost**	**Aggregate Depreciation**	**Net Book Value**
Premises	390,000	37,500	352,500
Motor vehicles	75,000	30,000	45,000
	465,000	67,500	397,500
Current assets			
Stock		105,000	
Debtors (less provision 5%)		128,250	
		233,250	
***Less* Creditors: amounts falling due within 1 year**			
Trade creditors	92,000		
Bank	34,500		
Expenses due	5,000	(131,500)	
Net current assets			101,750
Total net assets			**499,250**
Financed by			
Capital and reserves			
Authorised: 500,000 ordinary shares @ €1 each			
Issued: 380,000 ordinary shares @ €1 each		380,000	
Share premium		21,000	
Profit and loss balance		98,250	499,250
Capital employed			**499,250**

The following transactions took place during 20-5:

Jan. Coady Ltd brought an adjoining business, which included buildings €160,000, debtors €14,000, and creditors €54,000. The purchase price was discharged by granting the seller 100,000 shares in Coady Ltd at premium of 25c per share.

Feb. Coady Ltd decided to revalue premises at €600,000 on 28/2/20-5.

March Management decided that the provision for bad debts should be adjusted to 7% of debtors.

April Goods previously sold by Coady Ltd for €500 were returned. The selling price of these goods was cost plus 25%. Owing to a delay in returning these goods, a credit note was issued showing a 5% reduction as a restocking charge.

19

May	Received a bank statement on May 31 showing a direct debit of €3,000 to cover insurance for the year ended 31/4/20-6 and a credit transfer of €8,400 to cover ten months' rent in advance from May 1.
June	A payment of €3,080 was received from a debtor whose debt had previously been written off and who now wishes to trade with Coady Ltd again. This represents 70% of the original debt and the debtor has undertaken to pay the remainder of the debt in 20-6.
July	A creditor who was owed €7,800 by Coady Ltd accepted a delivery van, the book value of which was €7,400 in full settlement of the debt. The delivery van had originally cost €9,000.
Aug.	An interim dividend of 6c per share was paid on all issued shares.
Sept.	Received €25,000 from the issue of the remaining shares.
Nov.	Received the balance of the previously written-off bad debt as agreed in June.
Dec.	The buildings are to be depreciated at the rate of 2% per annum of value at 28/2/20-5. The total depreciation charge on delivery vans for the year was to be €9,000.

You are required to:

- Record on a tabular statement the effect of each of the above transactions on the relevant assets and liabilities.
- Show the total assets and liabilities on 31st December 20-5.

Q8 **From the following tabular statement of Meldrew Ltd, explain each transaction, clearly stating what is taking place and the effect if any it has on the profit and loss of the company.**

Assets	Jan.	Jan.	Feb.	Mar.	April	June	Sept.	Dec.	Dec.	Dec.	Total
Premises	320,000					160,000					480,000
Dpr premises	(16,000)					16,000		(9,600)			(9,600)
Vans	80,000						(24,000)				56,000
Dpr vans	(32,000)						12,800		(11,200)		(30,400)
Goodwill	25,600										25,600
Investments	32,000										32,000
Stock	56,000	8,800	(12,000)	(480)							52,320
Debtors	48,000		15,840								63,840
Bank	9,600				10,656		9,600				29,856
Prov. bad debts										(3192)	(3,192)
Total assets	523,200	8,800	3,840	(480)	10,656	176,000	(1,600)	(9,600)	(11,200)	(3,192)	696,424
Liabilities											
Capital	320,000										320,000
Premium	80,000										80,000
P & L	72,000		2,400				(1600)	(9,600)	(11,200)	(3,192)	48,808
Creditors	43,200	8,000		(432)							50,768
VAT	4,800	800	1,440	(48)							6,992
Rent receivable	3,200				10,656						13,856
Revaluation res.						176,000					176,000
Total liabilities	523,200	8,800	3,840	(480)	10,656	176,000	(1600)	(9,600)	(11,200)	(3,192)	696,424

Q9 From the following tabular statement of Gabby Ltd, explain each transaction, clearly stating what is taking place and the effect if any it has on the profit and loss of the company.

Assets	Jan.	Jan.	Mar.	May	June	Sept.	Dec.	Dec.	Total
Premises	300,000	112,000							412,000
Dpr premises	(15,000)								(15,000)
Office equipment	150,000						(950)		149,050
Dpr office equipment	(10,000)						210		(9,790)
Motor vehicles	60,000								60,000
Dpr vehicles	(20,000)								(20,000)
Stock	124,000			400					124,400
Debtors	56,000	18,000	1,400	(450)					74,950
Goodwill		2,500							2,500
Insurance					800			(600)	200
Total assets	645,000	132,500	1,400	(50)	800	0	(740)	(600)	778,310
Creditors	104,000	12,500					(900)		115,600
Expenses due	6,000								6,000
Bank	24,000		(600)		(1,000)	(180,000)			(157,600)
Ordinary share capital	350,000	100,000				150,000			600,000
Share premium	58,000	20,000				30,000			108,000
Profit and loss a/c	103,000		2,000	(50)			160	800	105,910
Rent receivable					1,800			(1,400)	400
Total liabilities	645,000	132,500	1,400	(50)	800	0	(740)	(600)	778,310

Exam Tips

- Use ruled paper for this question or lay out your table across two pages. Avoid turning the page sideways into landscape format.
- List the assets and liabilities, leaving two extra lines for each.
- Enter cost of assets and not the net book value. Treat depreciation as a negative asset.
- Deal with depreciation and adjustments for accruals and prepayments at the end of the year, even if they appear earlier in the question.
- After all changes the total assets and total liabilities must always be equal.
- Be sure to find the total assets and liabilities at the end of period.

20 Nature and Scope of Management Accounting

Objectives

On completion students should be able to:

- Understand the nature and scope of management accounting;
- Explain the role of the management (cost) accountant;
- Explain the relationship between management and financial accounting.

Introduction

Information is vital in order to make good decisions and to manage effectively. This information is useful only if it is accurate, up to date and relevant.

Management involves **planning**, **organising**, **controlling** and **decision-making**.

Planning: the setting of short-term and long-term goals and the policies decided on to achieve these goals.

Organising: putting the plans into action by co-ordinating the various activities and departments within the business.

Controlling: keeping a watchful eye on the plans and policies, making sure that the targets set are achieved and that corrective action is taken if necessary.

Decision-making: deciding among the different possible courses of action. This might involve, for example, sensitivity analysis (see Chapter 23).

DEFINITION

Management accounting is the area of accounting concerned with providing the management of a business with information which will form the basis on which they can make better-informed decisions.

Role of the management (cost) accountant

The management (cost) accountant will be involved in such areas as:

- trying to find the total cost of producing a single unit of product
- trying to the find the cost of running each department – for example, the finishing department, the production department, the polishing department
- trying to budget for the future costs of production and therefore selling prices
- the use of 'what if' or variance analysis to foresee and examine the different outcomes at different levels of production, different selling prices, different fixed costs, etc.
- controlling actual finances as against budget, rectifying any differences that may arise and trying to establish the causes of these variances.

Uses of management accounting information

- The information aids management in comparing actual costs with budgeted costs in order to control costs.
- The actual cost per unit can be used to find and fix selling prices.
- Budgeting is an essential tool in the planning, co-ordinating and controlling of the various activities of the business. It helps to show clearly what targets need to be achieved to the whole team.
- **Variance analysis** is used to show areas where actual costs are not in line with budgeted costs and identify where corrective action needs to be taken (see Chapter 24).
- It aids in capital investment appraisal and therefore ensures that the best use is made of funds available for investment. It will also determine whether growth can be achieved while ensuring that the risks to profitability are kept at acceptable levels.

20

The relationship between management and financial accounting

Financial accounting is concerned with recording, classifying and summarising transactions that have taken place. It reports on the effects of these transactions over the accounting period and various financial statements are produced, including standardised trading, profit and loss accounts, cash flow statements and balance sheets. It presents a true and fair view of the state of affairs of the business at the end of accounting period.

Management accounting, however, is concerned with the monitoring and controlling of the activities of the company and internal future planning and decision-making.

Management accounting *v* Financial accounting

Criterion	Management	Financial
Time	**Future** – focuses on future decisions such as selling price and production levels, trying to establish items for future accounting periods.	**Past** – records what happened in the previous accounting period, e.g. sales and purchases for the past year.
Users	**Internal** – management accounting information is primarily used by managers of each department, as well as the managing director.	**Internal and external** – financial accounting information is used by both internal and external users, such as potential shareholders.

Continued >

Criterion	Management	Financial
Frequency of reports	**Regular** – management accounting statements tend to be produced quarterly, half-yearly or monthly, e.g. cash budgets every six months or as often as the managers require them.	**Yearly** – financial statements are prepared on an annual basis, e.g. trading, profit and loss account for the year ended.
Information	**Departmental** – management accounting is done on a departmental basis, e.g. the production department, the marketing department, the sales budget.	**Total/overall** – financial reports are prepared for the business as a whole unit.
Regulation	**No legal requirements** – firms can prepare their management accounts in their own style.	**Legal requirements** – standards and presentation set down by Financial Reporting Statements (FRS) and Statements of Standard Accounting Practice (SSAPs).

In summary

- Management accounting is forward-looking; financial accounting records past events.
- Management accounting has an internal focus; financial accounting had both an internal and external focus.
- Management accounting reports are prepared regularly; financial accounts are prepared usually on an annual basis.
- Management accounting is micro accounting. financial accounting is macro accounting.
- Management accounting is not governed by legal requirements; financial accounting is.

Theory

Q1 Outline the role of the management accountant in an organisation.

Q2 What are the main uses of management accounting information?

Q3 What is the relationship between financial accounting and management accounting?

20

Exam Tip

- Know your theory extremely well.

21 Cost Classification

Objectives

On completion students should be able to:

- Classify costs under the various headings;
- Explain controllable, uncontrollable and period costs;
- Graphically represent costs;
- Separate mixed costs into fixed and variable elements.

The role of the management accountant is to gather information about costs. This information is more useful if it is classified. The type of classification is determined by the purpose for which it is required. This purpose is called the **cost objective**.

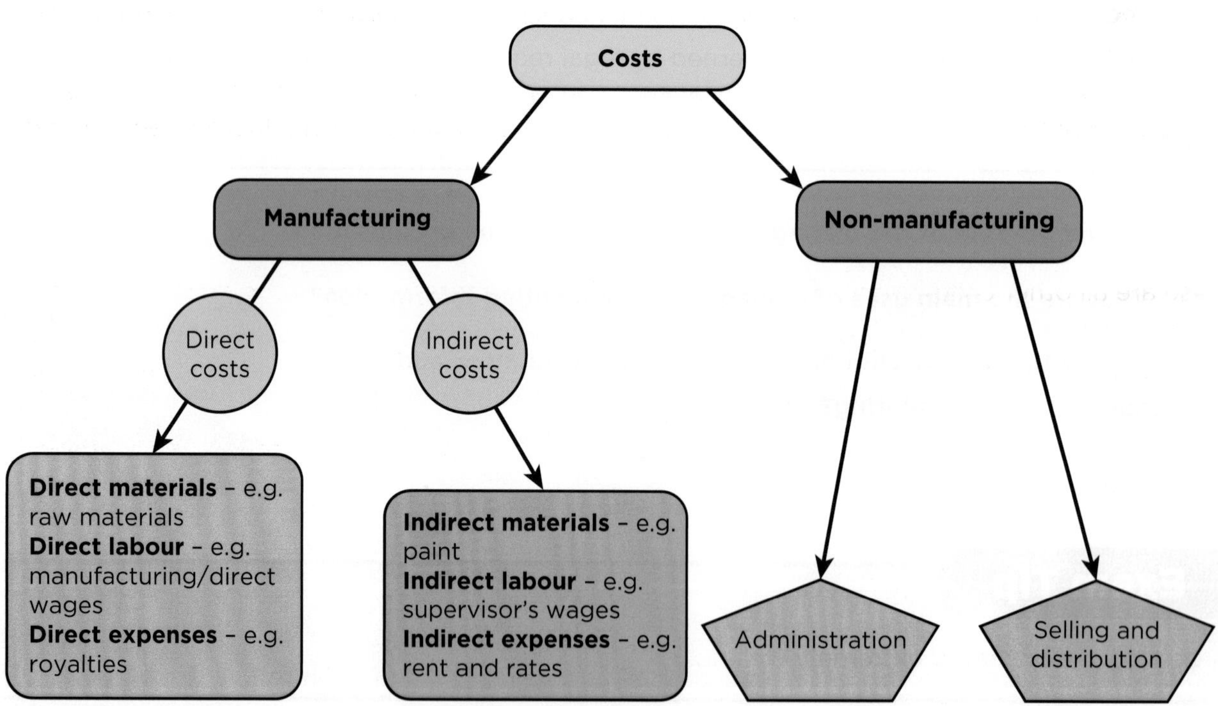

Manufacturing costs

The total cost of manufacturing a product consists of both direct and indirect costs.

Direct costs

Direct costs are those that are directly linked to a particular product or service. These costs are:

- **Direct materials** - raw materials used **directly** in the manufacturing process - for example, timber used in making tables.
- **Direct labour** - direct wages and manufacturing wages that can be **traced to each unit produced** - for example, where employees are paid on a piece rate (€x for each unit produced).
- **Direct expenses** - an expense that can be **traced to each unit produced** - for example, €1 paid in royalties for each unit produced or for the hire of special machines.

Indirect costs (overheads)

Indirect costs, or overheads, are costs which are **not directly linked** to the product or service. These costs must be included in the overall cost of production but cannot be traced directly to each unit produced. They include:

- **Indirect materials** - materials used in the production process but **difficult to quantify** - for example, varnish for varnishing the tables; lubricants.
- **Indirect labour** - for example, where employees are paid on a **time basis** or receive a salary (e.g. supervisor's wages).
- **Indirect expenses** - all other costs involved in the manufacturing process that **cannot be traced directly** - for example, light and heat, depreciation of machinery, factory rent and rates.

Non-manufacturing costs

These are all other costs involved in the running of the business outside of the manufacturing process. These can be classified as:

- **Selling and distribution** - overheads associated with the **sale and distribution of goods** - for example, delivery expenses, advertising, sales commission, showroom expenses.
- **Administration overheads** - overheads associated with **running the business** - for example, office expenses, office light and heat, depreciation of office equipment.

21

Fixed and variable costs

Costs can be further classified as **fixed** or **variable**.

All direct costs are variable but production overheads can have fixed and variable elements.

- A **fixed cost** is a cost which must be incurred regardless of the level of activity. Examples include depreciation of fixed assets, insurance for the year, fixed interest on a mortgage, rent and rates. **A fixed cost does not change as output increases.**
- A **variable cost** is one which increases as the level of activity increases. The more you produce the more in total it will cost. Examples include direct materials, direct labour and direct expenses. **Variable costs will change in total as output increases.**

Further cost classifications

Other classifications of costs include:

- **Controllable costs** *(Higher Level only)* are costs that can be controlled by the manager of a cost centre. She/he will make the decision about the amount of the cost or if the cost should be incurred and can be held responsible for variances in these costs. All variable costs are controllable. For example, commission to sales personnel can be controlled by the sales manager.
- **Uncontrollable costs** *(Higher Level only)* are costs over which the manager of a cost centre has no control and therefore cannot be held responsible for variances in them. For example, rates charged by the local authority are uncontrollable.
- **Period costs** relate to the accounting period rather than the level of production. These are primarily fixed costs and do not change with the level of activity - for example, insurance, rent and rates.
- **Mixed costs** are costs which have a fixed and a variable cost element - for example, telephone with line rental fixed and then charged per unit used.

Graphical presentation of costs

1. Fixed Costs

Fixed costs remain the same irrespective of the level of output.

Examples include:

- Rent
- Supervisor's salary
- Straight-line depreciation.

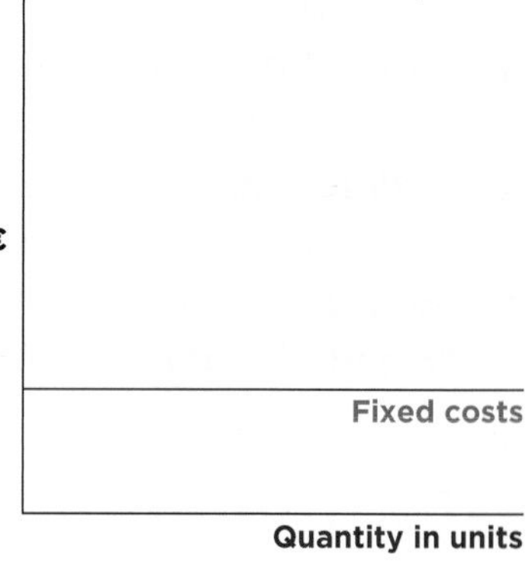

21

2. Variable costs

Variable costs vary directly with the level of production.

Example: 1 unit = €20
10 units = €200
50 units = €1,000

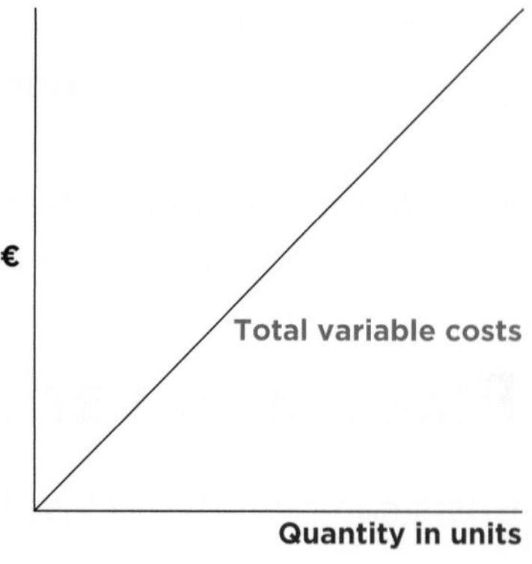

3. Step-fixed costs (Higher Level only)

In the long term all fixed costs are variable. Moreover, they only remain fixed within certain levels of activity. For example, if a machine is hired at €5,000 and has a capacity to produce 1,000 units, then if production reaches 1,001 units a second machine will have to be hired at another cost of €5,000.

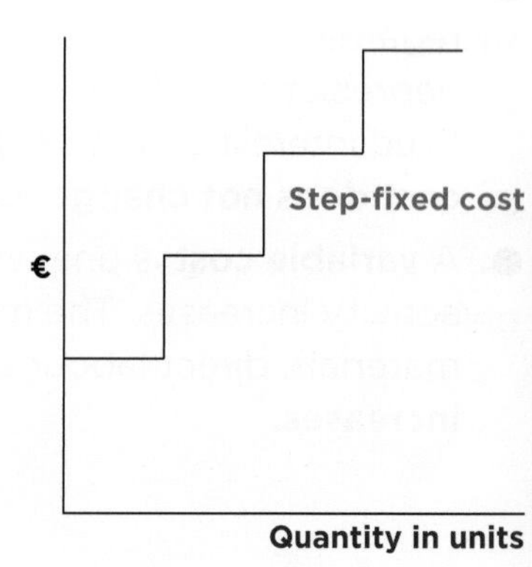

4. Step-variable costs (Higher Level only)

Variable costs can also be incurred in steps – for example, economies of scale, where discounts are given for bulk buying.

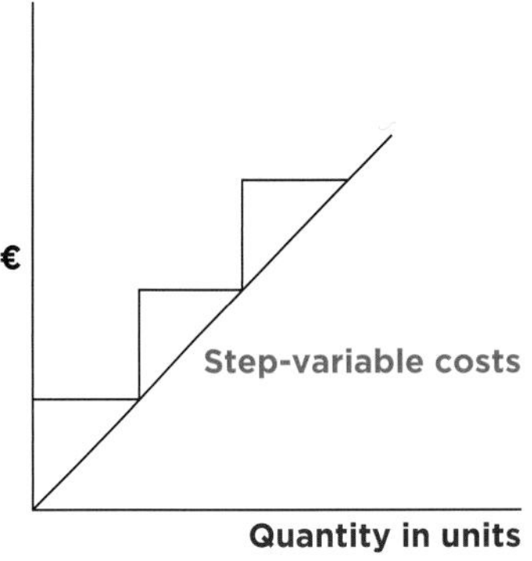

5. Mixed costs (Higher Level only)

These costs contain both a mixed part and a variable part – for example, an electricity bill is made up of a standing charge and a per-unit charge.

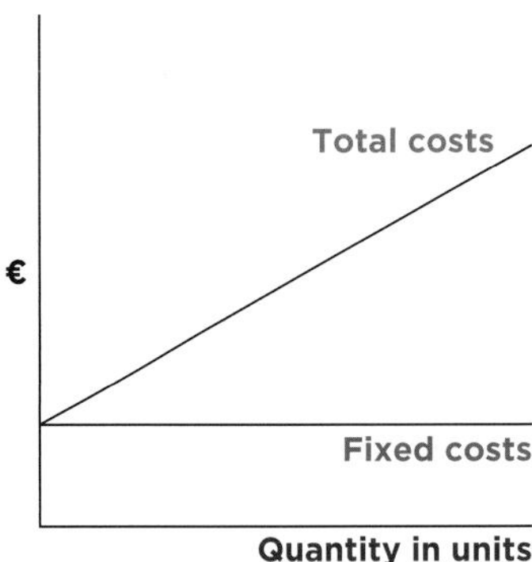

Separation of mixed costs into fixed and variable elements (Higher Level)

Mixed costs can be separated into their fixed and variable elements by using records of costs from previous periods and comparing them.

To separate mixed costs into fixed and variable elements we use what is known as the **high–low method**.

High–low method

Example

C. Lynch Ltd incurred the following costs during the month of October 20-1:

Week	Units of output	Total cost €
1	35,000	235,000
2	32,000	217,000
3	38,000	253,000
4	37,000	247,000

Separate the above costs into fixed and variable elements.

Solution

To solve this problem we use the high-low method.

Step 1

Take the highest and lowest level of output and their associated costs. Find the difference between them.

	Output	Cost €
Week 3 (high)	38,000	253,000
Week 2 (low)	32,000	217,000
Difference	6,000	36,000

21

Step 2

Use the following formula to work out the variable cost per unit:

$$\frac{\textbf{Difference in cost}}{\textbf{Difference in units}}$$

NOTE

This can be done at any level of activity and not just at the highest and lowest values.

Difference in cost is €36,000. Difference in units is 6,000. So:

$$\frac{36{,}000}{6{,}000} = \textbf{€6 variable cost}$$

Step 3

Now **substitute** this back into the total cost to find the fixed element.

	Total cost	-	Variable cost	=	Fixed costs
Highest level	253,000	-	228,000 (38,000 x 6)	=	**€25,000**
Lowest level	217,000	-	192,000 (32,000 x 6)	=	**€25,000**

The level of fixed costs **must be the same** when you substitute back the variable cost per unit.

Exercises – Higher level

21

Q1 **Tom Kehoe Ltd manufactures chips for the electronics industry. The following costs relate to different levels of activity.**

Output levels	8,000 units	13,000 units	14,500 units	15,000 units
Costs	**€**	**€**	**€**	**€**
Production overheads	100,000	145,000	158,500	163,000
Other overheads	60,000	85,000	92,500	95,000

You are required to:

- **Separate production overheads into fixed and variable elements.**
- **Separate other overheads into fixed and variable elements.**
- **Calculate the total cost of production overheads and other overheads at 11,000 units.**

Q2 **Edgar Morrissey Ltd manufactures steel shutters. The following costs relate to different levels of activity.**

Output levels	5,000 units	9,000 units	12,000 units	14,000 units
Costs	**€**	**€**	**€**	**€**
Production overheads	39,500	57,500	71,000	80,000
Other overheads	14,500	24,500	32,000	37,000

You are required to:

- **Separate production overheads into fixed and variable elements.**
- **Separate other overheads into fixed and variable elements.**
- **Calculate the total cost of production overheads and other overheads at 10,200 units.**

Q3 **Adele Murphy Ltd manufactures iPad stands and speakers. The following are the costs related to certain levels of activity.**

Output levels	7,500 units	9,000 units	10,500 units	12,000 units
Costs	€	€	€	€
Production overheads	23,000	26,900	30,800	34,700
Other overheads	11,000	12,200	13,400	14,600

You are required to:

- Separate production overheads into fixed and variable elements.
- Separate other overheads into fixed and variable elements.
- Calculate the total cost of production overheads and other overheads at maximum capacity if 10,500 units is 70% of the plant's capacity.

Q4 **Cricket Ltd manufactures components for the dairy industry. The following budgets have been prepared at 40%, 65%, 80% and 90% of the plant's capacity.**

Output levels	7,200 units (40%)	11,700 units (65%)	14,400 units (80%)	16,200 units (90%)
Costs	€	€	€	€
Production overheads	39,360	56,460	66,720	73,560
Other overheads	17,160	24,135	28,320	31,110

You are required to:

- Separate production overheads into fixed and variable elements.
- Separate other overheads into fixed and variable elements.
- Calculate the total cost of production overheads and other overheads at 100% capacity.
- Calculate the total cost of production overheads and other overheads at 25% capacity.

Q5 **Tiger plc manufactures a single component for the computer industry. The following production costs and output levels have been recorded for April, May and June 20-2.**

Output levels	24,000 units 60%	32,000 units 80%	36,000 units 90%
Direct materials	468,000	624,000	702,000
Direct labour	432,000	576,000	648,000
Production overheads	118,800	153,000	170,160
Other overheads	142,560	187,440	209,880
Administration expenses	80,000	80,000	80,000

You are required to:

- Separate production overheads into fixed and variable elements.
- Separate other overheads into fixed and variable elements.
- Find the number of units produced when the company operates at full capacity and all the costs incurred if Tiger plc was operating at full capacity.

Q6 **Draw a graph of step-fixed costs using the following payments at output levels shown.**

Hire of machines €	10,000	15,000	20,000	25,000
Output units	5,000	10,000	15,000	20,000

21

Theory

Q1 Explain the difference between:

(a) Direct and indirect cost

(b) Fixed and variable cost

(c) Controllable and uncontrollable cost.

Q2 Explain what is meant by a step-fixed cost and give one example.

Q3 Explain with examples:

(a) Mixed cost

(b) Period cost

(c) Non-manufacturing cost.

Q4 Graphically represent the following costs, giving an example of each:

(a) Fixed cost

(b) Step-fixed cost

(c) Mixed cost.

Exam Tips

- Be able to draw diagrams to represent costs.
- Make sure you draw and label all diagrams properly and to scale.
- Use the high–low method when asked to separate costs into fixed and variable elements.
- The high–low method is also asked about in other topics, e.g. flexible budgets.

21

22 Product Costing

Objectives

On completion students should be able to:

- Explain the purpose of product costing;
- Find the value of closing stock;
- Explain absorption costing and overhead recovery;
- Understand the three A's – absorption, apportionment and allocation;
- Calculate overhead absorption rates;
- Apportion and reapportion overheads;
- Cost a product;
- Show the effect of under- and over-absorption on profit.

Introduction

Product costing is the process of finding how much it costs to produce one unit of product. In order to do this one must collect and collate all the costs that are relevant to that product.

DEFINITION

A **product** is an item produced in a manufacturing concern.

Job costing

Job costing is carrying out work specifically at the request of a customer. This can be an individual item – for example, a tailor-made suit – or a batch of similar items – for example, Aer Lingus ordering five new planes from Airbus.

Each job will consist of direct materials, direct labour, direct expenses and overhead costs.

Reasons for product costing

1. **To set selling price** – the selling price of a product must reflect the cost of producing the product along with an anticipated profit.
2. **Control of costs** – to control costs it is necessary to compare budgeted costs with actual costs.
3. **Stock valuation** – in order to be able to complete the final accounts at the end of the financial period, it is necessary to know the value of opening and closing stock.
4. **To aid the planning and decision-making process.**

NOTE

When deciding on the selling price for a product it is necessary to work from budgeted and not actual figures.
Cost price + Profit = Selling price

Part A: Stock valuation

Stock valuation is important to both financial and management accounting.

Stocks should be valued at the **lower** of cost or net realisable value. The cost will normally be the lower but this may not always be the case. Sometimes it may be difficult to find out the exact cost of raw materials used in the production process – for example, where raw materials were purchased on different dates and at different prices.

Overvaluing stock will distort profits.

FIFO – first in, first out

This method of stock valuation assumes that the first items received into stock are the first items to be issued to production. For example, in the production of ice cream, the first stock of milk received from the creamery will be the first stock to be issued to the production process. Under this method the closing stock value will be at its most recent price.

Example 1

The following is the information for the receipts and issues of stock for the month of August 20-9:

August 1	Opening stock	4,000 units @ €2 each
August 3	Received	2,000 units @ €2 each
August 5	Received	1,000 units @ €2.20 each
August 10	Issued	3,300 units
August 12	Received	1,500 units @ €2.30 each
August 18	Issued	1,100 units
August 23	Received	2,000 units @ €2.40 each
August 26	Issued	1,800 units

(a) Calculate using FIFO the value of stock issued during August.

(b) Calculate using FIFO the value of closing stock on 31 August 20-9.

Solution

Using stores ledger card:

22

	Receipts			Issues			Stock (on hand)	
Date	**Quantity**	**Price €**	**Total €**	**Quantity**	**Price €**	**Total €**	**Quantity**	**Total €**
Aug 1	4,000	2.00	8,000				4,000	8,000
Aug 3	2,000	2.00	4,000				6,000	12,000
Aug 5	1,000	2.20	2,200				7,000	14,200
Aug 10				3,300	2.00	6,600	3,700	7,600
Aug 12	1,500	2.30	3,450				5,200	11,050
Aug 18				1,100	2.00	2,200	4,100	8,850
Aug 23	2,000	2.40	4,800				6,100	13,650
Aug 26				1,600	2.00	3,200		
				200	2.20	440	4,300	10,010
Total	10,500		22,450	6,200		12,440		

Value of stock issued: **€12,440**

Value of closing stock: **€10,010**

Example 2

Maddison Ltd had an opening stock of 1,800 units at €10 each on 1/1/20-6. The following are the details of the purchases and sales for the year ended 31/12/20-6:

Period	Credit purchases	Credit sales	Cash sales
1 Jan. - 31 March	1,200 units @ €10 each	800 units @ €20 each	400 units @ €20 each
1 Apr. - 30 June	3,000 units @ €12 each	1,100 units @ €22 each	1,000 units @ €20 each
1 July - 30 Sept.	7,000 units @ €14 each	4,000 units @ €26 each	1,000 units @ €24 each
1 Oct. - 31 Dec.	7,000 units @ €16 each	6,000 units @ €36 each	1,200 units @ €24 each

You are required to:

(a) Calculate the value of closing stock using FIFO.

(b) Prepare a trading account for the year ended 31/12/20-6:

Solution

(a) Closing stock

Always check that the purchase price is less than the selling price, as stock is valued at the lower of cost or net realisable value.

Step 1 Calculate the units received including opening stock.

1,800 + 1,200 + 3,000 + 7,000 + 7,000 = 20,000 units received

Step 2 Calculate the units issued (cash and credit).

1,200 + 2,100 + 5,000 + 7,200 = 15,500 units issued

Step 3 Subtract the issued from the received.

20,000 - 15,500 = 4,500 units left in stock

Step 4 Value stock working backwards until you reach 4,500 units

Closing stock: 4,500 @ €16 each = **€72,000**

(b) Trading account of Maddison Ltd for the year ended 31/12/20-6

	€	€
Sales (W1)		441,000
***Less* Cost of sales**		
Opening stock (1,800 x €10)	18,000	
Purchases (W2)	258,000	
Cost of goods available	276,000	
Less Closing stock	(72,000)	
Cost of goods sold		(204,000)
Gross profit		**237,000**

22

Workings

W1 Sales

Multiply all the issued units by the selling price.

(2,200 x 20) + (1,100 x 22) + (4,000 x 26) + (2,200 x 24) + (6,000 x 36) = **€441,000**

W2 Purchases

Total all the receipts.

(1,200 x 10) + (3,000 x 12) + (7,000 x 14) + (7,000 x 16) = **€258,000**

Exercises – Ordinary Level

Q1 The following is the record of receipts and issue of stock item no. 64 for the month of October 20-0:

Date	Receipts	Units	Unit price	Issued units
Oct. 1	Opening stock	2,500	€6.00	
Oct. 4	Receipts	1,500	€6.20	
Oct. 6	Receipts	3,000	€6.20	
Oct. 10	Issued			4,000
Oct. 23	Receipts	1,200	€7.00	
Oct. 29	Issued			2,200

You are required to:

- **Calculate using FIFO the value of stock issued during October.**
- **Calculate using FIFO the value of closing stock.**

Q2 The following is the record of receipts and issue of stock item no. ZD5 for the month of May 20-6:

Date	Receipts	Units	Unit price	Issued units
May 1	Opening stock	3,000	€3.00	
May 8	Receipts	3,500	€3.30	
May 10	Receipts	2,000	€3.60	
May 12	Issued			7,000
May 24	Receipts	3,000	€4.00	
May 31	Issued			3,500

You are required to:

- **Calculate using FIFO the value of stock issued during May.**
- **Calculate using FIFO the value of closing stock.**

Exercises – Higher Level

Q1 **Cassie Ltd had an opening stock of 2,200 units at €9 each on 1/1/20-9. The following are the details of the purchases and sales for the year ended 31/12/20-9:**

Period	Credit purchases	Credit sales	Cash sales
1 Jan. - 31 March	1,700 units @ €10 each	1,000 units @ €12 each	1,500 units @ €12 each
1 Apr. - 30 June	1,600 units @ €11 each	1,200 units @ €15 each	900 units @ €16 each
1 July - 30 Sept.	1,800 units @ €12 each	900 units @ €16 each	500 units @ €16 each
1 Oct. - 31 Dec.	2,000 units @ €13 each	1,200 units @ €17 each	950 units @ €17 each

You are required to:

- **Calculate the value of closing stock using FIFO.**
- **Prepare a trading account for the year ended 31/12/20-9.**

Q2 **Cropper Ltd had an opening stock of 1,900 units at €7 each on 1/1/20-5. The following are the details of the purchases and sales for the year ended 31/12/20-5:**

Period	Credit purchases	Credit sales	Cash sales
1 Jan. - 31 March	2,200 units @ €7 each	1,100 units @ €10 each	2,200 units @ €11 each
1 Apr. - 30 June	2,500 units @ €8 each	800 units @ €11 each	1,100 units @ €12 each
1 July - 30 Sept.	3,000 units @ €9 each	2,100 units @ €12 each	1,600 units @ €13 each
1 Oct. - 31 Dec.	3,100 units @ €11 each	1,500 units @ €12 each	600 units @ €13 each

You are required to:

- **Calculate the value of closing stock using FIFO.**
- **Prepare a trading account for the year ended 31/12/20-5.**

Q3 **Haley Ltd had an opening stock of 800 units at €6 each on 1/1/20-7. The following are the details of the purchases and sales for the year ended 31/12/20-7:**

Period	Credit purchases	Credit sales	Cash sales
1 Jan. - 31 March	2,400 units @ €6 each	600 units @ €12 each	1,200 units @ €12 each
1 Apr. - 30 June	2,800 units @ €7 each	900 units @ €11 each	1,000 units @ €11 each
1 July - 30 Sept.	3,900 units @ €8 each	1,000 units @ €12 each	1,500 units @ €13 each
1 Oct. - 31 Dec.	1,500 units @ €9 each	1,400 units @ €14 each	1,100 units @ €15 each

You are required to:

- **Calculate the value of closing stock using FIFO.**
- **Prepare a trading account for the year ended 31/12/20-7.**

22

Q4 **The following information relates to the purchases and sales (exclusive of VAT) of Baldwin Ltd for the year ended 31/12/20-2:**

Period beginning	Purchases	Sales on credit	Cash sales
1/1/20-2	3,400 @ €4.50 each	1,000 @ €6 each	1,900 @ €5 each
1/5/20-2	2,500 @ €5.00 each	1,200 @ €7.50 each	1,400 @ €7 each
1/9/20-2	1,600 @ €5.50 each	800 @ €8 each	500 @ €7.50 each

On 1/1/20-2 there was an opening stock of 600 units at €4.00 each.

You are required to:

- Calculate the value of closing stock, using first in, first out basis.
- Prepare a trading account for the year ended 31/12/20-2.

Q5 **The following information relates to the purchases and sales (exclusive of VAT) of Bridge Ltd for the year ended 31/12/20-3:**

Period beginning	Purchases	Sales on credit	Cash sales
1/1/20-3	2,000 @ €6 each	1,200 @ €8 each	1,000 @ €7.50 each
1/4/20-3	3,500 @ €7 each	2,400 @ €9 each	1,200 @ €8.50 each
1/7/20-3	4,000 @ €8 each	1,400 @ €10 each	1,200 @ €9.50 each
1/10/20-3	2,000 @ €9 each	1,800 @ €11 each	800 @ €10 each

On 1/1/20-3 there was an opening stock of 1,000 units at €5 each.

You are required to:

- Calculate the value of closing stock, using first in, first out basis.
- Prepare a trading account for the year ended 31/12/20-3.

22

Part B: Absorption Costing

When costing a product, both direct and indirect costs must be included. The direct costs can be allocated precisely to a product but indirect costs can't. Therefore these indirect costs must be divided up in a fair manner in order to include them in the cost of the product.

Absorption costing is the process of ensuring that the indirect costs of production are brought into the final cost of producing a product. It is sometimes referred to as **full costing** because it includes indirect fixed costs when calculating the cost of production.

Under absorption costing, the fixed overheads such as rent and other indirect costs are absorbed into the cost of the product. This process is called **overhead recovery**.

Overhead recovery can be done in three different ways - absorption, apportionment and allocation - the three A's.

1. Absorption

Overhead absorption means that the fixed overhead costs are included (absorbed) in the cost of producing a product. This is done by calculating pre-determined overhead absorption rates (OAR). These are usually calculated:

- per direct labour hour
- per machine hour
- per unit produced.

Note that the overhead absorption rate is based on the **budgeted figures** for the year and **not** the actual figures. This is because the actual figures may not be known until the end of the year.

NOTE

The overhead absorption rate is based on the **dominant activity**, e.g. labour hours in labour-intensive production processes.

Example calculation of an overhead absorption rate

Enterprise Ltd estimates (budgets) that the fixed production overheads for 20-8 will be €45,000 and during the year it will produce 9,000 units of product A which will incur 4,500 direct labour hours and 5,000 machine hours.

Direct labour hour $\frac{\text{Budgeted overheads}}{\text{Budgeted labour hours}} = \frac{45,000}{4,500} =$ €10 per direct labour hour

Machine hour $\frac{\text{Budgeted overheads}}{\text{Budgeted machine hours}} = \frac{45,000}{5,000} =$ €9 per machine hour

Per unit $\frac{\text{Budgeted overheads}}{\text{Budgeted units}} = \frac{45,000}{9,000} =$ €5 per unit produced

When a business produces a standard product (where all the units are of the same specification) each method of overhead absorption would give the same result for the overhead to be absorbed. However, if different products are being produced, for example shirts and ties, then using the labour hour or machine hour rate will be more suitable than a rate

22

per unit because the product that takes more time to produce will absorb more of the fixed overheads.

Sample Ordinary Level question

Absorption costing

Gigo Ltd is a small jobbing company that has the following budgeted costs for the coming year.

Direct materials	€252,800
Direct labour	€89,600
Factory overheads	€134,400

For the coming year, the company has also budgeted 11,200 labour hours and 19,200 machine hours.

The details of a customer's job number 65B are as follows:

Direct materials	€16,000
Direct labour	270 hours
Machine hours	400 hours

You are required to calculate:

(a) the overhead absorption rate per machine hour

(b) the overhead absorption rate per direct labour hour

(c) the cost of job number 65B using the overhead absorption rate per machine hour

(d) the cost of job number 65B using the overhead absorption rate per direct labour hour

(e) the selling price of job number 65B to the customer using both overhead absorption rates as calculated in (a) and (b) above and assuming a mark-up of 25% on cost.

Solution

(a) Overhead absorption rate per machine hour

$$\frac{\text{Budgeted overheads}}{\text{Budgeted hours}} = \frac{134{,}400}{19{,}200} = \textbf{€7} \text{ per machine hour}$$

(b) Overhead absorption rate per direct labour hour

22

$$\frac{\text{Budgeted overheads}}{\text{Budgeted hours}} = \frac{134{,}400}{11{,}200} = \textbf{€12} \text{ per direct labour hour}$$

(c) & (d) Cost of job number 65B

		Machine hours €	Labour hours €
	Direct materials	16,000.00	16,000.00
	Labour (89,600/11,200 = €8) 270 x 8	2,160.00	2,160.00
	Overheads using machine hours 400 x 7	2,800.00	
	Overheads using labour hours 270 x 12		3,240.00
	Total cost	**20,960.00**	**21,400.00**
(e)	Mark up 25%	5,240.00	5,350.00
	Selling price	**26,200.00**	**26,750.00**

Sample Higher Level question

OAR calculation and absorption costing

The monthly budgeted overheads for three departments of Ridge Enterprises are as follows:

	Variable €	Fixed €
Department 1	60,000	30,000
Department 2	20,000	10,000
Department 3	30,000	20,000

Ridge Enterprises estimates (budgets) that direct labour hours for each department are: Dept. 1 – 20,000 hours; Dept. 2 – 10,000 hours; and Dept. 3 – 5,000 hours.

(a) Calculate the overhead absorption rates for each department based on direct labour hours.

(b) If job no. 1961 spends 5 hours in Dept. 1, 12 hours in Dept. 2 and 3 hours in Dept. 3, calculate the total overheads to be absorbed by job no. 1961.

Solution

(a) Overhead absorption rates

	Variable	Fixed
Department 1	60,000/20,000 = €3 per hour	30,000/20,000 = **€1.50** per hour
Department 2	20,000/10,000 = €2 per hour	10,000/10,000 = **€1** per hour
Department 3	30,000/5,000 = €6 per hour	20,000/5,000 = **€4** per hour

(b) Job no. 1961

Department 1	Variable	5 x €3	€15.00	
	Fixed	5 x €1.50	€7.50	€22.50
Department 2	Variable	12 x €2	€24.00	
	Fixed	12 x €1	€12.00	€36.00
Department 3	Variable	3 x €6	€18.00	
	Fixed	3 x €4	€12.00	€30.00
Total overheads				**€88.50**

22

Under/over-absorption

Overhead absorption rates are based on budgeted figures (as the actual figures are not available). Businesses cannot wait until the actual figures are ready as they would not be able to calculate the selling price of the products as well as the actual costs involved in producing the products.

Under-absorption occurs when actual overheads are greater than the budgeted figures.

Over-absorption occurs when actual overheads are less than the budgeted figures.

NOTE

When the actual figures are prepared, then they are compared to the budgeted figures.

Example

The following information refers to the budgeted and actual costs of Frankie Ltd:

Budgeted	Direct labour hours	Machine hours	Total overheads €
Department 1	9,600	42,000	168,000
Department 2	54,000	12,000	43,200
Department 3	24,000		48,000
Actual	**Direct labour hours**	**Machine hours**	**Total overheads €**
Department 1	12,000	48,000	186,000
Department 2	44,400	18,000	36,000
Department 3	30,000		54,000

You are required to:

(a) Calculate departmental overhead absorption rates for Departments 1, 2 and 3.

(b) Show the under/over-absorption by department and in total for the period. Explain your answer.

Solution

(a) Departmental absorption rates

Department 1

$$\frac{168{,}000}{42{,}000}$$

= **€4.00** per machine hour

Department 2

$$\frac{43{,}200}{54{,}000}$$

= **€0.80** per direct labour hour

Department 3

$$\frac{48{,}000}{24{,}000}$$

= **€2** per direct labour hour

(b) Under/over-absorption

	Department 1	Department 2	Department 3	Total
Actual overheads	186,000	36,000	54,000	276,000
Overhead absorbed	192,000	35,520	60,000	287,520
Over/under absorbed	**6,000**	**(480)**	**6,000**	**11,520**
Workings	48,000 x 4 = 192,000	44,400 x 0.80 = 35,520	30,000 x 2 = 60,000	

22

Department 1: Costs incurred were €6,000 less than budgeted and therefore profits are €6,000 greater than expected.

Department 2: Costs incurred were €480 more than budgeted and therefore profits are €480 less than expected.

Department 3: Costs incurred were €6,000 less than budgeted and therefore profits are €6,000 greater than expected.

Overall costs incurred were €11,520 less than budgeted and therefore profits are €11,520 greater than expected.

2. Apportionment

Apportionment is the term used when dividing overheads which cannot be specifically identified with any one department. Overheads are divided among the different cost centres or departments using an equitable basis of apportionment.

The most common bases used for apportionment of overheads include:

- **Number of employees** Examples: Factory canteen, uniform costs
- **Volume in cubic metres** Examples: Light and heat of factory
- **Floor area (space)** Examples: Insurance, cleaning, etc.
- **Actual** Examples: Materials and direct labour
- **Book value or cost** Examples: Depreciation of machines, buildings, etc.

Reapportionment is where service department costs are allocated among the main production departments. Service departments are secondary to production and cannot recover costs. Therefore overheads can only be recovered through production, that is by being included as part of the cost of production.

Sample Ordinary Level question

The following information relates to Griffin Ltd for the coming year. The company had two production departments, 1 and 2, and one service department, A.

	Department 1	Department 2	Service A
Overheads costs	€20,000	€15,000	€14,000
Service A to be apportioned	80%	20%	
Machine hours	2,000 hours		
Labour hours		2,500 hours	

The details of a customer's job number 5H are as follows:

Direct materials	€2,400
Direct labour	€5,100
Hours in Dept 1	24 Hours
Hours in Dept 2	18 hours

You are required to:

(a) Apportion the costs of the service department between Departments 1 and 2.

(b) Calculate the overhead absorption for Department 1 using machine hours.

(c) Calculate the overhead absorption for Department 2 using labour hours.

(d) Calculate the cost of job number 5H.

(e) Calculate the selling price of job number 5H if mark-up is 25% of cost.

Solution

(a)

		Dept 1		Dept 2
Overhead costs		€20,000		€15,000
Service department	(14,000 x 80%)	**€11,200**	(14,000 x 20%)	**€2,800**
Total		€31,200		€17,800

22

(b) 31,200/2,000	=	**€15.60**	per machine hour
(c) 17,800/2,500	=	**€7.12**	per direct labour hour
(d) Direct materials		€2,400.00	
Direct labour		€5,100.00	
Department 1		€374.40	(24 x 15.60)
Department 2		€128.16	(18 x 7.12)
Total cost		**€8,002.56**	
(e) €8,002.56 x 1.25	=		**€10,003.20**

3. Allocation

This is used where overhead costs can be specifically identified and charged to a particular department (cost centre) and these overhead costs are allocated to that department.

Sample Higher Level question

Job costing (including an overhead analysis sheet)

Oggy Ltd has three departments: Purchasing, Production and Finishing. The following costs relate to 20-3.

	Total €	Purchasing €	Production €	Finishing €
Indirect materials	360,000	200,000	100,000	60,000
Indirect labour	230,000	100,000	90,000	40,000
Machine maintenance	60,000			
Plant depreciation	45,000			
Rent and rates	72,000			
Light and heat	52,500			
Factory canteen	28,000			

The following information relates to the three departments:

	Total	Purchasing €	Production €	Finishing €
Floor space (m²)	24,000	12,000	8,000	4,000
Volume (m³)	35,000	21,000	7,000	7,000
Plant valuation €	180,000	80,000	60,000	40,000
Machine hours	15,000	6,000	5,000	4,000
Employees	40	20	8	12
Labour hours	21,000	4,000	10,000	7,000

Job number 311 has just been completed. The details are:

	Direct materials €	Direct labour €	Machine hours	Labour hours
Purchasing	11,000	9,000	58	50
Production	10,900	4,500	35	90
Finishing	12,000	6,700	10	35

The company budgets for a profit margin of 25%.

You are required to:

(a) Calculate the overheads to be absorbed by each department, stating clearly the basis of apportionment used.

(b) Calculate a suitable overhead absorption rate for each department.

(c) Calculate the selling price of job number 311.

Solution

(a) Overhead analysis sheet

Overhead	Basis of apportionment	Total €	Purchasing €	Production €	Finishing €
Indirect materials	Actual	360,000	200,000	100,000	60,000
Indirect labour	Actual	230,000	100,000	90,000	40,000
Machine maintenance	Machine hours	60,000	24,000	20,000	16,000
Plant depreciation	Plant valuation	45,000	20,000	15,000	10,000
Rent and rates	Floor space	72,000	36,000	24,000	12,000
Light and heat	Volume	52,500	31,500	10,500	10,500
Factory canteen	Number of employees	28,000	14,000	5,600	8,400
Total overhead		847,500	425,500	265,100	156,900

(b) Overhead absorption rates for each department

Purchasing $\frac{\text{Budgeted overheads}}{\text{Budgeted machine hours}} = \frac{425{,}500}{6{,}000} =$ **€70.92** per machine hour

Production $\frac{\text{Budgeted overheads}}{\text{Budgeted labour hours}} = \frac{265{,}100}{10{,}000} =$ **€26.51** per direct labour hour

Finishing $\frac{\text{Budgeted overheads}}{\text{Budgeted labour hours}} = \frac{156{,}900}{7{,}000} =$ **€22.41** per direct labour hour

(c) Selling price of job number 311

	€	€
Direct materials		
Purchasing	11,000.00	
Production	10,900.00	
Finishing	12,000.00	33,900.00
Direct labour		
Purchasing	9,000.00	
Production	4,500.00	
Finishing	6,700.00	20,200.00
Overheads		
Purchasing (58 x 70.92)	4,113.36	
Production (90 x 26.51)	2,385.90	
Finishing (35 x 22.41)	784.35	7,283.61
Total cost		61,383.61
Profit		20,461.20
Selling price		**81,844.81**

22

Exercises – Ordinary Level

Q1 **The monthly budgeted overheads for three departments of The Moor Ltd are as follows:**

	Variable €	Fixed €
Planing	25,000	15,000
Polishing	10,000	20,000
Finishing	35,000	24,000

The Moor Ltd estimates (budgets) direct labour hours for each department are:

Planing department: 5,000 hours
Polishing department: 5,000 hours
Finishing department: 5,000 hours

You are required to:

- **Calculate the overhead absorption rates for each department based on direct labour hours.**
- **Calculate the overheads to be absorbed into job no. 1050 if it spends 23 hours in planing, 18 hours in polishing and 12 hours in finishing.**

Q2 **The monthly budgeted overheads for three departments of Brideswell Industries are as follows:**

	Variable €	Fixed €
Art and typesetting	40,000	20,000
Production	50,000	75,000
Polishing	15,000	10,000

Brideswell Industries estimates (budgets) direct labour hours for each department are:

Art and typesetting: 4,000 hours
Production: 25,000 hours
Polishing: 2,000 hours

You are required to:

- **Calculate the overhead absorption rates for each department based on direct labour hours.**
- **Find the total overheads to be absorbed by job no. 606 if it spends 10 hours in art and typesetting, 24 hours in production and 15 hours in the polishing department.**

Q3 **Gillian Ltd is a small company and has the following budgeted costs for the coming year:**

Materials (direct)	€540,000
Direct labour	€80,000
Factory overheads	€78,000
Labour hours	4,000 hours
Machine hours	12,000 hours

The details of a customer's order number 202 are as follows:

Direct materials	€12,000
Direct labour hours	460 hours
Machine hours	780 hours

You are required to calculate:

- the overhead absorption rate per direct labour hour
- the overhead absorption rate per machine hour
- the total cost of job number 202 using overhead absorption rate per direct labour hour
- the total cost of job number 202 using overhead absorption rate per machine hour
- the selling price of job number 202 using both overhead absorption rates and assuming a mark-up on cost of 20%.

Q4 Handy Ltd is a small company and its budgeted costs for the coming year are as follows:

Materials (direct)	€230,000
Direct labour	€50,000
Factory overheads	€80,000
Labour hours	2,000 hours
Machine hours	800 hours

The details of a customer's order OSO are as follows:

Direct materials	€15,000
Direct labour hours	24 hours
Machine hours	10 hours

You are required to calculate:

- the overhead absorption rate per direct labour hour
- the overhead absorption rate per machine hour
- the total cost of job OSO using overhead absorption rate per direct labour hour
- the total cost of job OSO using overhead absorption rate per machine hour
- the selling price of job OSO using both overhead absorption rates and assuming a mark-up on cost of 25%.

Q5 The following information relates to Kenny Ltd for the coming year. The company had two production departments, A and B, and one service department, 1.

	Department A	Department B	Service 1
Overheads costs	€12,000	€20,000	€10,000
Service 1 to be divided	60%	40%	
Machine hours	1,000		
Labour hours		1,200	

The details of a customer's job number 3R are as follows:

Direct materials	€4,000
Direct labour	€8,900
Hours in Dept A	36 hours
Hours in Dept B	40 hours

You are required to:

- Apportion the costs of the service department between Departments A and B.
- Calculate the overhead absorption for Department A using machine hours.

- Calculate the overhead absorption for Department B using labour hours.
- Calculate the cost of job number 3R under both overhead rates.
- Calculate the selling price of job number 3R if mark-up is 20% of cost.

Q6 The following information relates to Cole Ltd for the coming year. The company had two production departments, X and Y, and two service departments, 1 and 2.

	Department X	Department Y	Service 1	Service 2
Overheads costs	€55,000	€75,100	€20,000	€14,000
Service 1 to be divided	60%	40%		
Service 2 to be divided	80%	20%		
Machine hours	800			
Labour hours		1,150		

The details of a customer's job number 60X are as follows:

Direct materials	€5,600
Direct labour	€9,900
Hours in Dept X	54 hours
Hours in Dept Y	65 hours

You are required to:

- Apportion the costs of the Service 1 and 2 departments between Departments X and Y.
- Calculate the overhead absorption for Department X using machine hours.
- Calculate the overhead absorption for Department Y using labour hours.
- Calculate the cost of job number 60X.
- Calculate the selling price of job number 60X if mark-up is 12.5% of cost.

Exercises – Higher Level

22

Q1 McDonald Ltd is a small company with three departments. The following are the company's budgeted costs for the coming year.

Department	Variable costs	Fixed costs	Wage rate
X	€12 per hour	€5 per hour	€10 per hour
Y	€18 per hour	€7 per hour	€14 per hour
Z	€20 per hour	€8 per hour	€12 per hour

General administration overhead absorption rate is budgeted to be €6.50 per hour.

The following are the specifications for a quotation for job number 1790:

		Department	Hours
Material costs	€2,450		
Labour hours required in each department:		X	105
		Y	80
		Z	54

You are required to:

- Calculate the selling price of job no. 1790 if the profit is set at 20% of the selling price.

Q2 Fix It Ltd is a small company with three departments. The following are the company's budgeted costs for the coming year.

Department	Variable costs	Fixed costs	Wage rate
R	€8 per hour	€2 per hour	€12 per hour
S	€12 per hour	€9 per hour	€22 per hour
T	€9 per hour	€16 per hour	€30 per hour

General administration overhead absorption rate is budgeted to be €9.50 per hour.

The following are the specifications for a quotation for job number 1501:

		Department	Hours
Material costs	€3,400		
Labour hours required in each department:		R	80
		S	25
		T	32

You are required to:

- Calculate the selling price of job no. 1501 if the profit is set at 25% of the selling price.

Q3 The following are the specifications for a job quotation received from Mandy Ltd:

Material costs:	1,200 rolls @ €3.50 per roll	
Department:	Planing	40 hours
	Polishing	50 hours
	Finishing	10 hours

The company's budgeted overheads and hours for each department are as follows:

	Variable overheads	Fixed overheads	Hours
Planing	€15,000	€10,000	5,000
Polishing	€40,000	€12,000	8,000
Finishing	€60,000	€24,000	12,000

The wage rate for the planing department is €12 per direct labour hour, polishing department €14 per direct labour hour and finishing €15 per direct labour hour. General administration expenses are expected to be €12,500 for the month

You are required to:

- Calculate the variable and fixed overhead absorption rates for each department in direct labour hours.
- Calculate the administration overhead absorption rate in direct labour hours.
- Calculate the selling price of the job if the profit is set at 25% of selling price.

Q4 The following are the specifications for a job quotation received from Roxy Ltd:

Material costs:	900 rolls @ €18 per roll	
Department:	X	22 hours
	Y	26 hours
	Z	19 hours

22

The company's budgeted overheads and hours for each department are as follows:

	Variable overheads	Fixed overheads	Hours
X	€12,000	€24,000	6,000
Y	€45,000	€54,000	9,000
Z	€33,000	€77,000	11,000

The wage rate for the X department is €8 per direct labour hour, Y department €6 per direct labour hour and Z €4 per direct labour hour. General administration expenses are expected to be €5,200 for the month.

You are required to:

- Calculate the variable and fixed overhead absorption rates for each department in direct labour hours.
- Calculate the administration overhead absorption rate in direct labour hours.
- Calculate the selling price of the job if the profit is set at 12.5% of cost price.

Q5 Cuckoo Ltd has three departments, Purchasing, Production and Finishing. The following costs relate to 20-2.

	Total €	Purchasing €	Production €	Finishing €
Indirect materials	540,000	255,000	150,000	135,000
Indirect labour	900,000	540,000	216,000	144,000
Machine maintenance	90,000			
Plant depreciation	50,000			
Light and heat	200,000			
Rent and rates	480,000			
Factory canteen	49,000			

The following information relates to the three departments:

	Total	Purchasing	Production	Finishing
Floor space (m^2)	32,000	16,000	10,000	6,000
Volume (m^3)	40,000	24,000	8,000	8,000
Plant valuation €	100,000	60,000	30,000	10,000
Machine hours	60,000	15,000	30,000	15,000
Employees	70	40	20	10
Labour hours	70,000	10,000	40,000	20,000

Job number 909 has just been completed. The details are:

	Direct materials €	Direct labour €	Machine hours	Labour hours
Purchasing	23,000	4,500	100	90
Production	3,500	6,000	40	80
Finishing		2,000	8	22

22

The company budgets for a profit margin of 20%.

You are required to:

- Calculate the overheads to be absorbed by each department, stating clearly the basis of apportionment used.
- Calculate a suitable overhead absorption rate for each department.
- Calculate the selling price of job number 909.

Q6 Suite Ltd has three departments, Manufacturing, Tuning and Finishing.

	Total €	Manufacturing €	Tuning €	Finishing €
Indirect materials	360,000	220,000	80,000	60,000
Indirect labour	480,000	240,000	140,000	100,000
Machine maintenance	32,000			
Plant depreciation	160,000			
Rent and rates	54,000			
Light and heat	96,000			
Factory canteen	70,000			

The following information relates to the three departments:

	Total	Manufacturing	Tuning	Finishing
Floor space (m^2)	18,000	8,000	6,000	4,000
Volume (m^3)	48,000	24,000	16,000	8,000
Plant valuation (€)	800,000	480,000	200,000	120,000
Machine hours	100,000	50,000	25,000	25,000
Employees	140	60	60	20
Labour hours	208,000	80,000	96,000	32,000

Job number 482 has just been completed. The details are:

	Direct materials €	Direct labour €	Machine hours	Labour hours
Manufacturing	15,000	1,700	100	40
Tuning	4,500	7,800	30	180
Finishing	9,000	3,000	12	50

The company budgets for a profit margin of 20%.

You are required to:

- Calculate the overheads to be absorbed by each department, stating clearly the basis of apportionment used.
- Calculate a suitable overhead absorption rate for each department.
- Calculate the selling price of job number 482.

Q7 **Thorn Ltd has two production departments, A and B, and two ancillary service departments, 1 and 2. The following are the expected overhead costs for the next 6 months:**

Overhead	**Total (€)**
Depreciation of premises	40,000
Depreciation of machinery	2,000
Factory light and heat	12,000
Factory rent and rates	8,000
Factory canteen costs	4,000

The following information relates to the production and service departments:

	Production		**Service**	
	Dept A	**Dept B**	**Dept 1**	**Dept 2**
Volume in cubic meters	1,500	3,000	900	600
Floor area in square meters	1,200	900	600	300
Number of employees	270	150	105	75
Book value of machinery	€15,000	€22,500	€13,500	€9,000
Machine hours	25,000	37,500		

You are required to:

- **Calculate the overheads to be absorbed by each department, stating clearly the basis of apportionment used.**
- **Transfer the service department costs to production departments A and B on the basis of machine hours.**
- **Calculate a machine hour overhead absorption rate for departments A and B.**
- **Explain why it is necessary to transfer service department costs to production departments A and B.**

Q8 **The information below refers to the budgeted and actual costs of Mooney Ltd:**

Budgeted	**Direct labour hours**	**Machine hours**	**Total overhead €**
Department 1	20,000	50,000	200,000
Department 2	80,000	20,000	400,000
Department 3	50,000		100,000
Actual	**Direct labour hours**	**Machine hours**	**Total overhead €**
Department 1	21,000	56,000	220,000
Department 2	75,000	23,000	380,000
Department 3	48,000		105,000

You are required to:

- **Calculate departmental overhead absorption rates for Departments 1, 2 and 3**
- **Show the under/over-absorption by department and in total for the period and explain your answer.**

22

Theory

Q1 **What is meant by product costing?**

Q2 **Outline the main reasons for product costing.**

Q3 **Name two methods of valuing closing stock.**

Q4 **Name three overhead absorption rates and state why they are based on budgeted rather than actual figures.**

Q5 **Explain what is meant by 'reapportionment' of overheads.**

Q6 **Illustrate and explain 'over-absorption' of overheads.**

Exam Tips

- Ensure that you understand allocation, apportionment/reapportionment and absorption.
- When calculating the selling price of a product, make sure you identify correctly whether the profit is a percentage of cost or of selling price (mark-up or margin).
- Revise the layout of a trading account; it is often required as part of stock valuation.
- In overhead analysis sheets make sure you clearly state the basis of apportionment used.

22

23 Cost-Volume Profit Analysis (Marginal Costing)

Objectives

On completion students should be able to:

- Explain the principles of marginal costing;
- Show how CVP can help management in decision-making;
- Prepare a marginal costing statement;
- Calculate contribution, break-even point and margin of safety;
- Use sensitivity analysis to show the effects of changes in costs on profits;
- Know the limitations of CVP.

Introduction

DEFINITION

Cost-volume profit analysis is the term given to the study of the relationship between costs and volume (level of output) and their effect on profit at various levels of activity.

CVP analysis is used by management in decision-making and can aid managers in the following ways:

- to find the number of units that must be produced and sold for the business to break even
- to find the number of units that must be produced and sold in order to reach the company's target profit
- to decide between alternative courses of action
- to decide the most profitable volume of production
- to find what selling price the company should charge in order to break even and to reach a target profit
- to perform variance analysis ('what if') and to find the profit at different levels of activities
- to calculate the margin of safety
- to show the outcome of producing and selling one extra unit.

Marginal costing

DEFINITION

Marginal costing is an alternative method of costing to absorption costing. Both methods are used in CVP analysis.

Principles of marginal costing

- The total cost of producing a product can be clearly divided into fixed costs and variable cost elements.
- The fixed costs remain fixed and are not affected by the volume of output.
- When production increases by one unit, the unit cost of production will only increase by the variable cost of this extra unit.

If one extra unit is produced and sold then:

- Income will increase by the selling price of the unit sold.
- Costs will increase by the variable cost of this extra unit.
- Profits will increase by the selling price of the unit less the variable cost of the unit, i.e. **contribution** (see below).

NOTE

Variable cost is the **total variable cost** and not just the variable cost of production. For example, sales commission payable per unit sold would be included as a variable cost.

Marginal costing involves a number of essential elements:

1. Marginal costing statement
2. Contribution
3. Break-even point
4. Target profit
5. Contribution to sales ratio
6. Margin of safety
7. Break-even charts
8. Sensitivity analysis

1. Marginal costing statement

NOTE

You must be able to prepare a marginal costing statement.

Ordinary Level sample template

	Total cost	Per unit
Sales (units)	xxxxxx	xxxx
Less Variable costs	(xxxx)	(xxx)
Contribution	xxxxxx	xxxx
Less Fixed costs	(xxxx)	(xxx)
Profit	xxxxx	xxxxx

Contribution = Fixed costs plus profit

Higher Level sample template

		Total cost	Per unit
Sales (units)		xxxxxxxx	xxxxxxx
***Less* Variable costs**			
Direct materials	xxxxxxx		
Direct labour	xxxxxxx		
Direct expenses	xxxxxxx		
Other variable costs	xxxxxxx		
Commission if percentage based*	xxxxxxx	(xxxxxxx)	(xxxxx)
Contribution		**xxxxxxxx**	**CPU****
Less Fixed costs		(xxxxxx)	
Profit		**xxxxxxxx**	

See next page for notes.

*If commission is a percentage of selling price, list it as a separate variable cost – useful for questions involving a change in selling price. If commission is per unit, it can be included in other variable costs as it will remain constant and not change when selling price changes.

**CPU = contribution per unit

2. Contribution

Contribution is the amount each unit of sales contributes towards covering fixed costs and profits.

Selling price less variable costs = Contribution

The fixed costs must also be accounted for so when the variable costs are subtracted from the selling price the remainder **contributes** towards the fixed costs and the profits.

The concept of contribution is central to marginal costing theory.

Example

Graham Ltd sell their product for €120. The variable cost of the product is €80 and the fixed cost per unit is €10. Find the contribution using a marginal costing statement.

Solution

Marginal Costing Statement

	€
Sales	120.00
Less Variable costs	(80.00)
Contribution	40.00
Less Fixed costs	(10.00)
Profit	**30.00**

The contribution earned initially covers fixed costs and when these fixed costs are recovered the remaining contribution is profit.

23

3. Break-even point (BEP)

Break-even point is the point at which the profit is zero or the point at which the contribution equals all the fixed costs. It is the number of units that must be sold so that sales revenue equals total cost.

At break-even point, the business is making neither a profit nor a loss.

To calculate break-even point we use the following formula:

$$\text{Break-even point} = \frac{\text{Fixed costs}}{\text{Contribution per unit}}$$

Example

Tristan Ltd produces a single product. The following details relate to the product:

Selling price per unit	€20
Variable costs per unit	€12
Fixed costs	€6,400

(a) Calculate the contribution per unit.

(b) Calculate the break-even point.

(c) Prove that at the number of units from (b) the company is making neither a profit nor a loss.

Solution

(a) Marginal costing statement

	€
Sales	20.00
Less Variable costs	(12.00)
Contribution per unit	**8.00**

(b) Break-even point

$$\frac{\text{Fixed costs}}{\text{Contribution per unit}} = \frac{6,400}{8} = \textbf{800 units}$$

(c) Proof

	€
Sales (800 x 20)	16,000
Less Variable costs (800 x 12)	(9,600)
Contribution	6,400
Less Fixed costs	(6,400)
Profit/loss	**Nil**

NOTE

These figures show that if Tristan Ltd sells 800 units the company will break even, i.e. sales = total costs. It also means that if 801 units are sold the company will make a profit of €8. We can see that all the fixed costs have been charged to the first 800 units.

4. Target profit

Break-even analysis is also used to find the level of production and sales required to reach a required profit or target profit. This aids decision-making.

To find the number of units required to achieve this target, the target profit is treated like a fixed cost. The contribution required will need to cover this required profit as well as the fixed costs. The formula becomes:

$$\text{Level of sales required to reach profit target} = \frac{\text{Fixed costs + Target profit}}{\text{Contribution per unit (CPU)}}$$

23

Example

If Tristan Ltd above set its target profit for the year at €19,200, find the number of units required to achieve this profit and prove that at this level the target profit is achieved.

Solution

No. of units to achieve target profit = $\frac{6,400 + 19,200}{8} = \frac{25,600}{8} =$ **3,200 units**

Proof

	€
Sales (3,200 x 20)	64,000
Less Variable costs (3,200 x 12)	(38,400)
Contribution	25,600
Less Fixed costs	(6,400)
Profit	19,200

5. Contribution to sales ratio

This is another way to find the break-even point and the level of sales required to reach a target profit. The C/S ratio gives us the sales revenue for the break-even point. The break-even point in units is found by dividing the sales revenue by the unit selling price.

We use the contribution to sales ratio to find the break-even point when the variable cost per unit and the sales price per unit are not known or unavailable.

It shows the contribution per €1 of sales.

If the selling price per unit and the marginal cost per unit remain unchanged, then the C/S ratio is a constant.

Example

Slaney Way Engineering Ltd manufactures a single product. The following information is available:

Selling price	€100 per unit
Variable cost	€60 per unit
Fixed costs	€240,000

Using the contribution/sales ratio find:

- the break-even point
- the sales in units (volume) required to achieve a profit of €560,000.

Solution

Selling price	€100.00
Less Variable cost	(€60.00)
Contribution per unit	€40.00

Contribution/Sales ratio $\frac{\text{Contribution per unit}}{\text{Selling price}} = \frac{40}{100} = 40\%$

Break-even point $\frac{\text{Fixed costs}}{\text{Contribution/Sales ratio}} = \frac{240{,}000}{40\%} = €600{,}000$

In units $\frac{\text{Total sales €}}{\text{Selling price per unit}} = \frac{600{,}000}{100} =$ **6,000 units**

Target profit $\frac{\text{Fixed costs + Target profit}}{\text{Contribution/Sales ratio}} = \frac{240{,}000 + 560{,}000}{40\%} = €2{,}000{,}000$

In units $\frac{\text{Total sales €}}{\text{Selling price per unit}} = \frac{2{,}000{,}000}{100} =$ **20,000 units**

6. Margin of safety

The margin of safety is the amount by which sales can fall (from current activity level) before break-even point is reached. The margin of safety can be expressed in units, monetary value (€) or a percentage of budgeted sales.

Margin of safety = Sales – Break-even point

Example

If Slaney Way Engineering Ltd (above) sold 24,000 units, calculate its margin of safety:

- in units
- in euro
- as a percentage of sales.

Solution

From above, the break-even point is 6,000 units at a sales total of €600,000.

	Units	€	% of sales
Sales	24,000	2,400,000	
Less Break-even point	(6,000)	(600,000)	$\frac{1,800,000}{2,400,000}$ **= 75%**
Margin of safety	**18,000**	**1,800,000**	

7. Break-even charts

The relationship between revenues, variable costs, fixed costs and profit/loss can be represented in graph form using a break-even chart.

(a) Traditional break-even chart

Procedure for constructing a traditional break-even chart:

Step 1 Place the level of activity (units produced) on the X axis (horizontal).

Step 2 Place the costs and revenues on the Y axis (vertical).

Step 3 The fixed cost line will be parallel to the X axis as fixed costs remain constant at all levels of activity (assumption of marginal costing).

Step 4 The total cost line, beginning where the fixed cost line meets the Y axis, represents the total cost – that is, the variable cost and fixed cost. This line will be upwardly sloping to the right.

Step 5 The sales revenue line, beginning at the origin, represents the sales revenue from the units sold. This line will be upwardly sloping to the right.

Step 6 Where the total cost line and sales revenue line meet will be the break-even point.

23

Example

Buffy Ltd produces a single product which retails at €30 per unit. The variable cost per unit is €20 and fixed costs are estimated at €40,000. Using a break-even chart:

- Find the break-even point in units and sales value.
- The company is currently selling 6,000 units. Show the margin of safety.

Verify your answers with the use of formulae.

Solution

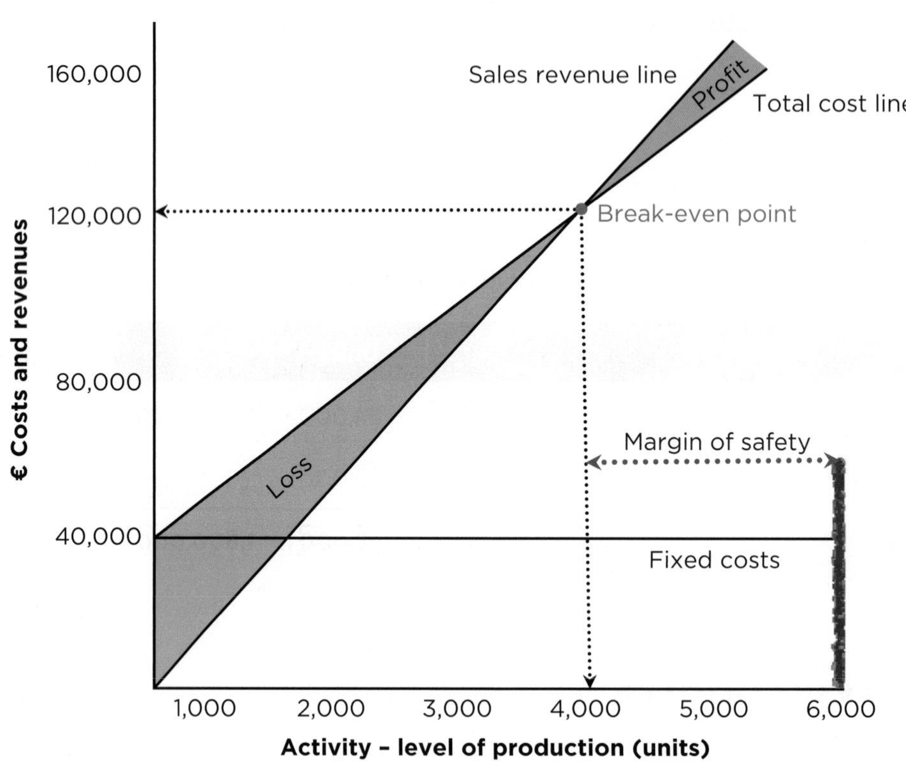

Verification

Sales price	€30
Less Variable cost	(€20)
Contribution per unit	€10

Break-even point using the formula

$$\frac{\text{Fixed costs}}{\text{Contribution per unit}} = \frac{40{,}000}{10} = 4{,}000 \text{ units}$$

In sales value 4,000 x 30 = **€120,000**

Margin of safety using the formula

Sales – Break-even point = Margin of safety
6,000 – 4,000 = 2,000 units
In sales value 2,000 x 30 = **€60,000**

To convert from units to sales value multiply the units by the selling price.

(b) Contribution break-even chart

The difference here is that a variable cost line is shown instead of a fixed cost line. This will show management the amount of contribution at the different levels of activity.

Contribution break-even chart – Buffy Ltd

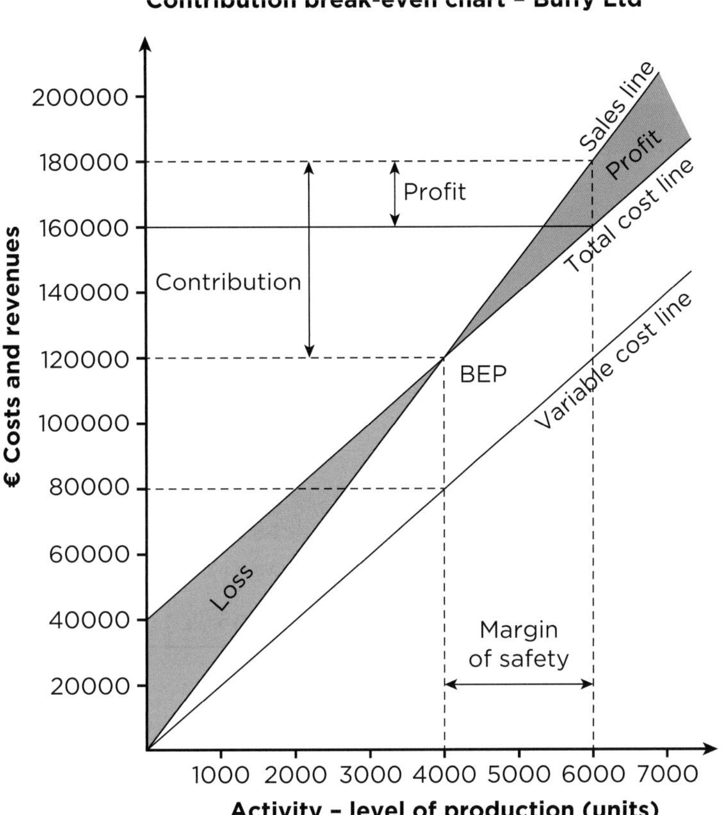

From the diagram, the break-even point (BEP) is at 4,000 units, at which point the difference between the sales line and the variable cost line is €40,000 (i.e. sales €120,000, less the variable costs, €80,000). The €40,000 is of course the fixed costs.

At sales of 4,000 units we can see:

	€
Sales (4,000 x 30)	120,000
Less Variable costs (4,000 x 20)	(80,000)
Contribution	40,000
Less Fixed costs	(40,000)
Profit	Nil

8. Sensitivity analysis

This analysis is often referred to as 'what if' analysis. It is a technique used by the management accountant to analyse and show the effect on profit brought about by change in:

- selling price/volume
- variable costs – direct materials, direct labour, direct expenses
- variable overheads
- fixed costs.

23

Example

If Buffy Ltd (see above) reduced its selling price by €2, and this resulted in an increase in sales volume of 10%, show the effect this would have on profits. All other cost levels remain the same. Would the company be better to make this change or retain the current selling price and activity level?

Solution

	Current situation	New situation
Selling price	€30.00	€28.00
Variable costs	€20.00	€20.00
Fixed costs	€40,000	€40,000
Sales volume	6,000 units	6,600 units (10% increase)

Prepare marginal costing statements:

	Current €	New €
Sales	(6,000 x 30) 180,000	(6,600 x 28) 184,800
Less Variable costs	(6,000 x 20) (120,000)	(6,600 x 20) (132,000)
Contribution	60,000	52,800
Less Fixed costs	(40,000)	(40,000)
Profit	20,000	12,800

Under the proposed new selling price, even though the company would sell more units, it will be less profitable as profits would fall by €7,200. The company should retain its current selling price and activity level.

Sample sensitivity analysis question

The following are the budgeted figures of Pyramid Ltd for the coming year

	€	€
Sales (80,000 units)		720,000
Direct materials	350,000	
Direct labour	130,000	
Fixed overheads	100,000	(580,000)
Profit		140,000

23

The maximum capacity of the firm is 100,000 units.

You are required to:

(a) Examine the following three options suggested to Pyramid Ltd after a market research campaign.

(b) Evaluate each option and suggest which plan the company should adopt. Give reasons for your answer.

Plan A: Reduce the selling price by €1.50 per unit and take out a new advertising campaign at a cost of €10,000. Sales volume will increase by 10%.

Plan B: Maintain the current selling price and increase capacity to 90%. This will incur an increase of 20% in factory overheads.

Plan C: Replace the machinery with new, more efficient motors which will reduce labour costs and materials costs by 10%, and increase capacity to 100% with no increase in overheads. The selling price would increase by 20% to cover the cost of the new machines. The company is to rebrand an improved product and engage in an advertising campaign at a cost of €300,000.

Solution

Step 1 Prepare a marginal costing statement for budgeted figures.

	€	€	Per unit
Sales (80,000 units)		720,000	9.00
***Less* Variable costs**			
Direct materials	350,000		
Direct labour	130,000	(480,000)	(6.00)
Contribution		240,000	3.00
Less Fixed overheads		(100,000)	
Profit		**140,000**	

Step 2 Prepare a marginal costing statement for each of the new plans.

Plan A

Selling price	9.00 - 1.50	=	€7.50
New sales volume	80,000 + 10%	=	88,000 units
New fixed overheads	100,000 + 10,000	=	€110,000

	€
Sales (88,000 x 7.50)	660,000
Less Variable costs (88,000 x 6)	(528,000)
Contribution	132,000
Less Fixed costs	(110,000)
Profit	**22,000**

Plan B

Selling price	Unchanged	=	€9.00
Capacity	90% (100,000)	=	90,000 units
New fixed overheads	100,000 + 20%	=	€120,000

	€
Sales (90,000 x 9.00)	810,000
Less Variable costs (90,000 x 6)	(540,000)
Contribution	270,000
Less Fixed costs	(120,000)
Profit	**150,000**

23

Plan C

Selling price	9.00 + 20%	=	€10.80
Direct materials	350,000 less 10%	=	€315,000
Direct labour	130,000 less 10%	=	€117,000
Capacity	Full	=	100,000 units
Variable cost per unit	(315,000 + 117,000)/100,000	=	€4.32
Fixed costs	100,000 + 300,000	=	€400,000

	€
Sales (100,000 x 10.80)	1,080,000
Less Variable costs (100,000 x 4.32)	(432,000)
Contribution	648,000
Less Fixed costs	(400,000)
Profit	**248,000**

Evaluation

Plan C should be chosen as the plan that the company should adopt. It will maximise profit at €248,000.

Existing plan	Profit	=	€140,000
Plan A	Profit	=	€22,000
Plan B	Profit	=	€150,000
Plan C	Profit	=	€248,000

Sample Ordinary Level question

Appleton Ltd manufactures a single item. The following is their proposed budget for the coming year:

	€	€
Sales (40,000 units)		800,000
Variable costs	240,000	
Fixed costs	100,000	(340,000)
Profit		460,000

1. **You are required to calculate:**
   - **(a)** selling price per unit
   - **(b)** fixed cost per unit
   - **(c)** variable cost per unit
   - **(d)** contribution per unit
   - **(e)** break-even point in units and sales value
   - **(f)** margin of safety in units and sales value
   - **(g)** the level of sales required to achieve a profit of €600,000.
2. If the company reduced its selling price by €1.50 and sold 15% more units would it fare better? Explain your answer.
3. Prepare marginal costing statements at the following activity levels: (a) 7,000 units; (b) 7,143 units; (c) 10,000 units; and (d) 50,000 units.

23

Solution

Marginal Costing Statement

	€
Sales (40,000 units)	800,000
Less Variable costs	(240,000)
Contribution	560,000
Less Fixed costs	(100,000)
Profit	460,000

1 (a) **Selling price per unit**

$$\frac{\text{Sales}}{\text{No. of units}} = \frac{800,000}{40,000} = \textbf{€20.00} \text{ per unit}$$

(b) **Fixed cost per unit**

$$\frac{\text{Fixed costs}}{\text{No. of units}} = \frac{100,000}{40,000} = \textbf{€2.50} \text{ per unit}$$

(c) **Variable cost per unit**

$$\frac{\text{Variable costs}}{\text{No. of units}} = \frac{240,000}{40,000} = \textbf{€6.00} \text{ per unit}$$

(d) **Contribution per unit**

Selling price – Variable cost €20.00 – €6.00 = **€14.00 per unit**

(e) **Break-even point in units and sales value**

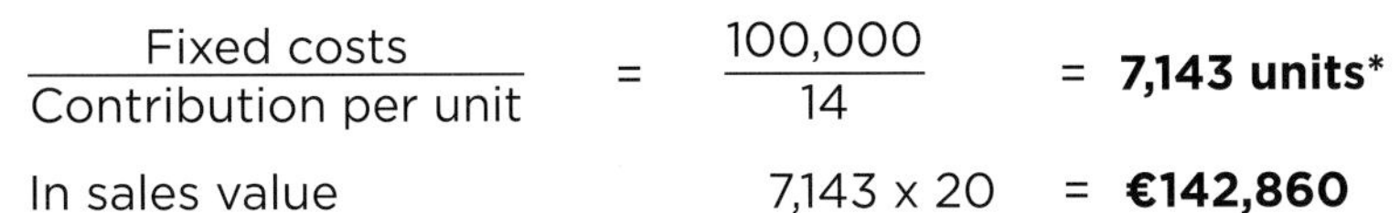

$$\frac{\text{Fixed costs}}{\text{Contribution per unit}} = \frac{100,000}{14} = \textbf{7,143 units*}$$

In sales value 7,143 x 20 = **€142,860**

NOTE

*The number of units must always be rounded up to the next full unit.

(f) **Margin of safety in units and sales value**

Current sales – Break-even point 40,000 – 7,143 = **32,857 units**

In sales value 32,857 x 20 = **€657,140**

(g) **The level of sales required to give a target profit of €600,000**

$$\frac{\text{Fixed costs + Target profit}}{\text{Contribution per unit}} = \frac{100,000 + 600,000}{14} = \textbf{50,000 units}$$

2 **Reducing selling price by €1.50 and selling 15% more units**

New selling price	€20 – €1.50	= €18.50
New sales volume	40,000 plus 15%	= 46,000 units

Marginal Costing Statement (under new conditions)

	€
Sales (46,000 x €18.50)	851,000
Less Variable costs (46,000 x €6.00)	(276,000)
Contribution	575,000
Less Fixed costs	(100,000)
New profit	**475,000**

Since the new profit is €15,000 greater than the existing position, the business would fare better if it reduced its selling price to sell 15% more units.

❸ **Marginal costing statements at different activity levels**

	7,000 units	7,143 units	10,000 units	50,000 units
Sales (units x selling price) (€20)	140,000	142,860	200,000	1,000,000
Less Variable costs (units x VC) (€6)	(42,000)	(42,858)	(60,000)	(300,000)
Contribution	98,000	100,002	140,000	700,000
Less Fixed costs	(100,000)	(100,000)	(100,000)	(100,000)
Profit (loss)	(2,000)	2	40,000	600,000

Sample Higher Level question

Shoesmith Ltd produces a single product. The company's profit and loss account for the year ended 31/12/20-2, when 50,000 units were produced and sold, was as follows:

	€	€
Sales (50,000 units)		300,000
Direct materials	95,000	
Direct labour	55,000	
Factory overheads	40,000	
Administration expenses	30,000	
Selling expenses	30,000	(250,000)
Profit		**50,000**

The materials, labour and 40% of the factory overheads are variable costs. Apart from sales commission of 5% of sales, selling and administration costs are fixed.

Before we look at any questions based on this business, the first step is to restate the budget given using marginal costing principles, i.e. prepare a marginal costing statement.

Marginal Costing Statement

	€	€	€ per unit
Sales (50,000 units)		300,000	6.00
***Less* Variable costs**			
Direct materials	95,000		
Direct labour	55,000		
Factory overheads (40% of 40,000)	16,000	(166,000)	(3.32)
Commission (300,000 x 5%)	15,000	(15,000)	(0.30)
Contribution		**119,000**	**2.38**
***Less* Fixed costs**			
Factory overheads (60% of 40,000)	24,000		
Administration expenses	30,000		
Selling expenses (30,000 - 15,000)	15,000	(69,000)	
Profit		**50,000**	

23

Now we can analyse this in more detail by answering the questions.

NOTE

When you restate the budget the profit figure must be the same as in the original budget.

Questions and Solutions

(a) Calculate the break-even point and margin of safety (in units and sales value)

Break-even point $\frac{\text{Fixed costs}}{\text{CPU}}$ $\frac{69{,}000}{2.38}$ = **28,992 units**

In sales value: 28,992 x €6 = **€173,952**

NOTE

To get the break-even point in sales value multiply the units by the selling price.

Margin of safety

Current activity - break-even point

50,000 - 28,992 = **21,008 units**

In sales value: 21,008 x €6 = **€126,048**

(b) Calculate the number of units that must be sold if the company is to increase its net profit by 20% over the previous year's figure, assuming the selling price and the cost levels and percentages remain unchanged.

Break-even point $\frac{\text{Fixed costs + Target profit}}{\text{Contribution per unit}}$

New target profit = Original profit (€50,000) + 20% = €60,000

Target sales = $\frac{69{,}000 + 60{,}000}{2.38}$ = **54,202 units**

(c) Calculate the profit the company would make if it reduced its selling price to €5.50, increased fixed costs by €12,000 and thereby increased the number of units sold to 55,000, with all other cost levels and percentages remaining unchanged.

NOTE

If selling price changes and commission is a percentage of selling price, then commission and variable cost total will also change.

Step 1 Write down all the changes.

Fixed costs increased by 12,000 per unit 69,000 + 12,000 = €81,000

Commission is 5% of €5.50 instead of €6 which makes commission €0.275 per unit

Number of units sold is now 55,000.

New selling price	€5.50	
Less Variable costs (excl. commission)	(€3.32)	(unchanged)
Less New commission	(€0.275)	
New contribution per unit	**€1.905**	

Step 2 Calculate the new profit (using contribution per unit).

Units (55,000 x CPU €1.905)	€104,775
Less Fixed costs	(€81,000)
New profit	€23,775

23

Alternatively you can prepare a full new marginal costing statement.

	€
Sales (55,000 x 5.50)	302,500
Less Variable cost (55,000 x 3.32)	(182,600)
Less Commission (55,000 x 0.275)	(15,125)
Contribution	104,775
Less Fixed costs	(81,000)
New profit	**23,775**

(d) Calculate the selling price the company must charge next year if fixed costs are increased by 10% but the volume of sales and profit remain the same.

Step 1 Set out new costs and profits.

New fixed costs 69,000 + 10% = 69,000 + 6,900 = €75,900

Profit required €50,000 (unchanged)

Number of units 50,000 units (unchanged)

Step 2 Find the contribution required.

Contribution = Fixed costs + Profit

Contribution = €75,900 + €50,000

Contribution = €125,900

Step 3 Find the contribution per unit required.

$$\frac{\text{Contribution (from above)}}{\text{Number of units}} = \frac{€125{,}900}{50{,}000} = €2.518$$

Step 4 Find the selling price (excluding commission).

Selling price – Variable cost per unit (excluding commission) = Contribution per unit

x – €3.32 = €2.518, therefore x = €5.838

Step 5 Find selling price including commission

In this example the commission is 5% of selling price. Since commission is 5% then the remainder must be 95%.

5.838 = 95%

Therefore 100% = 5.838/95 x 100 = **€6.15**

This is the new selling price to charge.

When the commission is a set price per unit, for example 40c per unit, then add on 40c to the answer from Step 4 above. In this example this would mean the selling price would be €5.838 + 40c = €6.238.

23

(e) Calculate the number of units that Shoesmith Ltd must sell at €7 per unit to provide a profit of 10% of the sales revenue received from these same units.

This involves the use of a formula:

$$\frac{\text{Fixed costs}}{\text{CPU – 10\% of selling price}}$$

NOTE

Because the selling price has changed and commission is a percentage of selling price, you must first find the new contribution per unit.

New Contribution

		€
New selling price	=	7.00
Less Variable costs (excluding commission)	=	(3.32)
Less New commission	=	(0.35)
New contribution	=	3.33

Now apply the formula:

$$\frac{\text{Fixed costs}}{\text{CPU - 10\% of selling price}} \qquad \frac{69{,}000}{3.33 - 0.70} \qquad = \qquad \textbf{26,236 units}$$

Alternatively, this can be calculated as follows:

Let n = number of units

Sales = Variable cost + Fixed cost + Profit

$7n = (3.32n + 0.35n) + 69{,}000 + 0.7n$

$7n - 3.32n - 0.35n - 0.7n = 69{,}000$

$2.63n = 69{,}000$

n = 26,236 units

Marginal costing compared to absorption costing

Marginal costing	Absorption costing
Fixed costs are charged in full to the period in which they are incurred.	A portion of fixed costs is carried into the next period, for example closing stock.
As the result of the above closing stock is valued lower.	As the result of the above closing stock is valued higher – i.e. closing stock includes fixed costs.
Used for decision-making purposes.	Must be used in financial accounts to comply with regulation.

NOTE

Both methods will give the same result if there is no opening or closing stock or if both stocks are the same.

23

Example

Stobart plc produced 24,000 units of a product during the year ended 31/12/20-9. During the year 18,000 of these units were sold at €7 per unit The production costs were as follows:

Direct materials	€1.20 per unit
Direct labour	€0.70 per unit
Variable overheads	€0.50 per unit
Fixed overhead costs for the year	€11,000

Show the profit and loss statements under marginal costing principles and absorption costing principles. Explain your answers.

Solution

Absorption Costing Statement

	€	€
Sales (18,000 x €7.00)		126,000
***Less* Production costs** (of 24,000 units)		
Direct materials (24,000 x €1.20)	28,800	
Direct labour (24,000 x €0.70)	16,800	
Variable overheads (24,000 x €0.50)	12,000	
Fixed overheads	11,000	
	68,600	
Less Closing stock (1/4 of 68,600)	(17,150)	
Cost of goods sold		(51,450)
Profit		**74,550**

Marginal Costing Statement

	€	€
Sales (18,000 x €7.00)		126,000
***Less* Production costs** (of 24,000 units)		
Direct materials (24,000 x €1.20)	28,800	
Direct labour (24,000 x €0.70)	16,800	
Variable overheads (24,000 x €0.50)	12,000	
	57,600	
Less Closing stock (1/4 x 57,600)	(14,400)	(43,200)
Contribution		82,800
Less Fixed costs		(11,000)
Profit		**71,800**

- There is a difference of €2,750 between the profits because the closing stock is valued differently.
- Marginal costing does not include fixed costs when costing a product, whereas absorption costing does. As a result, the closing stock figure is lower in marginal costing than it is under absorption costing.

Absorption costing should be used because it agrees with standard accounting practice and concepts, and matches costs with revenues.

23

Limitations of marginal costing (assumptions)

- It is assumed that variable costs are completely variable at all levels of output. It ignores economies of scale – for example, no discounts for bulk buying.
- It assumes that all fixed costs are fixed in the long term. However, most fixed costs are only fixed within a relevant range, e.g. step-fixed costs. In reality, all costs are variable in the long term.

- It assumes that all costs can be easily classified into fixed and variable costs. This means that all mixed costs can be easily separated into fixed and variable elements. The high-low method can be used for this purpose but it is not always possible to do this.
- It assumes that the selling price is constant and does not change, and there are no price-reduced sales or discounts given for large orders.
- It assumes that all stock produced is sold. Production in the period usually equals sales. Fixed costs are charged in total to a period and are not carried forward to the next period.
- It only works for one product. It assumes that the business produces a single product or that there is a constant product mix if two or more products are produced.

Exercises – Ordinary Level

Q1 **Curvage Ltd manufactures a single product which it sells for €23 per unit. All goods produced are sold so there is never any stock on hand. A costing analysis revealed the following:**

Variable costs per unit amount to:	€14 per unit
Fixed costs for the period amount to:	€45,000

You are required to:

- **Calculate the contribution for each unit sold.**
- **Calculate the break-even point in volume and sales value (revenue).**
- **Calculate the margin of safety in units and sales value if the budgeted level of production is 18,000 units.**
- **Prepare a marginal costing statement to show the profit/loss at the following production levels:**
  - (a) 4,000 units
  - (b) 5,000 units
  - (c) 6,800 units
  - (d) 7,500 units.
- **Calculate the level of production and sales revenue that will yield a profit of €50,000.**

Q2 **Radford Ltd manufactures a product which it sells at €25 per unit. All goods produced are sold so there is never any closing stock. A costing analysis has revealed the following:**

Variable costs:	€15 per unit
Fixed costs:	€20,000

You are required to:

- **Calculate the contribution for each item sold.**
- **Calculate the break-even point for this product using the data above.**
- **Prepare a marginal costing statement to show the profit/loss at the following production levels:**
  - (a) 1,000 units
  - (b) 2,000 units
  - (c) 3,000 units
  - (d) 4,500 units.
- **Calculate the level of production and sales revenue that will yield a profit of €30,000.**
- **Calculate the margin of safety in units and sales value if the profit was €30,000.**

23

Q3 **Mikado Ltd manufactures a product which it sells at €42 per unit. All goods produced are sold so there is never any closing stock. A costing analysis has revealed the following:**

Variable costs:	€26 per unit
Fixed costs:	€32,000

You are required to:

- **Calculate the contribution for each item sold.**
- **Calculate the break-even point for this product using the data above.**
- **Prepare a marginal costing statement to show the profit/loss at the following production levels:**
  - **(a)** **1,500 units**
  - **(b)** **2,000 units**
  - **(c)** **3,100 units**
  - **(d)** **4,000 units.**
- **Calculate the level of production and sales revenue that will yield a profit of €48,000.**
- **Calculate the margin of safety in units and sales value if the profit was €48,000.**

Q4 **Passage Plc manufactures a component for the computer industry. The product sells at €200 per unit. The unit variable cost is €120 per unit and fixed costs for the accounting period are expected to be €110,000.**

You are required to:

- **Calculate the contribution/sales ratio.**
- **Using this ratio find:**
  - **(a)** **the break-even point in units and sales value**
  - **(b)** **the volume of sales required to produce a profit of €126,000.**

Use marginal costing principles to prove your answer to both questions.

Q5 **Wenger Plc manufactures a component for the computer industry. The product sells at €90 per unit. The unit variable cost is €45 per unit and fixed costs for the accounting period are expected to be €180,000.**

You are required to:

- **Calculate the contribution/sales ratio.**
- **Using this ratio find:**
  - **(a)** **the break-even point in units and sales value**
  - **(b)** **the volume of sales required to produce a profit of €90,000.**

Use marginal costing principles to prove your answer to both questions.

23

Q6 **Gretna Ltd manufactures a single item. The following is their proposed budget for the coming year:**

	€	€
Sales (25,000 units)		150,000
Variable costs	75,000	
Fixed costs	51,000	(126,000)
Profit		24,000

You are required to calculate:

- the selling price per unit
- the variable cost per unit
- the contribution per unit
- the break-even point in units and sales value
- the margin of safety in units and sales value if budgeted sales for the period are 33,000 units
- the level of production that will yield a profit of €75,000
- the profit expected if the volume of sales increases by 10%, the company spend an extra €12,000 on advertising and sells its product for €7.50 per unit.

Exercises – Higher Level

Q1 **Tommy Ball Ltd produces a single product. The company's profit and loss account for the year ended 31/12/20-3 when 75,000 units were produced and sold was as follows:**

	€	€
Sales (75,000 units)		600,000
Materials	135,000	
Direct labour	95,000	
Factory overheads	60,000	
Administration expenses	22,000	
Selling expenses	80,000	(392,000)
Profit		**208,000**

The materials, labour and 30% of the factory overheads are variable costs. Apart from sales commission of 10% of sales, selling and administration costs are fixed.

You are required to:

- **Calculate the break-even point and margin of safety in units and sales value.**
- **Calculate the number of units that must be sold if the company is to increase its net profit by 15% in the following year, assuming the selling price and cost levels and percentages remain unchanged.**
- **Calculate the profit Tommy Ball Ltd would make if it reduced its selling price to €7, spent an extra €22,000 on advertising and thereby increased the number of units sold to 82,000, with all other cost levels and percentages remaining unchanged.**
- **Calculate the selling price the company must charge per unit if fixed costs increase by 15% but the volume of sales and profit remain the same.**
- **Calculate the number of units that must be sold at €10 per unit to provide a profit of 15% of the sales revenue received from these same units.**

Q2 Lisa Jones Ltd produces a single product. The company's profit and loss account for the year ended 31/12/20-4 when 95,000 units were produced and sold was as follows:

	€	€
Sales (95,000 units)		8,550,000
Materials	2,400,000	
Direct labour	1,300,000	
Factory overheads	850,000	
Administration expenses	300,000	
Selling expenses	900,000	(5,750,000)
Profit		**2,800,000**

The materials, labour and 45% of the factory overheads are variable costs. Apart from sales commission of 5% of sales, selling and administration costs are fixed.

You are required to:

- **Calculate the break-even point and margin of safety in units and sales value.**
- **Calculate the number of units that must be sold if the company is to increase its net profit by 30% in the following year assuming the selling price and cost levels and percentages remain unchanged.**
- **Calculate the profit Lisa Jones Ltd would make if it reduced its selling price to €80, spent an extra €40,000 on advertising and thereby increased the number of units sold to 98,000, with all other cost levels and percentages remaining unchanged.**
- **Calculate the selling price the company must charge per unit if fixed costs increase by 12% but the volume of sales and profit remain the same.**
- **Calculate the number of units that must be sold at €100 per unit to provide a profit of 10% of the sales revenue received from these same units.**

Q3 Agar Ltd produces a single product. The company's profit and loss account for the year ended 31/12/20-6 when 60,000 units were produced and sold was as follows:

	€	€
Sales (60,000 units)		1,380,000
Materials	470,000	
Direct labour	380,000	
Factory overheads	230,000	
Administration expenses	50,000	
Selling expenses	100,000	(1,230,000)
Profit		**150,000**

The materials, labour and 30% of factory overheads are variable costs. Labour costs include €40,000 salary paid to the factory supervisor. Apart from a sales commission of 5% of selling price the administration and selling expenses are fixed.

23

You are required to:

- Calculate the break-even point and margin of safety in units and sales value.
- Calculate the number of units that must be sold if the company is to increase its net profit by 10% in the following year assuming the selling price and cost levels and percentages remain unchanged.
- Calculate the profit Agar Ltd would make if it reduced its selling price to €20, spent an extra €10,000 on advertising and thereby increased the number of units sold to 70,000, with all other cost levels and percentages remaining unchanged except for sales commission which was to be increased to 6% of selling price.
- Calculate the selling price the company must charge per unit if fixed costs increase by 15% but the volume of sales remains the same and the company wants to increase net profit by 10% on the previous year's profit.
- Calculate the number of units that must be sold at €25 per unit to provide a profit of 25% of the sales revenue received from these same units.
- Construct a traditional break-even point chart showing total costs, fixed costs and revenue. Show the effect that an increase in sales price would have on the break-even chart.

Q4 Moynihan Ltd produces a single product. The company's profit and loss account for the year ended 31/12/20-8 when 80,000 units were produced and sold was as follows:

	€	€
Sales (80,000 units)		1,120,000
Materials	470,000	
Direct labour	290,000	
Factory overheads	150,000	
Administration expenses	40,000	
Selling expenses	100,000	(1,050,000)
Profit		**70,000**

Materials include a fixed element of €70,000 while labour includes the annual salary of the factory supervisor of €45,000. It is estimated that 40% of factory overheads are variable costs while apart from 40c per unit sales commission, administration and selling expenses are fixed.

You are required to:

- Calculate the break-even point and margin of safety in units and sales value.
- Calculate the number of units that must be sold if the company is to increase its net profit by 25% in the following year assuming the selling price and cost levels and percentages remain unchanged.
- Calculate the profit Moynihan Ltd would make if it reduced its selling price to €12, spent an extra €13,000 on sales promotional techniques and thereby increased the number of units sold to 86,000, with all other cost levels and percentages remaining unchanged.
- Calculate the selling price the company must charge per unit if fixed costs increase by 10%, the volume of sales increases by 5% and the profit the company requires to make increases by 8% on the previous year's profit figure.
- Calculate the number of units that must be sold at €16 per unit to provide a profit of 15% of the sales revenue received from these same units.

23

Q5 **Uniform Direct Ltd produces a single product. The company's profit and loss account for the year ended 31/12/20-2 during which 50,000 units were sold was as follows:**

	€	€
Sales		390,000
Materials	144,000	
Labour	76,000	
Factory overheads	37,000	
Administration expenses	18,000	
Selling expenses	20,000	(295,000)
Profit		**95,000**

The materials, direct labour and 30% of factory overheads are variable costs. Apart from sales commission of 5% of selling price, selling and administration expenses are fixed.

You are required to calculate:

- **The company's break-even point and margin of safety.**
- **The number of units that must be sold at €8.50 per unit to provide a profit of 10% of sales revenue from these same units.**
- **The profit the company would make in 20-3 if it reduced its selling price to €7.20 and increased fixed costs by €6,000 and therefore increased the number of units sold to 56,000, with all other cost levels and percentages remaining unchanged.**
- **The selling price the company must charge in 20-3 if fixed costs increase by 15% and the company wishes to maintain current profit levels with all other percentages remaining unchanged.**
- **The number of units that must be sold in 20-3 if the company wishes to increase its net profit figure by 12% above the current performance with all other cost levels and percentages remaining unchanged.**

Q6 **Cox Ltd is a manufacturing business and its budgeted financial statement is set out below. These figures are based on the business operating at 80% of capacity.**

	€	€
Sales (50,000 units)		2,000,000
Less **Cost of sales**		
Direct materials	720,000	
Direct wages	225,000	
Production overheads	678,000	(1,623,000)
Gross profit		377,000
Less Expenses		(210,000)
Profit		**167,000**

Expenses consist of administration and selling expenses and it is estimated that 40% of these are fixed with the remainder being variable.

23

Production overheads are mixed costs and in the past have behaved as follows:

Year	Production volume	Production overheads
1	60,000	€728,000
2	50,000	€678,000
3	40,000	€628,000

You are required to:

- Calculate the break-even point and margin of safety in units and sales revenue.
- Calculate the level of sales that will yield a profit of €400,000.
- Calculate the profit at full capacity if the present costs remain the same.

Market research has been conducted and the following options have been proposed. Consider each option by preparing a marginal costing statement for each and decide which option (if any) the business should adopt. Give reasons for your answers.

Option 1: Reduce the selling price to €34 which would result in sales volume reaching 90%. All other cost levels remain unchanged.

Option 2: Reduce the selling price by 10% and spend an extra €22,000 on a TV advertising campaign which would result in sales volume reaching full capacity.

Q7 Simpson Ltd manufactures a single product. The company has the following budgeted figures for 20-8:

	€	€
Sales (9,000 units)		1,008,000
Direct materials	252,000	
Direct labour	126,000	
Production overheads	70,000	
Administration expenses	120,000	
Selling expenses	60,000	(628,000)
Profit		**380,000**

The direct materials and direct labour are variable costs. Production overheads are a mixed cost including a variable cost per unit of €5.60. Apart from €4 per unit sales commission, administration and selling expenses are fixed.

You are required to:

- Calculate the break-even point and margin of safety in units and sales revenue.
- Calculate the number of units that must be sold to achieve a profit of €500,000.
- Calculate the number of units that must be sold to achieve a profit of 20% of sales revenue from these units.

From the plans set out below, which one would achieve maximum profits?

Option 1: Reduce selling price by 15% which would increase sales volume by 20%. A further €18,000 needs to be spent on advertising.

Option 2: Reduce the variable cost per unit by €3.20 by increasing the efficiency of the machines. This efficiency will cost 5% in extra fixed costs. All other costs, volumes and revenues will remain unchanged.

Option 3: If sales commission was increased to €4.40 per unit, sales would increase by 10% with all other cost levels and percentages remaining unchanged.

23

Q8 **Courtney Ltd produced 20,000 units of a product during the year ended 31/12/20-7. 16,000 of these units were sold at €12 per unit. The production costs were as follows:**

Direct materials	€3.50 per unit
Direct labour	€2.20 per unit
Variable overheads	€1.30 per unit
Fixed overheads	€3,600

You are required to:

- Prepare profit and loss statements under both marginal and absorption costing principles.

Theory

Q1 **Explain the contribution to sales ratio.**

Q2 **What is sensitivity analysis?**

Q3 **Outline the limitations of marginal costing.**

Q4 **For what purpose is the contribution to sales ratio regularly used? When is the use of the ratio essential?**

Q5 **Outline the differences between marginal and absorption costing and indicate which method should be used for financial accounting and why.**

Exam Tips

- Always start with the preparation of a marginal costing statement.
- Make sure you know the different formulae and write them out in your answer.
- Know the marginal costing equation:

Sales – Variable costs = Contribution – Fixed costs = Profits

- Always round **up** units.
- Know how to construct a break-even chart.
- Be careful with commission in questions – is it a percentage of sales, or fixed per unit?
- Know how to use sensitivity analysis.
- Learn the limitations (assumptions) of marginal costing.

24 Budgeting and Budget Planning and Control

Objectives

On completion students should be able to:

- Explain the reasons why budgets are prepared and the advantages of them;
- Explain the terms associated with budgets;
- Prepare all subsidiary budgets of the manufacturing/production budget;
- Prepare a cash budget;
- Prepare a flexible budget at different levels of activity.

Budgets

Budgets form part of the planning and control which are necessary in the management of any organisation. Budgetary control is necessary so that managers can:

- compare actual results with the budget
- identify any variances (differences) so that these can be further analysed
- take corrective action to ensure that all targets and objectives are achieved.

DEFINITION

A **budget** is a detailed short-term financial plan developed by an organisation for a definite period of time.

Advantages of preparing a budget

There are many reasons why organisations should prepare a budget:

- A plan of performance is drawn up.
- Areas of responsibilities are defined – this will improve the efficiency of personnel as they will each know what their responsibilities are.
- Staff are motivated as they have targets to achieve.
- The resources of the organisation are used as efficiently as possible.
- Comparisons can be made between the actual figures and budgeted ones and thus activities can be controlled and corrective action taken if necessary.
- It improves communication and encourages teamwork.

The principal budget factor

The **principal budget factor** is a factor that restricts activity or limits output and so prevents the company from expanding indefinitely.

Sales demand is the principal budget factor for most organisations. However, it can also be:

- the supply of materials
- the availability of labour
- the capacity of the plant
- the availability of capital.

There are a number of budgets that are prepared by organisations. We will examine these in three parts.

Part A:	**Manufacturing and related budgets**
Part B:	**Cash budgets**
Part C:	**Flexible budgets**

Part A: Manufacturing and Related Budgets

Budgets are prepared by manufacturing organisations so they can plan how many units of a product they need to manufacture and estimate the costs associated with producing these units.

1. Sales budget

The **sales budget** will show the quantities and the sales value of each product the company intends to sell.

A **sales forecast** for the budget period must be made before a sales budget can be prepared. The expected sales will be based on figures provided by the previous year's sales, the market research department, the opinion of the sales manager and sales representatives. Other sources would include trends/state of the economy, competition, the price to be charged/sales price, and consideration of whether the good is a luxury or a necessity.

The sales budget is prepared by the **sales manager**. This is a key budget as many of the other budgets are based on the sales budget. If this is inaccurate all other budgets will be inaccurate.

Example

ERT Ltd makes two types of processors, Extra and Extra Plus.

	Extra	**Extra Plus**
Budgeted sales	12,300 units	11,400 units
Expected unit selling price	€120	€140

Prepare a sales budget in units and euros.

Solution

Sales Budget

	Extra	Extra Plus
Budgeted sales (units)	12,300	11,400
x Expected selling price	x 120	x 140
Budgeted sales value	**€1,476,000**	**€1,596,000**

2. Production budget (including finished stock budget)

The **production budget** will decide the quantities of finished goods that must be produced to meet the expected demand (as from the sales budget) plus/minus the budgeted increase/decrease in closing stock levels of finished goods.

The production budget is prepared by the **production manager**. The production budget is expressed in quantities only. This budget shows how many actual units of product must be completed in the production process for the forthcoming budget period, for example the next four months.

Example

Quinn Ltd sells two products, Plum and Grape. All stocks are to be reduced by 20% from their opening levels by the end of 20-2. They are valued on a FIFO basis.

Budgeted sales in units:

Plum 2,000
Grape 3,000

Stocks of finished goods on 1 January 20-2 were as follows:

Plum 320 units
Grape 150 units

Prepare a production budget.

Solution

Production Budget

		Plum	Grape	
Budgeted sales		2,000	3,000	
Add Budgeted closing stock	(320 less 20%)	256	120	(150 less 20%)
Less Budgeted opening stock		(320)	(150)	
Budgeted production in units		**1,936**	**2,970**	

24

3. Direct materials usage budget

The **direct materials usage budget** is used to find the quantity of direct materials needed to meet the levels of production.

This budget is prepared by the **production manager** and is expressed in quantities only.

Example

Toby Ltd manufactures two types of product, Fone and Bone.

The material contents are as follows:	**Fone**	**Bone**
Material X	2 kg	3 kg
Material Y	3 kg	5 kg
The production budget is:	3,500 units	4,500 units

Prepare a materials usage budget for the above.

Solution

Materials Usage Budget

	Fone	Bone
Number of units to be produced	3,500	4,500
Number of kg of material X per unit	2 kg	3 kg
Budgeted material usage material X	7,000 kg	13,500 kg

Total amount of material X: **20,500 kg**

	Fone	Bone
Number of units to be produced	3,500	4,500
Number of kg of Material Y per unit	3 kg	5 kg
Budgeted material usage material Y	10,500 kg	22,500 kg

Total amount of material Y: **33,000 kg**

4. Direct materials purchases budget

When the quantities of required materials are known, a **materials purchases budget** can be prepared.

24

This budget is prepared by the **purchasing manager** and is expressed in both quantities and value. The materials purchase budget must be adjusted for opening and closing stocks of raw materials, in the same way as the production budget is adjusted in relation to finished goods.

Example

Tabs Ltd produces two products, Big Foot and Small Feet.

	Material D	Material S
Material usage for Big Foot (usage budget)	34,500 kg	38,900 kg
Material usage for Small Feet (usage budget)	45,600 kg	54,800 kg

(The above would have been calculated from the materials usage budget.)

The following information is also given:

- Stocks of raw materials at the beginning of the period:
  Material D 4,000 kg
  Material S 4,500 kg
- The expected purchase prices for the coming year are:
  Material D €2.30 per kg
  Material S €3.40 per kg
- Stocks are to be reduced by 20% from their opening levels by the end of the period and are valued using the FIFO method.

Prepare the raw materials purchases budget in units and euros.

Solution

Raw Materials Purchases Budget

	Material D (kg)	Material S (kg)
Required by production Big Foot	34,500	38,900
Required by production Small Feet	45,600	54,800
Total required for production	80,100	93,700
Add Budgeted closing stock	3,200	3,600
Less Budgeted opening stock	(4,000)	(4,500)
Budgeted purchase of raw materials	79,300	92,800
x Budgeted purchase price	x €2.30	x €3.40
Budgeted purchases	**€182,390**	**€315,520**

5. Direct labour budget

The **direct labour budget** is used to establish the number of direct labour hours and the related direct labour wage costs.

This budget is prepared by the **production manager** and is expressed in hours and value (cost). It is based on the number of units in production (from the production budget) and the required number of labour hours to make each unit. The direct labour wage rate must also be known.

Example

Wishbone Ltd produces two products, Strong and Weak.

	Strong	**Weak**
Number of units for production	3,500 units	5,000 units
Skilled labour requirements per unit	4 hrs	2 hrs
Expected labour rates per hour	€8	€8

Prepare the labour budget in hours and cost (€).

Solution

Labour Budget

	Strong	Weak
Number of units for production	3,500	5,000
x Number of labour hours	4	2
Number of budgeted labour hours	**14,000**	**10,000**
x Rate per hour in euro	x 8	x 8
Total cost of direct labour	**€112,000**	**€80,000**

6. Factory overhead budget

The **factory overhead budget** takes into account indirect materials, indirect labour and indirect expenses.

This budget is prepared by the **production manager** and is expressed in both quantity and value (€). Overhead absorption rates are calculated from this budget.

Overheads can be fixed or variable.

Example

Disk Ltd produces two products, Round and Square.

	Round	**Square**
Number of units for production	8,000 units	9,800 units
Skilled labour requirements	4 hrs	2 hrs
Expected variable labour rate	€2	€2

Prepare the variable overheads budget in hours and euro.

24

Solution

Variable Overheads Budget

	Round	Square
Number of units in production	8,000	9,800
x Number of labour hours	4	2
Total labour hours	**32,000**	**19,600**
x Variable overhead rate	€2	€2
Total budgeted variable overheads	**€64,000**	**€39,200**

7. Administration budget

The **administration budget** deals with all the administration expenses involved in the running of the business.

This budget is prepared by the **administration or office manager** and is expressed in financial terms. It is the sum of all administration expenses.

8. Selling and distribution budget

The **selling and distribution budget** deals with the costs that are likely to be incurred in the selling and distribution of the budgeted sales to customers.

This budget is prepared by the **sales manager** and/or the **distribution manager** and is expressed in financial terms. It is the sum of all selling and distribution expenses.

9. Capital budget

The **capital budget** deals with any planned capital expenditure.

Planned capital expenditure might include the purchase of fixed assets and planned capital receipts such as the sale of fixed assets. Decisions relating to these items would be the responsibility of the **board of directors**. The preparation of the capital budget is the responsibility of the **financial controller**.

10. Master budget

When all the budgets are ready (including the cash budget – see Part B of this chapter) a master budget is prepared. This provides an overview of the planned operations of the company for the budget period. This master budget will consist of:

- a budgeted profit and loss account
- a budgeted balance sheet.

In the case of a manufacturing business it will also include:

- a budgeted manufacturing account
- a budgeted trading account.

Sample Ordinary Level question

Bicycle Ltd manufactures two types of bike, Racer and Mountain. The sales of each type and other relevant figures for the year ended 31/12/20-2 are budgeted at:

Budgeted sales	Racer	Mountain
Budgeted sales	1,200 units	900 units
Expected selling price per unit	€160	€210
Expected stocks of finished goods	**Racer**	**Mountain**
Opening stock	300 units	150 units
Closing stock	320 units	170 units
Material content and costs	**Material Sun**	**Material Shine**
Racer	4 kg	5 kg
Mountain	3 kg	1 kg
Expected price per kg	€10	€14
Expected stocks of raw materials	**Material Sun**	**Material Shine**
Opening stock	200 kg	250 kg
Closing stock	230 kg	300 kg

Direct labour in hours

Racer 10 hours

Mountain 12 hours

Direct labour rate €13 per hour

You are required to prepare:

- sales budget in units and euro
- production budget
- materials usage budget
- materials purchases budget
- labour budget.

Solution

Sales Budget

	Racer	Mountain
Budgeted sales in units	1,200	900
Expected selling price	€160	€210
Budgeted sales value	€192,000	€189,000

24

Production Budget

	Racer (units)	Mountain (units)
Budgeted sales	1,200	900
Add Budgeted closing stock	320	170
Less Budgeted opening stock	(300)	(150)
Budgeted production in units	1,220	920

Materials Usage Budget

		Material Sun (kg)	Material Shine (kg)	
Racer	(1,220 x 4)	4,880	6,100	(1,220 x 5)
Mountain	(920 x 3)	2,760	920	(920 x 1)
Budgeted material usage		7,640	7,020	

Materials Purchases Budget

	Material Sun (kg)	Material Shine (kg)
Budgeted material needed for production	7,640	7,020
Add Budgeted closing stock of raw materials	230	300
Less Budgeted opening stock of raw materials	(200)	(250)
Budgeted purchase of raw materials	7,670	7,070
x Budgeted purchase price	€10	€14
Budgeted purchases	€76,700	€98,980

Labour Budget

	Racer	Mountain
Number of units for production	1,220	920
Number of hours in manufacture	10	12
Total number of hours required	12,200	11,040
x Direct labour hour rate	€13	€13
Total labour cost	€158,600	€143,520

Sample Higher Level question

A Cut Above Ltd has completed its budgeted sales forecast for 20-4. It makes two products, Hair and Dare, which it expects to sell at €380 and €400, respectively. All stocks are to be reduced by 12% from their opening levels by the end of 20-4 and stock is valued at the lower of cost or net realisable value on a FIFO basis.

	Hair	**Dare**
Budgeted sales	9,000 units	12,300 units

Stock of finished goods on 1/1/20-4 are budgeted as:

Hair 650 units @ €85 each

Dare 350 units @ €98 each

Both of these products use the same raw materials and labour but the quantity and hours vary. These are expected to be:

	Hair	**Dare**
Material G	6 kg	8 kg
Material O	5 kg	6 kg
Skilled labour	5 hrs	9 hrs

Stocks of raw materials on 1/1/20-4 are budgeted as:

Material G 700 kg @ €18 per kg

Material O 850 kg @ €21 per kg

24

The current market price of 1 kg of Material G is €19.50 and Material O is €22.50. The labour rate is to be €9.50 per direct labour hour.

Factory overhead costs are budgeted as:

Variable	€3.50 per direct labour hour
Fixed	€134,672 per annum.

You are required to:

- Prepare a sales budget.
- Prepare a production budget.
- Prepare a raw materials wage budget.
- Prepare a raw materials purchases budget in units and euro.
- Prepare a manufacturing budget.
- Prepare a budgeted trading account (if the budgeted cost of a unit of Hair is €96 and Dare is €99).

Solution

Sales Budget

	Hair	Dare
Expected sales (units)	9,000	12,300
x Expected selling price (€)	380	400
Total budgeted sales	€3,420,000	€4,920,000

Production budget

	Hair	Dare
Budgeted sales in units	9,000	12,300
Add Closing stock requirement (Opening stock less 12%)	572	308
Less Opening stock of finished goods	(650)	(350)
Budgeted production (units)	8,922	12,258

Raw materials usage budget

		Material G (kg)	Material O (kg)	
Hair	(8,922 x 6)	53,532	44,610	(8,922 x 5)
Dare	(12,258 x 8)	98,064	73,548	(12,258 x 6)
Total in kg		151,596	118,158	

Materials purchases budget

	Material G (kg)	Material O (kg)
Required for production	151,596	118,158
Add Closing stock requirement (Opening stock less 12%)	616	748
Less Opening stock of raw materials	(700)	(850)
Budgeted purchases of raw material	151,512	118,056
x Expected purchase price	€19.50	€22.50
Purchases in €	€2,954,484	€2,656,260

Manufacturing budget

Before we can prepare this we must first prepare:

- a labour budget
- a variable overhead budget.

Labour Budget

	Hair	Dare
Number of units for production	8,922	12,258
x Number of hours required	5	9
Total labour hours	44,610	110,322
x Skilled labour hour rate	€9.50	€9.50
Total cost of labour	€423,795	€1,048,059

Variable Overhead Budget

	Hair	Dare
Total labour hours (from above)	44,610	110,322
x Variable overhead rate	€3.50	€3.50
Variable overheads	€156,135	€386,127

Manufacturing Budget (production cost)

	€	€
Raw materials		
Opening stock of raw materials		
Material G (700 x 18)	12,600	
Material O (850 x 21)	17,850	30,450
Purchase of raw materials *(taken from materials purchases budget)*		
Material G	2,954,484	
Material O	2,656,260	5,610,744
Total raw materials available		5,641,194
Less Closing stock of raw materials		
Material G (616 x 19.50)	12,012	
Material O (748 x 22.50)	16,830	(28,842)
Cost of raw materials used		5,612,352
Direct labour *(taken from the labour budget)*		
Hair (44,610 x 9.50)	423,795	
Dare (110,322 x 9.50)	1,048,059	1,471,854
Prime cost		**7,084,206**
Variable overheads *(taken from the variable overhead budget)*		
Hair (44,610 x 3.50)	156,135	
Dare (110,322 x 3.50)	386,127	542,262
Fixed overheads		134,672
Cost of manufacture		**7,761,140**

Budgeted Trading Account

	€	€	€
Sales *(taken from the sales budget)*			
Hair		3,420,000	
Dare		4,920,000	8,340,000
***Less* Cost of sales**			
Opening stock of finished goods			
Hair (650 x 85)	55,250		
Dare (350 x 98)	34,300	89,550	
Cost of manufacture *(from the manufacturing account)*		7,761,140	
		7,850,690	
Less Closing stock of finished goods			
Hair (572 x 96)	54,912		
Dare (308 x 99)	30,492	(85,404)	(7,765,286)
Gross profit			**574,714**

Exercises – Ordinary Level

Q1 **Speed Ltd manufactures two types of toy trains, Greenline and Redline. The sales of each type and other relevant figures for the year ended 31/12/20-2 are budgeted at:**

Budgeted sales	**Greenline**	**Redline**
Budgeted sales	6,000 units	8,200 units
Expected selling price per unit	€17	€22
Expected stocks of finished goods	**Greenline**	**Redline**
Opening stock	800 units	700 units
Closing stock	760 units	650 units
Material content and costs	**Material OX**	**Material EN**
Greenline	2 kg	3 kg
Redline	4 kg	5 kg
Expected price per kg	€3	€4.50
Expected stocks of raw materials	**Material OX**	**Material EN**
Opening stock	4,000 kg	6,000 kg
Closing stock	3,600 kg	6,300 kg

24

Direct labour in hours

Greenline	3 hours
Redline	4 hours
Direct labour rate	€7 per hour

You are required to prepare:

- sales budget in units and euro
- production budget
- materials usage budget
- materials purchases budget
- labour budget.

Q2 **Berry Ltd manufactures two types of fruit juices, Straw and Blue. The sales of each type and other relevant figures for the year ended 31/12/20-2 are budgeted at:**

Budgeted sales	**Straw**	**Blue**
Budgeted sales	10,900 units	13,000 units
Expected selling price per unit	€3.60	€4.00
Expected stocks of finished goods	**Straw**	**Blue**
Opening stock	1,200 units	1,400 units
Closing stock	1,500 units	1,000 units
Material content and costs	**Material Currant**	**Material Black**
Straw	6 kg	8 kg
Blue	4 kg	6 kg
Expected price per kg	€5.90	€6.10
Expected stocks of raw materials	**Material Currant**	**Material Black**
Opening stock	6,000 kg	8,000 kg
Closing stock	6,500 kg	8,800 kg

Direct labour in hours

Straw	8 hours
Blue	9 hours
Direct labour rate	€7.95 per hour

You are required to prepare:

- sales budget in units and euro
- production budget
- materials usage budget
- materials purchases budget
- labour budget.

24

Q3 **Busy Bee Ltd manufactures two types of table, Side and Wide. The sales of each type of table and other relevant figures for the year ended 31/12/20-8 are budgeted at:**

Budget sales	**Side**	**Wide**
Budgeted sales	1,000 units	700 units
Expected selling price per unit	€200	€250
Expected stocks of finished goods	**Side**	**Wide**
Opening stocks	200	230
Closing stocks	180	240
Material content and costs	**Material F**	**Material G**
Side	8 kg	10 kg
Wide	9 kg	12 kg
Expected stocks of raw materials	**Material F**	**Material G**
Opening stocks	500 kg	480 kg
Closing stocks	550 kg	500 kg
Expected price per kg	€12	€14

Direct labour time in hours

Side **5 hours**

Wide **6 hours**

Direct labour hourly rate **€15**

You are required to prepare the following budgets:

- sales budget in units and euro
- production budget
- materials usage budget
- materials purchases budget
- labour budget.

Q4 **Focus Ltd manufactures two types of watch, Digital and Analogue. The sales of each type of watch and other relevant figures for the year ended 31/12/20-9 are budgeted at:**

Budgeted sales	**Digital**	**Analogue**
Budgeted sales	1,500 units	800 units
Expected selling price per unit	€90	€70
Expected stocks of finished goods	**Digital**	**Analogue**
Opening stocks	150	180
Closing stocks	200	220
Material content and costs	**Material J**	**Material K**
Digital	3 grams	4 grams
Analogue	2 grams	3 grams
Expected stocks of raw materials	**Material J**	**Material K**
Opening stocks	400 grams	300 grams
Closing stocks	380 grams	350 grams
Expected price per gram	€2.50	€3.00

Stocks of finished goods on 1/1/20-9 are expected to be:

Cookie	200 units at €24 each
Creme	150 units at €28 each

Both products use the same raw materials and skilled labour but in different quantities per unit as follows:

	Cookie	Creme
Material X	12 kg	8 kg
Material Y	10 kg	14 kg
Skilled labour	12 hours	14 hours

Stocks of raw materials on 1/1/20-9 are expected to be:

Material X	8,000 kg @ €0.80 per kg
Material Y	5,000 kg @ €1.00 per kg

The expected prices for raw materials during 20-9 are:

Material X	€1.00 per kg
Material Y	€1.20 per kg

The skilled labour rate is expected to be €6 per hour.

Production overhead costs are expected to be:

Variable	€1.50 per skilled labour hour
Fixed	€56,344 per annum

You are required to:

- Prepare a production budget in units.
- Prepare a raw materials purchases budget (in units and euro).
- Prepare a production cost/manufacturing budget.
- Prepare a budgeted trading account (if the budgeted cost of a unit of Cookie is €25 and Creme is €30).
- Explain what factors would be taken into account by Jacob Ltd in arriving at the expected sales in 20-9 of 16,000 units.

Q4 **Trident Ltd has recently completed its annual sales forecast to December 20-7. It expects to sell two products, Jed at €25 each and Ted at €36 each. All stocks are to be reduced by 20% from their opening levels by the end of 20-7 and are valued using the FIFO method.**

	Jed	Ted
Budgeted sales	14,000 units	5,880 units

Stocks of finished goods to be 1/1/20-7 are expected to be:

Jed	840 units at €15 each
Ted	630 units at €20 each

Both products use the same raw materials and skilled labour but in different quantities per unit as follows:

	Jed	Ted
Material R	5 kg	2 kg
Material S	2 kg	5 kg
Skilled labour	2 hours	3 hours 30 minutes

Stocks of raw materials on 1/1/20-7 are expected to be:

Material R	7,000 kg @ €0.40 per kg
Material S	4,200 kg @ €0.90 per kg

The expected prices for raw materials during the year 20-7 are:

Material R	€0.50 per kg
Material S	€1.00 per kg

The skilled labour rate is expected to be €8 per hour.

Production overhead costs are expected to be:

Variable	€2 per labour hour
Fixed overheads	€18,405

You are required to:

- Prepare a production budget (in units).
- Prepare a raw materials purchases budget (in units and euro).
- Prepare a production cost/manufacturing budget.
- Prepare a budgeted trading account (if the budgeted cost of a unit of Jed and Ted is €18.00 and €22.00 respectively).

Theory

Q1 **Explain what is meant by the principal budget factor.**

Q2 **Explain the term 'administration budget'. Illustrate your answer.**

Q3 **Explain what is meant by a capital budget.**

Q4 **Explain what is meant by a selling and distribution budget. Who prepares one? Illustrate your answer with an example.**

Q5 **Sales demand is the primary principal budget factor in most organisations. State two other items that could be considered to be the principal budget factor.**

Part B: Cash Budgets

> A **cash budget** is a plan that summarises the expected inflows and outflows of cash. The cash budget is prepared by the **management accountant** or **financial accountant**.

Cash is the lifeblood of any organisation and cash budgets are prepared in order to:

- ensure there is always enough cash available to meet the day-to-day needs of the organisation
- anticipate periods when the organisation will have cash surpluses
- anticipate periods when the organisation will have cash deficits.

When the organisation has a cash surplus it can arrange short-term investment opportunities in order to achieve maximum interest.

When the organisation has a cash deficit management can arrange alternative sources of finance such as a bank overdraft.

Preparing a cash budget will involve:

- allocating income from sales to the different months
- allocating expenditure to the different months
- finding net cash for each month
- finding the closing cash for the period.

> **Net cash = Total income – Total expenditure**
>
> **Closing cash = Net cash + Opening cash**
>
> **Closing cash for one month is the opening cash for the following month.**

Sample Ordinary Level question

G. Lee has the following assets and liabilities and capital at 1 January 20-2:

	€
Assets	
Fixed assets	490,000
Stock	20,000
Debtors	48,000
Cash	2,000
	560,000
***Less* Liabilities**	
Creditors	(60,000)
Capital	500,000

The expected sales and purchases for the next five months are as follows:

	Jan. €	Feb. €	Mar. €	April €	May €	Total €
Sales	90,000	80,000	75,000	90,000	65,000	400,000
Purchases	56,000	76,000	45,000	68,000	38,000	283,000

The following additional information is supplied:

(a) All sales are on credit and are paid one month after sale.

(b) All purchases are on credit except for €20,000 in April and are paid for one month after purchase.

(c) Lee rents the premises for €18,000 per annum payable each month.

(d) Wages are to be €2,400 per month.

(e) Equipment is to be bought in March for €12,000.

(f) Closing stock at 31/5/20-2 is expected to be €15,000.

(g) Net profit for five months is expected to be €92,500.

You are required to prepare:

- a cash budget showing Lee's expected monthly receipts and payments for the five months January to May 20-2
- a balance sheet as at 31/5/20-2.

Solution

Cash Budget

	Jan. €	Feb. €	Mar. €	Apr. €	May €	Total
Receipts						
Sales	48,000	90,000	80,000	75,000	90,000	383,000
Total receipts	**48,000**	**90,000**	**80,000**	**75,000**	**90,000**	**383,000**
Payments						
Purchases	60,000	56,000	76,000	65,000	48,000	305,000
Wages	2,400	2,400	2,400	2,400	2,400	12,000
Equipment			12,000			12,000
Rent	1,500	1,500	1,500	1,500	1,500	7,500
Total payments	**63,900**	**59,900**	**91,900**	**68,900**	**51,900**	**336,500**
Net cash	(15,900)	30,100	(11,900)	6,100	38,100	46,500
Opening cash	2,000	(13,900)	16,200	4,300	10,400	2,000
Closing cash	(13,900)	16,200	4,300	10,400	48,500	48,500

24

Budgeted Balance Sheet as at 31/5/20-2

	€	€
Fixed assets (+12,000)		502,000
Current assets		
Stock	15,000	
Cash	48,500	
Debtors	65,000	
***Less* Creditors: amounts falling due within 1 year**	128,500	
Creditors	(38,000)	
Net current assets		90,500
Total net assets		**592,500**
Financed by		
Capital 1/1/20-2		500,000
Net profit		92,500
Capital employed		**592,500**

Sample Higher Level question 1

Milly Ltd has the following assets and liabilities at 1st January 20-2.

Assets	Stock	€50,800	
	Debtors	€23,000	
	Cash	€1,500	
	Prepaid rates (3 months)	€900	€76,200
Liabilities	Capital		€76,200

Milly expects the sales for the next seven months will be as follows:

	Jan. €	Feb. €	Mar. €	Apr. €	May €	June €	July €
Sales	70,000	75,000	60,000	80,000	75,000	84,000	90,000

Note that:

- 80% of sales are cash and 20% are on credit collected one month after sale.
- Gross profit percentage of sales is 20%.
- Milly wishes to keep a minimum cash balance of €8,000 at the end of each month except in January when the minimum balance required is €12,000.
- All borrowings are in multiples of €1,000 and interest is at the rate of 12% per annum.
- Purchases each month should be sufficient to cover the following month's sales.
- Purchases are paid for by the end of the month.
- Equipment to be purchased on Feb. 1 for €16,000 (depreciation 15% per annum on cost).
- Milly rents premises for €36,000 per annum payable each month.
- Wages amounting to €8,000 are paid each month.
- Computer to be purchased for €2,800 on April 1 (depreciation is 25% of cost per annum).
- Rates paid for six months from 1 April were €2,400 (paid in April).
- One-fifth of the money borrowed on 31/1/20-2 is to be repaid at the end of June together with interest to date on the repaid amount.

You are required to:

- Prepare a cash budget for the six-month period from January to June 20-2.
- Prepare a budgeted profit and loss account (pro-forma income statement) for the six months ended 31/6/20-2.

Solution

Cash Budget

	Jan. €	Feb. €	Mar. €	Apr. €	May €	June €
Receipts						
Sales cash	56,000	60,000	48,000	64,000	60,000	67,200
Credit 1 month	23,000	14,000	15,000	12,000	16,000	15,000
Total receipts	**79,000**	**74,000**	**63,000**	**76,000**	**76,000**	**82,200**
Payments						
Purchases (Sales less 20% margin)	60,000	48,000	64,000	60,000	67,200	72,000
Equipment		16,000				
Rent	3,000	3,000	3,000	3,000	3,000	3,000
Wages	8,000	8,000	8,000	8,000	8,000	8,000
Computer				2,800		
Loan repayment						630
Rates				2,400		
Total payments	**71,000**	**75,000**	**75,000**	**76,200**	**78,200**	**83,630**
Loan	3,000		9,000		2,000	2,000
Net cash	8,000	(1,000)	(12,000)	(200)	(2,200)	(1,430)
Opening cash	1,500	12,500	11,500	8,500	8,300	8,100
Closing cash	12,500	11,500	8,500	8,300	8,100	8,670

Note on repayment:

Loan of €3,000 x 0.2 = €600

Add Interest 12% x 5/12 = €30

€630

Budgeted Profit and Loss Account for the six months ended 31/06/20-2

	€	€
Sales		444,000
***Less* Cost of sales**		
Opening stock	50,800	
Purchases	371,200	
	422,000	
Less Closing stock (80% of €90,000)	(72,000)	(350,000)
Gross profit		94,000

Continued >

	€	€
***Less* Expenses**		
Rent (3,000 x 6)	18,000	
Depreciation equipment (16,000 x 15% x 5/12)	1,000	
Depreciation computers (2,800 x 25% x 3/12)	175	
Rates (900 + 2400 x 3/6)	2,100	
Loan interest (150 + 270 + 20)*	440	(21,715)
Profit		**72,285**

*Loan interest: (3,000 x 12% x 5/12 = 150) + (9,000 x 12% x 3/12 = 270) + (2,000 x 12% x 1/12 = 20)

Sample Higher Level question 2

Heather Ltd set up a new business on 1/4/20-2 and has made the following forecast for the first six months of business. The shareholders invested €200,000 into the business bank account.

	Apr. €	May €	June €	July €	Aug. €	Sep. €	Total €
Sales	200,000	240,000	250,000	280,000	300,000	330,000	1,600,000
Purchases	145,000	156,000	167,000	180,000	195,000	212,000	1,055,000

The following additional information is provided:

(a) The expected selling price per unit is set at €25.

(b) The sales will be collected as follows:

- Cash sales: 30% of sales are for cash and a cash discount is given at 5%.
- Credit sales: 70% of sales are for credit and these debtors will pay their bills 60% in the month immediately after sale and 40% the second month after sale.

(c) Purchases will be paid for as follows:

- Cash purchases: 20% of purchases will be paid for immediately and a 4% cash discount will be received.
- Credit purchases: 80% of purchases are on credit and are paid for in the month immediately after purchase.

(d) The expenses of the business are expected to be as follows:

- Wages are to be €34,000 per month payable as incurred.
- Variable overheads are €1.20 per unit sold and are payable as incurred.
- Fixed overheads (including depreciation) are €9,500 per month and payable as incurred.

(e) New machinery was to be purchased in April costing €72,000 which will have a useful life of six years. To finance this purchase a loan of €84,000 was obtained and interest on this loan is 8% per annum. The capital sum is to be repaid in 40 equal instalments payable twice yearly beginning in 1st July 20-2. The interest for each month is to be paid on the last day of each month based on the amount of the loan outstanding at that date.

You are required to:

- Prepare a cash budget for the six months – April to September 20-2.
- Prepare a budgeted profit and loss account for the six months ended 30/9/20-2.
- Explain what is meant by an adverse variance and state why adverse variances may arise in direct materials costs.

Solution

Cash Budget, April – September 20-2

	April €	May €	June €	July €	Aug €	Sept €	Total €
Receipts							
Cash sales	57,000	68,400	71,250	79,800	85,500	94,050	456,000
Credit sales, 1 month		84,000	100,800	105,000	117,600	126,000	533,400
Credit sales, 2 months			56,000	67,200	70,000	78,400	271,600
Total receipts	**57,000**	**152,400**	**228,050**	**252,000**	**273,100**	**298,450**	**1,261,000**
Payments							
Purchases	27,840	29,952	32,064	34,560	37,440	40,704	202,560
Credit purchases, 1 month		116,000	124,800	133,600	144,000	156,000	674,400
Wages	34,000	34,000	34,000	34,000	34,000	34,000	204,000
Variable overhead	9,600	11,520	12,000	13,440	14,400	15,840	76,800
Fixed overhead	8,500	8,500	8,500	8,500	8,500	8,500	51,000
Loan interest	560	560	560	546	546	546	3,318
Machinery	72,000						72,000
Loan repayment				2,100			2,100
Total payments	**152,500**	**200,532**	**211,924**	**226,746**	**238,886**	**255,590**	**1,286,178**
Net cash	(95,500)	(48,132)	16,126	25,254	34,214	42,860	(25,178)
Loan	84,000						84,000
Opening cash	200,000	188,500	140,368	156,494	181,748	215,962	200,000
Closing cash	188,500	140,368	156,494	181,748	215,962	258,822	258,822

Budgeted Profit and Loss Account for the year ended 31/12/20-2

	€	€
Sales		1,600,000
***Less* Cost of sales**		
Purchases – materials	1,055,000	
Labour (6 x 34,000)	204,000	
Variable overheads	76,800	
Fixed overheads (8,500 x 6)	51,000	(1,386,800)
Gross profit		**213,200**
***Less* Expenses**		
Depreciation of equipment	6,000	
Discount allowed (1,600,000 x 30% x 5%)	24,000	(30,000)
		183,200
Add Discount received (1,055,000 x 20% x 4%)		8,440
		191,640
Less Loan interest (*see budget*)		(3,318)
Net profit		**188,322**

24

Adverse variance: In budgeting we compare actual costs with the budgeted costs. When the actual costs incurred are greater than the budgeted figures, the difference (variance) is said to be an adverse variance.

These variances can arise for a number of reasons. Perhaps the price paid for raw materials was higher than expected – as a result of, for example, a sharp rise in the price of oil.

Exercises – Ordinary Level

Q1 **Darragh Duff has the following assets and liabilities and capital at 1 January 20-3:**

	€	€
Assets		
Fixed assets	510,000	
Stock	40,000	
Debtors	50,000	
Cash	5,000	605,000
***Less* Liabilities**		
Creditors		(45,000)
Capital		**560,000**

The expected sales and purchases for the next five months are as follows:

	Jan. €	Feb. €	Mar. €	April €	May €	Total €
Sales	100,000	70,000	90,000	120,000	80,000	460,000
Purchases	78,000	56,000	80,000	74,000	65,000	353,000

The following additional information is provided:

(a) All sales are on credit and are paid one month after sale.

(b) All purchases are on credit except for €10,000 in March and are paid for one month after purchase.

(c) Duff rents the premises for €30,000 per annum payable each month.

(d) Wages are to be €7,000 per month.

(e) Equipment is to be bought in February for €24,000.

(f) Closing stock at 31/5/20-3 is expected to be €12,000.

(g) Net profit for five months is expected to be €31,500.

You are required to prepare:

- a cash budget showing Duff's expected monthly receipts and payments for the five months January to May 20-3
- a budgeted balance sheet as at 31/5/20-3.

Q2 **Eric Black has the following assets, liabilities and capital at 1 January 20-4:**

	€	€
Assets		
Fixed assets	700,000	
Stock	40,000	
Debtors	60,000	
Cash	10,000	810,000
Less **Liabilities**		
Creditors		(80,000)
Capital		**730,000**

The expected sales and purchases for the next five months are as follows:

	Jan. €	Feb. €	Mar. €	April €	May €	Total €
Sales	80,000	85,000	86,000	79,000	90,000	420,000
Purchases	35,000	45,000	55,000	65,000	75,000	275,000

The following additional information is provided:

(a) All sales are on credit and are paid one month after sale.

(b) All purchases are on credit except for €13,000 in April and are paid for one month after purchase.

(c) Black rents the premises for €6,000 per annum payable each month.

(d) Wages are to be €6,400 per month.

(e) Equipment is to be bought in March for €52,000.

(f) Closing stock at 31/5/20-4 is expected to be €18,000.

(g) Net profit for five months is expected to be €88,500.

You are required to prepare:

- a cash budget showing Black's expected monthly receipts and payments for the five months January to May 20-4
- a budgeted balance sheet as at 31/12/20-4.

Q3 **Kim Taylor had the following assets, liabilities and capital at 1 January 20-8:**

	€	€
Assets		
Fixed assets	1,000,000	
Stock	56,800	
Debtors	109,000	
Cash	4,200	1,170,000
Less **Liabilities**		
Creditors		(106,600)
Capital		1,063,400

24

The expected sales and purchases for the next five months are as follows:

	Jan. €	Feb. €	Mar. €	April €	May €	Total €
Sales	104,000	123,000	105,000	132,000	116,000	580,000
Purchases	98,000	56,000	67,000	95,000	49,000	365,000

The following additional information is provided:

(a) All sales are on credit and paid for one month after sale.

(b) All purchases are on credit except for €12,000 in February and are paid for one month later.

(c) Taylor rents the premises for €36,000 per annum payable monthly.

(d) Wages are to be €10,200 per month.

(e) Machinery is to be bought in April for €64,000.

(f) Closing stock at 31/15/20-8 is expected to be €54,900.

(g) Net profit for the five months is expected to be €147,900.

You are required to prepare:

- a cash budget showing Taylor's expected receipts and payments for the five months January to May
- a budgeted balance sheet as at 31/5/20-8.

Q4 Tom Shortt provides the following information for June 20-9:

	€
Debtors 1/7/20-9 (made up of May sales €104,000 and June sales €96,000)	200,000
Creditors 1/7/20-9	110,000
Bank overdraft 1/7/20-9	50,000

He expects sales, purchases and expenses for the next five months to be:

	July €	Aug. €	Sept. €	Oct. €	Nov. €
Sales	160,000	150,000	200,000	142,000	190,000
Purchases	80,000	100,000	121,000	106,000	140,000
Expenses	32,000	34,000	30,000	38,000	42,000

You are given the following additional information:

(a) Expenses are paid as they are incurred.

(b) All sales are in credit and paid for two months after the month of sale.

(c) All purchases are on credit except for €25,000 for cash in September and are paid for one month after the month of purchase.

You are required to:

- Prepare a cash budget on a monthly basis for the period July to November inclusive.
- Indicate what information Tom can get from the prepared cash budget.

Exercises - Higher Level

Q1 **Sasha Ltd has the following assets and liabilities at 1st January 20-3.**

	€	€
Assets		
Stock	34,500	
Debtors	45,000	
Cash	3,400	
Prepaid insurance (2 months)	800	83,700
Liabilities		
Capital		83,700

Sasha expects the sales for the next seven months will be as follows:

	Jan. €	Feb. €	Mar. €	Apr. €	May €	June €	July €
Sales	35,000	60,000	56,000	80,000	67,000	80,000	100,000

You are given the following additional information:

(a) 70% of sales are cash and 30% are on credit collected one month after sale.

(b) Gross profit percentage of sales is 25%.

(c) Sasha wishes to keep a minimum cash balance of €3,000 at the end of each month.

(d) All borrowings are in multiples of €500 and interest is at the rate of 10% per annum.

(e) Purchases each month should be sufficient to cover the following month's sales.

(f) Purchases are paid for by the end of the month.

(g) Purchased equipment on January 1 for €26,000 (depreciation 10% per annum on cost).

(h) Sasha rents premises for €18,000 per annum payable each month.

(i) Wages amounting to €12,000 are paid each month.

(j) Computer to be purchased for €4,000 on April 1 (depreciation is 20% of cost per annum).

(k) Insurance paid for six months from 1 March was €3,000 (paid in March).

(l) One quarter of the money borrowed on 31/1/20-3 was to be repaid at the end of June, together with interest to date on the repaid amount.

You are required to prepare:

- a cash budget for the six-month period from January to June 20-3
- a budgeted profit and loss account (pro-forma income statement) for the six months ended 31/6/2-3.

Q2 **Sky Ltd has the following assets and liabilities at 1st January 20-4:**

	€	€
Assets		
Stock	65,000	
Debtors	36,000	
Cash	8,900	
Prepaid rates (3 months)	900	110,800
Liabilities		
Capital		110,800

24

Sky Ltd expects the sales for the next seven months will be as follows:

	Jan. €	Feb. €	Mar. €	Apr. €	May €	June €	July €
Sales	70,000	90,000	100,000	160,000	135,000	160,000	180,000

You are given the following additional information:

(a) 80% of sales are cash and 20% are on credit collected one month after sale.

(b) Gross profit percentage of sales is 40%.

(c) Sky wishes to keep a minimum cash balance of €5,000 at the end of each month.

(d) All borrowings are in multiples of €1,000 and interest is at the rate of 12% per annum.

(e) Purchases each month should be sufficient to cover the following month's sales.

(f) Purchases are paid for by the end of the month.

(g) Purchased equipment on January 1 for €32,000 (depreciation 20% per annum on cost).

(h) Sky rents premises for €36,000 per annum payable each month.

(i) Wages amounting to €24,000 are paid each month.

(j) Computer to be purchased for €9,000 on April 1 (depreciation is 10% of cost per annum).

(k) Rates paid for six months from 1 April were to be €6,000 (paid in March).

(l) One quarter of the money borrowed on 31/1/20-4 was to be repaid at the end of June, together with interest to date on the repaid amount.

You are required to prepare:

- a cash budget for the six-month period from January to June 20-4
- a budgeted profit and loss account (pro-forma income statement) for the six months ended 31/6/2-4.

Q3 Tammy Ltd set up a new business on 1/1/20-3 and has made the following forecast for the first six months of business. The shareholders invested €100,000 onto the company.

	Jan. €	Feb. €	Mar. €	April €	May €	June €	Total €
Sales	350,000	380,000	400,000	450,000	460,000	440,000	2,480,000
Purchases	210,000	215,000	240,000	280,000	310,000	302,000	1,557,000

The following additional information is provided:

(a) The expected selling price per unit is set at €50.

(b) The sales will be collected as follows:

- **Cash sales:** 20% of sales are for cash and a cash discount is given at 8%.
- **Credit sales:** 80% of sales are for credit and these debtors will pay their bills 70% in the month immediately after sale and 30% the second month after sale.

(c) Purchases will be paid for as follows:

- **Cash purchases:** 10% of purchases will be paid for immediately and a 10% cash discount will be received.
- **Credit purchases:** 90% of purchases are on credit and are paid for in the month immediately after purchase.

(d) The expenses of the business are expected to be as follows:

- Wages are to be €36,000 per month payable as incurred.
- Variable overheads are €6 per unit and are payable as incurred.
- Fixed overheads (including depreciation) are €18,000 per month and payable as incurred.

24

(e) New machinery was purchased in January which cost €90,000 and this will have a useful life of five years. To finance this purchase a loan of €100,000 was obtained and interest on this loan is charged at 12% per annum payable monthly. The capital sum was to be repaid in one lump sum in 20-0. To provide for this the bank was instructed to transfer €2,400 each month into an investment fund. There was €110 interest earned by this fund by 31/7/20-3.

You are required to:

- Prepare a cash budget for the six months January to June 20-3.
- Prepare a budgeted profit and loss account for the six months ending 30/6/20-3.
- Explain the purpose of a cash budget and name two advantages of preparing them.

Q4 **Right on Track Ltd is a successful business which is expanding into the Irish market. On 1/7/20-3 the company has the following forecast for the first six months of trading.**

	July €	Aug. €	Sep. €	Oct. €	Nov. €	Dec. €	Total €
Sales	728,000	756,000	854,000	882,000	896,000	924,000	5,040,000
Purchases	352,000	384,000	432,000	448,000	576,000	608,000	2,800,000

The following additional information is provided:

(a) The expected selling price per unit is set at €70.

(b) The cash collection pattern from sales/debtors is expected to be:

- **Cash customers:** 50% of sales revenue will be for immediate cash and a cash discount of 5% will be allowed.
- **Credit customers:** 50% of sales revenue will be from credit customers. These debtors will pay their bills 50% in the month after sale and the remainder in second month after sale.

(c) The cash payments for purchases are expected to be:

- **Credit suppliers:** the purchases will be paid for 60% in the month after purchase when a 4% cash discount will be received. The remaining purchases will be paid for in the second month after purchase.

(d) Expenses of the business will be settled as follows:

- **Expected costs:** Wages €70,000 per month payable as incurred; variable overheads €14 per unit as incurred; fixed overheads (including depreciation) €84,000 per month payable as incurred.
- **Capital cost:** Equipment costing €75,600 with an estimated useful life of five years and nil residual value will be purchased on 1 July. This will be partly financed by a loan at 12% per annum. The capital sum is to be repaid in 24 equal instalments commencing on 1 August. The interest for each month is to be paid on the last day of each month based on the amount of the loan outstanding at that date.

You are required to:

- Prepare a cash budget for six months July to December 20-3.
- Prepare a budgeted profit and loss account for the six months ended 31/12/20-3.
- Explain what factors should be taken into account by the company in arriving at the expected sales of €5,040,000 for the last six months of 20-3.

Q5 **Full Stream Ahead Ltd is preparing to set up business on 1/1/20-9 and has made the following forecast for the first six months of trading.**

	Jan. €	Feb. €	Mar. €	April €	May €	June €	Total €
Sales	738,000	774,000	1,008,000	1,044,000	1,098,000	1,134,000	5,796,000
Purchases	342,000	378,000	432,000	450,000	594,000	630,000	2,826,000

The following additional information is provided:

(a) The expected selling price is €72 per unit.

(b) The cash collection pattern from debtors is expected to be:

- **Cash customers:** 60% of sales revenue will be for immediate cash and a cash discount of 10% will be allowed.
- **Credit customers:** 40% of sales revenue will be from credit customers. These debtors will pay their bills 50% in the month after sale and the remainder in second month after sale.

(c) The cash payments for purchases are expected to be:

- **Credit suppliers:** The purchases will be paid for 50% in the month after purchase when a 5% cash discount will be received. The remaining purchases will be paid for in the second month after purchase.

(d) Expenses of the business will be settled as follows:

- **Expected costs:** Wages €72,000 per month payable as incurred; variable overheads €18 per unit as incurred; fixed overheads (including depreciation) €81,000 per month payable as incurred.
- **Capital costs:** Equipment costing €86,400 with an estimated useful life of five years and no residual value will be purchased on 1 July. This will be partly financed by a loan of €79,200 at 6% per annum. Interest is to be paid monthly but capital loan repayments will not commence until September 20-9.

You are required to:

- Prepare a cash budget for six months January to June 20-9.
- Prepare a budgeted profit and loss account for the six months ended 30/06/20-9.
- Define 'cash budget' and describe **two** of its advantages.

24

Part C: Flexible Budgets (Higher Level)

Flexible budgeting is the process of adjusting (flexing) the original budget to the actual level of activity. This is necessary because the budget activity is often different from the actual activity. Flexible budgeting enables us to compare like with like. The original budget figures are adjusted to the actual level of activity.

NOTE

A main objective of budgeting is to control costs.

Flexible budgets are prepared to show the different costs at different production levels, up to and including maximum capacity.

Flexible budgets are prepared:

- to show management the cost levels associated with different levels of production
- to compare actual costs and budgeted costs so as to be able to identify any variances and take corrective action when necessary
- to compare budgeted costs and actual costs at the same level of activity
- to compare like with like
- to help in controlling costs or planning products levels.

Preparing a flexible budget

A flexible budget is prepared which will compare the costs for the accounting period with the budgeted costs for that period. It will show the differences (variances) between them.

This is easy to achieve when the actual level of activity is the same as the budgeted level.

Example:	Budgeted activity: 3,000 units @ €5 per unit	= €15,000
	Actual activity: 3,000 units @€5.50	= €16,500
	Difference	= €1,500

The adverse (unfavourable) variance in material costs can be clearly seen, with materials costing €1,500 more than expected.

However, when the actual level of activity also varies a comparison becomes more difficult.

Example:	Budgeted activity	3,000 units	Budgeted direct material costs	€9,000
	Actual activity	3,600 units	Actual direct material costs	€11,160

Budgeted material cost $\frac{9,000}{3,000}$ = €3.00 per unit

Actual material cost $\frac{11,160}{3,600}$ units = €3.10 per unit

24

This shows an adverse variance of 10c per unit.

Budgetary control

When a comparison has been made between the flexible budget and the actual results, management can study the variances (adverse and favourable) and as result can control costs. Management needs to look particularly at any adverse variances.

When analysing variances, it is important to remember that the individual or departmental manager may not be responsible for the total amount of the variance. Some costs are controllable and others are not. For example, the quantity of direct materials is the responsibility of the production manager and so would be controllable, but the price paid for these materials is the responsibility of the purchasing manager and would be uncontrollable as far as the production manager is concerned.

Cost behaviour

Costs can be classified into three main categories: variable, fixed and mixed. In summary:

- **Variable costs** will change in total with the level of production.
- **Fixed costs** remain the same in total.
- **Mixed costs** (semi-variable) are costs that have fixed and variable elements. The fixed part will not change but the variable part will change with the level of activity.

Example

Classify the costs below into fixed, variable and mixed costs.

Level of production	3,000 units	5,000 units	7,000 units	8,500 units
	€	€	€	€
Materials	27,000	45,000	63,000	76,500
Labour	15,000	25,000	35,000	42,500
Production overheads	17,000	25,000	33,000	39,000
Other overheads	10,000	14,000	18,000	21,000
Administration	15,000	15,000	15,000	15,000

NOTE

To determine if an expense is variable choose any **two** levels of production to see if the unit charge is the same.

Solution

We can start by looking at **materials**:

Cost of materials (€) / Level of production (units)	$\frac{27,000}{3,000}$	$\frac{45,000}{5,000}$	$\frac{63,000}{7,000}$	$\frac{76,500}{8,500}$
Material cost per unit	€9	€9	€9	€9

Since the answer remains constant at €9 per unit, we can see that the cost is changing in total directly with the level of production so we can see that is a **variable cost.**

We can do the same calculation with **labour** to determine if it is mixed or variable. We know it is not a fixed cost as the costs are different at each level of activity.

Cost of labour (€) / Level of production (units)	$\frac{15,000}{3,000}$	$\frac{25,000}{5,000}$	$\frac{35,000}{7,000}$	$\frac{42,500}{8,500}$
Labour cost per unit	€5	€5	€5	€5

24

Again, since we get a constant figure of €5 per unit, this cost varies directly with the level of production, so it is a **variable cost.**

Now let us look the **production overheads** and **other overheads**.

Use the same check system

Costs / number of units	17,000 / 3,000	25,000 / 5,000	33,000 / 7,000	39,000 / 8,500
Cost per unit	€5.66	€5	€4.71	€4.59

Since the production overheads are different per unit but the total is not the same, then these must be **mixed costs**.

NOTE

Use the **high-low method** to separate mixed costs into fixed and variable elements.

Production overheads	Units	€
High	8,500	39,000
Low	3,000	17,000
Difference	5,500	22,000

Therefore $\frac{22{,}000}{5{,}500}$ = **€4 per unit variable cost**

Substitute back in:		High (€)	Low (€)	
Total production overhead cost		39,000	17,000	
Less Variable costs	(8,500 x 4)	(34,000)	(12,000)	(3,000 x 4)
Therefore fixed costs		€5,000	€5,000	

Other overheads	Units	€
High	8,500	21,000
Low	3,000	10,000
Difference	5,500	11,000

Therefore $\frac{11{,}000}{5{,}500}$ = **€2 per unit variable cost**

Substitute back in:		High (€)	Low (€)	
Total production overhead cost		21,000	10,000	
Less Variable costs	(8,500 x 2)	(17,000)	(6,000)	(3,000 x 2)
Therefore fixed costs		€4,000	€4,000	

24

Since the **administration** costs are the same at all levels of production it is clear that these are fixed costs.

Summary

- Materials - variable cost
- Labour - variable cost
- Production overheads - mixed cost
- Other overheads - mixed cost
- Administration - fixed cost.

Restating the budget at a new level of activity

This will involve drawing up a new budget at the new level of activity.

Calculate:

1. the material cost per unit
2. the labour cost per unit
3. the production overheads variable cost per unit and fixed element (high-low method)
4. the other overheads variable cost per unit and fixed element (high-low method)
5. the fixed overheads (remain the same at all levels of production).

Example

From the example above we already know these figures:

Material cost per unit	€9
Labour cost per unit	€5
Production cost per unit	€4 variable and €5,000 fixed
Other overheads cost per unit	€2 variable and €4,000 fixed
Administration costs	€15,000

You are required to:

- Prepare a flexible budget at 10,000 units from the above data.

Solution

		€	€
Materials	10,000 units x 9		90,000
Labour	10,000 units x 5		50,000
Production overheads	Variable: 10,000 x 4	40,000	
	Fixed	5,000	45,000
Other overheads	Variable: 10,000 x 2	20,000	
	Fixed	4,000	24,000
Administration expenses			15,000
Total cost at 10,000 units			224,000

Restating the budget using marginal costing principles

This involves separating all the costs into either fixed or variable elements. Sales will be calculated based on a mark-up or margin of cost.

24

Example

Based on the budget above (10,000 units) and assuming a selling price of 25% mark-up on cost, restate the flexible budget using marginal costing principles, showing the contribution.

Solution

Flexible Budget at 10,000 units using marginal costing principles

	€	€
Sales (224,000 x 1.25)		280,000
***Less* Variable costs**		
Materials	90,000	
Labour	50,000	
Production overheads (variable)	40,000	
Other overheads (variable)	20,000	(200,000)
Contribution		**80,000**
***Less* Fixed costs**		
Production overheads	5,000	
Other overheads	4,000	
Administration expenses	15,000	(24,000)
Profit		**56,000**

Exercises – Higher Level

Q1 Wexford Plc manufactures a single product. The company has prepared the following flexible budgets at 5,000 units, 7,500 units and 9,000 units:

Output	5,000 units	7,500 units	9,000 units
	€	€	€
Materials	50,000	75,000	90,000
Labour	37,500	56,250	67,500
Production overheads	16,000	22,500	26,400
Other overheads	11,500	16,250	19,100
Administration	20,000	20,000	20,000

Profit is set at 25% of sales.

You are required to:

- **Classify the above costs as fixed, variable or mixed.**
- **Separate the production overheads into fixed and variable elements.**
- **Separate the other overheads into fixed and variable elements.**
- **Prepare a flexible budget at 10,400 units.**
- **Restate the above budget using marginal costing principles.**

24

Q2 Frost Ltd has prepared the following flexible budgets at 3,500 units, 6,000 units and 8,000 units:

Output	3,500 units	6,000 units	8,000 units
	€	€	€
Materials	28,000	48,000	64,000
Labour	38,500	66,000	88,000
Production overheads	16,500	24,000	30,000
Other overheads	18,750	30,000	39,000
Administration	19,000	19,000	19,000

Profit is set at 20% of cost of sales.

You are required to:

- Classify the above costs as fixed, variable or mixed.
- Separate the production overheads into fixed and variable elements.
- Separate the other overheads into fixed and variable elements.
- Prepare a flexible budget at 12,800 units.
- Restate the above budget using marginal costing principles.

Q3 Morse Ltd produces a single product. They have prepared the following flexible budgets at 4,000 units, 6,500 units and 9,000 units:

Output	4,000 units	6,500 units	9,000 units
	€	€	€
Materials	60,000	97,500	135,000
Labour	36,000	58,500	81,000
Production overheads	30,000	42,500	55,000
Other overheads	33,000	50,500	68,000
Administration	14,500	14,500	14,500

Profit is set at 20% of cost of sales.

You are required to:

- Classify the above costs as fixed, variable or mixed.
- Separate the production overheads into fixed and variable elements.
- Separate the other overheads into fixed and variable elements.
- Prepare a flexible budget at 95% plant capacity if 9,000 is 75% capacity.
- Prepare a flexible budget at 100% capacity using marginal costing principles.
- Explain what is meant by a fixed cost and give two examples. Illustrate by means of a graph.

Q4 **Lewis Plc produces a single product and has prepared flexible budgets at 3,400 units, 5,000 units and 7,300 units.**

Output	3,400 units	5,000 units	7,300 units
	€	€	€
Materials	40,800	60,000	87,600
Labour	20,400	30,000	43,800
Production overheads	7,800	11,000	15,600
Other overheads	11,200	16,000	22,900
Administration	4,000	4,000	4,000

Profit is set at 25% of sales.

You are required to:

- Classify the above costs as fixed, variable or mixed.
- Separate the production overheads into fixed and variable elements.
- Separate the other overheads into fixed and variable elements.
- Prepare a flexible budget at 9,000 units.
- Restate the above budget using marginal costing principles.

If the company spends an extra €3,000 on modernisation of the machinery, it will save 50c per unit in production overheads. Prepare a flexible budget at 12,000 units taking these new cost structures into account.

Q5 **Fletcher Ltd produces a single product and has prepared a flexible budget at 25%, 60% and 80% of the plant's capacity.**

Output	15,000 units	36,000 units	48,000 units
	€	€	€
Materials	202,500	486,000	648,000
Labour	118,500	284,400	379,200
Production overheads	40,500	93,000	123,000
Other overheads	68,000	156,200	206,600
Administration	54,000	54,000	54,000

Profit is set at 20% of sales.

You are required to:

- Classify the above costs as fixed, variable or mixed.
- Separate the production overheads into fixed and variable elements.
- Separate the other overheads into fixed and variable elements.
- Prepare a flexible budget at 90% and 100% of the plant's capacity.
- Restate the budget of 90% of the plant's capacity using marginal costing principles.
- Restate the budget of 100% of plant's capacity using absorption costing principles.

24

If the company spent an extra €16,000 on advertising and new machinery, other overhead costs would be reduced by 70c per unit, as well as a saving of 50c per unit for materials. Prepare a new flexible budget at full capacity using this new cost structure.

If the company bought new machinery this would increase the plant's capacity by 15% while reducing fixed overheads in all departments by 10%. Prepare a flexible budget at the new full capacity and new cost structure. Should the company go ahead with this project? (The cost of the new machinery is entered in the capital budget.)

Exam Tips

Manufacturing/Production budgets

- Ensure you know how to prepare all the subsidiary budgets.
- When calculating the number of units, add the closing stock and subtract the opening stock.
- Ensure you know how to prepare the production/cost manufacturing budget.
- Ensure you know how to prepare the budgeted trading, profit and loss account.
- Know how to calculate the value of closing stock – it may not be given in the question.

Cash budgets

- Identify what months the budget has to be prepared for.
- When preparing a cash budget it is important to remember that this shows actual cash paid and received.
- Don't include non-cash items in a cash budget.
- When preparing the schedule of payments to creditors and the schedule of receipts from debtors, you must take into account any opening and closing creditors/debtors.
- Don't forget any discounts: these must also be entered in the trading, profit and loss account.
- Check the date of loans received and be able to calculate the appropriate interest.
- When preparing the trading, profit and loss account, the sales and purchases figures are the actual sales and purchases and not the cash received/paid.

Flexible budgets

- Know the difference between fixed, variable and mixed costs, and be able to classify them.
- Revise the high-low method from Chapter 21.
- Flexible budgets can easily be integrated into cost-volume profit questions.

Summary of ratio analysis formulae (interpretation of accounts)

Ratio	Formula	Answer format
Return on capital employed (ROCE)	$\frac{\text{Profit before interest and tax} \times 100}{\text{Capital employed}}$	percentage
Return on shareholders' funds (ROSF)	$\frac{\text{Profit (after tax and preference dividend)} \times 100}{\text{Shareholders' funds}}$	percentage
Gross profit mark-up percentage	$\frac{\text{Gross profit} \times 100}{\text{Cost of sales}}$	percentage
Gross profit margin percentage	$\frac{\text{Gross profit} \times 100}{\text{Sales}}$	percentage
Net profit percentage	$\frac{\text{Profit before interest and tax} \times 100}{\text{Sales}}$	percentage
Stock turnover	$\frac{\text{Cost of sales}}{\text{Average stock}}$	times
Average stock	$\frac{\text{Opening stock + Closing stock}}{2}$	€
Average period of credit given to debtors	$\frac{\text{Debtors} \times 12 \text{ or } 52 \text{ or } 365}{\text{Credit sales}}$	months/weeks/ days
Average period of credit received from creditors	$\frac{\text{Creditors} \times 12 \text{ or } 52 \text{ or } 365}{\text{Credit purchases}}$	months/weeks/ days
Current ratio	Current assets : Current liabilities	X : Y
Acid test ratio (quick ratio)	Current assets – Closing stock : Current liabilities	X : Y
Gearing ratio	$\frac{\text{Fixed interest capital} \times 100}{\text{Capital employed}}$	percentage
Earnings per share (EPS)	$\frac{\text{Profit (after preference dividend)}}{\text{Number of ordinary shares issued}}$	cent
Dividend per ordinary share (DPS)	$\frac{\text{Ordinary dividends} \times 100}{\text{Number of ordinary shares issue}}$	cent
Price earnings ratio (PE ratio)	$\frac{\text{Market price of 1 share}}{\text{Earnings per share}}$	years
Price dividend ratio (period to recoup price at present payout rate)	$\frac{\text{Market price of 1 share}}{\text{Dividend per share}}$	years
Dividend yield	$\frac{\text{Dividend per share} \times 100}{\text{Market price of 1 share}}$	percentage
Dividend cover	$\frac{\text{Net profit (after tax and preference dividend)}}{\text{Ordinary dividend}}$	times
Interest cover	$\frac{\text{Profit before interest and tax}}{\text{Interest charges for the year}}$	times